Auditing:
A Systems Approach

Richard Scott Ph.D., C.P.A.

Professor
McIntire School of Commerce
University of Virginia

John Page Ph.D., C.P.A.

Associate Professor
University of New Orleans

Paul Hooper Ph.D.

Associate Professor and Department Chairman
University of New Orleans

Reston Publishing Company, Inc.
A Prentice-Hall Company
Reston, Virginia

Library of Congress Cataloging in Publication Data

Scott, Richard, 1935–
    Auditing, a systems approach.

    1. Auditing.   I. Page, John R., 1949–
II. Hooper, H. Paul.   III. Title.
HF5667.S345   657'.45   81-15888
ISBN 0-8359-0238-2   AACR2

Copyright 1982 by
Reston Publishing Company, Inc.
A Prentice-Hall Company
Reston, Virginia 22090

10   9   8   7   6   5   4   3   2   1

Printed in the United States of America

To   *Rita and Craig Scott*
     William and Jennifer Page
     Pam, Lisa, and Jody Hooper

Contents

Preface

Contemporary auditing reflects a change in the field that has taken place over recent years. The title, *Auditing: A Systems Approach,* is used to capture the essence of this new approach. A systematic approach to auditing is being taken, and the entity being audited is viewed as a collection of systems. The emphasis is upon transactions processing cycles and the controls incorporated into them. Auditing entails understanding systems and cycles, reviewing the controls embodied in the system, and testing transaction flows and the effectiveness of controls. Testing and review takes place throughout the period, not only at year-end. Auditors depend upon the design and functioning of the system. Reliance upon a system necessarily involves risk, and thus, risk analysis has become an important aspect of auditing. This philosophy has influenced how the text was constructed.

Auditing is a profession in the purest sense of the word. We hope to communicate that idea to students and help them develop a sense of respect and pride for the profession. The placement, in lead-off position, of an introduction to the profession and chapters on the ethical and legal environment reflects our regard for the "professionalism" of auditing.

Next, we turn to the transactions processing cycles and the accounting controls embodied in them. The concept of internal control is first developed, and applications described in language that attempts to concentrate on reasoning instead of jargon. Throughout the book, we have tried to balance the use of technical jargon with a need to introduce students to the language of the art. The entire audit from beginning to end is explained in Chapter 5. At the same time the theory of evidence, evidence gathering techniques, and the types of tests conducted are discussed. Chapters 6–10 concentrate on transactions cycles. Each cycle chapter breaks down the cycle into functions and describes the major operating and control activities. A flowchart illustrating functional and activity relationships is also positioned early in the chapter to visually convey the concept of a cycle. We believe that a major reason students find auditing difficult is because they are not well versed in the way firms are organized and transactions are processed. Consequently, these sections are comprehensive.

A second major section of the cycle chapters deals with the evaluation of internal control. First, audit objectives for the cycle are specified so that goals are immediately established and kept in mind throughout. Then the discussion swings to control objectives, risk analysis, and control strategies that are often employed in practice. Here we are viewing internal control from the firm's standpoint. This material ought to be of interest to those who design control systems, as well as those who review them for audit purposes. For example, internal auditors should be as interested in these materials as those who characteristically view the subject primarily from an independent auditor's vantage point. Finally, we turn to the auditor's evaluation of internal accounting controls. To the flowchart that was presented early in the chapter, we add an internal control questionnaire organized by cycle functions. The questionnaire, of course, relates directly to the preceding discussion on control objectives, risk analysis, and control strategies.

The third major section of the cycle chapters is devoted to compliance testing of controls and substantive testing of transactions details. Realistic audit programs are included in chapter appendices. In this way, we focus the discussion on concepts while preserving a sense of authenticity. Tests of details are contained in the audit program, discussed in the body of the chapters, and illustrated by flowcharts of audit procedures. We believe the flowcharting of audit procedures to be an innovative approach to this topic. The flowcharts tie in to the audit programs and conclude with an auditor's working paper that is illustrated immediately after. In class testing, we found students to be enthusiastic about this learning approach and about the "concept summaries" that are sprinkled throughout the book.

The final major section concentrates on substantive tests of balances and analytical review.

Chapters 11 and 12 examine the concluding phases of the audit and the variety of reports issued by auditors.

The subjects of statistical sampling and computers in auditing are divided among the final four chapters of the book. Our impression is that these topics are increasingly found in a second course in auditing. Placing them at the end of the book facilitates such an approach. On the other hand, they are free-standing and can be repositioned by the instructor if earlier treatment is desired. One or both topics, for instance, could be assigned after Chapter 5, just before the cycle chapters. A variety of chapter arrangements of the book is possible, in fact. Some instructors may prefer to postpone the topics of ethics and accountant's legal liability until later in the semester. This can be done without any loss of continuity.

End of chapter materials include a list of key terms, questions about the chapter, multiple choice questions, and problems from professional examinations, CPA firms, and the authors' experiences. A case study has been written to accompany this book. It is unique in that "mini-cases" are completed for each chapter as a student moves along. These can be graded or discussed piecemeal as the semester progresses, instead of being attacked as a massive undertaking at semester's end.

ACKNOWLEDGEMENTS

We are grateful to a number of people who helped us in one way or another with this book. We thank Emmie V. Hester, University of Virginia; Mary Jean Welsh, University of New Orleans; Jerry Babst, Deloitte, Haskins & Sells; Joe Ben Hoyle, University of Richmond; David Croll, University of Virginia; Milton Usry, Oklahoma State University; and John H. McCray, College of William & Mary.

We would especially like to thank Robert K. Elliott of Peat, Marwick, Mitchell & Co., Corine T. Norgaard of the University of Connecticut, James H. Stanley, Jr., of Gary, Stosch, Walls & Co., and Ann Kittler of Ryerson Polytechnical Institute for the invaluable comments they made in reviewing the manuscript.

The students of the McIntire School of Commerce of the University of Virginia cooperated in the class testing of this book. Their criticism and suggestions influenced the form of this book and improved it considerably.

We appreciate the materials provided us by Price Waterhouse & Co. and Peat, Marwick, Mitchell & Co. In addition, we recognize a debt to the American Institute of Certified Public Accountants, the Canadian Institute of Chartered Accountants, the Institute of Internal Auditors and The Institute of Management Accounting for problems and other materials.

A very substantial debt is owed by us to the staff of Reston Publishing for their help during the production of this book. We are particularly grateful to Diane Anderson for her creative efforts while production editor on the project.

A final and special word of thanks is reserved for Fred Easter, Executive Editor of Reston Publishing Company. His encouragement, patience, and support made writing this book much easier than it otherwise would have been.

Richard Scott

John Page

Paul Hooper

The Environment of Auditing

Auditing and the structure of the public accounting profession

Occupations in the United States are often classified into a hierarchy that denotes the social status of those who work in these occupations. A typical hierarchy of occupations would include:

professionals
managers and proprietors
clerical workers
skilled workers
laborers

The professions at the top of this hierarchy are separated from the remainder of occupations by two important features:

1. A common body of knowledge, which can be learned through formal education and applied in the work of the profession.
2. Standards of conduct higher than those imposed by law that are imposed by a national organization and voluntarily accepted by those practicing the profession.

The list of occupations generally regarded as professions includes accounting, architecture, engineering, law, and medicine. Accounting is the youngest of the professions listed. Public accounting became a full-time occupation only during the 19th century, a century after the other occupations listed above. Also, CPAs were the last group to formulate university schools to teach a common body of knowledge, to organize a national professional association, and to create and accept a code of professional ethics. There is no doubt, however, that public accounting has now assumed a position as one of the most influential and respected professions in the United States.

1.1 AUDITING AND TYPES OF AUDITORS

Auditing Defined

The primary activity of public accountants (CPAs in public practice) is auditing. Auditing has been variously defined by the American Institute of Certified Public Accountants (AICPA), the American Accounting Association (AAA), the U.S. General Accounting Office (GAO), and the Institute of Internal Auditors (IIA). The primary membership of each of these organizations and their definition of auditing is summarized in Exhibit 1–1.

A clear, concise definition of auditing can be distilled from these various approaches as follows:

> **Auditing is the process of determining and communicating whether the financial assertions of an individual or organization fairly represent the underlying facts and events on which the assertions are based.**

Several points in this composite definition are important.

Auditing is a Process

Auditing is an on-going activity rather than a static one-time check of the relationship between financial assertions and underlying events. This on-going process requires the gathering and analyzing of evidence as financial activities and events occur, even before financial assertions are made.

Determining and Communicating

The larger benefit of auditing derives from the increased credibility of financial assertions that results when the outcome of the audit process is communicated to groups who may rely on these assertions. This communication is called *attestation*. Attestation is the primary function of the audit process, and it usually takes the form of a report that expresses an opinion on the relationship between assertions and events.

Assertions Fairly Represent Events

The audit process focuses on the financial assertions made by an individual or business and on how well these assertions represent events that have occurred.

EXHIBIT 1-1 Approaches to Auditing

Organization	Primary Membership	Definition of Auditing
AICPA	CPAs in public practice	The objective of the ordinary examination of financial statements by the independent auditor is the expression of an opinion on the fairness with which they present financial position, results of operations, and changes in financial position in conformity with generally accepted accounting principles. The auditor's report is the medium through which he expresses his opinion or, if the circumstances require, disclaims an opinion. (Statement on Auditing Standards No. 1, 1973).
AAA	Academic accountants in teaching and research	Auditing is a systematic process of objectively obtaining and evaluating evidence regarding assertions about economic actions and events to ascertain the degree of correspondence between those assertions and established criteria and communicating the results to interested users. (AAA Committee on Basic Auditing Concepts, 1971).
GAO	Government accountants	The term "audit" may be used to describe not only work done by accountants in examining financial reports but also work done in reviewing: (a) compliance with applicable laws and regulations, (b) efficiency and economy of operations, and (c) effectiveness in achieving program results. (Standards for Audit of Governmental Organizations, Programs, Activities, and Functions, 1981).
IIA	Accountants employed full-time as auditors by industry	Internal auditing is an independent appraisal activity within an organization for the review of operations as a service to management. It is a managerial control, which functions by measuring and evaluating the effectiveness of other controls. (Statement of Responsibilities of the Internal Auditor, 1971).

No judgement is made on the wisdom of engaging in any of the events or whether or not the assertions depict "good" or "bad" fortune for the organization being audited. Such judgements are left to the users of audited information, who are given assurance by the audit process that the information fairly represents what really happened.

Types of Auditors

Individuals or groups who perform the audit function can be divided into three groups—independent auditors, government auditors, and internal auditors. Each of the following audit descriptions can be related to the definitions of auditing given in Exhibit 1–1.

Independent Auditors

Independent auditors are professionals who offer services to the public for a fee. The primary activity performed by independent CPAs is the examination of financial statements prepared by a client. This examination is made primarily for the benefit of creditors, owners and potential owners, and government agencies. Independent CPAs may also perform a number of other services such as tax work, management consulting, bookkeeping and accounting services, and the compilation and review of financial statements for clients.

Independent CPAs qualify to offer their services to the public by meeting a series of standards as to education and experience and by passing a uniform, national examination. Although the AICPA is the national professional organization of independent CPAs, the license to practice as a CPA is granted by individual states.

The main characteristic that separates independent CPAs from other types of auditors and from other professionals who offer services to the public for a fee (such as physicians and attorneys) is independence. Public accountants must be independent both in appearance and in fact from the clients they audit, while other professionals are considered advocates of the clients they serve. The primary beneficiaries of an independent audit may be individuals or organizations other than the CPA's client. This third-party beneficiary situation is seldom encountered in the work of other professions.

Government Auditors

Auditors are found in most areas of government activity. However, two agencies—the General Accounting Office and the Internal Revenue Service—employ most federal auditors. Government audits are performed to determine compliance with federal laws, statutes, policies, procedures, and rules. The government, and thus presumably society, benefits from these audits. Some government auditors hold CPA certificates, but education is the primary requirement for this type of work.

Auditors for the GAO may perform audits of other government agencies or programs or of companies with large government contracts. The results of these audits are usually made public and are often used as the basis for new laws and regulations.

IRS auditors are concerned with compliance with the federal tax laws (Internal Revenue Code). The results of these audits are confidential unless they become the basis for a court case between the IRS and a taxpayer.

Internal Auditors

Internal auditors are employees of private organizations (mostly businesses) and are concerned with determining whether organizational polices and procedures have been carried out and with safeguarding organizational assets. Internal auditors may also review the efficiency and effectiveness of operating procedures and controls and assess the reliability of data generated within an organization.

The management and board of directors of an organization are the most immediate users of the work of internal auditors. However, the work of internal auditors may ultimately affect the audit of a company's financial statements by independent CPAs, particularly in the area of internal control.

The Institute of Internal Auditors is the national professional association for internal auditors. This organization determines the criteria for certification as a certified internal auditor (CIA) and administers the national CIA examination. Although not all internal auditors are CIAs, the number is increasing. Additionally, some internal auditors are CPAs.

Audits of Financial Statements

Financial accounting activity is concerned with satisfying the information needs of those parties outside of the decision-making and control group of an organization. These external users may include creditors and potential creditors, owners and potential owners, government agencies, labor unions, law-makers, customers, suppliers, and even the general public. These external consumers of information on business activities have two common characteristics:

1. They are all consumers of financial information but not preparers of that information. They must accept and use information prepared by organization management.

2. Their most important source of financial information (for some groups the only source) is the financial statements of an organization.

Financial statements represent information prepared by management about management activities. Since these financial statements play a central role in the economic and social decision making of many groups, it is important that the inconsistencies and bias of the preparers of the information not affect the statements.

Audits of financial statements by independent CPAs determine that these statements have been prepared according to an objective set of criteria or rules called *generally accepted accounting principles* (GAAP) and that the statements fairly represent the underlying activities of the organization. In order to make this determination, an established set of standards called *generally accepted auditing standards* (GAAS) is applied.

Assumptions Behind Financial Statement Audits

The following statements about financial statement audits provide an overview of the process.

1. Financial statements are assertions by an organization's management and are, therefore, the responsibility of management.
2. These statements should be prepared consistently according to GAAP and, if so, will be relatively free of bias.
3. Whether or not financial statements have been prepared according to GAAP can be verified by the application of GAAS in the audit process.

Most of the remainder of this text will be concerned with financial statement audits and the independent CPAs who perform them.

1.2 ORGANIZATION OF THE PUBLIC ACCOUNTING PROFESSION

The organized accounting profession includes three different organizations—the American Institute of Certified Public Accountants, the State Societies of Certified Public Accountants and the State Boards of Public Accounting.

The AICPA

The American Institute of Certified Public Accountants (AICPA) is the national professional organization of CPAs. At mid-year 1980, its membership stood at approximately 150,000 of the estimated 200,000 CPAs in the United States. The AICPA traces its origins to the founding, in 1887, of the American Association of Public Accountants.

The objectives of the AICPA are stated to be (AICPA, By-Laws, 1974):

1. To unite certified public accountants in the United States.
2. To promote and maintain high professional standards of practice.
3. To assist in the maintenance of standards for entry into the profession.

CONCEPT SUMMARY
Types of Auditors

Auditor	Primary Publication	Type of Audits Performed
Independent CPA	*Journal of Accountancy*	Financial statement audits for the benefit of external third-party users of information.
GAO	*The GAO Review*	Compliance audits, which determine adherence to federal laws and statutes, policies, procedures, and rules by government agencies, programs, and contractors.
IRS	*The Federal Accountant*	Compliance audits which determine adherence to the Internal Revenue Code by taxpayers.
Internal	*The Internal Auditor*	Compliance audits, which determine adherence to organizational policies and procedures and safeguard assets. Operational audits, which review the effectiveness and efficiency of controls and the reliability of data.

---

4. To promote the interests of all CPAs.

5. To develop and improve accounting education.

6. To encourage cordial relations between CPAs and professional accountants in other countries.

The organization of the AICPA includes members, officers, the Board of Directors, the Council, and numerous boards and committees. The primary requirement for membership is the possession of a valid CPA certificate issued by a legally constituted authority.

Structure of the AICPA

The governing body of the AICPA is its Council, made up of more than two hundred members representing every state and territory, and weighted according to state membership. However, the Council is so large and diverse as to be unwieldy and is not a practical force in the day-to-day affairs of the AICPA. The Council does prescribe the make-up of the Board of Directors, which acts as the executive committee of the Council and controls and manages the activities of the AICPA including establishing major policies for the conduct of the organization's affairs.

The officers of the AICPA are a chairman of the Board of Directors, a vice-chairman of the Board, three volunteer vice-presidents, and a treasurer, all of whom are members in practice and consequently are part-time officials. The president, who is a member and full-time employee of the Institute, and a secretary, who is a full-time employee but need not be a member, actually carry on the day-to-day business of the Institute.

The pronouncements, statements, opinions, and bulletins of the committees and boards of the AICPA over the years since its formation now constitute the major portion of GAAP and GAAS. In addition, the AICPA has a Code of Professional Ethics, which enumerates acceptable standards of conduct for those CPAs who are Institute members.

The State Societies

In addition to a national professional organization, CPAs have formed voluntary organizations in each state. These state societies promote many of the same goals and aims of the AICPA.

The state societies have generally adopted the standards of practice and conduct promulgated by the AICPA. State societies have been particularly active in areas of professional development, such as continuing education, usually in cooperation with the AICPA. Most CPAs belong to both the AICPA and a state society.

The State Boards

The actual licensing of CPAs is the responsibility of the various state boards of accountancy. State boards have sole authority to grant CPA certificates upon completion of all prerequisites and to suspend or revoke certificates for proper cause. State boards also administer the uniform national CPA exam. These boards are public agencies of the state in which they operate and may consist of from five to twenty-four members, most of whom are from public practice.

It is important to differentiate between the voluntary national and state organizations, which have no legal function, and the state boards, which do. If a CPA violates the code of ethics of the AICPA or of a state society, these organizations may expel that person from membership. Although such an expulsion would certainly damage the professional reputation of a CPA, it would not directly affect his or her ability to practice public accounting with the CPA designation. Membership in either type of organization is not necessary to practice as a CPA.

On the other hand, a state board may suspend or revoke a CPA certificate for a violation of its regulations. Without this certificate it would be illegal to practice as a CPA within the state. Since each state grants its own license, however, it would be possible (although not frequent) for a person with a revoked CPA certificate in one state to practice as a CPA in another state under that state's certificate. At present, there is no national licensing of CPAs.

CPA Firms

Public accounting firms may be proprietorships, partnerships, or corporations (in some states). However, despite their organizational form, CPA firms are generally classified as local, regional, or national.

Local Firms

These firms are typically partnerships or corporations owned by a few CPAs. They generally have only one office and service clients within or close to one city or town. The independent audit work of local firms is limited since most companies with regular financial statement audits require larger CPA firms for this work. Local firms do a great deal of bookkeeping work, financial statement preparation, and tax work. They also perform management advisory services for clients.

Regional Firms

Regional firms may have offices in a few cities or even in adjacent states. These firms are characterized by more partners and a larger professional staff. Because of their larger size, regional firms do more auditing and less "write-up" work than local firms. Tax and management services are an important part of the activity of regional firms.

National Firms

These firms have offices in most major and many smaller cities. Some have offices throughout the world and are sometimes called international firms. National firms may have hundreds of partners and a professional staff in the thousands. Auditing generally accounts for most of the activity in these large firms, and write-up is only a small portion of the services provided.

The Big Eight

The largest of the international firms are called the "Big Eight." Almost all of the major corporations in the U.S. are audit clients of one of these firms. Exhibit 1–2 shows the Big Eight firms, their approximate U.S. and worldwide revenues and *Fortune* 500 clients as of the late 1970s, a statement of how each firm sees itself, and a general statement of how each firm is seen by its competitors. Since the Big Eight firms are all partnerships, they are not required to report publicly on their revenue, expense, and income activity or on their financial position. However, in recent years, many of the Big Eight have voluntarily begun producing and disseminating annual reports on their activities.

The national CPA firms and the Big Eight in particular are powerful forces in the public accounting profession. Thus, some familiarity with them is important to understanding the profession.

AN AUDIT OF THE BIG EIGHT

Firm	Worldwide Revenues	U.S. Revenues (in millions)	Number of FORTUNE 500 Clients (1977)	How They See Themselves	How Competitors See Them
Peat Marwick Mitchell	$516 (Fiscal 1977 in millions)	$365	67	Aggressive but not in an unprofessional way. We have the best people. Biggest weakness: too decentralized	Trying to recover from past problems with SEC. Very aggressive. Price cutter. Expanding scope of practice.
Coopers & Lybrand	$490	$256	50	Tough. We work harder. We've got a winner's kind of feeling. Our real strength is in the management team.	Has changed a lot. Most aggressive of the eight in handling business. Price cutter.
Price Waterhouse & Co	$479	$245	99	The premier accounting firm. We are to accounting what sterling is to silver. Our clients are the cream.	Not very aggressive. Staff getting steamed up after losing some clients.
Arthur Andersen & Co	$471	$351	72	Tough. Aggressive. We speak with one voice everywhere. Not well known outside the U.S.	Aggressive. Likes publicity. First to emphasize growth. No room for individual thought.
Deloitte Haskins & Sells	$410	$220	53	Not as aggressive as many of the Big Eight. Technical leader in the profession. The "auditor's auditor."	Nursery. Aggressive. Narrow in scope of services. Getting their act together. Strong individuals.
Arthur Young & Company	$390	$210	52	Tend to be less aggressive than others. Heavy emphasis on client service. We do not want to be the biggest.	Not as aggressive as other Big Eight firms. Widely respected. Super-professional.
Ernst & Ernst	$385	$285	61	A practical firm. Pragmatic. We put strong emphasis on quality service to our existing clients.	Sleepy. Not growing as fast except in certain industries. Lost their competitive edge. Loosed organization overseas.
Touche Ross & Co	$350	$185	24	We want to be the best. We're not as big as we want to be. We're not price cutters but we are price competitors.	Very aggressive in handling business. Enamored of size. Price cutter. Weak overseas.

EXHIBIT 1–2   An Audit of the Big Eight.* (July 17, 1978)

*The data on FORTUNE 500 Clients were prepared by Deloitte Haskins & Sells and Price Waterhouse. "The big accounting firms are private partnerships, and they have only recently begun releasing financial information about their own operations. Arthur Andersen was the first to issue an annual report, five years ago [1973]. Last year, [1977] Peat, Marwick, Mitchell and Price Waterhouse also published annual reports. Touche Ross has disclosed only its revenues. The other four firms released their revenue figures to FORTUNE—the first time they have let this information out. The Peat, Marwick figure for U.S. revenues is an estimate. The Touche Ross numbers do not reflect the firm's 1977 merger with J.K. Lasser." Reprinted from FORTUNE Magazine.

Hierarchy Within CPA Firms

The standard organization structure of a CPA firm is:

Partner
Manager
Senior
Assistant (or Junior)

This hierarchy is intended to be representative of most firms. Small firms may have fewer ranks, while larger firms may have more ranks or further breakdowns within each rank.

The basic ranks of CPA firms are summarized in Exhibit 1–3. It is not possible to draw an organization chart for a CPA firm as is done for most businesses because the managers, seniors, and juniors essentially form a pool for each audit, and the partner selects the appropriate sized audit team from the pool.

Naturally, the audit for a large business will require more people than the audit for a smaller one, and some audit procedures require more people than others. Thus, the same audit engagement may have a different number of people assigned to it at different states of its completion. As a result, when their assigned work on one audit is complete, auditors go back into the pool to be assigned to another audit and possibly another partner.

On any particular day, the CPA firm has an organization chart. However, this organization chart is never drawn because it changes every day as some audits begin, some audits conclude, and some auditors are released from one audit and join another.

EXHIBIT 1-3   Ranks Within a CPA Firm

Rank	Years with Firm	Annual Salary in 1980	Duties
Partner	10+	$50,000+	Relationship with client; overall responsibility for audit; signs audit opinion and management letter; billing and collection of fees.
Manager	6–9	$35,000 to $50,000	Supervisor of audit; helps senior plan audit program and time budgets; reviews working papers, audit opinion, and management letter.
Senior	3–5	$20,000 to $35,000	In charge of the audit on the job; holds costs and time within budget; directs and reviews work of the juniors.
Assistant (or Junior)	0–2	$12,000 to $20,000	Performs detailed audit procedures; prepares working papers documenting work accomplished.

Assistant

The first job for a young accountant right out of school will be as an assistant. The assistant is the most junior member of the firm and is sometimes called a junior rather than assistant. The assistant's primary tasks are to perform the detailed steps of the audit, such as mailing accounts receivable confirmations, reconciling bank accounts, footing columns to check accuracy, and verifying physical inventory. Additionally, the assistant must document these efforts in the working papers.

During his tenure as an assistant, the young accountant learns the nuts and bolts of auditing. In addition, he may work on a wide variety of jobs in a number of cities and towns and thus, gain an invaluable breadth of business experience.

Though much of his work is routine, the assistant should not do his work mechanically; he should be thinking of its implications. As an example, an assistant in one of the largest CPA firms prepared some confirmations for a client but did not mail them at the end of the day. The next day, the president of the client company reminded him twice of the importance of mailing the confirmations as quickly as possible. Becoming suspicious, the assistant opened some confirmations and discovered that the client had, during the previous evening, opened the envelopes and altered the confirmations. When the partner was informed, the CPA firm immediately resigned from the engagement. The client was subsequently found to have grossly overstated its assets, was eventually declared bankrupt, and was liquidated.

Senior

The senior is in charge of the audit field work. He will stay at the client's offices while the audit procedures are being conducted. The senior plans the assistants' work, reviews the working papers they prepare, and provides guidance in performance of their tasks.

The most difficult part of the senior's job is to get the audit work done in an adequate manner within the time constraints set by the partner. The partner and client establish a fee for the audit, and this fee establishes the amount of time the senior is given to perform the audit.

Manager

The manager is generally not at the client's office performing the audit on a day-to-day basis. His is a supervisory role. While the senior is usually involved in only one audit at a time, the manager supervises several audits simultaneously.

The manager's primary task is to ensure that his audits are progressing according to schedule and budget. He will guide and assist the senior as necessary. He also provides the required review of the work done in the field.

Partner

The partner has two primary tasks: (1) he deals with the client, and (2) he has overall responsibility for the audit. In dealing with the client, he must explain what the audit will involve, how much time it will take, what will be expected of the client, when the audited financial statements will be ready, and how much the audit fee will be. These negotiations are often difficult because the client wants the audit done quickly, with minimum disruption, and for a low cost—generally an impossible combination.

The partner has overall responsibility for the audit and must make any difficult decisions involving judgement. For example, suppose there were an uncertainty attached to a contingent liability, such as a lawsuit. The partner is the one who must ultimately decide whether the uncertainty requires a qualified opinion. Similar decisions are often faced in connection with other elements of financial statement disclosure or fairness of presentation.

Evolution of the Standards of the Profession

The organized profession, through its various committees and boards, has been promulgating standards since 1917. As early as 1932, the American Institute of Accountants (AIA—forerunner to the AICPA) established basic principles of accounting that were deemed applicable to companies listed on the New York Stock Exchange.

The standards of the public accounting profession are considered to be: (1) generally accepted accounting principles (GAAP), (2) generally accepted auditing standards (GAAS), and (3) the Code of Professional Ethics. The first two of these are discussed in this chapter, and the code of ethics is presented in Chapter 2.

Accounting Principles

In 1939, the AIA authorized its Committee on Accounting Procedure to issue formal pronouncements on accounting matters. These official pronouncements were called *Accounting Research Bulletins.* From 1939 to 1959, this committee issued 51 bulletins dealing with recommended accounting practices. In 1959, the Committee on Accounting Procedure and the Committee on Terminology (a second official committee) were replaced by the Accounting Principles Board (APB). This change was part of a move to emphasize research and theory in the development of accounting principles and to narrow inconsistencies and alternative acceptable principles. From 1959 through 1973, the APB issued 31 Opinions and 4 Statements, with the Opinions carrying more formal authority because they were assumed to represent "substantial authoritative support" for the particular principles covered. Throughout the life of both the Committee on Accounting Procedure and the Accounting Principles Board, the Institute relied on voluntary acceptance of its pronouncements because it lacked any basis for requiring compliance with these accounting principles.

The FASB

Widespread criticism of the APB from within and outside of the profession resulted in the creation of the Wheat Commission to study the process of establishing and communicating accounting principles. The recommendations of this commission, which included discontinuation of the APB and creation of a new body independent of the AICPA to develop accounting principles, were accepted by the Council of the Institute in 1972. The Financial Accounting Standards Board (FASB) was created with the hope that official pronouncements would have greater acceptability and respectability if the rule-making body were independent of the AICPA.

The FASB is independent of the AICPA and is made up of seven full-time members with four coming from public accounting. Members are appointed by the Board of Trustees of the Financial Accounting Foundation. These trustees are, in turn, appointed by the Board of Directors of the Institute. The FASB, then, is one step removed from the controlling body of the AICPA and is also funded independently.

The principles promulgated by the Committee on Accounting Procedure, the APB, and the FASB constitute GAAP from "within" the profession. The Code of Professional Ethics of the AICPA requires that members justify departures from these principles in their work. Exhibit 1–4 gives a comprehensive list of the Statements of the FASB as of June, 1981.

Auditing Standards

Formed in 1939 by the AIA, the Committee on Auditing Procedure was charged with the task of investigating and reporting on auditing matters (particularly the McKesson & Robbins, Inc., case discussed in Chapter 3). Shortly thereafter, this committee was given authority to issue guidelines for use by independent public accountants in conducting an audit. These guidelines were called *Statements on Auditing Procedure*.

The Committee on Auditing Procedure functioned as the major body empowered to issue guidelines on auditing and reporting for 33 years. Most major areas of auditing judgement and procedure have been a topic of a Committee on Auditing Procedure pronouncement.

From time to time, the committee summarized and codified all previous pronouncements into one statement. This occurred in 1951, for the first 24 statements, and again in 1963 for all statements through 32. Throughout this period, the strength of these guidelines rested upon their voluntary acceptance by AICPA members.

EXHIBIT 1-4 Pronouncements on Generally Accepted Accounting Principles

Date	Statement Number	Title
Dec., 1973	1	Disclosure of Foreign Currency Translation Information
Oct., 1974	2	Accounting for Research and Development Costs
Dec., 1974	3	Reporting Accounting Changes in Interim Financial Statements
Mar., 1975	4	Reporting Gains and Losses from Extinguishment of Debt
Mar., 1975	5	Accounting for Contingencies
May, 1975	6	Classification of Short-term Obligations Expected to be Refinanced
June, 1975	7	Accounting and Reporting by Development Stage Enterprises
Oct., 1975	8	Accounting for the Translation of Foreign Currency Transactions and Foreign Currency Financial Statements
Oct., 1975	9	Accounting for Income Taxes—Oil and Gas Producing Companies
Oct., 1975	10	Extension of "Grandfather" Provisions for Business Combinations
Dec., 1975	11	Accounting for Contingencies—Transition Method
Dec., 1975	12	Accounting for Certain Marketable Securities
Nov., 1976	13	Accounting for Leases
Dec., 1976	14	Financial Reporting for Segments of a Business Enterprise
June, 1977	15	Accounting by Debtors and Creditors for Troubled Debt Restructurings
June, 1977	16	Prior Period Adjustments
Nov., 1977	17	Accounting for Leases—Initial Direct Costs (Amendment of FASB Statement No. 13)
Nov., 1977	18	Financial Reporting for Segments of a Business Enterprise—Interim Financial Statements (Amendment of FASB Statement No. 14)
Dec., 1977	19	Financial Accounting and Reporting by Oil and Gas Producing Companies
Dec., 1977	20	Accounting for Foreign Exchange Contracts
Apr., 1978	21	Suspension of the Reporting of Earnings Per Share and Segment Information by Nonpublic Enterprises (Amendment of APB Opinion No. 15 and FASB Statement No. 14)
June, 1978	22	Changes in the Provisions of Lease Agreements Resulting From Refundings of Tax-Exempt Debt (Amendment of FASB Statement No. 13)
Aug., 1978	23	Inception of the Lease (Amendment of FASB Statement No. 13)
Dec., 1978	24	Reporting Segment Information in Financial Statements that are Presented in Another Enterprise's Financial Report (An Amendment of FASB Statement No. 14)
Feb., 1979	25	Suspension of Certain Accounting Requirements for Oil and Gas Producing Companies (An Amendment of FASB Statement No. 19)

EXHIBIT 1-4   (Continued)

Apr.,	1979	26	Profit Recognition on Sales-Type Leases of Real Estate (An Amendment of FASB Statement No. 13)
May,	1979	27	Classification of Renewals or Extensions of Existing Sales-Type or Direct Financing Leases (An Amendment of FASB Statement No. 13)
May,	1979	28	Accounting for Sales With Leasebacks (An Amendment of FASB Statement No. 13)
June,	1979	29	Determining Contingent Rentals (An Amendment of FASB Statement No. 13)
Aug.,	1979	30	Disclosure of Information About Major Customers (An Amendment of FASB Statement No. 14)
Sept.,	1979	31	Accounting For Tax Benefits Related to U.K. Tax Legislation Concerning Stock Relief
Sept.,	1979	32	Specialized Accounting and Reporting Principles and Practices in AICPA Statements of Position and Guides on Accounting and Auditing Matters
Sept.,	1979	33	Financial Reporting and Changing Prices
Oct.,	1979	34	Capitalization of Interest Cost
Mar.,	1980	35	Accounting and Reporting By Defined Benefit Pension Plans
Apr.,	1980	36	Disclosure of Pension Information
June,	1980	37	Balance Sheet Classification of Deferred Income Taxes
Sept.,	1980	38	Accounting for Preacquisition Contingencies of Purchased Enterprises
Oct.,	1980	39	Financial Reporting and Changing Prices: Specialized Assets—Mining and Oil and Gas
Oct.,	1980	40	Financial Reporting and Changing Prices: Specialized Assets—Timberlands and Growing Timber
Oct.,	1980	41	Financial Reporting and Changing Prices: Specialized Assets—Income-Producing Real Estate
Oct.,	1980	42	Determining Materiality for Capitalization of Interest Cost
Oct.,	1980	43	Accounting for Compensated Absences
Oct.,	1980	44	Accounting for Intangible Assets of Motor Carriers
Mar.,	1981	45	Accounting for Franchise Fee Revenue
Mar.,	1981	46	Financial Reporting and Changing Prices: Motion Picture Films
Apr.,	1981	47	Disclosure of Long-Term Obligations
June,	1981	48	Revenue Recognition When Right of Return Exists
June,	1981	49	Accounting for Product Financing Arrangements

Statements on Auditing Standards

In 1972, the Committee on Auditing Procedure was replaced by the Auditing Standards Executive Committee (AudSEC), and previous Statements on Auditing Procedure were incorporated into and superseded by *Statement on Auditing Standards No. 1*, the first of a new series on auditing and disclosure matters. At approximately this same time, the Code of Professional Ethics was revised to include a requirement that independent auditors adhere to the guidelines of these committees or be prepared to justify their departures from the Statements.

The Auditing Standards Executive Committee was renamed the Auditing Standards Board (ASB) in 1978. The functions of the ASB remained the same as those of its predecessor (AudSEC), although the number of members on the board was decreased, and certain other administrative changes were made within the AICPA.

Exhibit 1–5 gives a comprehensive list of auditing pronouncements as of June 1981. These have been codified by the AICPA and are contained in a book on *Professional Standards* that is updated each year. References hereafter such as AU 150 indicate the section in the professional standards where particular passages are to be found.

1.3 ATTESTATION—COMMUNICATING THE RESULTS OF AN AUDIT

The goal of financial statement auditing is a report that expresses the opinion of the independent auditor on the relationship between the financial statements and the underlying events and activities they represent. This relationship is expressed in terms of whether or not the financial statements present fairly the activities and position of the organization.

Auditor's Standard Report

The most common form of auditor communication to interested users is called the Auditor's Standard Report. Exhibit 1–6 presents three such reports for major U.S. corporations.

Two points should be noted about these standard reports before their specific content is examined.

1. The audit report is addressed to the owners or to the owners and directors of the business rather than to company management. This emphasizes the attestation function of the independent auditor.
2. The report is signed in the name of the CPA firm undertaking the audit rather than by the individual auditors or partners. This emphasizes that the entire firm has taken responsibility for the integrity of the audit.

EXHIBIT 1-5   Pronouncements on Generally Accepted Auditing Standards

Date	Statement Number	Title
		Statements on Auditing Standards
Nov., 1972	1	Codification of Auditing Standards and Procedures Statements on Auditing Procedures No. 1-54 (1939-1972)
Oct., 1974	2	Reports on Auditing
Dec., 1974	3	The Effects of EDP on the Auditor's Study and Evaluation of Internal Control
Dec., 1974	4	Quality Control Considerations for a Firm of Independent Auditors
July, 1975	5	The Meaning of "Present Fairly in Conformity with Generally Accepted Accounting Principles" in the Independent Auditor's Report
July, 1975	6	Related Party Transactions
Oct., 1975	7	Communications Between Predecessor and Successor Auditors
Dec., 1975	8	Other Information in Documents Containing Audited Financial Statements
Dec., 1975	9	The Effect of an Internal Audit Function on the Scope of the Independent Auditor's Examination
Dec., 1975	10	Limited Review of Interim Financial Information
Dec., 1975	11	Using the Work of a Specialist
Jan., 1976	12	Inquiry of a Client's Lawyer Concerning Litigation, Claims, and Assessments
May, 1976	13	Reports of Limited Review of Interim Financial Information
Dec., 1976	14	Special Reports
Dec., 1976	15	Reports on Comparative Financial Statements
Jan., 1977	16	The Independent Auditor's Responsibility for the Detection of Errors or Irregularities
Jan., 1977	17	Illegal Acts By Clients
May, 1977	18	Unaudited Replacement Cost Information
July, 1977	19	Client Representations
Sept., 1977	20	Required Communication of Material Weaknesses in Internal Accounting Control
Dec., 1977	21	Segment Information
Mar., 1978	22	Planning and Supervision
Oct., 1978	23	Analytical Review Procedures
Mar., 1979	24	Review of Interim Financial Information
Nov., 1979	25	Relationship of Generally Accepted Auditing Standards to Quality Control Standards
Nov., 1979	26	Association With Financial Statements
Dec., 1979	27	Supplementary Information Required by the Financial Accounting Standards Board
May, 1980	28	Supplementary Information on the Effects of Changing Prices
July, 1980	29	Reporting on Information Accompanying the Basic Financial Statements in Auditor-Submitted Documents

Continued on the following page

EXHIBIT 1-5 (Continued)

July,	1980	30	Reporting on Internal Accounting Control
Aug.,	1980	31	Evidential Matter
Oct.,	1980	32	Adequacy of Disclosure in Financial Statements
Oct.,	1980	33	Supplementary Oil and Gas Reserve Information
Mar.,	1981	34	The Auditor's Considerations When a Question Arises About an Entity's Continued Existence
April,	1981	35	Special Reports—Applying Agreed-Upon Procedures to Specified Elements, Accounts, or Items of a Financial Statement
April,	1981	36	Review of Interim Financial Information
April,	1981	37	Filings Under Federal Securities Statutes
April,	1981	38	Letters for Underwriters
June,	1981	39	Audit Sampling
			Statements on Standards for Accounting and Review Services
Dec.,	1978	1	Compilation and Review of Financial Statements
Oct.,	1979	2	Comparative Financial Statements
			Statement on Quality Control Standards
Nov.,	1979	1	System of Quality Control For a CPA Firm

The Scope Paragraph

Usually the first paragraph in the standard auditor's report, these sentences describe the particular financial statements examined and the nature of the examination. The nature of the examination is described in terms of generally accepted auditing standards and notes that any auditing procedures deemed necessary by the independent CPAs were carried out. This implies that the scope of the audit was not limited by company management.

The generally accepted auditing standards referred to in the scope paragraph consist of ten fundamental statements about the conduct of all audits. Nine of these were adopted by the AICPA in 1948 (one was added later), and they remain intact today. These standards should be differentiated from auditing procedures, which are specific tasks to be accomplished on a particular audit and may change from one audit to another.

Generally accepted auditing standards consist of ten guidelines divided into three groups:

General Standards

1. The examination is to be performed by a person or persons having adequate technical training and proficiency as an auditor.

Report of independent certified public accountants

To the Share Owners and Board of Directors of
General Electric Company

We have examined the statement of financial position of General Electric Company and consolidated affiliates as of December 31, 1978 and 1977, and the related statements of earnings, changes in financial position and changes in share owners' equity for the years then ended. Our examinations were made in accordance with generally accepted auditing standards, and accordingly included such tests of the accounting records and such other auditing procedures as we considered necessary in the circumstances.

In our opinion, the aforementioned financial statements present fairly the financial position of General Electric Company and consolidated affiliates at December 31, 1978 and 1977, and the results of their operations and the changes in their financial position for the years then ended, in conformity with generally accepted accounting principles applied on a consistent basis.

Peat, Marwick, Mitchell & Co

Peat, Marwick, Mitchell & Co.
345 Park Avenue, New York, N.Y. 10022
February 16, 1979

Report of Certified Public Accountants

To the Shareholders and Board of Directors of
Sears, Roebuck and Co.:

We have examined the Statements of Financial Position of Sears, Roebuck and Co. and consolidated subsidiaries as of January 31, 1979 and 1978, and the related Statements of Income, Shareholders' Equity and Changes in Financial Position for the years then ended. Our examinations were made in accordance with generally accepted auditing standards and, accordingly, included such tests of the accounting records and such other auditing procedures as we considered necessary in the circumstances.

In our opinion, the financial statements referred to above present fairly the financial position of Sears, Roebuck and Co. and consolidated subsidiaries at January 31, 1979 and 1978, and the results of their operations and changes in their financial position for the years then ended, in conformity with generally accepted accounting principles applied on a consistent basis.

Touche Ross & Co.

Chicago, Illinois, April 9, 1979

Report of Independent Accountants

To the Shareholders of Exxon Corporation

In our opinion, the consolidated financial statements appearing on pages 24 through 35 present fairly the financial position of Exxon Corporation and its subsidiary companies at December 31, 1978 and 1979 and the results of their operations and the changes in their financial position for the years then ended, in conformity with generally accepted accounting principles consistently applied. Our examinations of these statements were made in accordance with generally accepted auditing standards and accordingly included such tests of the accounting records and such other auditing procedures as we considered necessary in the circumstances.

153 East 53rd Street
New York, New York 10022
March 4, 1980

Price Waterhouse & Co.

EXHIBIT 1–6   The Auditor's Standard Report

2. In all matters relating to the assignment, an independence in mental attitude is to be maintained by the auditor or auditors.

3. Due professional care is to be exercised in the performance of the examination and the preparation of the report.

Standards of Field Work

1. The work is to be adequately planned and assistants, if any, are to be properly supervised.

2. There is to be a proper study and evaluation of the existing internal control as a basis for reliance thereon and for the determination of the resultant extent of the tests to which auditing procedures are to be restricted.

3. Sufficient competent evidential matter is to be obtained through inspection, observation, inquiries, and confirmations to afford a reasonable basis for an opinion regarding the financial statements under examination.

Standards of Reporting

1. The report shall state whether the financial statements are presented in accordance with generally accepted accounting principles.

2. The report shall state whether such principles have been consistently observed in the current period in relation to the preceding period.

3. Informative disclosures in the financial statements are to be regarded as reasonably adequate unless otherwise stated in the report.

4. The report shall either contain an expression of opinion regarding the financial statements, taken as a whole, or an assertion to the effect that an opinion cannot be expressed. When an overall opinion cannot be expressed, the reasons therefor should be stated. In all cases where an auditor's name is associated with financial statements, the report should contain a clearcut indication of the character of the auditor's examination, if any, and the degree of responsibility he is taking.

The general standards focus on the preparation, attitude, and professionalism of the independent auditor. These are the most philosophical of the GAAS and set the tone for the remaining standards. Field work standards broadly guide the conduct of the audit and have to do with work done while in contact with the client as the audit is under way. The reporting standards deal with attestation and the communication function of the auditor.

The Opinion Paragraph

The opinion paragraph is normally the second paragraph in the standard report. It deals with the basis for the preparation of the financial statements (generally accepted accounting principles, consistently applied) and gives the auditor's opinion on the fairness of the financial statement package. The auditor's opinion is an implicit statement of the responsibility he is assuming.

Unqualified Opinion

When the auditor states that the entire financial statement package "presents fairly" the position and activities of an organization, the opinion is *unqualified*. All three opinions illustrated in Exhibit 1–6 are unqualified opinions, as are the overwhelming majority of opinions issued by auditors. An unqualified opinion makes three basic statements about the audit and the financial statement package.

1. That the audit was conducted in accordance with GAAS and that the auditors determined the appropriate auditing procedures and tests for the situation.
2. That no major uncertainty exists in the auditor's mind as to the fairness of the financial statements.
3. That the financial statements were prepared and presented based on the consistent application of GAAP.

When one or more of these assertions cannot be made by the auditor, an unqualified opinion cannot be issued, and one of three other possible opinions must be chosen.

Qualified Opinion

Sometimes an auditor may feel that the financial statements taken as a whole do present fairly the financial circumstances of an organization, but he or she cannot make one or more of the three assertions necessary for an unqualified opinion. In this situation, a *qualified* opinion would be issued noting any material exceptions to the three assertions.

Disclaimer of Opinion

When the scope of an audit has been so limited or an unresolved uncertainty is potentially serious, an auditor may not be able to render an opinion (even qualified) on the financial statements. In these circumstances, a *disclaimer of opinion* (in other words, an inability to give an opinion) is necessary together with the reasons for the disclaimer. A disclaimer will almost certainly have a negative impact on the credibility of the financial statements.

Adverse Opinion

This opinion would be used if the auditor feels that the audit has uncovered material, serious departures from GAAP and, as a result, the financial statements do not present fairly the position and activities of the organization. An adverse opinion removes from the financial statements all credibility for external users.

Notice that a limitation of scope or a major uncertainty would not lead to an adverse opinion. Only a significant departure from GAAP that has an impact on the financial statements as a whole would result in an adverse opinion.

Auditor's reports will be discussed and illustrated in depth in Chapter 12.

Important Points in the Auditor's Standard Report

The following points summarize the important features of the auditor's standard report:

1. Although most standard reports contain a scope paragraph and an opinion paragraph, some combine the two into one paragraph and alter the order of the sentences (see, for example, the Exxon Report of Independent Accountants in Exhibit 1–6).
2. The balance sheet, income statement, retained earnings statement, and statement of changes in financial position are all audited.
3. These statements are prepared by management, and management assumes primary responsibility for them. A formal statement of this responsibility is sometimes included as part of the annual report. Exhibit 1–7 illustrates two of these "Reports of Management."
4. The financial statements are examined, but the accounting records are only tested rather than totally and completely examined.
5. GAAS are applicable to all audits.
6. Auditing procedures may vary from audit to audit.
7. The auditor expresses an opinion on the fairness of the financial statements taken as a whole. He does not guarantee or certify their correctness or absolute accuracy or that they are free from fraud.
8. All financial statements should be prepared according to the applicable GAAP, which are consistently applied.
9. GAAP includes adequate disclosure of all material information necessary to make the statements not misleading.

1.4 AUDITING DEVELOPMENTS IN THE 1980s

The environment in which the public accounting profession must function and the very nature of auditing itself has changed dramatically through the decade of the 1970s. However, public accounting is a dynamic profession and has responded positively to these changes. As CPAs face the challenges of the 1980s, two areas of critical importance to independent audits will occupy much of the time, thoughts, and energies of the members and official bodies of the profession. The 1980s will likely see a resolution to these new issues.

Report of management

To the Share Owners of
General Electric Company

We have prepared the accompanying statement of financial position of General Electric Company and consolidated affiliates as of December 31, 1978 and 1977, and the related statements of earnings, changes in financial position and changes in share owners' equity for the years then ended, including the notes and industry and geographic segment information. The statements have been prepared in conformity with generally accepted accounting principles appropriate in the circumstances, and include amounts that are based on our best estimates and judgments. Financial information elsewhere in this Annual Report is consistent with that in the financial statements.

Your Company maintains a strong system of internal financial controls and procedures, supported by a corporate staff of traveling auditors and supplemented by resident auditors located around the world. This system is designed to provide reasonable assurance, at appropriate cost, that assets are safeguarded and that transactions are executed in accordance with management's authorization and recorded and reported properly. The system is time-tested, innovative and responsive

to change. Perhaps the most important safeguard in this system for share owners is the fact that the Company has long emphasized the selection, training and development of professional financial managers to implement and oversee the proper application of its internal controls and the reporting of management's stewardship of corporate assets and maintenance of accounts in conformity with generally accepted accounting principles.

The independent public accountants provide an objective, independent review as to management's discharge of its responsibilities insofar as they relate to the fairness of reported operating results and financial condition. They obtain and maintain an understanding of GE's accounting and financial controls, and conduct such tests and related procedures as they deem necessary to arrive at an opinion on the fairness of financial statements.

The Audit Committee of the Board of Directors, composed solely of Directors from outside the Company, meets with the independent public accountants, management and internal auditors periodically to review the work of each and ensure that each is properly discharging its responsibilities. (See Audit Committee report on page 25.) The independent public accountants have free access to this Com-

mittee, without management present, to discuss the results of their audit work and their opinions on the adequacy of internal financial controls and the quality of financial reporting.

Your management has long recognized its responsibility for conducting the Company's affairs in a manner which is responsive to the ever-increasing complexity of society. This responsibility is reflected in key Company policy statements regarding, among other things, potentially conflicting outside business interests of Company employees, proper conduct of domestic and international business activities, and compliance with antitrust laws. Educational, communication and review programs are designed to ensure that these policies are clearly understood and that there is awareness that deviation from them will not be tolerated.

Reginald H. Jones
Chairman of the Board
and Chief Executive Officer

Howay
Senior Vice President, Finance
February 16, 1979

Responsibility for Financial Statements

The financial statements herein have been prepared under management direction from accounting records which management believes fairly and accurately reflect the transactions and financial position of the company. Management has established a system of internal control to provide reasonable assurance that assets are maintained and accounted for in accordance with its authorizations and that transactions are recorded accurately on the company's books and records.

The company's comprehensive internal audit program provides for constant evaluation of the adequacy and effectiveness of the internal controls and measures adherence to

management's established policies and procedures. The company's formally stated and communicated policy demands of employes high ethical standards in their conduct of its business.

The Audit Committee of the Board of Directors is composed entirely of directors who are not employes of the company. The committee meets periodically to review audit plans, internal controls, financial reports and related matters and has unrestricted access to the public accountants and to the internal auditors with or without management attendance.

Sears, Roebuck and Company

EXHIBIT 1–7   Report of Management

CONCEPT SUMMARY
The Four Auditor's Opinions

		OPINION			
		Unqualified	*Qualified*	*Disclaimer*	*Adverse*
CONDITIONS	SCOPE	Not limited	Limited	Significantly limited	—
	MAJOR UNCERTAINTY	None	Yes—minor impact on fairness	Yes—potentially serious impact on fairness	—
	GAAP	In accordance, consistently applied	Not in accordance or not consistently applied—minor impact on fairness	—	Not in accordance or not consistently applied—major impact on fairness

Detection of Fraud and Other Illegal Acts

The gap between expectations of regulatory agencies and financial statement users and the official position of the profession is probably wider here than on any other issue.

The following quotations from Ray Garrett, Jr., then Chairman of the Securities and Exchange Commission, sum up the views of many people in government regulatory agencies and many financial statement users.

> **A really successful fraud can scarcely be accomplished in our complex financial world without the help of accountants and lawyers. This may be active and intentional connivance or it may be more passive and subtle, but it is frequently essential. (***SEC News Digest,*** May 31, 1974).**

> **I think accountants should be willing to assume responsibility for the detection of management fraud. (Speech to AICPA Annual Meeting, 1973).**

This position on fraud detection seems at odds with the basic premise that ordinary audits cannot be relied upon to detect fraud because of the limited nature of the audit. An interpretation of the official position of the accounting profession on the detection of fraud given by an acknowledged leader of the profession is as follows:

1. Auditors accept the responsibility to uncover those material frauds that would be found by the application of generally accepted auditing standards (GAAS).

2. GAAS are designed in part to discover material fraud, particularly deliberate misrepresentations of management.

3. Frauds involving collusion, forgery or unrecorded transactions may not be detected by the application of GAAS.

4. There can be no absolute assurance that fraud will be detected.

5. Despite the limitations, auditors do provide substantial assurance of the reliability of financial statements.[1]

Categorical limitation of liability has been largely ignored by the public and the SEC. When a major fraud has gone undetected, the audit is automatically placed in an unfavorable light, and the auditor's best defense lies in showing that both his judgement and his work have been adequate. Official pronouncements on fraud detection provide guidelines for the auditor. However, responsibility for fraud detection will probably continue to be judged contextually based on the auditor's judgement and actions in a particular situation.

Judgement in Work and Disclosure

As the accounting profession began to come of age, interest in the professional judgement of auditors and how this judgement is applied began to grow. At the same time, an evolution in the definition of "adequate work" was taking place, and user expectations for "adequate disclosure" were undergoing substantial changes. Essentially, the disclosure requirements faced by auditors began evolving on two fronts. First, the adequacy of presentation by the auditor and the clarity of his communications became an issue. Second, the auditor's responsibilities for disclosure when irregularities are discovered began to expand significantly.

New Standards of Work and Disclosure

There have been rapid changes in what is expected of auditors in fulfilling their professional responsibilities. Specifically:

1. GAAP and GAAS have become the minimum standards of behavior to which auditors may be held.

2. Contextual decisions about the auditor's judgement on the applicability of GAAP and GAAS as well as his judgement in their application have become commonplace.

3. An auditor may be responsible for judgements where there are no professional standards if the judgements are unreasonable or carelessly made.

---

[1]Wallace E. Olson, "A Look at the Responsibility Gap," *The Journal of Accountancy* (January, 1975). Mr. Olson is a former president of the AICPA and was formerly executive partner of Alexander Grant & Company, as well as a member of the Study Group on Establishment of Accounting Principles, which recommended formulation of the FASB.

4. "Presents fairly" has begun to take on a meaning apart from GAAP, with that meaning applied to the totality of the auditor's work (the financial statements as a whole), not merely the individual judgements.

5. The auditor has begun to be viewed as communicator of meaningful, relevant information to the "average prudent person."

The profession's position on adequate work and disclosure is given in a number of official pronouncements. Generally, these pronouncements conclude that overall fairness in the presentation of financial statements requires: (1) that the substance of transactions be captured, (2) that GAAP are designed to report substance over form, and (3) that, in recording transactions in accordance with their substance, the auditor's judgement should be used to select the accounting principles most applicable to a particular circumstance.

In essence, the auditor is required to exercise his best judgement in the expression of an opinion as to whether:

1. Accounting principles selected and applied have general acceptance.

2. Accounting principles are appropriate in the circumstances.

3. Financial statements, including the related notes, are informative of matters that may affect their use, understanding, and interpretation.

4. Information presented in the financial statements is classified and summarized in a reasonable manner, that is, neither too detailed nor too condensed.

5. Financial statements reflect the underlying events and transactions in a manner that presents the financial position, results of operations, and changes in financial position stated within a range of limits that are reasonable and practicable to attain in financial statements.

The profession's responses to developments in the areas of fraud detection and professional judgement have been significant. The creation of the FASB represents an attempt to improve the quality of GAAP and the credibility of the process for their formulation. The new approach to statements on auditing matters and the substance of the statements themselves are designed to close the gap between public expectations and professional standards.

Auditing is a dynamic activity, and the environment of the public accounting profession has been in constant change over the past decade. Three of the major elements in this environment will be explored in the next two chapters. The ethical and regulatory environments of public accounting are the subjects of Chapter 2, and the legal environment will be discussed in Chapter 3.

Key Terms

adverse opinion

American Accounting Association (AAA)

American Institute of Certified Public Accountants (AICPA)

attestation

audit engagement

auditing

Auditing Standards Board (ASB)

auditor

Big Eight

certified public accountant (CPA)

disclaimer of opinion

Financial Accounting Standards Board (FASB)

General Accounting Office (GAO)

generally accepted accounting principles (GAAP)

generally accepted auditing standards (GAAS)

government auditor

independent auditor

Institute of Internal Auditors (IIA)

internal auditor

management report

opinion paragraph

qualified opinion

scope paragraph

standard report

state board

state society

unqualified opinion

Questions and Problems

Questions

1-1 Contrast the approaches to auditing taken by the AICPA, AAA, GAO, and IIA.

1-2 Discuss the primary assumptions underlying financial statement audits. Which of these assumptions may not always hold true?

1-3 What is the role of: (a) the AICPA, (b) the state societies, and (c) the state boards in the public accounting profession? How do the state boards differ from the voluntary societies?

1-4 Describe the evolution of GAAP citing the important committees and boards that have held rule-making authority and the reasons why these rule-making bodies were changed as GAAP evolved.

1-5 Describe the evolution of GAAS citing the important committees and boards that have held rule-making authority.

1-6 Discuss the function of the scope paragraph in the auditor's standard report. Discuss the function of the opinion paragraph.

1-7   Name the four possible types of auditor's opinions. Give the assertions an auditor must be able to make in order to issue an unqualified opinion.

1-8   Distinguish the conditions that justify giving a qualified opinion instead of a disclaimer of opinion. Do the same for a qualified opinion and an adverse opinion.

1-9   Summarize the official position of the public accounting profession on the auditor's responsibility for the detection of fraud and other illegal acts.

1-10 Summarize the official position of the public accounting profession that provides guidelines for the auditor's judgement in work and disclosure.

Multiple Choice Questions From Professional Examinations

1-11 Which of the following best describes the reason why an independent auditor reports on financial statements?

   a. A management fraud may exist, and it is more likely to be detected by independent auditors.
   b. Different interests may exist between the company preparing the statements and the persons using the statements.
   c. A misstatement of account balances may exist and is generally corrected as the result of the independent auditor's work.
   d. A poorly designed internal control system may be in existence.

1-12 The independent audit is important to readers of financial statements because it

   a. Determines the future stewardship of the management of the company whose financial statements are audited.
   b. Measures and communicates financial and business data included in financial statements.
   c. Involves the objective examination of and reporting on management-prepared statements.
   d. Reports on the accuracy of all information in the financial statements.

1-13 In comparison to the external auditor, an internal auditor is more likely to be concerned with

   a. Internal administrative control.
   b. Cost accounting procedures.
   c. Operational auditing.
   d. Internal accounting control.

1-14 Operational audits generally have been conducted by internal auditors and government audit agencies but may be performed by certified public accountants. A primary purpose of an operational audit is to provide

a. A means of assurance that internal accounting controls are functioning as planned.

b. A measure of management performance in meeting organizational goals.

c. The results of internal examinations of financial and accounting matters to a company's top-level management.

d. Aid to the independent auditor who is conducting the examination of the financial statements.

1-15 The auditor's opinion makes reference to generally accepted accounting principles (GAAP). Which of the following best describes GAAP?

a. The interpretations of accounting rules and procedures by certified public accountants on audit engagements.

b. The pronouncements made by the Financial Accounting Standards Board and its predecessor, the Accounting Principles Board.

c. The guidelines set forth by various government agencies that derive their authority from Congress.

d. The conventions, rules, and procedures that are necessary to define accepted accounting practices at a particular time.

1-16 Which of the following best describes what is meant by generally accepted auditing standards?

a. Acts to be performed by the auditor.

b. Measures of the quality of the auditor's performance.

c. Procedures to be used to gather evidence to support financial statements.

d. Audit objectives generally determined on audit engagements.

1-17 The auditor's judgement concerning the overall fairness of the presentation of financial position, results of operations, and changes in financial position is applied within the framework of

a. Quality control.

b. Generally accepted auditing standards, which include the concept of materiality.

c. The auditor's evaluation of the audited company's internal control.

d. Generally accepted accounting principles.

1-18 An opinion as to the "fairness" of financial statement presentation in accordance with generally accepted accounting principles is based on several judgements made by the auditor. One such judgement is whether the accounting principles used

a. Have general acceptance.

b. Are promulgated by the AICPA Auditing Standards Executive Committee.

c. Are the most conservative of those available for use.

d. Emphasize the legal form of transactions.

1-19 Which of the following is mandatory if the auditor is to comply with generally accepted auditing standards?

    a. Possession by the auditor of adequate technical training.

    b. Use of analytical review on audit engagements.

    c. Use of statistical sampling whenever feasible on an audit engagement.

    d. Confirmation by the auditor of material accounts receivable balances.

1-20 An investor is reading the financial statements of the Stankey Corporation and observes that the statements are accompanied by an auditor's unqualified report. From this the investor may conclude that

    a. Any disputes over significant accounting issues have been settled to the auditor's satisfaction.

    b. The auditor is satisfied that Stankey is financially sound.

    c. The auditor has ascertained that Stankey's financial statements have been prepared accurately.

    d. Informative disclosures in the financial statements, but not necessarily in Stankey's footnotes, are to be regarded as reasonably adequate.

1-21 If the auditor believes that required disclosures of a significant nature are omitted from the financial statements under examination, the auditor should decide between issuing

    a. A qualified opinion or an adverse opinion.

    b. A disclaimer of opinion or a qualified opinion.

    c. An adverse opinion or a disclaimer of opinion.

    d. An unqualified opinion or a qualified opinion.

1-22 An auditor is unable to determine the amounts associated with certain illegal acts committed by a client. In these circumstances the auditor would most likely

    a. Issue either a qualified opinion or a disclaimer of opinion.

    b. Issue only an adverse opinion.

    c. Issue either a qualified opinion or an adverse opinion.

    d. Issue only a disclaimer of opinion.

1-23 Which of the following best describes why publicly traded corporations follow the practice of having the outside auditor appointed by the board of directors or elected by the stockholders?

    a. To comply with the regulations of the Financial Accounting Standards Board.

    b. To emphasize auditor independence from the management of the corporation.

   c. To encourage a policy of rotation of the independent auditors.

   d. To provide the corporate owners with an opportunity to voice their opinion concerning the quality of the auditing firm selected by the directors.

1-24 The ultimate risk against which the auditor requires reasonable protection is a combination of two separate risks. The first of these is that material errors will occur in the accounting process by which the financial statements are developed, and the second is that

   a. A company's system of internal control is not adequate to detect errors and irregularities.

   b. Those errors that occur will not be detected in the auditor's examination.

   c. Management may possess an attitude that lacks integrity.

   d. Evidential matter is not competent enough for the auditor to form an opinion based on reasonable assurance.

1-25 The major reason an independent auditor gathers audit evidence is to

   a. Form an opinion on the financial statements.

   b. Detect fraud.

   c. Evaluate management.

   d. Evaluate internal control.

Problems

1-26 Johnson, a local real estate broker, is a member of the board of directors of Pennset Corporation. At a recent board meeting called to discuss financial plans, Mr. Johnson discovered two planned expenditures for auditing. In the controller's department budget, he found an estimate for internal audit activity, and in the treasurer's budget he found an estimate for the annual audit by a CPA firm.

   Mr. Johnson could not understand the need for two different expenditures for auditing. Since the CPA fee for the annual audit was less than the cost of the internal audit activity, he proposed eliminating the internal audit function. Required:

   a. Explain to Johnson the different purposes served by the two audit activities.

   b. What benefits does the CPA firm performing an audit derive from the existence of an internal audit function?

CMA

1-27 Feiler, the sole owner of a small hardware business, has been told that the business should have financial statements reported on by an independent

CPA. Feiler, having some bookkeeping experience, has personally prepared the company's financial statements and does not understand why such statements should be examined by a CPA. Feiler discussed the matter with Farber, a CPA, and asked Farber to explain why an audit is considered important.

Required:

a. Describe the objectives of an independent audit.

b. Identify ten ways in which an independent audit may be beneficial to Feiler.

AICPA

1-28 The following three statements are representative of attitudes and opinions sometimes encountered by CPAs in their professional practices:

1. Today's audit consists of test checking. This is dangerous because test checking depends upon the auditor's judgement, which may be defective. An audit can be relied upon only if every transaction is verified.

2. An audit by a CPA is essentially negative and contributes to neither the gross national product nor the general well-being of society. The auditor does not create; he merely checks what someone else has done.

3. It is important to read the footnotes to financial statements, even though they often are presented in technical language and are incomprehensible. The auditor may reduce his exposure to third-party liability by stating something in the footnotes that contradicts completely what he has presented in the balance sheet or income statement.

Required:

Evaluate each of the above statements and indicate:

a. Areas of agreement with the statement, if any.

b. Areas of misconception, incompleteness, or fallacious reasoning included in the statement, if any.

Complete your discussion of each statement (both parts a and b) before going on to the next statement.

AICPA

1-29 During the course of an audit engagement, an independent auditor gives serious consideration to the concept of materiality. This concept is inherent in the work of the independent auditor and is important for planning, preparing, and modifying an audit. The concept of materiality underlies the application of all generally accepted auditing standards, particularly the standards dealing with fieldwork and reporting.

Required:

a. Briefly describe what is meant by the independent auditor's concept of materiality.

b. What are some common relationships and other considerations likely to be used by the auditor in judging materiality?

c. Identify how the planning and execution of an audit might be affected by the independent auditor's concept of materiality.

AICPA (adapted)

1-30 Important organizations in the public accounting profession include:

the AICPA
the state societies of CPAs
the state boards of accountancy
the FASB
the ASB
the individual CPA firms

Following are duties or activities which may be associated with one or more of these important organizations.

1. Maintains standards for entry into the public accounting profession.
2. Carries out the practice of public accounting.
3. Promulgates standards of professional practice and conduct.
4. Issues official pronouncements on accounting principles (GAAP).
5. Licenses individuals to practice as CPAs.
6. Licenses firms to practice as CPAs.
7. Issues official pronouncements on auditing standards (GAAS).
8. Administers the uniform CPA exam.
9. Revokes, for proper cause, the license of individuals to practice as CPAs.
10. Operates as an official unit of the AICPA.
11. Regulates the reporting of companies whose securities are traded publicly.

Required:

Identify the organizations that are associated with each of these activities. Note any activity that is associated with an organization other than those mentioned and any activity that is not associated with any organization.

1-31 Leer, CPA, has discussed various reporting considerations with three of Leer's audit clients. The three clients presented the following situations and asked how they would affect the audit report.

1. A client has changed its concept of "funds" on its statement of changes in financial position. Both Leer and the client agree that the new concept of "funds" is a more meaningful presentation. In prior years, when Leer issued an unqualified report on the client's comparative financial statements, this statement showed the net change in working capital, whereas in the current year, the statement shows the net change in the cash balance. The client agrees that the change is material but believes it is obvious to readers and need not be discussed in the footnotes to the financial statements or in Leer's report. The client is issuing comparative statements but wishes only to restate the prior year's statement to conform to the current format.

2. A client has a loan agreement that restricts the amount of cash dividends that can be paid and requires the maintenance of a particular current ratio. The client is in compliance with the terms of the agreement, and it is not likely that there will be a violation in the foreseeable future. The client believes there is no need to mention the restriction in the financial statements because such mention might mislead the readers.

3. During the year, a client correctly accounted for the acquisition of a majority-owned domestic subsidiary but did not properly present the minority interest in retained earnings or net income of the subsidiary in the consolidated financial statements. The client agrees with Leer that the minority interest presented in the consolidated financial statements is materially misstated but takes the position that the minority shareholders of the subsidiary should look to that subsidiary's financial statements for information concerning their interest therein.

Required:

Each of the situations above relates to one of the four generally accepted auditing standards of reporting. Identify and describe the applicable standard of reporting in each situation, and discuss how the particular client situation relates to the standard and to Leer's report.

Organize your answer as follows:

Situation No.	Applicable GAAS of Reporting	Discussion of Relationship of Client Situation to Standard of Reporting and to Leer's Report

AICPA

1-32 Ray, the owner of a small company, asked Holmes, CPA, to conduct an audit of the company's records. Ray told Holmes that an audit is to be completed in time to submit audited financial statements to a bank as part of a loan application. Holmes immediately accepted the engagement and agreed to provide an auditor's report within three weeks. Ray agreed to pay Holmes a fixed fee plus a bonus if the loan was granted.

Holmes hired two accounting students to conduct the audit and spent several hours telling them exactly what to do. Holmes told the students not to spend time reviewing the controls but instead to concentrate on proving the mathematical accuracy of the ledger accounts and summarizing the data in the accounting records that support Ray's financial statements. The students followed Holmes' instructions and after two weeks gave Holmes the financial statements, which did not include footnotes. Holmes reviewed the statements and prepared an unqualified auditor's report. The report, however, did not refer to generally accepted accounting principles nor to the year-to-year application of such principles.

Required:

Briefly describe each of the generally accepted auditing standards and indicate how the action(s) of Holmes resulted in a failure to comply with each standard.

Organize your answer as follows:

Brief Description of Generally Accepted Auditing Standards	Holmes' Actions Resulting in Failure to Comply with Generally Accepted Auditing Standards

AICPA

1-33 Upon completion of all field work on September 23, 1982, the following "shortform" report was rendered by Timothy Ross to the directors of The Rancho Corporation.

To the Directors of The Rancho Corporation:

We have examined the balance sheet and the related statement of income and retained earnings of The Rancho Corporation as of July 31, 1982. In accordance with your instructions, a complete audit was conducted.

In many respects, this was an unusual year for The Rancho Corporation. The weakening of the economy in the early part of the year and the strike of plant employees in the summer of 1982 led to a decline in sales and net income. After making several tests of sales records, however, nothing came to our attention that would indicate that sales have not been properly recorded.

In our opinion, with the explanation given above, and with the exception of some minor errors that we considered immaterial, the aforementioned financial statements present fairly the financial position of The Rancho Corporation at

July 31, 1982, and the results of its operations for the year then ended, in conformity with pronouncements of the Accounting Principles Board and the Financial Accounting Standards Board applied consistently throughout the period.

Timothy Ross, CPA
September 23, 1982

Required:

List and explain deficiencies and omissions in the auditor's report. The type of opinion (unqualified, qualified, adverse, or disclaimer) is of no consequence and need not be discussed. Organize your answer sheet by paragraph (scope, middle, and opinion) of the auditor's report.

AICPA (adapted)

1-34 Brown, CPA, received a telephone call from Calhoun, the sole owner and manager of a small corporation. Calhoun asked Brown to prepare the financial statements for the corporation and told Brown that the statements were needed in two weeks for external financing purposes. Calhoun was vague when Brown inquired about the intended use of the statements. Brown was convinced that Calhoun thought Brown's work would constitute an audit. To avoid confusion, Brown decided not to explain to Calhoun that the engagement would only be to prepare the financial statements. Brown, with the understanding that a substantial fee would be paid if the work were completed in two weeks, accepted the engagement and started the work at once.

During the course of the work, Brown discovered an accrued expense account labeled "professional fees" and learned that the balance in the account represented an accrual for the cost of Brown's services. Brown suggested to Calhoun's bookkeeper that the account name be changed to "fees for limited audit engagement." Brown also reviewed several invoices to determine whether accounts were being properly classified. Some of the invoices were missing. Brown listed the missing invoice numbers in the working papers with a note indicating that there should be a follow-up on the next engagement. Brown also discovered that the available records included the fixed asset values at estimated current replacement costs. Based on the records available, Brown prepared a balance sheet, income statement, and statement of stockholder's equity. In addition, Brown drafted the footnotes but decided that any mention of the replacement costs would only mislead the readers. Brown suggested to Calhoun that readers of the financial statements would be better informed if they received a separate letter from Calhoun explaining the meaning and effect of the estimated replacement costs of the fixed assets. Brown mailed the financial statements and footnotes to Calhoun with the following note included on each page:

"The accompanying financial statements are submitted to you without complete audit verification."

Required:

Identify the inappropriate actions of Brown and indicate what Brown should have done to avoid each inappropriate action.

Organize your answer as follows:

Inappropriate Action	What Brown Should Have Done To Avoid Inappropriate Action

AICPA

1-35 Following are four statements that describe the auditor's potential responsibility for the detection of fraud in an ordinary audit engagement.

1. The auditor is responsible for the failure to detect fraud only when an unqualified opinion is issued.
2. The auditor is responsible for the failure to detect fraud only when such failure clearly results from nonperformance of audit procedures specifically described in the engagement letter.
3. The auditor must extend auditing procedures to actively search for evidence of fraud where the examination indicates that fraud may exist.
4. The auditor must extend auditing procedures to actively search for evidence of fraud in all audit situations.

Required:

a. Discuss each of the above statements. Distinguish: (1) the official position of the public accounting profession, (2) the apparent position of regulatory agencies, and (3) what seems to be the general feeling of users of audited financial statements.

b. Why do you think the positions of the profession and the public are so at odds in this area?

AICPA (adapted)

2

The ethical environment of public accounting

A man should *be* upright; not be *kept* upright.

Marcus Aurelius

A distinguishing mark of a professional is his acceptance of responsibility to the public. All true professions have therefore deemed it essential to promulgate codes of ethics and to establish means for ensuring their observance.[1]

Achieving and maintaining effective self-regulation is the hallmark of all professions. This self-regulation is usually characterized by standards of behavior that are promulgated and accepted by members of the profession, a system of preventative and corrective education, and an enforcement procedure.

The public accounting profession enjoys self-regulation because its members have met their responsibilities of professionalism in behavior and work. An important factor in meeting these responsibilities has been the creation and acceptance of a Code of Professional Ethics for public accountants. This code of ethics establishes standards of behavior for public accountants that are higher than those required by the law. Voluntary acceptance of these high standards gives independent CPAs the status and respect of belonging to a true profession and the right of self-regulation and social control of the profession.

Codes of Professional Ethics appear at all levels of the organized public accounting profession. The state societies and state boards of accountancy have each adopted codes of ethics. However, the most comprehensive and important code is that established by the AICPA. The AICPA Code of Professional Ethics has become the model for the ethics codes of the various states and is generally considered the code of ethics for the public accounting profession.

---

[1]AICPA, *Professional Standards Volume 2, Ethics, Bylaws, Quality Control*, Commerce Clearing House, Inc.

2.1 UNDERSTANDING THE CODE OF PROFESSIONAL ETHICS

The AICPA Code of Professional Ethics is divided into four parts. Each of the parts revolves around five fundamental areas of ethical responsibility for independent CPAs. These areas are:

1. Independence, integrity, and objectivity
2. Standards of performance (general and technical)
3. Responsibilities to clients
4. Responsibilities to colleagues
5. General conduct (other)

All aspects of the ethics code relate to one of these five areas. The four parts of the Code of Professional Ethics are:

1. *General Ethical Principles*—These are philosophical discussions of the standard of behavior independent CPAs should strive to achieve in each of the five areas of ethical responsibility listed above. These essays do not create enforceable standards to which CPAs will be held; instead they establish the atmosphere for ethical behavior beyond the minimum acceptable standards. The essays are approved by the Professional Ethics Division of the AICPA but not directly by AICPA membership.

2. *Rules of Conduct*—These are statements of the minimum acceptable standards of conduct to which independent CPAs should be held in each of the five areas of ethical responsibility. Rules are enforceable on members of the AICPA and on the members of other public accounting organizations that have adopted the AICPA code. Each of the rules of conduct has been directly approved by the membership of the AICPA.

3. *Interpretations of Rules of Conduct*—Often the scope and meaning of rules of conduct in each of the areas of ethical responsibility must be clarified. Interpretations provide guidelines to the application of the rules of conduct. Although these interpretations are not enforceable in the same sense as the rules of conduct, independent CPAs subject to the interpretations must justify departure from them in disciplinary matters. Interpretations are approved by the AICPA Professional Ethics Division after exposure to the state societies and state boards. AICPA members do not directly approve interpretations.

4. *Ethics Rulings*—These are the formal rulings of the AICPA Professional Ethics Division (after exposure to state societies and state boards), which apply the rules of conduct and interpretations to particular fact situations. Ethics rulings answer questions about proper conduct in a particular circumstance and are the most specific of the parts of the Code. Independent CPAs subject to the Code must justify behavior inconsistent with the ethics rulings in disciplinary matters.

The Code of Professional Ethics, then, has four levels of pronouncements (concepts, rules, interpretations, and rulings) in each of the five areas of ethical responsibility. These levels progress from the most general (concepts) to the most specific (rulings) in providing guidelines for the profession.

Exhibit 2–1 summarizes the fundamental behavioral principles applicable to each area of ethical responsibility together with the rules of conduct, interpretations, and rulings for each concept. This figure represents an overview of the AICPA Code of Professional Ethics.

The remainder of this chapter will present each of these components of the Code.

2.2 GENERAL ETHICAL PRINCIPLES

Rules of conduct can be best understood when interpreted against the background of the general ethical concepts since the rules do not exist in a vacuum independent of a unifying thread. The general ethical concepts give the rules of conduct a proper context and purpose.

The following five general ethical statements are taken directly from the AICPA Code of Professional Ethics and are quoted in their entirety.[2]

Independence, Integrity, and Objectivity

The public expects a number of character traits in a certified public accountant but primarily integrity and objectivity and, in the practice of public accounting, independence.

Independence has always been a concept fundamental to the accounting profession, the cornerstone of its philosophical structure. For no matter how competent any CPA may be, his opinion on financial statements will be of little value to those who rely on him—whether they be clients or any of his unseen audience of credit grantors, investors, governmental agencies and the like—unless he maintains his independence.

Independence has traditionally been defined by the profession as the ability to act with integrity and objectivity.

Integrity is an element of character which is fundamental to reliance on the CPA. This quality may be difficult to judge, however, since a particular fault of omission or commission may be the result either of honest error or a lack of integrity.

Objectivity refers to a CPA's ability to maintain an impartial attitude on all matters which come under his review. Since this attitude involves an individual's mental processes, the evaluation of objectivity must be based largely on actions and relationships viewed in the context of ascertainable circumstances.

---

[2]The complete Code of Professional Ethics is published as part of a volume entitled *AICPA Professional Standards Volume 2, Ethics, Bylaws, Quality Control*, Commerce Clearing House, Inc.

EXHIBIT 2-1   Overview of the AICPA Code of Professional Ethics

Area of Ethical Responsibility	Ethical Principle	Rules of Conduct	Interpretations	Ethics Rulings
Independence, Integrity, and Objectivity	A certified public accountant should maintain his integrity and objectivity and, when engaged in the practice of public accounting, be independent of those he serves.	Rule 101—Independence	8	approximately 60
		Rule 102—Integrity and Objectivity	none	
Standards of Performance (general and technical)	A certified public accountant should observe the profession's general and technical standards and strive continually to improve his competence and the quality of his services.	Rule 201—General Standards	2	approximately 10
		Rule 202—Auditing Standards	1	
		Rule 203—Accounting Principles	3	
		Rule 204—Other Technical Standards	1	
Responsibilities to Clients	A certified public accountant should be fair and candid with his clients and serve them to the best of his ability, with professional concern for their best interests consistent with his responsibilities to the public.	Rule 301—Confidential Client Information	1	approximately 15
		Rule 302—Contingent Fees	none	
Responsibilities to Colleagues	A certified public accountant should conduct himself in a manner that will promote cooperation and good relations among members of the profession.	none still in effect	none	none
General Conduct (other)	A certified public accountant should conduct himself in a manner that will enhance the stature of the profession and its ability to serve the public.	Rule 501—Acts Discreditable	2	approximately 45
		Rule 502—Advertising and Other Forms of Solicitation	4	
		Rule 503—Commission	1	
		Rule 504—Incompatible Occupations	1	
		Rule 505—Form of Practice and Name	2	

While recognizing that the qualities of integrity and objectivity are not precisely measurable, the profession nevertheless constantly holds them up to members as an imperative. This is done essentially by education and by the Rules of Conduct which the profession adopts and enforces.

CPAs cannot practice their calling and participate in the world's affairs without being exposed to situations that involve the possibility of pressures upon their integrity and objectivity. To define and proscribe all such situations would be impracticable. To ignore the problem for that reason, however, and to set no limits at all would be irresponsible.

It follows that the concept of independence should not be interpreted so loosely as to permit relationships likely to impair the CPA's integrity or the impartiality of his judgment, nor so strictly as to inhibit the rendering of useful services when the likelihood of such impairment is relatively remote.

While it may be difficult for a CPA always to appear completely independent even in normal relationships with clients, pressures upon his integrity or objectivity are offset by powerful countervailing forces and restraints. These include the possibility of legal liability, professional discipline ranging up to revocation of the right to practice as a CPA, loss of reputation and, by no means least, the inculcated resistance of a disciplined professional to any infringement upon his basic integrity and objectivity. Accordingly, in deciding which types of relationships should be specifically prohibited, both the magnitude of the threat posed by a relationship and the force of countervailing pressures have to be weighed.

In establishing rules relating to independence, the profession uses the criterion of whether reasonable men, having knowledge of all the facts and taking into consideration normal strength of character and normal behavior under the circumstances, would conclude that a specified relationship between a CPA and a client poses an unacceptable threat to the CPA's integrity or objectivity.

When a CPA expresses an opinion on financial statements, not only the fact but also the appearance of integrity and objectivity is of particular importance. For this reason, the profession has adopted rules to prohibit the expression of such an opinion when relationships exist which might pose such a threat to integrity and objectivity as to exceed the strength of countervailing forces and restraints. These relationships fall into two general categories: (1) certain financial relationships with clients and (2) relationships in which a CPA is virtually part of management or an employee under management's control.

Although the appearance of independence is not required in the case of management advisory services and tax practice, a CPA is encouraged to avoid the proscribed relationships with clients regardless of the type of services being rendered. In any event, the CPA, in all types of engagements, should refuse to subordinate his professional judgement to others and should express his conclusions honestly and objectively.

The financial relationships proscribed when an opinion is expressed on financial statements make no reference to fees paid to a CPA by a client. Remuneration to providers of services is necessary for the continued provision of those services. Indeed, a principal reason for the development and persistence in the professions of the client-practitioner relationship and of remuneration by fee (as contrasted with an employer-employee relationship and remuneration by salary) is that these arrangements are seen as a safeguard of independence.

The above reference to an employer-employee relationship is pertinent to a question sometimes raised as to whether a CPA's objectivity in expressing an opinion on financial statements will be impaired by his being involved with his client in the decision-making process.

CPAs continually provide advice to their clients, and they expect that this advice will usually be followed. Decisions based on such advice may have a significant effect on a client's financial condition or operating results. This is the case not only in tax engagements and management advisory services but in the audit function as well.

If a CPA disagrees with a client on a significant matter during the course of an audit, the client has three choices—he can modify the financial statements (which is usually the case), he can accept a qualified report or he can discharge the CPA. While the ultimate decision and the resulting financial statements clearly are those of the client, the CPA has obviously been a significant factor in the decision-making process. Indeed, no responsible user of financial statements would want it otherwise.

It must be noted that when a CPA expresses an opinion on financial statements, the judgments involved pertain to whether the results of operating decisions of the client are fairly presented in the statements and not on the underlying wisdom of such decisions. It is highly unlikely therefore that being a factor in the client's decision-making process would impair the CPA's objectivity in judging the fairness of presentation.

The more important question is whether a CPA would deliberately compromise his integrity by expressing an unqualified opinion on financial statements which were prepared in such a way as to cover up a poor business decision by the client and on which the CPA has rendered advice. The basic character traits of the CPA as well as the risks arising from such a compromise of integrity, including liability to third parties, disciplinary action and loss of right of practice, should preclude such action.

Providing advice or recommendations which may or may not involve skills logically related to a client's information and control system, and which may affect the client's decision-making, does not in itself indicate lack of independence. However, the CPA must be alert to the possibility that undue identification with the management of the client or involvement with a client's affairs to such a degree as to place him virtually in the position of being an employee, may impair the appearance of independence.

To sum up, CPAs cannot avoid external pressures on their integrity and objectivity in the course of their professional work, but they are expected to resist these pressures. They must, in fact, retain their integrity and objectivity in all phases of their practice and, when expressing opinions on financial statements, avoid involvement in situations that would impair the credibility of their independence in the minds of reasonable men familiar with the facts.

Standards of Performance—General and Technical

Since accounting information is of great importance to all segments of the public, all CPAs, whether in public practice, government service, private employment or academic pursuits, should perform their work at a high level of professionalism.

A CPA should maintain and seek always to improve his competence in all areas of accountancy in which he engages. Satisfaction of the requirements for the CPA certificate is evidence of basic competence at the time the certificate is granted, but it does not justify an assumption that this competence is maintained without continuing effort. Further, it does not necessarily justify undertaking complex engagements without additional study and experience.

A CPA should not render professional services without being aware of, and complying with, the applicable general or technical standards as interpreted by bodies designated by Council. Moreover, since published general and technical standards can never cover the whole field of accountancy, he must keep broadly informed.

Observance of the rule on general and technical standards calls for a determination by a CPA with respect to each engagement undertaken that there is a reasonable expectation it can be completed with the exercise of due professional care, with adequate planning and supervision and with the gathering of sufficient relevant data to afford a reasonable basis for conclusions and recommendations. If a CPA is unable to bring such professional competence to the engagement he should suggest, in fairness to his client and the public, the engagement of someone competent to perform the needed service, either independently or as an associate.

The standards referred to in the rules are elaborated and refined to meet changing conditions, and it is each CPA's responsibility to keep himself up to date in this respect.

Responsibilities to Clients

As a professional person, the CPA should serve his clients with competence and with professional concern for their best interests. He must not permit his regard for a client's interest, however, to override his obligation to the public to maintain his independence, integrity and objectivity. The discharge of this dual responsibility to both clients and the public requires a high degree of ethical perception and conduct.

It is fundamental that the CPA hold in strict confidence all information concerning a client's affairs which he acquires in the course of his engagement. This does not mean, however, that he should acquiesce in a client's unwillingness to make disclosures in financial reports which are necessary to fair presentation.

Exploitation of relations with a client for personal advantage is improper. For example, acceptance of a commission from any vendor for recommending his product or service to a client is prohibited.

A CPA should be frank and straightforward with clients. While tact and diplomacy are desirable, a client should never be left in doubt about the CPA's position on any issue of significance. No truly professional man will subordinate his own judgment or conceal or modify his honest opinion merely to please. This admonition applies to all services including those related to management and tax problems.

When accepting an engagement, a CPA should bear in mind that he may find it necessary to resign if conflict arises on an important question of principle. In cases of irreconcilable difference, he will have to judge whether the importance of the matter requires such an action. In weighing this question, he can feel assured that the practitioner who is independent, fair and candid is the better respected for these qualities and will not lack opportunities for constructive service.

Responsibilities to Colleagues

The support of a profession by its members and their cooperation with one another are essential elements of professional character. The public confidence and respect which a CPA enjoys is largely the result of the cumulative accomplishments of all CPAs, past and present. It is, therefore, in the CPA's own interest, as well as that of the general public, to support the collective efforts of colleagues through professional societies and organizations and to deal with fellow practitioners in a manner which will not detract from their reputation and well-being.

Although the reluctance of a professional to give testimony that may be damaging to a colleague is understandable, the obligation of professional courtesy and fraternal consideration can never excuse lack of complete candor if the CPA is testifying as an expert witness in a judicial proceeding or properly constituted inquiry.

A CPA has the obligation to assist his fellows in complying with the Code of Professional Ethics and should also assist appropriate disciplinary authorities in enforcing the Code. To condone serious fault can be as bad as to commit it. It may be even worse, in fact, since some errors may result from ignorance rather than intent and, if let pass without action, will probably be repeated. In situations of this kind, the welfare of the public should be the guide to a member's action.

While the Code proscribes certain specific actions in the area of relationships with colleagues, it should be understood that these proscriptions do not define the limits of desirable intraprofessional conduct. Rather, such conduct encompasses the professional consideration and courtesies which each CPA would like to have fellow practitioners extend to him.

It is natural that a CPA will seek to develop his practice. However, in doing so he should not seek to displace another accountant in a client relationship by any means which will lessen the effectiveness of his technical performance or lessen his concern for the rights of third parties to reliable information. Further, he should not act in any way that reflects negatively on fellow practitioners.

A CPA may provide service to those who request it, even though they may be served by another practitioner in another area of service, or he may succeed another practitioner at a client's request. In such circumstances it is always desirable and required in some situations before accepting an engagement that the CPA who has been approached should advise the accountant already serving the client. Such action is indicated not only by considerations of professional courtesy but by good business judgment.

A client may sometimes request services requiring highly specialized knowledge. If the CPA lacks the expertise necessary to render such services, he should call upon a fellow practitioner for assistance or refer the entire engagement to another. Such assistance or referral brings to bear on the client's needs both the referring practitioner's knowledge of the client's affairs and the technical expertise of the specialist brought into the engagement. If both serve the client best in their own area of ability, all parties are well served as is the public.

General Conduct—Other

In light of the importance of their function, CPAs and their firms should have a keen consciousness of the public interest and the needs of society. Thus, they should support efforts to achieve equality of opportunity for all, regardless of race, religious background or sex, and should contribute to this goal by their own service relationships and employment practices.

The CPA is a beneficiary of the organization and character of his profession. Since he is seen as a representative of the profession by those who come in contact with him, he should behave honorably both in his personal and professional life and avoid any conduct that might erode public respect and confidence.

Solicitation to obtain clients through false, misleading and deceptive statements or acts is prohibited under the Rules of Conduct because it will lessen the professional effectiveness and the independence toward clients which is essential to the best interests of the public.

Advertising, which is false, misleading and deceptive, is also prohibited because such representations will mislead some of the public and thereby reduce or destroy the profession's usefulness to society. A CPA should seek to establish a reputation for competence and character, through actions rather than words. There are many ways this can be done such as by making himself known through public service, by civic and political activities, and by joining associations and clubs. It is desirable for him to share his knowledge with interested groups by accepting requests to make speeches and write articles. Whatever publicity occurs as a natural by-product of such activities is entirely proper.

In his work, the CPA should be motivated more by desire for excellence in performance than for material reward. This does not mean that he need be indifferent about compensation. Indeed, a professional man who cannot maintain a respectable standard of living is unlikely to inspire confidence or to enjoy sufficient peace of mind to do his best work.

In determining fees, a CPA may assess the degree of responsibility assumed by undertaking an engagement as well as the time, manpower and skills required to perform the service in conformity with the standards of the profession. He may also take into account the value of the service to the client, the customary charges of professional colleagues and other considerations. No single factor is necessarily controlling.

Clients have a right to know in advance what rates will be charged and approximately how much an engagement will cost. However, when professional judgments are involved, it is usually not possible to set a fair charge until an engagement has been completed. For this reason CPAs should state their fees for proposed engagements in the form of estimates which may be subject to change as the work progresses.

Other practices prohibited by the Rules of Conduct include using any firm designation or description which might be misleading, or practicing as a professional corporation or association which fails to comply with provisions established by Council to protect the public interest.

A member, while practicing public accounting, may not engage in a business or occupation which is incompatible therewith. While certain occupations are clearly incompatible with the practice of public accounting, the profession has never attempted to list them, for in most cases the individual circumstances indicate whether there is a problem. For example, there would be a problem of conflict of interest if a practicing CPA were to serve on a tax assessment board since he would be open to accusations of favoring his clients whether this was done or not. Moreover, they might, under some circumstances, create a conflict of interest in the CPA's independence relationship with his clients.

Paying a commission to outsiders is prohibited in order to eliminate the temptation to compensate anyone for referring a client. Receipt of a commission is proscribed since practitioners should look to the client, and not to others, for compensation for services rendered. The practice of paying a fee to a referring CPA irrespective of any service performed or responsibility assumed by him is proscribed because there is no justification for a CPA to share in a fee for accounting services where his sole contribution was to make a referral.

Over the years the vast majority of CPAs have endeavored to earn and maintain a reputation for competence, integrity and objectivity. The success of these efforts has been largely responsible for the wide public acceptance of accounting as an honorable profession. This acceptance is a valuable asset which should never be taken for granted. Every CPA should constantly strive to see that it continues to be deserved.

The rules of conduct and interpretations, which follow, derive directly from these general ethical statements and are traceable back to them.

2.3 RULES OF CONDUCT AND INTERPRETATIONS

The 13 rules of conduct have been approved by the membership of the AICPA and represent the minimum standard of professional conduct for independent CPAs. The rules are less general than the ethical principles because they deal with specific types of conduct. Nevertheless, these rules must be phrased in terms sufficiently broad to encompass a wide range of situations. As a result, it is necessary that the meaning of particular rules be officially interpreted from time to time to avoid misinterpretation and misunderstanding. Official interpretations attempt to clarify ambiguities in the rules.

The Rules of Conduct are enforced by the internal disciplinary system of the AICPA, the state societies, and the state boards of accountancy. Departures by members from interpretations must be justified in the event of a disciplinary hearing.

Rules of conduct and interpretations will be presented in the five areas of ethical responsibility previously discussed. The rules are taken in their entirety from the Code of Professional Ethics.

Independence, Integrity, and Objectivity

Rule 101—Independence. A member or a firm of which he is a partner or shareholder shall not express an opinion on financial statements of an enterprise unless he and his firm are independent with respect to such enterprise. Independence will be considered to be impaired if, for example:

A. During the period of his professional engagement, or at the time of expressing his opinion, he or his firm
   1. (a) Had or was committed to acquire any direct or material indirect financial interest in the enterprise; or
      (b) Was a trustee of any trust or executor or administrator of any estate if such trust or estate had or was committed to acquire any direct or material indirect financial interest in the enterprise; or
   2. Had any joint closely held business investment with the enterprise or any officer, director, or principal stockholder thereof which was material in relation to his or his firm's net worth; or
   3. Had any loan to or from the enterprise or any officer, director, or principal stockholder thereof. This latter proscription does not apply to the following loans from a financial institution when made under normal lending procedures, terms, and requirements:
      (a) Loans obtained by a member or his firm which are not material in relation to the net worth of such borrower.
      (b) Home mortgages.
      (c) Other secured loans, except loans guaranteed by a member's firm which are otherwise unsecured.

B. During the period covered by the financial statements, during the period of the professional engagement, or at the time of expressing an opinion, he or his firm

1. Was connected with the enterprise as a promoter, underwriter or voting trustee, a director or officer or in any capacity equivalent to that of a member of management or of an employee; or

2. Was a trustee for any pension or profit-sharing trust of the enterprise.

The above examples are not intended to be all-inclusive.

Rule 102—Integrity and objectivity. A member shall not knowingly misrepresent facts, and when engaged in the practice of public accounting, including the rendering of tax and management advisory services, shall not subordinate his judgment to others. In tax practice, a member may resolve doubt in favor of his client as long as there is reasonable support of his position.

A summary of the current interpretations in effect on independence, integrity, and objectivity follows.

CONCEPT SUMMARY

Summary of Interpretations on
Independence, Integrity, and Objectivity

Rule	Interpretation
101—Independence	1. *Directorships*—an auditor may act as a director of a charitable, religious, civic, or other similar not-for-profit organization without impairing independence if he does not participate in or give advice on management functions and if the board is sufficiently large so that his membership might be viewed as honorary and is so identified.
	2. *Retired partners and firm independence*—a retired partner may have one of the types of relationships with a client of his former firm prohibited by Rule 101 if he is no longer active and not associated with his former firm and the fees he collects from the client are not material with respect to his own circumstances.
	3. *Accounting services*—a CPA performing accounting services for an audit client must retain his independence in fact and in appearance in the eyes of a reasonable observer by doing nothing to indicate that he is an employee of the client or is assuming management responsibility for the client.

Continued on the following page

	4. *Effect of family relationships on independence*—the financial and business interests of a family member in a client would presumably impair the CPA's independence as follows: (a) member's spouse, dependent children, or any other relative living with or supported by the CPA—independence impaired (b) other close kin—depends upon significance of interest or relationship and geographic proximity (c) remote kin—independence not impaired 5. *Meaning of the term "normal lending procedures, terms and requirements"*—the conditions under which an acceptable loan is made by a client financial institution to a CPA must be comparable to those of other loans of the same type made during the same period if independence is not to be impaired. 6. *The effect of actual or threatened litigation on independence*—the existence of or threat of litigation would impair the CPA's independence as follows: (a) litigation between client and auditor would normally impair independence unless the amounts involved were immaterial and not related to the quality of the audit work (such as billings for services resulting from non-audit activity) (b) litigation involving third parties would not normally impair independence unless material cross-claims are likely to result. 7. *Application to professional personnel*—the term "he and his firm" means: (a) all partners or shareholders, and (b) all full- and part-time professional employees participating in the engagement or located in the office handling the engagement. 8. *Financial interest in nonclient having investor or investee relationship with client*—a CPA's independence would be impaired if a direct or material indirect financial interest by the CPA exists in: (a) a nonclient investee in which a material investment is held by a client investor (b) a nonclient investor whose interest in a client investee is material.
102—Integrity and Objectivity	No interpretations have been issued.

Standards of Performance—General and Technical

Rule 201—General standards. A member shall comply with the following general standards as interpreted by bodies designated by Council, and must justify any departures therefrom.

A. *Professional competence.* A member shall undertake only those engagements which he or his firm can reasonably expect to complete with professional competence.

B. *Due professional care.* A member shall exercise due professional care in the performance of an engagement.

C. *Planning and supervision.* A member shall adequately plan and supervise an engagement.

D. *Sufficient relevant data.* A member shall obtain sufficient relevant data to afford a reasonable basis for conclusions or recommendations in relation to an engagement.

E. *Forecasts.* A member shall not permit his name to be used in conjunction with any forecast of future transactions in a manner which may lead to the belief that the member vouches for the achievability of the forecast.

Rule 202—Auditing standards. A member shall not permit his name to be associated with financial statements in such a manner as to imply that he is acting as an independent public accountant unless he has complied with the applicable generally accepted auditing standards promulgated by the Institute. Statements on Auditing Standards issued by the Institute's Auditing Standards Board are, for purposes of this rule, considered to be interpretations of the generally accepted auditing standards, and departures from such statements must be justified by those who do not follow them.

Rule 203—Accounting principles. A member shall not express an opinion that financial statements are presented in conformity with generally accepted accounting principles if such statements contain any departure from an accounting principle promulgated by the body designated by Council to establish such principles which has a material effect on the statements taken as a whole, unless the member can demonstrate that due to unusual circumstances the financial statements would otherwise have been misleading. In such cases his report must describe the departure, the approximate effects thereof, if practicable, and the reasons why compliance with the principle would result in a misleading statement.

Rule 204—Other technical standards. A member shall comply with other technical standards promulgated by bodies designated by Council to establish such standards, and departures therefrom must be justified by those who do not follow them.

Responsibilities to Clients

Rule 301—Confidential client information. A member shall not disclose any confidential information obtained in the course of a professional engagement except with the consent of the client.

CONCEPT SUMMARY
Summary of Interpretations on
General and Technical Standards

Rule	Interpretation
201—General Standards	1. *Competence*—a CPA who accepts an engagement implies that he possesses the necessary knowledge, technical skill, sound judgement and ability to supervise staff to complete the engagement. Additional research or consultation with specialists does not imply lack of competence, but if sufficient competence cannot be gained the client should be referred to another CPA.
	2. *Shopping for accounting or auditing standards*—before giving professional advice on accounting or auditing standards to the client of another CPA who has been retained to report on the client's financial statements, the new CPA must consult with the client's auditor to ascertain all facts relevant to the situation.
202—Auditing Standards	1. *Unaudited financial statements*—although this rule formally makes the Statements on Auditing Standards a part of the Rules of Conduct, it does not prohibit a CPA from becoming associated with unaudited financial statements. This interpretation cautions that the sections of SASs which deal with unaudited financial statements must govern in these circumstances.
203—Accounting Principles	1. *Departures from established accounting principles*—even though compliance with GAAP are required under Rule 203, this interpretation makes clear that the overriding accounting principle is that the financial statements should not be misleading. If the literal application of GAAP would result in misleading financial statements in a particular circumstance, the CPA should use professional judgement to determine the accounting treatment which would not result in misleading statements.
	2. *Status of FASB interpretations*—the FASB has been designated as the body to establish GAAP, and thus established accounting principles include Statements of Financial Accounting Standards by the FASB, as well as the Opinions of the APB and Accounting Research Bulletins which have not been superseded. These Statements, Opinions, and Bulletins will be construed in the light of any interpretations issued by the FASB.
	3. *FASB statements dealing with disclosure beyond the basic financial statements*—FASB statements which establish standards for disclosure outside of the basic financial statements are not covered by Rule 203. The FASB is designated to establish accounting principles dealing only with financial statements under Rule 203.
204—Other Technical Standards	1. *Forecasts*—a CPA may be associated with forecasts of future transactions by a client. However, full disclosure of the sources of information used, major assumptions made, the work performed, and degree of responsibility taken by the CPA must be made.

This rule shall not be construed (a) to relieve a member of his obligation under Rules 202 and 203, (b) to affect in any way his compliance with a validly issued subpoena or summons enforceable by order of a court, (c) to prohibit review of a member's professional practices as a part of voluntary quality review under Institute authorization or (d) to preclude a member from responding to any inquiry made by the ethics division or Trial Board of the Institute, by a duly constituted investigative or disciplinary body of a state CPA society, or under state statutes.

Members of the ethics division and Trial Board of the Institute and professional practice reviewers under Institute authorization shall not disclose any confidential client information which comes to their attention from members in disciplinary proceedings or otherwise in carrying out their official responsibilities. However, this prohibition shall not restrict the exchange of information with an aforementioned duly constituted investigative or disciplinary body.

Rule 302—Contingent fees. Professional services shall not be offered or rendered under an arrangement whereby no fee will be charged unless a specified finding or result is attained, or where the fee is otherwise contingent upon the findings or results of such services. However, a member's fees may vary depending, for example, on the complexity of the service rendered.

Fees are not regarded as being contingent if fixed by courts or other public authorities or, in tax matters, if determined based on the results of judicial proceedings or the findings of governmental agencies.

CONCEPT SUMMARY
Summary of Interpretations on
Responsibilities to Clients

Rule	Interpretation
301—Confidential Client Information	1. *Confidential information and technical standards*—the prohibition against the disclosure of confidential client information obtained by a CPA does not preclude the CPA from making all disclosures of information necessary to discharge all responsibilities under other professional standards. For example, the subsequent discovery of facts which existed, but were not known to the CPA, at the time of his auditor's report must be disclosed when discovered if they would have affected his report.
302—Contingent Fees	No interpretations have been issued.

Responsibilities to Colleagues

There are currently no rules of conduct in force on responsibilities to colleagues, and thus no interpretations or ethics rulings exist. The general ethical concepts presented in the previous section provide the sole guidance for the CPA in this area.

General Conduct—Other

Rule 501—Acts discreditable. A member shall not commit an act discreditable to the profession.

Rule 502—Advertising and other forms of solicitation. A member shall not seek to obtain clients by advertising or other forms of solicitation in a manner that is false, misleading, or deceptive.

Rule 503—Commission. A member shall not pay a commission to obtain a client, nor shall he accept a commission for a referral to a client of products or services of others. This rule shall not prohibit payments for the purchase of an accounting practice or retirement payments to individuals formerly engaged in the practice of public accounting or payments to their heirs or estates.

Rule 504—Incompatible occupations. A member who is engaged in the practice of public accounting shall not concurrently engage in any business or occupation which would create a conflict of interest in rendering professional services.

Rule 505—Form of practice and name. A member may practice public accounting, whether as an owner or employee, only in the form of a proprietorship, a partnership or a professional corporation whose characteristics conform to resolutions of Council.

A member shall not practice under a firm name which includes any fictitious name, indicates specialization or is misleading as to the type of organization (proprietorship, partnership or corporation). However, names of one or more past partners or shareholders may be included in the firm name of a successor partnership or corporation. Also, a partner surviving the death or withdrawal of all other partners may continue to practice under the partnership name for up to two years after becoming a sole practitioner.

A firm may not designate itself as "Members of the American Institute of Certified Public Accountants" unless all of its partners or shareholders are members of the Institute.

The ethical concepts, rules of conduct, and interpretations presented as a part of this chapter represent the essentials of the Code of Professional Ethics. The most specific components of the Code, ethics rulings, are also published by area of ethical responsibility. These rulings are quite numerous and can be found published in question and answer format in the Code of Professional Ethics (see footnote 1).

CONCEPT SUMMARY
Summary of Interpretations on General Conduct

Rule	Interpretation
501—Acts Discreditable	1. *Client's records and accountant's workpapers*—a CPA should not retain a client's records after demand has been made by the client for their return even though statutes may give him the legal right to do so. Copies of the records may be retained by the CPA, however. The CPA's workpapers are his own property and need not be turned over to the client unless they are an integral part of the client's records.
	2. *Discrimination in employment practices*— discrimination in hiring, promotion, or salary based on race, color, religion, sex, age, or national origin constitutes an act discreditable to the profession.
	3. *Failure to follow standards and/or procedures or other requirements in governmental audits*— When an engagement is accepted to perform certain government audits and an obligation is undertaken to follow specified government audit standards or procedures, failure to do so is an act discreditable to the profession in violation of Rule 501, unless the report discloses the fact that such requirements were not followed and the relevant reasons.
502—Advertising and Other Forms of Solicitation	1. *Informational advertising*—advertising that is objective, in good taste and professionally dignified is permitted without restriction on the type of advertising media, frequency, size, artwork, or type style. Information about a CPA or his firm including services offered, fees, and statements of policy or position about the practice of public accounting are permissible.
	2. *False, Misleading, or Deceptive Acts*—all forms of false, misleading, or deceptive advertising or other solicitation are prohibited, including self-laudatory statements not based on verifiable facts, comparisons with other CPAs, and certain testimonials or endorsements.
	3. *Self-designation as expert or specialist*—since an AICPA program for producing or recognizing competence in a particular specialty has not been developed, any self-designation as an expert or specialist is prohibited.
	4. *Engagement obtained through efforts of third party*—CPAs performing professional services for clients or customers of third parties must ascertain that the promotional efforts by the third party to obtain the client or customer are within the bounds of the rules of conduct.
503—Commissions	1. *Fees in payment for services*—although payment or receipt of a commission for referral of a client is prohibited, a referring CPA may receive a fee from a successor or from a client for professional services rendered to either.

Continued on the following page

Concept Summary (Continued)

504—Incompatible Occupations	1. *Incompatible occupations*—a CPA should not engage in an occupation inconsistent with his responsibilities under the Code of Professional Ethics while practicing public accounting. Incompatible businesses or occupations include those which would impair objectivity or would damage the image of public accounting on moral or legal grounds.
505—Form of Practice and Name	1. *Investment in commercial accounting corporation*—a CPA, while practicing public accounting, may have a financial interest in a nonprofessional corporation which performs similar services and does not meet the requirements for practice of the AICPA, if the CPA's interest in the corporation is not material and is only that of an investor.
	2. *Members who operate a separate business*—CPAs must observe all rules of conduct when participating in a separate business which offers one or more of the services normally offered by public accountants, whether or not they are also in public practice.

2.4 INTERNAL DISCIPLINARY MACHINERY OF THE PROFESSION

More than fifty committees and boards of the AICPA, made up mostly of members in practice, function in various areas of interest to public accountants. Two of these groups, the Professional Ethics Division and the Joint Trial Board, have responsibility for the internal disciplinary machinery. The Professional Ethics Division investigates potential disciplinary matters involving members and arranges for presentation of cases before the Trial Board, where it finds *prima facie* evidence of an infraction of the Code of Professional Ethics or the Bylaws of the AICPA. The Joint Trial Board adjudicates disciplinary charges brought against members of the Institute. It is the final arbiter on disciplinary matters.

The legal basis for the enforcement powers of the AICPA lies in the member's agreement upon joining to abide by the professional standards (ethics and bylaws) of the Institute.

The Professional Ethics Division

The Professional Ethics Division consists of an executive committee and subcommittees on technical standards, behavioral standards, and independence. It is supported by a small staff, most of whom are professionals. Each subcommittee may investigate alleged violations of professional standards, propose ethics interpretations of rules of conduct, and respond to the inquiries of members on matters of professional standards.

Although the Ethics Division may initiate investigations based on diverse sources ranging from news stories to information from government agencies, most of the division's work is triggered by formal complaints. The division attempts to act immediately on cases not in litigation but always defers its investigation on cases in litigation until these cases have been decided. Since the division lacks legal status or subpoena power to force cooperation, awaiting legal settlements and the availability of court-developed facts is the only reasonable path.

When the division judges a matter sufficiently serious to warrant public censure, suspension, or expulsion from the AICPA, and enough facts are present, the matter is referred to the Joint Trial Board for adjudication. For lesser offenses, the division has authority to issue administrative censures and require attendance at professional development courses.

The Joint Trial Board

The AICPA and the various state societies have begun to cooperate in enforcing the professional standards of public accounting. As of 1975, a Joint Trial Board structure has been in existence to adjudicate apparent violations. This structure consists of twelve Regional Trial Boards made up of CPAs from each of the state societies within the region and a National Review Board composed of members of the AICPA.

Regional Trial Boards

Cases are initially heard by a panel from the appropriate Regional Trial Board. Decisions from this panel simultaneously affect the AICPA and the state society and are final unless appealed in thirty days. Appeal to the National Review Board may be made on grounds of improper findings based on the facts by the regional board, improper interpretation of the applicable rules, the severity of the punishment, the availability of new evidence, and other similar reasons. An *ad hoc* screening committee of the National Review Board hears any petitions for appeals and petitions for a case to be initially heard by the board. This latter type of petition, however, is not normally granted by the screening committee.

The National Review Board

The National Review Board hears only cases cleared by the *ad hoc* screening committee, and the decisions of the Review Board are final and binding on the CPAs involved, the AICPA, and the state societies.

Under the Joint Trial Board plan a member CPA may be: (1) acquitted, (2) found guilty and censured, (3) found guilty and suspended from membership for a stipulated period of time, or (4) found guilty and expelled permanently. The names of all members found guilty of ethics violations are published periodically by the trial boards.

A CPA also may be suspended or terminated from the AICPA without a hearing if he or she is convicted in a court of law for any of the following:

1. A crime defined as a felony under the law of the convicting jurisdiction.
2. The willful failure to file any income tax return which the CPA as an individual taxpayer is required by law to file.
3. The filing of a false or fraudulent income tax return on his own or a client's behalf.
4. Willfully aiding in the preparation and presentation of the false and fraudulent income tax return of a client.

Also, suspension or termination from the AICPA without a hearing results when the CPA certificate or other license to practice is revoked or withdrawn by the appropriate State Board of Accountancy.

Preventative and Corrective Education

Education plays an important role in the self-regulation and internal disciplinary machinery of the public accounting profession. The following features of the preventative and corrective education program of the AICPA are particularly important.

1. Dissemination of the standards of the profession to as wide an audience as possible.
2. Continuing education home-study courses including one based on the Code of Professional Ethics.
3. A system for responding to telephone and written inquiries from members seeking guidance in applying professional standards to specific fact situations; 6,000 to 7,000 inquiries of various types are handled by the AICPA in a typical year.
4. The formulation of peer review and quality control units within the AICPA and the promulgation of standards in these areas.

This last component of the education program of the profession is particularly significant and will be discussed further.

AICPA Division for CPA Firms

In 1977, a new AICPA Division for CPA Firms was formed to bring firms into the membership of and under the influence of the professional standards and sanctions of the AICPA. The division has two sections: an SEC Practice Section (SECPS) for firms with clients subject to SEC regulation, and a Private Companies Practice Section for firms with private companies as clients.

Each section has its own executive committee and membership requirements, and each requires that its members participate in a mandatory peer review program. These peer reviews involve an examination of a firm's quality control standards and accounting and auditing services by a team of practitioners not associated with the firm under review. The results of these reviews must be reported to the section to which the firm belongs and are available in the section's public file.

A feature of the SEC Practice Section that is intended to add credibility is a Public Oversight Board. This five-member panel of distinguished individuals advises and oversees the activities of the SECPS, particularly the peer review program. Its emphasis is on the regulatory and sanctioning activities of the major committees that carry out the section's work.

The creation of the AICPA Division for CPA Firms was a major step by the public accounting profession in extending self-regulation to encompass firms as well as individual members.

AICPA Quality Control Review Division

In 1978, this division was established to develop quality control standards for CPA firms and to administer the AICPA voluntary peer review program. The goal of quality control standards is to provide guidelines for CPA firms to use in determining that GAAS are being met in their audit work.

Quality control policies and procedures have been formulated in nine specific areas:

1. Independence
2. Assigning personnel to engagements
3. Consultation with others when necessary
4. Supervision of professional staff
5. Hiring of professional staff
6. Professional development
7. Advancement of professional staff
8. Acceptance and continuance of clients
9. Inspection to assure effective application of other quality control policies and procedures

These quality control standards address the needs of CPA firms in each area rather than those of individual CPAs.

In addition to quality control guidelines, the Quality Control Review Division administers a voluntary peer review program. This program is designed for firms that choose not to join the Division for CPA Firms and is conducted in a manner similar to mandatory peer reviews. The results of the review must be filed with the AICPA and may be communicated to clients and staff by the reviewed firm.

CONCEPT SUMMARY

The Internal Disciplinary Machinery of Public Accounting

Unit	Primary Function
The Professional Ethics Division	Responds to inquiries about professional standards, proposes interpretations of rules of conduct, investigates alleged violations of professional standards, and refers cases to the Joint Trial Board for adjudication or issues administrative censure depending upon circumstances of case.
The Joint Trial Board	Hears those cases of alleged serious violations of professional standards and makes the final decision on whether the member should be acquitted, censured, suspended, or expelled from AICPA membership.
Division for CPA Firms	Consists of two sections, SEC Practice and Private Companies Practice, which function to bring member firms under the self-regulation of the AICPA primarily through the mandatory peer review provisions of each section.
Quality Control Review Division	Develops quality control standards for CPA firms which provide guidelines that GAAS are being adhered to in audit work and administers a voluntary peer review program for firms which are not members of either the SEC Practice or Private Companies Sections.
Practice Review Committee	Conducts confidential exchanges with practitioners and firms on deficiencies in work and reporting as part of the corrective education program of the AICPA.

Practice Review Committee

One of the oldest features of Institute self-regulation is corrective education. A committee of the AICPA, called Practice Review, conducts confidential exchanges with practitioners and firms on reporting deficiencies that have come to the attention of the committee. To encourage information on substandard work from as many sources as possible, the Bylaws of the AICPA originally prohibited the Practice Review Committee from referring its information or findings to the Professional Ethics Division or any other disciplinary body of the AICPA. Findings could be referred, however, to practice review programs in state societies when the firm involved was local rather than interstate.

In 1975, the Bylaws of the Institute were modified to permit the Practice Review Committee to send cases of non-cooperation and cases of repeated substandard work to the Professional Ethics Division for possible action.

2.5 FEDERAL REGULATION AND PUBLIC ACCOUNTING

Government entry into the area of securities regulation began with the passage of the first federal security law in 1933. This landmark legislation was followed in 1934 by another federal security law, and a new government agency charged with administering these laws became a part of the environment of public accounting.

The Securities and Exchange Commission

The primary interest of the Securities and Exchange Commission is to ensure the disclosure of all relevant information about the interstate issue and trading of securities and the companies issuing them, for use by investors in security decisions. The SEC is composed of five commissioners, who are appointed by the President and approved by the Senate for staggered terms of five years each. These commissioners supervise an agency made up of five major divisions and five major offices, each of which is designed to carry on a specific part of the SEC's responsibilities. The most important of these units for public accounting are the Office of the Chief Accountant and the Office of the General Counsel.

Office of the Chief Accountant

The chief accountant is the principal accounting and auditing authority for the SEC. The chief accountant and his staff draft the accounting rules and guidelines that govern the content and format of financial statements filed with the SEC, participate in administrative and court actions of the SEC involving accounting and auditing matters, recommend disciplinary actions against CPAs who practice before the SEC, and prepare Accounting Series Releases.

Although the Office of the Chief Accountant has cooperated with the rule-making bodies of the profession throughout its history, the chief accountant can exert substantial influence on GAAP.

Office of the General Counsel

The general counsel advises the Commission on legal problems that arise in connection with enforcement of laws the SEC is required to administer and conducts investigations for the SEC. Most of the investigations are concerned with the sale of securities without registration and with the misrepresentation or omission of material facts concerning securities offered for sale. The general counsel also carries out investigations dealing with market price manipulation and unethical and illegal activities by brokers. While conducting an investigation, the office of the general counsel has full power to subpoena witnesses, take evidence, and accumulate any other material relevant to the inquiry. If the Commission decides after a thorough investigation that a violation has occurred, it may pursue any of several legal channels open to it.

Major Pronouncements of the SEC

The major pronouncements of the SEC are its Regulation S–X and its Accounting Series Releases.

Regulation S–X is the primary accounting regulation of the SEC dealing with the form and content of financial statements filed with the Commission. Its requirements correspond closely with the GAAP and professional standards of the public accounting profession. Occasionally, Regulation S–X will require different treatment of a particular type of event or additional disclosure from that required under GAAP. Companies and their independent CPAs must comply with these additional requirements in statements filed with the SEC.

Professional standards of Regulation S–X are similar to those of the AICPA except in the area of independence. The SEC will not recognize a CPA or firm as independent if any accounting services are performed for an audit client. The AICPA Code of Professional Ethics allows accounting services to be performed for an audit client in certain situations (see Rule 101, Interpretation 3) without considering independence impaired.

The official communications of the SEC are called Accounting Series Releases (ASR). These pronouncements amend the Commission's own rules and regulations (including S–X) and promulgate new regulations. The subject matter of ASRs has ranged from accounting procedures and treatment required by the SEC to the results of administrative and quasi-judicial action by the Commission.

Federal Security Statutes

The SEC is charged with administering the following statutes:

The Securities Act of 1933
The Securities Exchange Act of 1934
The Public Utility Holding Company Act of 1935
The Trust Indenture Act of 1939
The Investment Company Act of 1940
The Investment Advisors Act of 1940

The Securities Acts of 1933 and 1934 are the most important for accountants and investors and will be discussed in the remainder of this section.

The Securities Act of 1933

This federal statute is designed to regulate all interstate securities issues to the public. Intrastate sales (the seller and all purchasers reside within one state) and certain private placements of securities are exempt from registration under the 1933 Act.

The act has two primary objectives:

1. To provide investors with financial and other information on securities offered for public sale.
2. To prevent fraudulent acts and practices in the sale of all securities.

All non-exempt security offerings must be registered with the SEC before the securities can be sold. This registration statement (primarily SEC Form S–1) must be filed with and accepted by the Commission, and potential investors must be provided with a prospectus. The prospectus provides information on the issuing company and the securities being offered as well as certified financial statements. All of the information in the prospectus is included in the S–1 Registration, which also provides additional information not given to investors.

Anyone associated with a registration statement (issuers, underwriters, attorneys, and independent CPAs) can be held responsible for the accuracy of the registration information with which they were associated.

The Securities Exchange Act of 1934

The 1933 Act focuses on the registration of new securities issues to the public and does not deal with the on-going activities of companies after the securities have been sold. The 1934 Act, on the other hand, is concerned with the continuous registration of companies whose securities are traded on organized stock exchanges as well as certain companies (those with $1 million or more in assets and 500 or more owners) whose securities are traded "over the counter." Continuous disclosure of relevant information from these companies is the goal of the act.

Registration under the 1934 Act is continuous because it must be updated each year by filing a registration statement with the SEC. The most important component of this registration statement is Form 10–K, which contains financial statements for the year that are examined by independent auditors.

Anyone associated with the registration statements of companies (including independent CPAs) can be held responsible for the information with which they were associated in the statements.

The Securities Acts of 1933 and 1934 and the Securities and Exchange Commission have been powerful forces in the environment of public accounting. In fact, the statutes were largely responsible for getting the auditing profession established. SEC pronouncements on accounting matters and professional standards have had a direct impact on practitioners, and the vital role of the independent CPA required by both securities acts has certainly contributed to the growth and stature of the profession. However, the benefits to public accounting of federal securities regulation have come at a cost. That cost is the expansion of the legal liability of independent CPAs. Chapter 3 will examine the legal environment.

Key Terms

Accounting Series Release (ASR)
Code of Professional Ethics
ethics
ethics rulings
general ethical principles
general standards
independence
integrity
interpretations
Joint Trial Board
objectivity
Practice Review Committee

Private Companies Practice Section
Professional Ethics Division
Quality Control Review Division
responsibility to colleagues
responsibility to clients
rules of conduct
SEC Practice Section
Securities Act of 1933
Securities and Exchange Commission (SEC)
Securities Exchange Act of 1934
technical standards

Questions and Problems

Questions

2-1 Give a brief description of each of the four components of the Code of Professional Ethics. Which of these components are enforceable upon AICPA members?

2-2 What are the five areas of ethical responsibility around which the Code of Professional Ethics is constructed? Why are each of these areas important to the practice of public accounting?

2-3 Discuss the thrust of the AICPA rule on independence, and indicate how this rule differs from the SEC rule on independence.

2-4 Describe Rule 202—Auditing Standards and give the practical implications of this rule and its interpretations for the independent CPA.

2-5 Describe Rule 203—Accounting Principles and give the practical implications of this rule and its interpretations for the independent CPA.

2-6 How might the rule on confidential client information come into conflict with other professional responsibilities? How should this conflict be resolved?

2-7 Discuss the thrust of the rule on advertising and the rationale for such a rule.

2-8 Contrast the functions of the Professional Ethics Division and those of the Joint Trial Board in enforcing professional standards.

2-9 What are the objectives of the Securities Act of 1933, and what types of securities are covered by the act? What types of securities are exempt from the provisions of the act?

2-10 What are the objectives of the Securities Exchange Act of 1934, and what types of companies are covered by the act? What types of companies are exempt from the provisions of the act?

Multiple Choice Questions from Professional Exams

2-11 Which of the following statements best describes why the profession of certified public accountants has deemed it essential to promulgate a code of ethics and to establish a mechanism for enforcing observance of the code?

    a. A distinguishing mark of a profession is its acceptance of responsibility to the public.

    b. A prerequisite for success is the establishment of an ethical code that stresses primarily the professional's responsibility to clients and colleagues.

    c. A requirement of most state laws calls for the profession to establish a code of ethics.

    d. An essential means of self-protection for the profession is the establishment of flexible ethical standards by the profession.

2-12 The AICPA Code of Professional Ethics derives its authority from the

    a. Bylaws of the American Institute of CPAs.

    b. Financial Accounting Standards Board.

    c. Federal government.

    d. Securities and Exchange Commission.

2-13 The AICPA Code of Professional Ethics states, in part, that a CPA should maintain integrity and objectivity. Objectivity in the code refers to a CPA's ability

    a. To maintain an impartial attitude on all matters which come under the CPA's review.

    b. To independently distinguish between accounting practices that are acceptable and those that are not.

    c. To be unyielding in all matters dealing with auditing procedures.

    d. To independently choose between alternate accounting principles and auditing standards.

2-14 The appearance of independence of a CPA, or that CPA's firm, could be impaired if the CPA

a. Owns a unit in a cooperative apartment house, where each unit has a vote in the cooperative, and the CPA, who does not participate in the management, has been retained as the auditor for the cooperative.

b. Joins a trade association, which is a client, and serves in a non-management capacity.

c. Accepts a gift from a client.

d. Serves as an executor and trustee of the estate of an individual who owned the majority of the stock of a closely held client corporation.

2-15 The AICPA Code of Professional Ethics requires compliance with accounting principles promulgated by the body designated by the AICPA Council to establish such principles. The pronouncements comprehended by the code include all of the following except

a. Opinions issued by the Accounting Principles Board.

b. AICPA Accounting Research Studies.

c. Interpretations issued by the Financial Accounting Standards Board.

d. AICPA Accounting Research Bulletins.

2-16 Richard, CPA, performs accounting services for Norton Corporation. Norton wishes to offer its shares to the public and asks Richard to audit the financial statements prepared for registration purposes. Richard refers Norton to Cruz, CPA, who is more competent in the area of registration statements. Cruz performs the audit of Norton's financial statements and subsequently thanks Richard for the referral by giving Richard a portion of the audit fee collected. Richard accepts the fee. Who, if anyone, has violated professional ethics?

a. Only Richard.

b. Both Richard and Cruz.

c. Only Cruz.

d. Neither Richard nor Cruz.

2-17 A CPA accepts an engagement for a professional service without violating the AICPA Code of Professional Ethics if the service involves

a. The preparation of cost projections for submission to a government agency as an application for a rate increase, and the fee will be paid if there is a rate increase.

b. Tax preparation, and the fee will be based on whether the CPA signs the tax return prepared.

c. A litigatory matter, and the fee is not known but is to be determined by a district court.

d. Tax return preparation, and the fee is to be based on the amount of taxes saved, if any.

2-18 Under the AICPA Code of Professional Ethics, a CPA is prohibited from performing which of the following actions?

a. Expressing an opinion on interim financial statements.

b. Permitting the CPA's college alumni magazine to report that the CPA has opened offices as "an accountant."

c. Making derogatory statements about the competence of the current CPA of a prospective client.

d. Assisting a client in preparing forecasts of the results of future transactions and events.

2-19 A CPA, who is a member of the American Institute of Certified Public Accountants, wrote an article for publication in a professional journal. The AICPA Code of Professional Ethics would be violated if the CPA allowed the article to state that the CPA was

a. A member of the American Institute of Certified Public Accountants.

b. A professor at a school of professional accountancy.

c. A partner in a national CPA firm.

d. A practitioner specializing in providing tax services.

2-20 Under the AICPA Code of Professional Ethics, which of the following characteristics is true for a professional corporation or association of CPAs?

a. The name may be impersonal as long as it does not indicate a speciality.

b. The shareholders must, in all cases, be jointly and severally liable for the acts of the corporation.

c. The corporation may provide services that are not compatible with the practice of public accounting.

d. A shareholder who ceases to be eligible to be a shareholder must dispose of all of his shares within a reasonable period.

2-21 A CPA examines the financial statements of a local bank. According to the AICPA Code of Professional Ethics, the appearance of independence ordinarily would not be impaired if the CPA

a. Serves on the bank's committee that approves loans.

b. Owns several shares of the bank's common stock.

c. Obtains a short-term loan from the bank.

d. Uses the bank's time-sharing computer service to solve client-related problems.

Items 22 through 25: Each of the following items begins with a statement of facts or an opening statement followed by two independent statements numbered I and II. You are to evaluate each statement and determine whether it is true. Your answer for each item should be selected from the following responses:

a. I only is true.
b. II only is true.
c. Both I and II are true.
d. Neither I nor II is true.

2-22 Williams, Inc., a one-man corporation, was in the business of underwriting unlisted, new-venture securities. Bonanza Mining Co., Ltd., engaged Williams to market $600,000 of its unregistered common stock.

I. The Bonanza Mining offering is subject to registration under the Securities Act of 1933.

II. If Williams, Inc., sells the Bonanza Mining securities in interstate commerce to unsuspecting purchasers, any purchaser is entitled to hold either Bonanza or Williams responsible for inaccurate information.

2-23 The partnership of Martinson & Co., CPAs, has been engaged to examine the financial statements of Boxphor, Inc., in connection with the registration of Boxphor's securities with the Securities and Exchange Commission.

I. Martinson & Co. is assuming much greater potential third-party liability than it assumes on engagements under common law.

II. If its examination is not fraudulent, Martinson & Co. may issue an appropriate disclaimer to the financial statements and thereby avoid liability.

2-24 The underlying purpose(s) of the Securities Act of 1933 is (are) to

I. Provide the investing public with the facts needed to evaluate the merit of the security being offered.

II. Provide a procedure to pass upon the merit of the securities being offered and the wisdom of investing in them.

2-25 The Securities Exchange Act of 1934 created the Securities and Exchange Commission. The Act also provides for the

I. Registration with the Securities and Exchange Commission of national securities exchanges and securities listed on exchanges.

II. Registration of certain companies whose securities are traded "over the counter."

Problems

2-26 Johnson, Inc., a closely held company, wishes to engage Norr, CPA, to examine its annual financial statements. Johnson was generally pleased with the services provided by its prior CPA, Diggs, but thought the audit work performed was too detailed and interfered excessively with Johnson's normal office routines. Norr asked Johnson to inform Diggs of the decision to change auditors, but Johnson did not wish to do so.

Required:

List and discuss the steps Norr should follow before accepting the engagement.

AICPA

2-27 The following cases relate to the CPA's management of his accounting practice:

Case 1

Judd Hanlon, CPA, was engaged to prepare the federal income tax return for the Guild Corporation for the year ending December 31, 1981. This is Mr. Hanlon's first engagement for the Guild Corporation.

In preparing the 1981 return, Mr. Hanlon finds an error on the 1980 return. The 1980 depreciation deduction was overstated significantly—accumulated depreciation brought forward from 1979 to 1980 was understated, and thus the 1980 base for declining balance depreciation was overstated.

Mr. Hanlon reported the error to Guild's controller, the officer responsible for tax returns. The controller stated: "Let the revenue agent find the error." He further instructed Mr. Hanlon to carry forward the material overstatement of the depreciable base to the 1981 depreciation computation. The controller noted that this error also had been made in the financial records for 1980 and 1981 and offered to furnish Mr. Hanlon with a letter assuming full responsibility for this treatment.

Required:

a. Evaluate Mr. Hanlon's handling of this situation.

b. Discuss the additional action that Mr. Hanlon should now undertake.

Case 2

Fred Browning, CPA, has examined the financial statements of the Grimm Company for several years. Grimm's president now has asked Mr. Browning to install an inventory control system for the company.

Required:

Discuss the factors that Mr. Browning should consider in determining whether to accept this engagement.

AICPA (adapted)

2-28 The Code of Professional Ethics requires that an auditor be independent in appearance as well as in fact.

Required:

a. Explain the concept of an "auditor's independence" as it applies to third-party reliance upon financial statements.
b. 1. What determines whether or not an auditor is independent in fact?
   2. What determines whether or not an auditor appears to be independent?
c. Explain how an auditor may be independent in fact but not appear to be independent.
d. Would a CPA be considered independent for an examination of the financial statements of a
   1. church for which the CPA is serving as treasurer without compensation? Explain.
   2. women's club for which a spouse is serving as treasurer-bookkeeper if there is no fee for the examination? Explain.

AICPA (adapted)

2-29 Alex Pratt, a retired partner of your CPA firm, has just been appointed to the board of directors of Palmer Corporation, your audit client. Pratt is also a member of your firm's Income Tax Advisory Committee, which meets monthly to discuss income tax problems of clients, including some competitors of Palmer Corporation. The CPA firm pays Pratt a fixed fee for each committee meeting he attends and a substantial monthly retirement benefit.

Required:

a. Discuss the effect of Pratt's appointment to the board of directors of Palmer Corporation on your independence in expressing an opinion on the Palmer Corporation's financial statements.
b. Might any other ethics problems arise from this statement? Discuss.

AICPA (adapted)

2-30 The Wanguard Corporation was formed on October 1, 1981, and its fiscal year will end on September 30, 1982. You audited the corporation's opening balance sheet and rendered an unqualified opinion on it. A month after rendering your report you are offered the position of secretary of the company because of the need for a complete set of officers and for convenience in signing various documents. You will have no financial interest in the company through stock ownership or otherwise, will receive no salary, will not keep the books, and will not have any influence on financial matters other than to provide occasional advice on income tax matters and similar advice normally given a client by a CPA.

Required:

a. Assume that you accept the offer but plan to resign the position prior to conducting your annual audit with the intention of again assuming the office after rendering an opinion on the statements. Can you render an independent opinion on the financial statements? Discuss.

b. Assume that you accept the offer on a temporary basis until the corporation has gotten under way and can employ a secretary. In any event you would permanently resign the position before conducting your annual audit. Can you render an independent opinion on the financial statements? Discuss.

c. Summarize the rules of conduct from the Code of Professional Ethics which have to do with CPA independence.

AICPA (adapted)

2-31 Gilbert and Bradley formed a corporation called Financial Services, Inc., each man taking 50 percent of the authorized common stock. Gilbert is a CPA and a member of the American Institute of CPAs. Bradley is a CPCU (Chartered Property Casualty Underwriter). The Corporation performs auditing and tax services under Gilbert's direction and insurance services under Bradley's supervision. The opening of the corporation's office was announced by a three-inch, two-column "card" in the local newspaper.

One of the corporation's first audit clients was the Grandtime Company. Grandtime had total assets of $600,000 and total liabilities of $270,000. In the course of his examination, Gilbert found that Grandtime's building, which had a book value of $240,000, was pledged as security for a ten-year term note in the amount of $200,000. The client's statements did not mention that the building was pledged as security for the ten-year term note. However, as the failure to disclose the lien did not affect either the value of the assets or the amount of the liabilities and his examination was satisfactory in all other respects, Gilbert rendered an unqualified opinion on Grandtime's financial statements. About two months after the date of his opinion, Gilbert learned that an insurance company was planning to loan Grandtime $150,000 in the form of a first-mortgage note on the building. Realizing that the insurance company was unaware of the existing lien on the building, Gilbert had Bradley notify the insurance company of the fact that Grandtime's building was pledged as security for the term note.

Shortly after the events described above, Gilbert was charged with a violation of professional ethics.

Required:

Identify and discuss the ethical implications of those acts by Gilbert that were in violation of the AICPA Code of Professional Ethics.

AICPA

2-32 An audit client, Oldtown Corporation, requests that you conduct a feasibility study to advise management of the best way the corporation can utilize electronic data processing equipment and which computer, if any, best meets the corporation's requirements. You are technically competent in this area and accept the engagement. At the completion of your study, the corporation accepts your suggestions and installs the computer and related equipment that you recommended.

Required:

a. Discuss the effect the acceptance of this management services engagement would have upon your independence in expressing an opinion on the financial statements of the Oldtown Corporation.

b. Instead of accepting the engagement, assume that you recommended Eve Mackey, of the CPA firm of Brown and Mackey, who is qualified in specialized services. Upon completion of the engagement, your client requests that Mackey's partner, John Brown, perform services in other areas. Should Brown accept the engagement? Discuss.

c. A local printer of data processing forms customarily offers a commission for recommending him as supplier. The client is aware of the commission offer and suggests that Mackey accept it. Would it be proper for Mackey to accept the commission with the client's approval? Discuss.

AICPA (adapted)

2-33 An auditor's report was appended to the financial statements of Worthmore, Inc. The statements consisted of a balance sheet as of November 30, 1982, and statements of income, retained earnings, and changes in financial position for the year then ended. The first two paragraphs of the report contained the wording of the standard unqualified report, and a third paragraph read as follows:

> The wives of two partners of our CPA firm owned a material investment in the outstanding common stock of Worthmore, Inc., during the fiscal year ending November 30, 1982. The aforementioned persons disposed of their holdings of Worthmore, Inc., on December 3, 1982, in a transaction that did not result in a profit or a loss. This information is included in our audit report in order to comply with certain disclosure requirements of the Code of Professional Ethics of the American Institute of Certified Public Accountants.

> BELL & DAVIS
> Certified Public Accountants

Required:

a. Was the CPA firm of Bell & Davis independent with respect to the fiscal 1982 examination of Worthmore, Inc.'s financial statements? Explain.

b. Do you find Bell & Davis' auditor's report satisfactory? Explain.

c. If no financial interest in Worthmore is or has ever been held by anyone connected with Bell & Davis, explain whether or not independence would be impaired in the following circumstances:

   1. Two directors of Worthmore, Inc., became partners of Bell & Davis on July 1, 1982, resigning their directorships on that date.

   2. During 1982, the former controller of Worthmore, now a Bell & Davis partner, was frequently called on for assistance by Worthmore. He made decisions for Worthmore's management regarding plant and equipment acquisitions and the company's product mix. In addition, he conducted a computer feasibility study for Worthmore.

AICPA (adapted)

2-34 Each of the following situations may involve violations of the AICPA Code of Professional Ethics.

   1. Triolo, CPA, has a small public accounting practice. One of Triolo's clients desires services that Triolo cannot adequately provide. Triolo has recommended a larger CPA firm, Pinto & Co., to his client, and, in return, Pinto has agreed to pay Triolo 10% of the fee for services rendered by Pinto for Triolo's client.

   2. Clark, CPA, wishes to express an opinion that the financial statements of Smith Co. are presented in conformity with generally accepted accounting principles. However, the financial statements contain a departure from an APB opinion and a departure from an FASB statement.

   3. Poust, CPA, has sold his public accounting practice to Lyons, CPA, and has turned over to Lyons all working papers and other documents relating to the auditing, tax, and other services of his practice.

   4. Adams is the executive partner of Adams & Co., CPAs. One of its smaller clients is a large non-profit charitable organization. The organization has asked Adams to be on its board of directors, which consists of a large number of the community's leaders. Membership on the board is honorary in nature.

   5. Pickens and Perkins, CPAs, decide to incorporate their practice of accountancy and have issued shares to all employees of the firm including professional and non-professional staff.

   6. Fenn & Co., CPAs, has time available on a computer, which it uses primarily for its own internal record-keeping. Aware that the computer facilities of Delta Equipment Co., one of Fenn's audit

clients, are inadequate for the company needs, Fenn offers to maintain on its computer certain routine accounting records for Delta. If Delta were to accept the offer, Fenn would continue to function as independent auditor for Delta.

7. Marquis, CPA, occasionally undertakes management advisory services engagements, although his practice deals primarily with auditing services. The Keller Corporation has recently asked Marquis to make a study of the company's executive compensation package. Marquis has no prior experience in this area.

8. Gutowski, a practicing CPA, has written an article, which is being published in a professional publication. The publication wishes to inform its readers about Gutowski's background including her academic degrees held, other articles she has published in professional journals, her CPA firm association, and the statement that she is an EDP expert and consultant.

Required:

a. Identify the Rule of Conduct applicable to each of the above situations.

b. For each situation, indicate: (a) whether or not an ethics violation has occurred and the reasons for your answer, and (b) the circumstances under which your decision would be different.

AICPA (adapted)

2-35 The AICPA Code of Professional Ethics consists of five ethical principles that are implemented by thirteen enforceable rules of conduct and twenty-six interpretations of these rules.

Required:

Summarize in your own words the thirteen rules of conduct, and give a specific example of CPA behavior that would be considered a violation for each of the twenty-six areas of interpretation.

The legal environment
of public accounting

> There is a significant gap between the thinking of the accounting profession
> and what the courts, and others are saying about auditors' responsibilities.[1]

So spoke the president of the AICPA in recognition of where the flood of legal
actions and adverse decisions had left the profession in 1975. It was a situation
of which most practicing public accountants were already acutely aware and one
which most feel must be solved if the profession is to continue its growth, high
level of performance, and place in society.

One of the most striking developments in public accounting over the past ten
years has been the change in the legal liability environment of the auditor.

3.1 THE BASIS OF LITIGATION AGAINST ACCOUNTANTS

Most legal actions in which public accountants are defendants revolve around
the concept of negligence. Typically, the plaintiff (the person or group with a
complaint) alleges that the accountant has been negligent in some fashion, and
the defendant-accountant strives to show he has not. A general appreciation of
negligence is helpful in understanding the position of the accountant and other
professionals under the law.

Society expects a certain reasonable standard of behavior from all persons,
and negligence is a departure from this standard. The behavior of professionals
in performing their work, however, is usually measured against a higher standard

---

[1]Wallace E. Olson, "A Look at the Responsibility Gap," *The Journal of Accountancy* (January
1975), p. 53.

in determining whether or not obligations and duties have been met. Those who hold themselves up to the public as possessing special expertise must exhibit the knowledge, skill, and judgement usually exhibited by members of their professions. It is clear that accountants must exhibit this high standard of duty and care in their work.

Legal Negligence

Legal liability for negligent conduct generally requires: (1) a duty to some standard of performance, (2) failure to meet that duty, (3) actual damage or loss, and (4) demonstrable cause and effect relationship between the failure to meet the standard and the damage or loss.

The standard of care owed by auditors to clients and other users of their work has often been at the center of litigation. The standard required depends upon the theory of liability chosen as the basis of the action, the proximity of the users, and the foreseeability of the damage or loss. Auditors may be required to demonstrate only slight care in some situations (failure of which is called gross negligence), while in other cases great care (failure of which is called mere negligence) is necessary.

An important factor in legal actions is alleged failure to meet whatever the required standard is determined to be. An important consideration has been the CPA's performance in meeting and applying the standards and procedures of the public accounting profession.

Negligence may be alleged against the auditor in any phase of his activities. CPAs may be found negligent in: (1) ascertaining the facts, (2) drawing inferences from the facts, and (3) communicating information so that it may be understood.

Classification of the Law

The law on which legal actions against accountants are based may be classified in a number of ways, with each division explaining the subject matter and mechanics from a different perspective. The best known classifications are the public-private and criminal-civil dissections of the law.

Public Law

Public law and criminal law tend to be synonymous, with both representing areas of legal dispute where society's interest is directly involved. Usually, "the people" are represented here by some government agency or agent who speaks for and protects the interests of the larger society. The state has an interest in and participates in these disputes. The entire area of public law is slightly broader than criminal law in that it may also include matters of constitutional and administrative law (such as rulings of the Securities and Exchange Commission).

Private Law

Private law, which is generally synonymous with civil law, includes those matters of legal dispute between private entities where society's interests are not directly involved. Private case law is usually divided into the law of contracts and the law of torts. The law of contracts is concerned with obligations, duties, rights, and privileges created between individuals by their own mutual agreement, while the law of torts is concerned with the rights and duties created by social custom and conceptions of equity. An agreement between an auditor and client as to the nature and scope of an audit would constitute a contract, and disputes between these two parties would be settled according to the law of contracts. On the other hand, disputes between the auditor and any outside users of his work who are not parties to the contract would have to be settled under the law of torts. Private law may also be written in the form of federal and state statutes.

Since areas of both public and private law make up the legal environment of public accounting, the boundaries and substance of each should be understood.

Types of Legal Actions

Legal actions against public accountants may be brought by clients under contract law, by third-party users of financial statements (such as creditors or stockholders) under tort law or statute law, or by the government under statute law. Contract and tort law are called *case law* or *common law*. Statute law is called *written law*. Actions brought by clients or third parties are always civil actions, which seek monetary damages or compensation from defendants. Actions brought by the government may be criminal and seek fine or imprisonment of those found guilty.

Exhibit 3–1 presents the types of legal liability faced by accountants and the parties or institutions to whom they may be liable. Also given are the major cases under each of the categories, which will be discussed in the remainder of this chapter.

3.2 LIABILITY UNDER COMMON LAW

Since at least the early twentieth century, public accounting in the United States has been recognized as a skilled profession subject to the same rules of liability as are members of other skilled professions. The question is not whether the usual theories of professional liability apply to public accountants but rather how these apply to the unique functions and circumstances of the CPA. Specifically, what are the expectations of society and the demands of the law with respect to public accountants in performing the audit function; what are the specific practices or omissions which have resulted in legal liability; and what are the limits of such liability?

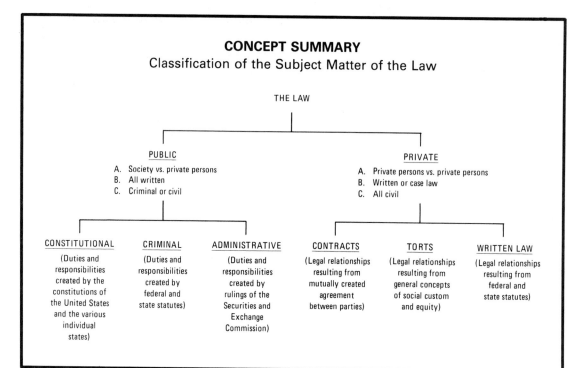

CONCEPT SUMMARY
Classification of the Subject Matter of the Law

THE LAW

PUBLIC
A. Society vs. private persons
B. All written
C. Criminal or civil

PRIVATE
A. Private persons vs. private persons
B. Written or case law
C. All civil

CONSTITUTIONAL
(Duties and responsibilities created by the constitutions of the United States and the various individual states)

CRIMINAL
(Duties and responsibilities created by federal and state statutes)

ADMINISTRATIVE
(Duties and responsibilities created by rulings of the Securities and Exchange Commission)

CONTRACTS
(Legal relationships resulting from mutually created agreement between parties)

TORTS
(Legal relationships resulting from general concepts of social custom and equity)

WRITTEN LAW
(Legal relationships resulting from federal and state statutes)

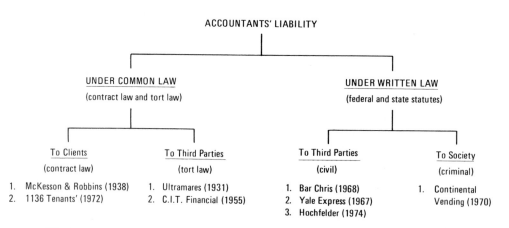

ACCOUNTANTS' LIABILITY

UNDER COMMON LAW
(contract law and tort law)

UNDER WRITTEN LAW
(federal and state statutes)

To Clients
(contract law)
1. McKesson & Robbins (1938)
2. 1136 Tenants' (1972)

To Third Parties
(tort law)
1. Ultramares (1931)
2. C.I.T. Financial (1955)

To Third Parties
(civil)
1. Bar Chris (1968)
2. Yale Express (1967)
3. Hochfelder (1974)

To Society
(criminal)
1. Continental Vending (1970)

EXHIBIT 3–1   Sources of Legal Liability of Accountants and Major Cases

80

As society's concepts of social and moral responsibility have evolved, the demands of the law upon the professions have changed. Public accounting has not been immune to these changes. In the past seventy-five years, auditors have seen their professional liability defined and then evolve and be redefined. To understand the current status of the civil liability of public accountants under common law, it is essential to examine the important legal decisions that affected the evolution of this liability.

Liability to Clients

The basis of the liability of auditors to clients lies essentially in the contractual relationship that exists between them. The contract creating this legal relationship should be formally written with all rights, duties, and obligations explicitly specified. More likely, however, the written agreement will be stated in general terms using non-technical language, or in some cases, there may be no written understanding at all between the parties. If a dispute arises in the former case, interpretation of the written agreement is necessary, while in the latter case the agreement must first be determined and then interpreted.

Analysis of important decided cases discloses that reconstructing non-written agreements between auditors and clients and interpreting agreements whether written or not, involves application of the law of contracts as well as accounting and auditing standards and procedures. It is in these areas that the most important auditor-client litigation has occurred.

McKesson & Robbins, Inc. (1938)

This case involved the discovery that inventory had been overstated by approximately $10 million and receivables by approximately $9 million in McKesson & Robbins, Inc., a wholesale drug company with assets of approximately $87 million. The financial statements had been audited, and the overstatement was undetected by the auditors. Although this action was settled without litigation (by the return of over $500,000 in audit fees by Price Waterhouse & Co.), the Securities and Exchange Commission investigation, which followed the disclosure of the fraud, overturned many existing pronouncements on auditor responsibility in the area of inventory and receivables.

The SEC investigation concluded that: (1) the auditors had not been as alert or vigilant as they should have been in performing the audit, (2) major overstatements of this type should have been discovered, (3) physical verification of inventories and direct confirmation of receivables should be a part of normal audit procedures, and (4) auditors should be elected by company stockholders (SEC Accounting Series Release No. 19, 1940).

Important Results

Before these results were published, the American Institute of Accountants (forerunner to the AICPA), rocked by the scandal, authorized a Committee on Auditing Procedure to examine auditing procedure and the limits of auditor responsibility. The committee issued its report in May 1939. This report became, in part, the first of a series of statements on auditing procedure in October 1939. The report recommended physical verification of inventories, direct confirmation of receivables, and stockholder approval of auditors selected by company directors. The first two recommendations of this report are now an established part of auditing practice. The latter recommendation has not yet become a requirement, although stockholder ratification of independent auditors selected by the board of directors is now a widespread practice.

This change in audit procedures was revolutionary rather than evolutionary and was brought about by the realization that the reasonably cautious and careful auditor could not always be counted on to detect even the most gross frauds. Recognizing that the courts would certainly hold public accountants to a duty of this magnitude, the SEC and the public accounting profession moved to include new procedures in audit work that would allow the auditor to meet his responsibilities and avoid potential legal liability. Although these new procedures were intended to aid the public accountant in satisfying his legal responsibilities to clients, they later became a factor in legal responsibility to third parties.

1136 Tenants' Corp. *v.* Max Rothenberg & Co., (1972)

This is an important case because it dealt with an area considered potentially troublesome for the profession (unaudited financial statements) and because one of the issues of contention was the auditor's contract itself. A corporate cooperative apartment house sued a firm of CPAs to recover losses which occurred while the defendant-accountants had performed "write-up" work (preparation of unaudited financial statements) for the cooperative. The plaintiff's managing agent had embezzled over $100,000 of cooperative funds, and this had gone unnoticed by the CPAs during their work. Two critical issues surfaced during the course of the litigation, and both were dealt with by the courts. First, the question of what had been contracted between the plaintiff and the defendant became a central issue because the agreement had been an oral one and was complicated by the fact that it took place between the managing agent (the embezzler) and the accountants. Second, the court considered the accountant's duties and obligations when dealing with unaudited statements.

In the early stages of the trial, both parties produced evidence supporting differing versions of what the oral contract entailed including proof by the accountants that the prepared financial statements were marked "no independent verifications." The accountants asked for dismissal of the case on the grounds that no audit was promised, no audit was undertaken, and therefore, no duty to discover misappropriation existed. The motion for dismissal was denied, and the denial was upheld by New York's Court of Appeals (the State's highest court). Interestingly, the appeals court felt that, even if there had been no agreement to perform an audit (still an open question at this point) an issue suitable for trial still remained. The court held that, even if the accountants "acted as but a robot, merely doing copy work," it still must be determined whether the suspicious actions of the agent were observed by the accountants thereby giving them the duty to inform the cooperative. Although the question of the contract was critical to this case, the court broadened the implications of the case for all public accountants by considering the duty owed by CPAs even without an audit.

Finally, in 1970, the case went to trial, and the verdict was for the plaintiff on the basis of negligent work. Damages of $237,278 were awarded. It was found that an audit was implied by the facts of the case in that the accountants admitted to doing more than mere "write-up" work. Once again, on appeal, the review court held that the accountants had been aware of certain suspicious facts and circumstances which created a duty for them to inform the plaintiff, no matter what the original agreement may have been. The decision was upheld by the Court of Appeals of New York.

Important Results

The 1136 Tenants' case changed the thinking of practicing CPAs in at least three important areas. First, several official pronouncements, including one SAS, resulted from this landmark case. Second, it was now clear that a public accountant has a duty to disclose to his client any facts or circumstances which may indicate the existence of fraud, no matter what the scope of his work is. In this case, the "suspicious circumstances" were a series of missing invoices discovered only after the accountants went beyond normal write-up procedures. The court's decision would seem to imply that at least some audit procedures are required, even in the most limited engagement.

Third, the 1136 case made clear the importance of care and clarity in defining the terms of an engagement and in communicating "association" with financial statements produced by audit work. In the light of this decision, written documentation is absolutely essential for every engagement, as is strict adherence to the profession's own standards for disclosing association with financial statements.

Liability to Third Parties

Inasmuch as the public accountant does not have a contractual relationship with third-party users of his work and report, the basis of his liability here differs from his liability to his client. Since the law of contracts does not apply to those without "privity" to the contract, the courts were at first uncertain as to which, if any, theory of liability to apply to third-party liability cases and to which standard of care the accountant must be held. As a result, there was reluctance on the part

CONCEPT SUMMARY

Auditor Liability to Clients Under Common Law

Case	Facts	Findings	Implications
McKesson & Robbins, Inc. (1938) (Case settled without litigation, but SEC investigation resulted)	1. Inventory overstated by $10 million. 2. Receivables overstated by $9 million. 3. Auditors returned $500,000 audit fee to client.	1. Overstatements should have been discovered. 2. Current auditing standards and procedures not adequate.	1. Physical verification of inventory now a part of normal audit procedures. 2. Direct confirmation of receivables now a part of normal audit procedures.
1136 Tenants' Corp. (1972) (Decision affirmed by New York State's highest court)	1. CPA firm performed bookkeeping work and prepared unaudited financial statements for client. 2. $100,000 embezzled by employee of client. 3. Oral agreement existed between CPA firm and client as to engagement.	1. Auditors found guilty of negligence and damages of $237,278 awarded. 2. Suspicious circumstances must be reported to client, even if outside of the agreed-upon work of the auditor.	1. Auditor has duty to disclose facts or circumstances that indicate fraud. 2. Some audit procedures may be required, even in the most limited engagement. 3. Written documentation is necessary in every engagement and "association" with financial statements must be carefully disclosed.

of courts to find any duty to third parties based on negligence no matter how gross. Eventually, however, a doctrine of third-party liability evolved based on a tort action, similar to malpractice.

The origins of this doctrine date to 1931 so that third-party liability for negligence under common law is still a new idea (in a legal sense) and is very much in a state of flux. Dramatic developments in this area have been, and will continue to be, more frequent than in the area of accountant-client liability.

This section will examine the important decided cases that have contributed to the evolution of third-party liability under common law.

Ultramares Corp. *v.* Touche (1931)

The Ultramares case is the most important American case dealing with the legal responsibility of accountants under common law. While Ultramares is no longer the most important case on accountants' legal liability (having been replaced by several securities law cases) it is still the most significant common law case.

The facts of this case were complex, and its process through the courts was involved. However, a brief description of the case gives an excellent view of how common law is created and settled. The defendant-accountants had audited the books of an importer in 1924 and given the client thirty-two copies of the certified balance sheet, knowing that these copies would be supplied to various creditors. The plaintiff was a creditor who made substantial loans to the importer based on the certified balance sheet. The balance sheet was extraordinarily inaccurate, showing a net worth of over one million dollars when, in fact, the firm's liabilities exceeded its assets by approximately $200,000. Overstatements of receivables and understatements of payables, which accounted for the difference, went undetected by the auditors. The plaintiff sued the auditors to recover his losses.

The plaintiff alleged causes of action based on negligence and fraud. The judge dismissed the fraud complaint and submitted the negligence question to the jury. The jury found for the plaintiff with damages of approximately $190,000, but the judge dismissed the verdict on grounds of law. The Appellate Division upheld the dismissal of the fraud action but narrowly reversed the negligence dismissal and upheld the jury's verdict. At this point, both parties appealed to the Court of Appeals, which reversed both decisions of the Appellate Division. The high court found evidence of negligence on the part of the accountants but ruled that it created no liability to the plaintiff. More importantly, it found reasonable basis to pursue the fraud action and ordered a new trial on this action. The trial was never held. The case was settled out of court.

The effect of this case on accountants was twofold. One part of the decision was viewed as favorable to the legal liability status of accountants, and the other was generally regarded as creating a new theory of liability for public accountants. The decision by the New York Court of Appeals held that there could be no third-party liability for mere negligence. This finding was of some comfort to accountants because it seemed to halt an apparent movement in the direction of liability for mere negligence.

It was in the second area, however, that the decision was to have its most lasting and significant impact upon public accountants. The court, in a landmark opinion, created a new third-party liability doctrine. This new concept, called *gross negligence,* seemed to bridge the gap between negligence and fraud. The court found that the existence of gross negligence on the part of an accountant may be taken by a jury as an indication or inference of the existence of fraud. It had long been clear that accountants would be held liable to third parties for fraud, but finding fraud required a willful intent to deceive. Such deceitful intent was seldom present and was difficult to show. With the Ultramares decision, deceitful intent was no longer necessary to the finding of fraud. Instead, accountants could be found guilty of fraud if, in the words of the court, ". . . their audit has been so negligent as to justify a finding that they had no genuine belief in its adequacy. . . ."

Important Results

The decision in Ultramares left the common law liability of accountants to third parties in the following condition.

1. The Court of Appeals held that "intent to deceive" was not necessary to a finding of fraud and that fraud could be inferred by a jury from gross negligence by accountants.

2. Gross negligence may be committed in the treatment of factual matters as well as by the expression of an opinion. If accountants "certified as a fact, true to their own knowledge" something about which they had no knowledge, and that certification was false, they may have committed gross negligence. Further, said the court, "they are not to be exonerated because they believed it to be true."

3. To avoid an inference of fraud, the auditor must not only believe in his opinion, he must have based the belief upon competent investigation and information.

The important cases at common law from 1931 to the present all trace their decisions to one aspect or another of the reasoning and logic in the Ultramares opinion. The common thread through these cases is a constantly broadening scope of liability as the theories created in Ultramares are refined and applied.

C.I.T. Financial Corp. v. Glover (1955)

This was another case of a creditor bringing suit against an auditing firm for alleged "fatal inadequacy" in the performance of audits for a firm that subsequently declared bankruptcy. The plaintiff had advanced approximately $1,500,000 to the firm and had not called in its loan because it relied on the results of the defendant's audits.

Five different causes of action were brought by the plaintiff including negligence, gross negligence, and fraud in concealment of errors. The case was tried in federal court because of the diversity of citizenship of plaintiff and defendant. The trial judge dismissed two of the counts, and the jury found for the defendants on the other three on the basis of the facts of the case, after establishing that the auditors did owe the plaintiffs the duty suggested by the causes of action. In other words, the verdict rested on the failure of the plaintiffs to prove that the auditors' work had been negligent or misleading in any material respect. The United States Court of Appeals heard an appeal by the plaintiffs based essentially on the findings of the jury. The dismissal of several counts by the judge was not contested. The verdict of the jury was affirmed, thus ending the litigation in favor of the accountants.

Important Results

The case is important for two reasons. First, it represents a successful defense by accountants in a close case that could have been decided either way. Second, the charge of the trial judge to the jury as they received the case is generally considered to be a fair and high quality statement of the law in the area of third-party liability by accountants.

The accountants' defense was based on several disclaimers in the audit report, which qualified their general statements concerning the financial stability of the debtor firm and disclosed the auditors' reliance on several assertions of management. In addition, the auditors established that the plaintiff possessed special knowledge of the business activities of the debtor firm, which made reliance on the audited statements unlikely.

As to the charge of the trial judge, reference was made to its quality in the opinion of the U.S. Court of Appeals. The charge discussed the duties of auditors in relation to the legal concepts of fraud, intent to deceive, gross negligence, and reliance and then addressed the area of third-party liability for ordinary negligence. One of the causes of action being submitted to the jury alleged such negligence and maintained that the defendants owed this duty of care to the plaintiffs. This portion of the charge has been widely quoted and is reproduced here in relevant part.

> Defendants are not to be held liable for mere negligence if their reports were made primarily for the benefit of Manufacturers Trading Corporation [the debtor firm and the client of the defendant-auditors] as a convenient instrumentality for use in the development of its business, and only incidentally or collaterally for the use of plaintiff. The test is then, did defendants know that the audits and certifications were being made for the primary benefit of plaintiff, and was plaintiff so specifically identified to the defendants? If this has not been established to your satisfaction by a preponderance of the credible evidence, your verdict shall be for the defendants on this third cause of action. If this has been established to your satisfaction by a preponderance of the credible evidence, then the defendants in preparing their audits would be liable to plaintiff for carelessness, blunders and errors in judgment, which were the result of failure to exercise that degree of care which a reasonably prudent accountant employed on a like and similar task would exercise. Apply, of course, when determining the degree of care required of the defendants, the standards of recognized accounting practice and procedure as you find them from the evidence which has been presented.[2]

These passages seem to extend to a specifically identified third party known by the accountant to be the primary recipient and beneficiary of the auditor's report the same rights as those in privity of contract.

The cases presented so far have illustrated critical points in the evolution of accountants' liability to clients and third parties at common law. These developments include significant extensions of auditing procedure and the establishment of new theories of liability by the courts.

---

[2]Taken from Roy E. Baker, *Cases in Auditing*, Englewood Cliffs, New Jersey: Prentice-Hall, Inc., 1969, pp. 34–35.

CONCEPT SUMMARY
Auditor Liability to Third Parties Under Common Law

Case	Facts	Findings	Implications
Ultramares (1931) (Original trial decisions appealed to New York State's highest court and reversed several times. Case never retried)	1. Certified balance sheet provided in multiple copies by auditors to be supplied by client to various creditors. 2. Balance sheet showed net worth of $1 million when, in fact, net worth was negative $200,000. 3. Creditor sued auditors to recover loans made on basis of balance sheet.	1. No liability to third parties can result from mere negligence on the part of the auditor. 2. Intent to deceive not necessary to sustain a fraud action against auditors. Court ordered that fraud action be pursued.	1. A new legal theory called gross negligence was created to bridge the gap between negligence and fraud. Certifying without knowledge may be gross negligence. 2. Fraud by auditor may be inferred by a jury from gross negligence on the part of auditors.
C.I.T. Financial Corp. (1955) (Case tried in federal court and decision upheld by U.S. Court of Appeals)	1. Audit performed for client which subsequently declared bankruptcy. 2. Creditor sued to recover $1,500,000 loan not called in prior to bankruptcy because of audit results.	1. Negligence and fraud actions were dismissed by trial judge. Jury found auditors not guilty of gross negligence. 2. Auditors defense based on disclaimers in the audit report and the special knowledge of the creditor which made reliance on financial statements unlikely.	1. It was a successful defense of auditors in a close case. 2. The charge to the jury by the trial judge, which was widely hailed as an excellent statement of the current status of the law, gave certain third parties the same rights as those in contract with the auditor.

3.3 CIVIL LIABILITY UNDER WRITTEN LAW

Statute law in the area of regulation of securities is relatively new in the United States, dating from 1933 with the passage of the first federal security law. Although many state laws regulating the sale of securities intrastate (called blue-sky laws) were in existence prior to this time, the stock market crash of 1929 brought to a head arguments for federal protection in interstate security transactions.

Several approaches to federal regulation were considered, but the full disclosure approach was chosen. Out of this approach came several federal statutes and the Securities and Exchange Commission, a government agency responsible for their administration. Of these new laws, only the Securities Acts of 1933 and 1934 are general in scope, and they provide most of the federal statute protection for investors. The remainder of this chapter will be concerned with the evolution of accountants' liability under these statutes.

Liability Under the 1933 Act

The 1933 Act is essentially a disclosure statute relating to *new* security issues offered to the public. It calls for filing certain information with the SEC prior to the issue of a new security. This information includes the primary business of the company; its officers, directors, and capital structure; details of the underwriting agreement for the security; and audited financial statements for the past three years. Taken together, this information is called the Registration Statement. This act's provisions encompass accountants through the requirement that independent CPAs audit the financial statements included in the filed registration statement.

Of the statutory defenses granted public accountants and others under the 1933 Act, only the defense commonly known as "due diligence" represents a generalized bar to liability. This defense has received the most attention in discussions of liability under the 1933 Act.

Escott *v.* Bar Chris Construction Corp. (1968)

This is the primary 1933 Act case to be tried and decided to date. It is often quoted and generally considered to be one of the most important cases dealing with accountants' liability under federal security statutes because: (1) there are few cases under the 1933 Act, (2) the standards of the profession (both accounting and auditing) and their application were a key factor in the case, (3) the matter of materiality was dealt with judicially, and (4) the "due diligence" defense was asserted by all defendants, including the accountants.

Plaintiffs in the case were approximately sixty purchasers of convertible bonds of Bar Chris Construction, which was engaged primarily in the construction of bowling alleys. Defendants included all persons who had signed the registration statement upon which the public offering of bonds had been made, all of the underwriters of the bond issue, and the company's auditors, Peat, Marwick, Mitchell & Co.

Begun as a partnership in 1946, the business grew rapidly, as a result of the advent of automatic pin setting machines, and was incorporated in 1955. Because of this rapid growth and its method of financing, Bar Chris was in constant need of working capital. A substantial public offering of stock was sold in 1959 and again in 1961. Needing still more cash in 1961, the firm also made a public offering of convertible debentures. It was the registration statement for this last issue of securities to the public upon which the case was based. This registration statement became effective on May 16, 1961. In late 1962, Bar Chris filed for bankruptcy and defaulted on interest payments due November 1, 1962. Action was begun in late 1962.

This case was extremely complex because of the number of plaintiffs and defendants,[3] although the action essentially rested on whether the registration statement contained false statements or misleading omissions. If so, were they material, and had the defendants exercised due diligence in their activities?

---

[3]So complex was the case that Judge McLean was moved to note in his opinion, "The testimony on many subjects in this case is confused. It is scattered over some 6,500 pages of stenographic minutes without any coherent explanation all in one place. To some extent this was inevitable, in view of the number of defendants, each of whom cross-examined the witnesses, plus the fact that plaintiffs, for the most part, were compelled to prove their case out of the mouths of hostile witnesses."

The presiding judge (there was no jury by agreement of the parties) found no fewer than ten material false statements or omissions ranging from an overstatement of earnings and current assets to several disclosure failures as to the nature of the company's activities.

Important Results

The most important aspect of the case deals with the due diligence defense and the requirements for its successful assertion by experts. Of concern here is the court's discussion of this defense as it pertained to the defendant-accountants and the conclusions to be drawn from this discussion.

The finding of the court that the auditors were unable to sustain the due diligence defense on all matters (although it was sustained on some matters) rested on their care in the application of accounting and auditing standards and their behavior when professional standards were vague or ambiguous.

The court held that Peat, Marwick, Mitchell & Co. failed to establish that "after reasonable investigation, [they had] reasonable ground to believe and did believe" that the statements were not misleading "at the time such part of the registration statement became effective." The court found that the Peat, Marwick approach to the audit met the test of generally accepted auditing standards but found negligence in the application of this program by the auditors on the job.

The judge found for the plaintiffs against all defendants, although many cross-claims among defendants remained. The case was settled, however, without appeal or determination of the cross-claims.

Bar Chris produced no startling new legal theories or extensions of liability beyond the clear meaning of the 1933 Act. Its importance rested in the fact that it was the first real test of the statute on all of its important provisions and thus could serve as a beacon for future litigation. An important statute was solidified, and a judicially determined preference among several acceptable alternative accounting principles was applied for the first time.

Liability Under the 1934 Act

The Securities Exchange Act of 1934 is concerned with the *continuing* registration and regulation of public securities exchanges and publicly traded securities, both on and off these exchanges. The act calls for annual reports, including certified financial statements, to be filed with the SEC by registered companies.

It is clear that liability under the 1934 Act was meant to be closer to liability at common law than the 1933 Act. This was so prior to any important decided cases under either statute.

As litigation activity increased under the federal security laws, a little-known provision of the 1934 Act emerged as the primary basis for the legal liability of accountants and others. This provision, known as Section 10(b) and Rule 10b-5, became the basis for most "implied liabilities" of the 1934 Act.

Fischer *v.* Kletz (1967)

Plaintiffs were stock and bond holders of Yale Express Systems, Inc., who filed suit against the officers and directors of Yale Express, the underwriters for Yale securities, and the firm's auditors for the years in question, Peat, Marwick, Mitchell & Co.

With the accountants as the principal defendants, the plaintiffs contended that damages had resulted from various errors and significant omissions in financial statements covering the years 1963–64. During these years, assets had been significantly overstated, and reported earnings of approximately $3 million actually turned out to be a loss of approximately $5 million. Although three sets of financial statements were involved in the action, only one set (December 31, 1963) had actually been audited by Peat, Marwick. The others were unaudited statements appearing in a prospectus in mid-year 1963 and unaudited interim statements for 1964.

Important Results

The case was important to the profession because: (1) it dealt with the subsequent discovery and disclosure of facts that existed but were unknown to the auditor at the time of the audit report, (2) the auditor's responsibilities under the 1934 Act, for unaudited, as well as audited statements were touched upon, and (3) the subsequent discovery actually took place while the auditors were acting as management consultants doing "special studies" for Yale Express.

The case rested upon the auditor's discovery in 1964 of certain information which allegedly showed that figures in the audited 1963 financial statements were substantially false and misleading. At issue in the case were questions of when this new discovery was made and the auditors' responsibilities for disclosure given their changed status from independent auditors to consultants for Yale. The plaintiffs contended that the discovery was made prior to the release of audited statements to the public and filing of the statements with the SEC, while the defendants claimed that the discovery took place after the filing. The new discoveries were not actually disclosed publicly or to the SEC until Peat, Marwick released the results of its management studies in May 1965.

In the only court decision to come out of this case, the U.S. District Court denied a motion by Peat, Marwick to dismiss certain parts of the complaint dealing with the unaudited statements on the basis that its liability to third parties could only be based on the audited statements and ended when these statements were filed. The court viewed the defendants as being potentially liable as independent accountants and as "aiders and abettors" for the unaudited work.

The major allegations of the case were never actually decided because Peat, Marwick, Mitchell & Co. and the other defendants settled prior to the trial for approximately $1 million.

Hochfelder *v.* Ernst & Ernst (1974)

This is an important recent case because it dealt with: (1) the accountants' responsibility for fraud detection, (2) accountants being charged as "aiders and abettors" under the 1934 Act for failure to detect and disclose such fraud, and (3) important considerations such as reliance by plaintiffs on the auditor's opinion.

The plaintiffs were clients of a Chicago brokerage firm, First Securities Company, which was registered with the SEC. Leston B. Nay, the firm's president and primary owner had, over a period of twenty-five years, advised clients to invest in several "escrow accounts," which he promised would yield high returns. In fact, the "escrow accounts" were non-existent and, according to a suicide note left in 1968 by Nay, the firm was bankrupt due to his thefts from these accounts. The firm's auditors since 1946, Ernst & Ernst, were charged as aiders and abettors to the fraud carried out at First Securities by virtue of the nature of their audit and their failure to uncover the fraud.

Important Results

Important implications of this case for accountants result from a decision made by the U.S. Supreme Court. In late 1972, the District Court ruled in favor of the defendants, dismissing the case on the grounds that wrongful conduct by the auditors had not been established by the facts presented to the court.

The appeals court reversed the lower court's decision with the finding that the plaintiffs had raised issues of material fact, which were appropriate matters for resolution by a jury, and that the case should be tried on the very issues on which the summary judgement was based.

In 1976, the Supreme Court reversed the finding of the U.S. Court of Appeals. The Court held in a six to two decision that ordinary negligence in the form of a failure by the accountants to conduct the type of audit that might have uncovered a client's fraud is not sufficient to sustain liability under the Securities Exchange Act of 1934.

As a matter of law, the Supreme Court decided that a showing of "intentional or willful" deceit was necessary for a finding that accountants were "aiders and abettors" to a fraud under the 1934 Act. According to the court, failure to uncover the existence of fraud in an audit, even if the audit was negligent, is not in itself sufficient to sustain liability. The Appeals Court had held that liability for such negligence constituted a matter of fact to be decided by a jury.

As a result of this decision, it was clear that the standard of care required by the 1934 Act to avoid liability was lessened and the scope of the statute significantly narrowed.

CONCEPT SUMMARY
Auditor Civil Liability Under Written Law

Case	Facts	Findings	Implications
Bar Chris (1968) (This is the primary case under the 1933 Act, and it was settled without appeal of the trial judge's findings—there was no jury by mutual agreement)	1. Registration statement including audited financial statements were filed with SEC pursuant to a public issue of bonds. 2. The company filed for bankruptcy the following year, and sixty bondholders sued everyone including the auditors.	1. Ten material false statements or omissions were found in financial statements. 2. Lack of due care in the application of accounting principles and auditing standards was found. 3. Approach to the audit was acceptable, but negligence was found in the application of the audit program.	1. First judicial interpretation of the important 1933 Act. 2. Judicially determined preference among alternative accounting principles was expressed for the first time. 3. Materiality was dealt with and decided upon by the court indicating an inclination on the part of the courts to deal with this matter.
Yale Express (1967) (Case was never actually tried but was settled out of court. Important law came from court decision on motion by defendants to dismiss certain parts of the case)	1. Three sets of financial statements were involved, although only one set had been audited. 2. Assets had been significantly overstated, and a loss of $5 million had been reported as a profit of $3 million. This was discovered after certification but not disclosed until later. 3. Bondholders and stockholders brought suit against the firm's auditors and others.	1. Information discovered subsequent to audit and certification which existed, but was not known, at the time of certification must be disclosed immediately by auditors. This is true even though this new information was discovered as the auditors were acting in a management service capacity. 2. Liability under the 1934 Act may extend beyond the certification date of statements.	1. Any information which makes previously certified financial statements untrue or misleading must be disclosed by auditors to anyone still acting on the original financial statements. This can be particularly troublesome when auditors act in more than one capacity. 2. Auditors may be held liable for unaudited work under the 1934 Act in certain circumstances.
Hochfelder (1974) (Major law in this case was set as U.S. Supreme Court reversed the ruling of Court of Appeals in interpreting the implied liability provisions for auditors under the 1934 Act)	1. Brokerage firm president encouraged clients to invest in escrow accounts that were non-existent. 2. This went on for 25 years and was not discovered by the firm's auditors. 3. The firm finally went bankrupt because of the president's thefts of these escrow amounts, and the clients sued the auditors for failure to discover the fraud.	1. Failure by auditors to conduct the type of audit which would have uncovered the fraud may be negligence. 2. Negligence is not sufficient basis for sustaining liability under the 1934 Act. 3. Intentional or willful deceit in the conduct of an audit is necessary for auditor liability under the 1934 Act.	1. The basis for liability under the 1934 Act was placed in approximately the same position as auditor liability to third parties under common law. 2. Gross negligence or fraud by auditors would be necessary to sustain liability. 3. The scope of a previously expanding statute was considerably narrowed by court interpretation.

3.4 CRIMINAL LIABILITY

No potential legal hazard has so surprised and alarmed the public accounting profession as the spector of criminal liability. So remote was this area of liability that early writings on accountants' liability contained no criminal liability cases involving accountants, and the topic was given no coverage or analysis.

The Securities Acts of 1933 and 1934, as well as several other federal statutes, have always contained provisions that could support criminal actions against accountants and others. Various provisions of the 1933 and 1934 Acts, the Federal False Statements Statute, and the Federal Mail Fraud Statute provide for penalties ranging from fines of $1,000 to $10,000 and/or imprisonment of one to five years. These statutes require that the accountant: (1) knowingly or willfully make a false or misleading statement; (2) conspire with others to make false or misleading statements; or (3) aid, abet, counsel, command, or induce others to make false or misleading statements to be criminally liable. Of course, the false or misleading statements must fall under the jurisdiction of the statutes—which includes any document "filed" with the SEC, and any document which has used the U.S. Postal Service—for criminal action to be sustained.

The relative immunity from criminal action based on allegations of fraud or conspiracy ended in 1970 with a landmark decision on accountants' liability in the Continental Vending Case. This case, a successful criminal prosecution by the government, will be discussed below.

United States *v.* Simon (1970)

Known as the Continental Vending Case, this is one of the major cases in the evolution of accountants' legal liability. For the first time in the United States, a federal grand jury brought indictments against auditors of a major public accounting firm. The case involved the Continental Vending Machine Corporation, which went into bankruptcy in 1963 shortly after its financial statements had been audited. At issue was a complicated scheme in which Harold Roth, a one-quarter owner of Continental, borrowed substantial sums from Continental for his personal stock market activities. The borrowings, dating from mid-1957, were made through an affiliated company, Valley Commercial Corporation, which Roth partially owned and completely operated. Continental would lend money to Valley which, in turn, would pass the money on to Roth.

At the time of the audit of Continental, these borrowings by Roth totaled $3.5 million. Before certification, representatives of Lybrand, Ross Brothers & Montgomery (now Coopers & Lybrand) learned that the loan could not be repaid by Valley because Roth could not repay Valley. With the approval of the auditors, Roth agreed to post collateral sufficient to secure the loan. However, the collateral consisted essentially of the securities of Continental held by Roth. In effect, Continental's receivable from Valley (Roth) was secured by its own securities. Even at that, the posted collateral fell short of the needed amount, so Continental netted a payable to Valley (from completely unrelated transactions and not involving Roth) against the receivable from Valley, thus making the value of the collateral more than that of the receivable.

The financial statements of Continental containing the above transactions, were certified by Lybrand in late 1962. Subsequently, a senior partner, junior partner, and manager of Lybrand were charged by the U.S. Attorney for the Southern District of New York with conspiracy to commit criminal fraud by "unlawfully, willfully, and knowingly" certifying false and misleading financial statements, and the accounting firm was named as a co-conspirator. The accountants were criminally charged under the Securities Exchange Act of 1934, the Federal False Statements Statute, and the Federal Mail Fraud Statute.

The case centered on the adequacy of the disclosure by the auditors of the Continental-Valley-Roth loan and collateral situation and on the auditor's responsibility for disclosing management misconduct which may have an adverse effect on financial statements. The auditor's defense was that of adherence to generally accepted accounting principles and auditing standards, although certain mistakes (such as netting the receivable and payable of two different parties) were admitted during the trial.

The first trial ended in a hung jury, but a second trial was held, and the accountants were convicted and fined. During the trials "expert witnesses" were called by both sides to testify as to whether the Lybrand audit was in accordance with applicable, generally accepted auditing standards. The experts disagreed on both the relevant standards and the matter of adherence.

In his charge to the jury, the judge asserted that, because of conflicting testimony, it was appropriate for the jury to determine if the financial statements were, as a whole, misleading. The judge also instructed that compliance with generally accepted accounting principles and auditing standards, while persuasive, was not conclusive.

Upon appeal of the conviction to the U.S. Court of Appeals, it became clear that the "experts" did not play a key role in the case and that, in the opinion of the Court, the case could have been decided without expert opinion. The Court of Appeals opinion, however, did not completely rule out compliance with generally accepted accounting and auditing standards as a defense. It also emphasized that conscious non-disclosure of relevant information could be criminal fraud.

The Supreme Court upheld the conviction by refusing to hear the appeal of the defendants. A companion civil suit was settled by Lybrand for approximately $1 million.

Important Results

The implications of this case are in the areas of: (1) the auditor as communicator and what constitutes adequate disclosure, and (2) adherence to generally accepted accounting principles and auditing standards as a defense to a criminal action. These issues are summed up by the following quotations:

The consideration you must ask yourself when you certify to a financial statement, or where you have something to do with other information which you
know is going to the public, is whether your statements communicate the true
financial condition which you supposedly are reporting upon; not whether
you can get away with it under accepted accounting principles, but whether
in fact it is misleading, because that in my estimation is truly the single accepted
accounting principle.[4]

. . . Judge Henry J. Friendly, . . . one of the most knowledgeable of federal
judges in financial and accounting matters, . . . said, in effect, that the first
law for accountants was not compliance with generally accepted accounting
principles, but rather full and fair disclosure, fair presentation, and if the
principles did not produce this brand of disclosure, accountants could not
hide behind the principles but had to go beyond there and make whatever
additional disclosures were necessary for full disclosure. In a word, "present
fairly" was a concept separate from "generally accepted accounting principles," and the latter did not necessarily result in the former.[5]

3.5 SUMMARY OF AUDITORS' LIABILITY

The legal liability exposure faced by public accountants has increased dramatically
in terms of the scope, frequency, and size of cases decided on established theories
of liability. Liability exposure has also expanded based on new or previously
inapplicable theories and new interpretations of statutes. The latter increase is
one of both scope and depth and is particularly troublesome for the profession.
The persons and groups to whom accountants may be held liable are rapidly
expanding, and the standard of care required of accountants has risen substantially. These changes have taken place since the Great Depression, with most of
the intensity and expansion occurring since the mid-1960s.

Factors, Events, and Attitudes Responsible for Increased Exposure

The variables responsible for these changes are many, varied, and complex.
Additionally, many of the factors interact to produce results not likely to occur
from any variable taken alone. Some of the factors, events and attitudes that have
been important in the evolution of accountants' legal liability are:

---

[4]Peter E. Fleming, who was the government prosecutor in the Continental Vending Case and
later successful defense attorney for accountants in another criminal case, was moved to render the
above advice to the accounting profession. Quotation taken from Denzil Y. Causey, Jr., *Duties and
Liabilities of the CPA,* the University of Texas at Austin: Bureau of Business Research, 1973, p. 107.

[5]A. A. Sommer, Jr., a member of the Securities and Exchange Commission spoke the above on
the implications of the Continental Vending Case to the American Bar Association in 1970. Quotation
taken from Abraham J. Briloff, *Unaccountable Accounting,* New York: Harper & Row, Publishers,
1972, pp. 21–22.

1. Increased government interest in and regulation of securities markets and all who play a role in their functioning.

2. Expansion of the law of negligence as new theories and interpretations were developed by the courts.

3. Changing concepts of the responsibility to the public of those who receive special privileges or recognition from society (professions and others).

4. Increased awareness by the public of litigation as a means of redressing grievances. The growth of class-action lawsuits coupled with an emerging feeling that someone should be responsible for the search and discovery of business fraud.

5. Dramatic increases in the complexities of business organizations and the necessary reporting for them.

6. Increased use of and importance attached to the services of public accountants.

7. Maturation of public accounting as a profession, and the growth in size, wealth, and liability insurance of CPA firms.

8. General misunderstanding on the part of users of public accounting services as to what the auditor does, what can be expected of him, and the meaning of his report. The failure of the profession to effectively educate users in those areas.

9. Inability of accountants, probably because of the structure of the profession, to respond quickly and decisively to emerging problem areas.

10. Some negligent work and/or improperly placed loyalties on the part of individual auditors.

The Current Status of Accountants' Legal Liability

Under some theories of law and some statutes, the legal liability of accountants has been greatly expanded, while in other areas the changes have been small or moderate. Generally, the specific exposure of accountants is a function of the basis for the liability (common law v. statute law), the proximity of the user or user group to the auditor (client v. third party), and the nature of the offense (civil v. criminal).

Common Law

Liability here (all civil) is a function of the proximity of a potential plaintiff to the accountant. The closer the proximity, the higher the duty of care owed. The ultimate in proximity arises from a contractual relationship with the accountant. Persons enjoying such privity of contract are customarily called *clients*. Courts have generally held that public accountants are liable for ordinary negligence where this proximity exists.

Ordinary negligence may be defined as the failure to use even ordinary care in the performance of one's work. The nature and clarity of the contractual agreement is important in the determination of the "care" required of the auditor. In actions for breach of contract, a showing of negligence is not necessary if non-performance by the auditor can be demonstrated.

As proximity decreases, the duty of care owed under common law lessens. Third parties (any users of audited financial statements not in privity of contract with the auditor) may enjoy proximity nearly as close as that of the auditor's clients or may be very far removed from the auditor. In addition to the closeness of legal relationship, the courts have begun to apply the test of foreseeability of specific third-party users by the auditor. This area of third-party liability has undergone major changes.

Public accountants have been held to be liable to third-party users for gross negligence or fraud (failure to use even slight care). If the work of the auditor is found to be for the "primary benefit" of the third party or if the auditor may reasonably foresee specific uses by identifiable classes of third parties relying on his work, ordinary care may be the applicable standard. In meeting the required duty of care, it is now clear that the accounting profession's own standards constitute minimum acceptable behavior.

Written Law

Under the Federal Securities Laws of 1933 and 1934, public accountants may be subject to civil or criminal liability. Civil liability to third parties differs markedly between the Acts of 1933 and 1934. The provisions of the 1933 Act are quite broad, exceeding those under common law in several important ways. Auditors may be found liable if certified financial statements required by the act are false or omit material facts. The statutory defense of due diligence is provided, but the wording of this defense requires freedom from even the slightest negligence.

Under the 1934 Act, liability provisions place public accountants in essentially the same position as at common law, with gross negligence as the test for liability.

Most disturbing to auditors has been the inception and expansion of criminal liability for fraud or conspiracy in their work. Various sections of both federal securities acts and conspiracy and mail fraud statutes provide the basis for criminal actions against public accountants. There have been only a few criminal cases decided, but several conclusions seem apparent from these cases.

1. All of the cases involved matters of adequate disclosure.
2. Adherence to GAAP and GAAS does not provide a complete defense to criminal charges.
3. Prosecution does not seem to pose a consistent threat. Confusion among jurors has been evident.

CONCEPT SUMMARY
Summary of Auditors' Liability

Type of Liability	To Whom Liable	Legal Basis of Liability	Behavioral Basis of Liability
Common Law	Clients and Others in Privity of Contract	Law of Contracts	Ordinary Negligence (failure to use ordinary care)
Common Law	Third Parties	Law of Torts	Gross Negligence (failure to use even minimum care) or Fraud (willful intent to deceive)
Written Law	Third Parties	Securities Act of 1933	Ordinary Negligence
Written Law	Third Parties	Securities Exchange Act of 1934	Gross Negligence or Fraud
Written Law	Society (criminal liability)	Securities Acts of 1933 and 1934 as well as other federal statues	Fraud

4. The threat of criminal prosecution provides regulatory agencies with substantial leverage on the profession and the practitioner.

The expansion of accountants' legal liability since the mid-1960s is most often seen as posing a threat to the very existence of public accounting. Actually, quite the contrary may be true. These legal liability developments can be a blessing in disguise to both the public accounting profession and independent CPAs. An amazingly prophetic viewpoint given in 1905 by one of the most respected early leaders of the profession sums up this position:

> In my opinion the quickest way to weed out the incompetent men who now hold themselves out as public accountants would be to make them understand the civil responsibility of a professional accountant. Naturally, an unreliable, incompetent man cares nothing about his moral responsibility, and so long as he knows that American courts have never laid down specific rules regulating the duties or obligations of public accountants, he probably feels safe from any legal responsibility. One sure and very desirable result of the weeding out process would be the raising of the professional standard, for a few irresponsible men can offset the good work of ten times their number.[6]

---

[6]Robert H. Montgomery, "Professional Standards: A Plea for Cooperation Among Accountants," *The Journal of Accountancy* (November 1905), p. 30.

Key Terms

aiders and abettors

C.I.T. Financial Corp. v. Glover (1955)

civil law

common law

criminal law

criminal liability

defendant

due diligence

Escott v. Bar Chris Construction Corp. (1968)

Fischer v. Kletz (Yale Express, 1967)

fraud

gross negligence

Hochfelder v. Ernst & Ernst (1974)

implied liability

McKesson & Robbins, Inc. (1938)

materiality

negligence

1136 Tenants' Corp. v. Max Rothenberg & Co. (1972)

ordinary negligence

plaintiff

private law

public law

registration statement

statute law

third-party liability

third-party user

Ultramares Corp. v. Touche (1931)

United States v. Simon (Continental Vending, 1970)

Questions and Problems

Questions

3-1 What is negligence in legal terms when applied to professionals? Distinguish between negligence and fraud.

3-2 Distinguish between: (a) public law and private law, (b) civil law and criminal law, and (c) common law and written law.

3-3 What major changes did the McKesson & Robbins discoveries bring about in auditing standards and procedures?

3-4 In which two important areas did the 1136 Tenants' Case change the thinking of practicing auditors?

3-5 What is the major significance of the Ultramares Case?

3-6 Contrast the intent and coverage of the 1933 and 1934 Securities Acts. Could a single legal action against auditors be brought simultaneously under both acts?

3-7 List three similarities between the Bar Chris and Yale Express Cases. List three differences between these cases.

3-8 How did the Hochfelder decision differ from the findings in the Ultramares Case? Did this disagreement change the precedent established in Ultramares?

3-9 Describe the major facts surrounding the Continental Vending Case, and discuss the implications of this case for CPAs in public practice.

3-10 What is the standard of behavior required of auditors to avoid liability under the 1933 Securities Act? The 1934 Act? Why are these standards different?

Multiple Choice Questions From Professional Examinations

3-11 The independent auditor of 1900 differs from the auditor of today in that the 1900 auditor was more concerned with the

    a. Validity of the income statement.

    b. Determination of fair presentation of financial statements.

    c. Improvement of accounting systems.

    d. Detection of irregularities.

3-12 The securities of Ralph Corporation are listed on a regional stock exchange and registered with the Securities and Exchange Commission. The management of Ralph engages a CPA to perform an independent audit of Ralph's financial statements. The primary objective of this audit is to provide assurance to the

    a. Regional Stock Exchange.

    b. Board of Directors of Ralph Corporation.

    c. Securities and Exchange Commission.

    d. Investors in Ralph securities.

3-13 For what minimum period should audit working papers be retained by the independent CPA?

    a. For the period during which the entity remains a client of the independent CPA.

    b. For the period during which an auditor-client relationship exists but not more than six years.

    c. For the statutory period within which legal action may be brought against the independent CPA.

    d. For as long as the CPA is in public practice.

3-14 When a CPA has concluded that action should be taken to prevent future reliance on his report, he should

    a. Advise his client to make appropriate disclosure of the newly discovered facts and their impact on the financial statements to persons who are known to be currently relying on or who are likely to rely on the financial statements and the related auditor's report.

    b. Recall the financial statements and issue revised statements and include an appropriate opinion.

c. Advise the client and others not to rely on the financial statements and make appropriate disclosure of the correction in the statements of a subsequent period.

d. Recall the financial statements and issue a disclaimer of opinion, which should generally be followed by revised statements and a qualified opinion.

3-15 The 1136 Tenants' case was chiefly important because of its emphasis upon the legal liability of the CPA when associated with

a. A review of interim statements.

b. Unaudited financial statements.

c. An audit resulting in a disclaimer of opinion.

d. Letters for underwriters.

3-16 One of the major purposes of federal security regulation is to

a. Establish qualifications for accountants who are members of the profession.

b. Eliminate incompetent attorneys and accountants who participate in the registration of securities to be offered to the public.

c. Provide a set of uniform standards and tests for accountants, attorneys, and others who practice before the Securities and Exchange Commission.

d. Provide sufficient information to investors who purchase securities in the marketplace.

3-17 The Securities and Exchange Commission is not empowered to

a. Obtain an injunction that will suspend trading in a given security.

b. Sue for treble damages.

c. Institute criminal proceedings against accountants.

d. Suspend a broker-dealer.

3-18 Under the Securities Act of 1933, subject to some exceptions and limitations, it is unlawful to use the mails or instruments of interstate commerce to sell or offer to sell a security to the public unless

a. A surety bond sufficient to cover potential liability to investors is obtained and filed with the Securities and Exchange Commission.

b. The offer is made through underwriters qualified to offer the securities on a nationwide basis.

c. A registration statement has been properly filed with the Securities and Exchange Commission, has been found to be acceptable, and is in effect.

d. The Securities and Exchange Commission approves of the financial merit of the offering.

3-19 Under which of the following circumstances is a public offering of securities exempt from the registration requirements of the Securities Act of 1933?

    a. There was a prior registration within one year.

    b. The corporation is a public utility subject to regulation by the Federal Power Commission.

    c. The corporation was closely held prior to the offering.

    d. The issuing corporation and all prospective security owners are located within one state, and the entire offering, sale, and distribution is made within that state.

3-20 The accuracy of information included in footnotes that accompany the audited financial statements of a company whose shares are traded on a stock exchange is the primary responsibility of

    a. The stock exchange officials.

    b. The independent auditor.

    c. The company's management.

    d. The Securities and Exchange Commission.

3-21 The most significant aspect of the Continental Vending case was that it

    a. Created a more general awareness of the auditor's exposure to criminal prosecution.

    b. Extended the auditor's responsibility for financial statements of subsidiaries.

    c. Extended the auditor's responsibility for events after the end of the audit period.

    d. Defined the auditor's common-law responsibilities to third parties.

3-22 In connection with the examination of financial statements, an independent auditor could be responsible for failure to detect a material fraud if

    a. Statistical sampling techniques were not used on the audit engagement.

    b. The auditor planned the work in a hasty and inefficient manner.

    c. Accountants performing important parts of the work failed to discover a close relationship between the treasurer and the cashier.

    d. The fraud was perpetrated by one client employee, who circumvented the existing internal controls.

3-23 When engaged to prepare unaudited financial statements, the CPA's responsibility to detect fraud

    a. Is limited to informing the client of any matters that come to the auditor's attention that cause the auditor to believe an irregularity exists.

b. Is the same as the responsibility that exists when the CPA is engaged to perform an audit of financial statements in accordance with generally accepted auditing standards.

c. Arises out of the CPA's obligation to apply procedures designed to bring to light indications that a fraud or defalcation may have occurred.

d. Does not exist unless an engagement letter is prepared.

3-24 When an independent auditor's examination of financial statements discloses special circumstances that make the auditor suspect that fraud may exist, the auditor's initial course of action should be to

a. Recommend that the client pursue the suspected fraud to a conclusion that is agreeable to the auditor.

b. Extend normal audit procedures in an attempt to detect the full extent of the suspected fraud.

c. Reach an understanding with the proper client representative as to whether the auditor or the client is to make the investigation necessary to determine if a fraud has in fact occurred.

d. Decide whether the fraud, if in fact it exists, might be of such a magnitude as to affect the auditor's report on the financial statements.

3-25 Which of the following best describes a trend in litigations involving CPAs?

a. A CPA cannot render an opinion on a company unless the CPA has audited all affiliates of that company.

b. A CPA may not successfully assert as a defense that the CPA had no motive to be part of a fraud.

c. A CPA may be exposed to criminal as well as civil liability.

d. A CPA is primarily responsible for a client's footnotes in an annual report filed with the SEC.

Problems

3-26 (a) "It is now doubtful if an auditor can defend a challenge to his opinion simply by having adhered to generally accepted auditing standards and by stating that the financial statements have been prepared in accordance with generally accepted accounting principles."

Required:

Discuss the above statement indicating its implications for the auditing profession.

(b) "The involvement of auditors with new types of financial presentation and disclosure brings with it the possibility of increased legal liability for auditors.

We believe that before auditors can accept the new responsibilities that flow from the broader concept of accountability, it is necessary to buttress their position of independence, remove fear of inordinate legal liability, and thus create the proper climate for change."

Required:

Discuss the above statement, considering the expanded role and responsibilities of auditors now being suggested.

CICA

3-27 Wendy Young, doing business as Wendy Young Fashions, engaged the CPA partnership of Small & Brown to examine her financial statements. During the examination, Small & Brown discovered certain irregularities which would have indicated to a reasonably prudent accountant that James Smith, the bookkeeper, might be engaged in a fraud. More specifically, it appeared to Small & Brown that serious defalcations were taking place. However, Small & Brown, not having been engaged to discover defalcations, submitted an unqualified opinion report and did not mention the potential defalcation problem.

Required:

What are the legal implications of the above facts as they relate to the relationship between Small & Brown and Wendy Young? Explain.

AICPA (adapted)

3-28 Watts and Williams, a firm of certified public accountants, audited the accounts of Sampson Skins, Inc., a corporation that imports and deals in fine furs. Upon completion of the examination, the auditors supplied Sampson Skins with 20 copies of the certified balance sheet. The firm was aware that Sampson Skins wanted that number of copies of the auditor's report to furnish to banks and other potential lenders.

The balance sheet in question was in error by approximately $800,000. Instead of having a $600,000 net worth, the corporation was insolvent. The management of Sampson Skins had "doctored" the books in the hope of avoiding bankruptcy. The assets had been overstated by $500,000 of fictitious and nonexistent accounts receivable and $300,000 of nonexistent skins listed as inventory when in fact Sampson Skins had only empty boxes. The audit failed to detect these fraudulent entries. Martinson, relying on the certified balance sheet, loaned Sampson Skins $200,000. He seeks to recover his loss from Watts and Williams.

Required:

State whether each of the following statements is correct or incorrect using common law principles, and give your reasons for each response.

1. If Martinson alleges and proves negligence on the part of Watts and Williams, he will be able to recover his loss.
2. If Martinson alleges and proves constructive fraud, (i.e., gross negligence on the part of Watts and Williams) he will be able to recover his loss.
3. Martinson does not enjoy privity of contract with Watts and Williams.
4. Unless actual fraud on the part of Watts and Williams could be shown, Martinson could not recover.
5. Martinson is a third-party beneficiary of the contract Watts and Williams made with Sampson Skins.

AICPA (adapted)

3-29 Donald Sharpe recently joined the CPA firm of Spark, Matts, and Wilcox. He quickly established a reputation for thoroughness and a steadfast dedication to following prescribed auditing procedures to the letter. On his third audit for the firm, Sharpe examined the underlying documentation of 200 disbursements as a test of purchasing, receiving, vouchers-payable, and cash-disbursement procedures. In the process, he found twelve disbursements for the purchase of materials with no receiving reports in the documentation. He noted the exceptions in his working papers and called them to the attention of the in-charge accountant. Relying on prior experience with the client, the in-charge accountant disregarded Sharpe's comments, and nothing further was done about the exceptions.

It was subsequently learned that one of the client's purchasing agents and a member of its accounting department were engaged in a fraudulent scheme whereby they diverted the receipt of materials to a public warehouse while sending the invoices to the client. When the client discovered the fraud, the conspirators had obtained approximately $70,000, $50,000 of which was after the completion of the audit.

Required:

Discuss the legal implications and liabilities to Spark, Matts, and Wilcox as a result of the above facts.

AICPA

3-30 A CPA firm has been named as a defendant in a class action by purchasers of the shares of stock of the Newly Corporation. The offering was a public offering of securities within the meaning of the Securities Act of 1933. The plaintiffs alleged that the firm was either negligent or fraudulent in connection with the preparation of the audited financial statements that accompanied the registration statement filed with the SEC. Specifically, they alleged that the CPA firm either intentionally disregarded, or failed to exercise reasonable care to discover, material facts which occurred subsequent to January 31, 1982, the date of the auditor's report. The securities were sold to the public on March 16, 1982. The plaintiffs have subpoenaed copies of the CPA firm's working papers. The CPA firm is considering refusing to relinquish the papers, asserting that they contain privileged communication between the firm and its client. The CPA firm will, of course, defend on the merits irrespective of the questions regarding the working papers.

Required:

Answer the following, setting forth reasons for any conclusions stated.
1. Can the CPA firm rightfully refuse to surrender its working papers?
2. Discuss the liability of the CPA firm in respect to events that occur in the period between the date of of the auditor's report and the effective date of the public offering of the securities.

AICPA

3-31 The Dandy Container Corporation engaged the accounting firm of Adams and Adams to examine financial statements to be used in connection with a public offering of securities. The audit was completed, and an unqualified opinion was expressed on the financial statements that were submitted to the Securities and Exchange Commission along with the registration statement. Two hundred thousand shares of Dandy Container common stock were offered to the public at $11 a share. Eight months later, the stock fell to $2 a share when it was disclosed that several large loans to two "paper" corporations owned by one of the directors were worthless. The loans were secured by the stock of the borrowing corporation, which was owned by the director. These facts were not disclosed in the financial report. The director and the two corporations are insolvent.

Required:

State whether each of the following statements is correct or incorrect based on federal securities laws, and give your reasons for each response.

1. The Securities Act of 1933 applies to the above described public offering of securities in interstate commerce.
2. The accounting firm has potential liability to any person who acquired the stock in reliance upon the registration statement.
3. An investor who bought shares in Dandy Container would make a *prima facie* case if he alleges that the failure to explain the nature of the loans in question constituted a false statement or misleading omission in the financial statements.
4. The auditors could avoid liability if they could show they were neither negligent nor fraudulent.
5. The auditors could avoid or reduce the damages asserted against them if they could establish that the drop in price was due in whole or in part to other causes.

6. The Dandy investors would have to institute suit within one year after discovery of the alleged untrue statements or omissions.
7. The SEC would defend any action brought against the auditors in that the SEC examined and approved the registration statement.
8. The auditor's responsibility for the fairness of the financial statements included in the registration statement is as of the financial statement date.

AICPA (adapted)

3-32 Gordon & Groton, CPAs, were the auditors of Bank & Company, a brokerage firm and member of a national stock exchange. Gordon & Groton examined and reported on the financial statements of Bank, which were filed with the Securities and Exchange Commission.

Several of Bank's customers were swindled by a fraudulent scheme perpetrated by Bank's president, who owned 90% of the voting stock of the company. The facts establish that Gordon & Groton were negligent but not reckless or grossly negligent in the conduct of the audit, and neither participated in the fraudulent scheme nor knew of its existence.

The customers are suing Gordon & Groton under the anti-fraud provisions of Section 10(b) and Rule 10b-5 of the Securities Exchange Act of 1934 for aiding and abetting the fraudulent scheme of the president. The customers' suit for fraud is predicated exclusively on the nonfeasance of the auditors in failing to conduct a proper audit, thereby failing to discover the fraudulent scheme.

Required:

Answer the following, setting forth reasons for any conclusions stated.

1. What is the probable outcome of the lawsuit?
2. What other theory of liability might the customers have asserted?

AICPA

3-33 The CPA firm of Bigelow, Barton, and Baron was expanding very rapidly. Consequently, it hired several new accountants, including a man named Smart. Shortly thereafter, the partners of the firm became dissatisfied with Smart's production and warned him that they would be forced to discharge him unless his output increased significantly.

At that time, Smart was engaged in audits of several clients. He decided that, to avoid being fired, he would reduce or omit entirely some of the standard auditing procedures listed in audit programs prepared by the partners. One of the CPA firm's clients, Newell Corporation, was in serious financial difficulty and had adjusted several of its accounts being examined by Smart to appear financially sound. Smart prepared fictitious working papers in his home at night to support purported completion of auditing procedures assigned to him, although he in fact did not examine the adjusting entries. The CPA firm rendered an unqualified opinion on Newell's financial statements, which were grossly misstated. Several creditors subsequently extended large sums of money to Newell Corporation relying upon the audited financial statements.

Required:

Would the CPA firm be liable to the creditors who extended the money in reliance on the erroneous financial statements if Newell Corporation should fail to repay them? Explain.

AICPA (adapted)

3-34 Jackson was a junior staff member of an accounting firm. He began the audit of the Bosco Corporation, which manufactured and sold expensive watches. In the middle of the audit, he quit. The accounting firm hired another person to continue the audit of Bosco. As a result of the changeover and time pressure to finish the audit, the firm violated certain generally accepted auditing standards when they did not follow adequate procedures with respect to the physical inventory. Had the proper procedures been used during the examination they would have discovered that watches worth more than $20,000 were missing. The employee who was stealing the watches was able to steal an additional $30,000 worth before the thefts were discovered six months after the completion of the audit.

Required:

Discuss the legal problems of the accounting firm as a result of this situation.

AICPA (adapted)

3-35 Risk Capital Limited, a Delaware corporation, was considering the purchase of a substantial amount of the treasury stock held by Florida Sunshine, a closely held corporation. Initial discussions with the Florida Sunshine Corporation began late in 1981.

Wilson and Wyatt, Florida Sunshine's accountants, regularly prepared quarterly and annual unaudited financial statements. The most recently prepared financial statements were for the year ended September 30, 1982.

On November 15, 1982, after protracted negotiations, Risk Capital agreed to purchase 100,000 shares of no par, Class A Capital stock of Florida Sunshine at $12.50 per share. However, Risk Capital insisted on audited statements for calendar year 1982. The contract for the purchase of the shares specifically provided:

> "Risk Capital shall have the right to rescind the purchase of said stock if the audited financial statements of Florida Sunshine for calendar year 1982 show a material adverse change in the financial condition of the corporation."

The audited financial statements furnished to Florida Sunshine by Wilson and Wyatt showed no such material adverse change. Risk Capital relied upon the audited statements, and purchased the treasury stock of Florida Sunshine. It was subsequently discovered that, as of the balance sheet date, the audited statements were incorrect and that there had been a material adverse change in the financial condition of the corporation. Florida Sunshine is insolvent, and Risk Capital will lose virtually its entire investment.

Risk Capital seeks recovery against Wilson and Wyatt.

Required:

a. Discuss each of the theories of liability that Risk Capital will probably assert as its basis for recovery.

b. Assuming that only ordinary negligence on the part of Wilson and Wyatt is proven, will Risk Capital prevail? Explain.

AICPA (adapted)

4

Internal control

The purpose of an auditor's examination is to give an opinion on the financial statements of a client. There are three basic reasons why financial statements may be unsatisfactory:

1. Improper application of accounting principles. For example, the firm might expense costs which should be capitalized, or vice-versa.

2. Mistakes in the accounting. For example, cash receipts could be recorded improperly or journal entries posted to the wrong account. However, a good accounting system should "catch" these errors and correct them.

3. Fraud in the accounting. For example, employees could be stealing from the company and covering the theft in the accounting records. A properly designed accounting system can help prevent fraud or detect its occurrence.

The auditor can never check every transaction. The number of transactions which must be examined will depend upon how well the accounting system detects and corrects mistakes and fraud.

4.1 BASIC CONCEPTS OF INTERNAL CONTROL

Accounting records are separate from the actual assets and operations of the business, but they should accurately reflect what is going on in the "real world" of assets and operations. Because of errors, the accounting records may not accurately reflect what happens to the business. Therefore, it is not sufficient for an accounting system to be simple, efficient, and provide management with the information it requires. The system must also accomplish two major aims:

1. To protect assets (especially cash and inventory) from being lost or stolen.
2. To ensure that the accounting records are accurate and complete.

These aims are so important that the techniques, methods, and procedures that help accomplish these goals are given a special name—*internal accounting control*. Internal accounting control is the total collection of means employed to accomplish the objectives stated above. The word "internal" serves to emphasize that these techniques are contained within the system.

Even a small business has so many transactions that they can never all be checked to determine that they were processed correctly. If a system is to be protected from errors, the system must protect itself from errors. Internal accounting control is the collection of methods and procedures with which a system protects itself from error.

Accounting Controls v. Administrative Controls

Because most firms deal in many transactions and have many employees, controls must be developed to ensure that top management's policies and directives are carried out. Thus, in addition to the two objectives listed previously, internal control has the following further objectives:

3. To promote efficient operations by reducing waste and duplication of effort.
4. To encourage compliance with company policies and procedures.

The first two objectives are "accounting controls," and the last two are "administrative controls."

Examples of Administrative Controls

Although the focus of this chapter is on accounting controls, examples of administrative controls will point up the differences between the two concepts. Some basic administrative controls are:

1. Personnel methods and procedures designed for hiring, training, and retaining employees.
2. Quality controls, which help guarantee that only high quality merchandise will be sold to customers.
3. Guidelines for determining whether salespersons are visiting an appropriate number of customers per day.
4. Ratios and other statistics (such as inventory turnover) developed by operating departments, which check to see if operations are running to form.

CONCEPT SUMMARY
Objectives of Internal Control

Objectives of Accounting Controls	1. Protect assets from being lost or stolen 2. Ensure that the accounting records are accurate and complete
Objectives of Administrative Controls	3. Promote efficient operations 4. Encourage the following of company policies and procedures

---

These methods and procedures promote efficient operations but do not protect assets or ensure record accuracy, at least directly.

The problem is that the best accounting system in the world might not get proper results, namely proper reflection in the accounts of the transactions to date. Assuming a system can work and is capable of handling all transactions, improper answers are the result of improper processing of transactions. These improper processings of transactions divide neatly into two types: accidental and intentional.

Detecting Accidental Errors

Accidental improper processings of transactions are simply mistakes. People will always make some errors, and no system can possibly prevent them all. However, the system should point out the existence of an error as soon as possible. Typical accounting systems contain a number of features designed to detect errors:

Double-Entry Method

The most important error-detecting feature is the double-entry method. The constant requirement that debits equal credits will point out numerous mistakes. The balancing of the special journals prior to posting and the taking of the trial balance are examples of attempts to catch errors as soon as possible. If debits do not equal credits, there is necessarily an error somewhere.

Audit Trail

The second most important error-detecting feature is the audit trail. The figures in the financial statements come from ledger balances. The ledger accounts indicate by their posting reference the journal source of all the debits and credits. Thus, it is possible to check the journal to see the original entries, and hence, find the supporting documents. Similarly, it is possible to go from the source documents forward through the ledger to their appearance on the financial statements by using the posting reference in each journal. This audit trail is absolutely essential for error detection. Whenever an error is discovered in an accounting number, it is necessary to go back to see where the record came from to determine the source of the mistake.

Suppose the balance in an asset account, such as inventory, is compared to the result of a physical count and pricing of the inventory. If the two do not balance, it must be possible to go back through the accounting records to see where the balance in the records came from and where the accounting records went wrong (assuming that the inventory is correct, and the accounting records are wrong). Even if an error is small in amount, it may be a symptom of a larger problem, the start of a growing problem, or the result of major (but offsetting) errors. Because of this, it always must be possible to get to the root of a problem; hence the audit trail.

Bank Reconciliation

Another error-detecting feature is the bank reconciliation. The cash balance given by the bank statement should reconcile with the cash balance given by the accounting records; any discrepancy should be explainable as a timing difference in the recording of cash transactions. A good bank reconciliation effectively tests that: (1) all checks were recorded properly; (2) all deposits were recorded properly; and (3) all miscellaneous charges such as bank service charges and checks returned NSF (i.e., not sufficient funds) were properly incorporated into the accounts.

Subsidiary Ledgers

A fourth error-detecting feature is the use of subsidiary ledgers. The control accounts in the general ledger for accounts receivable and accounts payable should always equal the total of the individual accounts in the respective ledgers. If the control does not agree with (or in accounting terminology, balance to) the total of the subsidiary ledger accounts, there is an error somewhere. It is quite possible for these totals not to agree. If a cash receipt on accounts receivable is entered properly in the cash receipts journal but is not posted to the individual account in the subsidiary ledger, the accounts receivable control account will be correct while the subsidiary ledger will be incorrect.

Billing Statements

An additional error-detecting feature is the use of billing statements for credit customers. It is certainly possible that a cash receipt on account or a credit sale could be posted to the wrong individual account. Both the control total and the total of the subsidiary ledger will be correct. The individual accounts will be incorrect; one account will be overstated by some amount, while another will be understated by the same amount. Since these two errors cancel each other out when totaling the subsidiary ledger, balancing is not effective in detecting this error. It is extremely likely, however, that if statements of account are sent to the customers, they will identify any incorrect entries. The customer whose balance due is higher than it should be, is more likely to complain than the customer whose balance is too low. However, there cannot be one without the other (or else the subsidiary ledger would not balance to the control).

Vendor Communications

Vendors do not receive statements as do customers; nevertheless, they will complain if not paid. Therefore, vendor communications act as an independent error-detecting check on the system. Suppose, for example, a firm paid one of its vendors, Fireplaces Unlimited, but debited the account of Fireworks Unlimited. The total of the subsidiary ledger will be correct: one balance will be understated, but another will be overstated an equivalent amount. Fireworks will not be paid because it appears they have already received payment. However, they will complain that they have not been paid. And if Fireplaces is paid again, it is at least possible that they will notice that they have been overpaid and will send a refund check.

CONCEPT SUMMARY
Basic Error-Detecting Features
of a Manual Accounting System

Double-entry Method	Points up errors, since rarely will an error in one-half of an entry be exactly offset by an equivalent error in the other half
Audit Trail	Allows the accountant to track backwards through the accounting records to the cause of an error
Bank Reconciliation	Provides an independent check that all checks, deposits, and miscellaneous charges were recorded properly
Subsidiary Ledgers	Provides cross checks of the general ledger control account with the subsidiary ledger
Customer Statements of Account	Provides independent check of accounts receivable subsidiary ledger account balances
Vendor Communications	Provides an independent check of accounts payable subsidiary ledger account balances

The Problem of Embezzlement

Attention now turns to the other side of accounting controls—deliberate mistakes. Writers discussing this topic generally employ euphemisms for what is really stealing. Stealing through the manipulation of accounting records does not usually involve physical violence, but it does involve the betrayal of trust. Two words are used in this context—embezzlement and defalcation.

They mean the same thing, namely, the fraudulent appropriation to one's own use of property entrusted to one's care. *Defalcation* is the term generally used in accounting. This problem can occur in any business. A defalcation in an international CPA firm involved the stealing of large sums from travel and expense money over a period of years by a bookkeeper in the main office. This fraud was discovered because the bookkeeper confessed; she had never been caught.

It is impossible to determine the amount of embezzlement precisely—most is never discovered—but estimates place such white-collar crime at well over forty billion dollars per year. Understandably, cash and inventory are the main targets of dishonest employees. Cash can buy almost anything. Inventory can either be used by the thief, or in many cases, readily converted into cash. One study showed that 88 percent of uncovered defalcations involved cash, with the remainder involving inventory. For cash embezzlements, the majority of individual incidents involved cash receipts, but the vast majority of dollar amounts (80%) involved cash disbursements.

Surprisingly, perhaps, the embezzler is usually a trusted employee who has been with his or her firm a long time. In one group of embezzlers studied, the people were employed an average of six and a half years before they started to steal. The embezzler usually finds either that it is impossible for him to live on his salary, or he feels unfairly treated.

4.2 CASH DEFALCATIONS AND INTERNAL CONTROL

Cash Disbursements Defalcations

Cash disbursements is the area of greatest dollar loss from embezzlement, so this subject should have particular emphasis.

Checks Payable to Other Firms

A bookkeeper can prepare checks payable to other firms so that the checks appear to be normal payments on account. After the checks are signed, he can divert the funds to himself by: (1) forging the endorsement of the check and cashing it, or (2) using a bank account which was especially created for depositing the funds.

The problem is getting an authorized signature on the checks. Techniques for doing this would depend upon whether he: (1) created the payee firm, or (2) used an existing, real firm. If he created the firm, he must also create false invoices for it, as well as any supporting documents required. If a real vendor is used, invoices could be resubmitted which have already been paid. However, there is then the problem of two checks relating to the same invoice. This can be resolved by intercepting the second, fraudulent check when it returns from the bank, and destroying it. The number and date of the original check can be changed and the altered check substituted in the files for the fraudulent check.

Checks Payable to Employees

Padding the payroll is another method of issuing checks and then appropriating them. Using this method, an employee might: (1) keep preparing checks for ex-employees after they have been terminated, or (2) add fake employees to the payroll. Padding can be accomplished by a number of people besides the book-keeper. If the foreman distributes paychecks, he might "forget" to inform the office that an employee has quit, and appropriate the check. Similarly, the person who adds employees might add a brother-in-law or cousin.

Checks Payable to Himself or Herself

Another possibility is for the embezzler to prepare checks to himself or herself using a check that was not prenumbered or a prenumbered check from the back of the checkbook. He can get the check signed by forging an authorized signature or by using checks which have been signed in blank (i.e., with the date, payee, and amount not yet filled in). Then he must intercept or control the bank statement so that the checks can be destroyed when the bank returns them. The cash balance per bank was reduced by the cleared check, but the general ledger balance was not. The general ledger balance can be reduced by increasing the recorded amount for another check and changing the check when the bank returns it. Alternatively, the embezzler can overfoot the cash column of the cash disbursements journal to reduce the general ledger cash balance. (Overfooting is the misadding of a column to get too large a total, while underfooting is the opposite.) However, credits will then exceed debits in the journal. He must then either decrease other credits by underfooting purchase discounts or increase debits by overfooting expenses.

Overpaying a Vendor

A further manipulation of cash disbursements is overpaying the amount due a vendor. Some vendors will send the firm a refund check for the amount overpaid; the embezzler then appropriates the refund check. The books are perfectly in balance: some asset or expense is simply overstated. This technique, however, does not often work since most vendors will carry a debit balance and not refund the money.

Defalcations of Cash Receipts

Stealing from Cash Sales

If the embezzler takes cash from cash sales, he can keep the books in balance by simply not recording the transaction or by recording an amount smaller than the actual sale. If a cash register or sales slip is part of the system, either can be used improperly. For example, in a bar the cash register need not be used at all since the customer does not expect a receipt.

In the case of a movie theatre where tickets are serially prenumbered, the cashier can sell the same ticket twice and pocket the amount received for the second sale. If ten tickets are resold at $3.50, that is $35.00 per night. The cashier can get used tickets back from the ticket taker. If the taker must tear the tickets and return half to each customer, he can take one of a couple's two tickets, tear it, and give the two halves back to the people. A complete ticket is then available for reuse. Conspiracy is necessary for this scheme to work, and the cashier will have to split the proceeds with the ticket taker.

Collections of Accounts Receivable

A major technique for stealing collections on accounts receivable is called lapping. Lapping consists essentially of stealing a payment from, for example, a person named Paul and paying Paul's account by using the next receipt, say that of Peter. Peter's account is paid by the next receipt, and the process continues indefinitely. Some people cannot believe that this is a prevalent practice because it is a process that never ends. But many embezzlers feel their theft is only temporary; they will put the money back, and everything will be covered.

Another possibility is to bill for a sale at the total amount due, while recording the sale at some lower amount. The embezzler can then appropriate the difference when the customer pays his bill.

A bolder method involves taking the cash, and recording the collection as usual in the cash receipts journal. The bank balance and the general ledger will not agree; the books being greater. The bank shortage can be covered by manipulating the bank reconciliation so that the books and bank statement appear to balance. Alternatively, the embezzler can improperly use the cash receipts journal by underfooting the cash column and overfooting the sales discounts column, thus keeping debits equal to credits. If a payment is ineligible, because the discount period has expired, the embezzler can still record the receipt as if it were and take the discount himself.

Finally, the embezzler may not record the cash receipt at all. Since the customer might complain of an incorrect bill, the embezzler must intercept the statement of account and any letters demanding payment. The debit balance continues on the books. To reduce it, a credit is created by credit memo or by writing off the debt as uncollectible.

CONCEPT SUMMARY
Defalcations of Cash

Area of Defalcation	How to Obtain Cash	How to Cover in Accounting Records
Cash Disbursements	A. Issue checks to others, appropriate the checks	1. Create false invoices 2. Use invoices twice for support 3. "Pad" the payroll 4. Pocket unclaimed wages and dividends
	B. Issue check to himself	1. Incorrectly foot the cash disbursements journal 2. Increase recorded amount of another check
	C. Overpay vendor, appropriate funds	1. Allow asset or expense to remain overstated
Cash Receipts	A. Take cash from cash sales	1. Record no amount 2. Record less than was received
	B. Take cash payments on accounts receivable	1. Lapping 2. Bill for full amount, but record sale at lower amount 3. Record cash receipt, but manipulate bank reconciliation 4. Record cash receipt but incorrectly use the journal 5. Do not record cash receipt but intercept statements of account 6. Do not record cash receipt but create credit memo or write off the amount 7. Pocket payment on an account which has been written off

Strategies for Detecting and Preventing Errors

Effective error detection and prevention is possible and desirable in all businesses. The remainder of this section will discuss what should be done in particular business situations to detect mistakes and to help prevent their occurrence. The system should consist of at least the following items.

Prenumber Checks

All cash disbursements should be made with prenumbered checks, with the exception of very small cash payments, such as postage due. Using checks for all major cash disbursements ensures that: (1) the disbursement is authorized, and (2) there is a permanent receipt. The check should be prenumbered to prevent the issuance of a check which is not recorded in the cash disbursements journal.

Keep Voided Checks

If someone makes a mistake preparing a check, it should be voided before pre-paring a new one. The voided check should be: (1) altered to prevent its use, and (2) filed to make sure all prenumbered checks are accounted for.

Prepare Bank Reconciliation

Someone should reconcile the bank statement to the accounting records on a monthly basis. If the bank reconciliation is to be effective, it should be performed by someone other than the person who controls the checkbook. The bank state-ment must be unopened when the person responsible for the reconciliation re-ceives it. Even in the smallest business, this division of labor is possible; the owner can and should reconcile the bank statement.

Use Cash Register

The system should utilize a cash register to record any cash transactions which occur over the counter. The cash register should make two records of all trans-actions; one kept internally and one given to the customer. Periodic comparisons should be made of the cash register totals, the cash receipts journal, and bank deposits. In situations where no receipt is given the customer and no receipt is expected, it is not uncommon for cash to be pocketed and no record made.

Deposit Cash Receipts Intact

Daily cash receipts should be deposited intact. This is essential to ensure that cash receipts are not being taken. If disbursements are made from cash receipts, the system will lose control; it will be difficult or impossible to distinguish proper from improper disbursements.

Restrict Check Signing

Check signing should be the responsibility of management who have no access to the accounting records. This step is necessary to ensure that the accounting records accurately reflect the checks written. In the smallest companies, this rule must be relaxed, as far as the owner is concerned.

Require Proper Support

Checks should only be drawn if there is proper support for them. This support should consist of at least: (1) a proper invoice, (2) evidence that the goods or services were received, and (3) evidence that the transaction was properly authorized. This is necessary to help ensure that only properly authorized and justified expenditures are made. Supporting documents should be cancelled once a disbursement is made to protect against paying the invoice twice.

Mail Checks Directly

All checks should be mailed promptly and directly to the payee. This ensures that the payee and only the payee receives the disbursement. Otherwise, an employee may appropriate the check.

Prenumber Invoices

There must be physical control over invoices so that they cannot be improperly used. Prenumbered invoices help ensure that all invoices will be accounted for.

List Mail Collections

When the mail is opened, a list of collections should be made. A responsible official should then compare the list with the journal entry and the bank deposit. This procedure helps ensure that all mail collections are retained and recorded.

Review Financial Statements and Approve General Journal Entries

Management (in a small company, the owner) should review monthly comparative financial statements. These statements ought to be sufficiently detailed to allow detection of any unusual revenue, expense, asset, or liability amounts. All general journal entries should be properly approved. Since these entries can affect all ledger accounts, they must be adequately supervised.

The strategies discussed so far are basic and certainly not all that could or should be used in any particular situation. Judgement is required to determine exactly what controls a particular system should contain.

4.3 INTERNAL CONTROL AND INVENTORY

Many small businesses, such as real estate firms and doctors' offices, are basically service-oriented and do not have significant amounts of inventory. The preceding discussion did not include inventory procedures because it was designed to apply to all businesses. But merchandising firms (such as retail stores and wholesalers that have significant amounts of inventory), must have controls to protect these valuable assets.

CONCEPT SUMMARY
General Control Strategies

Strategies	Control Objectives
1. Use only prenumbered checks for disbursements	Ensure all checks are accounted for
2. Void, but keep, spoiled checks	Ensure voided checks are not used and all checks are accounted for
3. Reconcile bank statements monthly	Ensure all checks are authorized and recorded and receipts deposited
4. Use cash register, check register daily	Ensure all cash receipts are recorded
5. Deposit cash receipts intact	Ensure all cash receipts are deposited
6. Check signing by management with no access to records	Ensure accounting records accurately reflect checks written
7. Have proper support for checks. Cancel supporting documents when paid	Only make properly authorized and justified expenditures. Only pay once
8. Mail check directly to payee	Ensure that payee, and only payee, receives disbursement
9. Use prenumbered invoices	Ensure all invoices are accounted for
10. List mail collections, compare with journal and deposit	Ensure all mail collections are retained and recorded
11. Review monthly comparative financial statements and approve all entries to general journal	Check any unusual revenues, expense, asset, or liability amounts. Ensure only authorized and proper journal entries are made

Business Documents

Most transactions are supported by some type of written evidence. This evidence signals that something important has occurred and provides the data for accounting. Whenever a business engages in an important activity, the record of that activity will take the form of a business document. Business documents, then, are the raw material of accounting transactions. All of the data processed by accounting systems should be traceable to one or more of these documents. Most journal entries are made directly from business documents, and these documents are usually kept and stored as support for financial statement information.

Although any given business may handle many different documents, five types are common and support most business activity.

Purchase Order

Most businesses prepare a *purchase order* as a formal offer to purchase inventory or other materials from a supplier. This document is, as the name implies, an order for goods or supplies from a specific vendor under specifically requested terms.

Debit Memorandum

When goods purchased on credit are not suitable and are returned to the supplier, the amount owed by the business (accounts payable) is decreased. A document is prepared which authorizes and explains the decrease in accounts payable.

Also, this document provides notification to the supplier that goods are being returned and that the amount owed is being reduced by the purchase price of the returned goods. The *debit memorandum* (debit memo) does these things, and it results in a debit to accounts payable.

Sales Slips

These may take many forms, but all of them are created to verify sales transactions. Often, the sales slip is simply a copy of a cash register tape (in the case of a cash sale), or it may be a credit card slip for credit sales. Sales slips identify the goods being sold, give the quantity and price of the goods, and supply information about the customer to whom the sale is made. Also, the salesperson will usually be identified on a sales slip so that commissions on sales can be calculated.

Credit Memorandum

If a customer returns goods that were sold on credit, the amount owed to the business (account receivable) is decreased. A document is prepared which verifies that the goods have been returned and that the amount owed by the customer should be reduced. This document, the *credit memo,* serves as the customer's verification that his bill should reflect the return of these goods. The credit memo is so named because it results in a credit to accounts receivable.

Invoice

The *invoice* is a billing statement for goods purchased or sold on credit. Businesses receive invoices from suppliers of goods for amounts owed to them (purchase invoices) and send invoices to customers for amounts they owe to the firm (sales invoices). The invoice notifies the buyer of terms of the purchase, the total amount owed, and the due date. Invoices are important because they trigger the inflow or outflow of cash for a business. When returned with payment, invoices also help the seller record the buyer's payment correctly.

Purchasing

Purchasing is the important task of buying the inventory a company needs at the best price possible. This function should be centralized under a responsible official, usually called the *purchasing agent.* Since inventory purchasing is one of the primary areas of many firms' operations, proper support for checks and cancellation of the support after payment become even more important. Purchase returns also become a major item and must be supervised to ensure that proper credit is obtained for returned merchandise. Finally, if an operating department requests that inventory be purchased, a requisition form should be filled out and approved so that all purchases are properly authorized.

Since inventory purchases involve large dollar amounts, there is a great potential for fraud because the purchasing agent can collude with suppliers. The purchasing agent will then act in the supplier's best interest, rather than his firm's best interest and either buy more goods than are actually needed or pay a higher price than is actually required. The supplier can make payments to the purchasing agent to reward this behavior. Such payments are usually called "kickbacks."

Custody

Custody of inventory involves receiving, storing, and eventually transferring the goods. Purchasing and receiving should be performed by different employees so that each can provide a check on the other. Similarly, receiving and storekeeping should be independent operations to provide additional checks. Further, there should be a physical inventory count taken on a regular basis by employees who are not in charge of the inventory. Finally, there should be physical control of the inventory. The value of the inventory should dictate the extent of physical control—unset one-karat diamonds require more control than two-penny nails. Locks, keys, guards, and authorization for withdrawal should be used as appropriate.

Record Keeping

Record keeping is the task of keeping track of the quantity of inventory. The person in charge of inventory should not keep the related accounting records. If the same person does both, a loss of merchandise could be covered in the accounting records. When merchandise is moved from the storeroom, a document should be prepared to assign responsibility and indicate receipt of the goods. As in the case of checks, all documents should be prenumbered to ensure their physical control. If practicable, a perpetual inventory system should be used. A perpetual system involves constantly keeping track of the receipts and withdrawals of each item of inventory as they occur.

4.4 BASIC CHARACTERISTICS OF INTERNAL ACCOUNTING CONTROL

It is impossible to memorize enough lists of internal control procedures and techniques to handle every situation. It is possible, however, to keep the general concepts in mind and be able to apply them to specific situations. The following control characteristics should be found in any system. To the extent any of them are not, the system is deficient.

Honest and Capable Employees

Any system is critically dependent on the people who staff it. If the people are dishonest or incompetent, even the finest system cannot perform properly. In contrast, honest and capable employees can function even in a situation where the other elements of internal control are lacking.

CONCEPT SUMMARY
Control Strategies for Inventory

Functions	Strategies
Purchasing	1. Centralize under a responsible official 2. Submit supporting documents with checks for payment 3. Cancel support when check is paid 4. Supervise all returned purchases 5. Use requisitions to initiate purchases
Custody	1. Separate purchasing from receiving 2. Separate receiving from storekeeping 3. Take physical inventory regularly 4. Use independent employee for physical inventory 5. Physically control access to inventory
Record Keeping	1. Separate record keeping from custody 2. Use material withdrawal slips. Require signatures. 3. Require all documents to be pre-numbered 4. Use a perpetual system, if possible 5. Compare results of physical inventory to records

---

However, even with honest and able employees, effective controls are needed. As discussed earlier, the embezzler is usually basically honest; the temptation proves too strong. The following strategies are helpful in deterring employee dishonesty:

1. Annual vacations should be taken by employees and jobs rotated periodically. In this way, fraud schemes that require constant attention will be discovered.

2. Employees in positions of trust should be bonded. A fidelity bond is essentially insurance protecting the company from loss resulting from employee dishonesty.

3. The firm should have a stated conflict of interest policy to prevent potential abuse. A conflict of interest occurs when an employee's self interest is contrary to the interest of the firm. An example would be a purchasing agent who owned stock in a supplier. The purchasing agent might buy more from that supplier than was justified because he personally would benefit financially. Such conflicts of interest should be avoided.

Clear Delegation and Separation of Duties

For a system to work properly, employees must know what they and others are to do. This can be partly accomplished by an organization chart, but that is not always sufficient. Job descriptions may be necessary for proper delegation.

Even more important is the clear separation of duties. Custody of assets must be separated from their record keeping. For example, if someone is in charge of inventory and keeps the inventory records, he may cover the theft of inventory by manipulation of accounting records. Authorizing transactions must be separated from recording transactions in the journals, and both must be separated from posting transactions to the ledgers. Finally, for inventory, it is important to separate the purchasing function from the receiving function.

Proper Procedures for the Processing of Transactions

Proper procedures start with proper authorization. Although a corporation's board of directors has ultimate authority, day-to-day operating authority is delegated to top management with specific guidelines to follow (e.g., the maximum amount to be borrowed without authorization by the directors). In turn, top management delegates specific responsibilities and authority to lower ranks of management such as authorization for credit sales as long as a credit limit is not exceeded. This delegation of authority, albeit necessary, must be suitable under the circumstances and must be checked to see that guidelines are followed. We have already described some review and authorization procedures. For example, examining proper support before signing any checks; reviewing entries to write-off customer accounts; and approval of requests to purchase materials.

A chart of accounts and procedures manuals are instruments that play a key role in controlling the processing of transactions. The chart of accounts contains a list of the account numbers and names for all asset, liability, owner's equity, revenue, and expense accounts. It also describes what goes into each account. The chart of accounts and operating and accounting procedures to be followed should be documented in procedures manuals. These manuals train new employees in the operation of the system and ensure that the same types of transactions are handled in the same way.

Suitable Documents and Accounting Records

Documents should be: (1) as simple and easy to use as possible to help cut down on error, (2) prenumbered to make it easier to keep physical control over the documents, (3) as few as possible to minimize confusion and form cost, and (4) designed to ensure that they will be properly filled out (e.g., providing blocks for approval signatures). Documents record that actions were authorized and properly carried out, and they fix responsibility. When a transaction occurs, a suitable document should promptly capture the salient features. One reason is to provide the input for the accounting system to record. Accurate and timely recording is vital to good control and prompt, meaningful reports. Comparative financial statements can signal that errors or irregularities have occurred by highlighting an extreme or unexpected change. Budgets act in the same way, particularly when compared to actual results. They also communicate management's plans and intentions, thereby contributing to unified actions.

Adequate Physical Control Over Assets and Accounting Records

Specific assets and accounting records dictate what represents adequate physical control. For example, most types of inventory should be kept in a stockroom, under the custody of one person, to allow the assignment of responsibility. Critical paper such as cash, certificates of deposit, marketable securities, accounting journals, and accounting ledgers should be stored in fireproof safes. Access to all of these articles ought to be limited to certain persons. It is always necessary to consider the cost of reconstructing documents or accounting records. If the risk of their loss is great enough, copies may be justified. A related problem is records retention and storage. The needs of the firm, the volume of the records to store, and the relevant state and federal rules on records all must be considered.

Independent Verification

No one is able to verify or evaluate his own performance very effectively. Thus, the verification must be done by someone independent of the subject and the system. Another area where independent verification works as a control is assets. Comparison of assets and accounting records is a sure way of discovering errors or irregularities. If the two do not agree, something is wrong. Agreement, however, does not mean that everything is right. Unrecorded cash sales that were diverted is a case in point.

Important means of independent verification were discussed earlier. Some examples were: (1) the bank reconciliation, if done by a person other than the one who controls cash or the related accounting records; (2) a list of cash receipts made when the mail is opened; (3) the physical counting of inventory to compare with perpetual inventory records; and (4) a separate group counting inventory. Perhaps the most common and best known independent verification is an audit by a CPA firm.

4.5 FLOWCHARTING AND EVALUATION OF INTERNAL CONTROL

Flowcharts are a basic means of studying internal control. A flowchart is a picture that shows the processing steps and document flows of a system—a picture of how the system works. You may have been exposed to flowcharting in a computer science or programming course. However, there is a distinction between a *program flowchart,* which is the flowchart of an individual computer program, and a *systems flowchart,* which is the flowchart of the entire system, including manual processing and document flows. System flowcharts describe complicated networks in a highly condensed and efficient format. They also force the flowchart analyst to completely understand how a system operates. The upshot is that this technique is an excellent means of studying and evaluating internal accounting

CONCEPT SUMMARY

Characteristics of Internal Accounting Control

Characteristics	Control Strategies
Honest and capable employees	1. Hire qualified people with good references 2. Require annual vacations 3. Bond employees in positions of trust 4. State conflict of interest policy
Clear delegation and separation of duties	1. Develop organization chart 2. Separate record keeping from custody of assets 3. Separate authorization from record keeping 4. Separate purchasing from receiving
Proper procedures for processing of transactions	1. Ensure proper authorization of transactions 2. Sign checks only with proper support 3. Employ a chart of accounts with account definitions 4. Describe operating and accounting procedures in manuals
Suitable documents and accounting records	1. Prenumber important documents 2. Develop comparative financial statements 3. Prepare budget of anticipated results; compare with actual results
Adequate physical control over assets and records	1. Limit access to inventory 2. Safeguard all important records 3. Deposit cash receipts intact daily 4. Keep paper valuables in fireproof containers
Independent verification of performance and assets	1. Reconcile bank statement independently 2. Prelist cash receipts 3. Take complete inventory regularly 4. Have an annual audit by a CPA firm

control. The symbols and logic of flowcharting have been standardized. Exhibit 4–1 shows the standard symbols. However, before introducing these symbols and discussing their application to a simplified sales system, some brief introductory comments describing this sales system may prove helpful.

The system begins when a customer sends in an order. The sales department takes this order, prepares a six-part invoice, and files the order by customer name. The invoice set then goes to the credit department for a credit check, comparing that customer's present balance and proposed sale with his or her credit limit. If the credit is rejected, the customer is informed, the invoice is filed by customer name, and the process is finished. If the credit is approved, the six copies of the invoice are used in a variety of ways: one goes to the customer as an acknowledgement of the order, another is used as an invoice, and a third is used as a packing slip. The other three copies are used in different phases of the transaction and are eventually filed by invoice number, date, and customer name. Many of the steps in a real system have been left out here, but this simplified system will serve to illustrate the flowchart symbols and concepts.

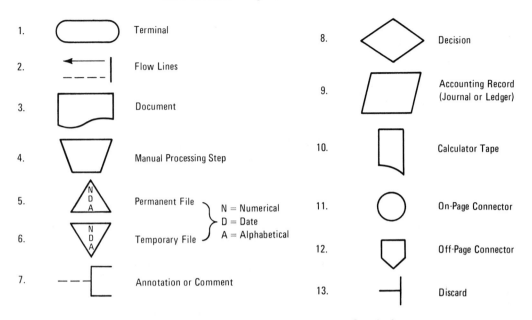

EXHIBIT 4-1   Standard Flowchart Symbols

1.   The first symbol is the oval, which stands for a terminal in the system—either a beginning or an end. The terminal generally shows something coming from outside the system in or from inside the system out. Thus, if a sale begins with a customer, the flowchart begins at an oval labelled CUSTOMER. In Exhibit 4–2 the beginning oval is at the top of the chart. A well-drawn flowchart reads from top to bottom.

2.   The second symbol is the flow line. The solid flow line indicates a document flow, while the dashed line indicates an information flow without a document. An example is the customer who generates an order. This is illustrated in Exhibit 4–2, with the order essentially flowing out of the customer. If, on the other hand, a foreman makes a verbal requisition (e.g., a request for parts), this would be shown as a dashed line as illustrated in Exhibit 4–3. Because English flows from top to bottom and left to right, a flowchart should flow in the same manner to make it as easy to read as possible. The flow lines not only indicate a flow, they also indicate the direction of the flow. In Exhibit 4–1, the dashed line is flowing from left to right. Sometimes a flow must go the other way and in those cases, we use an arrow to indicate the direction. Therefore, the horizontal document flow in Exhibit 4–1 is from right to left, and the vertical line is flowing from bottom to top.

3.   The third symbol is the document. This symbol represents any document, form, or report utilized by the system. Exhibit 4–2 illustrates the use of this

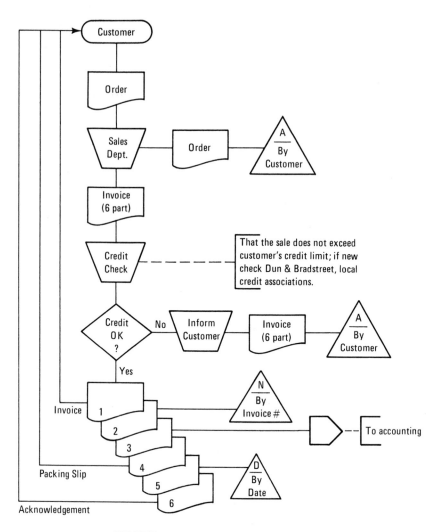

EXHIBIT 4–2   Simplified Sales System

symbol in a number of ways. Its first use is to show that the customer generates an order. Since this is a written order, the solid (i.e., document) flow line and the document symbol for the order are required.

4. The fourth symbol is the manual processing step. This symbol is a trapezoid, and it indicates any filling out of forms or adding up of numbers. In Exhibit 4–2 the customer order goes to the sales department, which prepares a six-part invoice. The next processing step is a credit check. Thus, the processing step box indicates any standard steps performed at any point in the system.

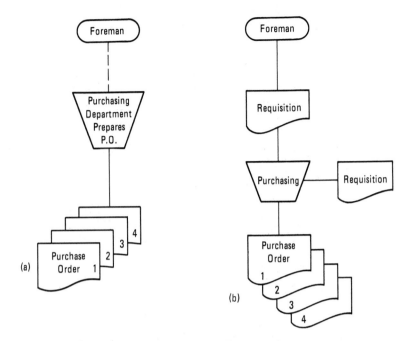

EXHIBIT 4–3 Verbal and Written Requisitions

5. The fifth symbol is the permanent file. After the sales department prepares the six-part invoice, the sales department still has the customer order. Exhibit 4–2 shows the customer order disappearing into the permanent file. But it is not enough just to know that something is filed, it is also important to know how the document is filed. The filing sequence should therefore be indicated within the file triangle. N signifies that filing is by number (e.g., by sales invoice number), D signifies filing by date, and A signifies filing alphabetically (e.g., customer's name).

6. The sixth symbol represents the temporary file; that is, documents only reside there for an interim period or until a specific event occurs. A file may always exist, but if documents only remain in the file for a temporary period it is a temporary file. For example, a file in the shipping department may contain a copy of an invoice that serves as a control on open orders which have not yet been shipped. The document will be removed from the file when the goods are shipped. Notice, the temporary file symbol is on its point, whereas the permanent file rests on its base.

7. The seventh symbol is the annotation or comment. This symbol is used to provide further explanation as necessary. For example, in Exhibit 4–2, the space in the manual step symbol for the credit check is insufficient to explain

the complete processing step. To provide a fuller explanation, the symbol for comment is used out to the side.

8. The eighth symbol is the decision. This important symbol is used for steps in the flowchart where alternative paths may be taken based upon some decision. An example appears in Exhibit 4–2 where the decision is whether or not credit is to be granted. There are two possible results—yes or no—and a different processing path is taken depending on the result. If the result is no, the customer is informed, the invoice is filed, and the process is over. If, on the other hand, the result is yes, the six parts of the invoice are processed in different ways.

9. The ninth symbol is the accounting record. The accounting record has a symbol separate from documents because it is not necessary to show the final disposition of an accounting record. The flowchart will simply assume the accounting records exist as complete entities in and of themselves. **Caution:** worksheets and financial statements are not part of the accounting records and should be represented by the document symbol.

10. The tenth symbol is the calculator tape or adding machine tape. This symbol is used when compiling a total; for example, from a batch of sales slips. Exhibit 4–4 depicts the preparation of a tape of the accounts receivable subsidiary ledger. The tape symbol is used in essentially the same way as the document symbol.

11. The eleventh symbol is the on-page connector. It sometimes happens that it is undesirable to connect all parts of a flowchart. The on-page connector indicates the point at which the flowchart is being left off, and another connector indicates where it is being picked up again. Exhibit 4–4 shows the use of an on-page connector. Another connector would be placed elsewhere on the flowchart to pick up what happens when the tape total does not equal the general ledger control.

12. The twelfth symbol is the off-page connector. Situations arise where the flowcharts of different systems are on different pages, and these systems must be tied together. The off-page connector is used to show where and how the flowcharts fit together. Exhibit 4–2 shows an invoice copy being sent to accounting for recording.

13. The thirteenth symbol is the discard symbol. There are three possible end results for every document processed by the system: (1) to be sent out of the system, symbolized by the oval; (2) to be filed, symbolized by the triangle; and (3) to be thrown away, symbolized by the discard symbol. Exhibit 4–4 shows how to indicate the discard of a tape after it is no longer useful.

Remember that the dashed flow line represents information flow, rather than the document flow illustrated by a solid flow line. Exhibit 4–3 illustrates these

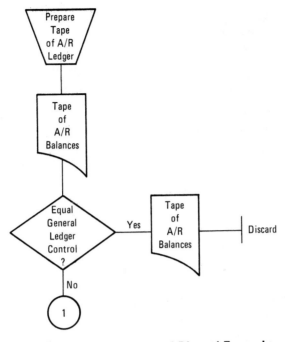

EXHIBIT 4–4   Tape and Discard Example

concepts. In section (a) there is a verbal request by the foreman for parts. Upon receiving this *verbal* request, the purchasing department will prepare a four-part purchase order and the system will continue from there. In (b) there is a *written* requisition prepared by the foreman and given to the purchasing department. Upon receiving this written request, the purchasing department prepares a four-part purchase order and proceeds as before.

It is very common in business systems to use multipart forms or to generate multiple copies of one report. Exhibit 4–3 flowcharts (a) and (b) are similar in that they actually show the four copies to make it apparent that there are multiple copies of the form. An advantage of this presentation is that lines can be drawn from each copy of the form to show where it goes. Exhibit 4–2 on the other hand, employs a more compact presentation for the six-part invoice. This format is useful when the set of forms is transported or used as a group rather than individually. The most appropriate presentation for any particular flowchart is a matter of judgement.

Once the system has been documented in a flowchart, the quality of internal control can be evaluated by applying the concepts and strategies discussed earlier in the chapter. This will be done extensively in Chapters 6–10. Additionally, any weaknesses should be pointed out to management for possible correction. This will be discussed in greater depth in Chapter 11.

Key Terms

accounting controls	footing (over-, under-)
administrative controls	internal control
audit trail	invoice
authorization	lapping
credit memorandum	padding
customer statements	physical inventory
debit memorandum	purchase order
defalcation	sales slip
embezzlement	systems flowchart
flowchart	

Questions and Problems

Questions

4-1 What are the four major goals of a system of internal control? Distinguish between accounting and administrative controls.

4-2 The double-entry system and subsidiary ledgers are two important characteristics of accounting systems which help detect errors. Describe how they accomplish this purpose.

4-3 Discuss two techniques for the embezzlement of cash receipts, and specify how these embezzlements could be prevented.

4-4 Discuss two techniques for the embezzlement of cash disbursements, and specify how these embezzlements could be prevented.

4-5 Discuss two techniques for the theft of inventory, and specify how these thefts could be prevented.

4-6 How can the use of prenumbered documents improve internal control? If checks were not prenumbered, what might happen?

4-7 Why is the separation of record-keeping from physical custody of assets an important internal control feature? Give three examples of areas where separation would be essential.

4-8 Explain why access to the general journal should be limited and all general journal entries properly authorized.

4-9 List the standard flowchart symbols.

4-10 Why are flowcharts used as a basis for the evaluation of internal control?

Multiple Choice Questions From Professional Examinations

4-11 Internal accounting control comprises the plan of organization and the procedures and records that are concerned with the safeguarding of assets and the

   a. Decision processes of management.
   b. Reliability of financial records.
   c. Authorization of transactions.
   d. Achievement of administrative objectives.

4-12 Which of the following is an invalid concept of internal control?

   a. In cases where a person is responsible for all phases of a transaction, there should be a clear designation of that person's responsibility.
   b. The recorded accountability for assets should be compared with the existing assets at reasonable intervals, and appropriate action should be taken if there are differences.
   c. Accounting control procedures may appropriately be applied on a test basis in some circumstances.
   d. Procedures designed to detect errors and irregularities should be performed by persons other than those who are in a position to perpetrate them.

4-13 Which of the following *best* describes the inherent limitations that should be recognized by an auditor when considering the potential effectiveness of a system of internal accounting control?

   a. Procedures whose effectiveness depends on segregation of duties can be circumvented by collusion.
   b. The competence and integrity of client personnel provides an environment conducive to accounting control and provides assurance that effective control will be achieved.
   c. Procedures designed to assure the execution and recording of transactions in accordance with proper authorizations are effective against irregularities perpetrated by management.
   d. The benefits expected to be derived from effective internal accounting control usually do *not* exceed the costs of such control.

4-14 To avoid potential errors and irregularities, a well-designed system of internal accounting control in the accounts payable area should include a separation of which of the following functions?

   a. Cash disbursements and invoice verification.
   b. Invoice verification and merchandise ordering.

    c. Physical handling of merchandise received and preparation of receiving reports.

    d. Check signing and cancellation of payment documentation.

4-15 Which of the following is a standard internal accounting control for cash disbursements?

    a. Checks should be signed by the controller and at least one other employee of the company.

    b. Checks should be sequentially numbered, and the numerical sequence should be accounted for by the person preparing bank reconciliations.

    c. Checks and supporting documents should be marked "Paid" immediately after the check is returned with the bank statement.

    d. Checks should be sent directly to the payee by the employee who prepares documents that authorize check preparation.

4-16 Internal control over cash receipts is weakened when an employee who receives customer mail receipts also

    a. Prepares initial cash receipts records.

    b. Records credits to individual accounts receivable.

    c. Prepares bank deposit slips for all mail receipts.

    d. Maintains a petty cash fund.

4-17 Which of the following procedures would best detect the theft of valuable items from an inventory that consists of hundreds of different items selling for $1 to $10 and a few items selling for hundreds of dollars?

    a. Maintain a perpetual inventory of only the more valuable items with frequent periodic verification of the validity of the perpetual inventory record.

    b. Have an independent CPA firm prepare an internal control report on the effectiveness of the administrative and accounting controls over inventory.

    c. Have separate warehouse space for the more valuable items with sequentially numbered tags.

    d. Require an authorized officer's signature on all requisitions for the more valuable items.

4-18 Which of the following is an internal control weakness for a company whose inventory of supplies consists of a large number of individual items?

    a. Supplies of relatively little value are expensed when purchased.

    b. The cycle basis is used for physical counts.

c. The storekeeper is responsible for maintenance of perpetual inventory records.

d. Perpetual inventory records are maintained only for items of significant value.

4-19 Which of the following is an effective internal accounting control measure that encourages receiving department personnel to count and inspect all merchandise received?

a. Quantities ordered are excluded from the receiving department copy of the purchase order.

b. Vouchers are prepared by accounts payable department personnel only after they match item counts on the receiving report with the purchase order.

c. Receiving department personnel are expected to match and reconcile the receiving report with the purchase order.

d. Internal auditors periodically examine, on a surprise basis, the receiving department copies of receiving reports.

4-20 Effective internal control in a small company that has an insufficient number of employees to permit proper division of responsibilities can *best* be enhanced by

a. Employment of temporary personnel to aid in the separation of duties.

b. Direct participation by the owner of the business in the record-keeping activities of the business.

c. Engaging a CPA to perform monthly "write-up" work.

d. Delegation of full, clear-cut responsibility to each employee for the functions assigned to each.

4-21 A well-designed system of internal control that is functioning effectively is most likely to detect an irregularity arising from

a. The fraudulent action of several employees.

b. The fraudulent action of an individual employee.

c. Informal deviations from the official organization chart.

d. Management fraud.

4-22 The use of fidelity bonds protects a company from embezzlement losses and also

a. Protects employees who make unintentional errors from possible monetary damages resulting from such errors.

b. Allows the company to substitute the fidelity bonds for various parts of internal accounting control.

c. Reduces the company's need to obtain expensive business interruption insurance.

d. Minimizes the possibility of employing persons with dubious records in positions of trust.

4-23 The normal sequence of documents and operations on a well-prepared systems flowchart is

a. Top to bottom and left to right.
b. Bottom to top and left to right.
c. Top to bottom and right to left.
d. Bottom to top and right to left.

4-24 Which of the following best describes the principal advantage of the use of flowcharts in reviewing internal control?

a. Standard flowcharts are available and can be effectively used for describing most internal company operations.
b. Flowcharts aid in the understanding of the sequence and relationships of activities and documents.
c. Working papers are not complete unless they include flowcharts as well as memoranda on internal control.
d. Flowcharting is the most efficient means available for summarizing internal control.

4-25 The auditor's study and evaluation of internal control is done for each of the following reasons *except*

a. To provide a basis for constructive service suggestions.
b. To aid in the determination of the nature, timing and extent of audit tests.
c. To establish a basis for reliance thereon.
d. To provide training and development for staff accountants.

Problems

4-26 Jerome Paper Company engaged you to revise its internal control system. Jerome does not prelist cash receipts before they are recorded and has other weaknesses in processing collections of trade receivables, the company's largest asset. In discussing the matter with the controller, you find he is chiefly interested in economy when he assigns duties to the fifteen office personnel. He feels the main considerations are that the work should be done by people who are most familiar with it, capable of doing it, and available when it has to be done. The controller says he has excellent control over trade receivables because receivables are pledged as security for a continually renewable bank loan, and the bank sends out positive confirmation requests occasionally based on a list of pledged receivables furnished by the company each week. You learn that the bank's internal auditor is satisfied if he gets an acceptable response on 70 percent of his requests.

1. Explain how prelisting of cash receipts strengthens internal control over cash.
2. Assume that an employee handles cash receipts from trade customers before they are recorded. List the duties which that employee should not do so that he does not have the opportunity to conceal embezzlement of cash receipts.
3. What are the implications for the bank if, during the bank auditor's examination of accounts receivable, some of a client's trade customers do not respond to his request for positive confirmation of their accounts?

AICPA

4-27 Discuss briefly the more important deficiencies in the system of internal control in the following situation. In addition, include a proper remedy for each deficiency. The cashier of the Easy Company intercepted customer A's check payable to the company in the amount of $500 and deposited it in a bank account that was part of the company petty cash fund, of which he was custodian. He then drew a $500 check on the petty cash fund bank account payable to himself, signed it, and cashed it. At the end of the month, while processing the monthly statements to customers, he was able to change the statement to customer A to show that A had received credit for the $500 check that had been intercepted. Ten days later, he made an entry in the cash received book which purported to record receipt of a remittance of $500 from Customer A, thus restoring A's account to its proper balance but overstating cash in bank. He covered the overstatement by omitting two checks that totalled $500 from the list of outstanding checks in the bank reconcilement.

AICPA

4-28 The town of Commuter Park operates a private parking lot near the railroad station for the benefit of town residents. The guard on duty issues annual prenumbered parking stickers to residents who submit an application and show evidence of residency. The sticker is affixed to the auto and allows the resident to park anywhere in the lot for twelve (12) hours if four quarters are placed in the parking meter. Applications are maintained in the guard office at the lot. The guard checks to see that only residents are using the lot and that no resident has parked without paying the required meter fee.

Once a week the guard on duty, who has a master key for all meters, takes the coins from the meters and places them in a locked steel box. The guard delivers the box to the town storage building, where it is opened. The coins are manually counted by a storage department clerk, who records the total cash counted on a "Weekly Cash Report." This report is sent to the town accounting department. The storage department clerk puts the cash in a safe, and on the following day, the cash is picked up by the town's treasurer, who manually recounts the cash, prepares the bank deposit slip, and delivers the deposit to the bank. The deposit slip, authenticated by the bank teller, is sent to the accounting department, where it is filed with the "Weekly Cash Report."

Required:

a. What internal control weaknesses do you see?

b. What recommendations do you have for strengthening the weaknesses over cash receipts?

AICPA (Adapted)

4-29 The Billon Company has an employee bond subscription plan under which employees subscribe to bonds and pay in installments through deductions from their salaries. The cashier keeps the supply of unissued bonds in a safe together with the records showing each employee's subscription and payments to date. The amounts of unissued bonds in the hands of the cashier and the balances due from employees are controlled on the general ledger—another department. However, the employees may, if they desire, pay any remaining balance to the cashier and receive their bonds.

When an employee makes a prepayment, the cashier notes the amount on his account, delivers the bond, and receives a receipt from the employee for the amount of the bond. The cashier deposits bond cash received in an employee bond bank account and submits a report showing the transaction to the general ledger department; this report is used as a basis for the necessary adjustments of the control accounts.

Periodic surprise counts of bonds on hand are made by independent employees, who check the amounts of unissued bonds and employees' unpaid balances with the control accounts. During the cashier's lunch hour, or at other times when he is required to be absent from his position, another employee, who has keys to the safe in which unissued bonds and employee bond payment records are kept, comes in and carries out the same procedures as enumerated above.

1. Point out the deficiencies in internal control, and describe the errors or manipulations that might occur because of each weakness.

2. Recommend changes in procedures to eliminate these weaknesses.

AICPA

4-30 A Canadian life insurance company maintains a large first mortgage investment portfolio. The mortgagors are all located in the province of the head office of the company. The president has advised CA, the company's auditor for many years, that the mortgage manager had suddenly disappeared.

He states that he feels the fees paid for the acquisition of mortgages are too high (i.e., finders' fees) and that there are possibilities that some mortgages have been granted for properties with appraised values which have been inflated. He then asks CA to investigate the possibility of fraud in the mortgage department.

From his working papers on the current internal control review, CA ascertains the following pertinent facts:

— All checks issued for finders' fees are prepared from check requisitions. These requisitions are prepared and signed by the mortgage manager. All requisitions are cross-referenced to the applicable checks.

— All finders' fees checks are prepared by the accounting department. They are prenumbered and signed by the vice-president of finance and the controller of the company after they review the finders' invoices.

— After the checks are signed, they are sent to the mortgage manager for distribution to the payees.

— All such checks are paid out of the company's general bank account. The finders' invoices are filed in the mortgage department.

— The amount authorized by the company for finders' fees is 1% of the principal amount of the mortgage loans.

— No other check requests are prepared by the mortgage department.

— All properties for which mortgage loans are granted are appraised by the mortgage manager. The mortgage manager decides on the mortgage loans to be granted.

— The company policy is not to grant mortgage loans on first mortgages in excess of 75% of the appraised value of the related property.

— The mortgage manager prepares all mortgage note documentation.

— Before the mortgage loan is granted, the finance committee board authorizes the mortgage loan amounts and interest rates and approves the mortgagors.

— The computer prepared mortgage ledger indicates the mortgage principal, unpaid interest, mortgage terms, interest rate, and aggregate balance due for each mortgage. Finders' fees are not indicated in this ledger.

— Finders' fees paid are recorded in a separate general ledger account. The general ledger is computerized, and the finders' fees account indicates the details of the date, check number and amount for each fee paid.

— All checks received from mortgagors are sent directly from the mailroom to the mortgage department for identification of the mortgagors. The checks are then submitted to the cash collections department for depositing.

CA's review of his files indicates that he has brought the internal control weaknesses, evident from the above described facts, to the attention of the company's management in a recent memorandum of recommendations to strengthen internal controls and procedures. Management's written response had been that they would review the procedures and take corrective action where they deemed it necessary.

Required:

Outline the recommendations and the reasons therefor which CA should have covered in his recent memorandum to the company's management.

CICA (adapted)

4-31 You have recently been engaged by the Alaska Branch of Far Distributing Company. This branch has substantial annual sales, which are billed and collected locally. As a part of your review, you find that the procedures for handling cash receipts are as follows:

a. Cash collections on over-the-counter sales and C.O.D. sales are received from the customer or delivery service by the cashier. Upon receipt of cash the cashier stamps the sales ticket "paid" and files a copy for future reference. The only record of C.O.D. sales is a copy of the sales ticket, which is given to the cashier to hold until the cash is received from the delivery service.

b. Mail is opened by the credit manager's secretary, and remittances are given to the credit manager for his review. The credit manager then places the remittances on a tray on the cashier's desk. At the daily deposit cut-off time the cashier delivers the checks and cash on hand to the assistant credit manager, who prepares remittance lists and makes up the bank deposit, which he also takes to the bank. The assistant credit manager also posts remittances to the accounts receivable ledger cards and verifies the cash discount allowable.

c. You also ascertain that the credit manager obtains approval from the executive office of Far Distributing Company, located in Chicago, to write off uncollectible accounts and that he has retained in his custody, as of the end of the fiscal year, some remittances that were received on various days during last month.

Required:

1. Describe the irregularities that might occur under the procedures now in effect for handling cash collections and remittances.

2. Give procedures that you would recommend to strengthen internal control over cash collections and remittances.

AICPA

4-32 At the Main Street Theater, the cashier, located in a box office at the entrance, receives cash from customers and operates a machine that ejects serially numbered tickets. To gain admission to the theater, a customer hands the ticket to a doorman stationed some 50 feet from the box office at the entrance to the theater lobby. The doorman tears the ticket in half, opens the door for the customer, and returns the stub to him. The other half of the ticket is dropped by the doorman into a locked box.

Required:

a. What internal controls are present in this phase of handling cash receipts?

b. What steps should be taken regularly by the manager or other supervisor to give maximum effectiveness to these controls?

c. Assume that the cashier and the doorman decided to collaborate in an effort to abstract cash receipts. What action might they take?

d. Continuing the assumption made in (c) above of collusion between the cashier and the doorman, what features of the control procedures would be likely to disclose the embezzlement?

AICPA

4-33 After completing the interim examination of the accounts of B. Ltd. a Canadian company CA sent a letter to the controller, commenting on several matters which he felt required improvement. The controller discussed the comments with his staff, then sent a reply rejecting all of CA's suggested improvements.

Excerpts from CA's letter are marked (L) below; excerpts from the controller's reply are marked (R).

1. *Petty cash:*

(L) The positions of petty cash custodian and cashier should be filled by different people. At present, the cashier controls the $500 petty cash fund—this situation results in weak internal control because of the possibility of cash being temporarily transferred between petty cash and cash receipts.

(R) A $500 fund is too small to warrant segregation of the duties. If the cashier, for example, were involved in a lapping operation of the cash receipts, and was using the petty cash fund to cover the shortage, $500 would not go very far. Similarly, if part of the $500 were borrowed by the cashier, the amount would not be significant. The cashier is covered by our blanket bond.

2. *Bank reconciliation:*
   (L) The bank reconciliation should be prepared by an employee who takes no part in the regular cash receipts or disbursements functions. The reconciliation is now prepared by the bookkeeper, who also prepares the cheques and is a signing officer.
   (R) We do not wish to segregate the duties with respect to the bank reconciliation and cash disbursements because the payroll cheques are included with the returned cheques. The confidential nature of the payroll amounts must be preserved.

3. *Purchase orders:*
   (L) A purchase order when accepted by the supplier is a binding agreement to purchase the merchandise or services ordered, and should therefore include unit prices. Approximately 75% of the purchase orders presently issued do not show unit prices.
   (R) As we deal with a limited number of suppliers and as all of their prices are published in catalogues (to which the accounts payable department checks invoice prices), entering the unit price on the purchase order is an unnecessary clerical step.

4. *Cancellation of documents:*
   (L) Suppliers' invoices and supporting documents should be cancelled by, or under the direct supervision of, a second cheque-signing officer. At present, vouchers are not cancelled; this could lead to a fraudulent or accidental duplicate payment of an invoice.
   (R) Our cash disbursement policy is that all invoices be paid within 15 days of receipt. The chance of a duplicate payment is minimal because a signing officer would notice an old invoice at the time the cheque was signed. The clerical effort to cancel the vouchers is therefore not warranted.

5. *Sales invoices:*
   (L) Sales invoices should be pre-numbered by the printer. Without the control provided by pre-numbering, the company has no assurance that employees are not suppressing invoices and misappropriating sales proceeds.
   (R) We discontinued pre-numbering sales invoices because we found that the time spent controlling them was quite significant. Sales invoices in our organization can originate in a number of places; accordingly, the clerk charged with the responsibility of accounting for the numbers had a very difficult time with the many numerical sequences. This problem was further aggravated when we switched to the present pre-billing system. The invoices are prepared before the merchandise is shipped, so the shipping department sometimes will hold an invoice for a considerable period of time awaiting receipt of the items from production or from an outside supplier.

6. *Vouchers payable:*

(L) The trial balance of vouchers payable should be reconciled monthly with the general ledger control account, by someone other than the accounts payable clerk. At the time of my examination there was a substantial difference between the accounts payable detail listing prepared by the accounts payable clerk and the control account in the general ledger.

(R) We have a new clerk in the accounts payable department; unfortunately your examination was conducted after she had been in the position for only two weeks. Our usual practice is to have the accounts payable clerk prepare a listing of unpaid vouchers at the month-end and pass this listing to the general ledger keeper, who reconciles it to the general ledger control account. At the time of your examination the listing had been returned to the clerk as a large number of errors had become apparent—she was instructed to locate the errors in her listing as a training exercise.

<u>Required:</u>

For each of the six matters above, suggest what CA's position should be in his reply to the controller, supporting the position you suggest by listing factors CA would consider in drafting his reply.

CICA

4-34 The partially completed credit sales systems flowchart on page 146 depicts the charge sales activities of the Bottom Manufacturing Corporation. A customer's purchase order is received, and a six-part sales order is prepared from it. The six copies are initially distributed as follows:

Copy No. 1— Billing copy—to billing department.
Copy No. 2— Shipping copy—to shipping department.
Copy No. 3— Credit copy—to credit department.
Copy No. 4— Stock request copy—to credit department.
Copy No. 5— Customer copy—to customer.
Copy No. 6— Sales order copy—file in sales order department.

When each copy of the sales order reaches the applicable department or destination, it calls for specific internal control procedures and related documents. Some of the procedures and related documents are indicated on the flowchart. Other procedures and documents are labeled with the letters *a* to *r*.

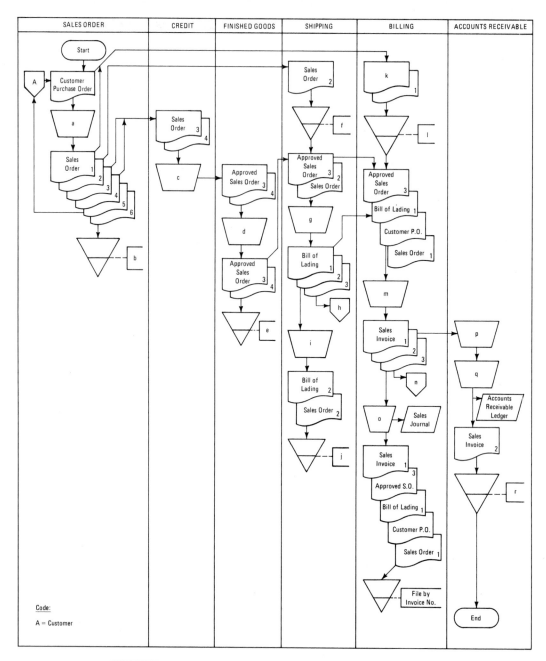

EXHIBIT 4-5 Bottom Manufacturing Company Flowchart

Required:

List the procedures or the internal documents that are labeled *c* to *r* in the flowchart of Bottom Manufacturing Corporation's charge sales system. Organize your answer as follows (note that explanations of the letters *a* and *b* in the flowchart are entered as examples):

Flowchart Symbol Letter	Procedures or Internal Document
a	Prepare six-part sales order.
b	File by order number.

AICPA

4-35 Anthony, CPA, prepared the flowchart on page 148 to portray the purchasing function of one of his clients, a medium-sized company, from the preparation of initial documents through the vouching of invoices for payment in accounts payable. The flowchart was a portion of the work performed to evaluate internal control.

1. Identify and explain the systems and control weaknesses evident from the flowchart.
2. Include the internal control weaknesses resulting from activities performed or not performed. All documents are prenumbered.

AICPA

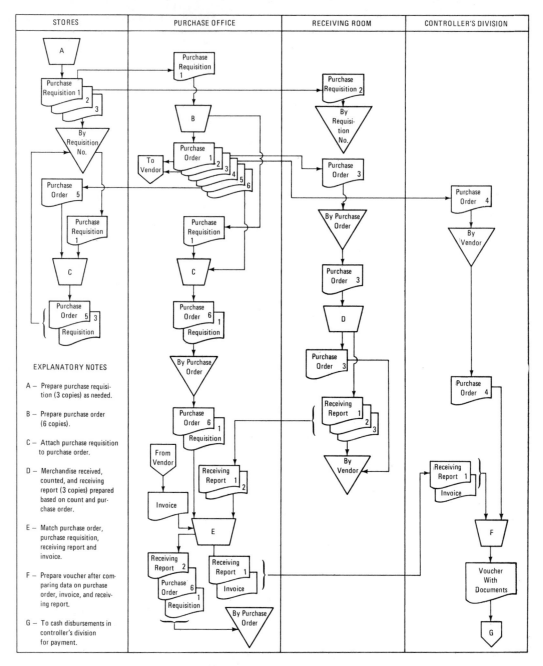

| STORES | PURCHASE OFFICE | RECEIVING ROOM | CONTROLLER'S DIVISION |

EXPLANATORY NOTES

A — Prepare purchase requisition (3 copies) as needed.

B — Prepare purchase order
(6 copies).

C — Attach purchase requisition
to purchase order.

D — Merchandise received,
counted, and receiving
report (3 copies) prepared
based on count and pur-
chase order.

E — Match purchase order,
purchase requisition,
receiving report and
invoice.

F — Prepare voucher after comparing data on purchase
order, invoice, and receiving report.

G — To cash disbursements in
controller's division
for payment.

EXHIBIT 4-6 Anthony's Flowchart

Auditing of Cycles—I

5

Systems approach to auditing

In this chapter, we will be following the progression of an audit from its inception to its conclusion. The concept of an audit and its major features will be introduced now and will be translated into implementation procedures and techniques in subsequent chapters. An audit is a purposive undertaking; it has a fundamental goal or audit objective. Never lose track of the fundamental purpose, and relate all other actions to it.

Associated with the audit objective is a responsibility to be knowledgeable about a client, its industry, and the environmental forces that have an impact upon it. Obtaining an appropriate background is "step one" in the overall planning for an engagement. A great deal of planning goes into an audit. A central issue involved is evaluating the client's system of internal controls and deciding to what extent they will be relied upon.

Evaluating a system of accounting controls calls for an analysis of the risks present, and reliance upon that system means taking a risk. Risk analysis and the audit tests that are to be conducted are facilitated by segmenting a firm into "cycles," a concept we will explore later. Audit tests gather evidence, which is documented in a formal manner in "working papers." Audit evidence furnishes support for the opinion that is ultimately expressed that the primary audit objective has (or has not) been achieved. As an audit draws to a close, a number of concluding steps are taken including preparation of the "auditor's report."

An overview of an audit, from planning through conclusion, is depicted in Exhibit 5–1. Now that a panorama of what stretches before us has been sketched, we can begin scrutinizing each major portion.

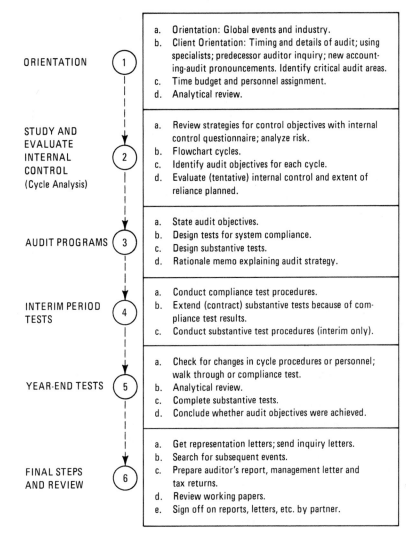

EXHIBIT 5–1 Overview of an Audit

5.1 AUDIT OBJECTIVES AND PLANNING

Audit Objectives

The central purpose, or primary objective, of all audits is to express an opinion on the fairness of representations contained in the client's financial statements. The auditor's report is the medium through which an opinion is expressed. The financial statements themselves are the representations of management.

Professional skill and care must be exercised in conducting an audit examination. Due professional care demands that the auditor maintain an attitude of professional skepticism and be alert to the possibility of illegal acts by clients. If an auditor believes that material errors (unintentional mistakes) or irregularities (intentional distortions) exist, audit procedures should be extended to obtain evidence rejecting or confirming that belief. Although the principal function of an audit is to report on the fairness of financial information and not to uncover fraud, illegal acts, or other irregularities, an auditor cannot ignore these possibilities. The responsibility to keep them in the forefront is clearcut. In addition to the primary audit objective, there are subsidiary, or secondary audit objectives. Secondary audit objectives are achieved by carrying out particular audit test procedures. For example, secondary audit objectives include: to establish the correctness of cash balances; to verify the existence of inventory and fixed assets; and to verify the workings of a specific procedure. When they are finally achieved, the total force of the secondary objectives comes together to accomplish the primary audit objective. Planning reflects the way that audit objectives are to be achieved and begins with orientation to the client, its industry, and the environment in which it operates.

Planning

The first standard of field work requires that, "The work is to be adequately planned and assistants, if any, are to be properly supervised." *Statement on Auditing Standards No. 22* elaborates on what is to be included in the planning phase of an audit. "Audit planning involves developing an overall strategy for the expected conduct and scope of the examination." (AU 311.03) The elements that have an impact on such a strategy are: conditions in the environment, industry characteristics, and particulars of a client's business.

Environment Conditions

A firm is dependent upon, and vulnerable to, the forces that constantly reshape the economic, political, and social environment in which it operates. An auditor must be aware of national and international conditions and events because of the impact they could have on a client. Keeping abreast of the news is a job-related responsibility. Raising questions about the consequences to a client of a revolution in Iran, a currency revaluation in West Germany, or a dockworkers strike on the U.S. east coast should become routine.

Industry Orientation

A similar responsibility holds for the industry in which the client firm operates. An auditor has to be knowledgeable about industry characteristics such as how it is affected by economic fluctuations, its technological sophistication, and the degree to which it is regulated by government, among other things. For instance, if a university were to become a new audit client, an understanding of the "education industry" would be essential. It would be wise to read the *Chronicle of Higher Education* for general information, as well as announcements of research grants and contracts. There is also an *Industry Audit Guide* that would be consulted.[1] If a CPA firm were to audit CETA or EPA grants awarded to a local government, they would keep an eye out for administrative requirements published in the *Federal Register* and the *Code of Federal Regulations* and be aware of the GAO's *Standards for Audit of Governmental Organizations, Programs, Activities, and Functions.* Not only is it necessary to learn about the industry, it is also important that special industry accounting principles, and government prescribed accounting practices be understood.

Other sources of industry information are: industry journals, newspapers, and newsletters (e.g., *Retail Outlook*); reports by investment and credit services (e.g., Standard & Poor's *Industry Guides,* Dun & Bradstreet) and brokerage houses; financial statements of competitor firms; and conferences with client management and specialists within the CPA firm. Background orientation materials are included in the working papers in the form of original references (or photocopies) and auditor memos.

Behind the demand for this orientation to the world in which the client functions stands a basic principle. If an opinion is to be formed concerning the fairness of an entity's financial statements, the auditor must understand his client's business, its position in the industry, and the setting in which all of this takes place.

Client Orientation

Client conferences, on-site tours, and reading through documents such as the charter, by-laws, and board minutes are the kinds of techniques employed in understanding a client's business. What does the firm do, and how is it organized? In what markets does it sell, and where are its locations? Broad questions that speak to fundamental matters provide an orientation to the client.

In the early stages of an engagement client meetings are held for orientation purposes and to discuss details of the audit and potential problem areas. Meanwhile, a time budget is being developed, and professional staff are assigned to the job. It is an accepted practice to send a letter to the client confirming the engagement, the type of work to be done, etc.

Questions are raised about numerous issues. What will the effect be of a new accounting or auditing pronouncement? What accounting policies are employed? Are general internal controls in place? Will it be necessary to use the work of a specialist, such as an actuary or a geologist? When will the audit be conducted?

---

[1]"Audits of Colleges and Universities," *Industry Audit Guide* (N.Y.: American Institute of CPAs, 1973).

These conferences, together with "analytical review" results, help identify *critical audit areas*. A critical audit area is a designation for which extra care and effort in testing is necessary.

Analytical Review

The first audit test takes place at this stage. As part of client orientation an analytical review is performed of significant ratios, operating statistics, and trends in financial data. Current period data and ratios are compared to: (1) their counterparts for the preceding period, (2) budgeted amounts for this period, and (3) industry averages.

If unusual or large differences turn up, the auditor tries to find an explanation. The abnormal and unexpected are investigated. The ratios of bad debts to credit sales or average inventory to cost of goods sold are often significant figures. If these ratios are substantially different from last year's, it may signal that problems exist with inventories. Product quality may have deteriorated, causing sales declines, inventory build-up, and irate customers who refuse to pay for their purchase. Valuation of inventory and accounts receivable then becomes an issue.

A trial balance, interim financial statements, and budgets are used in analytical review. Exhibit 5–2 is an auditor's working paper that contains a trial balance. Notice that last year's figures are included for comparison with this year's amounts to facilitate analytical review. Notice, too, the index column that references every account to another working paper. These working papers will be illustrated in the following chapters when the specifics of auditing are covered. Analytical review is a "substantive audit test" (discussed below) that is performed during the planning phase, and again at year-end.

Predecessor Auditor

When a change in CPA firms takes place, certain inquiries must be made by the "successor auditor." Communication with a predecessor auditor is a special kind of client orientation. The prospective client has to approve communication with the outgoing auditor, and he or she, in turn, is obliged under normal circumstances to respond to reasonable inquiries. Such matters as why the auditor switch is being made, management's integrity, and conflicts over accounting policies or auditing procedures are discussed.

The predecessor firm's working papers may be reviewed and copies made of parts that will continue to be important to the upcoming audit such as analyses of balance sheet accounts. A successor auditor may reject the engagement because of responses from the predecessor.

The client orientation activities of an auditor have an additional purpose—to provide the basis for forming an opinion on the quality of a client's system of internal accounting controls.

Scott Interspecial Industries
Trial Balance
12/31/X1

W.P. NO.	A-1
ACCOUNTANT	RKS
DATE	1/18/X2

WIP REF.	Account	Unadjusted Balances DR.	Unadjusted Balances CR.	Adjustments & Reclassifications DR.	Adjustments & Reclassifications CR.	Adjusted Balances DR.	Adjusted Balances CR.	Balance at 12/31/X0 DR<OR>
B-3	Cash	5011544 2				5011544 2		2417811 57
M-1	Securities - Treasury Bills	9862000				9862000		9794500
"	" - Southern Railway Notes	6000000 00				6000000		6000000 00
"	" - U.S. Treasury Notes	2565000 00				2565000 00		
M-1	Accrued Interest Receivable	943250				943250		2823 00
E-2	Accounts Receivable	477496755				477496755		427269957
G-1	Prepaid Insurance	1454000 00				1454000 00		1454000 00
H	Land	6500000 00				6500000 00		6500000 00
	Building	7256000 00				7256000 00		7256000 00
	Accum. Dep. - Building		1995400 00				1995400 00	<1633000 00>
	Factory Equipment	76747600 00				76747600 00		6557500 00
	Accum. Dep. - Factory Equip.		31964500 00				31964500 00	<2601800 00>
	Office Equipment	5579000 00				5579000 00		1964750 00
	Accum. Dep. - Office Equip.		3524600 00				3524600 00	<2476000 00>
	Autos & Trucks	5571900 00				5571900 00		5571900 00
	Accum. Dep. - Autos & Trucks		1235400 00				1235400 00	<1275800 00>
M-1	Investment - Rocket Ind. Stock	587500				587500		587500
"	- Shuttle Svcs. Stock	4775000 00		⑥ 13564700		4775000 00	13564700	—
M-1	Current Portion, L.T. Debt							105391 56
O-1	Accrued Payroll		1611378				1611378	161,378
M-1	Accrued Int. Payable - Mortgage		831320 0				831320 0	< 8498700 >
"	Accrued Int. Payable - Bank Note		150000				150000	—
M-1	Long Term Debt - Mortgage		285045200	⑤ 13564700			231460500	<285297200>
	- Bonds		10000000 0	Ⓐ 10000000 0			10000000 0	<10000000 0>
	- Bank Notes		10000000 0					—
M-1	Interest Income		2635050				2635050	< 1844575 85 >
G-1	Insurance Exp. - Mfg.	2540000 00				2540000 00		2274800 00
	- Admin.	1462176				1462176		1221050
M-1	Interest Expense	30210500				30210500		2494650
	⋯							
	Totals	126 984762 28	126 984762 28	13564700	13564700	126 984762 28	126 984762 28	-0-

EXHIBIT 5-2

5.2 INTERNAL ACCOUNTING CONTROLS AND TRANSACTION CYCLES

The second standard of field work specifies that internal control is to be studied and evaluated. How extensive the auditing test procedures will be is at question. Don't forget that auditing entails "testing," not 100 per cent duplicative review of every recorded transaction. The question can also be phrased, "To what extent will test procedures be *limited* because the system of controls is well designed and operating effectively, and therefore, can be trusted?" The more a system is relied upon the less testing is done to substantiate financial data. The extent of testing varies inversely with an auditor's reliance on internal control.

Complete reliance on internal controls, to the exclusion of all audit tests, is not permitted. Audit tests may be cut back or restricted when controls are good but never eliminated entirely. Here is where auditors take risks. They cannot be absolutely sure of anything when only tests are conducted and they must rely on a system or someone else. The exercise of judgement and risk-taking go hand in glove.

Throughout the process of studying and evaluating internal accounting controls, very basic issues are being explored. To what degree is an awareness of the need for controls present in the organization? Is there an atmosphere of control consciousness? Has management elevated control to a conspicuously important level, or is it relegated to a "back seat"? The attitude of an organization's members toward internal controls is an important clue to the quality of financial information that is to be audited. It will also ultimately set the tone for how the audit will be conducted; that is, the nature, extent, and timing of the work to be performed. If internal accounting controls are seriously deficient and have material weaknesses, that fact must be conveyed to the firm's management and the board of directors or its audit committee.

Studying Internal Accounting Control by Cycle Analysis

The firm is an amalgamation of complex systems organized to perform a variety of functions necessary to its existence. Systems are networks of individuals and departments linked together to carry out logically related activities. For example, there is a system for getting a firm's product to the customer. The functions involved in accomplishing that task are: marketing and order taking, credit approval, shipping, billing, customer accounts, and cash collections.

Each function is performed by a number of individuals attached to various departments. A number of specific activities will be carried out by them. Marketing and order taking, for example, includes advertising, market research, selling, and order entry and pricing. Some other systems are the "procurement system," which is designed to obtain the goods and services needed by a firm, and the "human resources system" that sees to the acquisition and utilization of personnel.

System networks are designed to react to certain events. They react by recognizing and processing transactions through a naturally organized sequence from beginning to end. Transactions are the subject matter of a system. They are economic events involving an exchange (or transfer) of assets or services. An exchange of assets/services with parties outside the firm, or a transfer within the firm, is measured in dollar terms and eventually ends up as recorded financial information. A transaction or economic event may also be activated by external forces (e.g., expropriation of assets by a foreign government) or by the passage of time (e.g., interest on debt; vesting of pension benefits).

In summary, transactions are economic events to be accounted for that are cycled through an organized system of logically related functional activities. Dividing a firm into segments along these lines is the key to a systematic methodology for studying internal accounting controls and conducting audit test procedures. We will hereafter refer to the segments of a business as *transaction cycles*. The system for getting a firm's product to the customer will be the "revenue and cash receipts cycle."

Steps in Cycle Analysis

Activities within a transaction cycle are designed to achieve certain *control objectives* as well as carry out operational functions. Transaction cycle control objectives are derived from the broad objectives of internal control to fit specific situations. For example, the first control objective expressed for the purchases and cash disbursements cycle is: "purchase requisitions are initiated by authorized personnel. All requests are reviewed and approved by management." The motive underlying internal accounting control objectives is to avoid or reduce the risk of asset losses, unintended employee actions, and errors.

Because controls are seldom perfect, the firm exposes itself to the risk of errors and irregularities. The seriousness of the risk varies from time to time and from situation to situation. Control objectives are expressed intentions to guard against the most significant kinds of risks. They are the *converse* of the types of errors and irregularities (i.e., risks) that could occur. The risks confronting an auditor are twofold. There is the risk of material errors or irregularities that may have occurred as transactions were processed. That is the realm of risk analysis. There is also the risk that misstatements contained in the financial statements will not be detected. That is the realm of risk-taking.

Certain techniques and procedures—we will refer to them as strategies—are employed to achieve the various control objectives. Strategies are drawn from the following arsenal of weapons:

1. *Supervision and review.* Only designated, approved actions are to be taken. These are authorized, supervised, and reviewed by an appropriate level of management. Management oversight is exercised over transactions and the control system itself.

2. *Restricted access* to assets, records, and information processing units. Enforce a "need to know, need to access" policy.

3. *Segregation of duties.* Separate incompatible activities; for example, asset custody and accounting. Divide transaction processing so that several persons are involved, each one handling only a phase of the total job. As division of duties becomes less and less feasible (e.g., in small departments), increase the degree of management oversight.

4. *Records and documentation.* As transactions are cycled through their appropriate networks, a record should be created. Upon conclusion of processing, the record is filed as documentary evidence supporting what took place. Serially numbered standardized forms collect vital information: date and time, persons processing and authorizing the transaction, nature of the task, and quantities handled.

5. *Formalized network designs and procedures.* How the firm is to be organized is spelled out in words and diagrams (organization chart). Jobs are described, responsibilities assigned, and authority delegated. Systems and procedures for processing transactions are specified, and information flows are planned. The documents and records to be used are indicated. Checks and balances are incorporated into the system such as:
   - Double checking (reperformance).
   - Validation (verifying correctness) by comparison with an independent source such as a vendor's invoice.
   - Supervisory approvals at key junctures in transaction processing.
   - Periodic comparisons between accounting records and physical counterparts (e.g., inventory cycle counts; fixed asset inventories; payroll verifications).
   - Checks on completeness: for numerical sequence of documents and forms; checks of control account totals against subsidiary account details; keeping "to-do" lists, due date lists, and holding files.

6. *Internal audit.* Existence of an internal auditing department is a powerful control strategy—particularly when it has direct access to the board of directors or its audit committee.

7. *Budgets and operating reports* that emphasize performance and responsibility reporting.

The control strategies just discussed are broad generalizations. The specific strategies devised by an individual firm will be more exactly designed to fit their particular conditions and circumstances.

Some of these strategies are intended to prevent, and others to detect errors and irregularities, but they are only effective to a degree. They can only give *reasonable assurance* of control over undesirable outcomes. Absolute assurance is probably not possible and is usually not attempted. Why? Because internal accounting controls are subject to these limitations:

- They are susceptible to management override.
- They are vulnerable to employee circumvention through collusion.

CONCEPT SUMMARY

Transactions Cycles and Internal Accounting Controls

Studying Internal Control by Transactions Cycles	*Purposes of Internal Control*	*Internal Control Strategies*	*Internal Control Limitations*

A. Revenue and Cash Receipts (Chapter 6)
B. Purchases and Cash Disbursements (Chapter 7)
C. Human Resources (Chapter 8)
D. Production (Chapter 9)
E. Capital Assets (Chapter 10) Part I
F. Financial Management (Chapter 10) Part II
	Prevent and Detect
	
	Errors and Irregularities
		1. Supervision and review
		2. Restricted access
		3. Segregation of duties
		4. Records and documentation
		5. Network designs and procedures (with checks and balances):
		  • reperformance
		  • validation by comparison
		  • supervisory approvals
		  • check accounting records vs. physical counterparts
		  • completeness checks
		6. Internal audit
		7. Budgets and operating reports
			• Management can override
			• Circumvention by employee collusion
			• Ordinary system break-downs
			• Adjustment lags to organizational change
			• Controls not perfect; cost-benefit balance

- System malfunctions can occur. Fatigue and misunderstood instructions can cause errors, for example.

- Instantaneous adjustment to the dynamics of organizational change is not possible.

- Controls may be incomplete or imperfect by design or omission because attempting absolute control is not cost-beneficial, i.e., the costs of control may exceed the benefits.

The steps in cycle analysis, in summary, follow this line: identify control objectives; analyze the risks inherent in the system of controls, and; evaluate the strategies that have been installed to counteract these risks. Be especially cautious about critical audit areas. By definition, they are the riskiest areas. They are significant because of the materiality of impact upon the financial statements or because of their sensitive nature.

Tools for Reviewing Internal Accounting Controls

Studying internal accounting control is accomplished by: (1) reviewing the strategies for achieving control that are incorporated into a transaction cycle and, (2) making *compliance tests* to see if controls are operating as planned. The two major tools used in a review of internal accounting controls are flowcharts and internal control questionnaires.

A flowchart is a sequential diagram. It visually portrays the network of activities that process transactions and related documents through a cycle. Each of the four cycle chapters that follow this one has a flowchart. In gathering information for the flowchart, auditors make oral inquiries, visual observations, and read job descriptions and systems and procedures manuals. To check their understanding of how the system operates, auditors may "walk through" one or more transactions. Tracing a transaction through the system is considered part of the compliance testing we will discuss shortly.

Internal control questionnaires have major divisions—one for general matters and one for each of the cycles. The questions are designed to inquire about control strategies that are customarily employed by businesses. Different questionnaires are used for firms that are in industries with unique characteristics such as banking, insurance, or railroading. Questions are structured so that a "yes" answer indicates the presence of a control strategy, or one that is satisfactory, while a "no" response reflects an unsatisfactory or missing control. A comments column is also included so that remarks can be made (particularly with "no" responses) and working paper references noted. Exhibit 5–3 is an example of the general matters section of a questionnaire. The other sections on specific controls for each cycle will appear in subsequent chapters.

Flowcharts are prepared and internal control questionnaires filled out for an initial engagement and only updated for subsequent engagements. Completion of the review tools (or updating them from last year) normally takes place during the interim period before year-end. At year-end, they would again be updated from the current interim period if any changes had taken place.

By now the secondary audit objectives have been identified for each cycle—at least in the auditor's mind. In addition, a tentative judgement has been made.

Tentative Evaluation of Accounting Controls

A tentative opinion is formed from the information gathered from client meetings, analytical review, sessions with a predecessor auditor, and by filling out an internal control questionnaire and preparing flowcharts. That opinion concerns the quality of the client's system of internal accounting controls and the extent to which it can be relied upon. As the audit work progresses through the interim period and year-end, the tentative opinion is subjected to reappraisal as the system is tested and more is learned about the actual state of affairs. But for now, there is sufficient information to develop an audit strategy and design audit programs.

Before we move on to designing audit programs the idea of evaluating controls needs to be refined. Essentially, a review of accounting controls is to see whether a firm's strategies are sufficient to accomplish their control objectives. In reviewing the system, auditors consider the kinds of errors and irregularities that could occur and determine the controls that should prevent or detect them.

The numerous specific controls that are built into transaction cycles are divided into: (a) those that are important, and in addition, seem to be suitable to the task, and (b) those that are irrelevant or unsatisfactory and clearly unreliable.

INTERNAL CONTROL QUESTIONNAIRE
General Matters

Client _____   Period _____

	Question	Yes	No*
1.	Is there an organization chart?		
2.	Do principal duties of officers conform to provisions of the by-laws?		
3.	Is there a systems and procedures manual with job descriptions?		
4.	Are prenumbered forms and documents used as a matter of firm practice?		
5.	Are duties of Treasurer and chief accounting officers (e.g., Controller) segregated?		
6.	Are accounting duties appropriately segregated from other major functions and those who are custodians of assets?		
7.	Are accounting employees and records at all locations under supervision of the chief accounting official? Is records access limited?		
8.	Is there an accounting procedures manual with a chart of accounts and account definitions?		
9.	Are accounting records kept up to date and balanced/reconciled monthly?		
10.	Are accounting reports prepared, checked, and revised by persons independent of the subject of the report?		
11.	Are journal entries adequately explained and properly approved?		
12.	Are reports comparing actual and budgeted expenditures prepared?		
13.	Are standard costs used?		
14.	Is there an Internal Audit Staff?		
15.	Does it have access to the audit committee or board of directors?		
16.	Do they use comprehensive audit programs appropriate to their objectives?		
17.	Are reports issued by Internal Auditors noting exceptions and recommendations?		
18.	Are Internal Auditors' reports reviewed and corrective action taken?		
19.	Are employees in a position of trust covered by a fidelity bond? Is the amount of coverage adequate?		
20.	Is there a policy and procedures to avoid employee-officer conflicts of interest?		
21.	Must all employees take an annual vacation, and are their duties then performed by others?		
22.	Is a periodic review of insurance coverage made by a responsible employee?		
23.	Are the firm's internal control policies documented?		

---

* Note: A "comments column" is also normally provided for on the questionnaire so that the auditor can include explanations, or working paper references—particularly when "No" answers are recorded.

EXHIBIT 5–3

If accounting controls are satisfactory, they can be relied upon. Consequently, less evidence needs to be gathered in reaching an opinion on the financial statements than would otherwise be the case. Recall that the degree of testing required to substantiate a client's financial representations varies inversely with the quality of internal accounting control. But are the control strategies that have been prescribed by management actually in place and working properly? Compliance tests must be conducted to answer these questions.

Accounting controls that are either absent or too weak to trust will, of course, not be relied upon. A *material weakness* must be reported to the firm's management and the board of directors or its audit committee, as we pointed out earlier. A material weakness is a condition where the system of controls could fail to detect or prevent, on a timely basis, material errors or irregularities that would have an impact on the financial statements. If a material weakness in accounting controls were discovered, the audit examination would be expanded to see if material errors or irregularities had in fact occurred or whether some other compensating strategies had effectively offset the weak ones. We are now ready to look at audit testing and evidence gathering.

5.3 AUDIT TESTING

During the planning phase and review of the accounting control system, the following was accomplished:

1. Critical audit areas and major transaction cycles were identified.
2. Secondary audit objectives were settled on.
3. Decisions were made concerning the accounting control strategies that would be relied upon.

The next series of actions begins with developing instructions for testing and evidence gathering. These instructions are called *audit programs*. One set of programs is primarily for compliance testing, and the other is for gathering evidence to substantiate monetary representations in the financial statements.

Audit programs are custom tailored to the client because every audit is different. Critical audit areas, for example, are different from one engagement to the next. Inventory is a critical audit area for a car dealer, but for a service business, such as a CPA firm, it is not. There are so many important variables that characterize a client and a particular audit that it has to be approached as a unique undertaking each time. The audit program that guides the auditor reflects each job's uniqueness. A memo explaining the audit strategy chosen, how it will achieve the secondary audit objectives, and why it was selected is advisable. Next, the control strategies are actually tested for compliance.

Compliance Testing

Economic events and related forms and records are processed through transactions cycles. The forms and records create an "audit trail." A documentary path can be traced from the earliest point when a recordable economic event is recognized to the general ledger account where it ultimately comes to rest by examining the system and record files. Earlier, in discussing flowcharting, we explained that one or more transactions might be traced, or "walked," through the system. That tactic was described as part of the compliance tests because it took the auditor along the route that transactions follow and provided some assurance that the system was operating according to plan. Compliance test procedures are conducted to see whether the operating network and control strategies are functioning effectively and as prescribed by management. Only those control strategies that are considered satisfactory and are to be relied upon are tested to see if they are in compliance.

If a control strategy is not important to the integrity of the financial statements or is too weak to trust, it is not tested. Other controls may not be tested because the costs outweigh the benefits, or it may be that other audit procedures can readily substantiate a significant portion of an account balance.

Remember that the purpose of compliance testing is to see whether prescribed operating procedures and controls are functioning effectively, not to verify the correctness of dollar amounts—that is the objective of substantive tests. As it so happens, it is often possible to do both things at once with "dual-purpose" procedures.

Dual-purpose procedures simultaneously test control strategies for compliance and substantiate monetary details of a sample of transactions that were processed through the cycle. Only a sample is tested generally because account balances, such as sales, purchases, and employee compensation, contain too many transactions to attempt a complete examination. Examination of a sample of documents to see that monetary amounts are correct and that they are charged to the proper accounts is a substantive test. It is referred to as a "test of details of transactions." An illustration of a dual-purpose test may be helpful.

Let's consider the purchases and cash disbursements cycle. A sample of paid purchase transactions is selected from the voucher register. It is traced to the accounts payable department to see if there is a filed copy for each transaction, of the: purchase requisition, purchase order, vendor's invoice, receiving report, and a voucher. In the process of following the audit trail, controls would be checked and transaction details tested. Transaction details, such as unit price, quantity, total cost, and accounts charged, would be examined and compared between one document and the next. At the same time, compliance of control strategies would be verified by checking for proper authorization on the requisition and receiving reports, by seeing that all of the necessary documents were collected before the vendor invoice was approved for payment, and by performing other procedures. A more extensive description of compliance and substantive tests is contained in later chapters where audit programs are illustrated. The results of compliance tests must now be assessed.

Assessing Compliance Test Results

Compliance tests are usually conducted early in the audit of the interim period before year-end to allow for modifications to the audit program that might be required. At year-end, inquiries are made to determine whether operating procedures or control strategies have been changed in the intervening period. If they have, a "walk-through" and compliance tests may be in order.

When the results of testing the various transaction cycle control strategies for compliance are known, they must be assessed. Professional judgement in evaluating the information is now called upon. There is no precise prescription for reacting to the results. Generally speaking, however, if adjustments are necessary, they will be made in the nature, extent, or timing of the ensuing audit procedures. We will explore several possibilities.

Control strategies may be operating as intended by management and effectively controlling against errors and irregularities. If so, the remaining substantive tests may be carried out when, and to the extent originally planned. If controls are even stronger than initially perceived, the type of testing might be changed, the extent of testing reduced somewhat, or some procedures performed in the interim period rather than at year-end.

Suppose, on the other hand, that the controls in a transaction cycle are weaker than originally thought. Audit program modifications might include the following: change the type of procedures to be used, increase the extent of testing, or shift the timing of testing, moving from interim to year-end. An extreme case might be encountered. Such material weaknesses might be discovered that it would be impractical or impossible to determine whether material errors or irregularities had occurred. In that event, the auditor's opinion concerning the financial statements would be qualified or an opinion disclaimed. Consideration might be given to withdrawing from the engagement as well.

When the necessary audit program modifications are made, the focus turns to substantive testing.

Substantive Testing

The management of an entity makes certain assertions in its financial statements concerning:

1. *Existence or occurrence:* Assets and liabilities exist at balance sheet date, and transactions occurred during the period.

2. *Completeness:* The financial statements include all transactions and accounts; none have been left out.

3. *Rights and obligations:* Assets are rights of the entity, and liabilities are obligations of the entity, at balance sheet date.

4. *Valuation or allocation:* Asset, liability, revenue, and expense components are stated at appropriate dollar amounts.

5. *Presentation and disclosure:* Financial statement components are properly classified, described, and disclosed.

Audit objectives are the auditor's statements concerning these assertions that can be tested. Substantive tests, in turn, gather evidence to achieve the audit objectives and support (or contradict) the assertions.

Most of these assertions, if incorrect, have an impact on the monetary amounts in financial statements. Consequently, substantive tests are aimed primarily at verifying dollar amounts—or conversely, at finding monetary errors. The search for monetary errors is made by (a) testing transactions systems and (b) testing account balances.

Testing transactions systems is customarily done in the interim period before year-end. Substantive tests of transactions details are conducted to verify a class or family of transactions such as purchases, payroll, sales, and cash receipts. This is the most efficient way of simultaneously substantiating numerous accounts, most of which are presented on the income statement. Many of these accounts are the total of high-volume transactions that do not lend themselves to complete verification. Auditors must look for persuasive evidence rather than absolute proof. Therefore, tests are carried out to see if: (a) the system is operating effectively and under control, and (b) the monetary amounts of a sample of transactions are correctly recorded and classified.

Tests of transactions details are often coupled with compliance tests in the form of dual-purpose procedures. Because dual-purpose tests start out under the assumption that the controls being tested are satisfactory, the concurrent substantive tests of details are also set at a minimum level. If controls are found to be unsatisfactory, additional substantive tests of details may be performed. Another possibility is that the original audit program for substantive tests of balances will be modified.

Substantive tests of balances concentrate on a single account balance rather than a class of transactions. They are, once again, concerned with the validity of monetary amounts. Tests of balances are normally performed as of year-end and focus mainly, although not exclusively, on balance sheet accounts. The following are some substantive tests of balances:

- Examining marketable securities and comparing aggregate cost to aggregate market value.

- Testing the physical inventory count.
- Counting coins and currency in vaults and petty cash drawers.

Another class of substantive testing is *analytical review*. Analytical review is a search for the abnormal or unexpected in financial statements. An auditor's expertise in general, plus orientation to a client and its industry in particular, are the bases for making the search. The financial statements are carefully read and compared with those of previous years and against budgets for the present and coming years. Absolute amounts of important items and trends in these items over time are examined. The relationship (e.g., ratios) between such items as sales to accounts receivable or inventory to cost-of-sales is scrutinized. If unusual amounts, fluctuations, or relationships are spotted, they are investigated and an explanation obtained.

These test procedures gather evidence that gradually builds up a sense of assurance. The weight of evidence eventually persuades the auditor that the principal audit objective has been fulfilled. We have already observed that risk-taking characterizes auditing. It should now be apparent that the type, amount, and quality of evidence is the keystone to risk-taking.

CONCEPT SUMMARY
Audit Testing

Types of Tests	Purpose	Example
1. Compliance Tests	To verify that accounting controls are working as intended.	• Select a sample of employees and: (a) Check personnel files for authorization to hire. (b) Check timecards (selected weeks only) for supervisor's initials approving jobs and hours.
2. Substantive Tests of Details	Verify financial statement assertions. Search for monetary errors in transactions systems.	• Recalculate gross salary and wages for a sample of employees. ($ rate × hours)
3. Dual Purpose Tests	Simultaneously verify controls and monetary amounts in systems.	• Select a sample of employees and: (a) check personnel files for authorized hiring and pay rates. (b) check timecards for approval and jobs and number of hours worked. (c) trace pay rate and hours worked to payroll register. Recalculate gross wages.
4. Substantive Test of Balances	Verify financial statement assertions. Search for monetary errors in account balances.	• Count marketable securities. • Examine broker's advice showing cost of securities. • Compare cost and market price.
5. Analytical Review	Identify exceptions. Search for unusual, unexpected, abnormal amounts or relationships.	• Compare this year's sales by geographic region to last year's. If the difference is unusual, investigate.

5.4 EVIDENCE

Evidence is the data or information that is assembled on which a judgement or conclusion is based. It encompasses any and all sorts of evidential matter, including material objects, documents, and verbal statements, by which proof or likelihood is established. There are two classes of evidence: (1) the underlying accounting data (e.g., ledgers, journals, working papers, cost allocations, reconciliations, etc.); and (2) corroborating information (i.e., supporting, confirming, reinforcing, strengthening the truth or accuracy of).

Are the client's financial statements fair representations? Reaching a conclusion on that question is a process of becoming progressively more assured of the condition of the financial statements. The statements are derived from underlying accounting data within the accounting system. Therefore, the underlying accounting data itself is a form of evidence. Alone, it is insufficient to support an opinion as to fairness. If an auditor is to be persuaded, evidence that corroborates the accounting data is necessary. For example, a Land account can be corroborated by inspecting the site and examining the deed and purchase contract. These audit procedures confirm that the land exists, who owns it, and the basis of valuation (cost).

The *sufficiency* of evidence is a matter of having enough. But whether there is enough is a question of the quantity of evidence and its quality or power to persuade. The third standard of field work requires that:

> Sufficient competent evidential matter is to be obtained through inspection, observation, inquiries, and confirmations to afford a reasonable basis for an opinion regarding the financial statements under examination.

Because it is seldom possible to be absolutely certain, an auditor must be persuaded. Substantial doubts must be eliminated by the weight of evidence. Evidence that is sufficient in authority and forcefulness is what persuades the auditor to take a risk in expressing an opinion. In summary, sufficiency is determined by the weight of evidence, which in turn, is related to the quantity and kind of evidence.

Competence is a word that epitomizes the quality, forcefulness, power to persuade, and authority of evidence. Competent evidence is relevant to whatever it is that is being substantiated. It is also valid and, therefore, reliable. These qualities are derived from the type of evidence and the technique employed in gathering it. Evidence obtained by direct personal knowledge or from an independent source outside the client firm has the greatest credibility.

The types of evidence relied upon by auditors follow. They are arrayed according to their power to persuade, starting with greatest and descending to lesser orders of forcefulness.

1. Physical presence of material objects (e.g., land, petty cash, inventory).
2. Documents:
    A. Created outside the client firm, and:
        (a) Received directly by the auditor (e.g., creditor confirmations, attorney's letters)
        (b) Received by client and given to the auditor (e.g., invoices, bank statements)
    B. Created inside the client firm, and:
        (a) Has circulated outside the firm, and is:
            *   received directly by the auditor (e.g., cancelled check with bank cut-off statement)
            *   received by client and given to the auditor (e.g., bank deposit slip)
        (b) Has remained within the firm (e.g., board of directors minutes, material requisition forms, inspection reports)
3. Underlying accounting data with:
    A. Excellent internal accounting control.
    B. Less than excellent accounting control.
4. Circumstantial evidence. Supplementary information that indirectly bears on the audit but usually not to the extent of substantiating a particular account, or transaction. This kind of information is accessory to the varieties above. (e.g., written or oral representations of the client such as in explanations and client representation letters; internal control; trade statistics, employee integrity; relationships between financial statement items.)

Greater assurance comes with using evidence of a higher order. It also tends to be more costly. Cost-benefit balance is an important consideration to keep in mind.

There are a variety of techniques employed in evidence gathering. Some furnish direct personal knowledge and others only indirect knowledge. Knowledge obtained indirectly, but from independent sources, is a potent form of evidence. When it comes from the client itself, it is only circumstantial. Reflect on the authority or competence of evidence that is gathered by each of the following techniques.

Observe, examine, inspect: Visual witnessing of actions, physical presence, or document content.

A. Observe actions to check on system compliance.
B. Count, observe, and examine material objects such as inventory, fixed assets, securities and cash-on-hand.

C. Inspect corroborative documents to substantiate accounting data. This is called *vouching*. It is used particularly with documents originated by an independent source. For example, inspect a vendor's invoice to verify that inventory or fixed assets were purchased by the client and properly recorded.

Obtain confirmations and written representations: Inquiries made of independent parties outside the client firm to verify significant account balances or transactions are referred to as *confirmations*. The inquiry and reply are in writing so that tangible evidence is created. Inquiries are customarily sent to customers, banks, attorneys, insurance companies, creditors, and trustees. If a reply is expected only in the event of a discrepancy or disagreement, it is a "negative" confirmation (e.g., cases where there are many accounts receivable with small balances). If a reply is required, it is a "positive" confirmation. An auditor must have complete control over the preparation, mailing, and receipt of confirmations.

Written representations must be obtained from a client's management (AU 333). They can include a variety of things, but they normally confirm management's oral representations made earlier, which were then subjected to corroboration where possible. Certain matters may not be susceptible to corroboration, such as plans to discontinue a segment of the business, or intentions to refinance short-term debt on a long-term basis. In these instances, a written representation is a vital piece of information.

Oral inquiry: This is verbal questioning that ordinarily serves as a starting point for further investigation. It does not produce a very forceful, competent form of evidence. Internal control questionnaires, for example, are filled in by auditors from client responses to oral inquiries.

Reperformance: Client calculations and summations are repeated, and transfers of amounts between accounting records (e.g., posting) is traced.

A. Recalculation of amounts such as depreciation, prepaid expenses, accrued liabilities, and income tax expense verify their correctness.

B. Column totals in journals and ledgers are checked by re-adding or "footing." Journals also have row totals because there are always several columns side by side. Adding them across is called "cross-footing."

C. A great deal of accounting information is transferred from one record to another, so tracing is necessary. Tracing starts from a recorded figure, or a form evidencing a transaction, and follows it through the accounting records to verify that it was recorded on time and in the proper accounts, allocation work papers, and cost records.

Analysis of accounts: This is a detailed, written explanation of the composition of an account, along with dollar amounts related to each item, e.g., the various insurance policies and premiums included in prepaid insurance. Individual items of material amount are usually vouched.

Reconciliation: Reconciliations are a special type of analysis. Two representations of an account balance from separate sources are compared and, if different are analyzed to discover why. Differences may be the result of time lags, as in the case of bank statements with checks outstanding, or deposits in transit. Other differences may be unrecorded items or errors that require adjustment to the accounts. Other examples of reconciliations are subsidiary ledgers to control accounts and reciprocal accounts, such as Home Office and Branch.

Review: Review describes a range of activities from being attuned to sense whether things are in order to the systematic methodology of analytical review. Auditors are constantly involved in observing what is taking place in a client firm. Professional inquisitiveness compels an auditor to register, at least mentally, anything that reflects on the firm and its financial statements. The same inquisitiveness is at work when books of account, financial statements, and other records are read, scanned, and compared to other data. These documents are given cursory examination to get impressions. For example, a quick flipping of the pages in a cash disbursement journal to see if check numbers appear to be in sequence is advisable. Is something out of order or unexpected? If not, evidence addressing the overall state of affairs is obtained.

Let's pause now and give some thought to the evidence and other materials that have been collected since the engagement began.

5.5 WORKING PAPERS AND CONCLUDING STEPS

Working Papers

The materials accumulated during planning, internal control study and evaluation, and audit testing and evidence gathering are assembled. These become the auditor's working papers. They include:

- Orientation materials: general and industry.
- An engagement letter.
- Client materials: conference memos, charter and by-laws, chart of accounts, pension plan contracts, etc.
- A time budget and summary of actual hours.
- Analytical review notes, interim financial statements, and budgets of the client.
- Internal control questionnaire and flowcharts.
- Audit programs: compliance and substantive.
- Rationale memo explaining the audit strategy used.
- A trial balance and adjusting-reclassifying entries.
- Evidence: analyses, reconciliations, confirmations, and representation letters, abstracts of minutes, photocopies of important client documents, and memos.

CONCEPT SUMMARY
Evidence

Classes	Characteristics	Kinds of Evidence (arrayed by competence)	Techniques for Gathering

1. Underlying Accounting Data:
  A. journals
  B. ledgers
  C. working papers
  D. reconciliations
  E. cost allocations
2. Corroborating Information:
  A. material objects
  B. documents
  C. verbal statements
	1. Sufficient.
	  The weight of evidence as derived from:
	  A. quantity
	  B. kind
	2. Competent. Established by:
	  A. quality
	  B. forcefulness
	  C. authority
	  D. power to persuade
	  Requirements for:
	  A. relevant
	  B. valid
	  C. reliable
		1. Physical presence
		2. Documents:
		  A. Third party origin:
		    (a) to auditor
		    (b) to client, to auditor
		  B. Client origin:
		    (a) circulated outside
		      • to auditor
		      • to client, to auditor
		    (b) remained in house
		3. Underlying accounting data, and:
		  A. excellent controls
		  B. sub-excellent controls
		4. Circumstantial:
		  A. client statements
		  B. internal controls
		  C. trade statistics
		  D. employee integrity
			1. Inspect, examine, observe.
			2. Request confirmations, written representations.
			3. Inquire verbally.
			4. Reperform:
			  A. recalculate
			  B. foot, cross-foot
			  C. trace
			5. Analyze accounts
			6. Reconcile
			7. Review

- A copy of the final financial statements.
- Review notes made by management level audit personnel when the working papers are reviewed (discussed below).

Materials that have importance for next year's engagement are often segregated and placed in a permanent file. The remaining materials, which have relevance to this year's job, are placed in a current file.

The style and format of working papers vary from firm to firm. Their content ought to include the client name and balance sheet date, the auditor's initials and date that the work was performed, a descriptive title for the document, an index number, notations of the audit procedures performed, and cross-indexing to other papers. There are many examples in the next five chapters. Guidelines for the content of working papers are contained in AU Section 338, "Working Papers."

Working papers legally belong to the auditor, not the client. Even so, their contents must be kept confidential, unless the client approves otherwise, because of provisions in the accounting profession's Code of Ethics. In the final analysis, working papers must support the opinion expressed in the auditor's report. They are proof that the principal audit objective has been achieved in accordance with generally accepted auditing standards.

Concluding Steps

As the audit winds down and field work is approaching completion, certain concluding steps are taken. Representation letters are requested from management and the secretary of the board of directors. An illustrative management representation letter for audit engagements,[2] and limited assurance "reviews"[3] appear in the authoritative literature.

The letter requested of the board's secretary certifies the authenticity of the minutes that were examined. Committees of the board (Finance, Executive) may also have minutes that are read as part of the audit. A letter certifying them may also be appropriate.

A letter is sent to the client's lawyer inquiring about "litigation, claims, and assessments."[4] The inquiry is to see if there are any unrecorded liabilities, or contingent gains or losses that might stem from a lawsuit. Infractions of the law might require disclosure.

Letters of inquiry are sent to "related parties" if material transactions with them have taken place. The existence, nature, and volume of related party transactions may require disclosure if the financial statements are to be fairly presented. Related parties are subsidiary or investee companies, major owners or management (and their immediate family), and entities under a common control. The relationship of the parties and the substance of their transaction(s) must be understood. This involves confirming the nature of the relationship, the transaction amount and terms, the manner of settlement, and the amounts due to and from the client firm.

Subsequent Events

Throughout this chapter we have referred to the "interim period," and "year-end." Actually, year-end is a convenient way of characterizing auditing activities that take place at year-end and during the subsequent period until the field work is done. Take, for example, financial statements for the calendar year 1983. It

---

[2]AU 333A. See also Exhibit 4 in Chapter 11 of this text.

[3]"Compilation and Review of Financial Statements," *Statement on Standards for Accounting and Review Services 1*, (AICPA, 1979), Appendix D. A "review" of financial statements involves performing inquiry and analytical procedures that provide a basis for expressing limited assurance that no material modifications to the statements are necessary. A review does not provide a basis for expressing an opinion on the fairness of the financial statements. It does not contemplate a study and evaluation of internal accounting control, tests of accounting records, or the gathering of evidence by inspection, observation, or confirmation, and certain other procedures ordinarily performed during an audit. In a "compilation", absolutely no expressions of assurance, or opinion are made; financial statements are simply prepared, or compiled for a client. Compilations and reviews are applicable to "nonpublic" firms only.

[4]AU 337. See also Exhibit 3 in Chapter 11.

would be best to conduct tests for proper cut-off in the early weeks of 1984. There is an added benefit from carrying over the audit into the subsequent period. Evidence may develop after year-end that casts a light on the condition of the financial statements. A note whose collectibility was in doubt may be collected or inventory sold that appeared obsolete.

Over and above the normal audit procedures that must necessarily take place in the subsequent period, there are special procedures applied in search of "subsequent events." There are two types of subsequent events that can have an impact on the financial statements. One is the discovery of new facts that shed light on a condition that existed at year-end, which we discussed above. The second type is an event that occurred after year-end, during the subsequent period. For example, a major casualty loss or the purchase of a business may have occurred.

If the financial statements have not been issued, they ought to be adjusted to reflect the first type of event. For the second type of event—assuming it is significant—disclosure in the notes would be necessary.

Certain audit procedures are performed in search of subsequent events, normally towards the end of field work. These include reading the latest interim financial statements, making inquiries of financial officers, and reading minutes of the subsequent period.

Responsibility to make inquiries or carry out audit procedures stops at the conclusion of field work.* However, if news of a subsequent event becomes known after the field work, but before financial statements are released, the adjustment or disclosure is still required. If news becomes known after financial statements are released, special steps must be taken.

In time, responses to the various letters are received, and field work is finished (including the search for subsequent events). The working papers and financial statements can then be reviewed by the engagement partner.

Review

Before the engagement partner starts reviewing, the in-charge accountant makes sure that the staff time summary for the job is up to date. It is the basis for billing the client, preparing next year's time budget, and evaluating the performance of the professional staff. Personnel evaluation forms are usually filled in at this time for everyone who worked on the engagement. A tentative auditor's report is drafted, along with a "management letter" suggesting improvements to control or operating systems that might be made. Tax returns are prepared, or those prepared by the client are reviewed.

The engagement partner reviews the working papers to see whether:

---

*Except for SEC registrations under the Securities Act of 1933 where it extends to the effective date of the registration.

1. Critical audit areas were properly investigated,
2. Secondary audit objectives were achieved,
3. Appropriate conclusions are stated, and the evidence supports them,
4. Details were properly attended to (indexing, initials, procedures stated, etc.) and the working papers are complete.

The working papers should justify the opinion expressed in the auditor's report and demonstrate that the auditor's primary objective was achieved.

The financial statements are reviewed for content, format, and completeness of disclosures. They may be part of a larger document such as an annual report. Financial information in the entire package must be checked for material inconsistencies or misstatements of fact.

If all is in order, the auditor's report and management letter are signed by the partner, discussed with the client, and released. The audit has been completed.

Key Terms

analytical review	management letter
assertions	predecessor auditor
audit objectives	reperformance
audit (test) procedures	representation letters
compliance tests	restricted access
control objectives and strategies	review
corroborating evidence	risk analysis
critical audit area	segregation of duties
cut-off	subsequent events
engagement letter	substantive tests
foot and cross-foot	sufficient, competent evidence
inquiry letters	transactions cycles
interim period	vouching
internal control questionnaire	working papers
irregularities	

Questions and Problems

Questions

5-1 What is required if an auditor discovers that an important control is not working properly and that, although nothing serious has yet occurred, substantial errors could be made that would affect accounting information to be recorded?

5-2 Why is it impossible to assure that a firm will not experience errors or irregularities?

5-3 Certain strategies are customarily employed to achieve internal control objectives. List and briefly describe them.

5-4 Briefly explain the difference between compliance and substantive testing. What is a "dual-purpose" test?

5-5 What is analytical review? When is it performed?

5-6 Describe the kinds of evidence relied upon by auditors. How is evidence related to auditor risk-taking?

5-7 The third standard of field work refers to sufficient competent evidential matter. Explain what evidence is and what the criteria *sufficient* and *competent* mean.

5-8 Indicate the variety of techniques employed in evidence gathering.

5-9 As an audit draws to a close, certain inquiry letters are sent and representation letters received by auditors. Describe them briefly.

5-10 What does a search for "subsequent events" refer to?

Multiple Choice Questions from Professional Examinations

5-11 Although the quantity, type, and content of working papers will vary with the circumstances, the working papers generally would include the

　　a. Copies of those client records examined by the auditor during the course of the engagement.

　　b. Evaluation of the efficiency and competence of the audit staff assistants by the partner responsible for the audit.

　　c. Auditor's comments concerning the efficiency and competence of client management personnel.

　　d. Auditing procedures followed and the testing performed in obtaining evidential matter.

5-12 Audit programs are modified to suit the circumstances of particular engagements. A complete audit program for an engagement generally should be developed

　　a. Prior to beginning the actual audit work.

　　b. After the auditor has completed an evaluation of the existing internal accounting control.

　　c. After reviewing the client's accounting records and procedures.

　　d. When the audit engagement letter is prepared.

5-13 At interim dates an auditor evaluates a client's internal accounting control procedures and finds them to be effective. The auditor then performs a substantial part of the audit engagement on a continuous basis throughout the year. At the minimum, the auditor's year-end procedures must include

a. Determination that the client's internal accounting control procedures are still effective at year-end.

b. Confirmation of those year-end accounts that were examined at interim dates.

c. Tests of compliance with internal control in the same manner as those tests made at the interim dates.

d. Comparison of the responses to the auditor's internal control questionnaire with a detailed flowchart at year-end.

5-14 One reason why the independent auditor makes an analytic review of the client's operations is to identify

a. Weaknesses of a material nature in the system of internal control.

b. Non-compliance with prescribed control procedures.

c. Improper separation of accounting and other financial duties.

d. Unusual transactions.

5-15 Audit evidence can come in different forms with different degrees of persuasiveness. Which of the following is the *least* persuasive type of evidence?

a. Documents mailed by outsiders to the auditor.

b. Correspondence between auditor and vendors.

c. Sales invoices inspected by the auditor.

d. Computations made by the auditor.

5-16 The confirmation of the client's trade accounts receivable is a means of obtaining evidential matter and is specifically considered to be a generally accepted auditing

a. Principle.

b. Standard.

c. Procedure.

d. Practice.

5-17 Which of the following *best* describes the primary purpose of audit-program procedures?

a. To detect errors or irregularities.

b. To comply with generally accepted accounting principles.

c. To gather corroborative evidence.

d. To verify the accuracy of account balances.

5-18 Engagement letters are widely used in practice for professional engagements of all types. The primary purpose of the engagement letter is to

   a. Remind management that the primary responsibility for the financial statements rests with management.

   b. Satisfy the requirements of the CPA's liability insurance policy.

   c. Provide a starting point for the auditor's preparation of the preliminary audit program.

   d. Provide a written record of the agreement with the client as to the services to be provided.

5-19 With respect to errors and irregularities, which of the following should be part of an auditor's planning of the audit engagement?

   a. Plan to search for errors or irregularities that would have a material or immaterial effect on the financial statements.

   b. Plan to discover errors or irregularities that are either material or immaterial.

   c. Plan to discover errors or irregularities that are material.

   d. Plan to search for errors or irregularities that would have a material effect on the financial statements.

5-20 An independent auditor has concluded that the client's records, procedures, and representations can be relied upon based on tests made during the year when internal control was found to be effective. The auditor should test the records, procedures, and representations again at year-end if

   a. Inquiries and observations lead the auditor to believe that conditions have changed significantly.

   b. Comparisons of year-end balances with like balances at prior dates revealed significant fluctuations.

   c. Unusual transactions occurred subsequent to the completion of the interim audit work.

   d. Client records are in a condition that facilitate effective and efficient testing.

5-21 Which of the following statements relating to compliance tests is most accurate?

   a. Auditing procedures cannot concurrently provide both evidence of compliance with accounting control procedures and evidence required for substantive tests.

   b. Compliance tests include physical observations of the proper segregation of duties that ordinarily may be limited to the normal audit period.

   c. Compliance tests should be based upon proper application of an appropriate statistical sampling plan.

    d. Compliance tests ordinarily should be performed as of the balance sheet date or during the period subsequent to that date.

5-22 The auditor's *best* course of action with respect to "other financial information" included in an annual report containing the auditor's report is to

    a. Indicate in the auditor's report, that the "other financial information" is unaudited.

    b. Consider whether the "other financial information" is accurate by performing a limited review.

    c. Obtain written representations from management as to the material accuracy of the "other financial information."

    d. Read and consider the manner of presentation of the "other financial information."

5-23 An audit program provides proof that

    a. Sufficient competent evidential matter was obtained.

    b. The work was adequately planned.

    c. There was compliance with generally accepted standards of reporting.

    d. There was a proper study and evaluation of internal control.

5-24 Analytical review procedures are

    a. Statistical tests of financial information designed to identify areas requiring intensive investigation.

    b. Analytical tests of financial information made by a computer.

    c. Substantive tests of financial information made by a study and comparison of relationships among data.

    d. Diagnostic tests of financial information which may *not* be classified as evidential matter.

5-25 Significant unexpected fluctuations identified by analytical review procedures will usually necessitate a (an)

    a. Consistency qualification.

    b. Review of internal control.

    c. Explanation in the representation letter.

    d. Auditor investigation.

Problems

5-26 Eric Jong, CPA, is auditing the financial statements of his client, the Fearless Flying School. Various audit procedures have been performed and evidence collected having different degrees of competence or authority. Rank each of the following from 1 to 6, using 1 for highest competence and 6 for lowest competence. Each case should be given a different ranking.

a. _____ Cancelled deposits and checks were received by Jong in a cut-off bank statement.

b. _____ A recently purchased airplane was examined.

c. _____ The vendor's invoice for the new airplane was vouched.

d. _____ A sample was drawn for conducting substantive tests of transactions details for the revenue and cash receipts cycle. The school's file copy of new student enrollment applications was vouched.

e. _____ The school has a substantial bank loan outstanding. Jong received a letter from the bank confirming the loan balance and terms.

f. _____ Jong raised a question about a substantial account receivable due from a former student. The account has shown no activity for six months. The school's president told Jong that he is certain the balance will be collected.

5-27 In late spring you are given a new assignment by the CPA firm for which you work. You will be the in-charge accountant on the annual audit of WAHOO Corp. for the year ending next December 31. This is a recurring engagement that has been performed for several years. The engagement letter for the upcoming audit is given to you, along with a list of personnel assigned to the job. It is your responsibility to plan and supervise the field work.

Required:

Discuss the necessary preparation and planning for the annual audit prior to beginning field work at the client's office. In your discussion, include the sources you should consult, the type of information you should seek, the preliminary plans and preparation you should make for the field work, and any actions you should take relative to the staff assigned to the engagement. Do not write an audit program.

AICPA (Adapted)

5-28 *Part a.* The first generally accepted auditing standard of field work requires, in part, that "the work is to be adequately planned." An effective tool that aids the auditor in adequately planning the work is an audit program.

Required:

What is an audit program, and what purposes does it serve?

Part b. Auditors frequently refer to the terms "standards" and "procedures." Standards deals with measures of the quality of the auditor's performance. Standards specifically refer to the ten generally accepted auditing standards. Procedures relate to those acts that are performed by the auditor while trying to gather evidence. Procedures specifically refer to the methods or techniques used by the auditor in the conduct of the examination.

Required:

List at least eight different types of procedures that an auditor would use during an examination of financial statements. For example, a type of procedure that an auditor would frequently use is the observation of activities and conditions. Do not discuss specific accounts.

AICPA

5-29 As an auditing supervisor, you assigned a staff auditor the responsibility for auditing a long-term construction project. The following events take place during the audit:

a. Prior to beginning the field work, the auditor submits an audit program and a proposed budget to you. The program does not include any tests of expenditure authorizations, work orders, or contract awards. Such tests are normally included in your audits of construction projects. However, audit files show that recent audits in these areas disclosed no significant problems or weaknesses. The proposed budget provides for what you consider to be excessive man-days compared to previous audits of a similar nature.

b. During the field work, the auditor submits weekly time and status reports to you. In one of the status reports, the auditor states that interim contract payments substantially in excess of the percentage of completion of construction work are being authorized and paid. Audit working papers and reference material are maintained in the auditor's file.

c. Following completion of field work, the auditor prepares a draft report for discussion with the auditee. After discussion with the auditee, the auditor completes and distributes the final audit report.

Required:

List three actions you would take as an auditing supervisor to administer each of the following audit phases:
1. Prior to the field work.
2. During the field work.
3. Following the completion of the field work.

IIA (Adapted)

5-30 Page Pooper, CPA, is examining the financial statements of the Diannah Corporation as of and for the period ended September 30, 1982. Pooper plans to complete the field work and sign the auditor's report on November 15, 1982. Pooper's audit work is primarily designed to obtain evidence that will provide a reasonable degree of assurance that the Diannah Corporation's September 30, 1982, financial statements present fairly the financial position, results of operations, and changes in financial position of that enterprise in accordance with generally accepted accounting principles

consistently applied. Pooper is concerned, however, about events and transactions of Diannah Corporation that occur after September 30, 1982, since
he does not have the same degree of assurance for such events as for those
that occurred in the period ending September 30, 1982.

Required:

a. Define what is commonly referred to in auditing as a "subsequent event,"
   and describe the two general types of subsequent events that require
   consideration by the management of Diannah Corporation and evaluation by Pooper.
b. Identify those auditing procedures that Pooper should follow to obtain
   the necessary assurances concerning subsequent events.

AICPA (Adapted)

5-31 Analytical review procedures are substantive tests that are extremely useful
in the initial audit planning stage.

Required:

a. Explain why analytical review procedures are considered substantive
   tests.
b. Explain how analytical review procedures may be useful in the initial
   audit planning stage.
c. Identify the analytical review procedures that a CPA might be expected
   to utilize during an examination performed in accordance with generally
   accepted auditing standards.

AICPA

5-32 The auditor should obtain a level of knowledge of the entity's business,
including events, transactions, and practices, that will enable the planning
and performance of an examination in accordance with generally accepted
auditing standards. Adhering to these standards enables the auditor's report
to lend credibility to financial statements by providing the public with certain
assurances.

Required:

a. How does knowledge of the entity's business help the auditor in the
   planning and performance of an examination in accordance with generally accepted auditing standards?
b. What assurances are provided to the public when the auditor states that
   the financial statements "present fairly . . . in conformity with generally
   accepted accounting principles applied on a consistent basis"?

AICPA

5-33 During the course of an audit, many test procedures are performed. A random list of some of these procedures follows. Identify them in two ways (using the codes given below): (1) Indicate the type of test, and (2) state which management assertion(s) the tests are attempting to verify:

C — compliance test
STD — substantive test of transactions details
DP — dual purpose test
SB — substantive test of balances
AR — analytical review

(a) Existence or occurrence
(b) Completeness
(c) Rights and obligations
(d) Valuation or allocation
(e) Presentation and disclosure

Test Procedure	Type of Test	Assertion Tested
1. Checked purchase requisitions for approval.		
2. Verified cash discounts taken for accuracy.		
3. Traced daily cash receipts totals to bank statements and to controller's department file copy of receipts list and duplicate deposit slip.		
4. Compared gross profit percentage for retail sales with industry average.		
5. Examined receiving reports for initials of quality control inspector.		
6. Confirmed outstanding bank note payable with creditor.		
7. Examined sales order for credit manager's approval.		
8. Compared prices on sales invoices with standard price list.		
9. Compared individual items on inventory count sheets with perpetual inventory records.		
10. Footed sales invoices and examined for initials of client's clerk responsible for checking arithmetic on invoices.		

5-34 Seven control techniques or strategies, such as "supervision and review," were discussed in this chapter. Which technique is at work in the following? For each situation, devise a compliance test.

1. Checks written by the firm require two signatures by authorized managers.

2. An accounting supervisor reconciles the bank account each month. He has no other responsibilities for cash.

3. All overtime work must be approved by the employee's immediate supervisor and his timecard initialed.

4. Mail is opened by the receptionist who has no other cash duties and no access to accounting records. Any cash received in the mail is listed and the cash given to the head cashier. The receipts list goes to the controller's office.

5. Sales invoices are checked for arithmetic accuracy by a clerk and initialed.

6. Internal auditors account for all sales invoices and checks each quarter.

7. The credit manager approves all sales made on credit.

5-35 The cash receipts system of the Jetta-Masters Force Field Co. are as follows. The mail department sends all cash receipts to an accounts receivable clerk, without a listing. The clerk keeps the cash receipts journal, prepares a bank deposit slip in duplicate, posts from it to the subsidiary accounts receivable ledger, and mails the deposit to the bank.

The firm's controller receives directly the validated deposit slip and a monthly bank statement, both unopened, and reconciles the statement.

Monthly, the accounts receivable clerk notifies the general ledger clerk of the totals entered in the cash receipts journal for that period so that they can be posted. The general ledger is posted with these amounts, as well as data from other sources that affect the cash account balance (e.g., funds borrowed from the bank).

Required:

a. List the controls included in the system.

b. List the weaknesses you see in the system.

c. For each control, devise a compliance test to check it.

Revenue and cash receipts cycle

The role of most organizations is to deliver some product and/or service to the marketplace. There an exchange transaction takes place, and cash or a promise to pay cash is received. When cash is received, the revenue cycle of the firm is complete. Not-for-profit entities do not engage in market exchange transactions in delivering their services. They do, however, experience similar asset flows and transaction cycles.

In addition to the mainstay revenue transactions of sales and/or services, other incidental earnings activities may occur. Incidental receipts from royalty agreements, rentals, and interest, for example, also pass through a revenue and cash receipts cycle.

Transactions are cycled through various departments where processing activities take place. The sequence of processing from beginning to end is the revenue and cash receipts cycle. Understanding what takes place in the revenue and cash receipts cycle is our first order of business. In the initial section of this chapter, we will describe the cycle functions and specific activities that are conducted in carrying out each function.

We will examine control objectives and the risks that are exposed if strategies are not deployed to protect against them. Finally, we will study how to audit in this setting. The evaluation of internal accounting controls will take center stage; then our focus will shift to audit procedures.

STUDYING THE CYCLE CHAPTERS

This chapter and the following four are devoted to transaction cycles and the auditing process. These chapters are all organized in the same way to facilitate your study. We suggest that you try the following approach in studying these chapters.

1. Learn how organizations are structured and transactions are processed. Do this by studying the flowcharts and the section on cycle functions and activities.

2. Study internal controls and strategies, noting how activities are organized to achieve control. Compare control strategies with the internal control questionnaire and the audit program for compliance testing.

3. Ask yourself how risk increases when controls are absent, and relate that to audit objectives and substantive testing.

6.1 CYCLE FUNCTIONS AND ACTIVITIES

The revenue and cash receipts cycle consists of a very fundamental set of activities. It involves bringing a product and/or service to the marketplace, selling it, and collecting its price. These economic events and transactions are logically related and form the start-to-finish sequence that we will study in evaluating internal accounting controls.

Certain functions must be performed in getting a product to the customer and collecting the price. They are illustrated in Exhibit 6–1. How these functions relate, and the activities that take place within each are explained in detail in a set of flowcharts. Exhibit 6–2 presents three examples of flowcharts that might be prepared in reviewing a client's internal accounting controls.

Keep in mind, however, that individual firms may be different from this model. A firm that deals in services (e.g., CPAs, banks) will not have a shipping function. Firms that sell only for cash will have no need for billing or credit administration. The amount of activity in a function, and the relative importance of one function versus another, can vary from company to company because of the firm's size and the type of product it sells. We have chosen to use a typical model of a firm that sells a product on credit terms and is large enough to have all of the separate functions shown in Exhibit 6–1. You may not always encounter the "typical firm," but you will find that the concepts developed here are readily transferred and adapted to "non-typical" cases.

FUNCTIONS

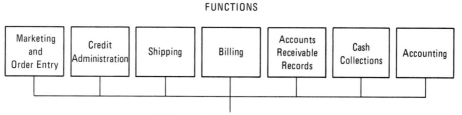

CUSTOMER MARKET EXCHANGES

EXHIBIT 6–1   Functions in the Revenue and Cash Receipts Cycle

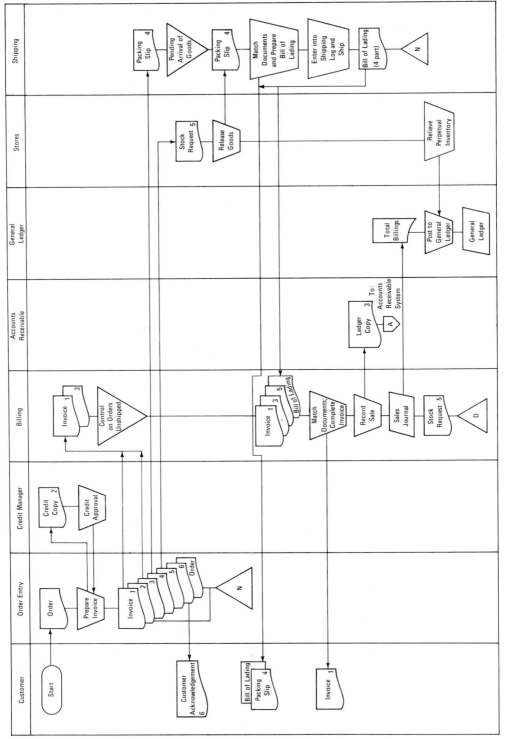

EXHIBIT 6-2   Sales System Flowchart

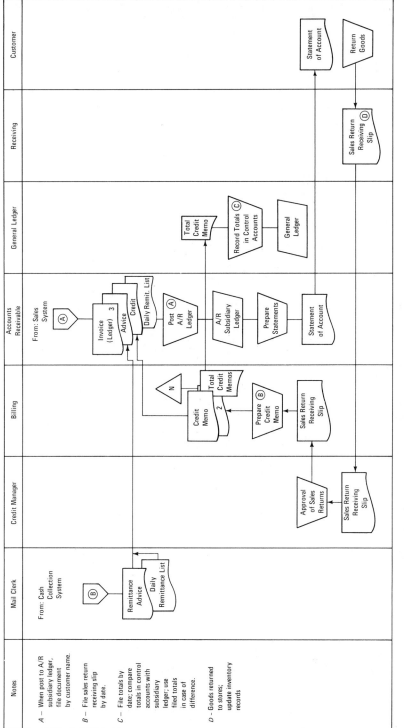

EXHIBIT 6-2 (Continued) Accounts Receivable System Flowchart

187

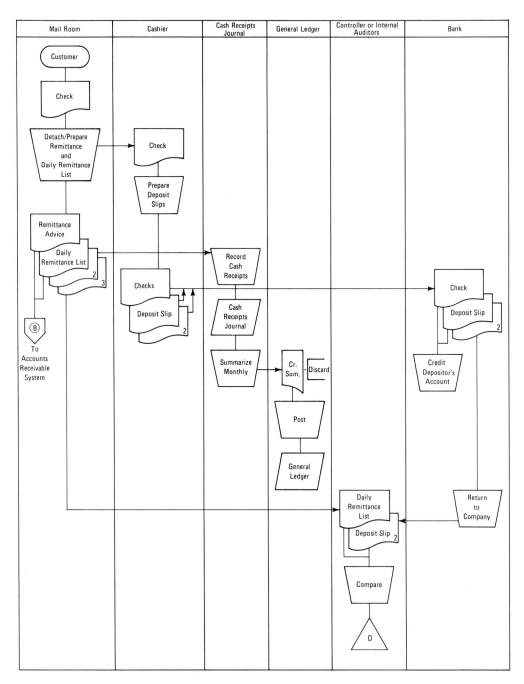

Mail Room	Cashier	Cash Receipts Journal	General Ledger	Controller or Internal Auditors	Bank

Customer

Check

Detach/Prepare Remittance and Daily Remittance List

Check

Prepare Deposit Slips

Remittance Advice

Daily Remittance List   2 3

Checks

Deposit Slip   2

B

To Accounts Receivable System

Record Cash Receipts

Cash Receipts Journal

Summarize Monthly

Cr. Sum. — Discard

Post

General Ledger

Check

Deposit Slip   2

Credit Depositor's Account

Return to Company

Daily Remittance List

Deposit Slip   2

Compare

D

EXHIBIT 6–2 (Continued) Cash Collection of Receivables Flowchart

188

You will find it helpful to trace through the flowcharts as you read the descriptions of cycle functions and activities that come next.

Marketing and Order Entry Function and Major Activities

Marketing is far-reaching in its scope. Advertising, promotion, sales forecasting, market and product research, and sales operations are some of the activities it encompasses. But these activities precede the point where an auditor's main interests begin. Once a customer's order is received and accepted, auditing concerns start. For that reason, we will shorten our title for this function to "order entry," even though it may embrace some earlier activities. Some earlier activities that continue to be of interest are: formulating product pricing policies; determining standard product lines (e.g., add or drop a product); and designing the means of communicating information about prices and products (e.g., catalogs).

A customer's order is taken by a salesman or received by mail. The order is reviewed for the type of products ordered, quantities, specifications, delivery dates, and requests for special prices, terms, or allowances. Other departments may be queried to see if merchandise is in stock or whether delivery deadlines can be met. Are requested engineering changes feasible? Then a sales invoice is prepared and the prices to be charged are entered on it. The credit manager is asked to approve sales to be made on open account. When credit approval is received, the multicopied sales invoice is separated and routed to departments that will need a copy to process the order. The customer is sent a copy to acknowledge the receipt and acceptance of the order.

There are other duties such as responding to customers' complaints. Customer requests to return merchandise are reviewed in collaboration with the credit manager. In addition, the order entry section cooperates with credit administration personnel in dealing with delinquent customers' accounts.

Credit Administration Function and Major Activities

Selling on credit terms is a fact of life in most modern businesses. Deciding who will get credit, how much, and for how long falls on the credit manager's shoulders. The volume of credit transactions is considerable, and the customer accounts that must be maintained represent a major undertaking. A common practice is to compile lists of approved customers and their credit limits. These lists aid in granting credit to existing customers. New customers must be investigated to determine whether credit should be extended and how much. The credit manager authorizes credit sales and merchandise returns for credit. When sales returns are approved, the billing department is notified to prepare a credit memo.

Monthly reviews are made of the accounts receivable aged trial balance. Pressure is then exerted to collect past due accounts. In extreme cases, delinquent accounts are turned over to lawyers or collection agencies.

Shipping Function and Major Activities

The exit point for merchandise leaving the firm is the shipping department. Depending on which mode of transportation is most commonly used for shipping, the loading dock can be found alongside railroad tracks, waterways, an airstrip, or an open area for trucks. The shipping department has personnel for handling the goods and specialists who make necessary arrangements for shipment by public carriers. It is not unusual for a firm to use an assortment of public carriers—such as railroads, airlines, and trucking firms—or combinations of them. Of course, a firm may have its own delivery vehicles that are used exclusively or in conjunction with public carriers.

Merchandise to be shipped normally comes to the shipping department from the packing department or directly from the warehouse if the goods are not to be packed. The goods are counted and a check made of details such as model numbers, customer name, special approvals (e.g., "no-charge orders") and destination. Arrangements are made for a public carrier or company transport, and a bill of lading is prepared. A daily log of shipments is also kept. When a shipment is transferred to the carrier, the billing department is notified.

Billing Function and Major Activities

The billing department actually performs two functions. One is sending a bill, or invoice, to customers to charge them for goods sold. The second is preparing credit memos when customers return merchandise or are given an allowance.

There are a variety of techniques used for billing a customer. For example, sometimes the customer is sent an invoice as soon as the order is received—in advance of shipment. In most cases, however, the goods are first shipped, and then the customer is billed. Sales invoices are frequently part of a multicopy form prepared by the order entry department or by computer. At the other extreme, a letter sent by a partner of a CPA firm may serve as an invoice.

Throughout this chapter, we have assumed a six-part form that is prepared by order entry when a customer's order is received. One copy goes to the credit department for approval, and another is used as the invoice when shipment is finally made. The other four parts are: an acknowledgement copy that goes to the customer to confirm the order; a packing slip that is shipped with the goods; a stock request copy that authorizes release of the goods from the warehouse; and a copy for accounts receivable to charge the customer's account.

Before an invoice is sent to a customer, its details are checked (prices, arithmetic, customer). It is then mailed and an entry made in the sales journal. A somewhat different routine is followed for sales returns. The sales return slip from the credit department is compared with a receiving report for returned merchandise. A credit memo is then prepared, one copy of which goes to accounts receivable for crediting the customer's account. A journal entry is made for sales returns and allowances from the credit memo.

Summary totals from the sales journal and returns and allowances journal are prepared (weekly or monthly) and transmitted to general ledger accounting. Entries are then made to the various control accounts that have been affected by that period's transactions.

The Accounts Receivable Records Function and Major Activities

For every customer who receives credit, an individual account must be created, maintained, and watched over. The sum of the accounts receivable records constitutes the subsidiary ledger. Entries to the detailed customer accounts are made from copies of sales invoices, credit memos, and customer remittance advices. With proper authorization, a specific account may also be written off if it is considered uncollectible. Maintaining the general ledger control account is not considered a part of this function. It is included in the accounting function that will be discussed shortly.

Vigilance must be exercised to prevent the accounts receivable records from falling out of balance with the general ledger control account. Because of the large volume and variety of transactions affecting accounts receivable, it is not difficult to lose control. To guard against this possibility, total customer account balances are reconciled monthly with the general ledger control account. In addition, each month's total debits and credits to the customer accounts are reconciled with amounts in the sales journal, cash receipts journal, and sales returns and allowances journal.

Monthly statements are prepared from the accounts receivable records and sent to customers showing the amounts due. This activity contributes to the effective operation of the cash collections and credit administration functions. An aged trial balance of accounts receivable is also prepared from the customer records to aid in the policing activities of the credit department.

Cash Collections Function and Major Activities

The firm receives payments from customers and other sources in the form of currency and checks. Cash may be collected by personnel in several different departments. It can be collected by salesmen, route delivery personnel, or a centralized cashier. In many cases payment comes through the mail. However cash is collected, great care must be exercised because cash is extremely vulnerable to theft. Endless ways of diverting cash have been devised by creative employees and enterprising professional criminals. It is a widely accepted practice to insure against losses from employee theft with a fidelity bond policy.

Payments usually represent revenue (cash sales) or receivables being paid off. Revenues can come from product sales; other sources, such as interest, dividends, rents; or miscellaneous transactions, such as sales of scrap, by-products, or surplus power and steam. Collections of receivables ordinarily come from customers owing on account or notes. Collections of cash can also come from income tax refunds, insurance proceeds, employees, officers, directors, or affiliated companies.

When checks are received through the mail, the attached remittance advice is separated and a restrictive endorsement stamped on the check's back (e.g., "for deposit only"). A remittance list is also prepared showing customers' names and amounts paid. Copies of the daily remittance list are distributed to:

a. Accounting, for entry into the cash receipts journal.

b. The controller's office, or internal audit department, for comparison with the duplicate deposit slip returned by the bank.

c. Accounts receivable for entry into the customers' accounts. The remittance advice itself is also transferred to accounts receivable.

Checks and currency are collected by the cashier, a bank deposit slip prepared, and the actual deposit made in the bank. Deposits of all cash receipts should be made on a daily basis. Entries to the cash receipts journal are summarized (weekly or monthly) and the totals transmitted for entry into the general ledger control accounts.

Accounting Function and Major Activities

The portion of the total accounting function that has a direct bearing on the revenue and cash receipts cycle has already been discussed as part of the billings, cash collection, credit administration, and accounts receivable records function. An entry is made in appropriate journals for sales, cash collections, and sales returns and allowances. These journals are periodically summarized and amounts posted to accounts in the general ledger. In addition, subsidiary ledgers are maintained for accounts and notes receivable. The amounts shown in journals, the general ledger, and subsidiary ledgers are checked and reconciled with one another. Accounts, such as sales and accounts receivable, that appear in more than one place should, of course, be in agreement.

Accounting responsibilities for journals, subsidiary, and general ledgers are commonly segregated from one another for reasons of control. Data recorded in each comes from a different, independent source. Due to this segregation of tasks, it is necessary to check and reconcile the amounts recorded.

6.2 INTERNAL ACCOUNTING CONTROL EVALUATION: OBJECTIVES, STRATEGIES, AND RISK ANALYSIS

Each of the activities just described is intended to carry out certain operational functions. Such activities are also designed to achieve certain control objectives. A firm's organizational structure is designed with two purposes in mind: (1) to deliver the firm's product and collect the customer's cash, and (2) to avoid or reduce the risk of asset losses, unintended employee actions, and errors.

We will discuss eight objectives of internal accounting control for this cycle. A variety of strategies (procedures and techniques) are recommended for achieving each of the control objectives. Study these carefully. You will have to identify them and understand their significance when conducting a review of a firm's internal control system. If you discover that control strategies are missing or working poorly so that control is inadequate, add that fact to the management letter. What are the consequences of a missing or improperly functioning strategy? The risk of losses, errors, and irregularities increases correspondingly. The kinds of risks that are exposed are explained for each control objective.

Examining control strategies and evaluating the firm's exposure to risk are for the purpose of assessing the potential impact on the audit objectives for this cycle. Audit objectives for the revenue and cash receipts cycle are to be satisfied that:

- Revenues (by segments for public corporations) and revenue deductions, cash collections, and receivables are properly accumulated, classified, and summarized in the accounts.
- All shipments are billed and recorded. Sales are distinguished from consignments and leases.
- Sales and cash receipts cut-off is proper.
- Cash inflows are controlled and safeguarded.
- Receivable balances represent valid, collectible amounts. Valuation of notes is proper.

As you study each of the control objectives, think about how much easier achieving the audit objectives will be if a firm's strategies are effectively achieving control.

CONTROL OBJECTIVE 1. *Customer orders are accepted only if the terms, prices, quantities, and product/service mix is satisfactory to the firm. All orders are reviewed for credit worthiness and approved before processing. Special terms, discounts, or concessions are authorized by an appropriate member of management.*

Risk Analysis

Control failures could result in undesirable outcomes. Orders might be accepted in violation of laws or export regulations or at prices that are disadvantageous. The specifications or size of an order might surpass the firm's capabilities or exceed warranty quality limits. Special terms, such as F.O.B. destination, might cause the firm to suffer a loss. Failure to comply with special terms, product specifications, delivery schedules, or quality requirements might cause loss of a customer or an uncollectible account receivable. Shipments to unauthorized customers or poor risks might prove uncollectible. These failures can be guarded against by defensive strategies.

Strategies

✔ Set policies in writing, defining the characteristics of acceptable orders (e.g., minimum lot sizes, quality specifications, standard prices, advertising allowances, delivery schedules) and the routing of sales orders.

✔ Use prenumbered documents (e.g., copy of sales invoice) to record order approval and credit authorization.

✔ Set policies in writing for the handling of special orders and sales to related parties.

✔ Prepare a means for communicating standard products, prices, warranties, and terms to customers (e.g., catalogs, bid-proposal forms, standard order forms and contracts). Include a date "in effect until."

✔ Compile approved customer lists with credit ratings and limits. Monitor credit limits for continuing applicability.

✔ Restrict access to customer credit lists, and set strict controls on additions, deletions, or changes to the list.

✔ Segregate order entry and credit administration and keep both separate from other cycle functions.

CONTROL OBJECTIVE 2. *Only approved customer orders are to be shipped. Orders are to be accurately filled and shipped within the promised time schedule.*

Risk Analysis

Control failures could result in undesirable outcomes. Last minute shipments might have to be made by expensive modes of transportation (e.g., air freight) and cause returns or receivables adjustments. Fictitious orders or amounts added to legitimate orders might be initiated and diverted when filled. Shipments of incorrect quantities or types of goods might be made. Shipments might be delivered late and customers alienated or lost so that receivables prove uncollectible. The following strategies guard against control failures.

Strategies

✔ Have shipping orders prepared by someone independent of the shipping department, based on an approved customer order.

✔ Release goods for shipment only when an authorized shipping order is presented.

✔ Maintain a "pending orders" file (backlog) organized by shipping date.

✔ Send customers an acknowledgement copy of their order once it is approved.

✔ Use prenumbered shipping orders and bills of lading. Control access to them. Have shipping department keep a file of bills of lading and a log of shipments with shipping order number.

✔ Have shipping department double check customer name, location, quantities and models being shipped against sales order.

✔ Keep shipping segregated from other functions in the revenue and cash receipts cycle. Restrict access to the shipping area.

CONTROL OBJECTIVE 3. *Every shipment is to be billed. Billings are to be based on shipments actually made to the customer. Sales invoices are to be promptly and accurately prepared according to the prices and terms of the customer order accepted.*

Risk Analysis

Several possible undesirable results can arise from control failures. Goods might be shipped and payment never received, or a kickback arrangement instituted for unbilled goods. Customers might be incorrectly billed and revenues correspondingly measured incorrectly. Invoice prices or quantities might not correspond to shipments, thereby causing customer dissatisfaction and disagreements. Billings might be delayed, causing delays in collecting cash and working capital tie-up. A variety of control strategies can prevent these things from happening.

Strategies

✔ Have shipping department notify billings department directly of completed customer orders.

✔ Keep billings segregated from other functions in the revenue and cash receipts cycle.

✔ Use prenumbered sales invoices. Require that an invoice be prepared for every shipment, including "no-charge" and C.O.D. shipments. Restrict access to invoices.

✔ Set up a review process to account for all shipping order numbers.

✔ Require special approval to process and ship "no-charge" merchandise (e.g., consignments, warranty replacements, promotional items).

✔ Maintain a master file of authorized prices for preparation of sales invoices. Control all price changes by appropriate authorization.

✔ Double check sales invoices for customer name, prices, allowances, and general clerical accuracy.

✔ Conduct regular supervisory reviews of backlog of unbilled shipments.

CONTROL OBJECTIVE 4.   *Subsequent adjustments to customer billings (e.g., returned merchandise, allowances granted for defects) are to be on legitimate grounds and with the authorization of management. Merchandise returned by customers is put back into inventory and reentered into the accounts.*

Risk Analysis

What can go wrong if controls fail here? Out-of-season or out-of-style merchandise might be returned for credit. Goods might be returned without reason or for reasons unacceptable to management. Credit memos might be issued to conceal unauthorized shipments of goods or customer payments that have been diverted. Merchandise might be returned to stores without knowledge of sales or purchasing personnel. Oversupply and eventual obsolescence might occur. The following strategies can defend against these malfunctions.

Strategies

✓ Returned merchandise is to be approved in advance by the sales manager and the credit manager.

✓ Receiving reports are prepared for all returned mechandise. Goods are inspected for quality, quantity, and agreement with customer's reason for the return.

✓ Use prenumbered credit memos. Prepare credit memos from sales return slip (credit manager approval) and receiving report.

✓ Segregate the preparation of credit memos from their approval.

✓ Have individuals who prepare credit memos forward a copy directly to subsidiary accounts receivable section and send, independently, a summary for entry to the general ledger control account.

✓ Prepare periodic summary reports of customer returns and distribute them to the sales manager and other appropriate members of management.

✓ Control custody and restrict access to unused receiving reports and credit memos.

CONTROL OBJECTIVE 5.   *Accounting for all revenue cycle transactions is to be complete, accurate, and timely. Every revenue item is to be recorded, properly classified, and summarized.*

Risk Analysis

Control failures can bring about the following. Accounting for revenues and adjustments to revenue might be incorrect (i.e., amounts, classification, or time period are not correct). An incorrect matching of revenues and expenses might occur with a corresponding misstatement of net income. Control accounts in the general ledger might not agree with transaction details and subsidiary accounts, thereby creating an out-of-control situation. The sales journal might be incorrectly recorded or totaled to conceal an irregularity, e.g., holding out amounts from cash sales. Strategies such as the following can minimize these dangers.

Strategies

- ✔ Employ a chart of accounts, written accounting procedures, account definitions, and standard journal entries.
- ✔ Set a routine for daily recording of sales invoices, cash register tapes, and credit memos.
- ✔ Set a routine for immediate recognition of cost-of-sales and sales commission expense when revenue is recorded.
- ✔ Check the numerical sequence of sales invoices and credit memos received by accounting.
- ✔ Require matching of sales invoices with documents evidencing shipment before entry in the sales journal.
- ✔ Require matching of credit memos with documents evidencing receipt of returned merchandise before journal entry for allowances.
- ✔ Verify amounts of sales invoices entered in the sales journal and customer accounts (e.g., batch totals).
- ✔ Reconcile sales journal with general ledger control accounts periodically.
- ✔ Institute special end-of-period procedures to ensure that all (and only actual) shipments are recorded (i.e., cut-off).
- ✔ Segregate the accounting for the sales journal, general ledger, and subsidiary accounts receivable. Restrict access to these books and records.

CONTROL OBJECTIVE 6. *Customer accounts and notes receivable are to be promptly set up and accurately maintained, with subsidiary and control accounts in balance.*

Risk Analysis

Inadequate controls over receivables create an opportunity for defalcation, e.g., writing-off a good customer account balance and diverting cash payments. In addition, failure to record individual accounts receivable might result in uncollectible amounts. Incorrect customer accounts might create ill-will. To ward off these prospects, employ strategies such as the following.

Strategies

- ✔ Have the billings department send a copy of every sales invoice directly to the individual who keeps the detail customer accounts for entry.
- ✔ Have daily remittance lists of payments received and customer remittance advices sent to subsidiary accounts receivable for entry.
- ✔ Reconcile both total daily billings and total daily cash collections with totals posted to customer accounts.
- ✔ Periodically reconcile receivables details to general ledger control accounts.
- ✔ Mail monthly account statements to customers.
- ✔ Conduct independent investigations of customer correspondence indicating disagreement with their account.
- ✔ Segregate the receivables accounting function from cash collections and other functions in the revenue and cash receipts cycle.

CONTROL OBJECTIVE 7. *Customer accounts and notes are to be regularly checked and evaluated for collectability and collection procedures administered vigorously.*

Risk Analysis

A gradual lengthening of the average collection period might occur with an increase in working capital tie-up and a danger of cash shortages. Increased risk of loss might occur as diligence in credit administration lessens. Failure to promptly recognize the deteriorating credit worthiness of a customer might result in larger losses than otherwise would have been the case. Poorly controlled write-offs might be used to cover up defalcations. Estimated collectible receivables might be overstated. Consider how the following strategies offset these risks.

Strategies

- ✔ Assign responsibility for credit collections to a specific individual.
- ✔ Periodically make customer credit reviews and evaluate credit limits in light of prevailing conditions.
- ✔ Prepare and evaluate aged trial balances of accounts and notes receivable. Reconcile them to general ledger control accounts.
- ✔ Investigate past-due accounts. Pursue delinquent accounts.
- ✔ Require management approval for writing off customer accounts or notes as uncollectible.
- ✔ Continue to attempt to collect accounts written off as bad.
- ✔ Place uncollectible accounts in the hands of a professional collection agency.

CONTROL OBJECTIVE 8. *Cash collections on accounts or notes receivable or from cash sales are to be immediately placed under control.*

Risk Analysis

If achieving this objective is not rigorously pursued, the following risks are faced. Cash collections might be diverted before ever being recorded or acknowledged. Customer accounts might not be credited for payments made. Cash sales might go unrecorded. Because cash is so easily stolen, theft is the greatest danger to guard against.

Strategies

✔ Use a central mailroom or name specific individuals to open the mail who have no asset custody or accounting duties.

✔ Compile a daily remittance list identifying all customer payments received by mail.

✔ Immediately place restrictive endorsements on all checks received (e.g., "for deposit only").

✔ Instruct the bank not to cash any customer check made out to the firm (i.e., it must be deposited).

✔ Deposit all cash in the bank at least daily following a double-counting.

✔ Have branch offices deposit all cash to an account restricted to the home office.

✔ Compare daily deposit slips with daily remittance lists and cash register tapes.

✔ Prepare "over and short" reports of cash register drawers.

✔ Have customer NSF checks investigated by an individual independent of cash handling and deposit personnel.

✔ Establish special controls operating outside the normal cash receipts function for cash from miscellaneous sources (e.g., scrap sales, sale of fixed assets).

✔ Have all employees handling cash covered by a fidelity bond.

Evaluating Internal Accounting Controls

Fundamental questions must now be asked, and critical decisions made, concerning the revenue and cash receipts cycle. Are the strategies for achieving control satisfactory, and to what extent will they be relied upon in planning audit test procedures? To answer these questions, a review of the control system is made. The major tools used in a review are an internal control questionnaire and flowcharts. With these tools, major errors or irregularities that could occur are pinpointed, and strategies that should control them are identified. The kinds of errors and irregularities that are possible have been described in the preceding

CONCEPT SUMMARY
Relationships of Cycle Functions and Controls

Function	Select Activities	Related Control Objective	Examples of Risks	Examples of Strategies
1. Order Entry	Takes orders, prepares sales invoices, sends copies to credit mgr. and customers	No. 1 Orders must be accepted No. 4 Adjustments are approved as valid	• Inability to fill accepted orders • Credit memos used to conceal thefts	• Policies defining acceptable orders • Receiving reports for all returns
2. Credit Administration	Checks customer credit worthiness, OKs sales invoices and returns, polices accounts receivable	No. 1 Credit approved beforehand No. 7 Follow up on customer accounts	• Uncollectible receivables • Working capital tie-up	• Customer credit limit lists • Aged trial balance of customer accounts
3. Shipping	Arrange for carriers, prepare bill of lading, transfer goods	No. 2 Ship only accurately filled approved orders	• Fictitious orders shipped and diverted	• Approved shipping orders • Check details of sales orders to goods.
4. Billing	Prepare credit memos, complete and send out sales invoices	No. 3 All shipments billed. All billings shipped. Invoices accurate.	• Kick-backs or lost revenues	• Prenumbered sales invoices • Double check invoices
5. Receivables Records	Maintain individual customer accounts, prepare monthly statements and trial balance	No. 6 Customer balances are accurate and up to date.	• Write-offs to divert cash • Alienated customers	• Separate copies of transactions documents for recording
6. Cash Collections	Transfer cash to cashier, distribute remittance list, deposit money in bank	No. 8 Place cash under control	• Cash stolen; not recorded	• Remittance lists • Restrictive endorsements
7. Accounting	Make entries to sales, cash receipts and sales returns and allowances journals. Post to general ledger. Reconcile books	No. 5 Transactions properly recorded	• Misstated net income • Irregularities concealed	• Approved and matched documents • Written procedures and chart of accounts

"risk analysis" sections. Specific control strategies that are critical in guarding against the unique risks of a particular firm then become the subject of compliance tests to see if they are actually operating as intended. When the results of compliance testing are known, they are assessed. A judgement on the reliance that will be placed upon the system is passed, and the audit program for substantive tests is approved or revised accordingly.

An internal control questionnaire is shown in Exhibit 6–3. When you study the questionnaire, notice how it directs an auditor's inquiries to the control strategies we examined earlier. Notice, too, that it is structured to focus attention on how the cycle functions are organized and how functional activities are divided.

INTERNAL CONTROL QUESTIONNAIRE
Revenue and Cash Receipts Cycle

Client _____   Period _____

	Yes	No*

Segregation of Functions

1. Are the functions listed below segregated from one another? (order entry, credit, etc.)

Order Entry

2. Are customer orders reviewed for terms (prices, quantities, allowances)?
3. Are customer orders reviewed for products/services offered by the client?
4. Are special orders authorized by appropriate management representatives?

Credit Administration

5. Is an approved customer list with credit ratings and limits used for approving credit?
6. Are changes to approved customer lists made only with management's authorization?
7. Does the credit department approve all returns of merchandise by customers?
8. Are merchandise returns authorized only when evidenced by a receiving report?
9. Are prenumbered sales return slips carrying the credit department's approval forwarded with the receiving report directly to the billings department?
10. Does the credit manager receive a monthly aged trial balance of accounts receivable?

Shipping

11. Are prenumbered shipping orders and bills of lading used?
12. Are blank bills of lading safeguarded and periodically checked?
13. Are shipments checked against the order for correctness of quantity, model, etc.?
14. Does shipping send a copy of the completed order to the billings department or otherwise notify them of shipment?
15. Are shipping orders prepared by someone independent of the shipping department?

Billing

16. Are prenumbered sales invoices and credit memos used?
17. Are blank sales invoices safeguarded and periodically checked?

---

*Note: A "comments" column is also normally provided for on the questionnaire so that the auditor can include explanations, or working paper references—particularly when "No" answers are recorded.

Continued on the following page

EXHIBIT 6–3

	Yes	No

18. Is a completed shipping order matched to each sales invoice and the two checked for quantities and numerical sequence?

19. Are other data on the invoice checked for correctness of details such as prices, special terms, allowances, extensions, and totals?

20. Are C.O.D. shipments treated like regular credit sales?

21. Are sales returns slips (authorization) compared with receiving reports for returned merchandise and checked for approval, quantity, condition?

22. Is management's authorization required before any customer allowances are given?

23. Are credit memos prepared only from properly authorized and documented returns and allowances?

24. Does the billings department forward a copy of all sales invoices and credit memos directly to the accounts receivable subsidiary ledger clerk?

25. Are summary totals of sales and sales returns and allowances sent to general ledger accounting separate from details provided to the customer accounts clerk?

Receivables Records

26. Is appropriate management approval required for customer account write-offs?

27. Do collection efforts continue after customer account write-offs?

28. Are customer accounts balances reconciled to the accounts receivable control accounts monthly?

29. Are monthly statements sent to customers?

30. Are monthly statement balances checked against the accounts receivable aged trial balance occasionally?

31. Is consignment inventory excluded from sales and regular customer accounts receivable?

32. Are claims for freight damages, insured losses, etc., properly recorded?

33. Are customer complaints over amounts due investigated by an independent party (e.g., internal auditors)?

34. Does management approve the accepting of notes for open accounts and extensions of time on matured notes?

35. Are notes receivable interest accruals properly made in advance of collection?

36. Is a notes receivable register used and periodically reconciled to the notes on file and the general ledger?

37. Is custody of notes receivable separate from accounting and adequately safeguarded?

Cash Collections

38. Are all cash receipts promptly turned over to the cashier and held until deposited?

39. Is a list made of all checks received and later checked against the bank deposit slip?

40. Is the bank deposit slip checked against the general ledger postings?

EXHIBIT 6–3 (Continued)

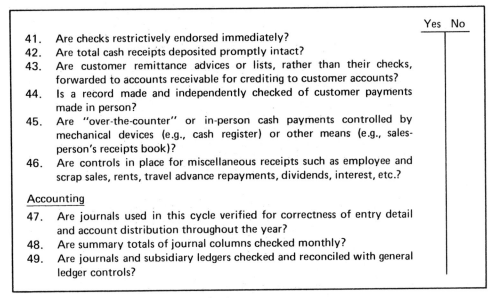

41. Are checks restrictively endorsed immediately?
42. Are total cash receipts deposited promptly intact?
43. Are customer remittance advices or lists, rather than their checks, forwarded to accounts receivable for crediting to customer accounts?
44. Is a record made and independently checked of customer payments made in person?
45. Are "over-the-counter" or in-person cash payments controlled by mechanical devices (e.g., cash register) or other means (e.g., salesperson's receipts book)?
46. Are controls in place for miscellaneous receipts such as employee and scrap sales, rents, travel advance repayments, dividends, interest, etc.?

Accounting

47. Are journals used in this cycle verified for correctness of entry detail and account distribution throughout the year?
48. Are summary totals of journal columns checked monthly?
49. Are journals and subsidiary ledgers checked and reconciled with general ledger controls?

EXHIBIT 6–3   (Continued)

Despite the fact that an internal control questionnaire is used, the review of accounting controls is not a mechanical process. The questionnaire is a preprinted form used for many engagements. Some questions will not be applicable for specific clients. The questions that are applicable will either be answered "no," indicating a control weakness, or "yes," indicating a strength. Neither type of answer immediately signifies anything. For example, if sales are primarily on a cash basis, it may not be significant that elaborate controls over credit administration or receivables records are missing. Conversely, the presence of elaborate controls for those activities will not be significant if credit sales and receivables are immaterial. Therefore, "yes" or "no" answers do not automatically lead to audit conclusions.

An auditor must be able to identify danger zones. These will vary from firm to firm. Only those areas or situations that can lead to material errors or irregularities are relevant—they are the danger zones! Furthermore, only controls that guard danger zones are important. If the controls are operating satisfactorily and can be trusted, audit tests can be cut back.

The internal control questionnaire is simply a guide in identifying important controls that may be trustworthy. A flowchart operates in the same capacity. Flowcharts such as those in Exhibit 6–2 help identify critical controls and provide a visual representation of how the cycle network is organized. Before any controls can be relied upon, additional proof is needed.

6.3 TESTING CONTROLS AND TRANSACTIONS DETAILS

Having singled out critical controls that might be relied upon, it now becomes necessary to test them. Compliance tests of the system of accounting controls verify that auditor reliance is, or is not, justified. Many tests will have a dual purpose, serving also to substantiate transaction details such as those for sales. The kinds of tests that may be appropriate are contained in an audit program in the appendix to this chapter. We recommend that you study it. When compliance testing is finished, and the actual condition of the control system is known, decisions can be made. Programmed substantive test procedures can be adjusted or approved. If adjusted, the audit program for substantive testing will be modified to reflect the conditions that were found to exist. The impact of such modifications will be felt on the nature, timing, and extent of test procedures.

Testing Controls for Compliance

Compliance testing involves following the transaction processing trail, observing the system in operation, and talking to employees to discover what is actually taking place. Do the control system descriptions contained in the flowcharts and internal control questionnaire conform to what is really happening?

By going from one department to the next, it is possible to observe a number of important control strategies. For example, you can witness segregated duties, management oversight in action, restricted access, and asset safeguarding devices. A variety of documents can also be observed, such as customer credit lists, price lists, written procedures, charts of accounts, and files of forms. Files can be examined to see if forms are prenumbered and matched, as required, with other forms (e.g., credit memos and receiving reports). Signatures, initials, or other symbols written on a form testify to double-checking routines and management authorization.

Verbal responses from duty-segregated employees can confirm a variety of matters. These responses can confirm the employees' awareness of responsibilities and of how they interface with others in the network. They can also confirm that checking and reconciliation procedures are being followed. By the time compliance testing is completed, the condition of the control system and the extent to which it can be relied upon should be known.

Substantiating Transactions Details

At the same time that compliance tests are being conducted, the auditor is performing tests to see whether the accounting for cycle transactions is proper. Account code numbers are examined to see if classification of the transaction is appropriate. To see if dollar amounts are correct, invoices are checked for unit prices, quantities, extensions, totals, discounts, and allowances. Proper timing is tested by matching shipping, billing, and recording dates. Journal entries, summary totals, and postings to subsidiary ledgers and general ledger accounts are checked for accuracy of recording. If a sample of transactions is accounted for correctly, and the control system is found to be satisfactory, we may conclude that the entire population (e.g., sales) has probably been accounted for fairly.

Selecting Samples and Audit Objectives

Many transactions may be handled in the revenue and cash receipts cycle during a year. In testing for compliance of the system and correctness of transaction details, it is customary to sample the total population of transactions. For example, two hundred sales transactions drawn at random might be selected from the much larger total for the year. A sample of sales invoices is ordinarily selected for making tests of the revenue phase of the cycle. They are traced through the audit trail while details are checked for evidence of compliance with controls and to substantiate monetary amounts. Exhibit 6–4 is a flowchart of these audit procedures. They are also specified in the audit program found in the appendix. Exhibit 6–5 is an illustration of the sales test working paper. Two other tests must be conducted in order for all of the audit objectives we described earlier to be achieved.

One audit objective is to be satisfied that all shipments are billed and recorded. Billings that are made but not shipped are generally not a problem because customers will react to them and advise the client of its error, but if a shipment were not billed and recorded, it would be omitted from the accounts. The accounts would be incomplete and understated. A *test for completeness* is best made by selecting sample shipping documents and tracing them to sales invoices and entries in the sales journal. This, then, would be a second sample chosen expressly to achieve a particular audit objective.

Another audit objective is to be satisfied that receivables are properly accumulated in the accounts. The sample of sales invoices will be used to accomplish that audit objective, but there is another possibility that must be explored. Are all of the receivables valid? Do they represent legitimate, collectible amounts? For example, a client might record fictitious sales and accounts receivable, without preparing invoices, in order to inflate revenues and net income. Or an employee might conceal an irregularity by making an entry to accounts receivable. *Tests of validity* are made by selecting a sample of entries posted to individual customer accounts in the subsidiary accounts receivable ledger. These are traced back to sales invoices, sales journal entries, and shipping documents.

The auditing principles just described have universal application. The same issues, for instance, are involved in the cash receipts phase of the cycle. Is all cash collected actually recorded? Do the amounts recorded in the cash receipts journal and the credits posted to customer accounts receivable records originate from a valid transaction? Exhibit 6–6 depicts the audit procedures and Exhibit 6–7 illustrates working papers for the test of cash receipts. The principles that address these questions can be summarized as follows:

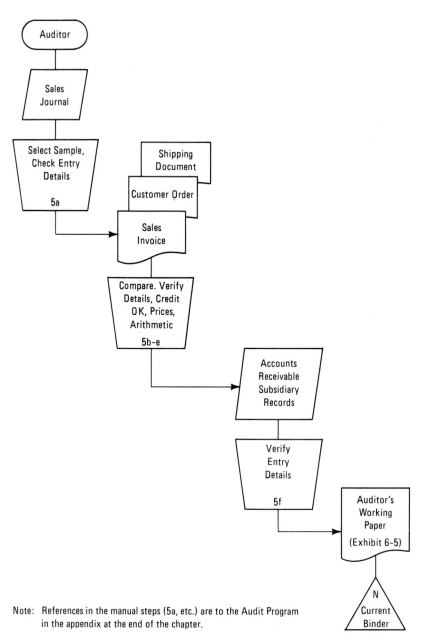

Note: References in the manual steps (5a, etc.) are to the Audit Program in the appendix at the end of the chapter.

EXHIBIT 6–4   Audit Trail for Sales Tests

45-105 EYE-EASE
45-405 20/20 BUFF
NATIONAL · Made in U.S.A.

Population — Sales invoices issued during 19X1: #'s 12892 – 23175.
Random sample of 200 — see w/p X-1A0 for selection criteria.

MONTH	INVOICE No.	AMOUNT	← AUDIT PROCEDURES →					MONTHLY SALES PER SALES JOURNAL	
JAN.	12947	8356214	√	น	∅	T	✗		1
⌡	13008	611787	√	น	∅	T	✗		2
	13089	6244	√	น	∅	T	✗		3
	13161	975502	√	น	∅	T	✗	14352901 16	4
FEB.	13464	78610	E₁	น	∅	T	✗	G/L	5
	13591	803572	√	น	∅	T	✗		6
	13616	12368709	√	น	E₃	T	✗		7
	13803	576138	√	น	∅	T	✗		8
⌡	14007	66704	√	น	∅	T	✗	1209194872	9
MARCH	14386	9172541	√	น	น	T	✗	G/L	10
⋮	⋮	⋮							11
DEC.	22965	800891	E₂	น	∅	T	✗		12
⌡	23075	7468114	√	น	∅	T	✗	2174782895	13
	TOTAL TESTED	947281305						G/L	14
	(≐ 4.7% of total sales)								15

Exceptions:

E₁ Credit approval missing. Appears to be a one-time error (no others noted as missing in sample) Pass further work.

E₂ Shipping approval missing. Located by client personnel — appears proper.

E₃ Footing error on invoice. Amount of error = $900. Client explained that temporary clerical help had been used in Feb. Traced to credit memo and adjustment made after customer reported error.

√ Invoice reviewed for proper approvals. No exceptions noted.

น Agreed prices per invoice to standard price list. No exceptions.

∅ Verified mathematical accuracy of invoice. No exceptions.

T Checked the entry in sales journal. No exceptions.

✗ Traced invoice to entry in subsidiary accounts receivable records. No exceptions.

G/L Agreed to general ledger. No exceptions.

EXHIBIT 6–5

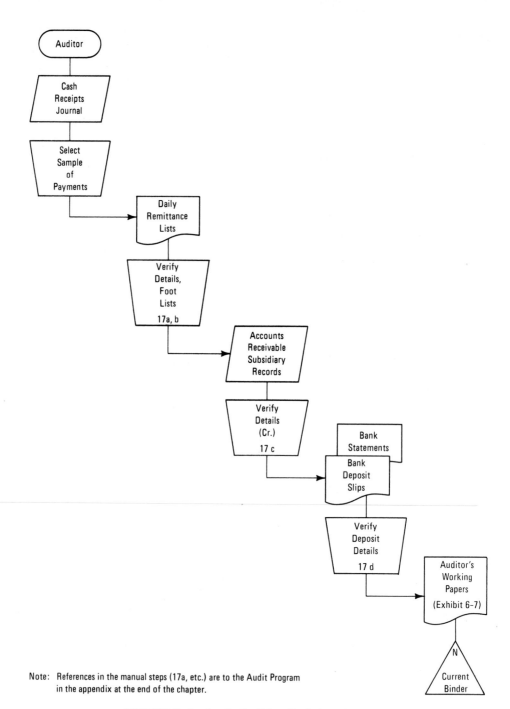

Note: References in the manual steps (17a, etc.) are to the Audit Program in the appendix at the end of the chapter.

EXHIBIT 6-6   Audit Trail for Cash Receipts Tests

	DATE	CUSTOMER	AMOUNT	DAILY C/R TOTAL	← AUDIT PROCEDURES →				
1	JAN. 8	ACME AIRLINES	472|93		√	ø	∧			
2		GALAXY TRAVELS	8604|21		√	ø	⊥	и	✗	
3	⊥	H. HUGHES	280|42	46238|91	√	ø	⊥	и	✗	(JAN. 9)
4									
5	JAN. 11	M. SPOCK	67099|04		√	ø	∧			
6	⊥	D. VADER	186217|55	695414|88	√	ø	⊥	и	✗	(JAN. 16)
7										Ⓐ
8									
9	DEC. 30	R2D2 INDUSTRIES	411|12		√	ø	∧			
10	⊥	TREKKIE TRAVELS LTD.	98804|56	1980604|13	√	ø	⊥	и	✗	(DEC. 31)

Ⓐ Investigated delay in deposit. Jan. 11 was a Friday. Cash
normally would have been deposited that night and
validated by bank on Monday (Jan. 14). Per client, cash
was delivered to bank on Friday. There was a major snowstorm
in City on Sunday night. All stores and banks closed Mon. &
Tues. Therefore, Jan. 16 validation appears reasonable.

√ Traced to daily remittance list, agreeing customer name, date, amount.

ø Agreed to credit in subsidiary accounts receivable ledger.

∧ Footed daily remittance list and agreed to daily cash
receipts journal total.

и Agreed daily total per cash receipt journal to general ledger.

✗ Agreed daily cash receipts total to validated deposit slip.
(Date noted is date of deposit per bank.)

(Population – Cash Receipts Journal for 19X1: 204 pages, 40 entries/page.
Random sample of 100 – see w/p E-1A for selection criteria.)

EXHIBIT 6–7

1. Samples for testing should be selected from different populations to achieve different audit objectives. The presence of several audit objectives ordinarily requires drawing more than one sample.

2. Tests for the completeness of accounting records should start with transaction documents. They should be traced forward through the audit trail to the accounting records.

3. Tests of validity for existence or occurrence should start with the accounting records and trace backward through the audit trail to the transaction documents.

Audit Consequences of Discovered Errors

There is a good possibility that errors will be detected by the tests of system compliance and transaction details. How serious they are depends on their kind and frequency. Some error is tolerated because no system is going to operate to perfection. It is difficult to designate a threshold beyond which the error rate is unreasonable. Tolerable levels of risk are matters settled by professional judgement, given the circumstances. We can describe auditor reaction in general terms, however, if discovered errors exceed a tolerable level.

The first reaction is to see if there were any extenuating circumstances present. If not, and the system is malfunctioning, several possibilities unfold. Errors discovered in transaction details cast doubt on the dollar information in the accounts (e.g., pricing errors, arithmetic errors in preparing invoices). They also indicate that internal accounting controls are deficient. On the other hand, errors may have occurred because of breakdowns in system controls but not have impugned the dollar information (e.g., failure to have all sales orders approved for credit or to check deposit slips against remittance lists). In either case, it is apparent that internal accounting controls are deficient.

When system controls are so deficient as to be unreliable, the next reaction is to expand year-end testing. The test procedures we have been discussing are performed primarily in the interim period. Another reaction is to change the type of test procedures. Thus, some tests may be added and others broadened in scope so that the extent of error can be determined. For example, planned confirmation of receivables balances might be expanded because of failure to have all orders approved for credit. In addition, positive rather than negative confirmations may be requested.

By changing year-end audit strategy, an auditor may be able to obtain assurances about financial statement balances using alternative measures. In an extreme case, if necessary assurances were not obtained, an adverse or qualified opinion might be issued.

CONCEPT SUMMARY

Relationship of Audit Samples, Procedures and Objectives

Type of Transaction	Kind of Test and Audit Objective	Audit Program Steps (see Appendix)	Sample of
Sales Recordings	Validity (overstatement). Sales are properly recorded.	5	Sales Journal Entries
Shipments	Completeness (understatement). All shipments are billed.	8	Shipping Log Entries
Cash Receipts Recordings	Validity (overstatement). Cash receipts are properly recorded.	17	Cash Receipts Journal Entries
Remittances Received	Completeness (understatement). Cash inflows are controlled.	21–23	Daily Remittance Lists

6.4 SUBSTANTIVE TESTS OF BALANCES AND ANALYTICAL REVIEW

Our study of substantive testing of account balances will concentrate on receivables and some related types of income. Tests of transaction details that substantiate revenue balances, such as sales, were examined in the preceding section. Tests of cash balances—the net amounts after cash receipts and cash disbursements are recorded—could be studied as part of this cycle but we will discuss them as part of the purchasing and cash disbursements cycle in Chapter 7.

A variety of receivables and related income accounts are encountered in practice. Such receivables include accounts, notes, lease contracts, installment contracts, tax refunds, rents, and royalties. The most common are accounts receivable and contracts receivable (leases, notes, installments). Other varieties are audited using the same basic techniques that are applied to accounts and contracts.

In all cases, the audit objective is to determine that receivables are properly accounted for and represent valid, collectible amounts. Tests of transactions details posted to receivable accounts have already been described in Exhibits 6–4 and 6–6. Now our focus turns to the ending balance of receivables and any contra allowance accounts.

Examine the audit program for receivables in the appendix at the end of this chapter and you will find a variety of procedures. There is inspection and vouching of notes, collateral, and lease contracts. Reperformance in the form of recalculation, footing, and tracing is carried out. Account analysis and confirmation of account balances with debtors are important techniques being used. An accepted practice is to confirm receivables. In fact, an auditor who does not do this has to justify his actions (AU 331.01).

Confirmations

Decisions must be made on which balances to confirm, how many to confirm, when to confirm them, and the type of confirmation to use. The questions of how many accounts or notes to confirm and which of these to choose are ideally settled by making a statistically random selection. Receivables are often composed of a few high-dollar accounts, thereafter tapering off to small balances. High-dollar balances are normally more important than small-dollar balances. To ensure that the more important balances are chosen, stratified sampling or dollar unit sampling selection methods (discussed in Chapters 13 and 14) may be used to determine the accounts to confirm. In addition, all questionable balances are usually confirmed.

When to confirm balances is influenced by the related internal accounting controls. If controls are good, confirming interim period balances is acceptable. When controls are not good, the timing shifts to year-end. There may also be an increase in the number of accounts to be confirmed and a switch made in the type of confirmation to be used. If interim balances are confirmed, supplementary tests are later made for the intervening period up to year-end. For example, checking entries to subsidiary accounts receivable and vouching of sales invoices and shipping documents on a sample basis may be performed.

The types of confirmations used are positive and negative. Either one or a combination of the two can be employed. The positive form requests debtors to reply whether or not they agree with the balance given. Positive confirmation requests are appropriate when:

1. Individual account balances are large.
2. The debtor can, and is likely to, respond.
3. Internal controls are weak, and the possibility of errors or irregularities is high.

A positive confirmation request is shown in Exhibit 6–8. Second and third requests may be sent if a customer does not reply to the first one. In the event that a response cannot be obtained, alternative procedures are used in order to verify that balance. For example, subsequent cash receipts may be checked or evidence of the original transaction (sales invoices and shipping documents) examined.

The negative form requests debtors to reply to the auditor only if they do not agree with the balance given. Negative confirmation requests are appropriate when:

1. There are many small account balances (e.g., a public utility).
2. Debtors can, and will, respond to the request.
3. Internal controls are effective.

(Prepared on Client's Letterhead Stationery)

I. Standard positive confirmation request*

Our auditors are making an examination of our financial statements and wish to obtain direct confirmation of the correctness of the amount owed to us as of the date indicated. Please compare the balance shown below with your records, noting details of any exceptions on the reverse side. Then sign this letter in the space provided and return it directly to our auditors. A reply envelope, which requires no postage, is enclosed for your convenience. This is not a request for payment, and remittance should not be made to our auditors.

Audit date _____   Account balance _____

The balance shown above was correct on the date indicated. (If not correct, check here _____ and indicate difference on reverse.)

II. Open invoice confirmation request*

Our auditors are making an examination of our financial statements and wish to obtain direct confirmation of the correctness of the invoice amount owed to us. Please compare the invoice amount shown below with your records, noting details of any exceptions on the reverse side. A copy of the invoice is enclosed to help you locate the requested information and identify any discrepancies. Then sign this letter in the space provided and return it directly to our auditors. A reply envelope which requires no postage is enclosed for your convenience. This is not a request for payment and remittance should not be made to our auditors. Your account balance with us may include other invoices; however, for purposes of confirmation, our auditors are interested in only this specific invoice.

Invoice no. _____

Invoice amount _____   Invoice date _____

The invoice amount shown above is correct. (If not correct, check here _____ and indicate difference on reverse.)

*The differences in content between the two confirmation requests are underscored.

EXHIBIT 6–8   Positive Confirmation Requests: Account Balances and Invoices

If a reply is not received, it is assumed that the balance is correct. The negative confirmation is considered to be a weaker form of evidence than the positive. To offset this weakness, a greater number of requests are sent to obtain the same degree of assurance. Any replies that dispute the balance are investigated, whether the original request was positive or negative.

Another issue to be resolved is whether to attempt to confirm balances at all. If customers are unable to get the information being requested, they cannot confirm a balance owed. Some information systems do not file invoices by creditor. They maintain files by invoice due date to provide for prompt payment and to secure the cash discount. In these situations, another confirmation technique is to inquire about specific invoices instead of balances. The procedure and underlying objectives are the same; only the data being confirmed are different. Confirming invoices is in its infancy, even though it has been officially sanctioned for some time (AU 331.07). Early indications are that it is a better, more efficient technique than confirmation of balances.[1]

Confirming account balances (or invoices) is a test procedure that contributes to achieving an important audit objective. It gives assurance that receivables are valid. Confirmations also aid in determining the collectability of accounts receivable. Customer acknowledgement of debt is an indication that it will be paid. Further assurance about the collectability of receivables comes from knowing that the allowance for doubtful accounts is adequate. Adequacy of the allowance can be judged by reviewing an aged trial balance of accounts receivable in light of surrounding circumstances. Of course, the ultimate sense of assurance comes with knowing that balances are paid. That fact can be ascertained by checking subsequent period cash receipts. Examine Exhibit 6–9 and notice how these objectives are met on a single working paper.

Substantive Testing of Income Account Balances

An income account balance and its associated receivable balance may represent an unusual transaction (e.g., a favorable legal judgement or insurance indemnification). Or it may represent an infrequently encountered transaction for that particular client; for example, accepting an interest-bearing note where open account credit would ordinarily be extended, loaning money to an employee, or renting idle facilities. The key feature of these transactions is their infrequency and small volume of recordings.

Testing to directly substantiate income balances of this sort is possible. Revenue transactions such as sales, on the other hand, often consist of too many transactions to attempt substantive testing of the account balance. Instead, tests of transaction details and reliance on the system of accounting controls (after

---

[1]For further information see: Jack L. Krogstad and Marshall B. Romney, "Accounts Receivable Confirmation—An Alternative Auditing Approach," *Journal of Accountancy* (February 1980), pp. 68–74. Exhibit 6–8 from the article.

Scott Interspacial Industries
Aging of Accounts Receivable (Trade)
12/31/X1

W.P. No. E-2
Accountant RKS
Date 2/28/X2

PBC

Customer Name	Current 0-30 Days	Past Due 31-60	61-90	Over 90	Total Balance			Cash Rec'd on Account, Jan X2
Acme Airlines	416.88				9482.12	✓		3266.41 ø
Blasto FF, Inc.	2692144	9265.23			29,867.65	M ✓		30000.00 ø
Cosmic Consignments			266.41	2841.136	3144.177		RC	2691.25 ø
Galaxy Travels	6851.34		9304.41		953259			6537.19 ø
H. Hughes	24008.99	6537.19	248126		35456.18	M ✓	e	
⋮								
R2 D2 Industries	7184921	6621193			15806.114	M ✓	e	6621193 ø
M. Spock		695.97	4010408		4079005	M ✓	RC	24003.86
Trekkie Travels, Ltd.	12646807				1264.857	✓	e	12646807 ø
D. Vader				4811.2716	4811.2716	✓	RC	
Zoomaway Weekender	76.14.88	40308			801.697	M		
Totals	3655.0431	10846922	2878.1366	12594136	47749.6755	✓ S/L		1,8220.756
% of Total	76.5	14.8	6.0	2.7	100%			✓
Aging in AR/O (per last yr. w/p)	3218764.08	19.884.797	42061.128	26080.4199	467126957			
% of Total	69.0	14.9	8.6	5.5	100%			

Improvement in aging appears to be due to more aggressive collection policy undertaken by new credit management 19 x 1. This also analyzed by allowance for doubtful accounts, w/p E-5.

✓ Footed
M Crossfooted
GL Agreed to general ledger
✓ Agreed account balance to subsidiary accounts receivable ledger
✓ Traced aging distribution to invoices, cash receipts, etc. (approved payer)
ø Agreed to February 19X2 cash receipts journal
R Account selected for further analysis concerning collectibility, see w/p E-3 for summary of discussions w/ credit manager and review of related correspondence.
c account selected for positive confirmation. see w/p E-4 for results of confirmation.

EXHIBIT 6-9

compliance testing) provide assurance that total sales are fairly stated.

Income account balances are analyzed, usually with the related receivable balances for principal and accrued income. The type of analysis and working paper format is similar to that for the Debt Summary in Chapter 10 (see Exhibit 10–7). Amounts such as interest income and accrued interest receivable are recalculated. Income and principal amounts for the year are traced to the cash receipts journal and general ledger control accounts. Contracts, notes, and reports from parties making payments are examined. Confirmation of the receivable balance is also appropriate if amounts are significant.

Analytical Review

The data that are reviewed analytically are contained in several documents:

1. Financial statements for the current and prior year and monthly statements in between.
2. Budgets. Sales projections by geographic and product-line segments are especially helpful. Cash budgets may also be useful.
3. Aged trial balance of accounts receivable at the end of the current and prior year.

Comparisons are made between the same accounts appearing in the financial statements of this year and last (e.g., sales, bad debts, receivables). Are the amounts drastically different? Is an amount seemingly inconsistent with some other known fact? Financial data are examined for unusual trends and patterns of change. Monthly financial statements are helpful in pinpointing peculiar fluctuations. Unexpected relationships may also wave a red flag. For example, sales of complementary products normally behave in a consistent manner. If fertilizer sales increase, seed sales would normally increase also. Contrary behavior alerts the reviewer to raise questions. Other relationships, such as gross profit percentages or the age distribution of customer accounts, can be equally revealing.

The following are some useful procedures for accounts connected with this cycle.

1. Compare receivable balances and their age distributions with the prior year's data (see Exhibit 6–9).
2. Compare current year's sales with the budget for the current period. Compare current year and last year's sales by segment and by month, if possible.
3. Reconcile credit sales, bad debt expense, the allowance for doubtful accounts, and average receivable balances in the current year.
4. Compare the ratio of cost-of-sales to sales and the gross profit percentage for this year with last year's figures.

If something out of the ordinary is encountered, further inquiry is made to find a satisfactory explanation. Constancy of a firm's activities over time is evidence of stability. That, in turn, provides an auditor with a degree of assurance that assets will be used to profit, that obligations will be met, and that equity investments are reasonably secure.

Key Terms

audit trail
bill of lading
cash receipts tests
confirmations
cut-off procedures
defalcation
fidelity bond policy
order entry

reconcile accounts
remittance advice and lists
restrictive endorsement
sales tests
shipping log
tests for completeness
tests of validity

APPENDIX

AUDIT PROGRAM
Tests of System Compliance and Transactions Details
Revenue and Cash Receipts Cycle

Client _____   Period _____

Sales Transactions

1. Obtain a list and specimen signatures of persons who authorize trans-actions at various stages (e.g., sales manager, credit manager, shipping manager).
2. Check the numerical sequence of sales invoices, shipping reports, and bills of lading kept on file for completeness.
3. Observe order entry for handling of customer orders and preparation of sales invoices.
4. Observe shipping department for handling of customer orders and preparation of shipping records.
5. Select a sample of sales transactions from the sales journal and perform the following steps:
   a. Check entries for promptness and accuracy of amounts and accounts.
   b. Trace to sales invoice and supporting documents. Check for approval to accept the order, to give credit, and to ship.
   c. Vouch data contained in the sales invoice to the customers' orders, shipping reports, and bills of lading to see if they are in agreement (name, address, models, quantity, terms, etc.).
   d. Vouch prices to standard price lists, catalogs, or contracts.
   e. Check for arithmetical accuracy (unit price × quantity extensions and invoice totals). Examine for signs of double-checking by client.
   f. Trace to entries to subsidiary accounts receivable records. Check for promptness and accuracy of amounts and customer being charged.
6. Scan the sales journal for unusual items. Scan the control account for sales in the general ledger for unusual items.
7. Check footings and cross-footings of the sales journal for a sample of months and trace postings to the general ledger.
8. Select a sample of shipments (e.g., from shipping log) and:
   a. Vouch to the bills of lading. Note shipping date.
   b. Trace to sales invoice and vouch for correspondence of details.
   c. Trace to sales journal for entry. Check for correctness of amounts, accounts, and dates.
9. At year-end, check shipments made just prior to, and shortly after, balance sheet date for proper cut-off. Check shipments against sales invoices and sales journal entries for the proper time period. Make the same kind of check for cut-off of cost of sales and inventory credits.

Sales Returns and Allowances

10. Select a sample of credit memos and perform the following steps:
    a. Check the numerical sequence of credit memos on file for completeness when selecting the sample.
    b. Examine for authorization and check for matching with receiving reports for returned merchandise.
    c. Check pricing of the credit and arithmetic (extensions and totals).
    d. Trace to journal entries and credits to customer accounts in the subsidiary accounts receivable ledger.
11. Foot and cross-foot the returns and allowances journal (sample if large volume), and trace totals to general ledger control accounts.
12. If returns are material, select a sample of returns from receiving department records. Vouch to credit memos and journal entries.
13. Check for material returns and allowances in the immediate post-balance sheet date period to determine if they should be taken into the current period, and for signs of fictitious sales.

Accounts Receivable

14. Check for evidence of monthly reconciliation of customer accounts total with general ledger control account.
15. Select a sample of debit postings to the subsidiary accounts receivable ledger. Trace and vouch sample to sales invoices, sales journal entries, and shipping documents.
16. Select a sample of credit postings to the subsidiary accounts receivable ledger. Trace and vouch sample to credit memos, daily remittance lists, journal entries, and receiving reports.

Cash Receipts

17. Select a sample of customer payments from the cash receipts journal and perform the following steps:
    a. Trace to daily remittance lists. Vouch for dates, customers, and amounts.
    b. Foot the remittance lists and compare totals with entries in the cash receipts journal.
    c. Trace cash receipts detail to credits made in subsidiary accounts receivable records.
    d. Compare daily remittance list amounts with duplicate bank deposit slips and bank statements (note dates).
18. Foot and cross-foot cash receipts journal and trace totals to general ledger control accounts (e.g., 3 months). Vouch all entries to cash not originating in the cash receipts journal.
19. Reconcile total cash receipts per the journal to the total deposits per the bank statements.
20. Review cash receipts records for unusual items.
21. Select a sample of daily remittance lists. Trace and vouch to duplicate deposit slips. Foot deposit slips.
22. Compare sample to bank statement for amounts and dates.
23. Trace sample to cash receipts journal. Compare amounts and dates.
24. Scan cash receipts journal for period immediately following balance sheet date. Investigate unusual items.
25. (If control is in question.) Intercept customer checks already recorded but not deposited. Foot deposit slip. Trace to subsidiary accounts receivable records and entries in cash receipts journal. Witness deposit to bank and later trace to bank statement. Investigate returned checks.

AUDIT PROGRAM
Substantive Tests of Balances
Receivables, Related Income, and Allowance
for Doubtful Receivables

Client _____   Period _____

Accounts Receivable and Contra

1. Obtain a list of accounts receivable balances at interim confirmation date or an aged trial balance of accounts at year-end, as deemed appropriate under existing conditions and controls.
2. Foot the list (trial balance) and agree total to the general ledger control.
3. Test the aging distribution and amounts against a sample of customer accounts.
4. Foot a sample of subsidiary ledger accounts.
5. Review the list (trial balance) and make sure that the following are correctly classified: current/noncurrent and amounts due from officers, owners, employees, affiliates, subsidiaries, parent company, installment accounts, and credit balances (reclassify if material).
6. Inquire whether any accounts are pledged or assigned.
7. Select a sample of accounts (or invoices) for confirmation.
8. Have (positive and/or negative) confirmation requests prepared and personally mail them.
9. If conditions are suspect consider:
   a. confirming accounts that had large balances which were written off during the year.
   b. testing for fictitious accounts by checking external sources (e.g., telephone directories) for customers.
10. Send second requests to customers not replying to positive confirmation requests.
11. Investigate customer replies that balances are incorrect, and obtain a satisfactory explanation.
12. Investigate positive confirmation requests not returned by customers and undelivered requests returned by the Post Office. Employ alternative auditing procedures to verify balances (e.g., check to payments made after year-end or interim confirmation date).
13. Scan general ledger control accounts for unusual items during the period and shortly thereafter.
14. Analyze the allowance for doubtful accounts. Reconcile it to bad debt expense and account write-offs.
15. Vouch accounts written off during the period for proper authorization. Inspect correspondence with customers, lawyers, and collection agencies.
16. Check cash receipts after year-end for payments by past-due accounts and customers with large balances at year-end.
17. Inquire into collectability of past-due accounts with an appropriate official and examine any related correspondence.

Notes and Lease Contracts Receivable

Done by:
Initial | Date

18. Obtain a list of notes and lease contracts receivable. Include those from customers, directors, owners, officers, employees, affiliated companies (subsidiaries, parent), and others. Foot the list, and agree to the general ledger control accounts.

19. Vouch list to subsidiary records of notes receivable for details such as maker, dates, amounts, etc.

20. Inspect notes and collateral on hand.

21. Examine lease contracts; vouch details against list. Evaluate treatment as financing, operating lease, etc. Prepare a schedule of future rental payments for disclosure.

22. Confirm note balances and collateral, including those discounted with recourse and any not on hand.

23. Evaluate adequacy of collateral in light of note amount.

24. Investigate any notes (interest and/or principal) or leases past due, under protest by the debtor, or extended at maturity.

25. Analyze interest income and lease rental income for the period and accrued rents and interest at year-end.

26. Determine current/noncurrent portions of notes receivable and lease contracts receivable at year-end, and analyze notes and leases for principal payments.

27. Trace interest, rents, and note principal payments to cash receipts journal for the period, and shortly after balance sheet date.

28. Determine the adequacy of allowance for doubtful notes and accounts receivable.

Questions and Problems

Questions

6-1 What are the major functions involved in the revenue and cash receipts cycle? Do all firms necessarily perform all of these functions?

6-2 Describe how duties are segregated to protect the integrity of customer accounts (i.e., subsidiary accounts receivable ledger).

6-3 Describe how segregation of duties and internal check points are organized to secure control over cash receipts.

6-4 What are the audit objectives for the revenue and cash receipts cycle?

6-5 List several important tests of transaction details for sales.

6-6 What actions would you likely take if you discovered errors in testing compliance of the system of accounting controls?

6-7 What tests procedures help determine the validity of accounts receivable?

6-8 Distinguish between tests for completeness and tests of validity. How are the two related to selection of samples for testing?

6-9 Under what circumstances would you send confirmation requests to customers

    a. using negative confirmation requests?

    b. using positive confirmation requests?

    c. asking for confirmation of invoices?

6-10 What analytical review procedures are appropriate for sales?

Multiple Choice Questions from Professional Examinations

6-11 An auditor is testing sales transactions. One step is to trace a sample of debit entries from the accounts receivable subsidiary ledger back to the supporting sales invoices. What would the auditor intend to establish by this step?

    a. Sales invoices represent bona fide sales.

    b. All sales have been recorded.

    c. All sales invoices have been properly posted to customer accounts.

    d. Debit entries in the accounts receivable subsidiary ledger are properly supported by sales invoices.

6-12 Which of the following is an effective internal accounting control over accounts receivable?

    a. Only persons who handle cash receipts should be responsible for the preparation of documents that reduce accounts receivable balance.

    b. Responsibility for approval of the write-off of uncollectible accounts receivable should be assigned to the cashier.

    c. Balances in the subsidiary accounts receivable ledger should be reconciled to the general ledger control account once a year, preferably at year-end.

    d. The billing function should be assigned to persons other than those responsible for maintaining accounts receivable subsidiary records.

6-13 To determine that sales transactions have been recorded in the proper accounting period, the auditor performs a cut-off review. Which of the following *best* describes the overall approach used when performing a cut-off review?

    a. Ascertain that management has included in the representation letter a statement that transactions have been accounted for in the proper accounting period.

b. Confirm year-end transactions with regular customers.

c. Examine cash receipts in the subsequent period.

d. Analyze transactions occurring within a few days before and after year-end.

6-14 Which of the following is *not* a principal objective of the auditor in the examination of revenues?

a. To verify cash deposited during the year.

b. To study and evaluate internal control, with particular emphasis on the use of accrual accounting to record revenue.

c. To verify that earned revenue has been recorded and recorded revenue has been earned.

d. To identify and interpret significant trends and variations in the amounts of various categories of revenue.

6-15 Which of the following might be detected by an auditor's cut-off review and examination of sales journal entries for several days prior to and subsequent to the balance sheet date?

a. Lapping year-end accounts receivable.

b. Inflating sales for the year.

c. Kiting bank balances.

d. Misappropriating merchandise.

6-16 The audit working papers often include a client-prepared, aged trial balance of accounts receivable as of the balance sheet date. This aging is *best* used by the auditor to

a. Evaluate internal control over credit sales.

b. Test the accuracy of recorded charge sales.

c. Estimate credit losses.

d. Verify the validity of the recorded receivables.

6-17 A CPA auditing a water utility wishes to determine whether all customers are being billed. The CPA's best direction of test is from the

a. Meter department records to the billing (sales) register.

b. Billing (sales) register to the meter department records.

c. Accounts receivable ledger to the billing (sales) register.

d. Billing (sales) register to the accounts receivable ledger.

6-18 Which of the following internal control procedures will *most likely* prevent the concealment of a cash shortage resulting from the improper write-off of a trade account receivable?

a. Write-offs must be approved by a responsible officer after review of credit department recommendations and supporting evidence.

b. Write-offs must be supported by an aging schedule showing that only receivables overdue several months have been written-off.

c. Write-offs must be approved by the cashier, who is in a position to know if the receivables have, in fact, been collected.

d. Write-offs must be authorized by company field sales employees, who are in a position to determine the financial standing of the customers.

6-19 In order to safeguard the assets through proper internal control, accounts receivable that are written off are transferred to a (an)

a. Separate ledger.

b. Attorney for evidence in collection proceedings.

c. Tax deductions file.

d. Credit manager since customers may seek to reestablish credit by paying.

6-20 For the purpose of proper accounting control, postdated checks remitted by customers should be

a. Restrictively endorsed.

b. Returned to the customer.

c. Recorded as a cash sale.

d. Placed in the joint custody of two officers.

6-21 Auditors sometimes use comparison of ratios as audit evidence. For example, an unexplained decrease in the ratio of gross profit to sales may suggest which of the following possibilities?

a. Unrecorded purchases.

b. Unrecorded sales.

c. Merchandise purchases being charged to selling and general expense.

d. Fictitious sales.

6-22 A company policy should clearly indicate that defective merchandise returned by customers is to be delivered to the

a. Sales clerk.

b. Receiving clerk.

c. Inventory control clerk.

d. Accounts receivable clerk.

6-23 Some firms which dispose of only a small part of their total output by consignment shipments fail to make any distinction between consignment shipments and regular sales. Which of the following would suggest that goods have been shipped on consignment?

a. Numerous shipments of small quantities.

b. Numerous shipments of large quantities and few returns.

c. Large debits to accounts receivable and small periodic credits.

d. Large debits to accounts receivable and large periodic credits.

6-24 Data Corporation has just completely computerized its billing and accounts receivable recordkeeping. You want to make maximum use of the new computer in your audit of Data Corporation. Which of the following audit techniques could *not* be performed through a computer program?

a. Tracing audited cash receipts to accounts receivable credits.

b. Selecting accounts to be confirmed on a random number basis.

c. Examining sales invoices for completeness, consistency between different items, valid conditions, and reasonable amounts.

d. Resolving differences reported by customers on confirmation requests.

6-25 It is sometimes impractical or impossible for an auditor to use normal accounts receivable confirmation procedures. In such situations, the *best* alternative procedure the auditor might resort to would be

a. Examining subsequent receipts of year-end accounts receivable.

b. Reviewing accounts receivable aging schedule prepared at the balance sheet date and at a subsequent date.

c. Requesting that management increase the allowance for uncollectible accounts by an amount equal to some percentage of the balance in those accounts that *cannot* be confirmed.

d. Performing an overall analytical review of accounts receivable and sales on a year-to-year basis.

Problems

6-26 The auditor for a pharmaceutical manufacturer was reviewing the accounts receivable activities. The auditor ascertained that controls provided reasonable assurance that:

- Sales are billed accurately and promptly.
- Accounts receivable are recorded properly.
- Accounts receivable are aged and followed up to ensure prompt collection.

Required:

For each of the three activities stated above, list three audit program steps to determine whether these activities are being carried out satisfactorily.

IIA (Adapted)

6-27 Cosmos Cosmetics uses advertising extensively in its marketing program. Elbert ("Buck") Rodgers, CPA, discovered the following situations in conducting the audit of Cosmos for the current period:

a. Billings from the advertising agency for insertions in magazines and newspapers are approved for payment without adequate review by advertising department personnel.

b. Purchases of advertising materials and artwork are made by one employee of the advertising department.

c. Company-owned materials, such as artwork, furniture, company products, and other items used for photographic sets, are retained by the advertising agency.

Required:

For each of the three situations, prepare four audit steps to be included in the audit program.

IIA (Adapted)

6-28 You are auditing the financial statements of Hardy Knox College. An initial step is to evaluate the student registration system. Based on interviews and a walk-through of the operation, you outline the major activities of this function.

Required:

From the following outline of major activities, list five internal control weaknesses (e.g., omissions of certain steps or measures) in the student registration procedures.

1. *Mail Room*
   - Opens all mail, prepares remittance advices, and remittance listings
   - Sends copies of advices and listings to:
     —Cashier (with cash and cheques)
     —Accounts receivable clerk
     —General bookkeeper
   - Destroys other copies of advices and listings

2. *Registration Clerk*
   - Receives three copies of completed registration forms from students
   - Checks for counselor's or similar approval
   - Records appropriate fee from official class catalog
   - If completed properly, approves forms and sends students with registration forms to cashier
   - If not completed properly, returns forms to student for follow-up and reapplication

3. *Cashier*
   - Collects funds or forwards two copies of registration forms to billing clerk
   - Records cash receipts in daily receipts record
   - Prepares and makes daily deposits
   - Forwards duplicate receipted deposit slips and daily receipts records to general bookkeeper
   - Destroys copies of daily receipts records
4. *Billing Clerk*
   - Receives two copies of registration form, prepares bill, and makes entries in registration (sales) journal
   - Forwards copies of billings and registration forms to accounts receivable clerk and forwards copies of bill to general bookkeeper
5. *Accounts Receivable Clerk*
   - Posts accounts receivable subsidiary ledger detailed accounts from remittance listings
   - Matches billings and registration forms and posts accounts receivable subsidiary ledger detailed accounts
6. *General Bookkeeper*
   - Journalizes and posts cash receipts and applicable registrations to general ledger
   - Enters registration (sales) journal data in general ledger

IIA (Adapted)

6-29 Dodge, CPA, is examining the financial statements of a manufacturing company with a significant amount of trade accounts receivable. Dodge is satisfied that the accounts are properly summarized and classified and that allocations, reclassifications, and valuations are made in accordance with generally accepted accounting principles. Dodge is planning to use accounts-receivable confirmation requests to satisfy the third standard of field work as to trade accounts receivable.

Required:

a. Identify and describe the two forms of accounts-receivable confirmation requests and indicate what factors Dodge will consider in determining when to use each.

b. Assume Dodge has received a satisfactory response to the confirmation requests. Describe how Dodge could evaluate collectibility of the trade accounts receivable.

IIA (Adapted)

6-30 There are several functions in the revenue and cash receipts cycle. Certain controls are built into these systems to assure proper performance of each step. One step is the acceptance of a customer's order. This step should be controlled by proper authorization.

Required:

List three additional steps in the sales (revenue) cycle. For each step, list one control an auditor would expect to find for that step.

IIA (Adapted)

6-31 You are the in-charge accountant examining the financial statements of the Krypton Company for the year ended December 31, 1983. During late October 1983, you, with the help of Krypton's controller, completed an internal control questionnaire and prepared the appropriate memoranda describing Krypton's accounting procedures. Your comments relative to cash receipts are as follows.

All cash receipts are sent directly to the accounts receivable clerk with no processing by the mail department. The accounts receivable clerk keeps the cash receipts journal; prepares the bank deposit slip in duplicate; posts from the deposit slip to the subsidiary accounts receivable ledger; and mails the deposit to the bank.

The controller receives the validated deposit slips directly (unopened) from the bank. He also receives the monthly bank statement directly (unopened) from the bank and promptly reconciles it.

At the end of each month, the accounts receivable clerk uses a journal voucher to notify the general ledger clerk of the monthly totals of the cash receipts journal for posting to the general ledger.

Each month, with regard to the general ledger cash account, the general ledger clerk makes an entry to record the total debits to cash from the cash receipts journal. In addition, the general ledger clerk occasionally makes debit entries in the general ledger cash account from sources other than the cash receipts journal, e.g., funds borrowed from the bank.

Certain standard auditing procedures have already been performed by you in the audit of cash receipts. The extent to which these procedures were performed is not relevant to the question.

- Total and cross-total all columns in the cash receipts journal.
- Trace postings from the cash receipts journal to the general ledger.
- Examine remittance advices and related correspondence to support entries in the cash receipts journal.

Required:

Considering Krypton's internal control over cash receipts and standard auditing procedures already performed, list all other auditing procedures which should be performed to obtain sufficient audit evidence regarding cash receipts. Give reasons for your choices. Do not discuss the procédures for cash disbursements and cash balances. Also, do not discuss the extent to which any of the procedures are to be performed. Assume adequate controls exist to assure that all sales transactions are recorded. Organize your answer sheet as follows:

Other audit procedures	Reasons for other audit procedures

AICPA (Adapted)

6-32 Required:

List five specific internal control measures you would expect to find in a well-controlled billing operation. EXAMPLE: Provision for notifying the Billing Department of all outgoing shipments.

IIA

6-33 In a large manufacturing organization supplying goods and services, several departments may be involved in the processing of customer complaints and the issuance of any resulting credit memos. Following is a list of such departments:

a. Receiving
b. Sales
c. Production
d. Customer service
e. Accounts receivable

Required:

Explain briefly the control function each department performs when processing complaints and issuing credit memos.

IIA

6-34 The monthly financial statements of a large municipal hospital show that the total of patients' accounts receivable has steadily increased over the past several months. The number of beds, however, has not changed, and the occupancy level and hospital billing rates have been stable. Moreover, there have been no significant changes in the hospitalization insurance contracts applicable to this hospital during the past twelve months. The most recent audit of the hospital was completed ten months ago.

Required:

List the questions you might ask as you inquire about this situation. These questions should reflect plausible explanations for the increase in accounts receivable.

IIA (Adapted)

6-35 The Art Appreciation Society operates a museum for the benefit and enjoyment of the community. During hours when the museum is open to the public, two clerks, who are positioned at the entrance, collect a five dollar admission fee from each nonmember patron. Members of the Art Appreciation Society are permitted to enter free of charge upon presentation of their membership cards.

At the end of each day, one of the clerks delivers the proceeds to the treasurer. The treasurer counts the cash in the presence of the clerk and places it in a safe. Each Friday afternoon, the treasurer and one of the clerks deliver all cash held in the safe to the bank and receive an authenticated deposit slip, which provides the basis for the weekly entry in the cash receipts journal.

The board of directors of the Art Appreciation Society has identified a need to improve the system of internal control over cash admission fees. The board has determined that the cost of installing turnstiles or sales booths or otherwise altering the physical layout of the museum will greatly exceed any benefits that may be derived. However, the board has agreed that the sale of admission tickets must be an integral part of its improvement efforts.

You have been asked by the board of directors to review the internal control over cash admission fees and provide suggestions for improvement.

Required:

Indicate weaknesses in the existing system of internal control over cash admission fees, and recommend one improvement for each of the weaknesses identified.

Organize the answer as indicated in the following illustrative example:

Weakness	Recommendation
1. There is no basis for establishing the documentation of the number of paying patrons.	1. Prenumbered admission tickets should be issued upon payment of the admission fee.

AICPA (Adapted)

Purchases and cash disbursements cycle

The purchases and cash disbursements cycle spans the internal system for procuring materials, supplies, and services. It also reaches across the management of trade credit and cash payments. In its broadest sense, purchasing extends to both assets and similar investments, hiring employees, and purchasing goods and services needed in daily operations. All but the last of these are covered in later chapters. Here we will concentrate on the acquisition of materials, supplies, and services. Most purchases are made on credit. That introduces the additional dimension of accounts payable and the disbursement system for payment of obligations.

There are certain characteristics of purchases that are worth remembering. The type of business influences their composition and relative importance. For example, a service-oriented business will normally have purchases of lesser amount than a merchandising or manufacturing firm. Purchases are often composed of many items of relatively low cost and only a few items of high cost. Many goods are stock catalog items. Others will be custom-made, such as subassemblies that the prime contractor for a space satellite might order. Purchases also include services. Examples include advertising, professional services of CPAs and attorneys, repair and maintenance contracts, and insurance policies. Most purchases are made in arm's length transactions, although buying from affiliated firms is not uncommon.

The history of business abounds with tales of irregularities that have occurred within this cycle. Kickbacks, bribes, and illicit wooing of employees with lavish gifts and entertainment are techniques that have worked successfully in the past. As a result, orders have been paid but never received. Substandard goods and orders with shortages have been delivered while employees looked the other way. Contracts have been awarded to vendors who were the highest bidder instead of the lowest. Embezzlement has been concealed by making disbursements to fictitious vendors. An unlimited variety of dirty tricks have been conjured up by creative employees. The point we are making is that an auditor needs to be especially alert to the possibility of fraud and other irregularities when auditing this cycle.

The functions and associated major activities in the purchases and cash disbursements cycle will be sketched out. Then control objectives and risks that are identified with the functions will be examined. Specific strategies designed to cope with these risks and achieve the control objectives will be described.

7.1 CYCLE FUNCTIONS AND ACTIVITIES

Procurement begins when a need for some item is recognized and ends when the supplier is paid. An elaborate network that ties together virtually all segments of the firm is involved. Coordination of its parts and carefully planned controls that are woven into the network fabric are essential.

Decisions have to be made to determine what to buy. That enters into the realm of planning and product engineering. A system is required to translate plans and decisions into action. Sources of supply must be identified and contacted. Materials must be inspected when they are received. When materials or services are accepted, the firm's obligation begins. Payables need to be recognized and prepared for payment, and payment must finally be made. The functions are illustrated in Exhibit 7–1. The network formed by these functions is pictured in Exhibit 7–2, which is a flowchart of activities and controls. A detailed description of functions and major activities follows.

Production Planning, Engineering, and Quality Control Functions

Production planning, engineering, and quality control are actually three separate functions. They are related insofar as they specify the quantity, quality, and source (i.e., make or buy) of goods and services that must be procured. When products are designed, quality and quantity standards and specifications are set. Bills of materials are made up detailing the type and amounts of product components. Schedules are set for production and purchasing. All of this is based on forecasted sales and budgeted production and inventory levels. Plans are converted into actions to ensure that the necessary materials, supplies, and services are available. Quality control also involves an inspection activity to see that specified quality levels are actually received.

Requisitioning Function and Major Activities

Requisitioning, or requesting that certain goods or services be purchased, is accomplished in a variety of ways. Bills of materials and schedules prepared by production planning and engineering can act as requests to obtain required goods and services. Some firms have an automatic requisitioning procedure that is ac-

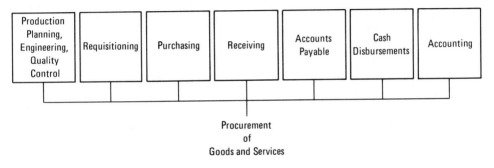

EXHIBIT 7-1 **Functions in the Purchases and Cash Disbursements Cycle**

tivated by inventory control personnel when levels drop to a reorder point. Retail store buyers decide what to buy and then buy it. Some goods and services are automatically delivered once they are initially ordered (e.g., electricity, fuel oil).

Requisitioning of goods and services is initiated by any one of several parties. Production planning, engineering, and stores personnel initiate most purchases of manufacturing materials and supplies. Operating supplies and services are often requested by departments that will use them. Some specialized goods or services are secured by individuals who are uniquely knowledgeable about them. For example, a firm's legal staff would arrange for outside legal counsel, and buildings and grounds would arrange for fuel oil to heat buildings.

A purchase requisition is prepared and forwarded to the purchasing agent, who is responsible for buying that commodity. The requisition form is approved by a supervisor, who is responsible for the request.

Purchasing Function and Major Activities

A central purchasing department is quite common. It may be organized so that buyers can specialize in purchasing a particular type or family of goods and services. Some firms, on the other hand, have decentralized purchasing. Individuals in each operating department are assigned the job of purchasing whatever is needed by the group.

Buyers have several responsibilities. They consolidate requisitions to be ordered from one vendor for the sake of efficiency and to take advantage of volume discounts. They shop around to get the best deal and to maintain or cultivate alternative sources of supply. Terms are negotiated with vendors, delivery schedules arranged, and orders placed. Buyers follow up on purchase orders when problems arise, such as late delivery or returns for credit. They also prepare debit memos in cases where unsatisfactory goods are returned to the vendor or a price concession is obtained.

Multi-copy purchase order forms are commonly used. A copy goes to the vendor, to accounts payable, to the requisitioning department, to receiving, and to an open order file. For high cost or custom made items, bid proposals may be

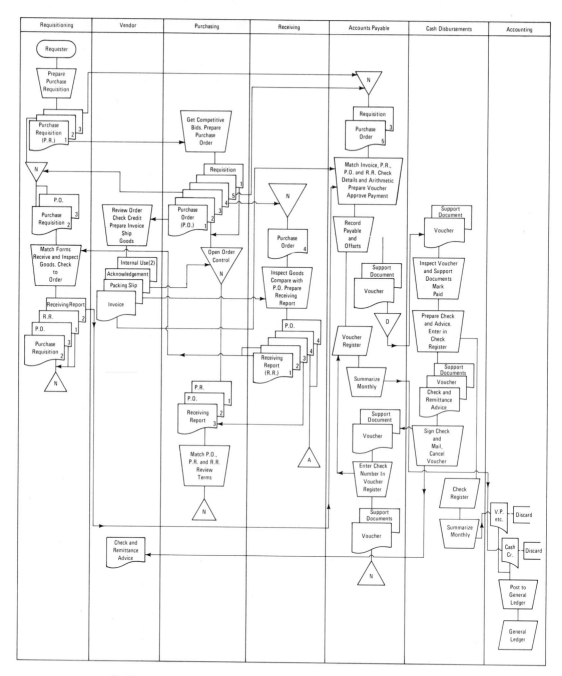

EXHIBIT 7–2   Purchasing and Cash Disbursements Flowchart

234

solicited or price quotations requested. Blanket purchase orders are sometimes used to handle purchases of large quantities of standard materials. For instance, a blanket order for monthly delivery of two hundred reams of photocopy paper might be issued to avoid repetitiously preparing purchase orders.

An important set of activities is concerned with the management and control of sources of supply. Data is accumulated reflecting the firm's experience with individual vendors. It may show prices—both current and trends—quality, and promptness of delivery. Vendor lists will also identify reliable sources (along with their particular specialties), lead times needed for delivery, and volume capacities.

Receiving Function and Major Activities

The receiving function is usually carried out by a separate department. Goods are delivered to the receiving department by a carrier (truck, boat, train, etc.). The delivery is checked for quantity by counting, weighing, or measuring. It is also inspected for quality and conformity to purchase order specifications (model number, colors, sizes, etc.). Shipments that are damaged, of inferior quality, or have shortages are immediately earmarked for action. An unsatisfactory shipment may be returned, or adjustments in price may be demanded.

A receiving report is prepared and distributed for deliveries that are accepted. The goods are then transferred to stores or the operating departments that will use them. Services and certain goods do not enter through the receiving department. They are delivered directly to the user department. A receiving report is not prepared in these cases. When an invoice is eventually received from a vendor for direct-delivery goods or services, it may be forwarded by accounts payable to the user department for confirmation and approval, or an internal acknowledgement form may be issued.

Accounts Payable Function and Major Activities

The accounts payable function is organized to process vendor invoices so that they are promptly paid, in the correct amount, for legitimate purchases of goods and services. Prompt payment is important in preserving a good credit rating and securing cash discounts. The function also includes processing data into the accounting system.

Copies of purchase requisitions, purchase orders, and receiving reports are collected and filed. A purchase order, however, is usually not prepared when professional services (CPAs, lawyers) or services such as insurance, utilities, and repairs are obtained.

Eventually, vendor invoices are received and matched with the supporting documents (purchase order, etc.). The invoice is checked to verify prices, quantities, items, and terms and to see whether the arithmetic is correct. Cash discounts and net amounts due are calculated. A voucher may be prepared, or the set of documents stamped with a voucher number, and submitted to a supervisor for review. Approved vouchers and supporting documents are then forwarded for entry in the voucher register or purchases journal. The vendor's invoice is filed until the date it is to be paid. Unpaid invoices can be filed by vendor, by due date, or simply controlled by due date in a computerized system. When the payment date arrives, the invoice, voucher, and other documents are forwarded to cash disbursements. Later, the paperwork is returned for filing.

Cash Disbursements Function and Major Activities

Activities that are connected with cash payments constitute the disbursement function. That function, however, is broader in scope than simply paying vendors. Satisfying obligations arising out of the purchase of goods and services is a substantial portion of total disbursements. But there are also payments for obligations that did not flow through the requisition-purchase system. We have already mentioned that professional services are usually secured without a purchase order. Other supplies and services (rent, electricity, fuel oil, telephone) are initially ordered, or contracted for, and thereafter are a recurring expenditure.

Disbursements are also made to discharge other liabilities, aside from accounts payable, such as income and property taxes and withheld payroll taxes. A disbursement is also made when funds are transferred to another bank account. For instance, a different account is customarily reserved for the month's payroll. Special payroll checks are then drawn against this account for each employee. Transfers may be made to fiscal agents for debt service and dividend payments. Petty cash outlays, loans, and requests for travel and other advances all involve disbursements.

The process of making disbursements starts when documents requesting payment are received. Supporting documents, vendor invoices, and vouchers are scrutinized and compared. Checks and remittance advices are prepared and signed, whereupon the voucher and supporting documents are stamped "paid," perforated, or otherwise cancelled. Large denomination checks may be signed by two officials. Check signing is often done by machine, using a signature plate. Entries recording the dates, amounts, and payees are made in the check register. Finally, checks are mailed and the cancelled voucher set returned to accounts payable for filing. Another activity related to cash disbursements is reconciling the bank statement cash balance to that in the general ledger on a monthly basis.

Accounting Function and Major Activities

Books of account and corresponding transaction processing procedures vary from one firm to the next. A voucher register system, for example, can be elected by any size firm, but it tends to be used principally by larger ones. With this system, every cash disbursement, except those out of petty cash, must first be recorded in a voucher register. Offsetting the vouchers payable credit entry is a distribution to the appropriate expense or asset account(s), i.e., the debit entry. A check register is employed to record the actual disbursement details; basically a debit to vouchers payable and a credit to cash. Check numbers are subsequently entered into the voucher register alongside the original payable entry.

An alternative is to use a purchases journal. In its pure form, the purchases journal records only merchandise purchases and accounts payable. It is a recording system associated with the merchandising trade. Other goods and services (supplies, utilities, professional services, etc.) are charged to an appropriate account when paid. At that time, an entry in the cash disbursements journal credits cash and distributes the debit to an asset, expense, or liability (e.g., reduction of payroll taxes withheld) account.

A hybrid form falls somewhere in between the voucher register and purchases journal systems. Some firms expand the purchases journal to include all credit purchases. This is sometimes referred to as a cost or expense journal, but it is more often called a purchases journal. In it is recorded the distribution of merchandise purchases, expenses, and assets to various debit accounts, with the offsetting credit made to accounts payable. A cash disbursements journal is still used, but it only distributes cash purchases, cash transfers and advances, and liability reductions.

Still another possibility exists. A small firm or a municipal government may use none of these systems. They may wait until the invoice is paid to record the purchase. A cash disbursements journal in these cases distributes the charge to the appropriate asset, expense, or liability (reduction) account.

Whichever system is in force, the transaction documents that provide the data to be recorded are the same. These are:

1. Documents describing the goods or services purchased and their cost, e.g., vendor invoices accompanied by purchase orders and receiving reports.

2. Vouchers reflecting supervisory review and authorization to pay. Vouchers may be used even if a voucher register system is not.

3. Internal requests for disbursements, e.g., transfers, advances, tax payments. These are self-assessed or self-determined. No invoice or request for payment is received from outside the firm.

4. Debit memos describing goods returned to vendors and associated details including price concessions obtained.

5. Checks and remittance advices evidencing the cash disbursement.

Every month, the journals are summarized and the totals transmitted to the general ledger for posting to various control accounts. These accounts are later reconciled to the journals and subsidiary ledgers to make sure that they all agree.

7.2 INTERNAL ACCOUNTING CONTROL EVALUATION: OBJECTIVES, STRATEGIES, AND RISK ANALYSIS

Acquiring goods and services is ordinarily a significant activity, although it varies in importance from firm to firm. It involves many departments and people and a large volume of transactions. Even a service firm has to buy goods and services. To a merchandising or manufacturing firm, however, purchasing is particularly important. Expenditures of major proportions made by these firms have a material impact on financial statements.

In the merchandising field there are wholesalers and retailers and variations of each stemming from the products they sell and their marketing philosophy. Merchandise characteristics and marketing philosophy join together in ways that have auditing implications. For example, merchandise can be characterized as being high-styled, seasonal, perishable, or created-demand items. All are marked by a limited life that poses the question of proper valuation. Some firms deal in high-priced, low turnover merchandise (jewelry, furs, sailboats); others deal in high volume, discount-priced goods. Internal accounting controls are somewhat different for each of these situations.

Manufacturing firms also have unique features that call for somewhat different controls. A job-order manufacturer may acquire many components and be labor intensive. A process manufacturer, on the other hand, may use only a few ingredients and be capital intensive. The extent of direct materials, indirect materials, and purchased overhead services going into a product also differs between firms. All of these variables influence the structure, organization, and controls used by a firm.

Because the prospects for errors and irregularities are excellent, this is a high risk cycle. Segregation of duties and use of operating checkpoints are essential. Accounts payable and cash disbursements are usually critical audit areas.

As you study the following sections, keep in mind that there are certain tendencies to watch out for. For example, firms tend to:

1. Understate expenses and liabilities at year-end by holding back invoices and by failing to recognize accruals.

2. Understate cash disbursements at year-end by improper dating of checks and cash journals.

3. Incorrectly classify transactions as either expenses or assets according to their desire to decrease or increase net income and/or taxable income.

In addition, the specter of fraud will occasionally surface as employees: (1) divert cash, (2) steal materials or obtain them for personal use, and (3) obtain bribes, graft, or kickbacks.

Consider the possibilities for irregularities and errors and the bearing they have on audit objectives as you proceed. Audit objectives for the purchases and cash disbursements cycle are to be satisfied that:

- Expenses, assets, and liabilities related to the cycle are properly valued and classified.
- Cash disbursements are for legitimate commitments and are properly recorded.
- Cut-off is correct for cash disbursements and purchases.
- All goods and services were received and are for legitimate business purposes.
- All purchases received and unpaid are reflected as liabilities.
- Intercompany transactions are clearly earmarked and eliminated from financial statements.
- Material long-term purchase order commitments, related party transactions, and contingencies are disclosed.

Immediately following are eight statements of internal control objectives for the cycle. Each is accompanied by control strategies that can be used to achieve the objectives. Inadequate control strategies expose the firm to risk of errors and irregularities.

The presence or absence of control strategies determine whether control objectives will be achieved to a satisfactory degree. Fewer and less potent controls increase risk. Evaluation of internal accounting controls and the degree to which they can be relied upon is a matter of analyzing risks and evaluating control strategies.

CONTROL OBJECTIVE 1. *Purchase requisitions are initiated by authorized personnel. All requests are reviewed and approved by management.*

Risk Analysis

If controls are not sufficient, a number of risks are exposed. Goods and services might be requested irrespective of price or other specifications or they might be requested well in advance of need, thereby causing unnecessary stockpiling. Requests might be initiated for goods or services that would be unacceptable if brought to management's attention. Purchases could exceed available resources and cause cash shortages and operating contractions. An imbalance of goods and services going to a particular segment (department, plant, or division) of the firm could occur, with corresponding shortages in other segments. Items might be purchased for non-business purposes (i.e., for personal use). Defensive strategies can be employed to offset these risks.

Strategies

- ✔ Furnish purchasing department with a list of personnel authorized to place requisitions.
- ✔ Order purchasing agents to reject requisitions from unauthorized personnel and for items that do not meet the firm's specifications.

- ✔ Have management review purchase orders before sending them to vendors.
- ✔ Prepare written policies and procedures for the requisitioning of goods and services.
- ✔ Use prenumbered purchase requisition forms.

CONTROL OBJECTIVE 2.   *Procurement is only made from vendors that have been evaluated and approved by management.*

Risk Analysis

Indiscriminate purchasing can cause these problems. Vendors might be unable to meet the firm's specified delivery date, price, quantity, quality, or material-service mix. Vendors might be selected, irrespective of price or other considerations, because they make gifts, provide lavish entertainment, or pay kickbacks. Fictitious vendors could be created in fraud schemes that siphon cash from the firm for undelivered goods or services. Import quotas might be violated when buying from foreign vendors. Contracts calling for purchases from minority businesses might be violated. Prices might be unfavorable if affiliated companies are unjustifiably favored. Purchases could represent a conflict of interest if made from a related party. Protecting against these dangers are control strategies such as the following.

Strategies

- ✔ Set prioritized criteria for vendors, e.g., quality control rejection rates, maximum delivery times, volume and cash discounts desired, etc.
- ✔ Require product-service evaluations of prospective vendors according to vendor selection criteria before placing an order.
- ✔ Maintain a master file of approved vendors. Update (i.e., add or delete) with authorized approval only.
- ✔ Establish a system of periodic review of approved vendors that incorporates latest experience, e.g., actual delivery times versus promised. Check whether they meet the latest vendor selection criteria.
- ✔ Design an early warning system to report on whether initial orders from new vendors are satisfactory.
- ✔ Institute a system that enables requisitioning departments to report back favorable and unfavorable experiences with vendors to the purchasing department.
- ✔ Prepare carefully documented analyses of decisions to purchase from affiliated companies or related parties. Require Board approval if transactions are significant.

CONTROL OBJECTIVE 3. *Goods and services are procured on the basis of authorized requisitions. Only goods and services that conform to specifications set by management are purchased. Purchase orders are reviewed and approved before being issued.*

Risk Analysis

Control failures make errors and irregularities possible. Materials and supplies that do not meet specifications might be purchased. Unnecessary quality might be wasted, or substandard goods might be unusable or unsalable. Amounts purchased might not be at "economic order quantity" levels. Situations requiring competitive bidding might be ignored or bypassed in error. Purchases could be made for personal use. Fictitious purchase orders could be issued for services that will not be rendered or for goods that will not be received. Purchase orders might be issued at inflated prices with the purchasing agent receiving a kickback from the vendor. In light of these possibilities, it is essential that controls are strategically placed.

Strategies

- ✔ Prepare written policies and procedures for purchasing of goods and services.
- ✔ Use prenumbered purchase orders and debit memos.
- ✔ Establish a separate purchasing department segregated from other cycle functions (e.g., receiving, accounting, etc.).
- ✔ Require that all purchases be made by the purchasing department unless specifically authorized by management.
- ✔ Conduct independent reviews of purchase orders for propriety of price, amount, style, and quantity purchased and to verify that vendors are approved (e.g., by internal auditors).
- ✔ Require that manufacturing materials be purchased in accordance with specifications on bills of materials or other engineering statements. Require that all purchases be in accordance with specifications set by management (e.g., quality, quantity, price, terms).
- ✔ Specify that purchases exceeding a predetermined dollar amount are to be based on competitive bids. Sole-source procurement is to be periodically reviewed by management and the rationale for buying this way documented.
- ✔ Stratify authority for approval of purchases, requiring higher levels as dollar amounts increase.
- ✔ Require stores personnel to alert purchasing in the event that inventory levels of major items surpass a prescribed level.

CONTROL OBJECTIVE 4. *Goods and services received conform to purchase specifications. Receipt is verified and promptly reported.*

Risk Analysis

Receiving is an important checkpoint. Without good controls, deliveries might be short of the amount ordered and accepted in full satisfaction of the quantity bought. Goods might be inadvertently placed in an area or department where they could be forgotten, damaged by the elements, or stolen. Duplicate requisitions might also be processed when the original shipment is not received. Substandard materials might be transferred to inventory instead of returned to the vendor. Orders that were cancelled or are received well after a reasonable delivery time might be accepted. Materials might be delivered to some location other than the receiving area where the order could be reloaded and stolen. A well-organized receiving function includes many of the following strategies.

Strategies

- ✔ Prepare written procedures for the receiving, inspection, acceptance (or rejection), and transfer of goods.
- ✔ Segregate receiving from other cycle functions, and reserve a physical location for the receiving department.
- ✔ Prepare a prenumbered receiving report for shipments accepted. Send copies to inventory control, purchasing, the requisitioning department, and accounts payable. (The latter may be transferred through the requisitioning department.)
- ✔ Send a copy of all purchase orders to receiving. Purchase orders should instruct vendors to deliver only to the receiving area. Purchase order details should be compared with the actual shipment received and the bill of lading.
- ✔ Set minimum standards for goods, which if not met, result in the goods being automatically returned to the vendor.
- ✔ Establish procedures calling for special authorization to accept goods delivered well behind schedule and for unusual items that deviate from the kind usually bought by the firm.
- ✔ Use internal acknowledgement forms for requisitioning department to report receipt of direct-delivery goods and services.
- ✔ Maintain a receiving log of incoming shipments indicating report numbers and dates.

CONTROL OBJECTIVE 5. *Vendor invoices are promptly processed when it is established that goods and services: (1) were actually received, (2) are correct* in specifications, (3) were authorized to be procured and invoice details are correct as to price, quantities, terms, and arithmetic.

Risk Analysis

If this control objective is not met, duplicate invoices might be received and processed for payment twice. Invoices could be processed for goods or services not received or for incorrect dollar amounts. Accounts payable might be recorded in the wrong time period or fail to be recorded. Purchase discounts could be lost because of delays in processing invoices. Processing delays at year-end might cause cut-off errors. Checks and balances become essential to guard against these risks.

Strategies

- Prepare written procedures for invoice processing.
- Segregate accounts payable from other cycle functions, especially accounting and cash disbursements.
- Have copies of purchase requisitions, purchase orders, and receiving reports forwarded directly to accounts payable.
- Match vendor invoices with supporting documents (e.g., P.O., P.R., R.R.) and examine for details before accepting them.
- Monitor invoice processing time by logging "in-out" times.
- Maintain due-date files of unpaid vendor invoices.
- Prepare numerically controlled vouchers for invoices and supporting documents and have them reviewed and approved by management.
- Check vendor invoices for the accuracy of arithmetic (extensions and totals).
- Reconcile total dollar amounts of vouchers transmitted for payment with total dollar amounts of checks written daily (or through weekly batch totals).

CONTROL OBJECTIVE 6. *Cash disbursements are for authorized purposes only. Checks are promptly prepared and signed by approved officials, based on proper authorization and supporting evidence.*

Risk Analysis

Cash transactions are subject to a high-risk exposure. Vouchers might intentionally or unintentionally be processed for payment more than once. Checks could be altered or prepared illicitly and signatures forged. Payments might be made for goods or services unacceptable to management. Purchase discounts could be lost because of processing delays. Disbursements might be made for goods or services that were not received. Consider how the following strategies guard against these dangers.

Strategies

✔ Segregate cash disbursements from invoice processing, purchasing, and accounting. Segregate check signing from check preparation.

✔ Have the Board of Directors designate personnel authorized to sign and co-sign checks. Bond these individuals.

✔ Require that an approved voucher with supporting documentation be furnished to check signers, and ask them to review the materials.

✔ Require that all disbursements except petty cash be made by check.

✔ Use prenumbered checks, signature plates, and check-protection devices for printing out amounts to be paid. Use a check-counter and reconcile the number of checks issued.

✔ Mark all vouchers and supporting documents paid or otherwise cancel them before returning to accounts payable for filing.

✔ Prohibit checks made out to "cash" or "bearer" and the signing of blank checks.

✔ Deface all spoiled checks. Keep them on hand for audit.

✔ Require dual signatures on checks exceeding some specified dollar limit.

✔ Have final signer of checks mail them to payees.

✔ Set up imprest petty cash funds, and have them restricted as to amount of expenditure.

✔ Review petty cash vouchers for proper support, and correct account distribution when funds are replenished.

✔ Insist that cashiers take vacations and rotate cashiers.

CONTROL OBJECTIVE 7. *Cash disbursements and accounts payable—and all offsetting accounts affected—are promptly recorded and summarized in the proper time period and correctly stated as to amount and account distribution. Subsequent adjustments to these accounts (e.g., purchase returns, allowances) are authorized by management.*

Risk Analysis

The consequences of accounting error are inaccurate data. Inaccuracies in account balances might become so great as to render financial statements meaningless or even misleading. Adjustments and reclassifications that are incorrect could cause accounts to be misstated. Improper cut-off might substantially understate liabilities and cash disbursements—as well as their offsetting accounts. Adjustments to accounts payable could be used to conceal diverted cash. Vendor credits or cash refunds for returned goods might go unrecorded, and cash could be diverted. Accounts payable balances might be increased or created by employees working in collusion with vendors. The following strategies can ward off these possibilities.

Strategies

✔ Prepare written procedures for the processing and recording of accounting information. Use a chart of accounts and account definitions.

✔ Double check documents coded with account numbers.

✔ Reconcile subsidiary accounts payable ledger to the general ledger control account and vendor statements periodically.

✔ Reconcile cash disbursements to reductions made in accounts payable periodically.

✔ Install checkpoints to verify the correctness of totals being transmitted (e.g., journal entries, machine tapes, etc.).

✔ Reconcile cash between the bank statement and general ledger control account each month. Have it reviewed.

✔ Require authorized approval before an account payable can be offset against a receivable from the same vendor.

✔ Require a debit memo for all goods returned to vendors.

CONTROL OBJECTIVE 8. *Critical materials, equipment, and records are to be safeguarded. Access to these items and to critical processing areas, such as data processing and receiving, is restricted to authorized personnel.*

Risk Analysis

Critical items include: blank checks, signature plates, check-signing machines, unused purchase orders, debit memos and other forms, accounting records, and data processing programs. In the wrong hands, any of these items could be put to illicit use. Materials could be stolen. Fraudulent forms, checks, or orders might be illicitly prepared. Fictitious vouchers and supporting documents might be inserted into the cash disbursements system and cash diverted. Records, files, and data processing programs could be altered or destroyed. Equipment and supplies might be damaged. Consequently, control strategies are put into service.

Strategies

✔ Keep data processing programs, unused checks, purchase orders, and other documents under lock and key. Review periodically.

✔ Place custody of signature plates and check-signing equipment under the control of a specific employee. Reconcile the number of checks issued with machine counter readings.

✔ Bond employees in positions involving cash and other liquid, disposable assets.

✔ Take precautions against fire, flooding, and other calamitous forces.

✔ Restrict access to receiving area and immediately transfer all goods to stores or user departments.

✔ Permit changes to master files (e.g., approved vendor lists) only with proper documentation and authorization.

Evaluating Internal Accounting Controls

There is an organizational network that performs the functions associated with the purchases and cash disbursements cycle. The people, procedures, and records are structured to accomplish these goals:

1. To process transactions (obtaining goods and services and paying for them).
2. To ensure the efficiency and effectiveness of operations (i.e., administrative controls).
3. To ensure the integrity and reliability of financial information and to safeguard assets (i.e., internal accounting controls).

A host of variables interact to shape the organizational network and its controls. Only when the network design is understood can the adequacy of controls be evaluated and an audit program planned. Flowcharts, narrative memos, and internal control questionnaires are the tools for analyzing a firm's organizational network and accounting controls.

The internal control questionnaire is filled out by making inquiries and personal observations. Flowcharts are based on inquiry, observation, job descriptions, procedures manuals, and systems diagrams of the client. On a repeat-engagement, both are simply updated. A questionnaire is shown in Exhibit 7–3 and a flowchart in Exhibit 7–2. Study both carefully.

Using an Internal Control Questionnaire

An illustration of how the internal control questionnaire might be used may be helpful. Assume a retail firm, fiscal year ending January 31, that buys a substantial amount of merchandise and operating supplies. The accounts payable function is a critical audit area because of the large number and dollar volume of transactions. A questionnaire has been completed.

Concentrate on questions 28 through 41 (see Exhibit 7–3), which pertain to accounts payable. Questions 34 and 35 are marked "N/A" because a voucher system is not employed. Question 40 is also "not applicable" because invoices are promptly recorded. Questions 30 shows a "no" answer. "No" responses are weaknesses in control and will be mentioned in the management letter. Although all merchandise purchases of this retailer enter through a central receiving department, there are some supplies delivered directly to the building maintenance

CONCEPT SUMMARY
Relationships of Cycle Functions and Controls

Function	Select Activities	Related Control Objective	Examples of Risks	Examples of Strategies
1. Production Planning, Engineering, and Quality Control	Specify standards and specifications for goods and services.	No. 3 Goods and services conform to the firm's specifications	• Unnecessary quality and higher prices.	• Purchases must conform to bill of materials.
2. Requisitioning	Initiate request for purchase of goods and services. Prepare form.	No. 1 Purchases are properly requisitioned and approved.	• Purchases of unacceptable goods, or for non-business purposes.	• Buyers reject unauthorized requisitions. • Prenumbered request forms.
3. Purchasing	Review requests. Prepare and place purchase orders. Maintain vendor lists.	No. 2 Buy from approved vendors. No. 3 Purchases based on requisitions.	• Partial or late deliveries. • Fictitious orders created to defraud.	• Master file of approved vendors. • Independent reviews of purchase orders.
4. Receiving	Receive goods. Check for conformity to order, quality specifications. Prepare report.	No. 4 Goods agree with orders. Receipts verified and reported. No. 8 Restrict access to receiving.	• Substandard materials or short amounts accepted. • Stolen or misapplied goods.	• Compare goods and purchase order. • Prenumbered receiving report. • Forbid entry to receiving dock without authorization.
5. Accounts Payable	Match and compare invoices with supporting documents. Prepare vouchers.	No. 5 Verify vendor invoices and promptly process. No. 8 Safeguard blank voucher forms.	• Cash discounts lost and cut-off errors. • Unrecorded liabilities • Fictitious vouchers prepared and cash diverted.	• Log invoices in and out. • Prepare prenumbered vouchers. • Keep voucher forms locked-up.
6. Cash Disbursements	Review cash requests. Prepare and issue checks. Make petty cash payments.	No. 6 Payments are for authorized purposes and prompt. No. 8 Safeguard checks and signature plates.	• Duplicate payments. • Forged checks.	• Segregate check signing. • Lock-up unused checks.
7. Accounting	Make entries to voucher register or purchases journal. Maintain accounts payable. Enter payments in disbursements journal. Post to general ledger.	No. 7 Transactions and accounts payable properly recorded.	• Misleading statements. • Adjustments used to conceal diverted cash.	• Reconcile bank statement monthly. • Written procedures and chart of accounts.

```
┌─────────────────────────────────────────────────────────────────────┐
│                                                                       │
│              INTERNAL CONTROL QUESTIONNAIRE                            │
│              Purchases and Cash Disbursements Cycle                    │
│                                                                       │
│        Client _____  Period _____         │
│                                                                       │
│  Segregation of Functions                                   Yes  No*  │
│  1.  Are the functions listed below segregated from one another?      │
│                                                                       │
│  Production Planning, Engineering, Quality Control                    │
│  2.  Are requirements for purchased materials and services tied in to │
│      the operating budget?                                            │
│  3.  Have quality standards been established, and does receiving use  │
│      them in materials inspection?                                    │
│  4.  Do make-or-buy decisions include production planning and         │
│      engineering input?                                               │
│                                                                       │
│  Requisitioning                                                       │
│  5.  Are there written procedures for the requisitioning of goods and │
│      services?                                                        │
│  6.  Must a purchase requisition or similar authorizing document      │
│      (e.g., a bill of materials) be prepared for purchases?           │
│  7.  Are account codes to be charged filled in on the purchase        │
│      requistion by the requesting department?                         │
│  8.  Are all purchase requisitions given authorized approval?         │
│  9.  Do requisitioning departments file a copy of the requisition and │
│      later compare goods received against it and the purchase order   │
│      and receiving report?                                            │
│                                                                       │
│  Purchasing                                                           │
│  10.  Are there written procedures for purchasing?                    │
│  11.  Are prenumbered purchase orders used and the forms kept under   │
│       numerical control?                                              │
│  12.  Must a purchase order be prepared for all purchases (except     │
│       from petty cash)?                                               │
│  13.  Is a purchase requisition required for a purchase order to be   │
│       made out?                                                       │
│  14.  Is there a purchasing department?                               │
│  15.  Are purchasing agents the only persons authorized to issue      │
│       purchase orders?                                                │
│  16.  Are competitive quotations required for large-dollar purchases? │
│  17.  Is there adequate documentation to provide reasons for          │
│       purchases from related parties, for not requesting bids or      │
│       price quotations, or for not accepting lowest prices?           │
│  ──────────────                                                       │
│  *Note: A "comments" column is also normally provided for on the      │
│         questionnaire so that the auditor can include explanations,   │
│         or working paper references—particularly when "No" answers    │
│         are recorded.                                                 │
│                                                                       │
└─────────────────────────────────────────────────────────────────────┘
```

EXHIBIT 7–3

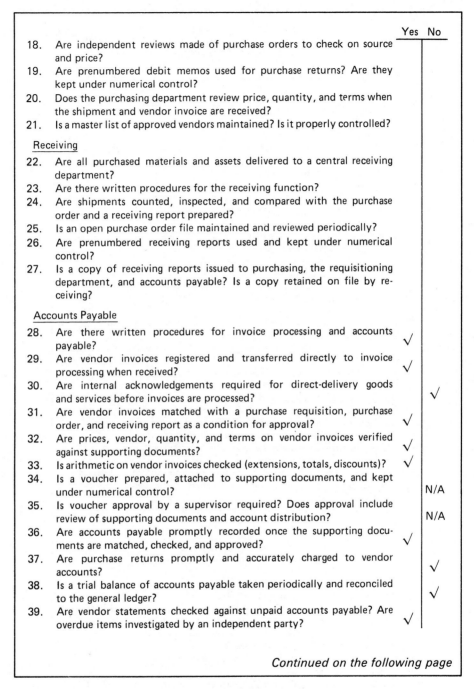

	Yes	No
18. Are independent reviews made of purchase orders to check on source and price?		
19. Are prenumbered debit memos used for purchase returns? Are they kept under numerical control?		
20. Does the purchasing department review price, quantity, and terms when the shipment and vendor invoice are received?		
21. Is a master list of approved vendors maintained? Is it properly controlled?		

Receiving

22. Are all purchased materials and assets delivered to a central receiving department?		
23. Are there written procedures for the receiving function?		
24. Are shipments counted, inspected, and compared with the purchase order and a receiving report prepared?		
25. Is an open purchase order file maintained and reviewed periodically?		
26. Are prenumbered receiving reports used and kept under numerical control?		
27. Is a copy of receiving reports issued to purchasing, the requisitioning department, and accounts payable? Is a copy retained on file by receiving?		

Accounts Payable

28. Are there written procedures for invoice processing and accounts payable?	√	
29. Are vendor invoices registered and transferred directly to invoice processing when received?	√	
30. Are internal acknowledgements required for direct-delivery goods and services before invoices are processed?	√	
31. Are vendor invoices matched with a purchase requisition, purchase order, and receiving report as a condition for approval?	√	
32. Are prices, vendor, quantity, and terms on vendor invoices verified against supporting documents?	√	
33. Is arithmetic on vendor invoices checked (extensions, totals, discounts)?	√	
34. Is a voucher prepared, attached to supporting documents, and kept under numerical control?	N/A	
35. Is voucher approval by a supervisor required? Does approval include review of supporting documents and account distribution?	N/A	
36. Are accounts payable promptly recorded once the supporting documents are matched, checked, and approved?	√	
37. Are purchase returns promptly and accurately charged to vendor accounts?		√
38. Is a trial balance of accounts payable taken periodically and reconciled to the general ledger?		√
39. Are vendor statements checked against unpaid accounts payable? Are overdue items investigated by an independent party?	√	

Continued on the following page

EXHIBIT 7–3 (Continued)

	Yes	No

40. If some obligations are unrecorded until paid (e.g., a cash disbursements journal distributes charges), is control adequate during the intervening period? — N/A

41. Are charges for freight-in reviewed, matched with the purchase order, and approved by traffic personnel? √

Cash Disbursements (General checking account and petty cash)

42. Has the Board of Directors approved persons who are authorized to sign checks? Are they bonded?

43. Are all disbursements (except petty cash) required to be made by check? Are payments out of cash register drawers prohibited?

44. Are prenumbered checks used and kept under numerical control?

45. Are checks made out to "cash" or "bearer" prohibited?

46. Are approved vouchers required for payment of purchases?

47. Does the person signing checks review the supporting documents?

48. Is check signing prior to preparing checks prohibited?

49. Does the last person signing a check see to its mailing?

50. Are voided checks defaced and kept on hand?

51. Are vouchers and supporting documents marked paid and cancelled by the person signing checks?

52. Are a signature plate, protectograph, and check-signing machine used?

53. Is a check counter on the signature machine used to reconcile to the number of checks issued?

54. Are employee advances authorized by an appropriate manager? Are amounts advanced reviewed periodically?

55. Is employee expense reimbursement adequately documented and reviewed?

56. Is cash per the general ledger reconciled to the bank statement monthly and reviewed by management?

57. Are bank statements with paid checks delivered directly to the person who reconciles the bank account?

58. Does bank reconciliation include an audit of checks (date, amount, endorsement, payee, signature) and entries in cash records?

59. Are stale checks outstanding automatically cancelled with the bank?

60. Are petty cash funds and freight funds imprest?

61. Are petty cash funds the responsibility of a specific individual? Is replenishment of the fund made to that person? Is that person required to take vacations?

62. Does every petty cash expenditure have a voucher signed by the payee to support it?

63. Are funds surprise-counted periodically?

64. Does a supervisor review petty cash expenditures?

65. Are maximum expenditure amounts set for petty cash?

Accounting

66. Are there written accounting procedures for this cycle?

67. Is there a chart of accounts? Is it available to requisitioning departments?

68. Are total disbursements during the month as recorded in the cash disbursements journal or check register reconciled to the reduction in accounts payable in the general ledger?

69. Is the subsidiary accounts payable ledger reconciled to the general ledger control monthly?

70. Are account distributions checked when petty cash is replenished?

71. Are budget vs. actual variance analyses conducted during the year?

EXHIBIT 7–3 (Continued)

250

department (e.g., lumber, acetylene, light bulbs, cement, paint, etc.). In addition, outside service repairmen normally proceed directly to the department needing help (e.g., photocopy machine and typewriter repair). Invoices are usually accepted at face value and processed without an internal acknowledgement.

The dollar magnitude of building maintenance expenses and repairs expenses in administrative departments is probably not material. Normally, little attention would be paid to these accounts. Because there are control weaknesses, however, the audit plan may be modified. Control objectives 3 and 5, above, are not being achieved by this firm. What risks are exposed? That is, what kind of errors or irregularities could have occurred? The section on risk analysis accompanying control objectives 3 and 5 suggests several dangers including the possibilities that: (1) the firm might be billed for goods and servies that were not received, and (2) materials may have been purchased for personal use by employees.

First, question whether any compensating controls are in place. In the case of outside repair services, we discover that a vendor time card is prepared and a receipt signature secured. A copy is mailed in with the vendor's invoice. Accounts payable personnel check for an approval signature before processing the invoice. There is, in fact, a compensating control.

No compensating controls are discovered in the case of materials that are delivered directly to the building maintenance department. A related question is whether a purchase requisition is prepared and submitted to a purchasing agent for an order to be placed. By looking at the responses to questions 6 and 15 and the working paper notes referenced by those questions, we discover that building maintenance buys its own materials. Accounting controls here are weak, and audit procedures will be affected.

One possible effect is to extend analytical review procedures for the building maintenance expense account(s). Relative dollar amounts and trends can be examined and comparisons made with similar figures for the industry. Actual amounts can also be compared with budget counterparts. Another possibility is to analyze the account(s) and vouch a sizable portion of its charges to vendor invoices and purchase orders. These documents can be examined for purchase approval, sequence of order numbers, agreement of document details, and reasonableness of items purchased (quantity and type). If nothing unusual is discovered, the account balance(s) will have been substantiated—at least to a level of reasonable assurance.

Turning back to the internal control questionnaire, we find that questions 37 and 38 have also been answered "No." While questioning the accounts payable supervisor, it was found that debit memos are usually very late in being processed, and a trial balance is not taken of unpaid invoices. Tardiness in processing debit memos signals a cut-off problem at year-end. Although debit memo processing would normally be checked for proper cut-off at year-end it will now be necessary to extend this procedure. It is decided to check the entire month of February for debit memos relating to purchase returns made in the fiscal period ended January 31.

Question 38 (no trial balance of unpaid invoices) is compensated for by several other controls. Incoming invoices are immediately registered, given a batch number, and numerically controlled for entry into the purchases journal. Vendor statements are checked to unpaid invoices, and delinquent items are investigated. At year-end a special trial balance will be requested from the client.

All other questions on the internal control questionnaire in the accounts payable section have been answered "Yes." In reviewing the system of controls for this function, a tentative evaluation has emerged. Generally, the system appears satisfactory and will be relied upon if it is operating effectively as planned. The next step, therefore, is to test the system strengths that are to be relied upon (the "yes" answers) for compliance.

7.3 TESTING CONTROLS AND TRANSACTIONS DETAILS

When the review of internal accounting controls is finished, audit programs are prepared. A preliminary judgement has been made about the control system, and its strengths have been identified. The kinds of tests, as well as their timing and extent, are selected. This is another facet of auditing that calls for judgement and experience.

Substantive tests of volume transactions, such as purchases, are earmarked for performance with the tests of compliance. These, of course, are the now familiar, dual-purpose tests.

Compliance testing is necessary for two reasons. First, preparation of the internal control questionnaire is based upon the client's statements. What is actually taking place may not correspond to those statements. The second reason is that control strategies may not be effective. They may not be achieving the control objective for which they were intended. It is fundamental to verify that the controls are in place and are operating effectively. Remember, only control strategies that are to be relied upon will be tested.

Test procedures follow the audit trail of transactions through the cycle using samples drawn from different sources. There are tests of completeness (e.g., are there unrecorded liabilities?) and tests of validity (e.g., were purchases made for legitimate purposes?). As controls and transactions details are tested, corroborative evidence is gathered using a variety of methods. Inquiries are made of various employees. Observations are made of asset and record safeguarding devices, duty-segregated employees, files, and departments in operation. Evidence-gathering techniques, such as vouching, tracing, recalculation, footing and reviewing, are employed, as in the test of vouchers illustrated in Exhibit 7—4. The illustration depicts step 3 in the audit program. (shown as an appendix to this chapter) These procedures in turn, result in the working paper in Exhibit 7—5.

Let's return to our earlier illustration. We reviewed the accounting control system for a retailer by filling out an internal control questionnaire. Then we zeroed in on the accounts payable function and made a tentative evaluation. Our

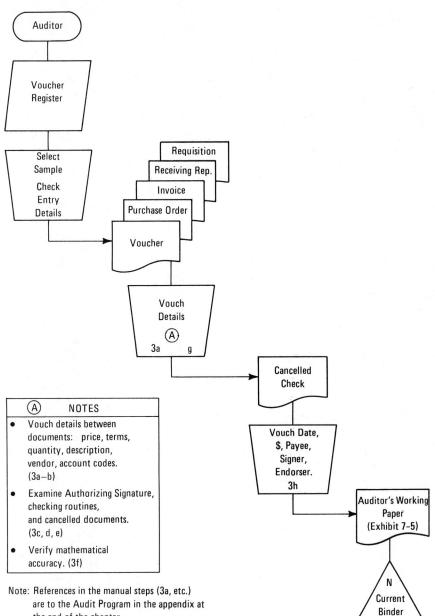

EXHIBIT 7–4 Audit Trail for Test of Vouchers

45-105 EYE-EASE
45-405 20/20 BUFF
Made in U.S.A.
NATIONAL

SCOTT INTERSPACIAL INDUSTRIES
TEST OF VOUCHERS
12/31/X1

MONTH	VENDOR	VOUCHER #	AMOUNT	MONTHLY VOUCHER REG. TOTAL	← AUDIT PROCEDURES →
JAN.	Scotty's Spare Parts, Inc.	57418	8930210		√ ⋃ ∅ ⩗ ✗ t
	Celestial Supplies	58003	76921		√ ⋃ ∅ ⩗ ✗ t
	Omar's Florist	58667	8918		√ ⋃ ∅ ⩗ ✗ t
	United Central Bank	59142	7805000 ①		√ ⋃ ∅ ⩗ ✗ t
	Four Seasons Deli	59837	6828	534120978 T∧	√ ⋃ ∅ ⩗ ✗ t
FEB.	Hartland Insurance	60005	982176		√ ⋃ ∅ ⩗ ✗ t
	Acme Office Supply	60604	285144		√ ⋃ ∅ ⩗ ✗ t
	Smith's Welding Co.	61013	90000		√ ⋃ E₁ ⩗ ✗ t
	Pinkerton's Service	61495	2691878		√ ⋃ ∅ ⩗ ✗ t
	Jones & Smith, CPA's	62530	4500000	693721488 T	√ ⋃ ∅ ⩗ ✗ t
	⋮				
	⋮				
DEC.	4th Nat'l. Bank	103867	100000 — ①		√ ⋃ ∅ ⩗ ✗ t
	Sloan's Service Co.	103988	630129		√ ⋃ ∅ ⩗ ✗ t
	United Steel Co.	104121	9839871		√ ⋃ ∅ ⩗ ✗ ⊗
	United Way	104360	200000	824168620 T∧	√ ⋃ ∅ ⩗ ✗ ⊗

(% of TOTAL VOUCHERS TESTED = 6.2%)

E₁ No authorization on invoice or voucher. Discussed with service mgr. He okayed payment, but failed to note approval. Appears to be isolated instance.

① Repayments of long-term debt. See w/p O-1.

√ Matched to and agreed with supporting documentation, including vendor invoice.

⋃ Reviewed account coding. Appears proper.

∅ Reviewed for proper authorization.

⩗ Verified mathematical accuracy.

✗ Agreed to voucher register and accounts payable subsidiary ledger.

t Traced to cancelled check, agreeing name and amount.

T Traced monthly voucher register total to general ledger.

∧ Footed monthly voucher register.

⊗ Not yet paid — traced to A/P trial balance

(POPULATION — Vouchers issued during year — #56901 through #104362)

(SAMPLE — 200 vouchers. See w/p N-1A for selection criteria.)

EXHIBIT 7–5

EXHIBIT 7-6 Control Strategies to be Tested for Compliance
Accounts Payable Function

Question No. from Internal Control Questionnaire (Exhibit 7-3)	Instruction No. from Audit Program (see Appendix)
28	By observation
29	11
30 ("NO" response will not be tested)	—
31, 32	3a
33	3d,f
34	3a
35	3c
36	11
37 ("NO." Tardy processing)	Extended version of 8
38 ("NO." Trial balance of accounts payable)	Get trial balance at year-end
39	10
40 ("Not Applicable," i.e., Nothing to test)	—
41	3a,c

conclusion was that the system of accounting controls appeared satisfactory. The only remaining issue was whether the control strategies to be relied upon (the "yes" answers) were operating effectively and as prescribed.

Control strategies are tested by following the audit program in the appendix. For example, the client has stated that vendor invoices are transferred directly to invoice processing and registered (Question 29). That statement is tested by following directive II from the audit program, which instructs the auditor to examine the register used to control vendor invoices. There are procedures contained in the same audit program for testing all of the controls. In Exhibit 7–6 the particular procedures to be followed are matched with the control strategy to be tested. They are identified by their respective number as taken from the audit program and the internal control questionnaire.

When compliance testing is finished and the condition of the controls is known, one of two courses of action will be taken. If the controls appear satisfactory, the program for substantive testing of balances will be finalized. If the controls have turned out to be unsatisfactory, further work to determine the extent and dollar magnitude of errors may be necessary. If monetary errors have been made, adjusting and/or reclassifying journal entries will be prepared to correct them. They will be posted to the trial balance and given to the client for entry into the accounts. A comment will be made in the management letter with suggestions for ways to correct the problem.

Proof-of-Cash

Deficiencies in the controls over cash may call for extraordinary measures. The possibility of embezzlement of cash is great, especially in the disbursements phase. If suspicions are aroused that fraud may have occurred, a proof-of-cash (a "4-column bank reconciliation") should be prepared. A proof-of-cash is a reconciliation of cash figures between the books of account and bank statements. Not only is the ending cash balance reconciled but also all of the cash receipts and disbursements as well. It can encompass a month, several consecutive months, or an entire year. An example is presented in Exhibit 7–7.

EXHIBIT 7-7   Proof-of-Cash

	Beginning Balance	Receipts	Disbursements	Ending Balance
per Bank Statement	600,466.47	4,546,901.70	4,551,841.62	595,526.55
Deposits in transit:				
beginning of period	3,650.00	(3,650.00)		
end of period		5,000.00		5,000.00
Outstanding checks:				
beginning of period	(10,450.69)		(10,450.69)	
end of period			79,372.13	(79,372.13)
Check returned for signature		(2,422.36)	(2,422.36)	
per Books	593,665.78	4,545,829.34	4,618,340.70	521,154.42

7.4 SUBSTANTIVE TESTS OF BALANCES AND ANALYTICAL REVIEW

As we turn to the topic of substantive testing of balances, cash and accounts payable immediately come to mind. Beyond that there are other balances that also must be tested. In addition, inquiries probing in search of contingent liabilities need to be made. We will examine these last two items shortly.

Cash On Hand and In Banks

A variety of accounts fall under this heading. Cash on hand includes petty cash and freight payment funds, cash register drawers, and money in vaults (e.g., hotels, gambling casinos). Cash in banks embraces checking accounts, savings accounts, certificates-of-deposit, money market certificates, and similar instruments. Some cash accounts are non-current (e.g., stock redemption funds, retirement funds, bond reserve funds) and cannot be used for current operating purposes.

Money on hand is substantiated by counting it. There are other procedures described in the audit program illustrated in the appendix, but they are incidental. Cash in the bank is tested by:

1. Preparing a bank reconciliation (or the client's is checked and then used). The concept and format of a bank reconciliation is the same as that found in introductory accounting textbooks.

2. Requesting a bank confirmation. See Exhibit 7–8 for an illustration of the standard confirmation form used by auditors.

3. Obtaining a "cut-off" bank statement and carrying out certain steps.

4. Inspecting passbooks, certificates of deposit, etc.

A standard bank confirmation inquiry is prepared, signed by the client, and personally mailed by the auditor. It is returned directly to the auditor, who compares it with cash balances on the bank reconciliation and any other analytical schedules that have been prepared. Notice that information about outstanding loans and contingent liabilities (e.g., guaranteeing another's debt) is also obtained. All cash accounts are confirmed: checking, savings, cash in the hands of a fiscal agent, etc.

Approximately two or three weeks after year-end, the client is requested to obtain a "cut-off bank statement" from its bank. The statement—with paid checks and deposit slips—is just like any other except that the bank makes it up right away instead of at month's end. It should be delivered unopened to the auditor. Paid checks and deposit slips are inspected and traced into the year-end bank reconciliation and the books of account. The statement's opening balance is verified to the "balance per bank" amount on the bank reconciliation. Dates on the paid checks are compared with those recorded in the cash disbursements journal to see if they agree. If a check is discovered that merely transferred cash to another of the client's cash accounts, a "red alert" is signalled. A cash transfer made right at year-end may be a ploy known as "kiting." It is used to either inflate cash balances or to cover money that has been embezzled.

Consider these facts. An embezzlement scheme has already siphoned off $10,000, and the general ledger account is now overstated. Normally, that situation would be detected by a bank reconciliation at year-end were it not for kiting. The cover-up proceeds as follows. A $10,000 check is drawn on the client's branch account in a Los Angeles bank. It is deposited on the last day of the year in the client's home-base bank in Washington, D.C. Neither the disbursement nor the deposit is recorded in the firm's cash journals. The Washington, D.C., bank reflects the deposit in its year-end statement, thereby increasing the balance by $10,000. Because of the "float" time in processing the check, it does not show as a payment in the year-end statement of the Los Angeles bank. Both accounts will now reconcile.

STANDARD BANK CONFIRMATION INQUIRY
Approved 1966 by
AMERICAN INSTITUTE OF CERTIFIED PUBLIC ACCOUNTANTS
NABAC, THE ASSOCIATION FOR BANK AUDIT, CONTROL
AND OPERATION

DUPLICATE
To be mailed to accountant

January 25 19X2

Dear Sirs:

Your completion of the following report will be sincerely appreciated. IF THE ANSWER TO ANY ITEM IS "NONE", PLEASE SO STATE. Kindly mail it in the enclosed stamped, addressed envelope **direct** to the accountant named below.

Report from

Yours truly,

Scott Interspacial Industries
(Account Name Per Bank Records)

(Bank) ___Mid-Marineland Bank___

By _Craig L. Scott_
Authorized Signature

___13 Poe Ave.___

___Hooksville , VA. 23229___

Bank customer should check here if confirmation of bank balances only (item 1) is desired. ☐

Clark Kent, CPA

1820 Grove Ave.

Richmond, VA. 23220

NOTE–If the space provided is inadequate, please enter totals hereon and attach a statement giving full details as called for by the columnar headings below.

1. At the close of business on _____Dec. 31 19X1_____ our records showed the following balance(s) to the *credit* of the above named customer. In the event that we could readily ascertain whether there were any balances to the credit of the customer not designated in this request, the appropriate information is given below:

AMOUNT	ACCOUNT NAME	ACCOUNT NUMBER	SUBJECT TO WITH-DRAWAL BY CHECK?	INTEREST BEARING? GIVE RATE
$595,526.55	CHECKING	7681057	yes	none
9,251.79	SAVINGS	SV 2303-3	no	5½%
100,000.00	MONEY MARKET CERTIFICATES	CD 6287-5	no	12.035 %

2. The customer was directly liable to us in respect of loans, acceptances, etc., at the close of business on that date in the total amount of $ __none__ , as follows:

AMOUNT	DATE OF LOAN OR DISCOUNT	DUE DATE	INTEREST RATE	PAID TO	DESCRIPTION OF LIABILITY, COLLATERAL, SECURITY INTERESTS, LIENS, ENDORSERS, ETC
$					

3. The customer was contingently liable as endorser of notes discounted and/or as guarantor at the close of business on that date in the total amount of $ __none__ , as below:

AMOUNT	NAME OF MAKER	DATE OF NOTE	DUE DATE	REMARKS
$				

4. Other direct or contingent liabilities, open letters of credit, and relative collateral, were *none*

5. Security agreements under the Uniform Commercial Code or any other agreements providing for restrictions, not noted above, were as follows (if officially recorded, indicate date and office in which filed):

Date _February 2_ 19X2

Yours truly, (Bank) MID-MARINELAND BANK
By D. R. Vader , Customer Service
Authorized Signature

FORM WP-681 (REV. 10/66)

EXHIBIT 7–8

When the paid check finally travels full-circuit and is returned with the cut-off bank statement, it will be caught. It will not be among the outstanding checks on the bank reconciliation, and its date will not agree with the cash disbursements entry that is eventually made in the next fiscal period. A proof-of-cash would also have uncovered this fraud, as would an analysis of interbank transfers.

Accounts Payable

Recall that there is a tendency to deliberately understate accounts payable. Time lags in processing purchase transactions can have the same effect. Compliance testing includes procedures to see if controls are bringing about a proper cut-off of purchases, returns, and cash disbursements. A by-product of these tests is detection of unrecorded liabilities.

Another test for unrecorded liabilities is sending requests for vendor confirmation of balances. It is often resorted to when accounting controls are weak. A letter similar to that used in confirming accounts receivable is prepared on client stationery asking if the stated balance is correct. It is sent to vendors with positive accounts payable balances as well as those with zero balances. Another approach is to ask vendors with whom the client has done a lot of business during the year to inform the auditor how much the payable is at year-end.

Other Balances

Earlier we mentioned that there are other balances associated with this cycle that must be tested. Specifically, these are:

1. Accrued liabilities: accruals at year-end of amounts due for rents, royalties, warranties, commissions, property taxes, and income taxes. (Accruals for debt interest and employee costs are covered in subsequent chapters.)
2. Prepaid expenses, deferred charges, and intangible assets.
3. Extraordinary losses, prior-period adjustments, and certain expenses that hold special significance. (e.g., insurance, charitable contributions, professional fees, miscellaneous, royalty and license payments, rent, income tax, travel and entertainment, and advertising) Some of these accounts are dealt with in conjunction with the corresponding accrued liability or prepaid asset balance.

Even though the expenses just mentioned were encompassed by earlier substantive tests of transactions details, there are reasons for going further. Some expenses are self-assessed. An invoice from an outside source does not establish the amount due (e.g., royalty, commissions, income taxes, and warranty expenses). They do not pass through the procurement phase of the cycle, only the cash disbursements phase. Tests of transaction details of the latter are concerned with payments, not expense measurement. To substantiate these balances, other steps must be taken.

Certain expenses involve complicated calculations or determinations. It is considered necessary to verify these by recalculation or redetermination. For example, income tax expense—current and deferred—is recalculated. Leases will be subjected to redetermination to verify that treatment as a capital or operating lease is correct. Extraordinary losses will be evaluated for infrequency of occurrence and unusual nature.

Some payments, e.g., debt service and dividend transfers to fiscal agents, are sensitive in nature and should be verified for correctness in amount and timing. Other expenses must be verified for compliance with contract agreements. Testing transactions for compliance with contract provisions is commonplace as, for instance, in the case of licensing and franchise agreements or rental contracts that require additional payments based on the volume of business done.

Determining the correctness of a prepaid or accrued expense balance often requires that the period's expenses be examined simultaneously (e.g., insurance). In addition, important data are obtained, such as that concerning employee bonding and the adequacy of insurance coverage. For example, see the analysis in Exhibit 7–9. An expense analysis may be necessary to extract details for filing special purpose statements such as tax returns, ERISA reports, SEC filings, and coverage on indebtedness reports.

Audit Procedures for Other Balances

First, accrued liabilities and the assets and expenses discussed above are analyzed. A schedule is prepared showing the additions and deductions during the year and the ending balance of the general ledger control account. Material and other important items are then scrutinized and one or more of these audit procedures employed:

1. Recalculate or test for reasonableness of amount.
2. Trace entries back to the originating document (e.g., an invoice, contract, working paper, or internal authorization form). Vouch for correctness of details and authorization.
3. Trace payments to the cash disbursements journal to see that amount, payee, and timing are correct.
4. Evaluate the accounting and classification for correctness (i.e., prepaid asset vs. expense; current vs. long-term; correct object code, etc.).
5. Request confirmation of balance (e.g., split-dollar life insurance) or send inquiry letters (e.g., to attorneys).

Contingent Liabilities

Professional fees are analyzed because they lead to attorney's charges. These bills are often in the form of a letter that refers to cases handled, legal research, and other work performed. That information, in turn, provides clues to contingent

Scott Interspacial Industries
Prepaid Insurance
12/31/X1

W. P. No. G-1
Accountant RCS
Date 1/31/X2

Prepared by Client

Policy #	Company	— Type of Coverage —	Amount of Coverage	Term Number Years	Policy Expiration Date	Balance Prepaid at 12/31/X0	Premiums Paid in 19X1	Expense During 19X1	Balance Prepaid at 12/31/X1
19670A	Ace Insurance Co.	80% Coinsurance – fire – Jackson building and contents	60,000,000 Bldg ø / 100,000,000 Contents ø	3 ø	3/31/X3 ø	8,100,000 √	—	3,600,000 ①	4,500,000 √
67209	Standard Insurance	fire – contents of office and equip	50,000,000 annex ø / 30,000,000 quarters ø	1 ø	1/31/X2 ø	—	982,176 u	982,176 ②	— Ⓐ
746	Trust Insurance Co.	Product liability insurance	100,000,000 each occurrence ø	2 ø	6/30/X2 ø	7,500,000 √	—	5,000,000 ①	2,500,000 √
5602	Certainty Insurance Co.	Blanket fidelity bond on employees in responsible positions	100,000,000 ø	2 ø	1/31/X2 ø	5,000,000 √	—	4,000,000 ②	1,000,000 √
9148 6X	Space Age Insurers	fire and extended coverage – inventory	20,000,000 ø / 30,000,000 ø	1 ø / 1 ø	4/30/X1 ø / 4/30/X2 ø	9,200,000 √	15,000,000 u / 1,592,176	9,200,000 ① / 7,500,000 ②	— √ / 7,500,000 √
						25,400,000 √	1,592,176	26,982,176	15,500,000
						^	^ GL	^	^ GL

√   Agreed to prior yr. w/p G-1
√A Footed, crossfooted.
√   Verified computation.
ø   Examined policy and agree information.
u   Examined voucher and supporting invoice.
GL Agree to general ledger.

Ⓐ Computation incorrect. Client should have set up 1/2 ($818.98) as prepaid insurance. Client concurrently approve all of the cost of this policy next year. Adjustment not considered necessary.

Breakdown of Expense:
Manufacturing   25,400,000 ⅀ ①
Admin & Selling   1,982,176 ⅀ ②
                  26,982,176

EXHIBIT 7-9

liabilities that might have to be disclosed or liabilities that ought to be recorded. A letter is sent to the attorneys on the client's stationery requesting information about litigation, claims, and assessments.

The minutes of the Board of Directors and its executive and finance committees are examined for the same reasons. In addition, other contingencies may be unearthed such as guarantees of debt for other parties. Information on long-term commitments, major raw material contracts, approval of agreements, and dividend declarations can be uncovered in a reading of the minutes.

Disclosure of contingent liabilities and major long-term commitments is necessary for fair presentation. Long-term purchase order commitments can also require loss recognition if market prices have fallen below the contract price.

CONCEPT SUMMARY
Cycle Accounts and Principal Audit Procedures

Cycle Accounts	Substantive Tests of Balances	Test of Transactions Details and Compliance
1. Cash (balances)	• Inspection; counting • Proof-of-cash or Bank Reconciliation • Bank confirmation • Cut-off bank statement	• Proof-of-cash
2. Intangible Assets and Deferred Charges	• Analyze accounts • Examine originating documents • Check amortization	
3. Accounts Payable	• Trial balance of unpaid invoices • Vouch invoices • Vendor confirmations	
4. Contingent Liabilities (note disclosures)	• Read Board's minutes • Lawyers' letters; verbal inquiry • Examine IRS tax audit reports	
5. Expenses* of special significance and related prepaid expenses, or accrued liabilities (if any). e.g., Royalties, Licenses and Franchise Fees, Advertising, Travel and Entertainment, Warranties, Commissions, Miscellaneous, Rents, Income Taxes, Property Taxes, Charitable Contributions, Insurance, Professional Fees.	• Analyze accounts (do expense and asset/liability (if any) together) • Check calculations • Vouch major entries to account • Examine contract, lease, policy, etc. • Verify compliance with agreements. • Evaluate accounting treatment • Inspect and confirm insurance policies	• Test of Vouchers
6. Other expenses having no special significance, e.g., Utilities, Postage, Office Supplies		• Test of Vouchers
7. Extraordinary Losses and Prior-period Adjustments	• Analyze accounts • Evaluate accounting treatment	
8. Purchases and Cash Disbursements*		• Test of Vouchers • Test of Receiving Reports • Cut-off Tests • Foot, Cross-foot Journals and Trace totals
9. Purchase Returns and Allowances		• Test of Debit Memos

*Audit procedures for debt service, employee costs and dividend payments are covered in later chapters. They are, however, basically the same as above.

Analytical Review

The host of expense and balance sheet accounts that have been described in this chapter are compared with their counterparts in other periods. Actual amounts are compared with those projected. In addition, there are a number of important relationships that are studied:

1. The gross profit percentage and relationship of cost-of-sales to sales is observed closely. Purchases are also related to cost-of-sales, and both are related to inventory levels.

2. Purchases and major expenses are related to the level of sales activity.

3. Purchase returns and allowances are related to aggregate purchases.

Key Terms

approved vendor list
bank confirmation
blanket purchase order
check counter
contingent liabilities
cut-off statement
debit memo
internal acknowledgement form

kiting
make-or-buy
proof-of-cash
purchase order
purchase requisition
receiving report
signature plate
voucher; voucher register

APPENDIX

AUDIT PROGRAM
Tests of System Compliance and Transactions Details
Purchases and Cash Disbursements Cycle

Client _____ Period _____

Acquisition Transactions

1. Obtain a list of persons and specimen signatures of those who are authorized to approve transactions at various stages (e.g., requisitioning, purchasing, receiving).
2. Check the numerical sequence of purchase orders, receiving reports, and debit memos.
3. Select a sample of paid invoices and perform the following steps:
   a. Vouch invoice data to supporting documents (voucher, purchase requisition, purchase order, and receiving report) for corresponding details such as price, vendor, quantity, description, terms.
   b. Check the accuracy of account codes charged (i.e., distribution).
   c. Examine supporting documents for authorizing signatures.
   d. Examine vendor's invoice for evidence of checking routines.
   e. Examine invoice and supporting documents for cancellation.
   f. Verify arithmetic accuracy of extensions and footings.
   g. Trace the entries in subsidiary accounts payable ledger (if one is used).
   h. Trace to cancelled check. Vouch amount, date, payee, signature, and endorsement.
4. Select a sample of receiving reports and:
   a. Vouch to purchase order for details.
   b. Trace to entry in purchase journal or voucher register.
   c. Trace to entry in perpetual inventory records.
5. Foot and cross-foot the purchase journal (or voucher register) for selected periods. Trace postings to the general ledger.
6. Scan the purchases journal (voucher register) for unusual items.
7. At year-end, check for proper cut-off of purchases:
   a. Trace final year-end receiving reports into the purchases journal and to vouchers.
   b. Examine purchases journal entries just prior to and shortly after year-end.
   c. Examine unrecorded invoices and unmatched receiving reports just prior to and shortly after year-end.
   d. Make similar checks for entries to perpetual inventory records.
8. Select a sample of debit memos and perform the following steps:
   a. Examine for authorization and reasons for the returns.
   b. Vouch to the shipping document and vouch for dates, item descriptions, and vendor.
   c. Trace into the subsidiary accounts payable ledger.

Accounts Payable

9. Check for evidence of monthly reconciliation of the total vendor accounts with the general ledger control account.

10. Check for evidence of reconciliation of vendor statements to subsidiary accounts payable.

11. Examine register used to control incoming vendor invoices. Check promptness of recording invoices.

Cash Disbursements

12. Test the numerical sequence of unused checks and checks recorded in the cash disbursements journal.

13. Examine voided checks. Trace to cash disbursements journal to see if omitted.

14. Foot and cross-foot the cash disbursements journal for selected periods. Trace postings to the general ledger.

15. Scan cash disbursements journal and bank statements for unusual items. Include the post-balance sheet period.

16. Scan the general ledger cash accounts. Vouch entries from unusual sources.

17. Scan petty cash reimbursement records for unusual amounts. If available, examine vouchers and supporting documents for approval and authenticity.

18. Review client bank reconciliations prepared during the year. Examine for supervisor's review.

Done by:
Initial | Date

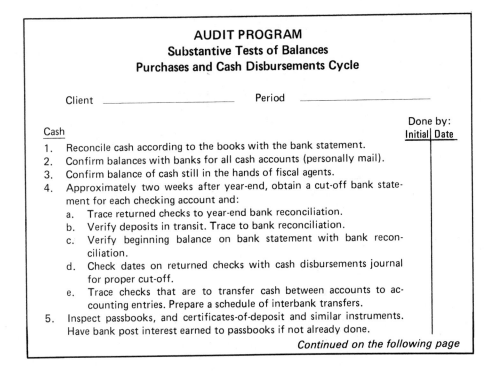

AUDIT PROGRAM
Substantive Tests of Balances
Purchases and Cash Disbursements Cycle

Client _____   Period _____

Done by:
Initial | Date

Cash

1. Reconcile cash according to the books with the bank statement.

2. Confirm balances with banks for all cash accounts (personally mail).

3. Confirm balance of cash still in the hands of fiscal agents.

4. Approximately two weeks after year-end, obtain a cut-off bank statement for each checking account and:

   a. Trace returned checks to year-end bank reconciliation.

   b. Verify deposits in transit. Trace to bank reconciliation.

   c. Verify beginning balance on bank statement with bank reconciliation.

   d. Check dates on returned checks with cash disbursements journal for proper cut-off.

   e. Trace checks that are to transfer cash between accounts to accounting entries. Prepare a schedule of interbank transfers.

5. Inspect passbooks, and certificates-of-deposit and similar instruments. Have bank post interest earned to passbooks if not already done.

Continued on the following page

6. Count and inspect all currency and checks on hand at year-end awaiting deposit.
7. Count petty cash, vault cash, and other funds on hand in the presence of custodians. Obtain a signature when returned. Trace balance to general ledger.
8. Confirm with custodians funds on hand that were not counted.

Prepaid Expenses, Other Assets

9. Analyze prepaid insurance and insurance expense and similar prepaid asset expenses. Note vital details.
10. Recalculate prepaid portion. Trace asset and expense balances to general ledger.
11. Vouch invoices for related expenses.
12. Inspect insurance policies. Watch for evidence of liens on insured properties.
13. Consider adequacy of insurance coverage.
14. Confirm major insurance policies. Ascertain cash surrender value and current period's equity portion of split-dollar premiums.
15. Review rented property leases. Collect data for disclosures. (Coordinate with capital asset audit program, step 19.)
16. Verify that properties are operating leases under FASB #13.
17. Vouch new deferred charges or intangible assets to originating documents.
18. Recalculate amortization of deferred charges or intangible assets. Reconcile interaction between asset and expense accounts.

Accounts Payable

19. Obtain a trial balance of accounts payable. Segregate amounts due to affiliates, owners, directors, officers, and employees from regular trade creditors. Foot.
20. Reclassify accounts with material debit balances.
21. Trace trial balance to general ledger control accounts.
22. Confirm account payable balances with vendors or request high-activity vendors to furnish a statement of unpaid invoices.
23. Vouch trial balance accounts to invoices on a sample basis.
24. Check vendor monthly statements against accounts payable balances.

Accrued Liabilities (excludes accrued employee compensation and benefits and related taxes, See Ch. 8, and accrued interest, see Ch. 10).

25. Check client calculations of income tax accruals and related expense. Consider timing differences and deferred tax effects.
26. Check client treatment of operating loss carry overs and investment and other tax credits.
27. Examine copies of tax returns filed in current period and IRS audit reports.
28. Vouch tax payments during period.

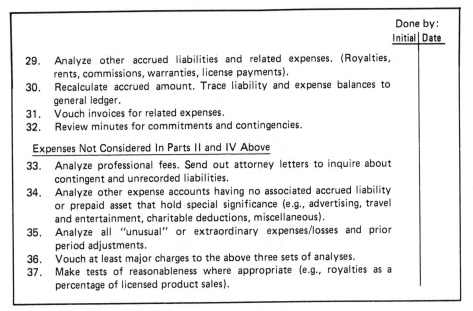

	Done by:	
	Initial	Date

29. Analyze other accrued liabilities and related expenses. (Royalties, rents, commissions, warranties, license payments).

30. Recalculate accrued amount. Trace liability and expense balances to general ledger.

31. Vouch invoices for related expenses.

32. Review minutes for commitments and contingencies.

Expenses Not Considered In Parts II and IV Above

33. Analyze professional fees. Send out attorney letters to inquire about contingent and unrecorded liabilities.

34. Analyze other expense accounts having no associated accrued liability or prepaid asset that hold special significance (e.g., advertising, travel and entertainment, charitable deductions, miscellaneous).

35. Analyze all "unusual" or extraordinary expenses/losses and prior period adjustments.

36. Vouch at least major charges to the above three sets of analyses.

37. Make tests of reasonableness where appropriate (e.g., royalties as a percentage of licensed product sales).

Questions and Problems

Questions

7-1 What are the audit objectives for the purchases and cash disbursements cycle?

7-2 An employee is considering removing a blank check from the back of a new supply of checks, making it out to a fictitious vendor, forging a signature, endorsing it, and cashing it at the bank. What accounting controls could detect or prevent this embezzlement?

7-3 What audit procedures might uncover the embezzlement described in Question 2?

7-4 Outline a dual-purpose test of vouchers.

7-5 Certain documents are normally required before making up a voucher. Which documents? Why is this so? Which department performs the task?

7-6 Only "Yes" responses to the internal control questionnaire are tested for compliance. Why? What is done if compliance testing turns up an unsatisfactory condition for these controls in actual use? What is done about "No" responses?

7-7 Describe year-end cut-off procedures for purchases.

7-8 What are the principal audit procedures for substantive testing of cash in banks?

7-9 What steps does an auditor take in searching for unrecorded liabilities?

7-10 How are contingent liabilities searched for, and what needs to be done if any are found?

Multiple Choice Questions from Professional Examinations

7-11 An important purpose of the auditor's review of the client's procurement system should be to determine the effectiveness of the procedures to protect against

    a. Improper materials handling.

    b. Unauthorized persons issuing purchase orders.

    c. Mispostings of purchase returns.

    d. Excessive shrinkage or spoilage.

7-12 If a client is using a voucher system, the auditor who is examining accounts payable records should obtain a schedule of all unpaid vouchers at the balance sheet date and

    a. Retrace voucher register items to the source indicated in the reference column of the register.

    b. Vouch items in the voucher register and examine related cancelled checks.

    c. Confirm items on the schedule of unpaid vouchers and obtain satisfaction for all confirmation exceptions.

    d. Compare the items on the schedule with open vouchers and uncancelled entries in the voucher register and account for unmatched items.

7-13 Which of the following is the *most* efficient audit procedure for the detection of unrecorded liabilities?

    a. Compare cash disbursements in the subsequent period with the accounts payable trial balance at year-end.

    b. Confirm large accounts payable balances at the balance sheet date.

    c. Examine purchase orders issued for several days prior to the close of the year.

    d. Obtain a liability certificate from the client.

7-14 Effective internal control over purchases generally can be achieved in a well-planned organizational structure with a separate purchasing department that has

    a. The ability to prepare payment vouchers based on the information on a vendor's invoice.

b. The responsibility of reviewing purchase orders issued by user departments.

c. The authority to make purchases of requisitioned materials and services.

d. A direct reporting responsibility to the controller of the organization.

7-15 Purchase cut-off procedures should be designed to test that merchandise is included in the inventory of the client company if the company

a. Has paid for the merchandise.

b. Has physical possession of the merchandise.

c. Holds legal title to the merchandise.

d. Holds the shipping documents for the merchandise issued in the company's name.

7-16 Jackson, the purchasing agent of Judd Hardware Wholesalers, has a relative who owns a retail hardware store. Jackson arranged for hardware to be delivered by manufacturers to the retail store on a C.O.D. basis thereby enabling his relative to buy at Judd's wholesale prices. Jackson was probably able to accomplish this because of Judd's poor internal control over

a. Purchase orders.

b. Purchase requisitions.

c. Cash receipts.

d. Perpetual inventory records.

7-17 To strengthen the system of internal accounting control over the purchase of merchandise, a company's receiving department should

a. Accept merchandise only if a purchase order or approval granted by the purchasing department is on hand.

b. Accept and count all merchandise received from the usual vendors.

c. Rely on shipping documents for the preparation of receiving reports.

d. Be responsible for the physical handling of merchandise but *not* the preparation of receiving reports.

7-18 Under which of the following circumstances would it be advisable for the auditor to confirm accounts payable with creditors?

a. Internal accounting control over accounts payable is adequate, and there is sufficient evidence on hand to minimize the risk of a material misstatement.

b. Confirmation response is expected to be favorable, and accounts payable balances are of immaterial amounts.

c. Creditor statements are *not* available, and internal accounting control over accounts payable is unsatisfactory.

d. The majority of accounts payable balances are with associated companies.

7-19 Which of the following internal accounting control procedures is effective in preventing duplicate payment of vendor's invoices?

a. The invoices should be stamped, perforated, or otherwise effectively cancelled before submission for approval of the voucher.

b. Unused voucher forms should be prenumbered and accounted for.

c. Cancelled checks should be sent to persons other than the cashier or accounting department personnel.

d. Properly authorized and approved vouchers with appropriate documentation should be the basis for check preparation.

7-20 The audit procedures used to verify accrued liabilities differ from those employed for the verification of accounts payable because

a. Accrued liabilities usually pertain to services of a continuing nature, while accounts payable are the result of completed transactions.

b. Accrued liability balances are less material than accounts payable balances.

c. Evidence supporting accrued liabilities is non-existent, while evidence supporting accounts payable is readily available.

d. Accrued liabilities at year-end will become accounts payable during the following year.

7-21 Which of the following is an internal control procedure that would prevent a paid disbursement voucher from being presented for payment a second time?

a. Vouchers should be prepared by individuals who are responsible for signing disbursement checks.

b. Disbursement vouchers should be approved by at least two responsible management officials.

c. The date on a disbursement voucher should be within a few days of the date the voucher is presented for payment.

d. The official signing the check should compare the check with the voucher and should deface the voucher documents.

7-22 Which of the following would detect an understatement of a purchase discount?

a. Verify footings and cross-footings of purchases and disbursements records.

b. Compare purchase invoice terms with disbursement records and checks.

c. Compare approved purchase orders with receiving reports.

d. Verify the receipt of items ordered and invoiced.

7-23 The standard bank cash confirmation form requests all of the following *except*

    a. Maturity date of a direct liability.

    b. The principal amount paid on a direct liability.

    c. Description of collateral for a direct liability.

    d. The interest rate of a direct liability.

7-24 An effective internal accounting control measure that protects against the preparation of improper or inaccurate disbursements would be to require that all checks be

    a. Signed by an officer after necessary supporting evidence has been examined.

    b. Reviewed by the treasurer before mailing.

    c. Sequentially numbered and accounted for by internal auditors.

    d. Perforated or otherwise effectively cancelled when they are returned with the bank statement.

7-25 Kiting is a technique that might be used to conceal a cash shortage. The auditor can *best* detect kiting by performing which of the following procedures?

    a. Examining the details of deposits made to all bank accounts several days subsequent to the balance sheet date.

    b. Comparing cash receipts records with the details on authenticated bank deposit slips for dates subsequent to the balance sheet date.

    c. Examining paid checks returned with bank statements subsequent to the balance sheet date.

    d. Comparing year-end balances per the standard bank confirmation forms with the like balances on the client's bank reconciliations.

Problems

7-26 You have completed an audit of activities within the purchasing department of your client. The department employs 30 buyers, seven supervisors, a manager, and clerical personnel. Purchases total about $500 million a year. Your audit disclosed the following conditions:

    1. Buyers select proposed sources without submitting the lists of bidders for review. Your tests disclosed no evidence that higher costs were incurred as a result of that practice.

    2. Buyers who originate written requests for quotations from suppliers receive the suppliers' bids directly from the mailroom. In your test of 100 purchases based on competitive bids, you found that, in 75 of the 100 cases, the low bidders were awarded the purchase orders.

3. Requests to purchase (requisitions) received in the purchasing department from other departments in the company must be signed by persons authorized to do so. Your examination of 200 such requests disclosed that three, all for small amounts, were not properly signed. The buyer who had issued all three orders honored the requests because he misunderstood the applicable procedure. The clerical personnel charged with reviewing such requests had given them to the buyer in error.

Required:

For each of the three conditions, state:
a. The risk, if any, which is incurred if each condition described above is permitted to continue.
b. The control, if any, you would recommend to prevent continuation of the condition described.

IIA (Adapted)

7-27 As an auditing manager, you assigned one of your supervisors to audit the acquisition and payment cycle of a client's new subsidiary. The key internal controls for acquiring goods and services appear adequate. However, the controls over cash disbursements concern you, so you give the supervisor special instructions. One objective of the audit is to determine if disbursements are recorded on a timely basis. One test to achieve this audit objective is to compare dates on a sample of cancelled checks to dates in the cash disbursements journal.

Required:

a. List three additional objectives for the audit of cash disbursements.
b. For each objective listed in (a), give one test to achieve the audit objective.

IIA (Adapted)

7-28 Mincin, CPA, is the auditor of the Raleigh Corporation. Mincin is considering the audit work to be performed in the accounts payable area for the current year's engagement.

The prior-year's working papers show that confirmation requests were mailed to 100 of Raleigh's 1,000 suppliers. The selected suppliers were based on Mincin's sample that was designed to select accounts with large dollar balances. A substantial number of hours were spent by Raleigh and Mincin resolving relatively minor differences between the confirmation replies and Raleigh's accounting records. Alternate audit procedures were used for those suppliers who did not respond to the confirmation requests.

Required:

a. Identify the accounts payable audit objectives that Mincin must consider in determining the audit procedures to be followed.

b. Identify situations when Mincin should use accounts payable confirmations and discuss whether Mincin is required to use them.

c. Discuss why the use of large dollar balances as the basis for selecting accounts payable for confirmation might not be the most efficient approach, and indicate what more efficient procedures could be followed.

AICPA

7-29 You are in charge of the audit of Cosmic Cloning, a corporation with total assets of $50 million. It manufactures its products in ten strategically located regional factories and sells, distributes, and services these products through a network of warehouses and branch offices located in most major cities.

You are preparing an audit work plan for the coming year that will utilize your audit staff in a manner that will maximize its effectiveness and minimize audit costs.

In the next year's work plan, you are considering auditing the company's numerous imprest cash funds. These funds, amounting to $1,000,000, are located in the home office, ten factories, and 110 warehouses and branch offices. The average balance of the cash funds in each of the warehouses and branch offices is $5,000.

Required:

List five factors you should consider in determining how to allocate next year's audit staff time to an audit of the company's cash funds. Briefly discuss the rationale supporting each of these five factors.

IIA (Adapted)

7-30 Retail Corporation, a ten-store men's haberdashery chain, has a written company policy which states that company buyers may not have an investment in nor borrow money from an existing or potential supplier. Chan, the independent auditor, learns from a Retail employee that Williams, a buyer, is indebted to Park, a supplier, for a substantial amount of money. Retail's volume of business with Park increased significantly during the year. Chan believes the debtor-creditor relationship of Williams and Park constitutes a conflict of interest that might lead Williams to perpetrate a material fraud.

Required:

a. Discuss what immediate actions Chan should take upon discovery of the above facts.

b. Discuss what additional actions Chan should take to be satisfied that Retail has no significant inventory or cost of sales problems as a result of the weakness in internal control posed by the apparent conflict of interest. Identify and discuss in your answer the specific problems, such as overstocking, which Chan should consider.

AICPA

7-31 Some of the audit objectives for the accounts payable function could be to determine whether controls and performance are adequate to assure that: (a) goods and services to be paid for have been received, (b) amounts billed are contractually authorized, (c) amounts billed are mathematically correct, (d) amounts approved for payment are distributed to the appropriate accounts, and (e) discounts earned have been deducted.

Required:

For each of the five audit objectives given above, state two key steps you would include in your audit program to determine whether the controls are operating effectively.

IIA

7-32 Lingham Company's fiscal year ends on April 30, and the company's certified public accountant, Sanders & Stein, conducts the annual audit during May and June. Sanders & Stein has prepared audit procedures for the different phases of the audit engagement with Lingham Company. Included among the audit program steps for cash on deposit with the Union State Bank are the following:

1. Obtain a bank confirmation as of April 30, 19X0, directly from Union State Bank.
2. Prepare a proof of cash for the month of April 19X0.
3. Obtain a cutoff bank statement directly from Union State Bank for a fifteen-day period (May 15) subsequent to the close of operations on April 30, 19X0.

Required:

a. Why should Sanders & Stein obtain a bank confirmation directly from the Union State Bank?
b. What is a "proof of cash," and why is it important in the audit of the cash in the bank account?
c. What is the purpose of obtaining a cutoff bank statement for a fifteen-day period after the end of Lingham Company's fiscal year?

CMA

7-33 Long, CPA, has been engaged to examine and report on the financial statements of Maylou Corporation. During the review phase of the study of Maylou's system of internal accounting control over purchases, Long was given the following document flowchart for purchases.

Required:

Identify the procedures relating to purchase requisitions and purchase orders that Long would expect to find if Maylou's system of internal accounting control over purchases is effective. For example, purchase orders are pre-

Maylou Corporation
DOCUMENT FLOWCHART FOR PURCHASES

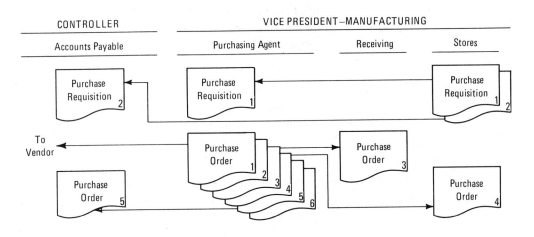

pared only after giving proper consideration to the time to order and quantity to order. Do not comment on the effectiveness of the flow of documents as presented in the flowchart or on separation of duties.

AICPA (Adapted)

7-34 The Patricia Company had poor internal control over its cash transactions. Facts about its cash position at November 30, 19X0, were as follows:

The cash books showed a balance of $18,901.62, which included undeposited receipts. A credit of $100 on the bank's records did not appear on the books of the company. The balance per bank statement was $15,550. Outstanding checks were: #62 for $116.25, #183 for $150, #284 for $253.25, #8621 for $190.71, #8623 for $206.80, and #8632 for $145.28.

The cashier abstracted all undeposited receipts in excess of $3,794.41 and prepared the following reconciliation:

Balance per books, November 30, 19X0		$18,901.62
Add: Outstanding checks:		
8621	$190.71	
8623	206.80	
8632	145.28	442.79
		$19,344.41
Less: undeposited receipts		3,794.41
Balance per bank, November 30, 19X0		$15,550.00
Deduct: unrecorded credit		100.00
True cash, November 30, 19X0		$15,450.00

Required:

a. Prepare a working paper showing how much the cashier abstracted.
b. How did he attempt to conceal his theft?
c. Using only the information given, name two specific features of internal control that were apparently lacking.

AICPA

7-35 During an audit engagement, Harper, CPA, has satisfactorily completed an examination of accounts payable and other liabilities and now plans to determine whether there are any loss contingencies arising from litigation, claims, or assessments.

Required:

What are the audit procedures that Harper should follow with respect to the existence of loss contingencies arising from litigation, claims, and assessments? Do not discuss reporting requirements.

AICPA

Human resources management cycle

This chapter deals with the acquisition of resources. We have already studied about goods and services purchased from vendors. Now we will focus on the acquisition of human resources, i.e., employees. The term "payroll" is often used when referring to the broader scope of activities involved in the management of human resources. Descriptions such as "manpower management" and "human resources" are more suitable for our discussion than "payroll." The fact that payroll is a critical function within the human resources cycle may account for widespread reference to it, even when describing functions over and beyond paying employees. We are interested in the entire cycle that deals with an entity's personnel.

Understanding the human resources cycle is a phase of the preliminary, orientation aspect of an audit. Understanding the client, and the industry and environment in which it operates, necessarily entails an analysis of the manpower management system. Our first step will be to identify the functions, and the major activities within them, that constitute the human resources management cycle. Next, we will lay out the dimensions of employee compensation and benefit plans and the wide array of forms these can take. After a review of several accounting matters, we will examine the variety of evidential matter available to an auditor. We will then concentrate on evaluation of internal accounting controls and auditing procedures.

8.1 CYCLE FUNCTIONS AND ACTIVITIES

The human resources management cycle runs the gamut from hiring to firing and includes all of the utilization and payment phases in between. Acquiring manpower resources activates a set of needs and requirements that extends beyond

FUNCTIONS

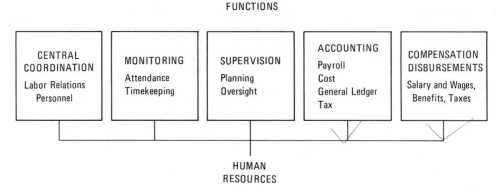

EXHIBIT 8–1   **Functions in the Human Resources Management Cycle**

departmental boundaries. These needs and requirements are satisfied by a variety of functions and activities. For example, designing compensation or benefit packages may be principally a task of the personnel department, but it will also involve the legal staff and financial officers. The functions comprehended by the human resources management cycle are illustrated in Exhibit 8–1 and are elaborated upon below.

To simplify our discussion we will refer to these functions as:

1. Personnel
2. Monitoring
3. Supervision
4. Accounting
5. Disbursement

They are also pictured in the flowchart in Exhibit 8–2.

Personnel Function and Major Activities

There are numerous activities involving the centralized coordination of the worker pool, including communications and employee relations. Most of these are either the personnel department's duty to perform or their responsibility to coordinate on behalf of other departments. Personnel interviews prospective employees and directs the most-likely candidates to operating departments where hiring decisions are made. They check references and create a file to document hiring decisions. New employees fill out federal and state government tax forms and any other payroll deduction authorization forms for withholdings they elect (e.g., union dues, charitable contributions). These facts are added to the employee master

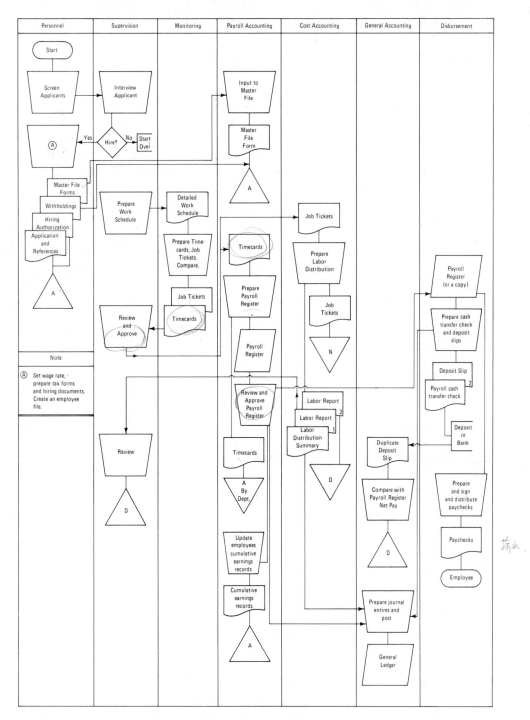

EXHIBIT 8–2 Human Resources Acquisition, Use, and Compensation Flowchart

file, thereby putting a new worker "on the payroll." The individual employee files are subsequently updated for promotions, transfers, payrate changes, and performance evaluations.

Other aspects of the personnel function involve broader activities. They begin with establishing personnel policies and procedures and incorporating them into personnel manuals and employee handbooks. Wage rates must be set, job requirements defined, and job descriptions prepared. Another activity is designing and administering employee benefit plans and incentive pay plans.

Administering these plans includes controlling the dispensing of fringe benefits. Records of employee eligibility are maintained, and records of backlog amounts of vacation, sick leave, vested pension benefits, etc., are kept. A liaison must be maintained with pension plan trustees and actuaries. They have to be notified of work force additions and retiring employees. A program has to be operated to check for deceased retirees. Liaison must also be maintained with insurance providers to notify them of changes in eligible members and to negotiate coverage amendments. Similarly, employee-related government reports have to be prepared and filed.

Employee counseling, recreation, and continuing education are additional personnel responsibilities in the modern firm. Finally, exit interviews are conducted with employees leaving the firm.

These activities are intended to accomplish certain results and to effect administrative and internal accounting controls. Notice that some are not carried out by the personnel department. Hiring decisions and setting of wage rates, for example, are responsibilities resting with operating departments or management.

Monitoring Function and Major Activities

Monitoring involves observing, or perceiving, and then recording the observation. For example, monitoring where, when, and for how long employees have been working is considered fundamental to good management. Monitoring serves as a basis for:

1. Directing and controlling personnel.
2. Planning and scheduling.
3. Billing and the preparation of bid proposals.
4. Determining compensation and product costs.

Specifically, the function entails identifying individual employees, taking attendance, and timekeeping. Detailed work schedules are prepared by management to assign employees to jobs and/or locations. Assignments may be made to clients' offices, delivery routes, departments, or construction sites. Transfers are noted (i.e., relocations to other departments or geographic regions). Lastly, performance data, such as units produced, miles driven, and chargeable hours, is gathered. Monitoring records and reports are distributed to supervisors and the payroll and cost accounting departments.

Supervision Function and Major Activities

When a management hierarchy is built into the organization structure, it is understood that there will be supervision of employees. Supervision entails the oversight and guidance of workers, with proper regard for efficiency, effectiveness, and employee welfare. It implies an assignment of appropriate authority along with a corresponding degree of responsibility. The direction and control of every phase of employee activities—beginning with job assignment and scheduling and ending with evaluation—is what characterizes the supervision function.

Supervision includes hiring, terminating, and laying-off employees. Assigning workers to specific jobs is another activity. Supervisors confirm worker output data and authorize the payroll department to pay incentive wages. Supervisors also approve overtime, "downtime," and relocation time, and oversee employees as they log in and out. Evaluating employees for merit pay raises and promotions is a supervisor's responsibility. Another responsibility is evaluating reported performance data by comparison with standards and investigating labor and other variances.

Accounting Function and Major Activities

The accounting function is an umbrella that covers virtually all aspects of an entity's operations. It encompasses the traditional tasks of recording, summarizing, classifying, and reporting financial information. Our discussion is confined to activities of the accounting function that have a direct bearing on human resources.

Cost accounting, tax accounting, financial accounting, and payroll accounting are specialities—often corresponding to departments—within the accounting function that have such a bearing. Their activities begin as soon as a new employee is hired. Copies of payroll deduction forms are sent to the payroll department and filed away, once the worker is added to the employee master file. The master file establishes who will be paid. Prior to payday, as soon as time cards are received, the payroll register (journal) is prepared. Gross pay, deductions, and net pay are calculated and recorded. This information is also added to the employees' cumulative earnings records. Unemployment taxes and the employer's portion of FICA taxes are determined. The payroll register is then forwarded to another department so that paychecks and/or (currency) envelopes can be prepared. Withheld and accrued payroll taxes are deposited into the bank accounts of the U.S. Treasury and state treasury, usually each month. In addition, several different payroll tax returns and forms have to be made out periodically and filed with the federal and state governments.

Meanwhile, the cost accounting department has received labor production data. Job tickets are sorted, and total labor costs are divided into categories such as direct labor and indirect labor. Direct labor, in turn, is assigned to jobs or processes in progress (WIP inventory) and to those that are finished (finished goods inventory). This labor distribution is used in preparing labor reports showing budget and standard cost variances and in constructing job order or process production cost reports reflecting unit product costs.

The data generated by payroll accounting and cost accounting are posted to the general ledger. Inventories, capital assets, and expenses are offset by withholdings, accrued liabilities, and cash when the pay is disbursed.

Disbursements Function and Major Activities

The disbursements function is straightforward and rather simple. Cash is paid out in return for employee services. Cash disbursements are also made for purchase of goods, services, and capital assets, as well as for debt service and other financing transactions. We will only deal with the portion of the disbursements function that concerns human resources. Normally the distinction is clear because a separate bank account is maintained exclusively for payroll; only payroll checks are drawn on that account. Prior to each payday, an amount equal to the total net pay for all employees is transferred from the general checking account to the payroll checking account. In this way, cash deposits and payroll disbursements are equal.

One of the paramount activities of this function to ensure that funds are available on time, in the right location, and in the needed amounts. Checks are prepared from the payroll register, signed, and dispensed to employees. Payroll is a very sensitive area. It is a cardinal rule, therefore, to always meet it on time. There are other disbursements besides net pay. Cash or checks must be distributed for:

1. Employee bonuses, commissions, and expense reimbursement.
2. Employee withholdings and employer payments for taxes.
3. Benefit plan fund transfers to trustees (e.g., pension plans).
4. Premiums to benefit providers, such as for health insurance and workmen's compensation insurance.

Another set of responsibilities of the disbursements function involves maintaining adequate supplies of checks and related supplies and safeguarding blank checks, signature plates, and check-signing equipment.

8.2 DIMENSIONS OF COMPENSATION AND BENEFITS

The human resources that an entity acquires are compensated by cash payments and fringe benefits. The mix of the two that is chosen by an organization is influenced by:

1. Its nature, size, location(s), and dispersion.
2. The characteristics of its product/service line(s).
3. The degree of labor or capital intensiveness it reflects.
4. Management's philosophy concerning its responsibilities.

Other factors can enter into the picture, but these are particularly significant. You can imagine how compensation packages will vary from a housebrand manufacturer of a standard commodity, to a marketing oriented cosmetics distributor, to a professional service organization such as a CPA firm.

Payment and reward structures have become very sophisticated and quite complex. Fringe benefits have grown at a more rapid rate in recent years than wages and salaries. Their cost in 1979 was approximately 33 percent of total payroll costs.[1] The major benefits paid and the related weekly costs per employee include:

	1969	*1979*	*Percentage Change*
FICA taxes, employer portion	$6.44	16.87	+162%
Insurance (life, hospital, surgical, etc.)	5.00	16.56	+231
Pensions	5.88	15.87	+170
Paid vacations	6.17	13.63	+121

The average total weekly benefit cost per employee was $39.46 in 1969 and $106.92 in 1979.

Employee compensation is a chessboard filled with pieces, each designed to do something different. The wide range of varieties is illustrated by the following list.

1. Salary and wages.
2. Incentive compensation:
   a. Executive retention programs:
      - Stock option and stock purchase plans.
      - Bonuses of cash or stock.
      - Deferred compensation and deferred profit-sharing arrangements, including "phantom" or "shadow" stock plans.
   b. Employee profit-sharing plans.
   c. Salesperson commissions.
   d. Piecework rates for production workers.

---

[1]U.S. Chamber of Commerce, *Employee Benefits—1979.*

3. Pension and retirement plans.

4. Insurance: life, hospitalization, dental, disability.

5. Compulsory programs: social security (FICA), state and federal unemployment taxes, and workmen's compensation insurance.

6. Paid holidays, vacation, sick leave, maternity leave.

7. Educational reimbursement, and in-house training courses.

8. Employee recreational activities.

9. Counseling services: financial, alcoholic, marriage, career.

10. Thrift plans: savings and stock purchase.

Payroll usually represents a significant, regularly recurring cash outflow. Because of this feature, management tends to be cautious about controls for payroll. The potential for loss is great, and the loss can be substantial. Another feature that contributes to control is the predilection of employees. They are very sensitive about receiving the correct amount of pay, on time, when it is due. Perk up your ears and tune in if you hear employee complaints; it could be a clue to a malfunctioning of the system.

Accounting Considerations

Several accounting matters concerning employee compensation and benefits ought to be reviewed at this point. Not all of the types of compensation and benefits listed previously are explicitly identified as compensation in financial statements or in the accounts. Some may not be recorded at all, as in the case of noncompensatory stock options (see *APB Opinion No. 27*). Another factor to keep in mind is the disclosure requirement for stock options (e.g., prices and number of shares exercised and exercisable) and pension plans. Pension plan expense, groups covered, and accounting/funding policies are some of the disclosures called for by *APB Opinion No. 8*. Those standards are for the firm that has established a pension plan and is funding it for its employees. Standards of financial accounting and reporting for defined benefit pension plans are prescribed by *FASB Statement No. 35*. The reporting standards specify format, content, and disclosure requirements for the statements of the plan itself.

Salaries are usually described as monthly or annual dollar amounts and are generally identified with office and supervisory personnel. *Wages* are expressed in hourly dollar amounts and associated with employees working in production and related activities. There are subdivisions of these classes. For example, a CPA firm is usually divided into professional staff and office staff, with the professionals being organized into audit, MAS, and tax departments. Ordinarily, there is an accounting and financial reporting counterpart to organizational divisions. As a result, salary and wages is seldom an aggregate figure in a solitary account. Instead, it is a set of figures—one for each unit of the firm. This splitting up of salary and wages is referred to as *distributing*. A significant portion may also be distributed to assets. For example, a manufacturing firm will distribute, or allocate, amounts to product cost accounts such as:

1. Work-in-process inventory—Direct labor.
2. Manufacturing overhead—Indirect labor.
3. Finished goods inventory, and cost of goods sold.

It is also possible to have portions of the cost allocated to self-constructed capital assets.

The payroll accounting and cost accounting systems are linked together. Both their separate and overlapping operations need to be appreciated because of the impact they have on inventory valuation and income determination. A sophisticated cost accounting system will be geared to furnish labor performance measurements based on standard times and costs, in addition to providing unit product cost data. Labor cost controls, such as productivity (efficiency) and rate (price) variances, are useful to an auditor in performing analytical reviews. They are also powerful administrative controls.

Manpower Records

There are many documents encountered during an audit that represent evidence auditors can use to corroborate accounting data. They can be found in a number of locations, so we have classified them by departments that commonly prepare or file the document.

Payroll Department

1. *Payroll register or journal*
2. *Cumulative employee earnings records.* A summation of gross salary and wages, itemized deductions, net pay, and related data such as number of exemptions, social security number, etc. It is built up from the payroll register and eventually becomes the basis for I.R.S. Form W-2.
3. *IRS Form W-2* (and the equivalent for states with individual income taxes). A report to the employee and to the Internal Revenue Service showing earnings data for the year, income taxes, and FICA taxes withheld.
4. *IRS Form W-4* (and the equivalent for states with individual income taxes). A form filled out by the employee stating exemptions claimed and marital status, which is used in determining the amount of income taxes the employer should withhold.
5. *Employee timecards and time reports.* A report showing regular and overtime hours worked and employee classification (office, production, etc.). The payroll department calculates gross pay by multiplying the appropriate rate by the hours reported.

Financial Accounting and/or Tax Departments

1. *IRS Form 941.* A quarterly report by employers showing employees' names, social security numbers, and the amount of income tax and FICA tax withheld. The employer's FICA tax expense is also added to the employee withholdings.

2. *IRS Form 940* (and state counterpart). The taxable base salary of employees is reported and an appropriate percentage rate applied to determine the unemployment tax to be paid by the employer.

3. *IRS Form 5500.* An ERISA (Employee Retirement Income Security Act of 1974) information return reporting on employee pension and welfare benefit plans. It has several variations and schedules for different types of plans and sizes of groups being covered. The report may be prepared and filed by a plan administrator (e.g., an insurance company) on behalf of the employer.

4. *Pension trustee reports.* Pension plans are ordinarily administered by banks or insurance companies. Trust agreements between the employer and the administrator (trustee) require that periodic financial statements be submitted to the employer. Information similar to that reported on IRS Form 5500 is included in the trustee's report (e.g., net fund assets, changes in net assets during the year).

5. *Workmen's compensation payroll reports.* An employer's insurance premium is calculated by applying certain percentage rates for office workers, factory workers, etc., to the respective gross salary and wages. The amounts and rates employed are reported to the employer.

Cost Accounting

1. *Production records.* Production labor costs are accumulated on job-order cost sheets or process cost production reports. The basis for direct and indirect labor production costs is the timecard or job ticket. It is often used for payroll purposes as well.

2. *Allocation workpapers.* Various workpapers are prepared to allocate costs to departments and products, e.g., service department allocations, overhead rate determinations, equivalent units/costs.

Personnel

1. *Employee personnel files:*
   a. *Active:* Includes authorization to hire, job criteria specifications data (skills, age, experience), pay rates, performance evaluations and pay increments, and promotion authorizations.
   b. *Inactive:* Exit interview forms and files of former employees.

2. *Union contracts.* Group compensation and benefit agreements.

3. *Employee handbooks:* contain information regarding eligibility and amounts of benefits available to employees.

4. *Retirement plan election statements.* Occasionally, employees are given a choice of how their retirement funds are to be invested (e.g., variable annuity, life insurance). Their election is recorded and filed.

5. *Voluntary election withholding statements.* A record evidencing employee approval for withholdings from pay. (e.g., union dues, savings bonds, parking fees, family hospitalization premiums, donations)

Other employee-related documents could conceivably be useful (e.g., salesman's reports, EEO, OSHA reports), but those listed above will be most commonly employed by auditors.

8.3 INTERNAL ACCOUNTING CONTROL EVALUATION: OBJECTIVES, STRATEGIES, AND RISK ANALYSIS

Soon we will begin to consider how to evaluate the system of internal accounting controls. A last step in preparing for that stage will be to identify the objectives that controls are expected to achieve. Eight "control objective" statements associated with the human resources management cycle will be identified. As in the previous chapters, risks inherent in certain operations and employee positions will be brought to your attention, and a number of strategies will be recommended. Some strategies are almost standard, e.g., segregation of duties, written-out documented routines, and management review. Some will serve to simultaneously accomplish two or more objectives. Basically, we are examining the functions, activities, and controls within the cycle for the potential impact they can have on the principal audit objectives, which are to be satisfied that:

- Compensation and benefit costs are properly recorded as to amount, timing, and classification. There is a proper allocation of costs between various classes of inventory, expenses, and self-constructed capital assets.

- Withholdings and accrued liabilities are recognized.

- All material facts have been disclosed (e.g., pensions, stock options, and deferred compensation data).

We will also be especially interested in the effectiveness of controls to safeguard assets because these assets are usually cash and very susceptible to defalcation.

CONTROL OBJECTIVE 1. *Personnel changes, and the accompanying changes in compensation, are authorized, documented, and correctly processed (e.g., new hires, transfers, terminations, promotions). Employee payroll deductions are also authorized, documented, and correctly processed.*

Risk Analysis

Exposure to the risk of fraud is considerable. Employees might be overpaid. The overpayment could become uncollectible or returned only begrudgingly. The excess might be diverted or subject to a kickback arrangement. Fictitious employees might be put on payroll and the salary payments diverted. Terminated employees not removed from the rolls promptly could receive amounts not due them, or their checks might be diverted. Federal or state laws might be violated because withholdings were incorrect, and fines or penalties could be incurred. Employee withholdings (authorized and unauthorized) might be diverted. These failures can be guarded against by defensive strategies.

Strategies

- Keep approval separate from payment and accounting.
- Place the power to authorize at an appropriate management level with someone situated in a position enabling oversight.
- Define responsibilities in writing, and explain how personnel processing networks are linked together.
- Use forms to record approvals, and keep them on file.
- Assign custody of authorization forms to someone who cannot improperly use them.
- Make periodic test checks of individual pay rates against authorization forms and union contracts.
- Compare manpower and compensation budgets with financial statements containing actual data.
- Have the internal audit department conduct employee census taking.

CONTROL OBJECTIVE 2.   *Labor use is to be for authorized business affairs. Personnel time/attendance is monitored, the data reviewed, and both the work and records approved. Monitoring records are promptly and correctly processed to: (a) the payroll department, (b) cost accounting, and (c) benefit plan trustees, actuaries, etc.*

Risk Analysis

Employee resources are wasted without monitoring. Employee time might be spent on projects that are not in the firm's best interest or lost on personal activities. Labor costs and inventory levels could exceed, or fall short of, planned-for levels. Unauthorized capital projects might cause a drain on funds. Labor usage might be inefficient with a lot of idle time and product quality problems. Workers might be paid for hours not worked or production not completed. Labor performance reports could be incorrect and mislead management. Payroll might be delayed and paychecks late. Financial statements could be delayed. A number of strategies protect against the risk of waste and inefficiency.

Strategies

✔ Have engineering prepare work orders specifying labor usage. Develop standard labor times and use employee scheduling systems.

✔ Require employees to prepare timecards or similar work records. Make these subject to review and approval by supervisors.

✔ Mark or otherwise cancel time records following their use to prevent having them processed a second time.

✔ Compare actual payroll amounts with those budgeted, and analyze labor variances.

✔ Require that large capital asset projects using company workers be approved by the Board of Directors.

✔ Station cost accounting clerks in major production areas to record employee time, collect job tickets, etc.

✔ Prepare idle-time reports to account for production down time, and have them reviewed by appropriate levels of management.

✔ Have supervisors observe timeclock punching in and out by workforce shifts.

✔ Set a schedule of delivery times and days for critical records such as timecards, idle-time reports, etc. Have delays investigated and explained.

✔ Provide written routines to follow for prompt processing of records through duty-segregated networks.

CONTROL OBJECTIVE 3. *Benefit plan obligations are based upon authorized and reviewed approvals.*

Risk Analysis

Employee benefits are more subject to error than irregularity. Unauthorized individuals might be added to benefit rolls. Unearned benefits could be obtained by employees. Benefit costs might not be accurately determined and reported. Coverage of eligible employees might not be started on time, or names could be omitted entirely. Funding might be excessive or inadequate to provide for benefits. Tax laws and regulations could be violated. With care, these possiblities can be avoided.

Strategies

✔ Have the personnel department send copies of authorization to hire forms, termination slips, etc. (or summaries) to accounting, payroll, actuaries, pension trustees, and insurance carriers.

✔ Prescribe the conditions that must be met by employees to become eligible for fringe benefits. Put these in writing.

✔ Require authorization for the dispensing of benefits, and keep a record of approvals, e.g., vacation schedules, approval forms for educational reimbursement.

✔ All benefit plan proposals or amendments ought to be reviewed by the Board of Directors.

✔ See to it that pension trustees add new employee names to their rolls only upon confirmation by the personnel department.

✔ Use independent actuaries for calculating current and (past) prior service cost.

CONTROL OBJECTIVE 4. *Payroll calculations are correct. Amounts are based on approved time/attendance data and authorized wage rates.*

Risk Analysis

If this control objective is not met, individual employee paychecks and associated withholdings could be wrong, thereby causing morale to suffer. Overtime premiums might not be recognized and paid. Salary, wages, and payroll tax expense could be incorrectly stated in the accounts. Benefits could be incorrectly determined, e.g., pension benefits, bonuses, profit sharing. The payroll register might contain deliberate misstatements (e.g., totals too large), and cash could be diverted. Consider how the following strategies can defend against these malfunctions.

Strategies

✔ Management established wage rates should be assigned to particular job positions by the personnel department.

✔ Reconcile total labor hours paid to attendance hours. In the case of incentive compensation plans, reconcile production reports and sales reports to the output figures used to calculate payroll.

✔ Make periodic tests of wage rates used for payroll calculations with those authorized.

✔ Double check the payroll register by recalculation (perhaps on a test basis) or by reconciling it to a predetermined control total.

✔ Establish special authorization procedures for overtime, bonuses, and other premium payments.

✔ Have a manager who is knowledgeable review the payroll to see if it appears correct. The reviewing manager should be segregated from the payroll department.

CONTROL OBJECTIVE 5. *Compensation and benefit costs are correctly distributed to the accounts. All liabilities for withholdings, accruals, and benefit plans are properly recognized.*

Risk Analysis

Misclassified costs might mislead management or outside parties basing their decisions on financial statements. The division of cost between assets and expenses might result in income being identified with the wrong period. Bid proposals might be too high or too low because of incorrect cost distributions to the accounts. Incorrect amounts might be billed under cost reimbursement-type contracts. Defalcations might be distributed to an expense account where they would tend to go undetected. Certain strategies minimize these dangers.

Strategies

- Record payroll deductions in separate accounts, and reconcile subsequent payments to them.
- Design the chart of accounts and accounting manual to provide for the necessary variety of inventories and expense categories and to direct the distribution process.
- Use standard forms, pre-coded with account numbers, for journal entries.
- Reconcile gross pay per the payroll register to payroll cash disbursed to verify recorded withholdings.
- Compare payroll tax amounts with liability control accounts.
- Have the labor cost distribution analysis reviewed and approved by a supervisor.

CONTROL OBJECTIVE 6. *Adjustments to payroll, account balances, and accounting distributions are only made with proper approval.*

Risk Analysis

Failure to have adjustments reviewed and approved can lead to these consequences. Incorrect amounts might be recorded. Incorrect amounts could also be paid out. Duplicate payments might be made. Changes that were not approved might be exploited to the personal advantage of an employee. Defalcations could be covered up by adjustments that conceal the irregularity. A variety of precautions are appropriate to offset these risks.

Strategies

- Specify a policy that adjusting journal entries are to be supported by evidence for the change and signed by an accounting supervisor.
- Require a manual signature (and a co-signature for large amounts) for special payroll or other unusual checks.
- Prepare written procedures explaining how changes are to be made and stipulating the approvals and reviews that are required.

- ✔ Use prenumbered standard forms for all adjustments.
- ✔ Restrict the distribution of passwords that give access to files to certain personnel on a "need-to-know" basis.

CONTROL OBJECTIVE 7.   *Compensation and benefit disbursements are made to eligible parties and in correct amounts.*

Risk Analysis

Risks run high when cash disbursements are involved. Fictitious employees might be put on the payroll. Checks for terminated employees could continue to be prepared and diverted. Payroll deductions might be overstated, net pay understated, and the excessive deductions misappropriated. Payroll register totals might be overstated and the excessive amount misappropriated. Fraudulent payroll checks could be drawn. Payments might be made to persons who are not in the firm's employ. To guard against these prospects, institute strategies such as the following.

Strategies

- ✔ Use an imprest payroll bank account, and compare deposits made to it with the payroll register.
- ✔ Reconcile the imprest payroll account on a regular basis.
- ✔ Assign internal auditors to investigate unclaimed payroll checks.
- ✔ Place a stop order on payroll checks outstanding for some specified time period. Notify internal auditors, and have them investigate.
- ✔ Assign internal auditors to investigate W-2 forms returned by the post office and employee complaints of discrepancies.
- ✔ Compare paid checks with payroll register entries and specimen signature cards for endorsement.
- ✔ Compare current period payroll with one from the recent past. Have differences reconciled.
- ✔ Rotate paycheck distribution personnel on a regular basis.
- ✔ Conduct occasional surprise payoffs.
- ✔ Make sure that all payroll check numbers are posted to the payroll register and the sequence accounted for.
- ✔ Require that employee identification cards be shown to obtain paychecks.

CONTROL OBJECTIVE 8.   *Custody is controlled, and access is restricted to: (a) employee master files, (b) data processing areas and programs, and (c) materials and equipment used in payroll (prenumbered checks, signature plates, check-signing machines, etc.).*

Risk Analysis

Failure to safeguard these articles can lead to records, files, and data processing programs being altered, lost, or destroyed. Equipment and supplies might be damaged. Confidential records might be stolen, or sensitive information could leak out. Substitute or duplicate records could be put into the files. Fraudulent records, reports, or checks might be illicitly prepared. The strategies below control these risks.

Strategies

- Keep payroll checks, signature plates, and data processing programs under lock and key.
- Keep computer facilities locked, and allow admittance only upon proof of identity.
- Have reports of changes in employee master files prepared monthly and reviewed by management.
- Restrict employee master files and data processing programs so that they are accessed by password only.
- Take periodic inventory of blank checks, payroll input forms, master file change forms, and payroll equipment.
- Use a special prenumbered set of checks for payroll.
- Assign responsibilities so that the signer of payroll checks, or the one who controls signature plates, is independent of the payroll department and operating department supervisors who approve and process employee time records.
- Require that voided checks be noted as such and placed on file.

Evaluating Internal Accounting Controls

The internal accounting control system for the human resources management cycle is studied and evaluated in the customary way—with a questionnaire and a flowchart. These are the key review devices. A walk-through the system to confirm the auditor's understanding that is reflected in the flowchart may also be included. Both the questionnaire and flowchart scrutinize and explore the specific strategies that have been chosen by management to achieve control. Whether the strategies are adequate is a fundamental question an auditor must address.

Evaluation of the internal accounting control system is an assessment or judgement made in two stages. At both stages, the judgement is whether the system is adequate to achieve the control objectives we have studied and to what extent it can be relied upon by an auditor. The first stage occurs at the time the control system review is finished. Material errors or irregularities that conceivably could occur are pinpointed, and the strategies that should control them are iden-

CONCEPT SUMMARY
Relationships of Cycle Functions and Controls

Function	Select Activities	Related Control Objectives	Examples of Risks	Examples of Strategies
1. Personnel	Screen applicants. Gather payroll data and set up employee files.	No. 1 Staffing and payroll changes authorized and documented. No. 3 Employee benefits authorized	• Fictitious employees added • Funding becomes excessive	• Segregate authorization and payroll. • Review by Board of Directors.
2. Monitoring	Record hours, location, output of employees and jobs worked.	No. 2 Worker time and output is monitored	• Production reports incorrect	• Area cost accounting clerks
3. Supervision	Hire employees, Schedule, direct, and control employee efforts. Evaluate and review performance.	No. 2 Labor for business use only.	• Unauthorized projects begun; time spent on personal matters.	• Engineering work orders. • Work schedules
4. Accounting	Prepare payroll. File tax returns. Distribute labor costs. Post to general ledger control accounts.	No. 4 Payroll is correct. No. 5 Costs correctly distributed and liabilities properly recognized No. 6 Adjustments approved	• Employee paychecks wrong • Mislead decisions • Incorrect entries made	• Double check payroll register. • Management review of labor distribution analysis. • Written procedures.
5. Disbursement	Prepare, sign and issue checks for compensation and benefit payments. Safeguard supplies and equipment	No. 7 Correct payments to eligible persons No. 8 Safeguard check-writing materials and equipment	• Fraudulent payroll checks drawn. • Confidential information leaks; stolen checks	• Reconcile imprest payroll account. • Keep articles locked up.

tified. Critical control strategies become the subject of compliance tests. The audit program is tailored to investigate these controls. The second stage occurs when compliance testing is completed. Any significant weaknesses in the system discovered during these two stages will have a bearing on the subsequent audit work to be done. Auditor judgements are also involved in determining the types of compliance tests that will be performed and how much and what kind of substantive testing needs to be carried out.

An internal accounting control questionnaire is illustrated in Exhibit 8–3. Notice that the questions are reminders of the various strategies that can be used in a system. The questionnaire directs us to ask how the cycle functions are organized and how the activities within functions are divided. If a personnel department does not exist, for example, and its activities are combined with other functional activities, controls may be inadequate.

Whether a system of controls is judged adequate or not will depend on responses to the questionnaire and the outcome of flowcharting. Few firms, if any, will attempt to employ all conceivable control strategies. They will select a set that best fits the existing conditions and cost factors. A decision not to use a particular strategy will result in either a compensating strategy or a void that increases risk. The latter possibility makes risk analysis a basic facet of an auditor's job. Recall the risks that are commonly associated with each of the control objectives. As you study the questionnaire raise the question in your mind: "What risks are exposed if this strategy is not employed (or is not operating although intended)?"

The flowchart in Exhibit 8–2 is a general description of how the functions and activities associated with compensation might be organized. In practice, of course, individual firms will design an organizational structure and procedural network to meet their own needs. Study the flowchart to reinforce your understanding of functional activities and to visualize how an optimum system might look. Consider how risk exposure would change if the system were structured in another way. What control strategies would be required to compensate for increased risk? Remember that risk analysis and evaluation of system controls are crucial facets in making decisions about compliance and substantive tests.

8.4 AUDIT TESTS

There are certain characteristics of compensation and benefit plans that influence how this cycle is audited. For one, cash disbursement is an important facet of the cycle, and cash is susceptible to fraud. Increasing the vulnerability to fraud is another characteristic. *Compensation* involves a great many transactions, each of which is relatively small compared to the total. Total compensation, in turn, is usually very large. *Benefit plans,* on the other hand, generally involve few transactions that occur infrequently. Because of materiality considerations, a greater emphasis is normally placed on auditing payroll.

Another influential characteristic is that balance sheet amounts associated with compensation and benefits are ordinarily not significant at year-end. An important exception is production labor content included in manufactured inventories. As a consequence, system compliance and transaction details hold greater significance than substantiating year-end balances of financial position.

These audit tests will involve observing the system in operation, making inquiries concerning what is taking place, and investigating the details of payroll and benefit plan transactions. Procedurally, auditors verify, recalculate and reconcile, follow the audit trail, and test the summarization and classification of data. The documents examined and vouched are manpower records, cancelled payroll checks, the books of account, and Board of Directors' minutes.

A random sample of transactions is chosen for the investigation of details that will reveal how the system is operating (i.e., compliance testing). This sample will also indicate how accurate and reliable are the accounting records (i.e., substantive testing). The appropriate tests of transactions details are carried out on the sample group. An audit program, such as the one in the chapter appendix, guides auditors as they seek to establish that employees are all legitimate; that

INTERNAL CONTROL QUESTIONNAIRE
Compensation and Employee Benefits

Client _____   Period _____

Segregation of Duties

Yes No*

1. Are the following activities segregated from one another and from custody of written authorization files?
   a. Payroll preparation and verification
   b. Approval of hours worked, and hiring-firing
   c. Distribution of payroll checks
   d. Custody of unclaimed paychecks. Are procedures adequate for later claims?
   e. Bank reconciliation of the payroll account

Personnel

2. Are written authorizations obtained and kept on file for:
   a. Persons added to and deleted from the payroll
   b. Salary and wage rates, rate changes, and job classifications
   c. Employee payroll deductions
3. Is information concerning authorizations transmitted to the payroll department promptly?
4. Is there a personnel department that maintains comprehensive individual employee files, including:
   a. Employee signatures
   b. Wage, salary, and payroll deduction information
5. Is the pension or retirement plan(s) administered by a trustee?
6. Does the client have controls to ascertain that pension benefit recipients are still living? Is the pension trustee notified promptly of deceased recipients?
7. Is an independent actuary used? Does the actuary make the calculations for current and (past) prior service costs?
8. Does the actuary and pension plan trustee receive employee data from the personnel department or some other source independent of payroll?

Monitoring and Supervision

9. Are timecards, or comparable records, prepared and used as a basis for making up the payroll and labor cost distributions?
10. Are timecards approved by responsible supervisors? Do supervisors approve overtime hours and sick leave?
11. Are employee advances authorized by management and reviewed periodically?

---

*Note: A "comments" column is also normally provided for on the questionnaire so that the auditor can include explanations, or working paper references—particularly when "No" answers are recorded.

EXHIBIT 8–3

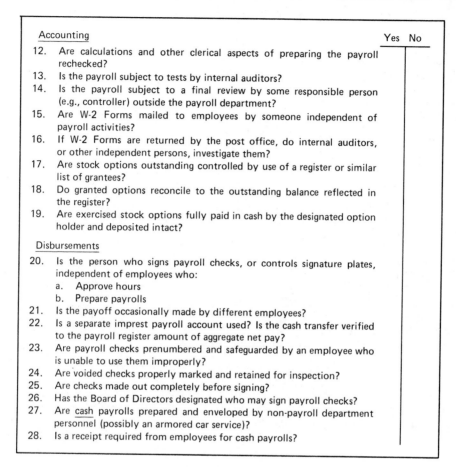

Accounting	Yes	No
12. Are calculations and other clerical aspects of preparing the payroll rechecked?		
13. Is the payroll subject to tests by internal auditors?		
14. Is the payroll subject to a final review by some responsible person (e.g., controller) outside the payroll department?		
15. Are W-2 Forms mailed to employees by someone independent of payroll activities?		
16. If W-2 Forms are returned by the post office, do internal auditors, or other independent persons, investigate them?		
17. Are stock options outstanding controlled by use of a register or similar list of grantees?		
18. Do granted options reconcile to the outstanding balance reflected in the register?		
19. Are exercised stock options fully paid in cash by the designated option holder and deposited intact?		

Disbursements

	Yes	No
20. Is the person who signs payroll checks, or controls signature plates, independent of employees who: a. Approve hours b. Prepare payrolls		
21. Is the payoff occasionally made by different employees?		
22. Is a separate imprest payroll account used? Is the cash transfer verified to the payroll register amount of aggregate net pay?		
23. Are payroll checks prenumbered and safeguarded by an employee who is unable to use them improperly?		
24. Are voided checks properly marked and retained for inspection?		
25. Are checks made out completely before signing?		
26. Has the Board of Directors designated who may sign payroll checks?		
27. Are cash payrolls prepared and enveloped by non-payroll department personnel (possibly an armored car service)?		
28. Is a receipt required from employees for cash payrolls?		

EXHIBIT 8-3 (Continued)

amounts paid, dispensed, and withheld are correct; and, that dollar amounts are promptly recorded in the proper accounts. Employees will see to it that the payroll is complete and no names are omitted. What the auditor must search for is the fictitious employee, payments to former employees, and irregularities.

In Exhibit 8-4, the sample is selected from the payroll register, and details are traced into cumulative earnings records. Personnel files are examined to verify the employees and their withholdings. Next, timecards are examined to see if the hours worked equal hours paid. Gross wages are recalculated and withholdings verified. Finally, the actual paycheck is vouched. Payroll tests culminate in a working paper, such as the one in Exhibit 8-5. Other tests are conducted on compensation and benefits transactions, as the audit program indicates.

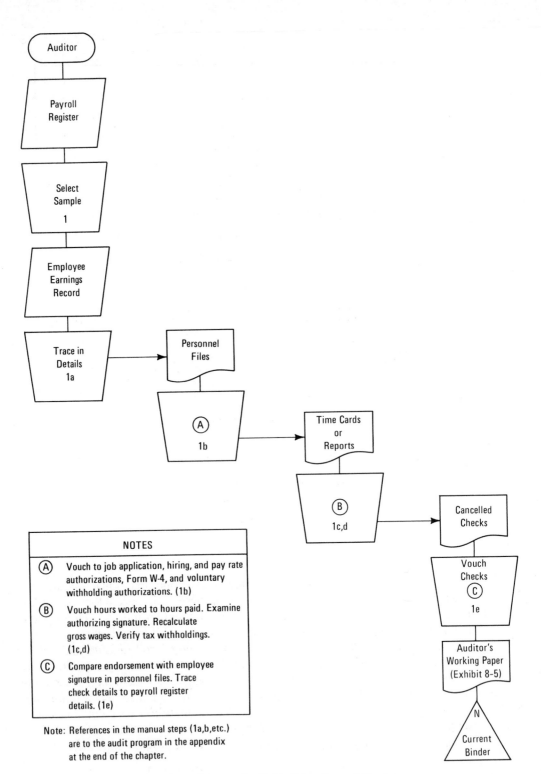

EXHIBIT 8–4 Audit Trail for Payroll Tests

The flowchart contains the following elements:

Auditor

Payroll Register

Select Sample 1

Employee Earnings Record

Trace in Details 1a → Personnel Files

(A) 1b → Time Cards or Reports

(B) 1c,d → Cancelled Checks

Vouch Checks (C) 1e

Auditor's Working Paper (Exhibit 8-5)

N Current Binder

NOTES

(A) Vouch to job application, hiring, and pay rate authorizations, Form W-4, and voluntary withholding authorizations. (1b)

(B) Vouch hours worked to hours paid. Examine authorizing signature. Recalculate gross wages. Verify tax withholdings. (1c,d)

(C) Compare endorsement with employee signature in personnel files. Trace check details to payroll register details. (1e)

Note: References in the manual steps (1a,b,etc.) are to the audit program in the appendix at the end of the chapter.

Scott Interspacial Industries
Payroll Test
12/31/X1

W.P. No. O-2
Accountant P
Date 1/16/X2

Payroll Period	Employee Name	Marital Status	Rate/Hr.	Regular Hours / O.T. Hours	Reg. Earnings / O.T. Earnings	Federal Income Tax	Deductions F.I.C.A.	Bonds & Insurance	United Way	Net	Check #
Feb. 16	James Mason	M-3 √	6/HR	40.0 X / 4.0 X	256.00 W / 38.40 W	71.15 ø	18.04 W	9.75 √	3.00 √	192.46 √	658
	Barbara Duncan	S-1 √	5.60/HR	40.0 X	224.00 W	83.90 ø	13.73 W	10.75 √	—	115.62 √	701
	Mark Johnson	M-2 √	30000/yr (salaried)	40.0	576.92 W	112.88 ø	35.36 W	5.25 √	1.00 √	422.43 √	704
	Karen Golden	M-0 √	36000/yr	40.0	692.30 W	204.50 ø	42.43 W	12.50 √	2.00 √	430.87 √	722
Aug. 31	Luke Skye	M-2 √	5.00/HR	36.0 X	180.00 W	38.81 ø	11.03 W	6.75 √	—	123.41 √	1561
	Amos Martin	S-1 √	5.60/HR	40.0 X	224.00 W	83.90 ø	13.73 W	5.25 √	1.00 √	120.12 √	1588
	Rick Rose	M-1 √	4.80/HR	40.0 X / 10.0 X	192.00 W / 72.00 W	40.55 ø	16.18 W	5.25 √	2.00 √	200.02 √	1593
	Lawrence Jenkins	M-4 √	24000/yr	40.0	461.53 W	60.08 ø	28.29 W	9.00 √	1.00 √	363.15 √	1604
Nov. 28	Deeba Varder	M-6 √	50000/yr	40.0	961.53 W	121.04 ø	Ⓐ	28.50 √	5.00 √	806.99 √	2009

Ⓐ Employee has passed FICA w/h ceiling; no deduction. Appears proper.

✓ Agreed hours worked to time card.

√ Agreed pay rate to personnel records.

√ Agreed to withholding form W-4.

ø Re calculated.

√ Agreed to a current withholding table traced to employee's request for withholding (in personnel file).

⊗ Examined cancelled check; agreed signature to employment application in personnel file.

W Agreed to payroll register; tested extensions.

∧ Footed payroll register; tested extensions.

σ Agreed total payroll amount to summary journal entry.

EXHIBIT 8-5

Observation of Payoff

Observation of the payday routine—especially when done unannounced—is an audit practice that provides assurances of system compliance and aids in fraud detection. It is often conducted only when the internal controls are weak. Observing the distribution of paychecks or pay envelopes can be conducted for the entire firm, a department, or just a sample of employees. Internal control evaluation, and the sheer numbers involved, usually determine which. The actual payoff of every employee must be witnessed, or investigated in the case of absent workers. All of the relevant details of the checks and the payroll register are verified and traced. A special audit program would be used if a payoff is to be observed.

Substantive Tests of Balances and Analytical Review

Substantive tests of balances for compensation and benefits are less extensive than the detailed tests of transactions, as shown in the audit program in the chapter appendix. The imprest payroll account is reconciled and confirmed, and a cutoff statement obtained. Cash procedures are the same as those usually conducted for checking accounts. Year-end accruals for payroll and benefit expenses are recalculated. For example, see Exhibit 8–6 for a payroll accrual recalculation.

If accounting controls are satisfactory, substantive tests of transactions details for payroll are normally sufficient to conclude that the audit objectives for compensation have been achieved. When a situation is encountered that is less than satisfactory, additional steps are taken. Total salary and wages recorded in the accounts may be reconciled to employee cumulative earnings records and/or to the comparable amounts reported in payroll tax returns. Exhibit 8–7 is an illustration of the latter. In that schedule, F.I.C.A. expense and withholdings are also reconciled.

Withholdings that are payable at year-end are verified by tracing to subsequent disbursements. Benefit plan expense calculations (bonuses, profit-sharing, pensions) of the client, pension plan trustee, or independent actuary, are examined and checked. Insurance benefits expenses may be analyzed. Payments to providers and pension plan trustees may be vouched. Disclosures for pension plans, stock option plans, and other compensation or benefit agreements are reviewed for completeness.

Some key operating statistics and ratios that would be examined in the analytical review process are:

1. Actual compensation and benefit costs of the current year compared to last year's actuals and this year's budgeted amounts

2. Total indirect labor to total overhead, with that percentage compared to last year's

Note: Employees are paid every Friday. Since December 31 fell on a Monday, client accrued 1/5 of the payroll for the week ending January 4. Since overtime during that week was minimal due to holidays, method appears proper.

PAYROLL PER REGISTER for
Week of January 4   8056892 ✓

Times   1/5   X 1/5
ACCRUED PAYROLL   1611378 ᴳᴸ

✓ Agreed to payroll register. scanned register - no unusual items noted.

ᴳᴸ Agreed to general ledger.

EXHIBIT 8–6

Scott Interspacial Industries	W. P. No.	O-3
Payroll Expense Reconciliation.	Accountant	R
12/31/X1	Date	1/27/X2

			FICA Withheld	
Amount of payroll per form 941 for 19X1:				
1st quarter	1,065,482.91 n		62,330.75	n
2nd quarter	1,159,008.07 n		67,801.97	n
3rd quarter	1,074,483.52 n		62,857.28	n
4th quarter	1,057,982.70 n		56,961.01	n
Total expense per form 941	4,356,957.20		249,951.01	✓
Salary expense:				
Admin. and selling	741,083.60 t			
Cost of sales	3,180,142.63 t			
Ending inventories	435,730.97 t			
	4,356,957.20			

n Per form 941
✓ agreed to employer's portion per books.
t Calculated by summarizing payroll entries to appropriate accounts or labor distribution sheets.

EXHIBIT 8–7

CONCEPT SUMMARY
Cycle Accounts and Principal Audit Procedures

Cycle Accounts	*Substantive Tests of Balances*	*Tests of Transactions Details and Compliance*
1. Cash–Payroll	• Bank reconciliation • Bank confirmation • Cut-off bank statement	• Payroll details test: disbursements phase. • Compare deposits with payroll register.
2. Withholdings Payable (taxes, contributions, savings plans, etc.)	• Reconcile to payroll tax returns • Trace to subsequent disbursements	• Payroll details test: check withholdings authorized and calculations.
3. Salary and Wages; Cash Incentive Compensation (Bonuses, profit-sharing, commissions, piece work)	• Reconcile to payroll tax returns and employee cumulative earnings records. • Recalculate year-end accrual.	• Payroll details test. • Review labor distribution. • Foot, cross-foot payroll register and trace totals. • Observe payoff.
4. Non-cash Incentive Compensation (Options, deferred compensation plans)	• Review disclosures and verify reserved shares.	
5. Pension Plan Costs	• Examine trustee's report and vouch payments. • Examine actuary's calculations and assumptions. • Review disclosures	
6. Insurance Expense (Life, hospitalization, etc.)	• Analyze accounts and vouch payments	
7. Payroll Tax Expense	• Reconcile to payroll tax returns	

---

3. Labor cost variances

4. The relationship of pension cost to gross salaries and wages

The next chapter deals with the production cycle. This chapter and the next interface because direct labor costs, and indirect labor and fringe benefit costs included in manufacturing overhead, are funneled into the cost accounting function.

Key Terms

benefit plans
employee cumulative earnings
    record
ERISA
Form 941; Form W-4
imprest payroll account
incentive compensation
job ticket
labor distribution
manpower records

master employee file
observation of payoff
payroll test
payroll register
pension plan disclosures
pension trustee reports
self-constructed assets
stock option disclosures
workmen's compensation insurance

APPENDIX

```
┌─────────────────────────────────────────────────────────────────────┐
│                          AUDIT PROGRAM                                │
│          Tests of System Compliance and Transactions Details          │
│                  Compensation and Employee Benefits                   │
│                                                                       │
│         Client  _____        Period  _____      │
│                                                                       │
```

Client _____   Period _____

Compensation	Done by:
	Initial | Date

Compensation

1. Select a sample of employees from the payroll register and perform the following steps:
   a. Verify details to entries on employee cumulative earnings records. Check to W-2 form at year-end.
   b. Trace into the personnel files and check:
      - Name, social security number, and authorization to hire/fire.
      - Authorized wage, commission, or piece rate used to calculate total compensation.
      - Withholdings authorized—voluntary and involuntary.
   c. Vouch hours worked used in payroll calculation to timecards or time reports. Vouch for supervisor's signature.
   d. Recalculate gross and net wages, and verify withholdings.
   e. Vouch cancelled payroll check for net pay, name, date, authorized signature, and check number. Examine employee endorsements and inspect check for alterations and suspicious details. For cash payrolls, examine receipts for employee signature, date, etc.
2. Scan remainder of payroll register for check number continuity and suspicious details. Verify that payroll has been reviewed/approved and double-checked for details.
3. Foot and cross-foot the payroll register for selected periods. Trace totals to summary journal entry, labor distributions, and to general ledger postings. Check that ledger postings are for correct number of pay periods.
4. Compare total net payroll with imprest fund deposit slip and/or bank statement posting of deposit.
5. Review distribution of labor costs for proper division between production labor (direct and indirect), general and administrative salaries, and selling salaries. Trace direct production labor to jobs/processes and indirect labor to manufacturing overhead.
6. Check court order for garnished wages.
7. Observe a print-out and machine signing of paychecks.

Benefit Plans

8. Secure and read documents describing benefit plan details. Analyze plan amendments (e.g., labor contracts, insurance contracts, pension trust agreements).
9. Verify that stock options granted, bonuses, and profit sharing are in accordance with authorizations by the Board of Directors.
10. Obtain detailed information that was submitted to trustee and actuary by the client (name and age of employees, salaries, etc.). Test for accuracy by tracing to appropriate manpower records.
11. Conduct tests to establish that retired employees receiving pensions are not deceased (or observe them being performed).

AUDIT PROGRAM
Substantive Tests of Balances
Compensation and Employee Benefits

Client _____   Period _____

Compensation

		Done by:
		Initial	Date

1. Review first post-balance sheet date payroll to ascertain that all year-end accruals have been made and to verify amounts.
2. Obtain cut-off bank statement; confirm and reconcile the imprest payroll bank account.
3. Take a total of nonmanufacturing salary and wages from employee cumulative earnings records and reconcile to general ledger control accounts.
4. Reconcile salary and wages, payroll tax expense, and payroll taxes withheld from the accounts to payroll tax returns.

Benefits

5. Check calculation of end-of-period accruals of vacation benefits, insurance premiums, pensions, etc.
6. Verify end-of-period payroll deductions to following period disbursements (e.g., checks sent to labor unions, insurance companies)
7. Vouch total disbursements made during the year to benefit plan providers and trustees.
8. Recalculate bonuses, profit sharing provisions.
9. Obtain actuary's and pension trustee's reports directly from the source and vouch all relevant amounts.
10. Check calculation of pension cost for conformity to APB Opinion No. 8. Examine actuarial methods and assumptions (cost method; actuarial gain/loss; unrealized appreciation) and consistency of application with prior periods. Obtain an independent consultant's verification of calculations if necessary.
11. Review (prepare) disclosures for pension plans and stock options.

Questions and Problems

Questions

8-1 Describe the major functions and key departments involved in the human resources management cycle.

8-2 Salary and wages can be distributed to a variety of accounts. Describe the type of accounts.

8-3 What are the principal sources of evidence concerning human resources that an auditor may encounter in conducting testing procedures?

8-4 A control objective relating to compensation and benefit disbursements is to ensure that payments are made to eligible parties in correct amounts. What risks are taken when control strategies are not adequate? How does a surprise payoff aid in achieving this control objective?

8-5 Internal controls for compensation and benefits include segregation of duties and the testing of payroll. What critical duties are typically segregated from one another? What tests are often made of the payroll by a firm's own personnel?

8-6 What kind of testing does an auditor usually perform in connection with compensation and benefits? Why?

8-7 What source would you turn to in selecting a sample for testing transaction details of payroll? How would you select the sample?

8-8 If you were conducting compliance tests of the *personnel* function, what activities would you tend to be particularly concerned with?

8-9 If you were conducting compliance tests of the *accounting* function as it relates to compensation and benefits, what activities would you tend to be particularly concerned with?

8-10 Describe several substantive tests of balances that you feel would be appropriate for (a) compensation and (b) benefits.

Multiple Choice Questions from Professional Examinations

8-11 Which of the following *best* describes proper internal control over payroll?

a. The preparation of the payroll must be under the control of the personnel department.

b. The confidentiality of employee payroll data should be carefully protected to prevent fraud.

c. The duties of hiring, payroll computation, and payment to employees should be segregated.

d. The payment of cash to employees should be replaced with payment by checks.

8-12 When examining payroll transactions, an auditor is primarily concerned with the possibility of

a. Overpayments and unauthorized payments.

b. Posting of gross payroll amounts to incorrect salary expense accounts.

c. Misfootings of employee time records.

d. Excess withholding of amounts required to be withheld.

8-13 An auditor decides that it is important and necessary to observe a client's distribution of payroll checks on a particular audit. The client organization is so large that the auditor *cannot* conveniently observe the distribution of the entire payroll. In these circumstances, which of the following is *most* acceptable to the auditor?

a. Observation should be limited to one or more selected departments.

b. Observation should be made for all departments, regardless of the inconvenience.

c. Observation should be eliminated, and alternative auditing procedures should be utilized to obtain satisfaction.

d. Observation should be limited to those departments where employees are readily available.

8-14 Which of the following procedures would normally be performed by the auditor when making tests of payroll transactions?

a. Interview employees selected in a statistical sample of payroll transactions.

b. Trace number of hours worked as shown on payroll to timecards and time reports signed by the foreman.

c. Confirm amounts withheld from employees' salaries with proper government authorities.

d. Examine signatures on paid salary checks.

8-15 Effective internal accounting control over the payroll function should include procedures that segregate the duties of making salary payments to employees and

a. Controlling unemployment insurance claims.

b. Maintaining employee personnel records.

c. Approving employee fringe benefits.

d. Hiring new employees.

8-16 A surprise observation by an auditor of a client's regular distribution of paychecks is primarily designed to satisfy the auditor that

a. All unclaimed paychecks are properly returned to the cashier.

b. The paymaster is *not* involved in the distribution of paychecks.

c. All employees have in their possession proper employee identification.

d. Names on the company payroll are those of bona fide employees presently on the job.

8-17 To check the accuracy of hours worked, an auditor would ordinarily compare timecards with

a. Personnel records.

b. Shop job time tickets.

c. Labor variance reports.

d. Time recorded in the payroll register.

8-18 Which of the following individuals is the most appropriate person to be assigned the responsibility of distributing envelopes that include employee paychecks?

a. The company paymaster.

b. A member of the accounting department.

c. The internal auditor.

d. A representative of the bank where the company payroll account is maintained.

8-19 It would be appropriate for the payroll accounting department to be responsible for which of the following functions?

a. Approval of employee time records.

b. Maintenance of records of employment, discharges, and pay increases.

c. Preparation of periodic government reports as to employee's earnings and withholding taxes.

d. Distribution of paychecks to employees.

8-20 A CPA reviews a client's payroll procedures. The CPA would consider internal control to be less than effective if a payroll department supervisor was assigned the responsibility for

a. Reviewing and approving time reports for subordinate employees.

b. Distributing paychecks to employees.

c. Hiring subordinate employees.

d. Initiating requests for salary adjustments for subordinate employees.

8-21 During 1979, a bookkeeper perpetrated a theft by preparing erroneous W-2 forms. The bookkeeper's FICA withheld was overstated by $500.00, and the FICA withheld from all other employees was understated. Which of the following is an audit procedure that would detect such a fraud?

a. Multiplication of the applicable rate by the individual gross taxable earnings.

b. Utilizing form W-4 and withholding charts to determine whether deductions authorized per pay period agree with amounts deducted per pay period.

c. Footing and cross-footing of the payroll register followed by tracing postings to the general ledger.

d. Vouching cancelled checks to federal tax form 941.

8-22 Effective internal control over the payroll function would include which of the following?

    a. Total time recorded on timeclock punch cards should be reconciled to job reports by employees responsible for those specific jobs.

    b. Payroll department employees should be supervised by the management of the personnel department.

    c. Payroll department employees should be responsible for maintaining employee personnel records.

    d. Total time spent on jobs should be compared with total time indicated on timeclock punch cards.

8-23 In testing the payroll of a large company, the auditor wants to establish that the individuals included in a sample actually were employees of the company during the period under review. What will be the *best* source to determine this?

    a. Telephone contacts with the employees.

    b. Tracing from the payroll register to the employees' earnings records.

    c. Confirmation with the union or other independent organization.

    d. Examination of personnel department records.

8-24 Which of the following is an effective internal accounting control used to prove that production department employees are properly validating payroll timecards at a time-recording station?

    a. Timecards should be carefully inspected by those persons who distribute pay envelopes to the employees.

    b. One person should be responsible for maintaining records of employee time for which salary payment is *not* to be made.

    c. Daily reports showing time charged to jobs should be approved by the foreman and compared to the total hours worked on the employee timecards.

    d. Internal auditors should make observations of distribution of paychecks on a surprise basis.

8-25 Which of the following is the *best* reason why an auditor should consider observing a client's distribution of regular paychecks?

    a. Separation of payroll duties is less than adequate for effective internal control.

    b. Total payroll costs are a significant part of total operating costs.

    c. The auditor did *not* observe the distribution of the entire regular payroll during the audit in the prior year.

    d. Employee turnover is excessive.

Problems

8-26 Two employees of the Loston Foundry were terminated for falsifying their time records. The employees had altered overtime hours on their timecards after their supervisors had approved the hours actually worked.

Several years ago, the company discontinued the use of timeclocks. Since then, plant supervisors have been responsible for manually posting the timecards and approving the hours for which their employees should be paid. The postings are usually entered in pencil by the supervisors or their secretaries. After the postings for the week are complete, the timecards are approved and placed in the mail racks outside the supervisors' offices for pickup by the timekeepers. Sometimes the timekeepers do not pick up the timecards promptly.

Required:

Assuming the company does not wish to return to using timeclocks, give three recommendations to prevent recurrence of the situation described above. For each recommendation, indicate how it will deter fraudulent reporting of hours worked.

IIA (Adapted)

8-27 A CPA's audit working papers contain a narrative description of a segment of the Croyden Factory, Inc., payroll system and an accompanying flowchart as follows:

Narrative

The internal control system with respect to the personnel department functions well and is not included in the accompanying flowchart.

At the beginning of each work week, payroll clerk No. 1 reviews the payroll department files to determine the employment status of factory employees and then prepares timecards and distributes them as each person arrives at work. This payroll clerk, who is also responsible for custody of the signature stamp machine, verifies the identity of each payee before delivering signed checks to the foreman.

At the end of each work week, the foreman distributes paychecks for the preceding work week. Concurrent with this activity, the foreman reviews the current week's employee timecards, notes the regular and overtime hours worked on a summary form, and initials the timecards. The foreman then delivers all timecards and unclaimed paychecks to payroll clerk No. 2.

Required:

a. Based on the narrative and accompanying flowchart, what are the weaknesses in the system of internal control?

b. Based on the narrative and accompanying flowchart, what inquiries should be made with respect to clarifying the existence of possible additional weaknesses in the system of internal control?

Note: Do not discuss the internal control system of the personnel department.

AICPA

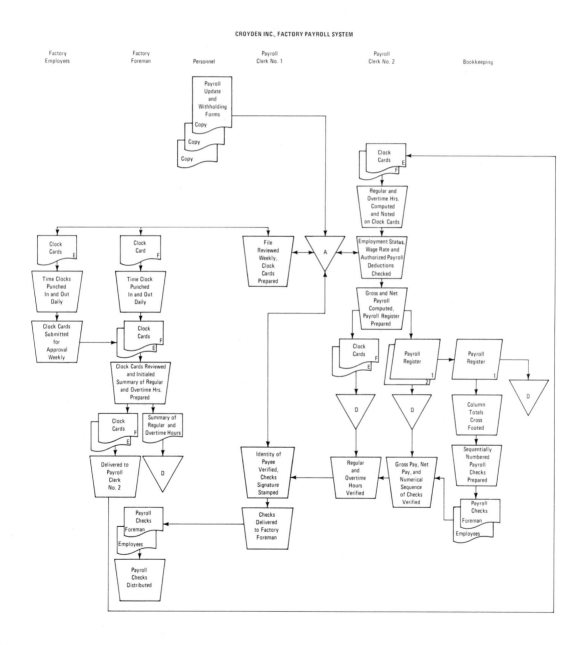

CROYDEN INC., FACTORY PAYROLL SYSTEM

8-28 James, who was engaged to examine the financial statements of Talbert Corporation, is about to audit the payroll. Part of the sample selected for audit by James includes the following input data and payroll register.

Talbert Corporation Payroll Input—Week Ending Friday, Nov. 23, 1979

Employee Data	*Permanent File*					*Current Week's Payroll Data*		
		W-4	*Hourly*	*Hours*		*Special Deductions*		
Name	*Social Security*	*Information*	*Rate*	*Reg*	*OT*	*Bonds*	*Union*	*Other*
A. Bell	999-99-9991	M-1	10.00	35	5	18.75		
B. Carr	999-99-9992	M-2	10.00	35	4			
C. Dawn	999-99-9993	S-1	10.00	35	6	18.75	4.00	
D. Ellis	999-99-9994	S-1	10.00	35	2		4.00	50.00
E. Frank	999-99-9995	M-4	10.00	35	1		4.00	
F. Gillis	999-99-9996	M-4	10.00	35			4.00	
G. Hugh	999-99-9997	M-1	7.00	35	2	18.75	4.00	
H. Jones	999-99-9998	M-2	7.00	35			4.00	25.00
J. King	999-99-9999	S-1	7.00	35	4		4.00	
New Employee								
J. Smith	999-99-9990	M-3	7.00	35				

Talbert Corporation Payroll Register—Nov. 23, 1979

	Social	*Hours*		*Payroll*		*Gross*	*Taxes Withheld*			*Other*	*Net*	*Check*
Employee	*Security*	*Reg*	*OT*	*Regular*	*OT*	*Payroll*	*FICA*	*Fed*	*State*	*Withheld*	*Pay*	*No.*
A. Bell	999-99-9991	35	5	350.00	75.00	425.00	26.05	76.00	27.40	18.75	276.80	1499
B. Carr	999-99-9992	35	4	350.00	60.00	410.00	25.13	65.00	23.60		296.27	1500
C. Dawn	999-99-9993	35	6	350.00	90.00	440.00	26.97	100.90	28.60	22.75	260.78	1501
D. Ellis	999-99-9994	35	2	350.00	30.00	380.00	23.29	80.50	21.70	54.00	200.51	1502
E. Frank	999-99-9995	35	1	350.00	15.00	365.00	22.37	43.50	15.90	4.00	279.23	1503
F. Gillis	999-99-9996	35		350.00		350.00	21.46	41.40	15.00	4.00	268.14	1504
G. Hugh	999-99-9997	35	2	245.00	21.00	266.00	16.31	34.80	10.90	22.75	181.24	1505
H. Jones	999-99-9998	35		245.00		245.00	15.02	26.40	8.70	29.00	165.88	1506
J. King	999-99-9999	35	4	245.00	42.00	287.00	17.59	49.40	12.20	4.00	203.81	1507
J. Smith	999-99-9990	35		245.00		245.00	15.02	23.00	7.80		199.18	1508
Totals		350	24	3,080.00	333.00	3,413.00	209.21	540.90	171.80	159.25	2,331.84	

Required:

a. Describe how James should verify the payroll input data shown above.

b. Describe (but do not perform) the procedures that James should follow in the examination of the November 23, 1979, payroll register shown above.

AICPA (Adapted)

8-29 The Heaven-Can-Help Health Care Association is a private-sector, not-for-profit health planning and coordination organization for metropolitan New Chicago. The association is a voluntary health association, which must report its expenses by program services (they have three) and supporting services (e.g., management, fund raising). Biggest of these expenses is salary and wages, which is divided into professional staff and administrative staff. Each of the two salary categories is allocated to the three program services and two supporting services on the basis of time logs. All 80 employees prepare a weekly time log on which their time spent in each area is recorded. Totals are transferred from the time log to a labor distribution summary sheet. At the end of each quarter, the summary sheet is totaled and percentages developed of time spent in each program or supporting service. There are separate percentages for professional staff and administrative staff. Salary expenses for the quarter are then multiplied by the appropriate set of percentages, giving ten salary figures in total. These ten salary figures appear in the financial statements.

What procedures would you perform in the audit of the labor distribution system of the association?

8-30 The Generous Loan Company has 100 branch loan offices. Each office has a manager and four or five subordinates who are employed by the manager. Branch managers prepare the weekly payroll, including their own salaries, and pay employees from cash on hand. The employee signs the payroll sheet signifying receipt of his salary. Hours worked by hourly personnel are inserted in the payroll sheet from timecards prepared by the employees and approved by the manager.

The weekly payroll sheets are sent to the home office along with other accounting statements and reports. The home office compiles employee earning records and prepares all federal and state salary reports from the weekly payroll sheets.

Salaries are established by home office job-evaluation schedules. Salary adjustments, promotions, and transfers of full-time employees are approved by a home office salary committee based upon the recommendations of branch managers and area supervisors. Branch managers advise the salary committee of new full-time employees and terminations. Part-time and temporary employees are hired without referral to the salary committee.

Based upon your review of the payroll system, how might funds for payroll be diverted?

AICPA (Adapted)

8-31 The Kowal Manufacturing Company employs about fifty production workers and has the following payroll procedures.

The factory foreman interviews applicants and either hires or rejects them. When the applicant is hired, he or she prepares a W-4 form (Employee's Withholding Exemption Certificate) and gives it to the foreman.

The foreman writes the hourly rate of pay for the new employee in the corner of the W-4 form and then gives the form to a payroll clerk as notice that the worker has been employed. The foreman verbally advises the payroll department of rate adjustments.

A supply of blank timecards is kept in a box near the entrance to the factory. Each worker takes a timecard on Monday morning, fills in his name, and notes in pencil on the timecard his daily arrival and departure times. At the end of the week, the workers drop the timecards in a box near the door to the factory.

The completed timecards are taken from the box on Monday morning by a payroll clerk. Two payroll clerks divide the cards alphabetically between them, one taking the A to L section of the payroll and the other taking the M to Z section. Each clerk is fully responsible for his or her section of the payroll. The clerks compute the gross pay, deductions and net pay, post the details of the employee's earnings records, and prepare and number the paychecks. Employees are automatically removed from the payroll when they fail to turn in a timecard.

The paychecks are manually signed by the chief accountant and given to the foreman. The foreman distributes the checks to the workers in the factory and arranges for the delivery of checks to workers who are absent. The payroll bank account is reconciled by the chief accountant, who also prepares the various quarterly and annual payroll tax reports.

Required:

a. List the potential errors and irregularities that are possible in this system.

b. What control strategies could offset the risks you have identified?

AICPA (Adapted)

8-32 Henry Brown is a large independent contractor. All employees are paid in cash because Brown believes this arrangement reduces clerical expenses and is preferred by his employees. You find in the petty cash fund approximately $200, of which $185 is stated to be unclaimed wages. Further investigation reveals that Brown has installed the procedure of putting any unclaimed wages in the petty cash fund so that the cash can be used for disbursements. When the claimant to the wages appears, he is paid from the petty cash fund. Brown contends that this procedure reduces the number of checks drawn to replenish the fund and centers the responsibility for all cash on hand in one person inasmuch as the petty cash custodian distributes the pay envelopes.

1. Does Brown's system provide proper internal control of unclaimed wages? Explain fully.

2. Because Brown insists on paying wages in cash, what procedures would you recommend to provide better internal control over unclaimed wages?

AICPA

8-33 The Polaris Probes Co. manufactures satellite navigation units for commercial and pleasure craft. The units employ the U.S. Navy's Navigational Satellite System ("TRANSIT"), which transmits three signals from five orbiting space satellites. The signals are received and processed by the Polaris MAG-III, a high-speed microcomputer, to fix a ship's position. Product manufacturing is the largest segment of the firm. A payroll system, which operates as follows, is in place for manufacturing personnel.

Department supervisors send timecards to a payroll clerk at the end of each pay period. The clerk summarizes regular and overtime hours for each employee and inserts an hourly rate provided by the personnel department onto the timecards. The clerk then sends the timecards to the data processing center, where a paycheck is printed and a payroll register prepared. The checks, timecards, and payroll register are returned directly to the payroll clerk. Payroll register details (hours and rate) are then compared to the timecards. If an error is found, the clerk voids the check, prepares a new one for the correct amount, and adjusts the payroll register. A signature plate is then obtained from the accounting department, and a signature is applied to the checks by the clerk. Finally, someone from personnel picks up the checks and holds them until payday, when they are delivered to the department supervisors for distribution to the employees.

Required:

The review and evaluation of internal accounting controls entails identifying the risks that are inherent in a system and appraising the control strategies that counteract the risks. What risks do you see in the payroll system above, and what control strategies would counteract them?

8-34 In conducting an evaluation of internal accounting controls for the human resources management cycle, a questionnaire is used. Questions are asked such as:

a. Are timecards approved by responsible supervisors? Are overtime hours and sick leave approved?

b. Are written authorizations obtained for persons added to and deleted from the payroll?

c. Are calculations and clerical aspects of preparing the payroll rechecked?

d. Does the actuary and pension plan trustee receive employee data from the personnel department or from some other source independent of payroll?

Required:

1. For each question above, indicate the control objective(s) being aided if the strategy is working satisfactorily.

2. In addition, indicate risks that are exposed if the strategy is not working satisfactorily.

3. Lastly, indicate the compliance test(s) that verify whether the strategy is working satisfactorily.

8-35 You are about to perform a test of payroll details for a medium-sized manufacturer of football equipment and industrial abrasives. Labor cost represents a substantial portion of the total dollars spent by the BUMP and GRIND Corporation. A working paper with the following column headings has been prepared for you by the client onto which you will enter the data from a sample of hourly employees already selected.

Column Heading

1. Employee number	9. FIT withheld
2. Employee name	10. Union dues
3. Job classification	11. Hospitalization
4. Hours worked—straight line	12. Net pay
5. Hours worked—overtime	13. Check number
6. Hourly rate	14. Account number charged
7. Gross pay	15. Account title charged
8. FICA withheld	

Required:

a. How would you verify the information in each of the columns above?

b. In addition to the test of payroll details, list five other tests of payroll transactions.

Auditing of Cycles—II

9

Production cycle and inventories

Production is comprised of a series of functions that combines resources or factors of production and transforms them into a product. The production cycle is the link that joins together the other cycles we have studied. It interfaces with the purchases cycle and the human resources cycle. These cycles make available materials, supplies, services, and manpower to carry out production. There is also an interface with the revenue cycle. Products that are created in the production cycle may be stored for a while but are soon sold. At that point, the revenue cycle begins.

The production cycle is not a continuous flow. The factors of production (inputs) are not always obtained in a regular and consistent pattern. This is particularly true of materials. Consequently, some stockpiling is necessary to avoid production stoppages and slowdowns. By the same token, it is considered necessary to stockpile finished goods because customers desire almost immediate delivery. Inventory stockpiling represents an interlude in the cycle flow. Inventory itself has many ramifications. It must be managed, guarded, accounted for, and counted. Information systems for keeping track of quantities and locations and for determining product costs are as elaborate as any found in the firm.

Inventory is tangible personal property held for sale or for use in producing articles for sale. The categories into which it can be classified are:

1. On Hand:
    A. Raw materials, purchased parts, and subassemblies in stores.

    B. Work-in-process.

    C. Finished goods:

     a. principal products.

     b. by-products.

     c. replacement parts.

     d. seconds, irregulars, and out-of-season or obsolete goods.

  D. Manufacturing supplies.

  E. Scrap.

2. Off-Premises:

  A. Consignments-out; out for customer trial.

  B. Loans and demonstrator models.

  C. At public warehouses.

  D. On customer's premises (e.g., construction sites).

  E. At processor's or subcontractor's to be worked on.

  F. In-transit (from suppliers; to customers F.O.B. destination).

A network of functions constitutes the production cycle and inventories. Our next step is to examine the major activities taking place in each function.

9.1 CYCLE FUNCTIONS AND ACTIVITIES

The production cycle and inventories include the functions represented visually in Exhibit 9–1. Production planning and control is a continuation of the function that began by initiating materials purchases. It involves making plans for production, issuing orders for work to start, and monitoring results.

    The stores function begins where receiving ended. Withdrawals are subsequently made from stores of raw materials, manufacturing supplies, purchased parts, and subassemblies. A product is manufactured, inspected, and returned to

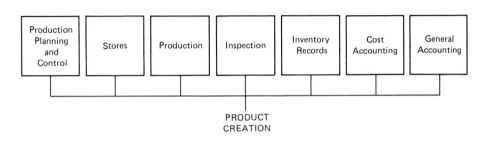

EXHIBIT 9–1 Functions in the Production Cycle

stores as finished goods. The cost of this activity and the end-product is determined by the cost accounting system. The quantities (and possibly the costs) of inventory are kept track of by an inventory records system. The costs of acquiring and transforming resources into products are reflected in the accounts as inventory. When finished goods are sold, costs are transferred from inventory to cost of sales accounts, and the revenue cycle takes over. Now that the cycle has been briefly sketched, a more detailed description of each function will be presented to show how the various functions relate to each other. As you read these sections, trace through the production cycle flowchart in Exhibit 9–2.

Production Planning and Control Function and Major Activities

Planning for the manufacture of a product involves making choices about the quantities and qualities of manpower, materials, supplies, and facilities that will be blended together. Products are designed and engineered, blueprints made, and materials specified for their manufacture. In addition, there are considerations such as plant layout and methods and sequencing of fabrication, assembly, and packaging. The product creation process is broken down into steps that define the sequence of operations and their timing and locations. Details are hammered out concerning required materials (bills of materials), manpower, and equipment. Standards are set for both the quantities and prices of labor, materials, and over-head. These become the nucleus for a standard cost accounting system using analyses of variances for control.

Production has to be initiated. This is done by issuing production orders to the departments where the work will be performed. Subsequent follow-up on these orders is made to monitor their progress. Inventory also has to be managed. How much material is on hand and how much needs to be purchased for completion of major new orders must be determined. Requests have to be made for materials purchases and letting of contracts. Standards are set for the types of items to carry, the levels to be maintained, and economic order quantities and reorder points for replenishing stock. All of these activities make up production planning and control.

Stores Function and Major Activities

The principal function of stores is to provide areas for stockpiling materials and finished goods. These areas may be warehouses, rooms, or enclosures. Goods are stored in predetermined spots where they can be readily located and withdrawn when needed. Raw materials are issued when authorized requests are received from production departments, and finished goods are released when shipping orders are received. When standard stock items fall to the reorder point, purchase requisitions are prepared and sent to the purchasing department. Additions to stores are verified and moved to their assigned locations.

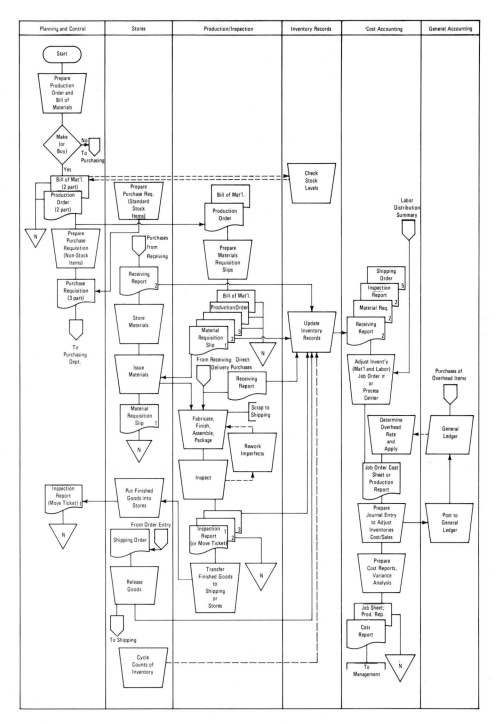

EXHIBIT 9–2 The Production Cycle

Access to storage areas is restricted to safeguard assets. Stores are policed to inhibit unauthorized entry and prevent the illicit removal of materials.

Verification of the inventory on hand is accomplished by counting the stock. This is known as "taking" or "counting" inventory, although physical quantities are also translated into dollar valuations by "pricing." Inventory counting may take place once a year or once a day, depending on the kind of inventory. It may be taken in segments on a rotating basis that eventually results in all items being counted. Alternatively, the firm may stop operations and count the entire inventory at one time. We will elaborate on the verification process later in the chapter when substantive testing is discussed.

If obsolete, spoiled, or damaged items are discovered, they are segregated from the regular stock, and management is alerted. Goods that are not owned by the firm are also segregated (e.g., sold goods, customer materials). Some firms have the added problem of having to control goods at other locations such as public warehouses, construction sites, and vendor processing plants.

Production Function and Major Activities

The function of production is to create a product. At one extreme, production is an integrated process that turns out a flow of products. At the other, discrete units are custom built to order. Many business firms combine characteristics of each and, therefore, fall somewhere in between. Product creation begins by assembling the necessary inputs and making preparations for carrying out the production order. Machines, jigs, and dies are set up and equipment and tools made ready. Raw materials and supplies are requested from stores for fabrication. Fabricated components, purchased parts, and subassemblies bought from subcontractors are assembled into a product. Painting, finishing, and packaging complete the sequence, whereupon a final inspection is made.

Standards are employed throughout production. They provide guidelines for the quantity and quality of inputs for each unit of output. Quality standards are also used to guide production in achieving a desired level of quality of product. Products that fail to meet quality standards must be either reworked, recycled, cannibalized for parts, scrapped, or sold as "seconds."

Inspection Function and Major Activities

Quality control activities are often so integrated with production that they seem to be one, but they are different functions. Inspection is oversight to ensure that prescribed levels of product quality are achieved. It has already been exercised in acceptance of purchased materials when they were received. Quality control standards can be expressed in numerous ways, depending on the product and process involved. They are specified in terms of product performance, appearance, or tolerances, as well as labor or material inputs and safety features. Quality control inspectors can be strategically placed throughout the production process as well as at its finish. In every case, they are testing to see that standards of quality are met. Products that do not meet standards of quality are rejected. Inspection reports are prepared and summarized, and the results are communicated to management.

Inventory Records Function and Major Activities

Keeping track of what is in stores and how much of each item is there, is the purpose of an inventory records system. A detailed running record of inventory is a worthwhile control tool. Not all firms have a system of inventory records. Some find it infeasible, as in the case of a discount retail store carrying many different items of low-cost, high-turnover merchandise. Others feel it is too expensive and elect not to maintain any records.

An inventory records system shows the quantity, type, and location of every item of raw materials and finished goods in stock. Manufacturing supplies are sometimes included. Unit costs for each item may be shown, making the inventory records a subsidiary ledger that ties into the control accounts. On the other hand, they may only show quantities and not costs. Increases are reflected in the inventory records for purchases, production, and sales returns. Decreases stem from transfers out, sales, and purchase returns. Adjustments are also made to the records for differences discovered when physical counts are taken. Inventory records are often kept by either the production control department or stores.

Cost Accounting Function and Major Activities

Simply put, the function of cost accounting is to provide information for management planning and control and to determine unit costs. The most important unit cost is that of products. It is used in the valuation of finished goods inventory and cost of sales, as well as for control purposes. Other units for which costs are assembled are: cost, profit and investment centers, product-line (industry) segments, and geographic segments.

Some firms have virtually no cost accounting function. Others employ very elaborate cost systems that include standard costs and variance analysis. The configuration of production systems vary as much as the degree of cost accounting sophistication. Manufacturers may produce for stock or by customer order only. The production process may be short or lengthy. A stream of products may be created through an integrated process (e.g., chemicals), or a large discrete product may be created as an individual job.

A variety of acceptable practices exists for determining valuations and assigning them to products and time periods. Market values may be used for inventory and cost of sales in some industries (e.g., meat products, gold mining, securities of a broker). Market value, in the form of net realizable value (ceiling) or replacement/reproduction cost, may be introduced in the event that lower-of-cost-or-market is required. Cost itself is a bird of many colors. Standard cost may be used instead of "actual" cost. Overhead may be actual or based on predetermined rates. Departmental overhead rates may be used instead of a single plantwide rate. Variances may be charged entirely to cost of sales or allocated between inventory and cost of sales. In short, both the production and cost systems are subject to numerous variations and modifications. Understanding the possibilities is critical in auditing this cycle.

A sophisticated cost system tied in with a perpetual inventory system involves the following activities.

- Recording materials inventory purchases: raw materials, supplies (if not immediately expensed), purchased parts, and subassemblies. Detail records are adjusted, and journal entries are prepared to debit inventory in the accounts.

- Recording transfers of materials from stores to production departments. Journal entries are prepared to charge WIP inventory and relieve raw materials inventory. (manufacturing supplies inventory would be charged to overhead expense.) Variance accounts would also be affected for usage and price (if not isolated when purchased) if standard costs were employed.

- Charging direct labor cost to WIP inventory and indirect labor cost to overhead accounts by journal entry. Variances may be involved once again.

- Recording transfers between WIP inventory accounts based on move tickets (e.g., from one processing center to another).

- Gathering cost data for developing an overhead rate or rates. Applying overhead to job order cost sheets or process production reports and in the accounts as well. Variances may be involved.

- Recording completed production transferred to finished goods stores or to customers. Preparing journal entries to charge finished goods inventory or cost of sales and relieve WIP inventory.

- Updating, at least monthly and at the conclusion of a job (batch or run), job order cost sheets or process production reports.

- Preparing journal entries for transfers out of finished goods inventory for goods sold.

- Preparing and distributing cost reports for management showing quantities produced and in process and corresponding costs (and variances if standard costs are used. Variances would also have to be distributed by journal entry to cost of sales alone or between cost of sales and inventory).

General Accounting Function and Major Activities

Only that part of the general accounting function that directly bears on the production cycle and inventories is discussed here. Various expenses identified as belonging to the overhead pool are posted in the general ledger. Input comes from the purchases and cash disbursements journals (or voucher register), the labor distribution summary, and journal entries for manufacturing supplies withdrawn from inventory and cost allocations such as amortization and depreciation. Overhead data are then provided for cost accounting to develop overhead rates. Adjustments are also posted to raw materials, WIP, finished goods (and possibly supplies) inventories and cost of sales as balances change over time. Once again, a cost system tied into a perpetual inventory system is assumed. If absent, a purchases account and various expense accounts would accumulate costs during the year. Inventories would then be adjusted and cost of sales determined at year-end.

9.2 INTERNAL ACCOUNTING CONTROL EVALUATION: OBJECTIVES, STRATEGIES, AND RISK ANALYSIS

Accounting controls concentrate on production and inventories and the information systems associated with them. The objectives of control are concerned with the safeguarding of inventory and its efficient use. Safeguarding also extends to forms, documents, and records. Efficiency begins with production planning and control, continues through the various manufacturing processes, and ends with inspection. The information systems so important to accounting control are designed to provide detailed information on production quantities and costs. They also permit comparison and reconciliation with physical stocks.

The cost of carrying inventory itself is considerable. Controls are intended to minimize these costs, consistent with the need to keep some stock on hand. In addition to the outright cost of materials and supplies, there are expenses for insurance, storage facilities, protection devices, and stores personnel. Beyond that, there are labor and overhead costs incurred in creating finished products. All told, the investment in working capital is high.

Inventory is made up of so many items at so many locations, that physical verification by counting is necessary, even if perpetual inventory records are kept. An associated danger that must be controlled is one of imbalanced or overstocked inventory items and the risk of obsolescence. Whether inventory values can be realized is a consideration that needs to be kept in the limelight. Finally, there is a substantial risk of loss possible through theft, mishandling, and mismanagement.

Eight internal accounting objectives for the production cycle and inventories are expressed in the following pages. Control strategies that will aid in achieving these objectives are outlined. Risks that arise when control strategies are incomplete or inadequate are also enumerated. Knowledge of control objectives, strategies, and risks is the foundation for reviewing and evaluating a firm's internal accounting controls.

Equally important is having a solid understanding of the audit objectives for the production cycle and inventories. An auditor wants to be satisfied that:

- The valuation and classification of inventory and cost of sales is appropriate and consistently applied.
- Inventory is salable and carried at no more than net realizable value.
- Inventory is safeguarded, all of it is accounted for, and non-owned goods are excluded.
- Inventory liens and pledges are disclosed.

CONTROL OBJECTIVE 1.　*Production details (volume, mix, specifications, timing, location) and the composition and levels of inventory are to conform to the firm's plans.*

Risk Analysis

Control failures could result in a number of undesirable outcomes. Excess quantities or the wrong types of inventories might be produced or purchased. Storage capacity might be exceeded. Inventory carrying costs could become excessive and working capital tie-up create financial problems. Imbalances of inventory between different plants could occur. Subsequent inventory level adjustments might require lay-offs or overtime work. The following defensive strategies can counteract these risks.

Strategies

- Require an approved production order before manufacturing can be initiated.
- Prepare sales forecasts as a basis for production planning and setting inventory levels.
- Set standards for inventory levels by classes. Establish reorder points and economic order quantities.
- State policies concerning make or buy decisions.
- Check inventory levels before releasing production orders and purchase requisitions.
- Prohibit custom production unless a firm customer order is held.

CONTROL OBJECTIVE 2.　*Management of inventory is to provide for: (a) dividing the inventory into groups and assigning it to specific locations, (b) controlling and efficient handling of materials, and (c) enforcing of policies restricting the use of inventories to authorized purposes.*

Risk Analysis

If this objective is not met, substantial risks unfold. Disorganized stock could cause production delays and unnecessary purchase requisitions or production runs. Scattered, decentralized stores areas might cause inventory levels to surpass those actually required because of needless duplication. Failure to isolate goods that are obsolete, damaged, or out-of-season could obscure the extent of these items and forfeit the chance to dispose of them at special prices. Materials consumed might be for unauthorized purposes or represent duplicate quantities being used to make up for inferior work. Movement of materials might not be communicated to inventory records and cost accounting, thereby making them inaccurate. Large adjustments to the accounts might have to be made unexpectedly. Consider how the following strategies defend against these malfunctions.

Strategies

- Confine stores to a single specific area or building.
- Organize inventory by bins, shelves, compartments, etc., and label with part numbers and descriptions.
- Remove obsolete, damaged, and out-of-season items to a separate area.
- Create a special records system for off-premises inventory (e.g., consigned-out, in public warehouses).
- Tag or otherwise label non-owned materials (e.g., to be processed or repaired).
- Prohibit release of materials without an authorized materials requisition slip or shipping order.
- Segregate storekeeping from other cycle functions (e.g., record keeping).
- Use prenumbered forms for acquiring, transferring, or withdrawing inventory.

CONTROL OBJECTIVE 3. *Inventories, inventory records, and forms and documents associated with production and inventories are to be safeguarded. Access to these articles and to processing and storage areas is to be restricted to authorized personnel.*

Risk Analysis

What can go wrong if controls fail here? Inventory and cost records might be altered, damaged, or destroyed. Inventory could be stolen. Materials might be taken from stores and used for unauthorized purposes. Finished goods might be cannibalized for parts by service personnel. Fraudulent forms could be illicitly prepared. These possibilities can be guarded against by certain strategies.

Strategies

- Store inventory in special enclosures, rooms, or warehouses.
- Assign custody of stores areas and inventory to specific individuals.
- Prohibit admission to stores and production areas to all but authorized personnel. Use employee badges and sign-in sheets.
- Employ guards, physical barriers, and detection devices.

✔ Keep records, forms, and other documents under lock and key.

✔ Take precautions against fire and other natural calamities.

✔ Periodically review unused (and used) prenumbered forms for completeness of sequence (e.g., move tickets, materials requisition slips).

CONTROL OBJECTIVE 4. *Inventory quantities, by item, are to be physically verified periodically. Items that are obsolete, damaged or overstocked are to be identified and reported to management.*

Risk Analysis

If controls fail, theft or damage might go undetected. Inventory records could become hopelessly inaccurate without physical counts to verify them. Inventory would be misstated on financial statements. Critical shortages of materials and production backlogs might develop. Strategies such as those below can minimize these dangers.

Strategies

✔ Conduct a complete physical count annually.

✔ Divide the inventory into sectors, and count each on a rotating basis (i.e., cycle count).

✔ Assign special count crews to the physical verification job.

✔ Have stores personnel count remaining items at low levels when withdrawals are made. Record quantity and date on bin cards.

✔ Prepare lists to be used in checking stock of obsolete items, discontinued styles, and maximum quantities allowed for major items.

✔ Use rotating piles for materials such as sand, chemicals, etc., and draw down one at a time.

✔ Earmark base stock levels of inventory items.

✔ Request confirmation of quantities stored in public warehouses and compare to records.

CONTROL OBJECTIVE 5. *Manufacturing areas are to assemble and prepare resources to carry out production orders on schedule. Resources consumed are to be within standards set for inputs. Outputs produced are to be inspected and transferred out of production if quality specifications are met.*

Risk Analysis

Without proper controls these risks are incurred. Jobs might be finished behind schedule so customers would refuse delivery. Inputs might be inefficiently employed with respect to production outputs. Unauthorized substitution of direct materials could be made to the detriment of the product. Inferior quality products might be transferred out of production and remain in stores unsalable. Materials might be requisitioned, diverted, and masked as defective discards. Scrap might be understated or unreported, sold, and the proceeds diverted. Good products might be smuggled out in scrap. Combating these risks are defensive strategies.

Strategies

✔ Require that production materials, parts, and subassemblies be requisitioned on the basis of production orders and bills of materials.

✔ Prepare work schedules well in advance to integrate various open production orders. Establish a system for setting job priority.

✔ Prepare backlog and production output reports for management.

✔ Set direct material and direct labor standards to control factor inputs.

✔ Require that products be inspected for conformity to quality control specifications.

✔ Use prenumbered inspection reports or move tickets for transferring products between departments and to finished goods stores.

✔ Establish a policy for determination and treatment of rework, discards, and "seconds."

✔ Segregate and inspect scrap to ensure that nothing else is included and to gain control of quantities. Prepare scrap reports.

CONTROL OBJECTIVE 6. *Detailed records of inventory are to be maintained. Materials acquired and used and products produced and sold are to be promptly and accurately recorded.*

Risk Analysis

The risks exposed by control failures in this area are related to inventory. Unnecessary purchasing or production could occur if records were not available to indicate stock levels. Inventory might be stolen or improperly used in the absence of detailed records to point out discrepancies. Frequent, complete physical counts, with attendant high costs and production stoppages, might be necessary. Imbalances of individual inventory items could occur. Slow-moving items might not be identified in time to take corrective action. However, these possibilities can be avoided with strategic controls.

Strategies

✔ Organize an inventory records department. Segregate it from storekeeping and production.

✔ Set up a perpetual inventory record for every item of raw materials, purchased parts, subassemblies, and finished goods.

✔ Assign serial numbers to all inventory items and location addresses for all stores areas.

✔ Require that every addition and withdrawal of inventory be supported by a document that is forwarded to inventory records.

✔ Reconcile and adjust inventory records to agree with periodic physical counts. Investigate major discrepancies.

✔ Require that adjustments to inventory records be approved by management.

CONTROL OBJECTIVE 7.   *Production costs are to be accurately and promptly accumulated and classified. The cost of goods produced is to be accurately and promptly determined. Cost valuations are to be consistently applied in accordance with prescribed cost flow assumptions and evaluated against market prices periodically.*

Risk Analysis

If these objectives are not met, the following problems may arise. Information for comparison of actual results with standards might be unavailable. Interim financial statements might be impossible to prepare, or highly unreliable. An improper division of period and product costs and improper matching of costs and revenues could occur. Inventory valuation might be incorrect. Pricing policy might be misguided by poor cost information. Bid proposals based on cost data could result in unprofitable contracts. Cost information might be inadequate for management control purposes (e.g., inability to explain where and why excessive costs were incurred). A variety of mitigating strategies can be employed.

Strategies

✔ Prepare written procedures and policies for recording and assigning cost data.

✔ Issue account codes and descriptions for WIP inventory and overhead detail accounts.

✔ Employ cost records for individual jobs or production runs.

✔ Reconcile production costs added to cost records with the sources of cost data (e.g., payroll, purchases).

✔ Set predetermined departmental overhead rates. Revise as needed to keep them current.

✔ Use a standard journal entry register and prenumbered standard journal entry forms for transmitting and recording cost data.

✔ Analyze cost variances and investigate unusual amounts.

✔ Have cost reports prepared showing input costs, variances, and product costs.

CONTROL OBJECTIVE 8. *Transactions affecting inventory, cost of sales, overhead applied, and detailed overhead expenses are promptly recorded, classified, and summarized in the accounts in the proper time period.*

Risk Analysis

The risks faced here concern financial accounting. Accounts might be incorrectly stated and have to be adjusted by substantial amounts. Subsidiary records could fall out of balance with control accounts. Cut-off at year-end might be incorrect, thereby causing financial information to be wrong. To offset these risks, strategies such as the following can be inaugurated.

Strategies

- ✔ Reconcile WIP inventory control accounts to cost records periodically.
- ✔ Reconcile raw materials and finished goods inventory control accounts to perpetual inventory records (if unit costs are kept).
- ✔ Reconcile offsetting changes in control accounts (e.g., credits to finished goods inventory with cost-of-sales debits).
- ✔ Require that adjustments to the accounts be reviewed and approved by management.
- ✔ Adjust the accounts to agree with physical count of inventory.
- ✔ Set up a manufacturing overhead control account and reconcile to detail expense accounts periodically.

Evaluating Internal Accounting Controls

Evaluation of internal accounting controls focuses on those strategies that should prevent or detect errors and irregularities. An initial step is to isolate the types of errors and irregularities that could occur with production transactions and related assets. Of chief interest are possible malfunctions that are both likely and significant. Then, accounting controls are searched for that should prevent or detect these errors and irregularities. Both steps are facilitated by:

1. Being aware of control objectives and strategies that are commonly employed.
2. Understanding the risks that are exposed when control strategies are inadequate or absent.
3. Systematically analyzing the accounting controls that are present.

A systematic analysis of accounting controls is accomplished by flowcharting and completing an internal control questionnaire. Every firm has some combination of internal controls for production and inventory. However, the networks that are

CONCEPT SUMMARY
Relationships of Cycle Functions and Controls

Function	Select Activities	Related Control Objective	Examples of Risks	Examples of Strategies
1. Production Planning and Control	Select manufacturing, processes and standards. Issue production orders.	No. 1 Production and inventory details should conform to plans.	• Excessive or wrong types of goods produced.	• Sales forecasts and production orders. • Standards for inventory levels.
2. Stores	Stockpile and control materials and finished goods. Make periodic counts of stock.	No. 2 Inventory in stores is to be organized and controlled. No. 3 Safeguard inventory. No. 4 Verify inventory.	• High stock levels and production delays. • Inventory stolen. • Undetected theft, losses.	• Physical compartments and prenumbered requisition forms. • Employee badges; guards. • Cycle counts.
3. Production	Assemble inputs and create products.	No. 5 Produce goods efficiently and on time.	• Delivery delays; lost customers; wasted materials.	• Production orders and work schedules. • Standards for labor, materials, and scrap.
4. Inspection	Test products for quality.	No. 5 Approve products if quality standards are met.	• Inferior, unsalable goods.	• Quality control standards. • Inspection reports.
5. Inventory Records	Maintain details of materials and products in stock.	No. 3 Safeguard inventory records. No. 6 Keep track of all inventory items.	• Altered or lost records. • Unnecessary purchases or production.	• Keep records locked up. • Perpetual inventory records.
6. Cost Accounting	Determine unit costs. Provide planning and control information.	No. 7 Record accurate, timely production costs.	• Incorrect inventory values. • Misguided pricing policy.	• Detailed costs records by job or process. • Predetermined overhead rate(s).
7. General Accounting	Make entries for inventories, overhead costs, and cost of sales.	No. 8 Inventory and production transactions are properly recorded.	• Incorrect accounts requiring large adjustments. • Misstated income.	• Reconcile control accounts to detail records every month.

designed to process production transactions and achieve control are unique in the way they combine various features. They use physical safeguards, procedural checks and balances, an accounting infrastructure, and segregation of duties in different ways. Each cycle function must be placed under the microscope. Details of how the system is structured are the object of our search.

Are activities in the various functions segregated so that incompatible duties are not assigned to one individual? For example, inventory custody and inventory record keeping should not be the responsibility of the same person. Inquiries guided by the internal control questionnaire pinpoint duties that are properly segregated as well as those that are not. Study Exhibit 9–3 to get a better idea of relevant questions that should be asked. Notice too, how the flowchart in Exhibit 9–2 integrates the many parts of a system into a whole. Appropriately segregated

INTERNAL CONTROL QUESTIONNAIRE
Production Cycle and Inventories

Client _____ Period _____

Segregation of Functions Yes No*

1. Are the functions listed below segregated from one another?

Production Planning and Control

2. Are production budgets prepared?
3. Are production orders based on:
   a. projected needs for stock
   b. customer orders received
4. Are bills-of-materials revised often enough to be current?
5. Are make-or-buy decision procedures systematically followed?
6. Are affiliates given advantages in make-or-buy decisions?
7. Is purchasing of materials based on bills of materials?
8. Are production backlog and available productive capacity reports prepared?

Stores

9. Is custody of inventory assigned to a specific individual?
10. Are physical safeguards against the elements, theft, and unauthorized withdrawal of inventory adequate?
11. Is access to stores areas restricted?
12. Are additions to inventory verified against supporting documents for quantity, kind, and condition?
13. Are inventory withdrawals prohibited without an approved shipping order or materials requisition slip?
14. Are material requisition slips and shipping orders forwarded to inventory records for adjustment?
15. Are storekeepers instructed to report items that are overstocked, damaged, or unsalable?
16. Is management approval required for disposal of unusable or unsalable items?
17. Is control over off-premises (e.g., public warehouses, consigned-out) items adequate?
18. Are non-owned items (e.g., for repair or processing) readily identifiable and adequately controlled?
19. Is inventory counted on a cycle basis during the year?
20. Are cycle counts supervised and conducted by independent persons?
21. Are the client's written instructions for physical counts sufficiently comprehensive?

---

*Note: A "comments" column is also normally provided for on the questionnaire so that the auditor can include explanations or working paper references—particularly when "No" answers are recorded.

continued on the following page

EXHIBIT 9-3

	Yes	No

22. Are prenumbered count tags or count sheets used? Are they initialed by the employees taking the count?
23. Are assignment sheets used for physical counts and all tags accounted for?
24. Are inventory records adjusted for discrepancies discovered by the counting?
25. Are counts and arithmetic on count sheets and summaries checked by a second person?
26. Are goods owned but not on the premises either confirmed or counted at least annually?

Production and Inspection

27. Are quality control standards set in writing?
28. Have production standards been set for materials, scrap, labor?
29. Is preparation of materials requisition slips by anyone other than production supervisors prohibited?
30. Is an inspection report or move ticket prepared for goods transferred from production to stores?
31. Are quantities of scrap recorded by production and then promptly transferred for recycling or sale?

Inventory Records

32. Is a perpetual inventory system used?
33. Does it include costs, not just quantities?
34. Are cost records reconciled with general ledger controls periodically?
35. Are stock levels checked against bills-of-materials prior to placing purchase requisitions?
36. Are records promptly adjusted to cycle counts of amounts on hand if differences exist?
37. Are physical count–book amount differences usually of reasonable size?
38. Is management approval required for adjustments to inventory records?
39. Do records satisfactorily identify owned inventory items off premises?
40. Are non-owned goods satisfactorily identified by the inventory records?
41. Are changes to inventory records made only from properly authorized documents (e.g., materials requisition slips, shipping orders, receiving reports, journal entries)?
42. Are records reviewed periodically for slow-moving and obsolete items?

EXHIBIT 9–3 (Continued)

Cost Accounting	Yes	No
43. Are standard costs employed? Are they integrated with the accounting records?		
44. Are standards reviewed at least annually?		
45. Are cost variances calculated and reported?		
46. Is the disposition of variances reasonable?		
47. Are data entered into the cost system from prenumbered, approved documents only (e.g., receiving reports, shipping orders, materials requisition slips, move tickets)?		
48. Are subsidiary cost records (job order sheets/production reports) reconciled to general ledger controls for WIP inventory?		
49. Are bases for valuation (e.g., actual cost) and method of determining cost flows (FIFO, LIFO) consistent with prior years?		
50. Does inventory cost include freight, duty, and insurance and exclude rebates, discounts, and allowances?		
51. Is the composition of overhead reasonable (e.g., full absorption)?		
52. Is the basis for applying overhead reasonable and consistent with prior years?		
53. Are overhead rates adjusted frequently enough to reflect current conditions?		
54. Is intercompany profit on inventory transfers clearly identified?		
55. Are periodic cost-production reports distributed to management?		
General Accounting		
56. Are journal entries to reflect receipts, transfers, and withdrawals to inventory and cost of sales accounts reviewed and approved?		

EXHIBIT 9–3 (Continued)

duties are control strengths; inadequately segregated duties are weaknesses. A weakness provides little assurance that errors and irregularities will be promptly detected. In fact, a weakness at a critical point should prompt an investigation to see whether errors or irregularities have already occurred. It should also be pointed out in the management letter.

What controls exist for safeguarding inventory? Measures such as special rooms, warehouses, and enclosures are important. Equally important are policies that restrict access to stores and production areas. Assigning custody of materials to specific persons is a basic, but effective, tactic. If these individuals physically verify materials coming into or exiting from stores, controls are enhanced even more.

A series of questions is asked about procedural controls and the accounting system. The cost system should provide valid and consistent valuations for goods that are produced. A system of inventory records contributes immensely to control because it reflects materials and finished goods on hand and their movements. How do these systems operate and how sophisticated are they? Procedural controls such as review, authorization, and the creation of documents to move materials are also the subject of auditor inquiry.

By the time a review of accounting controls is finished, it will be clear what systems, safeguards, and procedures exist and how duties are segregated. A judgement can then be made about strengths and weaknesses of the client's internal accounting controls. Strengths that can be relied upon will be tested for compliance. That is our next subject.

9.3 TESTING CONTROLS AND TRANSACTIONS DETAILS

An audit program is now constructed to test the control strengths that were identified in the review of internal accounting controls. Compliance tests and concurrent tests of transactions details concentrate on:

1. the product creation system (planning and control; manufacturing and inspection; stores).
2. the inventory records system.
3. the cost system.

In distinguishing between these systems, the following ideas are important. The product creation system is a transformation process, combining and converting quantities of manpower, materials, services, and facilities (factors of production) into units of product. Both inputs and outputs are quantities expressed in real terms.

The cost system gathers cost data generated by the product creation system and develops unit costs of product. In other words, dollar counterparts (payroll and purchases costs, cost allocations) of real manufacturing inputs are accumulated using job order or process cost systems and reduced to a unit cost basis.

The inventory records system maintains detailed information on quantities of materials. These data reflect raw materials, purchased parts and subassemblies (inputs ready to enter production), and finished goods that have emerged from production. Unit costs may be included for each physical item, but that is not a necessary condition. If unit costs are maintained, their source will be vendor invoices for inputs ready to enter production and unit costs developed by the cost system for finished goods coming out of production. Standard costs can be used in lieu of actual costs.

The cost system and inventory records system (with unit costs) are vital to asset valuation and income determination and the consistent measurement of both. To start with, some costs are accumulated (inventoried), while others are immediately charged to expense. That demarcation is important because it affects the periodic measure of income. Costs that are accumulated are then assigned to cost of sales and inventories. Cost of sales for public corporations must be

CONCEPT SUMMARY
Systems On Which Tests of Details Focus

Production Cycle System	*Relationship to Production*
Product Creation System	Combines factors of production: labor, materials, etc. (expressed in real terms: lbs. hrs. units of product.)
Cost System	Costs from the product creation system (expressed in dollar terms: labor, materials, and overhead costs invested in work-in-process inventory.)
Inventory Records System	I. Raw Materials: Waiting transfer into product creation system. (expressed in quantities and possibly costs from vendors) II. Finished Goods: Emerged from product creation system. (expressed in quantities and possibly costs from the cost system.)

further divided into segment data by industry and geographic region. Inventory costs are also divided into classes—raw materials, WIP and finished goods. Lastly, valuation of the WIP and finished goods ending inventory count depends completely on unit cost data generated by the cost system. If management's representations of inventory and income—in the aggregate and by subdivisions—are to be acceptable, these systems must be operating well.

There is an audit program for compliance tests and substantive tests of transactions details in the appendix to this chapter. Production transactions are substantiated by testing to see whether:

1. The cost system properly reflects product costs by element and assigns them to jobs (or process centers), units of product, and classes of inventory according to prescribed cost flow assumptions consistently applied.

2. The inventory records system accurately reflects all additions and withdrawals of raw materials and finished goods. Furthermore, that unit costs are correct in amount and assigned according to prescribed cost flow assumptions consistently applied.

Test No. 19 from the audit program accomplishes the first objective. Cost records are vouched to supporting documents and into the inventory records where unit cost data are maintained. Exhibit 9–4 illustrates the audit tests that culminate in the working paper illustrated in Exhibit 9–5.

The second objective is accomplished by audit program tests 6 through 9. There are several kinds of documents that result in entries being made to the inventory records. These transaction documents (receiving reports, material requisition slips, inspection reports or move tickets, and shipping orders) are traced to the inventory records on a sample basis.

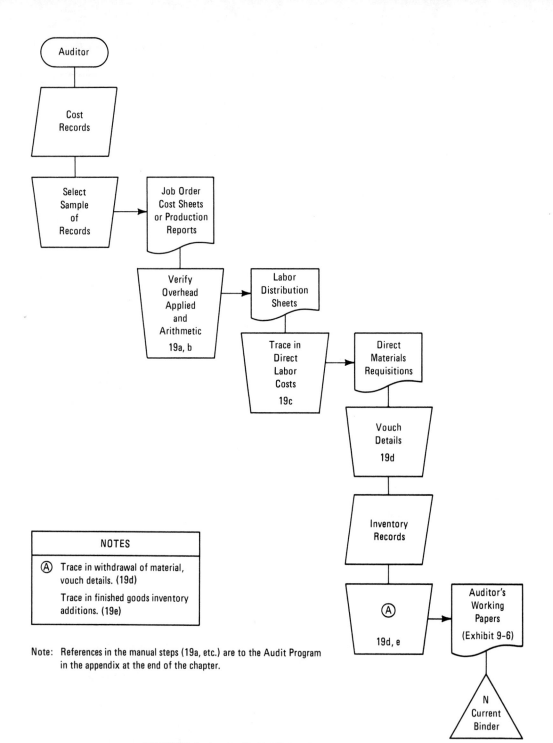

Auditor

Cost Records

Select Sample of Records

Job Order Cost Sheets or Production Reports

Verify Overhead Applied and Arithmetic
19a, b

Labor Distribution Sheets

Trace in Direct Labor Costs
19c

Direct Materials Requisitions

Vouch Details
19d

Inventory Records

Ⓐ
19d, e

Auditor's Working Papers
(Exhibit 9-6)

N
Current Binder

NOTES

Ⓐ Trace in withdrawal of material, vouch details. (19d)

Trace in finished goods inventory additions. (19e)

Note: References in the manual steps (19a, etc.) are to the Audit Program in the appendix at the end of the chapter.

EXHIBIT 9–4   Audit Trail for Test of Cost Reports

W. P. No.	F-1
ACCOUNTANT	RKS
DATE	11/10/X1

Scott Interspacial Industries
Test of Cost Reports
12/31/X1

Production Period	Job Order No. / Model No.	Materials	Direct Labor	Applied Overhead (150%)	Total Cost
Feb.	B-4-X9J / X9J	241050 ✓	68156 n	102234 t	411440 ⌀ a
Feb.	B-1-R3D3 / R3D3	6080975 ✓	1288193 n	1932740 t	9302208 ⌀ a
June	F-18-B2Q / B2Q	62100 ✓	84806 n	127209 t	274115 ⌀ a
Sept.	J-7-R3D3 / R3D3	7648000 ✓	1388912 n	2083368 t	11120280 ⌀ a

✓ Traced direct materials cost per report to materials requisition slips. Vouched for authorization, job number, quantity and description. Traced material requisition into detail inventory records. Vouched for quantity and cost. No errors noted.

n Traced direct labor charges to labor distribution sheet for the period.

t Tested application of overhead to direct labor $. Treatment appears proper and consistent with prior years. See w/p F-6 for review of overhead rate calculation.

⌀ Verified mathematical accuracy of cost report. No errors noted.

a Traced job cost to detail inventory records.

EXHIBIT 9–5

The two sets of audit tests are further illustrated in Exhibit 9–6. Materials flows and materials usage by laborers generate transactions documents. Transactions documents supply data to the inventory records and cost systems. Various audit procedures (Nos. 6 through 9 and 19) are carried out to test the processed transactions documents and their recordings. All of these relationships are portrayed in the illustration.

Pricing of the physical count of ending inventory depends on these systems for cost information. Let's turn to that topic now.

9.4 SUBSTANTIVE TESTS OF BALANCES AND ANALYTICAL REVIEW

Substantiation of account balances sets focus on year-end inventories. Already completed auditing procedures have gathered evidence about (a) the inputs to production, (b) the products exiting from production, and (c) the transformation process that goes on in production. Additional evidence gathering would almost seem redundant, but it is not. The scope, complexity, and exceptions that characterize production and inventories make it necessary to do more. Physical existence and quantities need to be checked, valued, and reconciled to accounting records. The question of utility of inventory (i.e., salability) also has to be explored.

Inventory is subject to obsolescence, spoilage, deterioration, evaporation, breakage and damage, spillage, shrinkage, and other processing losses. Add these possibilities to a high probability of errors, plus the chance of irregularities, and the reasons for physical verification become clear.

Physical verification can be accomplished:

1. By a complete annual count at or about year-end with no perpetual inventory records maintained in between.

2. By a complete annual count at or about year-end which is checked against perpetual inventory records.

3. By complete counts at different intervals of time according to inventory value. For example, "high priced" items might be counted monthly, "medium priced" items annually, and "low priced" items every two years.

4. By an ongoing cycle count of segments of the inventory that eventually succeeds in counting the entire stock. Cycle counts are usually employed together with perpetual inventory records. The records are adjusted if they do not agree with the physical count.

5. Based upon a statistical sample of items that are counted and priced. An inference is then made about the entire inventory population.

6. By requesting confirmation from other parties that are holding inventory off premises (e.g., in public warehouses).

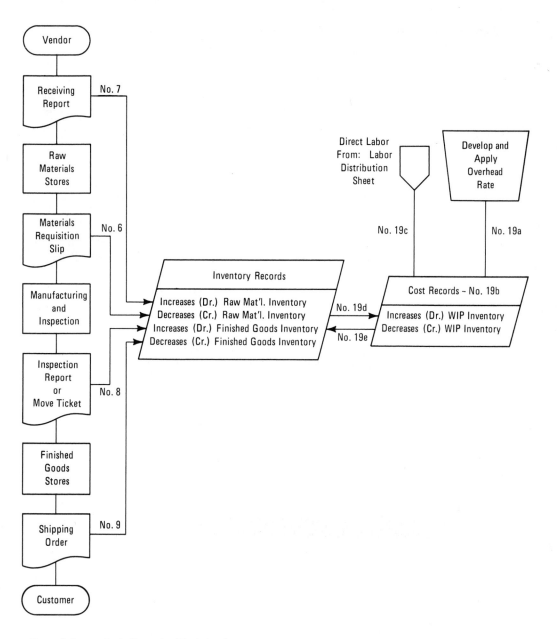

Note: References in the illustration (No. 6-9, 19) are to the
      audit program in the appendix at the end of
      the chapter.

**EXHIBIT 9-6   Relationship of Materials Flows, Transactions Documents, and
Audit Tests**

Employees of the firm usually conduct the physical count, but occasionally a firm of specialists is hired to do it instead. Quite often, one encounters a complete annual count conducted by the firm's employees at year-end. This variety of physical verification will be discussed in detail below. The chances of a manufacturer having a perpetual inventory system are good, particularly with larger firms.

Client Counting of Inventory

A physical count is preceded by careful planning that begins well before year-end. At year-end, the inventory is actually counted. Finally, the pricing, extending, and summarizing process takes place, stretching for several weeks beyond year-end. Each of these stages involves a number of unique activities.

Planning

Written instructions are prepared by the client to explain the details of counting and checking. These duties are assigned to specific individuals. Time schedules are set for the counting, and preparations are made for plant shut-down or overtime work. Receiving and shipping are coordinated with the counting to ensure a proper cut-off. Inventory count tags or count sheets are obtained. Obsolete and other questionable-value inventory is identified, and the inventory and stores areas are arranged for the actual count.

Counting

The entire inventory that is not held by others off premises is "counted." Actually, the inventory is expressed in quantities by weighing, measuring, counting, and estimating. Methods such as photographic surveys are used to estimate inventories that are widely scattered (e.g., cattle), difficult to count (e.g., logs in a river), or which cannot be weighed (e.g., a hill of gravel). Production orders in process may be estimated for the percentage completed by engineers or production supervisors.

The amount on hand is recorded on an inventory tag along with other essential details such as stock number, unit of measure (e.g., dozen, board feet, barrel), description, and location. A second individual double checks the count, and supervisors review the work. Independent auditors make tests and inquiries, whereupon individual areas are approved as having been completed. When the entire inventory is counted and approved, all of the tags are assembled sequentially by tag number. Tags that were used, voided, and unused are accounted for.

Pricing and Summarizing

Data from the inventory tags are transcribed onto inventory sheets or entered into computer readable form. Off-premises inventory is added, and precautions are taken to exclude non-owned materials. The pricing process then begins.

Inventory pricing is actually a matter of selecting an appropriate cost and applying it to the item listed on the inventory sheet. Costs are selected from different sources: invoices and cost records, perpetual inventory records, and standard cost sheets. Actual costs selected must reflect designated cost flow assumptions if specific identification is not applicable. Costs of major items are compared with net realizable values and replacement/reproduction costs for lower-of-cost-or-market valuation in the event that "utility" has declined. Unit costs are multiplied by quantities, and the total cost for each item is extended on the sheets. These total costs per item are then added together by inventory class (e.g., raw materials, WIP, finished goods) to produce the aggregate dollar inventory.

Quantities obtained from the physical count are compared with perpetual inventory records, and the records are adjusted for differences. The general ledger accounts are also adjusted by journal entry to agree with the physical count results.

Audit Procedures

There are auditor activities that correspond to those of the client. They are: (1) planning, (2) observation, and (3) verification of summarized results. The audit program in the chapter appendix for substantive tests of balances follows this sequence.

Planning

Facts are gathered and decisions made in anticipation of the counting of inventory. Basic facts that must be known include location, types, and approximate quantity and value of inventory. Unfamiliar locations where inventory is stored may need to be visited. The client's written instructions are reviewed to make sure that all necessary arrangements have been made. Decisions are made concerning staffing, inventory observation, and testing. Specific matters are decided upon, such as the locations to be covered, amounts of inventory to be tested, and how items are to be selected for testing. Professional staff requirements are scheduled and instructions prepared for assistants.

Observation

Since the McKesson & Robbins fraud of 1938, observation of inventories has been a generally accepted auditing procedure. It is always necessary for an auditor to make or observe some physical counts of the inventory. This standard holds equally for clients who use cycle counting procedures or statistical sampling or employ a firm of specialists to do the counting. Failure to observe inventory is considered an audit scope limitation. Depending on the materiality of the amounts involved, the auditor's report would either disclaim an opinion or contain one that is qualified.

One purpose of observing the inventory count is to ascertain that the assets exist. A second is to witness the counting system in action. Being present at the time of counting allows one to see if employees understand their written instructions and are faithfully following them. Independent auditors are not expected to be expert appraisers of inventory worth. They can, however, formulate reasonable judgements about the condition and level of stock.

Auditor control over inventory tags used in the count is established by recording the tag numbers issued to individuals responsible for counting stock in each area. Unused and voided tags are reconciled with those actually used. Later, tests are made to see that only the used tags were entered into the inventory pricing sheets. A working paper for tag control and subsequent procedures is illustrated in Exhibit 9–7.

Client counts are tested by recounting some items and comparing the results to the attached tags. Other details written on the tags are also verified, e.g., stock number, description, and location. The state of completion of WIP inventory is discussed with production supervisors to determine reasonableness. A record is made for the working papers of a representative number of inventory items that were tested (see Exhibit 9–8). Later, these items are traced to the inventory sheets to check for accuracy of the client's records. Inventory that is damaged, obsolete, or in some way appears to be of questionable value is noted. Any materials moved during the counting are also noted to make sure that double counting or omission did not occur. The receiving department is visited, and the last receiving report number of the year is noted, along with a description of materials purchased. The same is done with shipping. A record is made of the goods sold and the final shipping order number used in the year. This information is used in the cut-off tests of purchasing and sales described in earlier chapters. When the tests, inquiries, and inspection of inventory areas are finished, the accounting for all tags is checked.

Inventory that is off premises is often verified by confirmation. Observing a physical count is certainly permissible, if feasible. However, some inventory is not even physically identifiable (e.g., fungibles such as grains, chemicals, or oils). Materials stored in a public warehouse, for example, would be verified by direct confirmation. In addition, the warehouse receipts would be inspected and certain other supplemental inquiries might be made (AU 901.28–.32). If warehouse

Scott Interspacial Industries
Inventory Tag Control
12/31/X1
Location #001- Main Plant

W. P. No.	F-2
ACCOUNTANT	RKS
DATE	1/1/X2
	1/21/X2

AREA	TAG NUMBERS		
	ISSUED	USED	UNUSED Ⓐ
Raw Materials Warehouse	0001 – √ 0099 ⊥	0001 – ⊘ 0046 ⊘	0047 – 4 0099 4
Assembly Department	0100 – √ 0199 ⊥	0100 – ⊘ 0149 ⊘	0150 – 4 0199 4
Finished Goods Warehouse	0200 – √ 0299 ⊥	0200 – ⊘ 0248 ⊘ and 0256 ⊘	0249 – 4 0255 4 and 0257 – 4 0299 4

√ Observed issuance of tags to inventory counters. No other tags issued.

⊘ Accounted for numerical sequence of tickets used during observation and test counts. No discrepancies noted.

4 All unused tickets were marked "Void." Numerical sequence accounted for.

Ⓐ Verified that these tag numbers were not listed on the inventory summary printout. No errors noted.

EXHIBIT 9-7

Scott Interspacial Industries
Inventory Test Counts
12/31/X1
Location # 001 - Main Plant

W. P. No.	F-3
ACCOUNTANT	RKS
DATE	1/1/X2
	1/21/X2

Tag #	Item	Count Per Client	Count Per RKS (if different)		
	RAW MATERIALS WAREHOUSE				
0001	PART # QY2Z	503 n ∅			
0018	NAILS - Size 3	30 lb. n ∅			
0046	PART # 00X4	2376	2386 ① n ∅		
	ASSEMBLY DEPARTMENT				
0100	Model XX01	27 n ∅			
0122	Model B2Q	408 n ∅			
	FINISHED GOODS WAREHOUSE				
0200	Model R3D3	742	737 ① ∅		
0201	Model XJ36	67 n ∅			
0204	Model X19Y	12 n ∅			
0256	Model X9J	941 n ∅			

Note: A significant number of other test counts were made which are not recorded here. No discrepancies were noted. Test counts were concentrated in finished goods warehouse due to materiality.

n Agreed to inventory summary printout by location and tag #.

① Client adjusted tag to agree to   count.

∅ Agreed to clients' detail inventory records. No exceptions noted.

EXHIBIT 9-8

receipts were pledged as collateral for loans, a confirmation would be requested from the lender. A narrative memo describing the inventory observation is frequently included in the working papers.

Verification of Summarized Results

When the client has finished pricing, extending, and summarizing the inventory, the final phase of testing begins. Three series of tests are conducted. The first series of tests is devoted to inventory quantities.

Inventory sheets are examined to see whether tag numbers listed agree with the control sheet of used, voided, and unused tags. Then, items that were test-counted are traced from the working papers into the inventory sheets. Goods in transit uncovered during cut-off tests, and materials that were transferred between locations during the counting, are checked against the inventory sheets for proper treatment. Confirmations of off-premises inventory are also traced to the inventory sheets. Some cross-testing between the inventory sheets and the tags is performed. In each of the tests, all details should agree, although the quantities are of paramount importance. These tests provide assurance that the client's inventory sheets are fair representations of quantity. A sample of items is then traced into the perpetual inventory records and another sample traced from them back to the inventory lists.

The second series of tests is devoted to inventory pricing. A sample of items is selected from the inventory sheets. Supporting documents are vouched for the validity of the assigned costs and the proper, consistent application of cost flow assumptions. Purchased items such as raw materials are vouched to vendor invoices. Manufactured items such as finished goods are vouched to cost records or standard cost sheets. Major inventory items are tested for loss of utility and application of lower-of-cost-or-market valuations. An inventory price test is shown in Exhibit 9–9.

The last series of tests is devoted to arithmetical accuracy of the inventory lists. Extensions and footings are tested by recalculation. Totals are traced to summary sheets, and they, in turn, are tested for footing. Finally, if there is a perpetual inventory system, the total inventory dollars are traced from the summary sheets to the general ledger control accounts.

Cycle Counts and Statistical Inference of Inventory

The preceding discussion centered around a complete annual count made at year-end. There are two ways of verifying physical quantities that do not require a complete annual count. With one technique, portions of the inventory are counted in a rotating cycle that eventually results in all items being tallied. The entire inventory is not taken altogether at one time, however. For financial statement purposes, an inventory figure is obtained from the perpetual inventory records.

Scott Interspacial Industries
Inventory Price Test
12/31/X1
Location #001 Main Plant

W. P. No.	F-4
ACCOUNTANT	RKS
DATE	1/29/X2

Item	Cost Per Inventory Summary		Total Cost Per Inventory Summary	% of Dept. Total Price-Tested
Raw Materials				
Part # QY2Z	105 each		32315 ∜	
Nails - size 3	42 per lb.		1260 ∜	
Part #0X21	7895 each		1776375 ∜ Ⓑ	
⋮				13.7%
Assembly Department				
Model XX01 - 100% complete	9856 each		266112 ∜	
Model B2Q - 100% complete	19229 each		5805432 ∜ Ⓐ	
⋮				68.4%
Finished Goods Warehouse				
Model R3D3	421250 each		311303750 ∜ Ⓐ	
Model X19Y	6643 each		797116 ∜	
⋮				
Model X9J	69802 each		65683682 ∜ Ⓐ	78.2%

% of total inventory price-tested for location #001 = 65.4%

∜ Recalculated total cost. No errors noted.
4 Agreed unit cost to vendor's invoice.
Ⓑ Agreed unit cost to November cost reports. Recalculated client computations on a test basis. (Note: cost reports were tested during our interim work - see w/p F-1.)
Ⓐ Cost compared with net realizable value. No write-down required.
Ⓑ Cost compared to replacement cost. No write-down required.

EXHIBIT 9-9

Auditing procedures are substantially the same as those we have already discussed—namely, planning, observation, and verification. One or more physical cycle counts are observed and test counts recorded. Client count records are reviewed to verify that the majority of inventory was counted during the past year. Test count and client cycle count work sheets are traced to perpetual inventory records, which in turn, are tested for pricing and arithmetic. At year-end, some additional cross-tracing is done between perpetual inventory records and the physical inventory to check on agreement, and cut-off is tested.

A second technique that avoids a complete physical count is based on statistical sampling. It is called "estimation sampling for variables." A random sample of inventory is chosen from classes of similar items. The sample is counted and priced, producing a sample value. The average unit sample value is then extended to determine the total population value. Auditing procedures include examining the sampling plan for statistical validity. The degrees of precision and reliability specified by the client are also evaluated for their reasonableness in the circumstances. Sample counts are observed and tested, and procedures in general are evaluated for proper application.

Beginning Inventory and the First-Time Audit

A first-time audit of a client brings with it certain problems. The prior-period inventories will not have been subject to observation and testing by the new auditor. Prior-year inventory balances are often a significant amount on balance sheets being presented for comparative purposes. They are also a significant element in the determination of current year income.

A qualified opinion or disclaimer can be avoided if alternative procedures can be applied satisfactorily and the *current* inventory is observed and counted. SEC filings include financial statements for three years to which the auditor must attest. The auditor's report must be unqualified, or the filing is considered defective and will not be approved. Alternative procedures would be critical in this situation if it were a first-time audit. If the statements have been audited by a predecessor auditor and inventories are fairly presented, that opinion can be relied upon. A review of the predecessor auditor's working papers relating to inventories would be made and the client's count records examined.

In the event that the prior years' inventories were not subject to audit, alternative procedures are employed. These would include reviewing the client's written instructions, inventory sheets, and tags. Tracing, cross-tracing, and arithmetical accuracy tests would be made. Inventory pricing would be tested if possible. Subsequent period test counts would be traced to perpetual inventory records. Sales and production records for the post-balance sheet date period would be examined and reconciled back to the prior-period inventory. Gross profit tests would be made to determine the reasonableness of inventories. If alternative procedures are used to substantiate opening inventory balances of a new client, that fact need not be mentioned in the auditor's report.

Other Matters

Certain large public enterprises are required to disclose information about the effect of changing prices on inventory and fixed assets.[1] *Statement on Auditing Standards 28* prescribes certain special review procedures, inquiries, and comparisons concerning these disclosures.[2] Inquiries about the data on inventories expressed in constant dollars and current costs would include, for example, the appropriateness of sources of information used and how they were chosen and assumptions and judgements made in the calculations. This review can be made following the verification of summary results.

Even in cases where a complete physical count of inventory is made annually, it may not be timed to fall at the balance sheet date. On occasion, the annual count takes place shortly before or shortly after year-end. Once again, auditing procedures are substantially the same as they are for a year-end count. In addition, an analysis is made of the inventory accounts for receipts, transfers, and withdrawals made in the intervening period. These are vouched to supporting documents (invoices, shipping orders, etc.) to verify that the changes were legitimate and properly recorded. The objective is to reconcile from the inventory count to the general ledger amounts at year-end. Analytical review procedures, such as making gross profit tests, are also used.

Analytical Review

Certain relationships and account balances that are important in analytical review of the purchases cycle are equally important here. Gross profit percentages and the relationships between purchases, inventory levels, cost-of-sales, and sales are very telling. These are even more revealing if segment data (e.g., industries) are available. Changes in any of these proportions usually reflect strong undercurrents.

Inventory levels and inventory turnover by class (raw materials, WIP, finished goods) are compared with their counterparts from prior years. Where there are numerous locations, such as plants manufacturing consumer durables or retail chain stores selling them, data by location are very helpful. Production cost data—both unit and aggregate—are reviewed. Standard cost variances, the ratio of indirect to direct labor, overhead rates and over/underapplied overhead are examined and compared with expectations and prior period figures.

Balances and relationships that have changed significantly stimulate inquiry and a search for reasonable explanations. Amounts that have not changed but should have, given the surrounding facts and circumstances, also initiate auditor search.

---

[1]"Financial Reporting and Changing Prices," *Statement of Financial Accounting Standards No. 33* (Stamford, Conn: Financial Accounting Standards Board, September, 1979).

[2]"Supplementary Information on the Effects of Changing Prices," *Statement on Auditing Standards 28* (N.Y.: American Institute of CPAs, June, 1980), par. 3, 4.

Key Terms

bill of materials
cost system
cycle counts
inspection report
intervening period
inventory count sheets
inventory records system

move ticket
observation of inventory
pricing inventory
production order
public warehouse receipts
quality control

APPENDIX

AUDIT PROGRAM
Tests of System Compliance and Transactions Details
Production Cycle and Inventories

Client _____   Period _____

Production

1. Review production budget and backlog reports.
2. Review make-or-buy decision documentation. Watch for related party transactions.
3. Examine recent bills of materials and production orders.
4. Inquire when production standards were last revised.
5. Review standard costs by element for reasonableness.
6. Select a sample of material requisition slips and:
   a. Trace raw materials withdrawals into inventory records. Vouch for description, date, quantity, requesting department, approval, stated purpose, and cost.
   b. Trace to production order and/or bill of materials.

Stores

7. Select a sample of receiving reports. Trace additions into raw materials inventory records. Vouch for accepting signature by stores, quantity, cost, description, and date.
8. Select a sample of inspection reports or move tickets for transfers from production. Trace additions into finished goods inventory records. Vouch for accepting signature by stores, date, quantity, description, and cost.
9. Select a sample of shipping orders. Trace withdrawals into finished goods inventory records. Vouch for date, quantity, description, and cost.
10. Review physical safeguards in stores areas and the conduct of guards and other employees responsible for restricting access and for custody of inventory.
11. Examine documents evidencing management's approval to dispose of significant amounts of obsolete, damaged, overstocked, or end-of-season inventory.
12. Review client's controls for off-premises inventory. Examine confirmations if obtained during the year.
13. Review client's controls for non-owned materials (e.g., being processed, repaired, or consigned-in).
14. Review client's written instructions for cycle counting inventory.
15. If inventory is cycle counted during the year, examine count sheets. Examine for double check of count, pricing, and arithmetic. Trace to perpetual inventory records for adjustments. Verify that personnel counting, supervising, and pricing are independent of storekeepers.

Verifying Inventory Summarization and Pricing

16. Obtain detail lists and summary sheets of inventory after it has been priced.
17. Verify that tag numbers that were unissued, unused, or voided are not included.
18. Test (quantity × price) extensions.
19. Test footing and detail to summary sheets.
20. Trace totals from detail to summary sheets.
21. Check items that were test-counted from working papers to inventory sheets for agreement of details.
22. Check inventory sheets for in-transit items discovered during purchases cut-off tests.
23. Test detail inventory sheets back to inventory tags for agreement of details. Test tags into inventory sheets also.
24. If requests for confirmation of off-premises inventory were received, check that items are listed on inventory sheets and details are correct.
25. Trace inventory quantities from inventory sheets to perpetual inventory records, and vice versa. Include non-owned and off-premises items.
26. Select a sample of items from the inventory lists and do the following:
    a. Vouch the cost of purchased materials (raw materials, supplies) to vendor invoices (layer increments only with LIFO).
    b. Vouch the cost of manufactured items (finished and WIP) to job order cost sheets, production reports or standard cost sheets.
    c. Verify that inventory pricing conforms to methods used to assign cost during the year (e.g., LIFO, FIFO, etc.).
27. Verify that valuation bases and methods are consistent with those used for opening inventories.
28. Check for loss of utility and application of lower of cost or market by doing the following:
    a. Make inquiries of marketing personnel concerning softening demand, intensified competition, and falling prices.
    b. Review current price schedules.
    c. Scrutinize perpetual inventory records and inventory lists for obsolete, slow-moving, or overstocked items.
    d. Review contracts in progress for potential losses (contract price less costs to complete vs. carrying value).
    e. Examine subsequent period sales for prices, unusual discounts, or extended terms.
29. Reconcile year-end inventory balance between general ledger controls, inventory summary of physical count, perpetual inventory records, and cost records (e.g., job order cost sheets). Investigate significant differences.
30. Inquire whether inventory liens or pledges exist. Review loan agreements for liens or pledges.
31. Examine consignment agreements.
32. Obtain necessary information on intercompany profits that will be eliminated from inventory valuations.
33. Obtain and review replacement cost information for large public clients making disclosures under FASB No. 33 (see SAS No. 28).

AUDIT PROGRAM
Substantive Tests of Balances
INVENTORY

Client _____ Period _____

Preparation

1. Determine the location of inventories. Get an approximate idea of types, quantities, and values of items to be counted.
2. Review written instructions for physical count.
3. Tour locations that are unfamiliar or that should be examined before the physical count.
4. Make decisions concerning observing and testing physical counts of inventory (e.g., location, types, selection process, amounts).
5. Evaluate whether physical count must be:
   a. Complete, i.e., can reliance be placed on system controls and cycle counts or client use of statistical sampling procedures?
   b. At an interim-date or at year-end.
6. Prepare instructions for assistants and summarizing memo for working papers.

Verifying Inventory Quantities

7. Observe the counting of inventory by the client. Make appropriate inquiries to verify that instructions are being followed.
8. Select certain items and test count. Compare description, stock number, location, quantity, and unit of measure to the information recorded on count tags. Examine tags for counter's and checker's initials.
9. Record a representative number of items test-counted. List essential details on working papers (tag number, quantity, unit of measure, location, stock number). Note items that appear damaged, obsolete, overstocked, etc.
10. Record all goods transferred in or out during counting. Verify later that double-counting or omission was avoided.
11. Obtain document numbers and descriptions of the last goods received and shipped for cut-off verification of purchases and sales.
12. Verify that non-owned goods (consignments, repairs, processing) are counted and labeled properly.
13. Obtain a control list of issued (including unused and voided) tags or count sheets by number.
14. Tour areas when counts are finished to check that all inventory is tagged.
15. For off-premises inventory (public warehouses, consignments-out, etc.) either:
    a. Observe and test physical counts if material, or,
    b. Request direct confirmation.

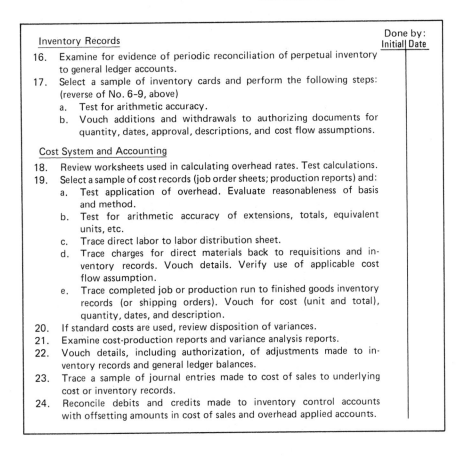

Inventory Records	Done by: Initial Date
16. Examine for evidence of periodic reconciliation of perpetual inventory to general ledger accounts.	

17. Select a sample of inventory cards and perform the following steps: (reverse of No. 6-9, above)
  a. Test for arithmetic accuracy.
  b. Vouch additions and withdrawals to authorizing documents for quantity, dates, approval, descriptions, and cost flow assumptions.	

Cost System and Accounting

18. Review worksheets used in calculating overhead rates. Test calculations.
19. Select a sample of cost records (job order sheets; production reports) and:
  a. Test application of overhead. Evaluate reasonableness of basis and method.
  b. Test for arithmetic accuracy of extensions, totals, equivalent units, etc.
  c. Trace direct labor to labor distribution sheet.
  d. Trace charges for direct materials back to requisitions and inventory records. Vouch details. Verify use of applicable cost flow assumption.
  e. Trace completed job or production run to finished goods inventory records (or shipping orders). Vouch for cost (unit and total), quantity, dates, and description.
20. If standard costs are used, review disposition of variances.
21. Examine cost-production reports and variance analysis reports.
22. Vouch details, including authorization, of adjustments made to inventory records and general ledger balances.
23. Trace a sample of journal entries made to cost of sales to underlying cost or inventory records.
24. Reconcile debits and credits made to inventory control accounts with offsetting amounts in cost of sales and overhead applied accounts.

Questions and Problems

Questions

9-1 Describe the relationship between the inventory records and cost systems. How do they relate to inventory?

9-2 What responsibilities does an auditor have as far as inventory held in a public warehouse is concerned?

9-3 A perpetual inventory record of inventory quantities is maintained by a manufacturing firm. What tests of details and compliance would you perform if controls appear good?

9-4 What are the audit objectives for the production cycle and inventories?

9-5 Outline the principal audit procedures conducted in the verification of physical inventory (i.e., quantities on hand).

9-6 Indicate the tests of inventory pricing that are appropriate for manufactured inventory.

9-7 What procedures would you follow in checking for loss of utility of inventory, i.e., to apply lower of cost or market valuations?

9-8 If a client does not take a complete physical count but uses cycle counts and prepares inventory figures from its perpetual records, how would audit procedures be different?

9-9 What special procedures are necessary in auditing beginning inventory for the first time?

9-10 A client has to make a substantial adjustment for underapplied overhead at year-end. What explanations might be reasonable for the adjustment? How might audit procedures be affected?

Multiple Choice Questions from Professional Examinations

9-11 From which of the following evidence-gathering audit procedures would an auditor obtain *most* assurance concerning the existence of inventories?

a. Observation of physical inventory counts.
b. Written inventory representations from management.
c. Confirmation of inventories in a public warehouse.
d. Auditor's recomputation of inventory extensions.

9-12 Which of the following is the *best* audit procedure for the discovery of damaged merchandise in a client's ending inventory?

a. Compare the physical quantities of slow-moving items with corresponding quantities from the prior year.
b. Observe merchandise and raw materials during the client's physical inventory taking.
c. Review the management's inventory representation letter for accuracy.
d. Test overall fairness of inventory values by comparing the company's turnover ratio with the industry average.

9-13 Lust, CPA, succeeded Krave, CPA, as auditor of Crude Oil Corporation. Krave had issued an unqualified report for the calender year 1980. What can Lust do to establish the basis for expressing an opinion on the 1981 financial statements with regard to opening balances?

a. Lust may review Krave's working papers and thereby reduce the scope of audit tests Lust would otherwise have to do.
b. Lust must apply appropriate auditing procedures to account balances at the beginning of the period so as to be satisfied that they are properly stated and may *not* rely on the work done by Krave.

c. Lust may rely on the prior year's financial statements since an unqualified opinion was issued and must make reference in the auditor's report to Krave's report.

d. Lust may rely on the prior year's financial statements since an unqualified opinion was issued and must refer in a middle paragraph of the auditor's report to Krave's report of the prior year.

9-14 When verifying debits to the perpetual inventory records of a non-manufacturing company, an auditor would be most interested in examining a sample of purchase

a. Approvals.
b. Requisitions.
c. Invoices.
d. Orders.

9-15 A client's physical count of inventories was lower than the inventory quantities shown in its perpetual records. This situation could be the result of the failure to record

a. Sales.
b. Sales returns.
c. Purchases.
d. Purchase discounts.

9-16 An inventory turnover analysis is useful to the auditor because it may detect

a. Inadequacies on inventory pricing.
b. Methods of avoiding cyclical holding costs.
c. The optimum automatic reorder points.
d. The existence of obsolete merchandise.

9-17 The auditor tests the quantity of materials charged to work-in-process by tracing these quantities to

a. Cost ledgers.
b. Perpetual inventory records.
c. Receiving reports.
d. Material requisitions.

9-18 Which of the following procedures would *best* detect the theft of valuable items from an inventory that consists of hundreds of different items selling for $1 to $10 and a few items selling for hundreds of dollars?

a. Maintain a perpetual inventory of only the more valuable items with frequent periodic verification of the validity of the perpetual inventory record.

b. Have an independent CPA firm prepare an internal control report on the effectiveness of the administrative and accounting controls over inventory.

c. Have separate warehouse space for the more valuable items with sequentially numbered tags.

d. Require an authorized officer's signature on all requisitions for the more valuable items.

9-19 Effective internal control over the purchasing of raw materials should usually include all of the following procedures *except*

a. Systematic reporting of product changes that will affect raw materials.

b. Determining the need for the raw materials prior to preparing the purchase order.

c. Obtaining third-party written quality and quantity reports prior to payment for the raw materials.

d. Obtaining financial approval prior to making a commitment.

9-20 When an auditor tests a client's cost accounting system, the auditor's tests are *primarily* designed to determine that

a. Quantities on hand have been computed based on acceptable cost accounting techniques that reasonably approximate actual quantities on hand.

b. Physical inventories are in substantial agreement with book inventories.

c. The system is in accordance with generally accepted accounting principles and is functioning as planned.

d. Costs have been properly assigned to finished goods, work-in-process and cost of goods sold.

9-21 Although the validity of evidential matter is dependent on the circumstances under which it is obtained, three general presumptions have some usefulness. The situations given below indicate the relative reliability a CPA has placed on two types of evidence obtained in different situations. Which of these is an *exception* to one of the general presumptions?

a. The CPA places more reliance on the balance in the scrap sales account at plant A, where the CPA has made limited tests of transactions because of good internal control, than at plant B, where the CPA has made extensive tests of transactions because of poor internal control.

b. The CPA places more reliance on his or her computation of interest payable on outstanding bonds than on the amount confirmed by the trustee.

c. The CPA places more reliance on the report of an expert on an inventory of precious gems than on the CPA's physical observation of the gems.

d. The CPA places more reliance on a schedule of insurance coverage obtained from the company's insurance agent than on one prepared by the internal audit staff.

9-22 An auditor would be most likely to learn of slow-moving inventory through

a. Inquiry of sales personnel.

b. Inquiry of stores personnel.

c. Physical observation of inventory.

d. Review of perpetual inventory records.

9-23 Which one of the following procedures would *not* be appropriate for an auditor in discharging his responsibilities concerning the client's physical inventories?

a. Confirmation of goods in the hands of public warehouses.

b. Supervising the taking of the annual physical inventory.

c. Carrying out physical inventory procedures at an interim date.

d. Obtaining written representation from the client as to the existence, quality, and dollar amount of the inventory.

9-24 Zonker has an inventory of parts consisting of thousands of different items of small individual value but significant total value. Zonker could establish effective internal accounting control over the parts by requiring

a. Approval of requisitions for inventory parts by a company officer.

b. Maintenance of inventory records for all parts included in the inventory.

c. Physical counts of the parts on a cycle basis rather than at year-end.

d. Separation of the store-keeping function from the production and inventory record-keeping functions.

9-25 The primary objective of a CPA's observation of a client's physical inventory count is to

a. Discover whether a client has counted a particular inventory item or group of items.

b. Obtain direct knowledge that the inventory exists and has been properly counted.

c. Provide an appraisal of the quality of the merchandise on hand on the day of the physical count.

d. Allow the auditor to supervise the conduct of the count so as to obtain assurance that inventory quantities are reasonably accurate.

Problems

9-26 In developing the audit program for an accounts payable function, some of the audit objectives could be to determine whether controls and performance are adequate to assure that: (a) goods and services to be paid for have been received, (b) amounts billed are contractually authorized, and (c) amounts billed are mathematically correct.

Required:

Identify three key objectives for each of the following activities.
a. Purchasing
b. Traffic (shipping)

IIA (Adapted)

9-27 CA and his staff were recently sent to the offices of a new client, a manufacturer of furniture. CA's firm had been engaged to perform an audit for the year ended August 31, 1982. E Ltd. has not had an audit before, and its unaudited financial statements and income tax returns for previous years were prepared by a non CA external accountant. In the course of the audit, one of CA's junior staff raised the following points with CA: "E Ltd. uses a standard cost system based on standards set for maximum efficiency. It also employs direct costing for fixed factory overhead. Won't we have to convert their cost of goods sold to actual costs and closing inventory to the lower of actual costs or replacement costs? That will be a big job! If we don't, we'll have to qualify our report as to the valuation of closing inventory—and the client doesn't want this. And didn't we give the client a rough estimate of the cost of an audit? He'll have to do the converting schedules for us. . . . We'll lose money on the job if we have to do them. . . ."

CA asked his junior staff member to wait for an answer until the matter could be discussed with the client. CA thereupon raised the issue with the client and received the following response: "Look, Revenue Canada has accepted that we cost our inventory at standard using direct costs for income tax purposes; I'm certainly not going to change them and have to pay more income taxes—we need the cash for expansion. Also, we set up our present costing system for our internal uses. We need the variances in order to judge foremen's performance, and direct costing helps with pricing, and so on. We can't operate without the system, and I'm not going to mess it up for an auditor. Besides, our accounting staff is grossly overworked and cannot handle more needless bookkeeping. . . . I think that you are being unreasonable and are ignoring the basics of what makes this business successful."

Required:

As CA, what response would you give to your client? What additional comments would you give to your junior staff member?

CICA (Adapted)

9-28 As part of the examination of the production cycle, a CPA is reviewing a parent company's practices and procedures for allocating overhead costs to wholly owned subsidiaries. This process is similar in nature to the allocation of overhead to manufactured products.

Required:

List five possible audit steps that the auditor should include in the audit program for this assignment.

IIA (Adapted)

9-29 Following the observation of a physical inventory, an auditor compared the physical inventory counts with the perpetual inventory records and noted that there were apparent shortages. These shortages were materially greater than those found at the end of the previous year.

Required:

a. Identify four possible causes, other than theft, for the differences between the physical counts and the perpetual inventory records.
b. Assuming that the cause of the differences was theft, give three recommendations to prevent theft.

IIA

9-30 An auditor found that three of the eight cost centers in a manufacturing plant had accumulated large credit balances. Services performed by the cost centers were charged to production at predetermined rates.

Required:

List three audit steps that the auditor should apply to investigate the large credit balances.

IIA (Adapted)

9-31 You are auditing the inventory control function of a large maintenance operation for city-owned vehicles. At this point in your audit, the following information has been discovered:

a. Vehicle maintenance records indicate that the number of inoperative trucks waiting for spare parts is increasing, even though the total number of trucks is decreasing.
b. Stockroom employees have been unable to find some parts, even though the perpetual inventory system shows them as being on hand.
c. The investment in spare-parts inventory has remained at about the same level since the last audit.
d. Many of the spare parts can be used for passenger cars.
e. The perpetual inventory is maintained on inventory record cards by a clerk in the parts warehouse office.

Required:

Prepare two audit steps to be included in the audit program for each of the five items above.

IIA (Adapted)

9-32 During the performance of cut-off tests for purchases, Ms. Perspicacious Fox, CPA, examined the paid invoices file of Timely Remittances, Inc. Several invoices were discovered that appear to have been improperly recorded. The firm uses the periodic method of determining inventories and had made a physical count on December 31, 1983—the close of business. The entry to adjust inventory to its year-end balance has already been made by entering a credit to Cost of Goods Sold. Other accounts are still open.

Required:

a. Prepare any adjusting entries you believe are necessary relating to the invoices listed below.

b. What additional audit procedures do you feel are necessary relating to the following purchases?

Items Purchased	F.O.B.	Invoice Date	Invoice Amount	Receiving Report Date	Entered in the Accounts
1. Raw materials	Shipping point	12/25/83	$14,200	12/31/82	1/4/84
2. Raw materials	Shipping point	12/28/83	3,450	1/4/84	12/31/83
3. Factory supplies	Destination	12/28/83	12,825	12/31/83	1/4/84
4. Raw materials	Destination	12/29/83	3,470	1/4/84	12/31/83
5. Electrical power		12/28/83	1,750	1/4/84	1/6/84
6. Factory supplies	Shipping point	12/30/83	4,400	12/31/83	1/4/84
7. Raw materials	Destination	12/28/83	13,250	1/4/84	12/31/83
8. Raw materials	Shipping point	12/29/83	3,810	1/5/84	1/6/84

9-33 Your audit client, Apollo Appliances, Inc., operates a retail store in the center of town. Because of lack of storage space, Apollo keeps inventory that is not on display in a public warehouse outside of town. The warehouseman receives inventory from suppliers and, on request from your client by a shipping advice or telephone call, delivers merchandise to customers or to the retail outlet.

The accounts are maintained at the retail store by a bookkeeper. Each month, the warehouseman sends to the bookkeeper a quantity report indicating opening balance, receipts, deliveries, and ending balance. The bookkeeper compares book quantities on hand at month-end with the warehouseman's report and adjusts the books to agree with the report. No physical counts of the merchandise at the warehouse were made by your client during the year.

You are now preparing for your examination of the current year's financial statements in this recurring engagement. Last year you rendered an unqualified opinion.

Required:

a. Prepare an audit program for the observation of the physical inventory of Apollo Appliances, Inc.: (1) at the retail outlet, and (2) at the warehouse.

b. As part of your examination, would you verify inventory quantities at the warehouse by means of: (1) A warehouse confirmation? Why? (2) Test counts of inventory at the warehouse? Why?

c. Since the bookkeeper adjusts books to quantities shown on the warehouseman's report each month, what significance would you attach to the year-end adjustments if they were substantial? Discuss.

AICPA (Adapted)

9-34 Mesospheric Morsels, Inc. a processor of frozen foods carries an inventory of finished products consisting of fifty different types of items valued at approximately $2 million. About $750,000 of this value represents stock produced by the company and billed to customers prior to the audit date. This stock is being held for the customers at a monthly rental charge until they request shipment, and it is not separated from the company's inventory.

The company maintains separate perpetual ledgers at the plant office for both stock owned and stock being held for customers. The cost department also maintains a perpetual record of stock owned. The above perpetual records reflect quantities only.

The company does not take a complete physical inventory at any time during the year since the temperature in the cold storage facilities is too low to allow one to spend more than fifteen minutes inside at a time. It is not considered practical to move items outside or to defreeze the cold storage facilities for the purpose of taking a physical inventory. Due to these circumstances, it is impractical to test count quantities to the extent of completely verifying specific items. The company considers as its inventory valuation at year-end the aggregate of the quantities reflected by the perpetual record of stock owned, maintained at the plant office, and priced at the lower of cost or market.

Required:

a. What are the two principal problems facing the auditor in the audit of the inventory? Discuss briefly.

b. Outline the audit steps that you would take to enable you to render an unqualified opinion with respect to the inventory. (You may omit consideration of a verification on unit prices and clerical accuracy.)

AICPA (Adapted)

9-35 The Roisterous Robots Company is engaged in the manufacture of command androids with analog capabilities under specific contracts and in accordance with customers' specifications. Customers are required to advance 25 percent of the contract price. The company records sales on a shipment basis and accumulates costs by job orders. The normal profit margin over the past few years has been approximately 5 percent of sales, after providing for selling and administrative expenses of about 10 percent of sales. Inventory is valued at the lower of cost or market.

Among the jobs you are reviewing in the course of your annual examination of the company's December 31 financial statements is one for Android Q2–U2 at a firm contract price of $50,000. Costs accumulated for the job at the year-end aggregated $30,250. The company's engineers estimated that the job was approximately 55 percent complete at that time. Your audit procedures have been as follows:

1. Examined all contracts, noting pertinent provisions.
2. Observed physical inventory of jobs in process and reconciled details to job order accounts.
3. Tested input of labor, material, and overhead charges into the various jobs to determine that such charges were authentic and had been posted correctly. The month of September was selected for test.
4. Confirmed customers' advances at year-end.
5. Balanced work-in-process job ledger with control account.

Required:

With respect to Android Q2–U2:

a. State the additional audit procedures, if any, you would employ, and explain the purpose of the procedures.
b. Indicate the manner and the amount at which you would include Android Q2–U2 in the balance sheet.
c. Comment on the method of choosing cost transactions for the month of September for test.

AICPA (Adapted)

10

Capital assets and financial management cycles

There are two more transactions cycles to study. When we have concluded, our audit of financial statements will be virtually finished. The capital assets cycle is designed to procure tangible properties that provide supporting facilities for the operating functions of the firm. These assets are used in the principal business of the firm and in secondary ventures, such as the rental properties of a manufacturer. The acquisition phase of the capital assets cycle interfaces with the cash disbursements system or the financial management cycle, depending on the source of payment.

Financial management is the second cycle. It has much in common with the capital assets cycle. Both are marked by a concentration of responsibilities in the hands of a few high-level officials. Both process relatively few transactions, and the span to completion is short. There are other similarities that we will underscore later.

The financial management cycle is portrayed in Exhibit 10–1. Plans for new capital from various sources are made, and steps to secure it are taken. Capital funds are then divided up among competing demands. In between, short-term investments are made with temporary surpluses of funds. These, in turn, are eventually funneled back into the capital flows mainstream. Capital asset acquisitions are a major use of capital funds. Here is where the two cycles interface. The financial management cycle contains four major audit areas: short-term investments, long-term investments, and the two principal sources of capital—debt, and equity. First we will study the capital assets cycle, and then we will concentrate on financial management.

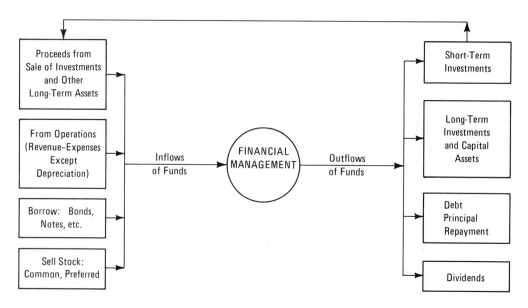

EXHIBIT 10–1   The Financial Management Cycle

I   CAPITAL ASSETS

10.1   CYCLE FUNCTIONS AND ACTIVITIES

The capital assets cycle begins with the preparation of a request or proposal to acquire fixed assets. It continues through the review and approval of the capital investment proposal and on to the actual acquisition and installation or construction. At this juncture, the cycle branches off into a payment segment and an operating segment. The payment segment is either accomplished by the cash disbursement system or by the financial management system, depending on the amount of funds involved. Purchases of minor equipment or furniture and fixtures would usually flow through the cash disbursements system and be paid out of operating funds. Major asset acquisitions, such as a building, would probably involve some sort of financing arrangement.

The operating segment continues with the use and maintenance of assets. Concurrently, detailed accounting records keep track of each item's cost and depreciation, in addition to other vital data. Eventually an asset reaches the end of its useful life and is retired and scrapped, sold, or traded.

The term capital assets is intended to include plant, property and equipment, rental properties, and assets of this variety held for future use. It includes owned assets, (capital) leased assets, and borrowed assets such as the U.S. Government sometimes provides to its contractors. Assets can be standard or custom-made items and can be purchased or self-constructed.

Capital asset functions and major activities are briefly described below.

Preparation of Proposals

The operating unit that will use the asset ordinarily prepares a formal request. Funds may have been budgeted for it specifically or for capital expenditures in general. Modern capital budgeting techniques may be used to assist in evaluating the proposal. Before being released for authorization, the operating unit's management will review and approve the proposal. Then the proposal goes to a higher level of management or, in some cases, even to the Board of Directors.

Review and Approval

The level of management that a proposal rises to varies directly with the magnitude of its cost. A modest request for a new desk would be reviewed by a relatively low-rung manager. A substantial expenditure would require approval by a higher level of management—perhaps even the president. Major undertakings would probably go before the Board of Directors.

The review and authorization process is a very important one. Considerable care and attention is paid to it. The nature and configuration of a firm's business is established by the capital assets it buys. Approved proposals are authorizations to proceed with the acquisition and possibly, funding. Rejected proposals are sent back to the initiator.

Acquisition and Installation

Many capital assets are acquired by the purchasing department. Other assets that are specialized, very complex, or have to be constructed, will be handled by those in the firm technically able to do so. Outside engineers, architects, and consultants may be engaged to assist. Activities include selecting a source and negotiating contract terms, monitoring progress and costs, and inspecting the finished article. A project number may be assigned to the item and used for accumulating costs. Installation can include a wide range of preparatory efforts involving foundations, electrical wiring, plumbing, and structural rearranging of buildings. Testing, "break-in" periods and training of operators may also be considered a part of installation.

Use and Maintenance

Once past the installation period, assets are put to use. Over its useful life an asset will very likely require some repair. In addition, periodic maintenance and refurbishment will be called for. It is often difficult to distinguish between repairs and maintenance that only keep an asset going and betterments and additions that extend or broaden its capabilities. Describing the specific activities associated with the use of capital assets is virtually impossible because of the variety of assets encountered. Fundamentally, the activities are devoted to productive application of assets in carrying out the firm's economic mission.

Detailed Property Records

Every capital asset requires a detailed record. The set of property records is a subsidiary ledger to the general ledger control accounts for fixed assets. The two are periodically reconciled. Information contained in the record includes: asset description and identification number; location; date of acquisition; total cost; whether owned, leased, or borrowed; supplier; estimated useful life and salvage value; and depreciation method. The detailed property records are amended when new assets are acquired, assets are transferred within the firm, or assets are retired. Expenses of repair and maintenance are sometimes posted to the detailed property records. A routine practice is to take a physical inventory of fixed assets periodically and compare results with the detailed property records. Control over capital assets is enhanced considerably by this check.

Retirement and Disposal

There are three facets to retirement and disposal of capital assets. A decision has to be made on when and how to get rid of an asset. Disposals should be approved by management so that they can give consideration to replacing it or doing without. The second facet is to notify accounting. The detailed property record is then removed from the active asset file, and accounts are adjusted in the general ledger. Many retired assets have scrap, salvage, or trade-in value. Monitoring the disposal to see that this value is received and recorded in the accounts is the final facet.

10.2 INTERNAL ACCOUNTING CONTROL EVALUATION: OBJECTIVES, STRATEGIES, AND RISK ANALYSIS

The acquisition of capital assets resembles the purchase of inventories and supplies, and control objectives, strategies, and risks are similar for both. There are relatively fewer transactions in the capital asset cycle, and each stands alone and more readily identifiable than materials purchases. As a result, internal accounting controls are simpler. This is not a high-risk area. In the majority of cases, capital assets are not considered a critical audit area.

In the following section, there are four control objectives for capital assets and strategies to achieve these objectives. An analysis is also made of risks that attend each control objective. We have not repeated many of the objectives, strategies, or risks that were explained in connection with purchases, even though they apply to capital assets equally. Nor have we duplicated our discussion of the cash disbursements phase of the cycle. Payments for capital assets are subject to the same considerations as are purchases of inventory. They enter into the mainstream of the disbursement system and become simply another transaction to process. What follows, therefore, are unique or more important facets of internal accounting controls for capital assets.

Audit objectives for the capital assets cycle are to be satisfied that:

- All capital asset acquisitions—purchased and leased—are recorded, and a distinction is correctly made between assets and expenses.

- Capital assets are properly valued, and cost is assigned to time periods in accordance with accepted methods, using reasonable estimates of asset life and salvage value.

- Capital asset disposals, and associated gains or losses, are promptly and accurately reflected in the accounts.

CONTROL OBJECTIVE 1. *Capital asset acquisitions are initiated by authorized personnel in accordance with the firm's plans and specifications. Requests are reviewed by management or the Board of Directors.*

Risk Analysis

Control failures could result in resource allocation by the firm that is dysfunctional. Capital assets that are not needed might be acquired. Imbalances of capital assets within the firm could occur, with some segments having too little and some too much. Properties might unknowingly be acquired from related parties. Cost overruns and overpayments to contractors might occur. Assets might be purchased that should have been leased. Counteracting these risks are strategies such as the following.

Strategies

- ✔ Prepare written policies and procedures for requesting property additions and extraordinary repairs or maintenance.
- ✔ Require management at the requesting department or division level to review and approve all capital investment proposals.
- ✔ Establish guidelines and limits of authority, in dollar terms, for initiating and approving property acquisition requests.
- ✔ Devise special approval procedures for cost overruns.
- ✔ Employ capital budgeting techniques for evaluation of proposals.

CONTROL OBJECTIVE 2. *Capital assets and detailed property records are to be safeguarded to prevent unauthorized use or removal or loss from damage or deterioration. Access to capital assets and records is limited to authorized personnel for approved purposes.*

Risk Analysis

The most immediate danger faced is that assets might be stolen, lost, damaged or destroyed. Property records might be altered, lost or destroyed. Unnecessary capital demands might be made due to premature replacement of assets that were stolen, lost, damaged or destroyed. Inability to locate assets might result in unneeded duplicates being purchased. Safeguards against these risks include the following.

Strategies

- ✔ Assign custody and responsibility for capital assets and property records to specific individuals.
- ✔ Have properties independently appraised for evaluating adequacy of insurance coverage.
- ✔ Restrict access to portable capital assets by enclosures and physical barriers. Employ requisitioning procedures, and maintain records of assets issued to personnel.
- ✔ Limit access to buildings, and control movements of visitors.
- ✔ Keep deeds, agreements, leases, and contracts under lock and key. Restrict access to detailed property records.

CONTROL OBJECTIVE 3. *Accounting for capital assets is to meet the firm's specifications for recording and classification. Depreciation and tax credits are to be allocated to the time periods and in accordance with the methods selected by management.*

Risk Analysis

If controls were to fail, tax benefits might be lost, or tax assessments levied, because of improper accounting treatment of capital assets and associated expenses. Property taxes and insurance premiums might be paid on assets that have been disposed of or retired. It might not be possible to determine the cost, accumulated depreciation, investment tax credit recapture, and deferred income tax adjustment associated with an asset that is sold. Asset valuation and income determination could be improper and lead to inappropriate decisions. Strategies such as those listed below guard against these risks.

Strategies

- ✔ Prepare written policies and procedures on accounting matters such as dollar capitalization limits, depreciation and investment tax credit methods, and distinguishing betterments from repairs.

- ✔ Maintain a detailed record for every owned, leased, and borrowed capital asset indicating description, location, I.D. number, total cost, vendor, date of acquisition, useful life, salvage value, and depreciation method.

- ✔ Take a physical inventory of capital assets periodically and compare it with detailed records.

- ✔ Reconcile detailed property records with general ledger control accounts on a regular basis.

- ✔ Use standard journal entries for depreciation and amortization.

CONTROL OBJECTIVE 4. *Sales and other asset disposals are to be approved by management and promptly and accurately reported.*

Risk Analysis

If controls are inadequate a variety of risks unfold. Salvage value proceeds could be diverted. Illicit sales of assets might be made by dishonest employees. Assets might be sold to poor credit risks or competitors. Assets that were needed in another segment of the firm might be sold. Asset and expense accounts could be overstated. Pledged assets might be sold in violation of loan agreements. Offsetting these risks are defensive strategies.

Strategies

- ✔ Prepare written policies and procedures for retirements and disposals of capital assets.

- ✔ Require a level of approval above that of the department or division using the asset.

- ✔ Require that officials authorizing asset disposals notify accounting directly.

- ✔ Forbid removal of assets from the premises without signed authorization on prenumbered forms.

Evaluating Internal Accounting Controls

Up to this point, internal accounting controls have been evaluated in order to select controls to rely upon. If compliance testing justified reliance upon controls, the nature, timing, and extent of the audit procedures that followed were influenced. The capital asset cycle is different, and it warrants a different audit approach.

The majority of business firms have relatively few capital asset transactions. Asset acquisitions are generally of significant dollar value and represent items essential to the firm's operations. Planning for acquisitions and disposals of properties is an intensive procedure that precedes the actual event by a considerable length of time. Close management oversight is exercised during the planning and execution phases. Another consideration is that many assets, once put into service, could not be removed without leaving a conspicuous void. Lastly, data on capital assets must be scrupulously collected for filing tax returns. Depreciation and investment tax credits on newly acquired assets are significant matters to the firm. Under the circumstances just described, less attention is devoted to auditing the system and more to substantiating balances.

This is not to say that evaluation of internal controls is relinquished entirely. It is still carried out using an internal control questionnaire such as in Exhibit 10–2. Flowcharting is rarely justified for the capital asset cycle. There are three main reasons for inquiring about internal controls:

1. To fulfill the auditing standard requiring that all material weaknesses in internal accounting controls be reported to management and the Board of Directors.

2. To search for possible areas where operating improvements could be made, i.e., management letter comments.

3. To decide on the extent of substantive testing of balances.

CONCEPT SUMMARY
Relationship of Capital Asset Cycle Functions and Controls

Function	Related Control Objective	Examples of Risks	Examples of Strategies
1. Prepare Proposals 2. Review and Approval	No. 1 Authorized persons initiate and review requests. Requests conform to plans.	• Unneeded assets are acquired. • Asset imbalances within the firm.	• Capital budgeting forms and procedures. • Stratified dollar limits of authority.
3. Acquisition and Installation	(see Chapter 7, Purchasing)		
4. Use and Maintenance	No. 2 Safeguard capital assets.	• Assets stolen or misplaced.	• Restrict access to assets.
5. Detailed Property Records	No. 2 Safeguard property records. No. 3 Proper recording of assets and subsequent allocations.	• Property records altered. • Lost tax credits.	• Keep deeds, leases, etc. locked-up. • Reconcile records to general ledger control accounts. • Standard journal entries for depreciation.
6. Retirement and Disposal	No. 4 Disposals are approved by management and promptly recorded.	• Salvage proceeds diverted. • Sale of needed assets.	• Special disposal forms. • Next higher level management approval.

INTERNAL CONTROL QUESTIONNAIRE
Capital Assets Cycle

Client _____   Period _____

	Yes	No*

1. Are capital investment proposals prepared by initiating departments or divisions for:
   a. Fixed asset acquisitions (purchase or lease)?
   b. Extraordinary repairs or maintenace of fixed assets?
2. Is there a written company policy and procedures for:
   a. Preparing capital investment proposals?
   b. Distinguishing between capital assets and repairs and maintenance expenses?
3. Does the firm employ a system of stratified authorization for approval of capital investment proposals?
4. Are procedures in effect to assure that assets are delivered or constructed and that they conform to specifications? Is accounting promptly notified of newly leased and purchased fixed assets?
5. Are actual purchase prices compared to authorized amounts? Is approval obtained for excess amounts?
6. Are expenditures for assets constructed by the firm's personnel, or installed by them, accounted for and controlled by procedures similar to those for manufactured inventory (work order number, etc.)?
7. Does the firm designate personnel to watch over and control costs, specifications, and time schedules of construction work done by contractors?
8. Are detailed property records kept for fixed assets? Are fully depreciated assets still in use included?
9. Are detailed property records reconciled to the general ledger control account at least annually?
10. Is detailed record keeping segregated from custody and responsibility for properties?
11. Is a periodic count of properties made and compared with detailed property records?
12. Are adjustments made to the detailed property records as a result of physical counts approved by a responsible official?
13. Are assets leased or loaned to others subject to periodic inspection?
14. Are assets owned by others and loaned to the firm controlled by detailed records and physically inspected periodically?
15. Are disposals and transfers of properties promptly reported to accounting for adjustment of the detailed asset records?
16. Is formal authorization required for disposal of properties?
17. Do asset acquisition and disposal authorizations contain data on assets being replaced and their estimated salvage value? Is the latter monitored to ensure receipt?
18. Are properties appraised for insurance purposes and adequacy of coverage evaluated?
19. Are depreciation rates and methods compared with actual patterns of asset consumption?
20. Are asset safeguards and restricted access to assets and property records in force?

---

*Note: A comments column is also normally provided for on the questionnaire so that the auditor can include explanations or working paper references—particularly when "No" answers are recorded.

EXHIBIT 10–2

10.3 SUBSTANTIVE TESTING

The audit approach, then, is to concentrate on substantiating capital asset balances and directly related accounts, such as depreciation expense, accumulated depreciation, and repairs and maintenance expense. Rent expense would also be substantiated in connection with this cycle if it had not already been audited together with accrued liabilities or prepaid assets.

An analysis, such as the one in Exhibit 10–3, is made of the various capital asset accounts: equipment, furniture and fixtures, vehicles, etc. The beginning asset balances are verified by tracing to last year's working papers. Normally, it is not necessary to do more than check that the cumulative capital asset balances have been carried forward correctly. On an initial audit, the predecessor auditor's working papers would be examined to make sure that capital assets were handled properly. If there has never been an audit, the prior years' records have to be examined or a qualified opinion expressed.

Asset acquisitions and disposals in the current year are vouched to supporting documents such as invoices. Authorizations for major asset acquisitions are looked for in the minutes of the Board of Directors. Details of the transaction, such as cost, item description and dates, and proof of ownership, are established by vouching. If there are liens or other encumbrances on the property, they can usually be detected at this time. Disposals of capital assets are reviewed to see whether the treatment of gains/losses or trade-in values is proper and to determine that proceeds (if any) were received and recorded.

Repairs and maintenance expense is also analyzed. Substantial charges that were made to the account are vouched to underlying invoices to make sure that the charges are legitimate and properly recorded. Another objective is to establish that none of the transactions charged to expense should have been capitalized. Similarly, rent expense is analyzed and rental agreements examined to make sure that capital leases have not been incorrectly treated as operating leases. Capital leases that have been recorded as assets are checked to see that they meet the criteria for capitalization. Improper accounting for any of these cases is corrected by making an adjusting journal entry.

Capital asset acquisitions are traced into depreciation schedules and the detailed property records. Cost should be recorded and used in the calculation of depreciation and the investment tax credit. Material interest costs incurred during construction or development of capital assets acquired for use, sale, or lease should be included in cost.[1] Calculations of capitalized interest costs, depreciation expense, and the investment tax credit are reviewed and tested. If a different depreciation method is used for tax purposes, those calculations, and the related deferred income tax effect, are also reviewed and tested. The determination of

---

[1] "Capitalization of Interest Cost," *Statement of Financial Accounting Standards No. 34* (Stamford, Conn.: Financial Accounting Standards Board, October, 1979).

Scott Interspacial Industries

Summary – Fixed Assets & Depreciation w Depreciation A/c's

12/31/x1

W. P. No. I
ACCOUNTANT R
DATE 1/04/x2

Description	Fixed Assets				Depreciation		Accumulated Depreciation			
	Balance, 12/31/x0	Additions	Retirements	Balance, 12/31/x1	Rate	Method	Balance, 12/31/x0	Expense	Disposals	Balance, 12/31/x1
Land	650000 √	—	—	650000 GL Λ	N/A	N/A	—	—	—	—
Building	7256000 √	—	—	7256000 GL Λ	5%	SL	1632600 √	362800	—	1995400 GL Λ
Equipment – factory	6854200 √	984560 I-1	164000	7674760 GL Λ	10%	SL	2601200 √	746450	131200	3196450 GL Λ
– Office	496750 √	88240 I-2	17090	557900 GL Λ	20%	SL	267000 √	102750	17090	352660 GL Λ
Autos and Trucks	379800 √	265700 I-3	88310	557190 GL Λ	20%	SL	1227800 √	126040	80000	1239840 GL Λ
	15626750 Λ	1338500 Λ	269400 Λ	16695850 Λ	same as prior years		4637600 Λ	1263040 GL	229290	5668350 Λ

Λ, M Footed, crossfooted.
√ Agreed to beginning balance per general ledger and prior yr. w/p's.
√√ Recalculated depreciation expense and depreciation associated with disposal. Appears proper.
GL Agreed to general ledger.
T Additions tested on w/p noted beside each category.
φ Disposals and related accumulated depreciation tested on w/p I-4.

AX1 Investment Tax Credit # 106400 I-5
(net of recapture)

EXHIBIT 10-3

CONCEPT SUMMARY

Accounts Analyzed, Audit Procedures, and Matters To Watch For

Analysis of	Major Audit Procedures*	Watch For
Capital Asset Additions, Disposals and Balances	1. Verify beginning balances 2. Vouch additions and disposals 3. Read Board minutes for authorization	1. Liens on property 2. Interest capitalized 3. Treatment of gains/losses and trade-ins 4. Capital leases meet criteria
Accumulated Depreciation	1. Verify beginning balances 2. Reconcile with depreciation expense and disposals	1. Fully depreciated assets
Depreciation Expense	1. Test calculations 2. Trace in asset additions and disposals 3. Recalculate deferred tax effect	1. Consistency of depreciation method employed 2. Determination of useful life and salvage value.
Repairs and Maintenance Expense	1. Vouch major charges to invoices	1. Expenses that should be capitalized
Rent Expense	1. Examine rental agreement	1. Leases that should be capitalized.

*See the audit program in the Appendix to this chapter for more extensive procedures.

---

salvage values, the setting of estimated useful lives, and the methods of depreciation employed are reviewed for consistency when the expense calculation is tested.

Accumulated depreciation is audited by checking the opening general ledger balance against last year's working papers and verifying additions and deductions made to the account. Additions to the account are verified as a byproduct of the depreciation expense procedures. Once they have been completed, total depreciation expense is reconciled to the accumulated depreciation additions. The majority of account deductions can be verified by the analysis of capital asset disposals—the two merely have to be reconciled.

A detailed audit program can be found in the appendix to this chapter.

Disclosure and Analytical Review

There are a host of disclosure requirements associated with the capital asset family of accounts we have been discussing. The facts that have to be disclosed in the financial statements or accompanying notes include:

1. The balances of major classes of capital assets.
2. Basis of valuation for capital assets.
3. Depreciation expense for the period, accumulated depreciation balance, and a description of depreciation methods.
4. The amount of assets recorded under capital leases and related depreciation.

5. Total rent expense for the period from operating leases.

6. Liens on capital assets.

7. Amount of interest capitalized and the total interest cost for the period.

8. Investment tax credit for the period and the method for its accounting (deferral vs. flow-through).

9. Total identifiable assets by segment for public enterprises, along with depreciation expense and capital asset additions for the period.

10. Supplementary information concerning changing prices (general and specific price level changes). Certain large public enterprises must measure the effects of changing prices on property, plant, and equipment, in addition to depreciation, depletion, and amortization expense.

Because of the extensive substantive testing of balances associated with this cycle, the need for analytical review procedures is limited. Where it is used, analytical review involves comparison of this year's and the prior year's amounts of expenses (repairs and maintenance, rent, depreciation), capital assets, and accumulated depreciation. Comparison of actual capital expenditures with those budgeted may also be made. Relating the level of repairs and maintenance to capital asset balances is also considered useful.

II FINANCIAL MANAGEMENT

10.4 CYCLE FUNCTIONS AND ACTIVITIES

The financial management cycle begins with planning and continues on through the securing and use of financial resources. Competing uses need to be weighed and balanced, and resource allocations made among them. One such use is investments. Advances to affiliates is a fairly common account that is classified in the investments category of the balance sheet. It is a type of receivable. Auditing its balance and associated income—accrued and earned—is no different from other types of receivables. The investments we will concentrate on are securities. Then we will turn to sources of capital.

Securities: Investments, Collateral, and Treasury Stock

Securities are classified as short-term, or "marketable securities," and long-term, or "investments." These terms are ambiguous and overlapping. However, in practice, it is relatively easy to distinguish between the two categories based on management's intention. What one finds is that:

1. Securities are held to earn a return on funds that are in excess of immediate needs or are investments of accumulated funds designated for some special purpose, such as a construction project or debt and preferred stock redemptions. It is common to find relatively short-maturity, fixed income securities, such as U.S. Treasury Bills, being held for this purpose. Common or preferred stocks are ordinarily not suitable as short-term investments because of their greater vulnerability to market price changes. If securities' proceeds are to be returned to the working capital mainstream at maturity, the investment is classified as short-term marketable securities (i.e., current assets). If proceeds from securities are reserved for some other purpose and are unavailable for working capital, the securities are long-term investments.

2. Securities are acquired to enable an investor firm to control, or significantly influence, another firm. A long-term relationship is intended. These securities include common and preferred stock of subsidiary firms, "investee firms," and joint venture corporations. Occasionally, one comes across a partnership interest that represents the same sort of relationship. Most preferred stock investments are carried at cost. Common stocks, partnership interests, and participating preferred stocks are carried on an equity basis.

Although exceptions will be found in practice, these rules generally hold true. It is not unknown, for example, for long-term investments in bonds to be made or for stock investments to be carried as a short-term or long-term speculation. Securities are held under two other circumstances.

1. They may be collateral held against a loan or similar credit transaction made with another firm.

2. A firm may purchase some of its own stock and hold it in the treasury or sell it to employee trusts under employee stock ownership plans (ESOPs) or to employees under stock purchase plans.

It is not unusual to find firms that have few, or even none, of the above transactions. Therefore, definition of responsibilities, procedures for authorization and execution, and segregation of duties may not be well established. Each transaction that comes along is treated as needed, in a unique fashion. Exhibit 10–4 illustrates the investment phase of the financial management function.

Sources of Capital

The financial management function is also responsible for securing capital and servicing its sources. Capital is available from many sources and in many forms. Some is transitory and imposes an immediate commitment to repay the principal amount. Other forms can be considered standing sources of capital, carrying no commitment to repay. The risks and costs of each are different; each has its

EXHIBIT 10-4   Securities in the Financial Management Function

Balance Sheet Classification	Usual Types	Associated Accounts
Marketable Securities (Current Assets)	U.S. Governments, Commercial Paper, CDs. Fixed income with short maturity.	a. Interest Income b. Accrued Interest Receivable

Investments* (Non-Current Assets)	1. Construction funds, Preferred stock or debt redemption funds. Same types as above.
	2. *Common stock of affiliates
	3. **Reacquired common (i.e., Treasury) stock held for deferred compensation.
	4. **Reacquired common (i.e., Treasury) stock held for resale under Stock Purchase Plans or to ESOP Trusts.
		1. a. Interest Income
		   b. Accrued Interest Receivable
		2. a. Equity in Earnings of Affiliates
		   b. Deferred Income Taxes (Cr.) on distributable but as yet undistributed earnings of affiliates carried at equity.
		   c. Amortization of "excess cost" (Goodwill).*
		3. Accrued compensation (liability).
		4. See AICPA Statement of Position—SOP 76-3 for ESOPs. Otherwise, none.

Owners' Equity (Contra)	Reacquired common stock held in the Treasury.	None.
Notes on Collateral	Various types of securities used. Can be fixed income securities or stocks (the debtor firm's or a third firm).	Accounts or Notes Receivable from the debtor that has given securities as collateral.

*Investments in common stock of subsidiary firms would not appear in *consolidated* financial statements. The Investment elimination made in consolidation may cause amortizable Goodwill to emerge. Similarly, amortization of "excess cost" often occurs with Investments in Common Stock of "investee" firms. There is no deferred income tax effect arising out of amortization of Goodwill or comparable "excess cost" amounts. There is a deferred income tax effect, however, from accruing the Equity in Earnings of Investees and Subsidiaries (to the extent that the latter's income is not permanently invested).

**These securities may also be classified in Owners' Equity as a contra item.

advantages and disadvantages. Financial management decides upon the amounts and composition of capital, as well as the risks, terms, and costs that are acceptable.

Capital can be borrowed from owners, institutional lenders, and vendors. Borrowings are usually contractual agreements in the form of notes, bonds, mortgages, or acceptances. Capital leases and convertible debentures are among the more exotic varieties. Assets are often pledged or used to secure borrowings. Inventory, accounts receivable, securities, and fixed assets are the leading candidates to protect loans.

Capital contributed or donated by owners and earnings retained on their behalf are standing sources. Contributed capital is evidenced by certificates or contractual-type agreements and may come from a sole proprietor, partners, or shareholders. Stock held by shareholders can be common, preferred, or Class A and B. "Minority interest" is simply a combination of contributed capital and retained earnings associated with the outside shareholders of a consolidated subsidiary firm. Options and warrants are a potential source of capital, although detachable warrants can have a recordable value when issued. Their immediate significance is a possible impact on EPS calculations and the disclosure requirements that have to be met concerning terms. The issuing firm must have sufficient shares of stock reserved to satisfy holders who wish to exercise their warrants or options.

Each of these sources of capital expects a return. Cash disbursements that represent returns on investment are interest, dividends, or drawings against profits. Amounts are either specified by contract or declared by the Board of Directors. Firms can perform all of the tasks associated with securing capital and servicing its sources, or agents can be engaged to do it for them. Major public corporations hire the services of banks or trust companies to do the following:

1. Register newly issued securities and cancel reacquired securities. The registrar signs and registers new securities (stocks or bonds) when issued initially or upon a purchase-sale transfer in the open market.

2. Record the names and number of shares or bonds held by investors. This record becomes the subsidiary ledger for capital stock or bonds payable. A financial institution serving in this capacity is referred to as a transfer agent.

3. Pay interest or dividends to individual investors. A check is written by the client to the fiscal or disbursing agent for an amount to cover the total payout. Individual checks are then written and distributed by the fiscal agent (except for interest on coupon bonds where coupons have to be redeemed). The same bank usually acts as transfer and disbursing agent.

It can now be seen that financial management is concerned with both investments and sources of capital. The major activities connected with both areas of responsibility are briefly described below. Keep in mind that the activities are basically the same for the investments phase and the capital sources phase.

Planning and Approval

Cash and total financial resources needs are assessed and expressed in the form of budgets. The supply and demand for funds is identified, and decisions are made about securing additional amounts if needed. Temporary surpluses of cash are foreseen through the medium of budgets, and plans are laid for their temporary investment. Commitments to longer-term investments are also made during the planning process. If capital is inadequate, provision is made for expansion through borrowings or equity issues. When the time comes to proceed with these plans, review and approval is involved—often at the highest management levels. Particulars are decided upon, such as types of securities to acquire (issue), price, rates of return, and maturity. Authorization is given to move ahead with purchases or sales of investments and obtaining new capital.

Buying and Selling

Consummating some types of transactions is elementary, as, for example, when purchasing U.S. Treasury bills. A purchase or sale can be made with a single telephone call to a bank or brokerage house. In other cases, such as when a long-term investment is made to gain control of another firm or new securities are to be issued, the proceedings are lengthy, complicated, and expensive. They may involve many intermediaries, including lawyers; "finders," who locate prospective acquisition candidates; CPAs; and investment bankers.

Certificates evidencing a transaction are received when the price is paid or surrendered when proceeds are received in the case of a sale. A certificate can be made out to the investor, to the name of the brokerage house where it is held, or to the previous owner who has, in turn, endorsed it over to the buyer. Some securities are not registered and do not specify the owner. They are "bearer" securities, negotiable by anyone who possesses them.

Custody and Safeguarding

Some securities are held by brokerage houses in the "street name," as we mentioned a moment ago. Physical safeguarding is their responsibility. If the investor takes possession of securities, the problem of their safeguarding arises. That problem is usually solved by either keeping them in a safe deposit box at a bank or locking them in a safe on the premises. Access to the securities is limited, often requiring two designated parties to be present.

A firm may hold its own securities that have been purchased for the treasury or for resale. It may also hold securities that have been given as collateral to secure a loan or other credit transaction. Safeguarding these securities and keeping them separate from owned investments is an added responsibility.

Protecting legal documents, such as loan agreements, bond indentures, lease contracts, and unissued securities, is an important activity. Some debt securities are negotiable and have to be treated just like cash.

Recordkeeping

Detailed records of all borrowings, securities issued, investments, treasury stock, and securities held as collateral are necessary. These records contain information such as description, certificate number, cost or other valuation, date of acquisition or issue, denomination, location, and interest or dividend rates. Entries are made for purchases, sales, and changes in terms or location, as well as for stock dividends or splits. The detailed records are subsidiary accounts to the general ledger control accounts.

General Accounting

Investments, treasury stock, and sources of capital have to be measured and recorded in the general ledger. They also have to be defined as current or noncurrent in classified balance sheets.

Cost or its equivalent is usually the basis of valuation of investments and includes all outlays incurred in the transaction. A long-term investment in stock effected as a pooling of interests, however, would be valued at the acquired firm's underlying equity. Expenses such as finder's fees, registration costs, and professional fees stemming from a pooling of interests are immediately charged to income and not included in the investment cost. Cost may be modified, however. For example, certain marketable equity securities are carried at the lower of aggregate cost or market. Common stock investments in subsidiaries and investee firms are maintained on an equity basis. That, in turn, can have an effect on deferred income taxes.

Complicated measurements are encountered in accounting for sources of capital. Amortization of premiums and discounts—sometimes based on imputed interest rates—is involved in measuring debt expense. The treatment of capital leases is even more difficult. Debt that is restructured or is to be refunded presents other unique problems. As a result of the complexity of accounting for investments, treasury stock, and sources of capital, these areas are susceptible to error.

10.5 INTERNAL ACCOUNTING CONTROL EVALUATION: OBJECTIVES, STRATEGIES, AND RISK ANALYSIS

Investments

Investments, treasury stock, and collateralized securities are generally well controlled. Management is aware that securities can be almost as good as cash and are vulnerable to the same risks. Several control objectives and strategies to achieve them follow. They do not include the investment activities that interface with the cash disbursements or cash receipts phases of operations. Everything that we have studied concerning cash remains unchanged.

CONCEPT SUMMARY
Relationship of Cycle Functions and Controls:
Investments (I) and Sources of Capital (SC)

Function	Select Activities	Related Control Objective	Examples of Risks	Examples of Strategies
1. Planning and Approval	Prepare cash and capital budgets, plan for capital expansion.	No. 1 Investment and capital expansion is planned and authorized. Execution is according to plan.	(I) Inappropriate investments made. (SC) Increased cost of capital.	(I) Board Approval Required. (SC) Short- and long-term budgets.
2. Buying and Selling	Place orders, exchange consideration			
3. Custody and Safeguarding	Protect securities, loan agreements, leases, etc.	No. 2 Securities and documents are safeguarded. Access is restricted.	(I) Investments stolen. (SC) Unissued stock stolen.	(I) Keep in bank vault. (SC) Employ independent registrar.
4. Recordkeeping	Keep detailed records of securities held, borrowings, and stock issued	No. 3 Detailed records provide control.	(I) Poor decisions based on inaccurate information. (SC) Late dividend or interest payments.	(I) Detailed schedules for management. (SC) Employ a transfer and disbursing agent.
5. General Accounting	Make entries, maintain accounts, classify, and measure items	No. 4 Accounting is complete, prompt, and according to GAAP.	(I) Investments and related income misstated. (SC) Delayed public security issues.	(I) Assign responsibility to a technically competent person. (SC) Have an expert review statements.

The audit objectives for investments, treasury stock, and securities held as collateral are to be satisfied that:

- They physically exist and are owned by the firm (or clearly identified and segregated if held as collateral).
- Their valuation and classification is correct.
- Income from investments is properly recorded as to amount, type, and time period.

CONTROL OBJECTIVE 1. *All investment transactions are to be authorized by the Board of Directors or a designated official. Amounts, terms, security type and risk, and timing of investments are to be in accordance with criteria set by the firm.*

Risk Analysis

Without review and authorization, securities held as collateral or for resale to employees might be sold. Inappropriate or untimely investments might be made resulting in capital losses, cash flow problems, or unsatisfactory returns. Fictitious or inflated prices might be paid for securities. Unauthorized transactions might be entered into for personal gain—to the company's detriment. To avoid these risks, the following strategies could be used.

Strategies

- ✔ Set investment policies in writing, defining acceptable credit ratings and rates of return and requirements for maturity, diversification, and liquidity.
- ✔ Specify the individuals authorized to buy and sell securities and the dollar limits of their authority. Prepare written procedures for approval of transactions.
- ✔ Segregate payment for purchases and receipt of proceeds from the individual doing the buying and selling of investments.
- ✔ Require Board approval for acquisition or disposal of an equity interest in affiliates.
- ✔ Have an independent comparison made of executed transactions with the Board's minutes and buy/sell orders.

CONTROL OBJECTIVE 2. *Securities are to be safeguarded from theft and misappropriation and access restricted to authorized personnel.*

Risk Analysis

If precautions are not taken, securities might be stolen, lost or destroyed. Stock splits or dividends could be diverted. Individuals might remove securities for their personal use such as to obtain loans. The following strategies guard against these risks.

Strategies

- ✔ Keep all securities in a vault or safe-deposit box.
- ✔ Require two signatures from authorized personnel to gain admission to securities. Maintain a log of admissions.
- ✔ Segregate custodianship from investment decision making and accounting.
- ✔ Reconcile custodian reports for securities not kept on hand, with detailed records periodically.

CONTROL OBJECTIVE 3. *Securities are to be controlled through detailed records, which are themselves safeguarded.*

Risk Analysis

Control failures could have these adverse consequences. Unauthorized transactions might be entered into that alter the approved composition of the investment portfolio into a highly undesirable mix. Buy or sell decisions could be made on the basis of inaccurate information. The detailed records and investment portfolio composition might fall into disagreement. Various strategies ward off these risks.

Strategies

- ✔ Maintain a log of buy and sell orders issued to brokers.
- ✔ Reconcile transactions recorded for the period with brokers' statements.
- ✔ Periodically count securities on hand, and reconcile details to subsidiary records.
- ✔ Prepare detailed schedules of investments periodically, and issue them to management.

CONTROL OBJECTIVE 4. *Accounting (recording, classifying, and valuation) for investments, related income, and subsequent adjustments of investment balances is to be prompt and in accordance with generally accepted principles.*

Risk Analysis

Some of the errors and irregularities possible include: Investment balances and income might be measured incorrectly or in the wrong time period. Transactions might go unrecorded. Returns on investments (gains, interest, dividends) could be diverted. Misclassification of investments could occur. Non-taxable income might be improperly treated as taxable. Defensive strategies follow.

Strategies

- ✔ Assign responsibility for proper accounting to a specific individual. Have adjusting entries reviewed.
- ✔ Reconcile general ledger control accounts periodically to the detailed records.
- ✔ Compare income from investments for interim periods (e.g., every six months) with projected amounts. Accrue income based on amounts indicated by detailed records.
- ✔ Employ forms for executing transactions and accounting. Prohibit entries to the accounts unless a completed, authorized form is submitted.

Sources of Capital

On the surface, the control objectives for sources of capital seem almost the same as for investments. They focus on authorization, safeguarding, detailed records, and accounting. There are differences, however—differences in emphasis and in the strategies employed to achieve control objectives. The relative importance of one control versus another is different when it comes to sources of capital. Servicing debt and keeping track of the various individual providers of capital are the paramount concerns. If a transfer and disbursing agent are assigned these responsibilities, the control objectives are virtually achieved. In the realm of investments, on the other hand, authorization and safeguarding of securities is of greater importance.

The caveats we issued before are worth repeating because they are equally true here. Remember that transactions that expand sources of capital are infrequent and usually controlled at upper-management levels. Once capital is obtained, servicing it leads us into the cash disbursements system and a separate set of objectives and strategies.

The audit objectives for sources of capital are to be satisfied that:

- All sources of capital are recorded and their valuation, classification, and necessary disclosures are proper.
- Returns of capital and returns on capital are correctly demarcated and properly recorded and classified in the appropriate time period.
- Commitments to future capital transactions (stock options, warrants, contingent issues of stock) are properly reflected in the financial statements.

CONTROL OBJECTIVE 1. *Expansion of capital is only to be undertaken after planning and coordination with short- and long-term needs. Authorization is to come from the Board of Directors and is to include specifications of type, permanence, cost, and capital structure balances.*

Risk Analysis

The risks associated with this objective are very serious. Control over the firm might be lost to creditors or outsiders. Financing might have to be accepted under unsatisfactory terms. Costs of capital could increase to unacceptable levels, and a decline in credit standing take place. An imbalance of debt to equity could arise, carrying with it the risk of default. Severe consequences such as these call for rigorous controls.

Strategies

- Specify individuals authorized to negotiate and carry out borrowings and equity issues, including the dollar limits of their authority. Require dual signatures on all notes, leases, and mortgages.
- Prepare cash, financing, and capital expenditure budgets for near-term operations and long-term planning.
- Set policies in writing concerning: debt-equity ratio; dividend payout ratio; the portion of stock in public hands, and acceptable loan agreement restrictions.
- Review all prospective capital expansion transactions to see that existing agreements are not violated, and proposed restrictions are tolerable.
- Prepare a checklist of restrictive covenants and review for compliance periodically.

CONTROL OBJECTIVE 2. *Documents, certificates, and contracts relating to sources of capital are to be safeguarded. Custody is to be controlled and access restricted to authorized personnel.*

Risk Analysis

The risks faced in this case are obvious. Unissued or retired security certificates might be put to unauthorized use, lost, or stolen. Legal documents pertaining to borrowings or stock issues might be lost, stolen, or destroyed. To protect against these possibilities, the following strategies are employed.

Strategies

- ✔ Use the services of an independent registrar of securities.
- ✔ Assign responsibility for custody to a specific party. Keep this duty segregated from detailed record keeping.
- ✔ Use prenumbered certificates for stocks, bonds, stock options, warrants, etc.
- ✔ Keep contracts and security certificates under lock and key and restrict access to them.
- ✔ Require submission of a surrendered certificate, or a stockholder affidavit for a lost certificate, before a new one can be issued.

CONTROL OBJECTIVE 3. *Detailed records are to supply information on the amount and identity of individual providers of capital, as well as conditions attaching to each source.*

Risk Analysis

If this information were not readily available, dividend or interest payments might be made late, or to the wrong party. Payments claimed to be for dividends or interest could be diverted. Proceeds from borrowings or stock issues or from the exercise of options or warrants could also be diverted. Defensive strategies follow.

Strategies

- ✔ Employ a transfer and disbursing agent.
- ✔ Use an imprest cash account for paying dividends if a disbursing agent is not employed. Reconcile the account.
- ✔ Have someone independent of the disbursing function redeposit unclaimed dividend checks immediately.
- ✔ Make tests of reasonableness to see if interest and dividend payments agree with balances and terms of outstanding sources of capital.
- ✔ Periodically count unissued stocks and bonds on hand and reconcile details to subsidiary records and, in turn, to general ledger control accounts.

✔ Segregate detailed record keeping from cash disbursements and document custodianship.

CONTROL OBJECTIVE 4.   *Accounting (recording, classification, valuation, and cut-off) for sources of capital and related returns to providers is to be complete, prompt, and correct.*

Risk Analysis

Accounting errors could result in unrecorded liabilities. Sources of capital might be misstated. Security issues could be delayed because of failure to comply with SEC regulations. Disclosures associated with sources of capital might not be made. Interest expense and dividends paid could be incorrectly measured or reported in the wrong time period. E.P.S. calculations might be incorrect. A sampling of strategies that are appropriate in these circumstances is given below.

Strategies

✔ Establish procedures for reporting Board actions to accounting concerning dividends declared, new borrowings, lease contracts, and stock issues or retirements.

✔ Routinely reconcile reports of registrar, transfer, and disbursing agents to general ledger control accounts.

✔ Set up standard journal entries based on debt contracts, for amortization of discounts or premiums and accrual or prepayment of interest.

✔ Have new securities offering statements prepared for the SEC or state authorities reviewed by an independent expert.

Evaluating Internal Accounting Controls

Infrequent transactions are typical of both investments and sources of capital. As a result, firms have an unsystematic approach to dealing with them. Flowcharting is seldom warranted in evaluating accounting controls because of these characteristics. A questionnaire such as the one in Exhibit 10–5 serves in searching for material control weaknesses, and learning how transactions are handled. Compliance testing is not attempted because substantive testing easily satisfies our audit objectives without having to rely on the system of accounting controls.

High-level authorization and oversight is the key to control in this audit area. Authorization to borrow, to expand owners' equity, and to make major investments generally comes from the Board of Directors and is recorded in their minutes. Considerable planning and negotiating is involved, and investment bankers, CPAs, and lawyers are consulted along the way. Preparation is lengthy and complicated. Concluding the transaction and recording it in the accounts, on the other hand, is swift and simple.

INTERNAL CONTROL QUESTIONNAIRE
Financial Management Cycle

Client _____   Period _____

Investments   Yes   No*

1. Does the Board of Directors (or its Finance or Executive Committee) either:
    a. Approve all securities transactions (type and price)?
    b. Or assign authorization powers to the Treasurer or a comparable official?

2. Is authorization from the Board or an official required for:
    a. Receipt or release of securities?
    b. Release of collateral?
    c. Changes in terms of securities?
    d. Write-offs of worthless securities?

3. Are the following segregated from one another?
    a. Cash receipts and disbursements.
    b. Detailed records of securities.
    c. Securities custodians.

4. Are registered securities made out in the firm's name or restrictively endorsed to them?

5. If securities are in the possession of an independent custodian (e.g., a bank), has the Board of Directors approved the appointment?

6. If securities are kept on hand, are they in a safe or similar locked and restricted device?

7. Is safeguarding securities the joint responsibility of two or more officials, and is access permitted only in the presence of both?

8. Is a surprise inspection and count of securities made periodically (or a direct confirmation obtained from independent custodians and collateralized debtors) by internal auditors or officials who do not have custody or access to them? Is the count/confirmation compared with the securities records?

9. Are records of securities kept in detail (including certificate number and dollar amount)?

10. Are detailed securities records periodically reconciled with the general ledger control accounts?

11. Does the detail of securities records reflect:
    a. Prompt entry of purchases and sales of securities owned?
    b. Prompt entry of receipt and release of securities held as collateral?
    c. Prompt receipt of proceeds from sale or maturity of securities?

12. Are securities held as collateral and treasury stock recorded, segregated, and controlled in the same way as investment securities?

13. Is income (dividends or interest) verified to data in financial publications or other sources?

---

*Note: A comments column is also normally provided for on the questionnaire so that the auditor can include explanations or working paper references—particularly when "No" answers are recorded.

continued on the following page

EXHIBIT 10–5

Sources of Capital

Yes   No

1. Is all borrowing authorized by the Board of Directors? Do they specify officers who can borrow, and maximum commitments they can make?
2. Are subsidiary company borrowings reviewed by the Board of the parent company?
3. Does an official review the terms of prospective borrowings and outstanding obligations to ensure compliance with restrictive convenants?
4. Are the terms of borrowings eventually negotiated, compared with the Board's authorization?
5. Are two authorized signatures required on all notes, leases, and mortgages?
6. Is a bank or trust company acting as the client's registrar, transfer agent, interest/dividend paying agent?
7. If so, are reports of the agents periodically reviewed and reconciled to general ledger controls by an independent person?
8. If the firm acts for itself in registering and transferring stock/bonds and paying dividends/interest:
    a. Is an imprest bank account used for interest/dividend payments, subject to satisfactory controls for cash disbursements?
    b. Are unissued certificates (stocks/bonds) kept in custody by an official?
    c. Are stock/bond certificates or cremation certificates kept on file to evidence retirements?
9. Are unclaimed dividends promptly recognized as liabilities and checks redeposited?
10. Are detailed records of borrowings kept by an employee who is not authorized to sign debt instruments or checks?
11. Is a shareholders' register kept showing details by class of stock?

EXHIBIT 10–5 (Continued)

An important set of controls are those that watch over restrictive covenants. Debt and equity contracts often have strings tied to the capital to protect investors. Failure to comply with a restriction may be an event of default. It can cause loans to immediately come due or give voting rights to preferred shareholders, who otherwise have none. Restrictive covenants constrain the client in various ways. They can limit dividend payouts and purchases of fixed assets, require that redemption or sinking funds be accumulated, prohibit or subordinate future borrowings, and impose working capital or interest coverage minimums.

Once again, the purpose of evaluating internal controls is to search for material weakness and improvements that might be recommended and to decide on the extent of substantive testing. Substantive testing is the next step.

10.6 SUBSTANTIVE TESTING

Ordinarily, compliance testing is bypassed in favor of substantive testing of balances, which include investments and related income, sources of capital balances, and associated dividends and interest accounts. The accounts relating to investment securities are considered first.

To achieve the first audit objective, examine the securities to ascertain their existence and ownership. If they are held by a custodian, a confirmation request is sent. Vouching buy and sell transactions and comparing carrying values to market values establishes the correctness of valuations. Analysis and vouching of interest income, dividend income, gains and losses, equity accruals, and write-downs to market values does two things. It substantiates investment income earned and accrued and investment balances. A detailed audit program describing these substantive tests of balances is shown in the appendix to this chapter. A working paper illustrating the audit procedures we have just discussed is shown in Exhibit 10–6. It is an analysis of marketable securities, gains and losses, and interest income earned and accrued. The kind of procedures used to substantiate source of capital balances depend on whether independent agents are employed.

If agents handle the details of stock, bonds, and disbursements of dividends and interest, a confirmation letter is sent. A written request for confirmation is also sent to creditors and trustees representing all other major forms of debt. For example, if you re-examine Chapter 7, you will see that the standard bank confirmation requests information on bank borrowings. Terms of the loan, interest rates, and assets pledged are confirmed in addition to the balance owed. Virtually all of the audit objectives for this area can be accomplished with one procedure.

Even if there is no agent, corroborating evidence can be readily collected from other sources. The steps to be taken are reflected in the audit program depicted in the chapter appendix. A schedule of borrowings and related interest, such as Exhibit 10–7 is first prepared. New sources of capital are added to beginning balances, and principal payments are subtracted. Interest accruals or prepayments are combined with interest payments and amortization of premiums and discounts. This analysis facilitates checking the correctness of calculations and accounting treatment. Then the transactions of the period are vouched to cash receipts and disbursements and documents such as loan agreements, Board minutes, and security certificates. This evidence demonstrates that the transactions were authorized, carried out as ordered, and recorded properly. A conclusion that the financial representations are (or are not) fair can then be drawn.

Analysis and auditing of equity sources of capital is basically the same as for borrowings. A detailed schedule is prepared to describe the changes that took place during the year and the balances which remain. Each change is examined and corroborated by some sort of evidence. Registrars and transfer agents are sent confirmation letters.

When analysis and testing of borrowings and equity is finished, several questions are posed. Are there any signs of unrecorded liabilities? Interest expense

Scott Interspacial Industries
Marketable Securities
12/31/X1

W. P. No.	C-1
Accountant	R
Date	1/16/X2

Classification	Description	At Cost — Balance, 12/31/X0	Additions	Sales	Balance, 12/31/X1	Market Price, 12/31/X1	Gain or <Loss> on Sale	Interest — Accrued 12/31/X0	Receipts	Accrued, 12/31/X1	19X1 Income
N/A	U.S. Treasury Notes, 8.5%, maturing 8/31/X5 ($100,000 face)	97845 GL	—	97945	—	—	621 >	2833 GL	4250 t / 1416 t	—	2833 ∧
CURRENT	U.S. Treasury Bills, 12.00%, maturing 3/15/X2 ∅	—	97000 α	—	1620 / 97000 GL / 98620 ⑧	98200 √ / 98200	—	—	—	1620 √ ⑧	1620 ∧
CURRENT	(A) Southern Railway Notes, 9%, 12/31/X2 ∅	60000 GL	—	—	60000 GL	59210 √	—	—	5400 t	—	5400 ∧
CURRENT	U.S. Treasury Notes, 12.5%, 3/31/X2 ($250,000 face) ∅	—	256500	—	256500 / 316500	257300 √ / 315410	—	—	1603125 t / 8000 > /b	781250 √ /b	15843.75 ∧
NON-CURRENT	Common Stocks: Recess Ind., 1000 sh. ∅	58750 GL	42750 α	—	58750 GL	87500 √	—		293375 R t	—	293375 ∧
	Shuttle Service Ltd., 9000 sh. ∅ / 1000 sh. ∅	—	5000 α	—	47750 GL / 53625 / 4687745	50500 √ / 53525 / 472860		2833	360 t 8 / 197751	9432.50	360 ∧ / 12235050

(A) Reclassified from non-current to current due to maturity in coming year.
∅ Examined security during yr. end count.
√ Agreed yr. end market value to 12/1/X2 Wall St. Journal.
GL Agreed balance to general ledger; also prior yr. w/p.
u Recalculated; traced to sales proceeds in cash receipts journal.
t Traced amounts to cash receipts journal.
√ Recalculated; amount of accrued appears proper.
b Accrued interest paid when note was purchased.
α Reviewed purchase documents; recorded at proper amount.
R Agreed to dividends declared per published investment service.
∧, ∧ Footed, crossfooted.

EXHIBIT 10-6

Scott Interspacial Industries
Debt Summary
12/31/X1

	W. P. No.	M-1
	ACCOUNTANT	R
	DATE	1/8/X2

| Debt / Terms | PRINCIPAL | | | | INTEREST | | | | |
	Balance, 12/31/X0	Additions	Payments	Balance, 12/31/X1	Current Portion	Non-Current Portion	Accrued, 12/31/X0	Payments	Expense	Accrued, 12/31/X1
C Mortgage										
R Chase Manhattan, 30 yr, 8¾%, semi-annual payments of $146,140, 3/1 and 9/1, secured by factory bldg., orig. amt. = $3,000,000 2@= 142,140 √ 2@= 142,140 ±	2,922,972 √	—	3/1 146,010 ① 9/1 146,710 ② √	2,850,252 ✗ G.L.	35,647 √	2,814,605	84,087 √	3/1 126,130 ② √ 9/1 125,930 ① √	250,905 √	83,132 ✗ G.L.
C Bonds										
R Series A, term, 20 yr., maturing 12/31/X9, int. at 5%, pd. 6/30 and 12/31. Issued at face. Bond trustee - Celestial Trust Co.	1,000,000 √	—	—	1,000,000 G.L.	—	1,000,000 √	—	6/30 25,000 √ 12/31 25,000 √ ±	50,000 √	—
C Bank Note										
R $100,000, 90 day, 12%, due 2/14/X2. Unsecured. Jefferson National Bank	—	100,000	—	100,000 G.L.	100,000 √	—	—	—	1,500 √	1,500 ✗ G.L.
Totals	3,922,972	100,000	3,2,720	3,950,252 ✗	135,647	3,814,605	84,087	3,0,560	302,105	84,632 ✗
	∧	∧	∧	∧	∧	∧	∧	∧	G.L.	∧

A,M Footed, cross-footed.
G.L. agreed to general ledger.
√ agreed to ending balance on prior yr. w/p.
W uncollateralized a-l/or agreed to permanent file amortization schedule.
C confirmed with debt holder or trustee.
± examined cancelled check.
a examined rate and agreed terms.
R reviewed debt covenants for compliance; no problems noted.

R.J.E. ⑥ DR. CR.
Long-Term Debt - Mortgage 35,647
Long-Term Debt - Bank Note 100,000
  Current Portion L.T. Debt 135,647

To reclassify current portion of L.T. debt for financial statement purposes.

EXHIBIT 10-7

might be disproportionately large, for instance, suggesting that outstanding debt is not reflected in the accounts. Have any restrictive covenants been violated? A question of whether the client is a going concern might be raised if an extreme event of default has occurred. Lastly, which securities are common stock equivalents or have a dilutive effect on EPS? The securities of "public" firms must be identified and their impact measured. The number of shares reserved for stock options, convertible securities, etc., must also be checked.

Analytical review of sources of capital and related accounts is generally unnecessary except for the relationship between interest expense and average outstanding debt during the period. That relationship is helpful in searching for unrecorded debt.

Sources of capital have a far-reaching effect stretching across many years. That is why documents and data such as loan agreements, schedules analyzing stock and debt, lease contracts, bond indentures, and option and stock purchase plans are carried forward from year to year in a permanent file.

We started this chapter by saying that our audit of financial statements was virtually finished. The last of the cycles has now been covered. The few concluding steps to be taken will be described in the next chapter. Then the auditors' report will be drafted. That is discussed in Chapter 12.

Key Terms

capital expenditure proposal	registrar
capitalized interest cost	registration costs
capital lease	restrictive covenants
debt service	self-constructed assets
event of default	shareholder's register
finder's fee	standard journal entry
fiscal agent	standing sources of capital
held in the street name	stratified dollar limits of authority
imprest dividend account	transfer agent
pooling of interests	transitory sources of capital
property records	

APPENDIX

AUDIT PROGRAM
Substantive Tests of Balances
Capital Assets Cycle

Client _____   Period _____

Done by:

Initial | Date

1. Reconcile the general ledger control account balances to the summary list of capital assets.
2. Check summary list of capital assets against detailed property records.
3. Analyze changes in the various general ledger capital asset control accounts.
4. Vouch additions to invoices, titles, deeds, timecards, etc.
5. Determine whether interest cost has been properly capitalized.
6. Inspect significant asset acquisitions.
7. Analyze repairs and maintenance expenses, and examine supporting documents to see if any items should be capitalized.
8. Verify calculation of the investment tax credit for qualifying assets.
9. Trace capital asset deductions to disposal authorization and associated documents (e.g., bill of sale).
10. Examine the general ledger and detailed property records to check that disposals were properly removed from the asset and accumulated depreciation accounts and that the amount of gain or loss or treatment of trade-in value is correct.
11. Verify calculation of the investment tax credit recapture and deferred income tax credit adjustment (if any) on disposals.
12. Review with management whether fully depreciated assets should be written off.
13. Review the reasonableness of estimated useful lives and depreciation rates.
14. Compare depreciation methods and estimated useful lives employed this year with prior periods to determine consistency.
15. Determine whether any assets are pledged or carry a lien and whether any material purchase commitments existed at year-end.
16. Verify that the beginning general ledger balances for accumulated depreciation are correct.
17. Test depreciation calculations for the current year's expense.
18. Reconcile depreciation expense to additions made to the accumulated depreciation accounts.
19. Obtain a schedule of new capital leases and reconcile to the general ledger control account. Vouch to the lease contract. Review the additions for correct treatment as a capital lease. Check related calculations.

AUDIT PROGRAM
Substantive Tests of Balances
Financial Managment Cycle

Client _____   Period _____

Investments

1. Obtain or prepare a schedule of securities, including transactions and related income for the year. List details and identify items as short-term, long-term, affiliates, treasury stock, or collateral.
2. Check schedule for arithmetical accuracy and trace totals to general ledger control accounts.
3. Inspect securities on hand in the presence of the custodian. Compare with schedule for certificate numbers and other details.
4. Confirm securities held by others.
5. Determine whether any owned securities are pledged.
6. Vouch transactions of the period; verify gains and losses.
7. Verify investment income using published sources. Check related accruals and unamortized premium/discount.
8. Compare market values of securities with carrying values. Consider write-downs to aggregate market or for permanent impairment of value.
9. Review and recalculate equity in earnings of investees and subsidiaries, and related goodwill amortization.
10. Trace treasury stock to the stock register and collateralized stock to loan agreements.

Sources of Capital

A—BORROWINGS

1. Obtain and prepare a schedule of borrowings, including transactions for the period and related interest. List details and identify as to type (lease contracts, bonds, notes, etc.) and classification (current or non-current). Segregate debt to owners and affiliates.
2. Check schedules for arithmetical accuracy and trace totals to general ledger control accounts.
3. Request confirmation of borrowings from lenders, trustees and lessors. Include request for terms, interest, and security pledged.
4. Vouch transactions for the period. Examine new debt agreements and trace principal payments on outstanding debt.
5. Examine cancelled debt securities retired during the period and account for unissued bonds.
6. Check calculations for interest (expense, accrued, or prepaid) on all borrowings and leases and unamortized discount or premium.
7. Vouch selected interest payments. Check for reasonableness of the year's interest expense and whether there might be any unrecorded debts.
8. Review convenants of debt agreements for compliance or events of default.

B—OWNERS' EQUITY

Done by:
Initial | Date

9. Obtain or prepare a schedule of various categories of owners' equity (capital stock, partners' capital, additional paid-in-capital, drawings, retained earnings).

10. Check schedule for arithmetical accuracy, and trace totals to general ledger control accounts.

11. Request confirmation of capital stock details from transfer agent and registrar (authorized and issued shares, etc.), or see No. 12.

12. If client keeps its own records, verify unissued and retired stock certificates, and vouch transactions during the period that changed owners' equity.

13. Foot the shareholders' register, and trace totals to general ledger control accounts.

14. Check for correct accounting treatment of entries made to retained earnings, such as prior period adjustments and stock dividends.

15. Check for proper recording and payment of dividends on common and preferred stock.

16. Reconcile dividends paid to rate authorized and outstanding shares on date of record.

17. Secure information on convertible securities, options, warrants, stock purchases plans, etc. for needed disclosures and EPS calculations.

Questions and Problems

Questions

10-1 Why is flowcharting and compliance testing of capital asset and financial management transactions usually not warranted?

10-2 In the audit of capital assets, certain expense accounts are analyzed in search of assets. Which accounts are these? Which items should be reclassified and capitalized if encountered?

10-3 Securities in the possession of a firm can be classified in a number of ways. Enumerate these and indicate the audit procedures you would follow in verifying that the classification of each was correct.

10-4 What are the audit objectives for capital assets?

10-5 What are the audit objectives for investments in securities?

10-6 Describe the audit procedure(s) you would follow to identify assets that have been pledged to secure borrowings. How would you ascertain that the terms of a debt are as stated by a client?

10-7 Distinguish between a transfer agent, a registrar, and a disbursing agent. What is the primary substantive test procedure employed with these agents?

10-8 What safeguards do you consider most appropriate for securities?

10-9 An analysis of borrowings includes several types of accounts. What are they, and why are they brought together on the same schedule?

10-10 Describe the audit procedures applied to dividends.

Multiple Choice Questions From Professional Examinations

10-11 An auditor determines that a client has properly capitalized a leased asset (and corresponding lease liability). As part of the auditor's procedures, the auditor should

    a. Substantiate the cost of the property to the lessor and determine that this is the cost recorded by the client.

    b. Evaluate the propriety of the interest rate used in discounting the future lease payments.

    c. Determine that the leased property is being amortized over the life of the lease.

    d. Evaluate whether the total amount of lease payments represents the fair market value of the property.

10-12 Which of the following best describes the independent auditor's approach to obtaining satisfaction concerning depreciation expense in the income statement?

    a. Verify the mathematical accuracy of the amounts charged to income as a result of depreciation expense.

    b. Determine the method for computing depreciation expense, and ascertain that it is in accordance with generally accepted accounting principles.

    c. Reconcile the amount of depreciation expense to those amounts credited to accumulated depreciation accounts.

    d. Establish the basis for depreciable assets, and verify the depreciation expense.

10-13 Which of the following is a customary audit procedure for the verification of the legal ownership of real property?

    a. Examination of correspondence with the corporate counsel concerning acquisition matters.

    b. Examination of ownership documents registered and on file at a public hall of records.

    c. Examination of corporate minutes and resolutions concerning the approval to acquire property, plant, and equipment.

    d. Examination of deeds and title guaranty policies on hand.

10-14 Tennessee Company violated company policy by erroneously capitalizing the cost of painting its warehouse. The CPA examining Tennessee's financial statements would most likely learn of this error by

    a. Discussing Tennessee's capitalization policies with its controller.

    b. Reviewing the titles and descriptions for all construction work orders issued during the year.

    c. Observing, during the physical inventory observation, that the warehouse has been painted.

    d. Examining in detail a sample of construction work orders.

10-15 A normal audit procedure is to analyze the current year's repairs and maintenance accounts to provide evidence in support of the audit proposition that

    a. Expenditures for fixed assets have been recorded in the proper period.

    b. Capital expenditures have been properly authorized.

    c. Noncapitalizable expenditures have been properly expensed.

    d. Expenditures for fixed assets have been capitalized.

10-16 When a company has treasury stock certificates on hand, a year-end count of the certificates by the auditor is

    a. Required when the company classifies treasury stock with other assets.

    b. Not required if treasury stock is a deduction from stockholders' equity.

    c. Required when the company had treasury stock transactions during the year.

    d. Always required.

10-17 A company has additional temporary funds to invest. The Board of Directors decided to purchase marketable securities and assigned the future purchase and sale decisions to a responsible financial executive. The best person(s) to make periodic reviews of the investment activity should be

    a. The investment committee of the Board of Directors.

    b. The treasurer.

    c. The corporate controller.

    d. The chief operating officer.

10-18 In order to avoid the misappropriation of company-owned marketable securities, which of the following is the best course of action that can be taken by the management of a company with a large portfolio of marketable securities?

a. Require that one trustworthy and bonded employee be responsible for access to the safekeeping area where securities are kept.
b. Require that employees who enter and leave the safekeeping area sign and record in a log the exact reason for their access.
c. Require that employees involved in the safekeeping function maintain a subsidiary control ledger for securities on a current basis.
d. Require that the safekeeping function for securities be assigned to a bank that will act as a custodial agent.

10-19 A company guarantees the debt of an affiliate. Which of the following best describes the audit procedure that would make the auditor aware of the guarantee?

a. Review minutes and resolutions of the Board of Directors.
b. Review prior year's working papers with respect to such guarantees.
c. Review the possibility of such guarantees with the chief accountant.
d. Review the legal letter returned by the company's outside legal counsel.

10-20 The auditor's program for the examination of long-term debt should include steps that require the

a. Verification of the existence of the bondholders.
b. Examination of any bond trust indenture.
c. Inspection of the accounts payable subsidiary ledger.
d. Investigation of credits to the bond interest income account.

10-21 During the course of an audit, a CPA observes that the recorded interest expense seems to be excessive in relation to the balance in the long-term debt account. This observation could lead the auditor to suspect that

a. Long-term debt is understated.
b. Discount on bonds payable is overstated.
c. Long-term debt is overstated.
d. Premium on bonds payable is understated.

10-22 A company issued bonds for cash during the year under audit. To ascertain that this transaction was properly recorded, the auditor's best course of action is to

a. Request a statement from the bond trustee as to the amount of the bonds issued and outstanding.
b. Confirm the results of the issuance with the underwriter or investment banker.

   c. Trace the cash received from the issuance to the accounting records.

   d. Verify that the net cash received is credited to an account entitled "Bonds Payable".

10-23 An audit program for the examination of the retained earnings account should include a step that requires verification of the

   a. Gain or loss resulting from disposition of treasury shares.

   b. Market value used to charge retained earnings to account for a two-for-one stock split.

   c. Authorization for both cash and stock dividends.

   d. Approval of the adjustment to the beginning balance as a result of a write-down of an account receivable.

10-24 Florida Corporation declared a 100% stock dividend during 1975. In connection with the examination of Florida's financial statements, Florida's auditor should determine that

   a. The additional shares issued do not exceed the number of authorized but previously unissued shares.

   b. Stockholders received their additional shares by confirming year-end holdings with them.

   c. The stock dividend was properly recorded at fair market value.

   d. Florida's stockholders have authorized the issuance of 100% stock dividends.

10-25 If a company employs a capital stock registrar and/or transfer agent, either one or both should be requested to confirm directly to the auditor the number of shares of each class of stock

   a. Surrendered and cancelled during the year.

   b. Authorized at the balance sheet date.

   c. Issued and outstanding at the balance sheet date.

   d. Authorized, issued, and outstanding during the year.

Problems

10-26 You are the in-charge auditor of Astro Aeronautics, a public corporation with total assets of over $1 billion. Included in the assets are short-term marketable securities and long-term security investments. The financial management function is located at executive headquarters in Lexington, Massachusetts, and performed by high-ranking officials of the company. List six questions you would ask in reviewing internal controls concerning custodianship of securities.

10-27 Rivers, CPA, is the auditor for a manufacturing company with a balance sheet that includes the caption "Property, Plant, and Equipment." Rivers has been asked by the company's management if audit adjustments or reclassifications are required for the following material items that have been included or excluded from "Property, Plant, and Equipment."

1. A tract of land was acquired during the year. The land is the future site of the client's new headquarters, which will be constructed in the following year. Commissions were paid to the real estate agent used to acquire the land, and expenditures were made to relocate the previous owner's equipment. These commissions and expenditures were expensed and are excluded from "Property, Plant, and Equipment."

2. Clearing costs were incurred to make the land ready for construction. These costs were included in "Property, Plant, and Equipment."

3. During the land-clearing process, timber and gravel were recovered and sold. The proceeds from the sale were recorded as other income and are excluded from "Property, Plant, and Equipment."

4. A group of machines was purchased under a royalty agreement that provides royalty payments based on units of production from the machines. The cost of the machines, freight costs, unloading charges, and royalty payments were capitalized and are included in "Property, Plant, and Equipment."

Required:

a. Describe the general characteristics of assets, such as land, buildings, improvements, machinery, equipment, and fixtures, that should normally be classified as "Property, Plant, and Equipment," and identify audit objectives (i.e., how an auditor can obtain audit satisfaction) in connection with the examination of "Property, Plant, and Equipment." Do not discuss specific audit procedures.

b. Indicate whether each of the four items above requires one or more audit adjustments or reclassifications, and explain why such adjustments or reclassifications are required or not required.
Organize your answer as follows:

Item Number	Is Audit Adjustment or Reclassification Required? Yes or No	Reasons Why Audit Adjustment or Reclassification is Required or Not Required

AICPA

10-28 The following covenants are extracted from the indenture of a 20-year bond issue. The indenture provides that failure to comply with its terms in any respect automatically advances the due date of the loan to the date of noncompliance:

1. "The debtor company shall endeavor to maintain a working capital ratio of 2 to 1 at all times, and, in any fiscal year following a failure to maintain said ratio, the company shall restrict compensation of officers to a total of $100,000. Officers for this purpose shall include Chairman of the Board of Directors, President, all vice presidents, Secretary, and Treasurer."

2. "The debtor company shall keep all property which is security for this debt insured against loss by fire to the extent of 100 percent of its actual value. Policies of insurance comprising this protection shall be filed with the trustee."

3. "The debtor company shall pay all taxes legally assessed against property which is security for this debt within the time provided by law for payment without penalty and shall deposit receipted tax bills or equally acceptable evidence of payment of same with the trustee."

4. "A sinking fund shall be deposited with the trustee by semiannual payments of $300,000, from which the trustee shall, at his discretion, purchase bonds of this issue."

Required:

a. Indicate the audit procedures you would perform for each covenant.
b. Comment on any disclosure requirements that you believe are necessary.

AICPA

10-29 In connection with a recurring examination of the financial statements of the Louis Manufacturing Company for the year ended December 31, you have been assigned the audit of the Manufacturing Equipment, Manufacturing Equipment—Accumulated Depreciation, and Repairs to Manufacturing Equipment accounts. Your review of Louis' policies and procedures has disclosed the following pertinent information:

1. The Manufacturing Equipment account includes the net invoice price plus related freight and installation costs for all of the equipment in Louis' manufacturing plant.

2. The Manufacturing Equipment and Accumulated Depreciation accounts are supported by a subsidiary ledger, which shows the cost and accumulated depreciation for each piece of equipment.

3. An annual budget for capital expenditures of $1,000 or more is prepared by the budget committee and approved by the Board of Directors.

Capital expenditures over $1,000 that are not included in this budget must be approved by the Board of Directors, and variations of 20 percent or more must be explained to the board. Approval by the supervisor of production is required for capital expenditures under $1,000.

4. Company employees handle installation, removal, repair, and rebuilding of the machinery. Work orders are prepared for these activities and are subject to the same budgetary control as other expenditures. Work orders are not required for external expenditures.

Required:

a. Cite the major objectives of your audit of the Manufacturing Equipment, Manufacturing Equipment—Accumulated Depreciation, and Repairs of Manufacturing Equipment accounts. Do not include in this listing the auditing procedures designed to accomplish these objectives.

b. Prepare the portion of your audit program applicable to the review of current-year additions to the Manufacturing Equipment account.

AICPA (Adapted)

10-30 You were engaged to examine the financial statements of Ronlyn Corporation for the year ended June 30. On May 1, the corporation borrowed $500,000 from Second National Bank to finance plant expansion. The long-term note agreement provided for the annual payment of principal and interest over five years. The existing plant was pledged as security for the loan.

Due to unexpected difficulties in acquiring the building site, the plant expansion had not begun by June 30. To make use of the borrowed funds, management decided to invest in stocks and bonds, and on May 16, the $500,000 was invested in securities.

Required:

a. What are the audit objectives in the examination of long-term debt?

b. Prepare an audit program for the examination of the long-term note agreement between Ronlyn and Second National Bank.

c. How could you verify the security position of Ronlyn on June 30?

d. In your audit of investments, how would you
   1. Verify the dividend or interest income recorded?
   2. Determine market value?
   3. Establish the authority for security purchases?

AICPA

10-31 Hardware Manufacturing Company, a closely held corporation, has operated since 1960 but has not had its financial statements audited. The company now plans to issue additional capital stock to sell to outsiders and wishes to engage you to examine its current transactions and render an opinion on the financial statements for the year ended December 31.

The company has expanded from one plant to three plants and has frequently acquired, modified, and disposed of all types of equipment. Fixed assets have a net book value of 70 percent of total assets and consist of land and buildings, diversified machinery and equipment, and furniture and fixtures. Some property was acquired by donation from stockholders. Depreciation was recorded by several methods using various estimated lives.

Required:

a. May you confine your examination solely to current-year transactions of this prospective client whose financial statements have not previously been examined? Why?

b. Prepare an audit program for the January 1 opening balances of the Land, Building and Equipment, and Accumulated Depreciation accounts at Hardware Manufacturing Company. You need not include tests of current transactions in your program.

AICPA (Adapted)

10-32 As a result of highly profitable operations over a number of years, Eastern Manufacturing Corporation accumulated a substantial investment portfolio. In his examination of the financial statements for the year ended December 31, 19X0, the following information came to the attention of the Corporation's CPA:

1. The manufacturing operations of the corporation resulted in an operating loss for the year.

2. In 19X0, the corporation placed the securities making up the investment portfolio with a financial institution, which will serve as custodian of the securities. Formerly, the securities were kept in the corporation's safe deposit box in the local bank.

3. On December 31, 19X0, the corporation sold and then repurchased on the same day a number of securities that had appreciated greatly in value. Management stated that the purpose of the sale and repurchase was to establish a higher cost and book value for the securities and to avoid the reporting of a loss for the year.

Required:

a. List the objectives of the CPA's examination of the investment account.

b. Under what conditions would the CPA accept a confirmation of the securities on hand from the custodian in lieu of inspecting and counting the securities himself?

c. What disclosure, if any, of the sale and repurchase of the securities would the CPA recommend for the financial statements?

AICPA

10-33 In connection with his examination of the financial statements of Belasco Chemicals, Inc., Grande Mack, CPA, is considering the necessity of inspecting marketable securities on the balance sheet date, May 31, 19X1, or at some other date. The marketable securities held by Belasco include negotiable bearer bonds kept in a safe in the treasurer's office and miscellaneous stocks and bonds kept in a safe deposit box at The Merchants Bank. Both the negotiable bearer bonds and the miscellaneous stocks and bonds are material to proper presentation of Belasco's financial position.

Required:

a. What factors should Mr. Mack consider in determining the necessity for inspecting these securities on May 31, 19X1, as opposed to other dates?

b. Assume that Mr. Mack plans to send a member of his staff to Belasco's offices and The Merchants Bank on May 31, 19X1, to make the security inspection. What instructions should he give to this staff member as to the conduct of the inspection and the evidence to be included in the audit working papers? (Note: Do not discuss the valuation of securities, the income from securities, or the examination of information contained in the books and records of the company.)

c. Assume that Mack finds it impracticable to send a member of his staff to Belasco's offices and The Merchants Bank on May 31, 19X1. What alternative procedures may he employ to assure himself that the company had physical possession of its marketable securities on May 31, 19X1, if the securities are inspected on May 28, 19X1? on June 5, 19X1?

AICPA

10-34 The controller of AB Limited has presented CA, the shareholders' auditor, with the financial statements for the year ended June 30, 1983. The statements include the statement of contributed surplus and retained earnings for the year on page 407.

Required:

Outline audit procedures that CA would apply to verify the items presented in the statement of contributed surplus and retained earnings. *Ignore procedures related to "Net income for the year".*

CICA (Adapted)

AB LIMITED

Statement of Contributed Surplus and Retained Earnings

for the year ended June 30

	1983	1982
Contributed surplus		
Incentive grants (note 4)	$ 94,200	—
Deduct:		
Cost of redemption of preferred shares in		
excess of their par values	40,000	—
Balance at end of year	$ 54,200	
Retained earnings		
Balance, beginning of year	$1,025,000	$ 980,000
Net income for the year	128,000	105,000
	$1,153,000	$1,085,000
Deduct:		
Dividend on preferred shares	$ 30,000	$ 60,000
Extraordinary adjustments to company		
pension plan (note 5)	73,000	—
	$ 103,000	$ 60,000
Balance at end of year	$1,050,000	$1,025,000

AB LIMITED

Notes to Financial Statements

for the year ended June 30, 1983

Note 4

During the year the company received the following grants from the Government of Canada.

Grant received relating to wage expenses of the year and future
years for new jobs created by plant expansion $44,200
Grant received relating to the acquisition of fixed assets for plant
expansion 50,000

The Federal government has approved additional grants totalling $30,000 relating to fixed asset acquisitions. These grants have not been received at June 30, 1983 and, accordingly, are not recorded in the accounts in the year then ended.

Note 5

During the year the benefits payable under the company's pension plan were modified. Accordingly, the company made past service payments to the trustees of the plan totalling $53,000.

The consulting actuaries carried out the normal biennial actuarial revaluation which is required by the company's pension plan. Accordingly, the company made payments to the trustees of the plan totalling $20,000.

10-35 You are a CPA engaged in an examination of the financial statements of Pate Corporation for the year ended December 31, 19X3. The financial statements and records of Pate Corporation have not been audited by a CPA in prior years.

The stockholders' equity section of Pate Corporation's balance sheet at December 31, 19X3, follows:

Stockholders' equity:

Capital stock—10,000 shares of $10 par value authorized; 5,000 shares issued and outstanding	$ 50,000
Capital contributed in excess of par value of capital stock	32,580
Retained earnings	47,320
Total stockholders' equity	$129,900

Pate Corporation was founded in 19X0. The corporation has ten stockholders and serves as its own registrar and transfer agent. There are no capital stock subscription contracts in effect.

Required:

a. Prepare the detailed audit program for the examination of the three accounts comprising the Stockholders' Equity section of Pate Corporation's balance sheet. (Do not include in the audit program the verification of the results of the current year's operations.)

b. After every other figure on the balance sheet has been audited by the CPA, it might appear that the retained earnings figure is a balancing figure and requires no further verification. Why does the CPA verify retained earnings as he does the other figures on the balance sheet? Discuss.

AICPA

11

Completing the audit

Chapter 5 presented the systems approach to auditing. Exhibit 5–1 gave an overview of an audit by breaking it down into six steps. The first five steps were described in Chapters 5 through 10. This chapter will go through the details of the last step, namely, concluding audit procedures, preparing the auditor's report, and reviewing working papers. The primary topics of interest will be contingent liabilities, lawyers' letters, management representation letters, and subsequent events. After these topics are discussed, the chapter will review the steps to show the importance of quality review in all phases of an audit. Finally, the chapter will discuss the normal conclusion in most audits—an unqualified opinion accompanied by a management letter.

11.1 CONTINGENCIES AND COMMITMENTS

The financial statements represent the output of the accounting process. As such, they reflect the accounting events that have occurred. However, much important financial information is not reflected in the financial statements. For full and complete disclosure, this information is generally given in notes to the statements.

Contingent Liabilities

The most common liabilities involve a known amount and have a fixed date when payment is due. For example, when inventory is purchased, the amount of the liability "accounts payable" is known—it is simply the amount of the invoice. The invoice also states when the payment is due, usually in 30 days.

There are, however, liabilities which do exist but whose amounts are uncertain. For example, when a plane crashes, the insurer of an airline definitely owes money to survivors and the families of the victims. However, the amount owed is uncertain, pending negotiation and litigation. Since the amount to be paid out is large, to omit it entirely from the financial statements would be extremely misleading. On the other hand, to include it presents two problems: (1) the accounting problem of assigning a dollar figure, and (2) the legal problem of possibly prejudicing negotiations.

Even more difficult are liabilities which may or may not exist. An example would be a lawsuit against the company alleging negligence and asking for damages. The company may contend that there was no negligence and that the suit has no merit. However, the judge or jury may hold the company responsible and award damages anyway. Further, a more subtle possibility exists. The company may publicly claim that the suit has no claim but privately realize that the company very well might lose. This type of situation presents all the difficulties of the earlier problem, but there is added uncertainty.

In circumstances like this, there is no mechanical rule which can be clearly applied in every situation. The accounting treatment of such events necessarily involves judgement. However, the generally accepted procedure laid out in *Statement of Financial Accounting Standards No. 5,* "Accounting for Contingencies," requires three steps. The first step is to determine the liability to be: (1) probable, (2) reasonably possible, or (3) remote. The second step is to determine if the amount of the potential liability: (1) can be reasonably estimated, or (2) cannot be reasonably estimated. The third step is to apply the following rules:

1. An accrual is required when the liability is probable *and* the amount can be reasonably estimated. In all other cases an accrual is not required.
2. A note is required if the liability is only reasonably possible or if the amount cannot be estimated.
3. A note is permitted, but not required, if the liability is only remote.

Product Warranties

There is a fairly straightforward accrual of a contingent liability in the case of product warranties. Many companies agree to fix products if they break within a certain time from the date of sale. All of the sales revenue is recognized in the period of sale. In order to match expenses with revenues, the company must recognize related warranty expense in the same period. Since products do break, the likelihood of incurring warranty costs in the future is a virtual certainty. Further, companies can often predict the future costs associated with warranties. Thus, this situation meets the requirements for an accrual.

Guaranteed Notes

There are two cases where the amounts are known for certain and are generally disclosed even if the likelihood is remote. These are: (1) discounted notes receivable, and (2) guaranteed notes payable of other companies. In both cases, the company will pay the creditor only if the debtor does not pay. Discounted notes receivable can be shown on the balance sheet as a contra-asset to the notes receivable account or disclosed in a note. As a practical matter, disclosure by note is always used.

The disclosure by Hercules, Inc., is typical: "At December 31, 1978, Hercules was contingently liable as guarantor of notes payable of affiliated companies aggregating $26,400,000."

Lawsuits

The accrual of a contingent liability does not occur very frequently in the case of lawsuits. Even if the liability is probable, the amount cannot be reasonably estimated, and thus no accrual is made. A note to the financial statements will describe the suit and perhaps mention the potential impact on the company.

Exhibit 11–1 provides three examples of notes for contingent liabilities involving lawsuits. The first note concerns the General Motors Corporation. This is the most common type where the company acknowledges that it is involved in a number of lawsuits but reassures the users of the financial statements that their effect will not be material. As a practical matter, given the current legal climate, every major corporation will be involved in lawsuits. Thus, the mere existence of lawsuits should not be cause for alarm—they are part of doing business today.

The second note in Exhibit 11–1 concerns the Gillette Company. As is the case for all major corporations, the company acknowledges that it is involved in a number of lawsuits. But for Gillette, the potential liability *may* be material in relation to earnings, though it would not be material in relation to the company's financial position. The auditor evidently believes this note is adequate disclosure because the auditor's opinion does not refer to it.

The third note in Exhibit 11–1 concerns the St. Regis Paper Company. The company pleaded no contest (*nolo contendere*) to a federal antitrust indictment, which is in essence an admission of guilt. This has evidently spawned a number of civil suits by private individuals and corporations claiming damages. Since St. Regis has already pleaded no contest in the federal case, the plaintiffs in these civil cases have a very good chance to win. But the amount of liability is still unknown. Because the amount of liability cannot be reasonably estimated, it can only be disclosed in a note—not on the financial statements. Because the amount could be quite large, the auditor must qualify his opinion with respect to these lawsuits.

Commitments

Corporations may sign contracts committing themselves to buy or sell certain goods in the future. These commitments are often normal means to ensure a steady flow of raw materials or a reliable level of sales. In most cases, these commitments are not of concern to the auditor.

General Motors Corporation: The standard note to the financial statements concerning contingent liabilities.

Note 14. Contingent Liabilities

There are various claims and pending actions against the Corporation and its subsidiaries with respect to commercial matters, including warranties and product liability, governmental regulations including environmental and safety matters, civil rights, patent matters, taxes and other matters arising out of the conduct of the business. Certain of these actions purport to be class actions, seeking damages in very large amounts. The amounts of liability on these claims and actions at December 31, 1979, were not determinable but, in the opinion of the management, the ultimate liability resulting will not materially affect the consolidated financial position or results of operations of the Corporation and its consolidated subsidiaries.

The Gillette Company: Liability from lawsuits is not expected to materially affect financial position, but may materially affect earnings. The auditor's opinion does not refer to this uncertainty.

Gillette is subject to additional legal proceedings and claims which involve both private and governmental parties and cover a wide range of matters, including antitrust and trade regulation, product liability, contracts, collection, customs, tax, patent and trademark matters and three purported class actions alleging discrimination in employment practices. In some misleading advertising and antitrust violations in connection with a television commercial for a Gillette product. Management believes that it has meritorious defenses to this action and that even if liability were found, it would be far less than the amount sought. Management after review, including consultation with counsel, considers that any ultimate liability which could arise from these proceedings and claims would not materially affect the consolidated financial position of the Company, although it could be material in relation to the earnings of any period in which any such determination were to occur.

St. Regis Paper Company: Lawsuits are pending and the need for a provision for any liability cannot be assessed. The auditor's opinion is qualified with respect to these.

In 1976, St. Regis Paper Company was indicted by Federal grand juries in Chicago and Philadelphia, which charged violations of the Sherman Act because of alleged participation in conspiracies to fix, raise, maintain, and stabilize the prices of folding cartons and the prices and terms and conditions of sale of consumer bags. The company pleaded *nolo contendere* in Chicago and was fined. The company was tried and acquitted in Philadelphia. In 1975, an investigation into the container industry was commenced in Texas. Indictments were voted, but the company was not named. In 1977, an investigation of antitrust violations in the sale of primary papers was commenced in Philadelphia. The company has been named as a defendant in many private treble damage actions charging violations of the antitrust laws in the same industries as those investigated. In addition, on August 1, 1977, an arbitration proceeding commenced with respect to monetary and other equitable relief sought by an owner against St. Regis under an exclusive timber cutting contract between St. Regis and the owner. The proceeding was concluded in December 1977. The company cannot now assess the extent of its exposure for damages in the above actions or the damages and cost of complying with any injunction which may be issued in the arbitration proceeding. Accordingly, no provision for any liability has been made in the 1977 and 1976 financial statements.

EXHIBIT 11-1

CONCEPT SUMMARY
Treatment of Contingent Liabilities

| Likelihood | – TREATMENT – | |
	Can Estimate Amount	Cannot Estimate Amount
Probable	Accrual	No accrual; note required
Reasonably possible	No accrual; note required	No accrual; note required
Remote	No accrual; note permitted	No accrual; note permitted

However, the corporations make these commitments based upon certain expectations of the future that may turn out to be wrong. The corporation may then be locked in to a commitment that could produce a loss. In the case of a prospective loss, there must be disclosure of the commitment and its probable effect. The rules for disclosure are the same as those for contingent liabilities. Two examples of commitments disclosures are shown in Exhibit 11–2.

Audit Procedures

The audit must deal with contingencies from the beginning. The audit programs for each of the cycles must attempt to uncover any loss contingencies related to that cycle. There is, then, no separate audit program for contingencies. There are four primary audit procedures:

Discussion With Management

The auditor should discuss with management the firm's policies and procedures used to identify and account for contingencies. The auditor should also inquire whether there are any undisclosed contingencies. The workpapers must include documentation of these discussions and identification of the personnel consulted. The management representation letters (presented in Section 11.2) will later confirm these discussions in writing.

Review of Legal Expense

The auditor should analyze legal expense for the year to determine: (1) the lawyers paid by the firm, and (2) evidence of contingent liabilities, such as cases lawyers may be working on.

Du Pont: Disclosure of purchase commitments in excess of present requirements. However, the effects are expected to be immaterial.

The Company and its consolidated subsidiaries have various purchase commitments for materials, supplies, and items of permanent investment incident to the ordinary conduct of business. In the aggregate such commitments are not at prices in excess of current market. While certain of these commitments are for quantities in excess of the Company's present requirements, they are not expected to have any material adverse effect on the consolidated financial position or results of operations of the Company.

Lykes Corporation: Disclosure of purchase commitments in excess of anticipated production requirements. In this case, commitments could result in a possible loss.

In connection with certain agreements, Youngstown has commitments to purchase iron ore in quantities which substantially exceed its present needs and as a result, may be required to invest funds in excess inventory, or sell the excess, perhaps at a loss. Under the agreements, Youngstown may refuse to accept the iron ore, however, such action would result in substantial cost penalties, the amount of which depend on various circumstances and operating levels at the iron ore mines.

EXHIBIT 11- 2

Audit Inquiry Letter

The auditor is not a legal expert and cannot be expected to judge the expected outcome of a lawsuit. A lawyer, preferably the one involved in the suit, must make such judgements. However, if the auditor were to ask the lawyer's opinion on the lawsuit, the lawyer would hide behind the "confidentiality" of the lawyer-client relationship.

As a result, the auditor must have the client direct their lawyer to give his or her professional judgement to the auditor. The client sends this instruction, in writing, to the lawyer by means of the audit inquiry letter. Exhibit 11–3 provides an example of such a letter (AU 337A). There are several important points in this letter:

1. The lawyer must discuss all matters up to the date of his response, not just the end of the year.

2. The letter includes a list of pending lawsuits which is prepared by management. In the example, there was only one case, but for a larger business, there could easily be more.

3. The client sends an audit inquiry letter to every lawyer dealing with material lawsuits.

4. The client specifically requests the lawyer's professional judgement about the outcome of the lawsuit, including the range of possible loss.

5. The letter requests that the lawyer specifically identify any limitations on his response.

6. The letter requests a judgement on possible unasserted claims, i.e., lawsuits which could be filed but have not been. An example would be a possible suit for patent infringement. This area is particularly delicate because disclosure of the fact itself may actually trigger the lawsuit.

In response to the client's audit inquiry letter, the lawyer sends a letter of confirmation to the auditor. This letter documents the lawyer's professional judgement of pending lawsuits and unasserted claims.

Review of Minutes and Reports

The fourth and final primary audit procedure is to review minutes of the Board of Directors and reports that may suggest contingencies. Regulatory agency and Internal Revenue Service reports may bring to the surface matters such as additional tax assessments and rate reimbursement orders.

11.2 REPRESENTATION LETTERS

The auditor must obtain a written management representation letter from client management in every audit. This letter documents the oral representations that management normally makes during an audit. The management representation letter is part of the evidence the auditor accumulates, but it cannot substitute for other audit procedures. For example, even if management claims that inventory is properly stated, this does not mean that it is, in fact, properly stated. For this reason, inventory must be substantiated by other procedures.

Intent of Management

However, the intent of management is sometimes the controlling factor in determining proper accounting treatment. For example, the same equity security could be classified as either a current asset or a long-term asset. The deciding factor is the intent of management. If management intends to sell the security within the next year, the security is a current asset; if management intends to hold the security, the security is a long-term asset.

Scott Interspacial Industries
1000 Launch Pad Lane
Richmond, Virginia 23222

January 31, 19X2

McGlinchey, Stafford, Mintz, and Wolbrette
800 E. Main Street
Richmond, Virginia 23221

Dear Sirs:

In connection with an examination of our financial statements at December 31, 19X1, and for the year then ended, management of the Company has prepared, and furnished to our auditor,

Clark Kent, CPA
1820 Grove Avenue
Richmond, Virginia 23220

a description and evaluation of a contingency, as set forth below involving matters with respect to which you have been engaged and to which you have devoted substantive attention on behalf of the Company in the form of legal consultation or representation. This contingency is regarded by management of the Company as material for this purpose. Your response should include matters that existed at December 31, 19X1, and during the period from that date to the date of your response.

Pending Litigation

On October 15, 19X1 a major competitor, Galactic Enterprises, Inc., filed suit in federal court alleging misleading advertising in connection with newspaper advertisements which mentioned their products and seeking damages of $600,000. The case is scheduled for trial on April 1, 19X2. Management intends to contest this case vigorously. Management believes this suit is without merit and that the Company will prevail. Even if liability were found, the amount would be less than $50,000.

EXHIBIT 11–3

TO: McGlinchey, Stafford, Mintz, and Wolbrette

Page 2

Please furnish to our auditor such explanation, if any, that you consider necessary to supplement the foregoing information, including an explanation of those matters as to which your views may differ from those stated and an identification of the omission of any pending or threatened litigation, claims, and assessments or a statement that the list of such matters is complete.

We understand that whenever, in the course of performing legal services for us with respect to a matter recognized to involve an unasserted possible claim or assessment that may call for financial statement disclosure, if you have formed a professional conclusion that we should disclose or consider disclosure concerning such possible claim or assessment, as a matter of professional responsibility to us, you will so advise us and will consult with us concerning the question of such disclosure and the applicable requirements of Statement of Financial Accounting Standards No. 5. Please specifically confirm to our auditor that our understanding is correct.

Please specifically identify the nature of and reasons for any limitation on your response.

Very truly yours,

SCOTT INTERSPACIAL INDUSTRIES

Craig L. Scott

Craig L. Scott, President

CLS:eng

EXHIBIT 11–3 (Continued)

Such classifications can be extremely important. If the security is a current asset, any decline in the market value is represented on the income statement, thus reducing net income. If the security is a long-term asset, any decline in market value does not affect income. The effect can be substantial.

In a case such as this, the representation of management is the primary audit evidence. If the effect is material, the auditor may want to see these intentions approved by the Board of Directors. But even this is merely a statement of intention. The auditor, therefore, must sometimes rely on the representations of management unless other audit procedures have uncovered contradictory evidence.

Types of Representations

Exhibit 11–4 provides a typical management representation letter (AU 333A.05). In it there are four basic representations.

Proper Conduct by Employees

The letter states that management and other employees have acted properly in the conduct of their duties. Specifically, management and the other employees did not violate any laws and did not commit any irregularities.

Irregularities refer to intentional distortions of the financial statements. These intentional distortions can result from either management fraud or defalcations. Chapter 4 discussed some of the most common defalcations of cash and inventory. Management fraud would include the following:

1. Omitting significant accounting events from the financial records
2. Altering documents
3. Recording of transactions without substance
4. Misapplying accounting principles intentionally.

Adequate Provision for Losses

The letter states that the financial statements make adequate provision for losses. This would include the proper treatment of contingent liabilities, unasserted claims, excessive purchase commitments, or unfavorable sales commitments. Section 11.1 of this chapter discussed these items in greater detail.

Adequate Disclosure

The letter also states that the financial statements provide adequate disclosure. In other words, the form, arrangement, and content of the financial statements and notes is satisfactory. Included is the terminology used, the amount of detail given, the classification of items, and the bases of valuation used in the statements.

Scott Interspacial Industries
1000 Launch Pad Lane
Richmond, Virginia 23222

March 3, 19X2

Mr. Clark Kent, CPA
1820 Grove Avenue
Richmond, Virginia 23220

Dear Mr. Kent:

In connection with your examination of the balance sheet of Scott Interspacial Industries as of December 31, 19X1, and the related statements of income and retained earnings and changes in financial position for the year then ended for the purpose of expressing an opinion as to whether the financial statements present fairly the financial position, results of operations, and changes in financial position of Scott Interspacial Industries in conformity with generally accepted accounting principles, we confirm, to the best of our knowledge and belief, the following representations made to you during your examination:

1. We are responsible for the fair presentation in the financial statements of financial position, results of operations, and changes in financial position in conformity with generally accepted accounting principles.

2. We have made available to you all
   (a) financial records and related data, and
   (b) minutes of the meetings of stockholders, directors, and committees of directors, or summaries of actions of recent meetings for which minutes have not yet been prepared.

3. There have been no
   (a) irregularities involving management or employees who have significant roles in the system of internal accounting control;
   (b) irregularities involving other employees that could have a material effect on the financial statements; or
   (c) communications from regulatory agencies concerning noncompliance with, or deficiencies in, financial reporting practices that could have a material effect on the financial statements.

EXHIBIT 11–4

4. We have no plans or intentions that may materially affect the carrying value or classification of assets and liabilities.

5. The following have been properly recorded or disclosed in the financial statements:
   (a) related party transactions and related amounts receivable or payable, including sales, purchases, loans, transfers, leasing arrangements, and guarantees;
   (b) capital stock repurchase options or agreements or capital stock reserved for options, warrants, conversions, or other requirements;
   (c) arrangements with financial institutions involving compensating balances or other arrangements involving restrictions on cash balances and line-of-credit or similar arrangements; and
   (d) agreements to repurchase assets already sold.

6. There are
   (a) no violations or possible violations of laws or regulations whose effects should be considered for disclosure in the financial statements or as a basis for recording a loss contingency; and
   (b) except for the lawsuit by Galactic Enterprises discussed in the audit inquiry letter and the attorney's letter of confirmation, no other material liabilities or gain or loss contingencies that are required to be accrued or disclosed by Statement of Financial Accounting Standards No. 5.

7. There are no unasserted claims or assessments that our lawyer has advised us are probable of assertion and must be disclosed in accordance with Statement of Financial Accounting Standards No. 5.

8. There are no material transactions that have not been properly recorded in the accounting records underlying the financial statements.

9. Provision, when material, has been made to reduce excess or obsolete inventories to their estimated net realizable value.

10. The company has satisfactory title to all owned assets, and there are no liens or encumbrances on such assets nor has any asset been pledged.

EXHIBIT 11–4   (Continued)

11. Provision has been made for any material loss to be sustained in the fulfillment of, or from inability to fulfill, any sales commitments.

12. Provision has been made for any material loss to be sustained as a result of purchase commitments for inventory quantities in excess of normal requirements or at prices in excess of the prevailing market prices.

13. We have complied with all aspects of contractual agreements that would have material effect on the financial statements in the event of noncompliance.

14. No events have occurred subsequent to the balance sheet date that would require adjustment to, or disclosure in, the financial statements.

Very truly yours,

SCOTT INTERSPACIAL INDUSTRIES

Craig L. Scott

Craig L. Scott, President

Randolph Scott

Randolph Scott, Treasurer

CLS:RS:eng

EXHIBIT 11–4 (Continued)

If information that is required by GAAP were to be omitted, a qualified or adverse opinion would be expressed by the auditor. (SAS 32). The representations include certain matters such as transactions with related parties. Related parties are all who might not fully pursue their own interests in making agreements with the firm. These would include: (1) a company under common control, (2) owners of a significant amount of stock, (3) management, (4) members of their immediate families, and (5) companies accounted for by the equity method.

General Representations

The letter further gives a number of general representations. This would include the availability of necessary data, such as accounting records and the minutes of Board of Director meetings. There would also be broad representations that the company properly recorded all transactions and complied with all contractual agreements.

11.3 SUBSEQUENT EVENTS

The auditor's responsibility does not cease with the balance sheet date. Certainly, the auditor is primarily concerned with events of the period reported on by the financial statements. However, events can occur after the balance sheet date which affect the financial statements and their use. When this happens, the auditor cannot take a "head-in-the-sand" approach and deny responsibility for those events which are subsequent to the balance sheet date. The auditor is presumed to work on an audit up until the date of the audit report. Thus, the financial statements should reflect all relevant events up to that date, even those "subsequent events" which occurred after the balance sheet date but before the date of the audit report.

Adjustment of Financial Statements

Many of the figures on the financial statements are estimates—a "best guess" at the true state of affairs. For example, the balance of accounts receivable, net of the allowance for uncollectible accounts, is an estimate of the net realizable value of those receivables. Many factors contribute to determining the best possible estimate. The primary factors are: (1) the age of the account, since older accounts are less likely to be collected; and (2) the past experience the firm has had in collecting accounts receivable.

No matter how much effort the firm expends on developing this estimate, it still remains an estimate, and it is not necessarily correct. Furthermore, events may occur after the balance sheet date that can improve the estimate. For example, a major customer may go bankrupt and its account receivable become worthless.

If a subsequent event can refine an estimate in the financial statements, the auditor must insist that the firm make an adjustment to improve the estimate.

Contingent Liabilities

Contingent liabilities are other examples where subsequent events can help refine estimates. For example, the firm may settle a lawsuit for a fixed sum. Then there is no need for an estimate. Similarly, a contingent liability, such as a guaranteed note, can become an actual liability.

Sale of Long-Term Assets Below Cost

A resource is an asset only if that resource has future value for the business. This future value is assumed to equal or exceed the unexpired cost of the asset. If this assumption is proven unjustified by the sale of the asset below unexpired cost, then the financial statements should be adjusted.

Disclosure in the Financial Statements

Important events may occur after balance sheet date that are not reflected in the financial statements, not even as estimates. Though they occurred after the balance sheet date and thus cannot affect the financial statements themselves, the footnotes can and should disclose the effect of these events. Exhibit 11–5 provides examples of the three basic types of disclosure which are often necessary:

1. A major issue of debt or equity capital
2. A major purchase or sale of a business segment
3. A major loss or any major achievement, such as a significant product breakthrough or new discovery.

Audit Program

The auditor must review subsequent events to determine if they require adjustment or disclosure in the financial statements. Since the auditor is responsible for all events up to the date of the audit report, he or she usually performs a subsequent events review at the end of the audit. The review consists of the following steps.

Read Interim Financial Statements

The auditor should obtain the latest interim financial statements and compare them with the statements being examined. The auditor must investigate any substantial deviation from expected performance to determine if adjustments or disclosures are required.

INA Corporation: The Company guarantees debentures of a subsidiary which are sold subsequent to the balance sheet date.

On February 22, 1978, the corporation completed the sale of £20,000,000 (equivalent to $38,950,000) of 10% Sterling Foreign Currency Notes of its subsidiary, INA International Holdings, Ltd. The debentures are guaranteed by the corporation. The proceeds are being invested in securities of the United Kingdom government to support the property and casualty insurance business to be conducted in the United Kingdom. The notes are due March 1, 1988 and are not redeemable before March 1, 1982, except in the event of certain changes affecting United States taxation.

UAL, Inc. (parent of United Airlines):   Footnote discloses a subsequent purchase of a major hotel.

UAL purchased all of the outstanding capital stock of Mauna Kea Beach Hotel Corp. on February 1, 1978 for $51,500,000 less an amount equal to the acquired company's outstanding mortgage of approximately $14,900,000 plus a supplemental payment to be made in early March based on the acquired company's net current assets as of January 31, 1978. Properties of the hotel company consist of the Mauna Kea Beach Hotel, a resort located on the island of Hawaii, and leasehold interests in hotel land, an 18-hole championship golf course and certain adjacent undeveloped land. The hotel and golf course are being managed by Western International.

Household Finance Corporation: Footnote discloses the effect of a decline in the Canadian dollar subsequent to the balance sheet date.

The Canadian foreign exchange rate decreased from .9142 at December 31, 1977 to .9004 at February 10, 1978, the latest date available prior to the date of this report, resulting in a pretax unrealized foreign exchange loss of approximately $6,600,000 during this period.

EXHIBIT 11- 5

CONCEPT SUMMARY
Subsequent Events

Required Action	Description	Examples
ADJUSTMENT OF FINANCIAL STATEMENTS	Events that clarify the true state of affairs on the balance sheet date. These events help refine the estimates made as of the balance sheet date; thus the estimates should be adjusted.	1. Bankruptcy of a customer with a large receivable balance. 2. Settlement of a lawsuit at a figure different from that recorded. 3. Sale of investments or equipment for less than book value.
DISCLOSURE IN FINANCIAL STATEMENTS	Significant events that arose subsequent to the balance sheet date. These events cannot be reflected in the financial statements but should be disclosed because of their importance	1. Major issues of debt and equity securities. 2. Purchase or disposition of business segments. 3. Losses arising from some important event.

Inquire of Management

The auditor should discuss with management: (1) the current status of items in the financial statements that were accounted for on the basis of tentative, preliminary, or inconclusive data, and (2) any unusual adjustments that have been made since the balance sheet date.

Read Minutes of Stockholders' and Directors' Meetings

The auditor should obtain a copy of the minutes of meetings of the stockholders and the Board of Directors in the new fiscal year. The auditor must review these minutes and consider major events for adjustment or disclosure.

Obtain Confirmation and Management Representation Letters

Letters of confirmation from the client's attorney and management representation letters were discussed in detail earlier.

Discoveries After the Audit Report Date

Auditors are responsible to search for subsequent events that occurred between the balance sheet date and the date of auditor's report. But even after the audit report is dated, their responsibilities have not ended, only their obligation to search. Facts may later be discovered that actually existed at the audit report date but were unknown at that time. If discovery of existing facts is made before the financial statements are issued (although after the date of the auditor's report), the statements should be adjusted or disclosures made, just as for the subsequent events already described.

After the financial statements and auditor's report are issued, facts may be discovered that actually existed at the audit report date but were unknown at that time. If these facts make the financial statements materially misleading, a different course of action is necessary.

Once the auditor determines that issued financial statements are materially misleading, he must inform the client and insist that the client issue revised financial statements immediately. If the company is publicly held, it should contact the SEC; if it is a regulated industry, the client should contact the regulatory agency. In the most common case, the company should contact any banks who are depending upon the financial statements in making loans to the company. The auditor must check to ensure that the client has contacted these outside parties.

If the client refuses to take all of these steps, the auditor must contact each member of the Board of Directors and anyone who may be relying on the financial statements. This would include, as appropriate, the SEC, any regulatory agencies, or banks.

The auditor is not responsible after the audit for discovering facts that existed but were unknown as of the date of the audit report. However, if these facts come to his attention, he cannot ignore them; he must investigate.

Implicit in the above discussion is that only the discovery of facts *that existed at the time of the audit report* need cause the reissue of financial statements. If a development arises *after* the audit report, there is no need for reissued financial statements.

Subsequent Events After Field Work

All of the previous discussions concerned subsequent events that took place between balance sheet date and the date of the auditor's report. Only the time when the event was learned about was in question. There is one remaining possibility to discuss. Consider a subsequent event that occurs after field work is concluded (auditor's report date) and is discovered after field work is concluded, but financial statements have not yet been issued.

The client's financial statements should be adjusted or a disclosure added.* If the statements are adjusted, with an explanation given or a note inserted to disclose the event, the auditor's report is affected. Dual-dating is normally used in these cases. The date of the subsequent event being explained or disclosed is added to the auditor's report, while the normal field work ending date remains. An *adjustment* that is not explicitly explained in the financial statements does not affect the auditor's report.

---

*In all of the situations involving material subsequent events, it was implied that the client's financial statements were revised as needed. Failure to do so would force the auditor to express a qualified or adverse opinion or disclaim an opinion.

11.4 AUDIT REVIEW AND QUALITY CONTROLS

A CPA firm is required to have a system of quality controls to ensure that their accounting and auditing work meets professional standards. There are nine elements of quality control. Each must be considered in developing policies and procedures leading to reasonable assurance of conforming to professional standards. The elements and the objectives that are to be met by each set of policies and procedures include:

1. *Independence.* Members of the firm must maintain independence to the extent required by Rule 101 of the rules of conduct.

2. *Assigning Personnel to Engagements.* This relates to supervision. Work is to be performed by persons with the necessary technical training and proficiency.

3. *Consultation.* Personnel should seek assistance when needed from persons having appropriate levels of knowledge, competence, judgement, and authority.

4. *Supervision.* The performance and oversight of work should be sufficient to result in quality work.

5. *Hiring.* Recruiting and hiring policies should result in securing employees of integrity and high technical competence.

6. *Professional Development.* Personnel should acquire and maintain the knowledge needed to fulfill their responsibilities and advance within the firm.

7. *Advancement.* Those selected for advancement are to possess the necessary qualifications to assume new responsibilities (character, intelligence, judgement, motivation, etc.).

8. *Acceptance and Continuance of Clients.* The likelihood of association with a client whose management lacks integrity is to be minimized (i.e., be selective in determining professional relationships).

9. *Inspection.* Inspection of the other eight elements of quality control is to be made periodically by the firm itself. Are they effectively applied?

In short, a CPA firm must have policies and procedures for the nine elements that bring about quality work. They must communicate them to the firm's personnel and monitor the system's effectiveness. Review and supervision is critical at all stages of the audit in bringing about quality work.

Evidence is collected by the audit team, with much of it developed by staff auditors. Staff auditors usually have only up to three years of experience. An "in-charge" senior auditor, therefore, reviews the evidence and working papers prepared by junior members as the audit progresses. Later, a management-level auditor (supervisor or manager) will ordinarily review the working papers and drafts of the auditor's report and management letter. The engagement partner also reviews the financial statements, auditor's report, and working papers with emphasis on the overall results, rather than minor details. Many firms then have a second partner perform a "preissuance" review of the financial statements and auditor's report alone. From this description of the review process, it should be apparent that independent auditors take great care to turn out a quality product.

Steps in Conducting an Audit Engagement

Exhibit 11–6 provides a summary of the steps in conducting an audit engagement. Going through these steps will provide an overview of an entire audit and will emphasize the importance of quality review at every stage of the audit.

Notice how much effort and attention is devoted to planning, supervision, and review of the audit work. Great care is taken to see that audit objectives are defined and achieved. Audit conclusions have to be supported by sufficient competent evidence, and the working papers must support the opinion expressed in the auditor's report.

Working papers should be sufficient to show that the accounting records agree or reconcile with the financial statements, or other information being reported on, and that the standards of field work have been complied with. Working papers ordinarily should include documentation showing that:

1. The work has been planned, supervised, and reviewed, indicating observance of the first standard of fieldwork.

2. The system of internal accounting control has been studied and evaluated as a basis for reliance thereon and for determining the extent of tests to which the auditing procedures are to be restricted, indicating observance of the second standard of field work.

3. The audit evidence obtained, auditing procedures followed, and the testing performed, provided sufficient competent evidential matter to afford a reasonable basis for an opinion, indicating observance of the third standard of field work.

The principal products of an audit are the auditor's report and the management letter. Let us examine each more closely.

11.5 STANDARD AUDITOR'S REPORT

There are two basic results from the majority of audits:

1. The issue of a standard auditor's report. This is a signed statement from the auditor that the financial statements are presented fairly in accordance with GAAP, consistently applied.

2. The preparation of a management letter. This is a letter from the auditor to the client identifying deficiencies and opportunities for improvement in the client's systems.

Planning

1. Engagement partner prepares engagement letter and requests an audit team for the engagement. Submits estimated timing for engagement.
2. Audit team (manager, senior, and assistants) assigned to engagements based on experience, independence, past evaluations, and time availability.
3. Audit team reviews permanent files, workpaper files, correspondence files, and prior year's financial statements, audit report, and management letter.
4. Preplanning meeting with engagement partner.
5. Planning conference with client.
6. Manager/senior prepares detailed planning memo identifying critical audit areas, and time budget.

Interim Work

7. Commencement of interim field work:
   Evaluation of internal control
   Compliance tests
   Substantive tests and analytical review
8. Senior discusses progress of work and any engagement problems with audit team.
9. Review of interim workpaper files by senior.
10. Interim performance evaluation of assistants.

Year-End Work by Audit Team

11. Year-end work:
    Substantive tests and analytical review
    Conclusion memoranda
    Lawyers' letters
    Representation letter
    Certificate of minutes
    Search for subsequent events
    Consultation with industry specialist on reporting problems
    Draft of financial statements, auditor's report, and management letter
    Disclosure checklist
    Time summary and analysis.
12. Throughout engagement, senior monitors the assistants' work.
13. Senior and manager review workpapers, report, and management letter. Initial all workpapers as evidence of review.
14. Audit team clears all review notes.
15. Hold exit conference with client.

Partner Review of Work by Audit Team

16. Engagement partner reviews workpapers, auditor's report, and management letter. Initials the covers of all workpaper files and permanent files, report, and management letter as evidence of review.
17. Audit team clears engagement partner review notes.
18. Second partner review of report. Reviewer's checklist completed. Initials report.

continued on the following page

EXHIBIT 11–6

Production of Report

19. Report and management letter submitted to report department. Before report is processed, it is checked to see that two partners have approved it.
20. Report and management letter typed and proofread. Report also checked for mathematical accuracy.
21. Engagement partner signs report and management letter and submits them to client.
22. Final audit team performance evaluations.
23. Billing of client. Collection of fees.
24. Workpaper files and copies of the report and management letter sent to file department. Notification to managing partner that engagement was completed and available for in-house inspection.

EXHIBIT 11-6   (Continued)

Auditor's Report

Exhibit 11–7 presents an example of a standard auditor's report (AU 509.07). The report has five parts:

1. *Address.* Because the auditor's responsibility is to the client company, the address of the report should be the stockholders of the company and/or its Board of Directors. The report should not be addressed to the company's management.

2. *Scope paragraph.* This paragraph is a statement describing the nature of the examination. It specifically states that the auditor only tests the accounting records.

3. *Opinion paragraph.* This paragraph expresses an unqualified opinion. Further, the wording of the paragraph satisfies all four reporting standards, as discussed in Chapter 1.

4. *Signature.* The firm's name is signed to the audit report, regardless of the partner in charge of the audit. This indicates that the entire firm takes responsibility for the audit report.

5. *Date.* The date of the audit report is the date of the last day of field work. This is the date through which the auditor must take responsibility.

Conditions That Must Be Satisfied

As mentioned above, the standard auditor's report is issued in most audits because an unqualified opinion is by far the best possible result from the client's viewpoint. Any other opinion will very possibly reduce its stock price or cause difficulties

[1] Address	To the Shareholders and Board of Directors Scott Interspacial Industries
[2] Scope Paragraph	We have examined the balance sheet of Scott Interspacial Industries as of December 31, 19X1, and the related statements of income, retained earnings, and changes in financial position for the year then ended. Our examination was made in accordance with generally accepted auditing standards and, accordingly, included such tests of the accounting records and such other auditing procedures as we considered necessary in the circumstances.
[3] Opinion Paragraph	In our opinion, the financial statements referred to above present fairly the financial position of Scott Interspacial Industries as of December 31, 19X1, and the results of its operations and the changes in its financial position for the year then ended, in conformity with generally accepted accounting principles applied on a basis consistent with that of the preceding year.

[4] Signature

[5] Date   March 3, 19X2

EXHIBIT 11–7   Standard Auditor's Report

in borrowing money. Therefore, client firms will almost always cooperate with their auditor to ensure that a standard audit report can be issued.

To issue a standard audit report, the following conditions must be satisfied:

1. There can be no scope limitation. No conditions can preclude the application of any auditing procedures that the auditor considers necessary in the circumstances.

2. There can be no material departure from a generally accepted accounting principle.

3. There can be no inconsistency in the application of accounting principles i.e., from one year to the next.

4. There can be no unusual uncertainties.

If any of these conditions are not satisfied, the auditor cannot issue a standard auditor's report. Chapter 12 discusses the audit reports necessary in those circumstances.

CONCEPT SUMMARY
Basic Letters for an Audit

Type	From	To	Purpose	Whether Required
Engagement Letter	Auditor	Client	Record agreement between auditor and client about the audit, especially when it will be done and how much it will cost	Optional, but usually sent to record terms of the engagement.
Audit Inquiry Letter	Client	Client's Attorneys	Direct the attorneys to inform the auditor of the status of pending lawsuits and unasserted claims	Required if the attorney deals with material matters
Attorneys' Letters of Confirmation	Client's Attorneys	Auditor	Document the attorneys' professional judgement of pending lawsuits and unasserted claims	Considered appropriate by legal profession
Management Representation Letter	Client	Auditor	Document the oral portrayals of events given by management to the auditor	Always required
Management Letter	Auditor	Client	Advise the client of the deficiencies and potentials for improvement identified by the auditor during the audit	Optional, but usually sent to improve relationship with client
Communication of Weaknesses in Internal Control	Auditor	Client	Inform the client of any material weaknesses in internal accounting control discovered during the audit	Required only if such weaknesses are found

Management Letter

As mentioned above, the auditor prepares a management letter at the same time as the audit report. A management letter contains recommendations, such as those in Exhibit 11–8, concerning possible improvements in the client's operations. An auditor is not required to prepare a management letter, but he does so for three reasons:

1. To improve service to the client. Since the auditor takes an independent look at the company's operations and spends many hours examining its systems, he can often identify possibilities for improvement that can substantially help the client.

2. To improve the image of the auditor. Since the auditor may be engaged at the insistence of the SEC or a creditor bank, the client often views the auditor as a disturbance. The management letter is an opportunity to portray a more positive role.

3. To increase the accounting practice. The client's staff may be adequate only for operation of the existing system. As a result, even if suggested improvements are desirable, the company's employees will not be capable of effecting them. This is an excellent opportunity for the CPA firm's management advisory services staff.

CLARK KENT, CPA
1820 Grove Avenue
Richmond, Virginia 23220

March 3, 19X2

Mr. Craig L. Scott, President
Scott Interspacial Industries
1000 Launch Pad Lane
Richmond, Virginia 23222

Dear Mr. Scott:

In the course of our examination of the financial statements of Scott Interspacial Industries, we have identified a number of areas where improvements appear possible. Following is a list of items that we feel should be brought to your attention.

Bonding of Employees

Employees, including those who handle large amounts of cash and inventory, are not bonded. This practice exposes the company to a substantial risk.

The company should bond employees who handle cash and inventory. Experience has shown that bonding provides a psychological deterrent and another independent check on backgrounds, in addition to protection in case of loss.

Vague Policy or Procedure

1. There is no stated conflict of interest policy giving guidance on employees' dealings with related firms, such as suppliers and customers.
2. There is no chart of accounts detailing which accounts to use in specific cases.
3. There is no basis of comparison to judge good or bad performance. As it is, there is no budget with which to compare actual performance, nor do the monthly financial statements provide any comparative figures.
4. There is no stated policy for the determination of uncollectible accounts, i.e., those accounts for which payment will not be received, either due to bankruptcy or other reasons.

EXHIBIT 11–8

TO: Mr. Craig L. Scott, President
Scott Interspacial Industries

Page 2

5. There is no stated procedure for the return of defective merchandise and no control to ensure that the proper amount reduces the total owed the vendor. Related to this, the company does not have a debit memorandum to document and control the return of damaged or defective goods.

The company should develop a policies and procedures manual to provide guidance and direction to employees in their duties. The manual would additionally have the benefit of providing easier training for new employees. This manual should detail company policy concerning conflicts of interest, amount of paid vacation, sick leave, maternity leave, hiring and firing of employees, the length of time to keep records, issuing credit, and writing off uncollectible accounts. The manual should also detail company procedures, including return of defective merchandise, as well as guidelines for transaction processing. This should include a chart of accounts that will detail the appropriate use of each account.

The financial statements should provide a comparison of this month's and this year's performance to those of last year. Additionally, the monthly financial statements should include an aged trial balance of accounts receivable instead of simply a schedule of accounts receivable. This report should help indicate the collectibility of these accounts. Eventually, the company should develop a budgeting system to better plan and control operations.

Weak Procedures
1. Paid invoices are not perforated or cancelled and thus, potentially, could be used more than once.
2. The receiving report and credit memorandum are not prenumbered. This practice allows the possibility that documents could be lost or misplaced without that fact becoming apparent.
3. The procedure for approval of vouchers for payment is weak. It is not clear that a corporate officer will review the support and approve it before the check is prepared, signed, and mailed.
4. Important accounting records, such as the accounts receivable subsidiary ledger, are not kept in a safe and could be lost in a fire or other accident.

EXHIBIT 11–8 (Continued)

434

TO: Mr. Craig L. Scott, President
    Scott Interspacial Industries

Page 3

    These procedures should be changed to provide increased efficiency and improved internal control. Paid invoices should be perforated to prevent their reuse. All documents, including the receiving report, the (new) debit memorandum, and the credit memorandum, should be prenumbered to allow better physical control. The controller should review a voucher and related support in order to authorize payment; his signature should be required before payment is made. Important documents should be kept in a safe for better physical control.

    We would be pleased to discuss these comments with you. Further, if we can provide any assistance in implementing these recommendations, please do not hesitate to contact us.

Very truly yours,

Clark Kent, CPA

Clark Kent,
Certified Public Accountant

CK:eng

EXHIBIT 11–8   (Continued)

Communication of Weakness in Internal Control

Even though the auditor is not required to prepare a management letter, he or she must communicate material weaknesses in internal control to both company management and the Board of Directors. A material weakness is a situation where a material error or irregularity could occur and not be discovered by the company's employees. Exhibit 11–9 provides the required form of this communication of a material weakness in internal control (AU 323.08).

We have examined the financial statements of Scott Interspacial Industries for the year ended December 31, 19X1 and have issued our report thereon dated March 3, 19X2. As a part of our examination, we made a study and evaluation of the Company's system of internal accounting control to the extent we considered necessary to evaluate the system as required by generally accepted auditing standards. Under these standards, the purposes of such evaluation are to establish a basis for reliance on the system of internal accounting control in determining the nature, timing, and extent of other auditing procedures that are necessary for expressing an opinion on the financial statements and to assist the auditor in planning and performing his examination of the financial statements.

Our examination of the financial statements made in accordance with generally accepted auditing standards, including the study and evaluation of the Company's system of internal accounting control for the year ended December 31, 19X1, that was made for the purposes set forth in the first paragraph above, would not necessarily disclose all weaknesses in the system because it was based on selective tests of accounting records and related data. However, such study and evaluation disclosed the following conditions that we believe to be material weaknesses, excluding those which were corrected before they came to our attention.

[A description of the material weaknesses that have come to the auditor's attention would follow.]

The foregoing conditions were considered in determining the nature, timing, and extent of audit tests to be applied in our examination of the financial statements, and this report of such conditions does not modify our report dated March 3, 19X2, on such financial statements.

EXHIBIT 11–9

Key Terms

assistant (or junior)
commitment (sales and purchase)
communication of weakness in
    internal control
contingent liabilities
dual-dating
engagement partner

lawyers' letter
management letter
management representation letter
preissuance review
quality controls
senior
subsequent events

Questions and Problems

Questions

11-1 Define a contingency, and briefly discuss accounting for contingencies. Distinguish between a contingency and a commitment.

11-2 Give the purpose and basic contents of an audit inquiry letter. Why is the audit inquiry letter sent by the client rather than the auditor?

11-3 What is the purpose of a management representation letter? Who sends it? Who receives it?

11-4 List five basic representations in a management representation letter.

11-5 Describe the types of events occurring after the balance sheet date that require adjustment of the financial statements. Give three examples of such events.

11-6 Describe the types of events occurring after the balance sheet date that require disclosure in the financial statements. Give three examples of such events.

11-7 What makes up a system of quality control for a CPA firm? What is the objective of such a system?

11-8 Summarize the basic steps in conducting an audit engagement.

11-9 List the conditions that must be satisfied before the auditor can issue an unqualified opinion. Why is an unqualified opinion important to the client?

11-10 Discuss the purpose and basic contents of a management letter. Why does the auditor send it? How can it be useful to the client?

Multiple Choice Questions From Professional Examinations

11-11 Management furnishes the independent auditor with information concerning litigation, claims, and assessments. Which of the following is the auditor's primary means of initiating action to corroborate such information?

    a. Request that client lawyers undertake a reconsideration of matters of litigation, claims, and assessments with which they were consulted during the period under examination.

    b. Request that client management send a letter of audit inquiry to those lawyers with whom management consulted concerning litigation, claims, and assessments.

    c. Request that client lawyers provide a legal opinion concerning the policies and procedures adopted by management to identify, evaluate, and account for litigation, claims, and assessments.

    d. Request that client management engage outside attorneys to suggest wording for the text of a footnote explaining the nature and probable outcome of existing litigation, claims, and assessments.

11-12 Which of the following audit procedures would be least effective for detecting contingent liabilities?

    a. Abstracting the minutes of the meetings of the Board of Directors.

    b. Reviewing the bank confirmation letters.

    c. Examining confirmation letters from customers.

    d. Confirming pending legal matters with the corporate attorney.

11-13 A company guarantees the debt of an affiliate. Which of the following *best* describes the audit procedure that would make the auditor aware of the guarantee?

    a. Review minutes and resolutions of the Board of Directors.

    b. Review prior year's working papers with respect to such guarantees.

    c. Review the possibility of such guarantees with the chief accountant.

    d. Review the legal letter returned by the company's outside legal counsel.

11-14 A charge in the subsequent period to a notes receivable account from the cash disbursements journal should alert the auditor to the possibility that

    a. a contingent asset has come into existence in the subsequent period.

    b. a contingent liability has come into existence in the subsequent period.

    c. a provision for contingencies is required.

    d. a contingent liability has become a real liability and has been settled.

11-15 An auditor generally obtains a formal written statement from a client concerning the accuracy of inventory. This particular letter of representation is used by the auditor to

    a. Reduce the scope of the auditor's physical inventory work but not the other inventory audit work that is normally performed.

    b. Confirm in writing the valuation basis used by the client to value the inventory at the lower of cost or market.

    c. Lessen the auditor's responsibility for the fair presentation of balance sheet inventories.

    d. Remind management that the primary responsibility for the overall fairness of the financial statements rests with management and not with the auditor.

11-16 An auditor must obtain written client representations that normally should be signed by

    a. the president and the chairman of the board.

    b. the treasurer and the internal auditor.

    c. the chief executive officer and the chief financial officer.

    d. the corporate counsel and the audit committee chairperson.

11-17 As part of an audit, a CPA often requests a representation letter from the client. Which one of the following is *not* a valid purpose of such a letter?

    a. To provide evidence.

    b. To emphasize to the client the client's responsibility for the correctness of the financial statements.

    c. To satisfy the CPA by means of other auditing procedures when certain customary auditing procedures are not performed.

    d. To provide possible protection to the CPA against a charge of knowledge in cases where fraud is subsequently discovered to have existed in the accounts.

11-18 Subsequent events affecting the realization of assets will ordinarily require adjustment of the financial statements under examination because such events typically represent

    a. the culmination of conditions that existed at the balance sheet date.

    b. the final estimates of losses relating to casualties occurring in the subsequent events period.

    c. the discovery of new conditions occurring in the subsequent events period.

    d. the preliminary estimate of losses relating to new events that occurred subsequent to the balance sheet date.

11-19 An auditor performs interim work at various times throughout the year. The auditor's subsequent events work should be extended to the date of

a. a post-dated footnote.
b. the next scheduled interim visit.
c. the final billing for audit services rendered.
d. the auditor's report.

11-20 Which event that occurred after the end of the fiscal year under audit, but prior to issuance of the auditor's report, would not require disclosure in the financial statements?

a. Sale of a bond or capital stock issue.
b. Loss of plant or inventories as a result of fire or flood.
c. A major drop in the quoted market price of the stock of the corporation.
d. Settlement of litigation when the event giving rise to the claim took place after the balance sheet date.

11-21 On January 28, 1977, a customer of Tom Corporation suffered a total loss as a result of a major casualty. On March 1, 1977, Tom wrote off as uncollectible a large receivable from this customer. The auditor's report on Tom's financial statements for the year ended December 31, 1976, has not yet been issued. The write-off in the subsequent period requires

a. disclosure in the 1976 financial statements.
b. adjustment to the 1976 financial statements.
c. presentation of the 1976 financial statements with a prior-period adjustment.
d. no adjustment or disclosure in the 1976 financial statements but disclosure in the 1977 financial statements.

11-22 The independent auditor lends credibility to client financial statements by

a. stating in the auditor's management letter that the examination was made in accordance with generally accepted auditing standards.
b. maintaining a clearcut distinction between management's representations and the auditor's representations.
c. attaching an auditor's opinion to the client's financial statements.
d. testifying under oath about client's financial information.

11-23 Which of the following would be an inappropriate addressee for an auditor's report?

a. The corporation whose financial statements were examined.

b. A third party, even if the third party is a client who engaged the auditor for examination of a non-client corporation.

c. The president of the corporation whose financial statements were examined.

d. The stockholders of the corporations whose financial statements were examined.

11-24 The standard short-form auditor's report is generally considered to have a scope paragraph and an opinion paragraph. In the report, the auditor refers to both generally accepted accounting principles (GAAP) and generally accepted auditing standards (GAAS). In which of the paragraphs are these terms used?

a. GAAP in the scope paragraph and GAAS in the opinion paragraph.

b. GAAS in the scope paragraph and GAAP in the opinion paragraph.

c. GAAS in both paragraphs and GAAP in the scope paragraph.

d. GAAP in both paragraphs and GAAS in the opinion paragraph.

11-25 Although there is *no* professional requirement to do so on audit engagements, CPAs normally issue a formal management letter to their clients. The primary purpose of this letter is to provide

a. evidence indicating whether the auditor is reasonably certain that the system of internal accounting control is operating as prescribed.

b. a permanent record of the internal accounting control work performed by the auditor during the course of the engagement.

c. a written record of discussions between auditor and client concerning the auditor's observations and suggestions for improvements.

d. a summary of the auditor's observations that resulted from the auditor's special study of the system of internal control.

Problems

11-26 Beta Manufacturing Limited is a public company; 60% of its shares are owned by Alpha Ltd. Beta buys all its raw materials and leases its plant and equipment from Alpha. Beta has also obtained from Alpha a substantial loan at a low interest rate and pays Alpha royalties and management fees. Beta sells 30% of its production to Delta Ltd., a company in which the president of Alpha has a controlling interest.

Required:

a. How do the recommendations of the Auditing Standards Board (or the Accounting Research Committee in Canada) on related party transactions improve the comparability of Beta's performance with that of other companies?

b. What auditing considerations face Beta's auditor as a result of the Board's (Committee's) recommendations on related party transactions, and how might the auditor deal with these problems?

CICA (adapted)

11-27 The major written understandings between a CPA and client, in connection with an examination of financial statements, are the engagement (arrangements) letter and the client's representation letters.

Required:

a. 1. What are the objectives of the engagement (arrangements) letter?
   2. Who should prepare and sign the engagement letter?
   3. When should the engagement letter be sent?
   4. Why should the engagement letter be renewed periodically?
b. 1. What are the objectives of the client's representation letters?
   2. Who should prepare and sign the client's representation letters?
   3. When should the client's representation letters be obtained?
   4. Why should the client's representation letters be prepared for each examination?

AICPA (adapted)

11-28 You are in the process of "winding up" the field work on the Big Buck Stove Corporation, a company engaged in the manufacture and sale of kerosene space heating stoves. To date, there has been every indication that the financial statements of the client present fairly the position of the company at December 31 and the results of its operations for the year then ended. The company had total assets at December 31 of $4 million and a net profit for the year (after deducting federal and state income tax provisions) of $285,000. The principal records of the company are a general ledger, cash receipts record, voucher register, sales register, check register, and general journal. Financial statements are prepared monthly. Your field work will be completed on February 20, and you plan to deliver the report to the client by March 12.

Required:

a. Prepare a brief statement as to the purpose and period to be covered in a review of subsequent events.
b. Outline the post-audit review program that you would follow to de-

termine what transactions involving material amounts, if any, have occurred since the balance sheet date.

AICPA (adapted)

11-29 Lancaster Electronics produces electronic components for sale to manufacturers of radios, television sets, and phonograph systems. In connection with his examination of Lancaster's financial statements for the year ended December 31, 1982, Don Olds, CPA, completed field work two weeks ago. Mr. Olds is now evaluating the significance of the following items prior to preparing his auditor's report. Except as noted, none of these items have been disclosed in the financial statements or footnotes.

Item 1

Recently, Lancaster interrupted its policy of paying cash dividends quarterly to its stockholders. Dividends were paid regularly through 1981, discontinued for all of 1982 in order to finance equipment for the Company's new plant, and resumed in the first quarter of 1983. In the annual report, dividend policy is to be discussed in the president's letter to stockholders.

Item 2

A ten-year loan agreement, which the Company entered into three years ago, provides that dividend payments may not exceed net income earned after taxes subsequent to the date of the agreement. The balance of retained earnings at the date of the loan agreement was $298,000. From that date through December 31, 1982, net income after taxes has totaled $360,000 and cash dividends have totaled $130,000. Based upon these data, the staff auditor assigned to this review concluded that there was no retained earnings restriction at December 31, 1982.

Item 3

The Company's new manufacturing plant building, which cost $600,000 and has an estimated life of 25 years, is leased from the Sixth National Bank at an annual rental of $100,000. The Company is obligated to pay property taxes, insurance, and maintenance. At the conclusion of its ten-year noncancelable lease, the Company has the option of purchasing the property for $1. In Lancaster's income statement, the rental payment is reported on a separate line.

Item 4

A major electronics firm has introduced a line of products that will compete directly with Lancaster's primary line, now being produced in the specially designed new plant. Because of manufacturing innovations, the competitor's line will be of comparable quality but priced 50% below Lancaster's line. The competitor announced its new line during the week following completion of field work. Mr. Olds read the announcement in the newspaper and discussed the situation by telephone with Lancaster executives. Lancaster will meet the lower prices, which are high enough to cover variable manufacturing and selling expenses but will permit recovery of only a portion of fixed costs.

Required:

For each item 1 to 4 discuss:

a. Any additional disclosure in the financial statements and footnotes that the CPA should recommend to his client.
b. The effect of this situation on the CPA's report upon Lancaster's financial statements. For this requirement, assume that the client did not make the additional disclosure recommended in part (a).

AICPA

11-30 You have completed your audit of Carter Corporation and its consolidated subsidiaries for the year ended December 31, 1982, and were satisfied with the results of your examination. You have examined the financial statements of Carter Corporation for the past three years. The Corporation is now preparing its annual report to shareholders. The report will include the consolidated financial statements of Carter Corporation and its subsidiaries and your standard auditor's report. During your audit the following matters came to your attention:

1. The Internal Revenue Service is currently examining the Corporation's 1980 federal income tax return and is questioning the amount of a deduction claimed by the Corporation's domestic subsidiary for a loss sustained in 1980. The examination is still in process, and any additional tax liability is indeterminable at this time. The Corporation's tax counsel believes that there will be no substantial additional tax liability.

2. A vice president, who is also a stockholder, resigned on December 31, 1982, after an argument with the president. The vice president is soliciting proxies from stockholders and expects to obtain sufficient proxies to gain control of the board of directors so that a new president will be appointed. The president plans to have a footnote prepared that would include information of the pending proxy fight, management's accomplishments over the years, and an appeal by management for the support of stockholders.

3. In 1982, the Corporation changed its method of accounting for the investment credit. An investment credit of $121,000 deferred in prior

years was credited to retained earnings, and the full 1982 investment credit of $50,000 was recorded as a reduction of income tax expense. As a result, net income after taxes for 1982 was increased by $45,000. You approved of this change as an acceptable alternative accounting treatment.

Required:

a. Prepare the footnotes, if any, that you would suggest for the items listed above.

b. State your reasons for not making disclosure by footnote for each of the listed items for which you did not prepare a footnote.

AICPA (adapted)

11-31 In connection with your examination of the financial statements of Olars Manufacturing Corporation for the year ended December 31, 1982, your post-balance sheet date review disclosed the following items:

1. *January 3, 1983:* The state government approved a plan for the construction of an express highway. The plan will result in the appropriation of a portion of the land area owned by Olars Manufacturing Corporation. Construction will begin in late 1983. No estimate of the condemnation award is available.

2. *January 7, 1983:* The mineral content of a shipment of ore enroute on December 31, 1982, was determined to be 72 percent. The shipment was recorded at year-end at an estimated content of 50 percent by a debit to raw material inventory and a credit to accounts payable in the amount of $20,600. The final liability to the vendor is based on the actual mineral content of the shipment.

3. *January 31, 1983:* As a result of reduced sales, production was curtailed in mid-January, and some workers were laid off. On February 5, 1983, all the remaining workers went on strike. To date, the strike is unsettled.

4. *February 10, 1983:* A contract was signed whereby Mammoth Enterprises purchased from Olars Manufacturing Corporation all of the latter's fixed assets (including rights to receive the proceeds of any property condemnation), inventories, and the right to conduct business under the name "Olars Manufacturing Division." The effective date of the transfer will be March 1, 1983. The sale price was $500,000 subject to adjustment following the taking of a physical inventory. Important factors contributing to the decision to enter into the contract were the policy of the board of directors of Mammoth Industries to diversify the firm's activities and the report of a survey conducted by

an independent market appraisal firm that revealed a declining market for Olars products.

Required:

Assume that the items described above came to your attention prior to completion of your audit work on February 15, 1983, and that you will render a standard auditor's report for *each* item:

a. Give the audit procedures, if any, that would have brought the item to your attention. Indicate other sources of information that may have revealed the item.

b. Discuss the disclosure that you would recommend for the item, listing all details that should be disclosed. Indicate those items or details, if any, that should not be disclosed. Give your reasons for recommending or not recommending disclosure of the items or details.

AICPA (adapted)

11-32 In connection with his examination of Flowmeter, Inc., for the year ended December 31, 1982, Hosch, CPA, is aware that certain events and transactions which took place after December 31, 1982, but before he issues his report dated February 28, 1983, may affect the company's financial statements.

The following material events or transactions have come to his attention.

1. On January 3, 1983, Flowmeter, Inc., received a shipment of raw materials from Canada. The materials had been ordered in October 1982 and shipped F.O.B. shipping point in November 1982.

2. On January 15, 1983, the Company settled and paid a personal injury claim of a former employee as the result of an accident that occurred in March 1982. The Company had not previously recorded a liability for the claim.

3. On January 25, 1983, the Company agreed to purchase for cash the outstanding stock of Proter Electrical Co. The acquisition is likely to double the sales volume of Flowmeter, Inc.

4. On February 1, 1983, a plant owned by Flowmeter, Inc., was damaged by a flood, and an uninsured loss of inventory resulted.

5. On February 5, 1983, Flowmeter, Inc., issued and sold to the general public $2,000,000 in convertible bonds.

Required:

For each of the events or transactions above, indicate the audit procedures that should have brought the item to the attention of the auditor, and the form of disclosure in the financial statements, including the reasons for such disclosures. Arrange your answer in the following format.

Item No.	Audit Procedures	Required Disclosure and Reasons

AICPA (adapted)

11-33 The major result of a financial audit conducted by an independent accountant is the expression of an opinion by the auditor on the fairness of the financial statements. While the auditor's report containing the opinion is the best known report issued by the independent auditor, other reports are often prepared during the course of a normal audit. One such report is the management letter (informal report).

Required:

a. What is the purpose of a management letter?
b. Identify the major types of information that are likely to be covered in a management letter. Support your answer with a detailed example of one of the types identified above.

CMA

11-34 Tuloak Manufacturing Company is a small manufacturer of oak porch swings. It was organized as a proprietorship in 1950 by its current president and majority stockholder, Samuel Lawten. Tuloak was incorporated in 1970 when growth of the company necessitated the raising of additional capital.

The accounting system of Tuloak is quite simple. The system has evolved over the years in response to external reporting requirements, and a strong emphasis has not been placed on internal control. The firm's relatively small size (49 employees) also makes effective internal control more difficult than in a larger firm.

The CPA firm of Deber & Associates has been hired to perform the audit of Tuloak for the fiscal year ending October 31, 1982. This is the first time that Deber has been engaged to audit Tuloak's financial statements. The partner-in-charge of the audit has reminded his staff that material weaknesses in internal control must be communicated to audit clients. The partner has concluded that a management letter should be issued to Tuloak following the audit for the year ended October 31, 1982. The management letter sent by Deber to Tuloak follows on page 448.

Upon receipt of the management letter, Mr. Lawten asked his chief accountant, Charles Earl, to respond to the management letter. Mr. Earl's response is given on page 449.

Deber & Associates, CPAs
Oak Park, North Carolina

Samuel Lawten, President
Tuloak Manufacturing Company

In connection with our audit of the financial statements of Tuloak Manufacturing Company of October 31, 1982, we reviewed various internal procedures and controls of the company in order to plan the scope of the audit. We did not make a comprehensive review for the purpose of submitting detailed recommendations. However, as a result of our review, we did observe certain areas where material weaknesses in internal controls and procedures exist. These weaknesses are itemized below and should be corrected.

Cash. Control over cash disbursements for purchases of materials is inadequate due to the fact that creditor checks are prepared by the accounts payable bookkeeper, signed by the treasurer, and then returned to the accounts payable bookkeeper for mailing to creditors.

We recommend that the checks be mailed by the treasurer rather than by the accounts payable bookkeeper.

Accounts Receivable. The extension of credit to customers is approved by the sales manager, who also authorizes the write-off of delinquent accounts.

We recommend that the write-off of delinquent accounts be approved by the chief accountant.

Inventory. Purchases of raw materials are made only upon receipt of a purchase requisition signed by the production supervisor. When shipments of raw materials are received, a receiving report is signed by any available production worker in the vicinity of the receiving dock.

We recommend that the production supervisor be the only employee permitted to sign the receiving report; then the supervisor will know that the materials requisitioned have arrived.

Marketable Securities. Stock certificates related to marketable securities are kept in Mr. Lawten's office desk drawer to facilitate prompt settlement when the expected holding period is relatively short.

We recommend that all stock certificates be held in a bank safety deposit box accessible only by Mr. Lawten.

Payroll. Hourly production workers are required to punch in on a mechanical timeclock each morning, and then punch out at the end of the day. Presumably, they take a one-hour lunch break. Occasionally, a worker might not return from lunch, have a friend punch his card at the end of the day, and receive a full day's pay for a half-day's work.

To prevent this from happening in the future, we recommend that each employee be required to punch out and back in for lunch and that each supervisor initial the daily timecards of each employee under his/her control, thereby verifying the presence of workers for the full day.

Sincerely,

Deber & Associates

Memorandum

TO: Samuel Lawten, President
FROM: Charles Earl, Chief Accountant
SUBJECT: Response to management letter from Deber & Associates

Pursuant to your request, I am writing this memo in response to the management letter of our independent accountants, Deber & Associates. My comments related to each of their recommendations are presented below.

Cash. I do not believe that the change in procedure recommended is necessary because the accounts payable bookkeeper cannot possibly benefit from handling the signed checks made payable to our material suppliers. Each check is supported by an approved purchase requisition, purchase order, receiving report, and vendor's invoice.

Accounts Receivable. The current system of having the sales manager approve the write-off of delinquent accounts is preferable because the sales manager is more familiar with each of the customers having delinquent accounts and thus can more accurately determine the appropriate time to write-off their accounts. In addition, as chief accountant, I should not be required to approve the write-off of accounts which I am responsible for maintaining.

Inventory. The auditors' recommendation that the production supervisor alone sign receiving reports is impractical because the supervisor is often supervising employees physically removed from the vicinity of the receiving dock. Such a requirement would reduce the production supervisor's effectiveness. I suggest we continue with the present system of receiving report approvals.

Marketable Securities. All stock certificates related to marketable securities are registered in the company name, so putting such certificates in a bank safety deposit box is unnecessary. In addition, your desk drawer may be locked, and the advantage of convenient access more than offsets any improvement in control.

Payroll. The recommendation that hourly production workers punch out and back in for their lunch breaks would necessitate new timecards to accommodate twice as many clock entries as are currently required. In addition, if an employee is going to miss a half-day's work by having a friend punch his or her card at the end of the day under the current system, only one additional erroneous entry will be required by the friend after lunch under the proposed system.

Required:

For each of the weaknesses of internal controls and procedures identified by Deber & Associates, discuss whether:

a. The weakness identified by Deber & Associates is substantive and should be brought to Tuloak's attention.

b. The recommendation proposed by Deber & Associates is a reasonable and appropriate solution.

c. The response of Charles Earl of Tuloak Manufacturing Company is satisfactory under the circumstances.

CMA

11-35 As part of your annual audit of Call Camper Company, you have the responsibility for preparing a report on internal control to management. Your workpapers include a completed internal-control questionnaire and documentation of other tests of the internal-control system which you have reviewed. This review identified a number of material weaknesses; for some of these, corrective action by management is not practicable in the circumstances.

Required:

Discuss the form and content of the report on internal control to management based on your annual audit and the reasons or purposes for such a report. Do not write a report.

AICPA (adapted)

12

Communicating results

All organizations in society require a system for measuring and reporting the results of their financial activities. Information on the financial activities of public and non-public businesses, governments, political parties, universities and other schools, churches, hospitals, and other organizations is necessary for informed decisions by members of a society. The flow of objective and reliable information in the form of financial statements makes possible the allocation of scarce resources in a reasonable manner.

The most important function of independent auditing is attestation. This attestation takes the form of an auditor's report, which lends credibility to financial statements. This chapter is concerned with the types of auditor's reports that communicate the results of the work of independent CPAs and the use of these reports.

12.1 TYPES OF AUDIT OPINIONS AND REPORTS

The fourth reporting standard described in Chapter 1 focuses on the responsibilities of independent CPAs in their report communications. Four types of auditor opinions and reports are consistent with the letter and spirit of this reporting standard. The four types of opinion which may result from an independent audit of financial statements are (in the order of their frequency of occurrence):

1. Unqualified opinion (discussed in Chapters 1 and 11)
2. Qualified opinion
3. Disclaimer of opinion
4. Adverse (negative) opinion

Qualified Opinion

Sometimes an auditor may feel that the financial statements do present fairly the financial circumstances of an organization, but cannot make one or more of the assertions necessary for an unqualified opinion. In this situation, a qualified opinion would be issued that addresses the financial statements as a whole while noting any material exceptions to the assertions.

If the audit has not been conducted according to GAAS and the scope of the audit has been limited, or GAAP have not been followed or consistently applied, or a major uncertainty exists which cannot be resolved, a qualified opinion may be appropriate. It is important to note that a qualified opinion would be used only if the auditor feels that an opinion can be rendered on the financial statements in spite of these problems.

Qualified opinions are communicated by the use of "except for" or "subject to" phrases in the audit report with explanatory comments.

Except for

The phrase "except for" is intended to communicate an objection to something about the financial statements being presented. "Except for" with an accompanying explanation is used if: (1) the scope of the audit has been limited, (2) the financial statements contain a departure from GAAP, or (3) GAAP were not consistently applied. In other words, if any of the first three assertions necessary for an unqualified opinion cannot be made but the fairness of the financial statements taken as a whole is not materially affected, the auditor may take objection and qualify his report by the use of the "except for" phrase with an explanation of the objection.

Subject to

The "subject to" phrase communicates a contingency, uncertainty, or unresolved situation that may affect the financial statements. The existence of this uncertainty is communicated by the use of "subject to" in the audit report with an accompanying explanation. Thus, if the fourth assertion necessary for an unqualified opinion cannot be made but the financial statements do otherwise present fairly the currently determinable circumstances, a "subject to" qualification is appropriate. The Canadian Institute of Chartered Accountants dropped the "subject to" opinion requirement effective November 1980. As long as contingencies or going concern problems are satisfactorily accounted for and disclosed, an unqualified opinion can be issued by chartered accountants.

Writing a Qualified Opinion

When a qualified opinion is necessary, it is usually written as a three-paragraph report. The scope paragraph is standard unless the qualification results from a limitation of the scope of the audit. An explanatory paragraph, which discusses the objection or uncertainty, is added between the scope and opinion paragraphs. This explanatory paragraph is not used, however, when the qualification is due to the inconsistent application of GAAP. Changes in accounting principles are explained as a part of the "except for" statement in the opinion paragraph. The opinion paragraph is always modified by the "except for" or "subject to" phrase.

Disclaimer of Opinion

When an auditor is not independent or the scope of an audit has been severely limited or there is an unresolved uncertainty that is far-reaching and serious, an auditor should not render an opinion on the financial statements. A disclaimer of opinion (in other words, inability to give an opinion) is necessary together with an explanation of all substantive reasons for the disclaimer. A disclaimer should never be expressed if an opinion has been formed, especially to avoid giving an adverse opinion. Nor should a "piecemeal opinion" be expressed on certain identified items if a disclaimer or adverse opinion is being issued on the statements as a whole.

Notice that a limited scope or a major uncertainty may result in either a qualified opinion or a disclaimer of opinion. The major difference is whether or not the auditor feels that an opinion on the statements taken as a whole can be given, even with the limited scope or major uncertainty. This will depend on whether or not sufficient evidence has been produced by the audit examination and on the materiality of the scope limitation or the unusual uncertainty. If an auditor is not independent, he should always disclaim an opinion and state specifically that his independence is lacking.

Disclaimers of opinion that result when an audit has not been performed (compilations and unaudited financial statements) will be discussed in a later section of this chapter.

Adverse Opinion

This opinion would be used if the auditor feels that the audit has turned up material, serious departures from GAAP and, as a result, the financial statements do *not* present fairly the position and activities of the organization.

A limitation of scope or a major uncertainty cannot lead to an adverse opinion. Only a significant departure from GAAP which impacts the financial statements as a whole would result in an adverse opinion. Thus, the choice between an

CONCEPT SUMMARY
Qualified Audit Reports

Auditor's Report	Scope Limitation	Departure from GAAP	Inconsistent Application of GAAP	Major Uncertainty
Scope Paragraph	Modify second sentence dealing with GAAS and scope of audit	No change	No change	No change
Explanatory Paragraph	Yes	Yes	No	Yes
Opinion Paragraph	"except for" with reference to explanatory paragraph	"except for" with reference to explanatory paragraph	"except for" followed by appropriate explanation	"subject to" with reference to explanatory paragraph

"except for" qualification and an adverse opinion rests on the auditor's judgement of the materiality of the departure on the fairness of financial statements taken as a whole. A middle paragraph, must give the reason for an adverse opinion and show the impact on the statements, if possible. The opinion paragraph should leave out any reference to consistency (the consistency phrase implies use of GAAP).

Adverse opinions are extremely rare in that most auditors succeed in convincing the client to revise the financial statements in accordance with GAAP before they are issued. If this cannot be done, the only alternative to an adverse opinion is withdrawal from the engagement by the auditor.

12.2 DEPARTURES FROM THE STANDARD AUDIT REPORT

The four broad circumstances which bring about a substantive change in the wording of the standard auditor's report have been discussed. This section will present more detail on conditions within each of these broad areas that may result in a qualified or adverse opinion, a disclaimer, or some other wording change from the standard audit communication.

Departures from the wording of the standard report would be necessary in the following situations:

1. The scope of an examination is restricted by the client or by circumstances.
2. The scope of an examination is affected because part of the work has been performed by other auditors.
3. The financial statements contain departures from GAAP.
4. The financial statements contain inadequate disclosure.
5. The financial statements contain inconsistent application of GAAP.

6. Major unusual uncertainties exist that may have an impact on the financial statements.

7. The auditor wishes to emphasize an important matter affecting financial statements.

Scope Restricted by Client or Circumstances

Restrictions on the scope of the auditor's examination that are imposed by the client most often involve refusal to allow: (1) the direct confirmation of receivables, or (2) the observation of physical inventory.

Circumstances such as inadequate accounting records or an initial audit by a newly hired auditor may make certain procedures impossible to perform. In the case of scope limitations, an auditor may be able to satisfy himself by applying other auditing procedures and issue an unqualified opinion. If alternative procedures cannot be employed, a qualified opinion or disclaimer will be issued. Where audits have been limited in scope, negative assurances should not be given, e.g., "Nothing was found to indicate that statements are not fairly stated."

If a qualified report is released it: (1) describes the scope limitation, and (2) contains an "except for" opinion. Examine the following report.

(Scope paragraph)

We have examined the balance sheet of Limitations, Ltd. as of December 31, 19XX, and the related statements of income and retained earnings and changes in financial position for the year then ended. Our examination was made in accordance with generally accepted auditing standards and, accordingly, included such tests of the accounting records and such other auditing procedures as we considered necessary in the circumstances, except as stated in the following paragraph.

(Middle paragraph)

In accordance with the terms of our engagement, we did not examine records supporting the company's investment in a foreign company, stated at $......, as described in Note B to the financial statements. Accordingly, we do not express an opinion as to this investment.

(Opinion paragraph)

In our opinion, except for the effect of the matter referred to in the preceding paragraph, the aforementioned financial statements. . . .

Note B: During the year the corporation acquired an eight per cent interest in a foreign company. . . .

A qualified opinion is based on the materiality of the item(s) involved rather than the scope limitation itself. This distinction is important. Another distinction to remember is that an engagement to audit only one financial statement—say, a balance sheet—is not a scope limitation.

If the scope limitation had a far-reaching impact, a disclaimer would be in order. For example, a newly engaged auditor might not have witnessed the physical counting of inventory at year-end. Although alternative procedures could have solved the problem of not having observed the beginning inventory, the ending inventory quantities must be tested. If that were impossible, a disclaimer of opinion would be issued.

(Scope Paragraph)

. . . . Our examination was made in accordance with generally accepted auditing standards, and accordingly included such tests of the accounting records and such other auditing procedures as we considered necessary in the circumstances, except as stated in the following paragraph.

(Middle Paragraph)

We did not observe the taking of the physical inventory as of December 31, 19X0, because that date was prior to our appointment as auditors for the company, and we were unable to satisfy ourselves regarding inventory quantities by means of other auditing procedures.

(Opinion Paragraph)

Because the inventory at December 31, 19X0, is a material factor in the determination of financial position, and because we did not observe the taking of physical inventories, as noted in the preceding paragraph, the scope of our work was not sufficient to enable us to express, and we do not express, an opinion on the aforementioned financial statements.

February 18, 19X1

CONCEPT SUMMARY
Alternatives to the Standard Auditor's Report

Effect on Examination or on Financial Statements	Scope Limitation	Departure from GAAP	Inconsistent Application of GAAP	Major Uncertainty
Concentrated	Qualified Opinion "except for" with reference to explanatory paragraph	Qualified Opinion "except for" with reference to explanatory paragraph	Qualified Opinion "except for" followed by appropriate explanation	Qualified Opinion "subject to" with reference to explanatory paragraph
Widespread (Impacts statements as a whole)	Disclaimer of Opinion with explanatory paragraph	Adverse Opinion with explanatory paragraph	—	Disclaimer of Opinion with explanatory paragraph

Examination Made by Other Auditors

When client activities include subsidiaries, divisions, branches, or components that are geographically and operationally widespread, different auditors may be responsible for examining various parts of client operations. Here, one firm must assume the role of principal auditor. The principal auditor would usually be most familiar with the overall financial statements of the client and would likely have audited a material part of company activities.

If the principal auditor assumes responsibility for the overall fairness of the financial statements in his audit report, no reference to other auditors need be made. A standard unqualified opinion may be issued if the principal auditor is satisfied. On the other hand, if the principal auditor is unwilling to accept overall responsibility for the work of another auditor, a change in the standard report is necessary. The report of the principal auditor must then make reference to the work of others and carefully communicate the division and extent of responsibility between auditors.

An example of a principal auditor's report that refers to the work of another auditor (and therefore divides responsibility) is given below.

To the Board of Directors
The Black and Decker Manufacturing Company
Towson, Maryland

We have examined the consolidated statement of financial condition of The Black and Decker Manufacturing Company and subsidiaries as of September 30, 1979, and September 24, 1978, and the related consolidated statements of earnings, changes in stockholders' equity, and changes in financial position for the fiscal years then ended. Our examinations were made in accordance with generally accepted auditing standards and, accordingly, included such tests of the accounting records and such other auditing procedures as we considered necessary in the circumstances. We did not examine the financial statements of certain consolidated subsidiaries located outside the United States which statements reflect total assets and revenues constituting 17% and 18% in 1979 and 32% and 37% in 1978, respectively, of the related consolidated totals. These statements were examined by other independent accountants whose reports thereon have been furnished to us and our opinion expressed herein, insofar as it relates to the amounts included for these subsidiaries, is based solely on the reports of the other independent accountants.

In our opinion, based upon our examinations and the reports of the other independent accountants, the financial statements referred to above present fairly the consolidated financial position of The Black and Decker Manufacturing Company and subsidiaries at September 30, 1979 and September 24, 1978, and the consolidated results of their operations and changes in their financial position for the fiscal years then ended, in conformity with generally accepted accounting principles consistently applied during the period, except for the change, with which we concur, in the method of determining the cost of United States inventories as described in the notes to the consolidated financial statements.

Notice that, even when the principal auditor decides to refer to the examination of other auditors, the opinion is not considered to be qualified. The departure from the wording of the standard report simply alerts readers that the audit work was divided, and therefore, so is the responsibility. The extent of divided responsibilities is usually expressed in terms of the percentage of revenue and assets audited.

Deciding Whether or Not to Make Reference

The principal auditor's decision to assume responsibility for the financial statements as a whole should be based on a number of considerations including:

1. The materiality of the examination of the other auditor to the financial statements as a whole.
2. The reputation, professional standards, and competence of the other auditor.
3. The independence of the other auditor.
4. Whether or not the work of the other auditor was supervised by the principal auditor.

If the principal auditor decides that he cannot rely on the examination of another auditor as that work affects his own report, he should issue a qualified opinion or, if the other work is extremely material to the financial statements as a whole, a disclaimer of opinion.

Predecessor and Successor Auditors

When one auditor replaces another, the new auditor should establish a proper basis for his opinion in the first audit, including the consistent application of GAAP. In the process, consultations with the predecessor auditor are usually necessary. Ordinarily, predecessor auditors are expected to make themselves and their working papers available to those who succeed them for reasonable review. If the prior year's portion of comparative statements was audited by a predecessor auditor whose report is not presented, the successor's report is affected. The scope paragraph must then indicate: (1) that the prior year's statements were audited by other auditors, (2) the date of their report, (3) the type of opinion issued, and (4) explanations, if an unqualified opinion was not expressed.

Departures from GAAP

The first reporting standard requires that the auditor's report state whether the financial statements are presented in accordance with GAAP. Material departures from GAAP in financial statements must be noted by an "except for" qualification or an adverse opinion, with the basis for the departure from an unqualified opinion clearly explained as in the following examples. The dollar effect on the financial statements should also be indicated if possible.

Qualified Opinion

(Middle paragraph)

Although the proceeds of sales are collectible on the installment basis, revenue from such sales is recorded in full by the Company at time of sale. However, for income tax purposes, income is reported only as collections are received, and no provision has been made for income taxes on installments to be collected in the future, as required by generally accepted accounting principles. If such provisions had been made, net income for 19... and retained earnings as of December 31, 19..., would have been reduced by approximately $...... and $......, respectively, and the balance sheet would have included deferred income taxes of approximately $......, and current liabilities would have been increased and working capital would have been reduced by the same amount.

(Opinion paragraph)

In our opinion, except that provision has not been made for additional income taxes as described in the preceding paragraph, the aforementioned financial statements present fairly. . . .

Adverse Opinion

(Same Middle paragraph as above)

(Opinion paragraph)

Because of the materiality of the amounts of omitted income taxes as described in the preceding paragraph, we are of the opinion that the aforementioned financial statements do not present fairly the financial position of X Company at December 31, 19..., or the results of its operations or the changes in its financial position for the year ended in conformity with generally accepted accounting principles.

GAAP include not only the broad principles of accounting but also the rules, procedures, and conventions used to apply these principles. As such, there is no one comprehensive list of GAAP that can be used as a handy reference. The following are well-recognized sources of GAAP:

1. Statements and Interpretations of the FASB
2. Opinions of the APB (Accounting Principles Board)
3. Accounting Research Bulletins of the AICPA
4. Pronouncements of the SEC and other regulatory agencies
5. Pronouncements of professional organizations such as the AAA (American Accounting Association)
6. Other pronouncements of the AICPA, such as industry audit guidelines

Since in most cases more than one accounting principle or procedure is available (LIFO vs. FIFO, accelerated depreciation vs. straight line), the auditor must determine both that the principle or procedure chosen by the client is applicable to the current circumstance and that it is generally accepted.

Departures Due to Fairness

There is one principle that governs over all: *financial statements should be not misleading*. Departures from GAAP may be accepted by auditors in certain unusual circumstances. If the use of an established principle or procedure would cause financial statements to be misleading, an alternative acceptable principle or procedure may be used to remedy the situation. In these unusual circumstances, an auditor may issue an unqualified opinion with an explanation of why the more established principle or procedure would result in misleading financial statements. Such circumstances are rare, however.

Inadequate Disclosure

The third standard of reporting deals directly with adequate and informative disclosure. Adequate disclosure is a part of conformity to GAAP. Disclosure has to do with the form and content of financial statements and the accuracy and clarity of accompanying footnotes. Adequate disclosure involves not only the completeness and correctness of financial statements and notes but also an element of effective communication. When this level of disclosure is not present in financial statements, the auditor must: (1) provide, if possible, the information necessary (except for certain specific exclusions) to make the disclosures adequate in an explanatory paragraph of his opinion, and (2) issue a qualified or an adverse opinion (SAS 32). Following is an example of an opinion qualified because of inadequate disclosure:

(Middle paragraph)
On January 15, 19..2, the company issued debentures in the amount of $...... for the purpose of financing plant expansion. The debenture agreement restricts the payment of future cash dividends to earnings after December 31, 19..1.

(Opinion paragraph)

In our opinion, except for the omission of the information in the preceding paragraph, the aforementioned financial statements present fairly. . . .

Inadequate disclosure may involve omission of one of the basic financial statements. If the statements purport to present financial position and results of operations (i.e., to be complete) the auditor should note in an explanatory paragraph that a required statement is not being presented and issue a qualified or adverse opinion. It is considered inappropriate for an auditor to prepare a basic financial statement that management has refused to prepare.

Inconsistent Application of GAAP

The second standard of reporting requires that the auditor state whether GAAP have been consistently applied. Two important questions must be answered if a change in accounting principle occurs:

1. How is the change to be expressed in the financial statements?
2. What is the period of time to which the consistency reference applies?

A change in accounting principle can be expressed by restating the financial statements of prior years or by reporting the cumulative effect only in the year of change. Also, the auditor may be reporting on only one year's statements or on comparative statements for several years.

Change in Accounting Principle Requiring Restatement

When financial statements are retroactively restated for a change in GAAP (e.g., a change from LIFO) the auditor's report in the year of change should note that the statements are consistent after the restatement. The auditor's explicit agreement with the change should also be given.

The Board of Directors and Stockholders Chock Full O'Nuts Corporation:

(Standard Scope Paragraph)

In our opinion, the aforementioned financial statements present fairly the consolidated financial position of Chock Full O'Nuts Corporation and subsidiaries at July 31, 1979 and 1978, and the results of their operations and the changes in their financial position for the years then ended, in conformity with generally accepted accounting principles applied on a consistent basis after restatement for the change, with which we concur, in the method of accounting for leases as described in note 3 to the financial statements.

The same type of report is used when changing from a principle that is not generally accepted to one that is. Reports in years subsequent to the year of change need not mention the change in GAAP or the restatement.

Change in Accounting Principle Not Requiring Restatement

For changes in GAAP that are reported as a cumulative effect when they occur, a slightly different wording is used. In the year of the change, a report would be phrased as follows.

> To the Shareholders and Board of Directors, Whittaker Corporation
>
> (Standard Scope Paragraph)
> In our opinion, the aforementioned consolidated financial statements present fairly the consolidated financial position of Whittaker Corporation and consolidated subsidiaries as of October 31, 1979 and 1978, and the consolidated results of their operations and changes in financial position for the years then ended, in conformity with generally accepted accounting principles applied on a consistent basis, except for the change, with which we concur, to the last-in, first-out (LIFO) method of valuing certain inventories as described in Note 3 of Notes to Consolidated Financial Statements.—

For a later year after the change, but still part of the comparative statements, the auditor's report would state:

> (Opinion paragraph)
> . . . in conformity with generally accepted accounting principles consistently applied during the period subsequent to the change, with which we concur, made as of November 1, 1978, in the method of valuing certain inventories as described in Note X to the financial statements.

A change in GAAP which does not affect the financial statements for the years being reported on by the auditor need not be mentioned in his report.

The following points about the effect of inconsistencies on the auditor's report should be noted.

1. Inconsistency in the application of GAAP can only result in a qualified opinion, never a disclaimer of opinion or an adverse opinion.

2. The consistency reference in the auditor's report refers to the immediately preceding year, if one year's financial statements are presented, or to all year's financial statements presented in the case of comparative statements.

3. The consistency reference does not apply to the initial examination of a new company but does apply to the initial examination of an established company by a newly hired auditor.

4. Inconsistency in the application of GAAP is the foremost reason for the use of qualified opinions by auditors.

5. A change in accounting principle must be reasonably justified. If not, the auditor's report should state that fact.

Unusual Uncertainties

From time to time, a business may find itself in the midst of circumstances whose outcome cannot be reasonably determined as of the date of the auditor's opinion. These uncertainties usually involve tax matters, lawsuits, and certain other contingencies whose final outcome is in the hands of parties other than the client.

When one or more unusual uncertainties exist whose effect on financial statements cannot be determined, the auditor may:

1. Issue an unqualified opinion, if there is little probability that the resolution of the uncertainty will have a material effect on the financial statements.
2. Issue a "subject to" qualified opinion with an explanatory paragraph, if there is a reasonable probability that the resolution of the uncertainty will have a material effect on the financial statements.
3. Disclaim an opinion, if there is a reasonable probability that the resolution of the uncertainty will have a disastrous effect on the financial statements and the client. The language of an uncertainty disclaimer is similar to the disclaimer illustrated earlier under "scope limitations." They are rare in practice, however.

A fascinating auditor's report with a "subject to" qualification is the one in Exhibit 12–1 for the Chrysler Corporation.

Emphasis of a Matter

Occasionally, an auditor may wish to emphasize a matter that has already been adequately reported on and disclosed in the financial statements. This can be accomplished by the use of a middle paragraph to call attention to the matter being highlighted. Since the explanation is one of emphasis rather than disclosure, the opinion is not considered qualified because of it.

To make this point very clear, the standard unqualified scope and opinion paragraphs are used with no reference to the explanatory emphasis paragraph between them. This type of opinion has not been widely used by auditors, but it can be helpful for matters such as related party transactions, changes in accounting estimates, and changes in operating conditions.

Reports on Comparative Statements

Comparative statements often show current and last year's data side by side. At times, three-to-five year's data are presented. We have already illustrated and discussed some features of auditor's reports on comparative financial statements. A few additional points need mentioning. The degree of responsibility assumed

Shareholders and Board of Directors
Chrysler Corporation
Detroit, Michigan

We have examined the accompanying consolidated balance sheet of Chrysler Corporation and consolidated subsidiaries at December 31, 1979 and 1978, and the related consolidated statements of operations and changes in financial position for the years then ended. Our examinations were made in accordance with generally accepted auditing standards and accordingly included such tests of the accounting records and such other auditing procedures as we considered necessary in the circumstances.

As more fully described in Note 2, during 1979 the Corporation encountered substantial problems resulting in a loss of $1,097.3 million which has significantly weakened its financial condition. Consequently, the Corporation is currently in violation of loan covenants with certain lenders which permits the acceleration of substantially all debt including the long-term debt (see Note 3). In addition, the Corporation recognized the need to expend an initially estimated $13.5 billion (subject to continual review) for product programs for the period 1979-1985, including $7.8 billion for capital expenditures. Because Chrysler determined that it would be unable to sustain its losses and raise such total capital requirements through conventional funding sources, it requested federal government assistance in the form of loan guarantees which resulted in the Chrysler Corporation Loan Guarantee Act of 1979. The Operating Plan submitted to the government on December 17, 1979 anticipates resolving these financial needs through the continued availability of existing financing, an additional $2.1 billion from the sale of assets, concessions from interested parties, and other financing arrangements, and the remainder from cash flow from operations. This Plan, under continual review and refinement to deal with changing conditions, also projects a reduced operating loss in 1980, a profit in 1981 and substantially improved profits thereafter. The availability of a commitment for federal loan guarantees for new borrowings of up to $1.5 billion depends upon meeting the requirements of the Chrysler Corporation Loan Guarantee Act of 1979, as discussed in Note 2. It is the Corporation's objective to have all conditions met by April 1, 1980, and to be in a position to obtain the Board's guarantee of the first loan under the Act shortly thereafter. Prior to the finalization of arrangements with the Loan Guarantee Board and with current lenders to modify the terms of various existing loan agreements, significant interim financing is necessary to meet the Corporation's financial obligations until federally guaranteed loans are available.

The Corporation anticipates completing commercial and industrial arrangements with PSA Peugeot-Citroen ("Peugeot") by May 31, 1980 (see Note 5). Such arrangements are contemplated as part of the Corporation's ongoing operations, and its 14% ownership of Peugeot continues to be valued as a long-term investment. However, the basis for the valuation of the Peugeot stock may be different if the nature of this investment changes because of failure to reach the commercial and industrial arrangements.

The ability of the Corporation to operate in accordance with its operating and financing plans is dependent on many factors, some of which are beyond the Corporation's control, including the effect of government energy, safety, and emissions policies, the availability and price of gasoline, overall automobile industry market conditions, acceptance of the Corporation's products, and the impact of world economic and political developments. Because the achievement of these plans is dependent upon future events, there can be no assurance that the necessary interim or long-term financing can be arranged, that future operations will occur as planned, that there will be no need to significantly restructure Chrysler's product programs, or that the anticipated commercial and industrial arrangements with Peugeot will be achieved. The accompanying financial statements have been prepared on the basis of accounting principles applicable to a going concern and accordingly they do not purport to give effect to adjustments, if any, that may be appropriate should the Corporation be unable to continue as a going concern and therefore be required to realize its assets and liquidate its liabilities, contingent obligations and commitments in other than the normal course of business and at amounts different from those in the accompanying financial statements.

In our report dated February 26, 1979, our opinion on the 1978 financial statements was unqualified; however, in view of the uncertainties arising in 1979 as referred to in the preceding paragraphs, our opinion on the accompanying 1978 financial statements, expressed in the next paragraph, replaces our previous opinion.

In our opinion, subject to the effects of such adjustments, if any, as might have been required had the outcome of the uncertainties described above been known, the financial statements examined by us present fairly the financial position of Chrysler Corporation and consolidated subsidiaries at December 31, 1979 and 1978, and the results of their operations and changes in their financial position for the years then ended, in conformity with generally accepted accounting principles applied on a consistent basis.

EXHIBIT 12–1   Qualified Report for Uncertainty with an Updated Opinion on Last Year

464

by an auditor for all of the years presented in comparative statements should be clearly stated. This entails the following:

1. Identifying all of the statements audited. Audited current-year statements can be shown in comparison to compiled or reviewed statements of the prior year(s).
2. Expressing an appropriate opinion, assurance, or disclaimer for each year's statements. Different opinions may be expressed for a series of consecutive years. A prior year's opinion may be updated if a different opinion becomes appropriate (e.g., resolution of an uncertainty).
3. The opinion paragraph consistency phrase is different from the one used with single-year statements. For comparative statements, all of which are audited, the language used is, "applied on a consistent basis."
4. The auditor's report is dated as of the end of field work of the current year.

Exhibit 12–2 is another fascinating auditors' report. It is rare for a report to be signed by partners of four CPA firms. Notice that the auditors' report on the City of New York refers to other auditors, points out a departure from GAAP, emphasizes a matter, and is qualified for uncertainty. Comparative statements are being presented.

12.3 SPECIAL REPORTS

The term "special reports" refers to auditor communications issued in connection with examinations for which the standard opinion paragraph is not applicable. The opinion paragraph of the standard report may be inappropriate in the following circumstances.

1. The financial statements being examined are prepared on a basis other than GAAP (such as cash basis statements or statements based on regulations of a government agency).
2. The auditor is examining and reporting only on specific elements, accounts, or items of a financial statement (such as the determination of rentals, royalties, profit-sharing bonuses, or provisions of bond indentures).
3. The examination is concerned with monitoring compliance with contractual agreements or regulatory requirements that are related to audited financial statements.
4. The financial statements being examined are prepared on the prescribed forms or schedules of an agency and require a prescribed form of auditor's opinion.

The general auditing standards and standards of field work are as applicable to examinations that result in special reports as they are to all general-purpose

PEAT, MARWICK, MITCHELL & CO.

And

RICHARD A. EISNER & COMPANY   MITCHELL, TITUS & CO.   STEWART, BENJAMIN & BROWN, P.C.

CERTIFIED PUBLIC ACCOUNTANTS

The City of New York:

We have examined the financial statements of the General, Capital Projects and Debt Service Funds and the Statement of Long-term Obligations of The City of New York as of and for the years ended June 30, 1979 and 1978. Our examinations were made in accordance with generally accepted auditing standards, and accordingly included such tests of the accounting records and such other auditing procedures as we considered necessary in the circumstances. We did not examine the fiscal 1978 expenditures and encumbrances of the Board of Education included in the General and Capital Projects Funds ($2.6 billion and $40 million, respectively), nor did we examine the accounts and transactions of the Municipal Assistance Corporation For The City of New York included in the Debt Service Funds and Statement of Long-term Obligations (see Note C to the financial statements). These expenditures, encumbrances, accounts and transactions were examined by other auditors whose reports thereon have been furnished to us, and our opinion expressed herein, insofar as it relates to the fiscal 1978 amounts included for the Board of Education and to the amounts included for the Municipal Assistance Corporation, is based solely upon the reports of the other auditors.

The City does not maintain complete records of its general fixed assets and, therefore, a Statement of General Fixed Assets is not presented in the accompanying financial statements as required by generally accepted accounting principles.

As discussed in Note I, in recent years the City has experienced severe financial difficulties including substantial recurring operating deficits and loss of access to the public long-term credit market. The City has embarked on a comprehensive four-year program to balance its revenues and expenditures in conformity with generally accepted accounting principles and obtain long-term and seasonal financing. While the City thus far has been able to meet many of the objectives of the program, its ability to accomplish the overall program objectives depends on the realization of numerous assumptions and the occurrence of future events, many of which cannot be assured.

As indicated in Note J, numerous real estate tax certiorari proceedings are presently pending against the City on the grounds of alleged inequality of assessment. While an adverse decision involving this issue could have a substantial financial impact on the City, its ultimate outcome cannot presently be determined, and no provision for this potential exposure, if any, has been made in the financial statements.

In our opinion, based upon our examinations and the reports of the other auditors, subject to the effect of such adjustments, if any, as might have been required had the ultimate resolution of the real estate tax issue discussed in the preceding paragraph been known, the aforementioned financial statements present fairly the financial position of the General, Capital Projects and Debt Service Funds and the Statement of Long-term Obligations of The City of New York at June 30, 1979 and 1978, and the results of operations of such funds for the years then ended, in conformity with generally accepted accounting principles applied on a consistent basis.

Peat Marwick, Mitchell & Co.

Richard A. Eisner & Company

Mitchell, Titus & Co.

Stewart, Benjamin & Brown, P.C.

New York, New York
October 31, 1979

EXHIBIT 12-2

466

CONCEPT SUMMARY

Departures from the Standard Audit Report

Caused By	Example	Type of Report
Scope restricted by client	Physical inventory not observed	Qualified or disclaimer
Scope restricted by circumstances	Initial audit engagement	Qualified or disclaimer on some statements
Examination by other auditors	Different auditors for branches or subsidiaries	Unqualified opinion which may or may not make reference to other auditor's work
Departures from GAAP	Failure to record provision for income taxes on installment sales	Qualified or adverse
Inadequate disclosure	Dividend restriction not disclosed	Qualified or adverse
Inconsistent application of GAAP	Change in depreciation method	Qualified
Unusual uncertainties	Contested income taxes or pending lawsuit	Qualified or disclaimer
Emphasis of a matter	Changes in accounting estimates	Unqualified with explanatory paragraph

examinations. Also, the third and fourth standards of reporting apply to special reports. The first and second standards of reporting do not apply to special reports since GAAP are usually not a consideration in these examinations. However, the first standard of reporting is satisfied by the disclosure that the financial statements are not intended to conform to GAAP together with an opinion as to whether the statements are in conformity with whatever basis is being used.

Basis of Accounting Other than GAAP

Reporting by an auditor under the "special reports" provision for a basis of accounting other than GAAP is permissible only if one of the following applies:

1. The basis is prescribed by a government regulatory agency that has jurisdiction over the client.
2. The basis used is the same as that used by the client to file income tax returns for the period.
3. The cash basis or modified cash basis is used.
4. The approach has substantial support and is applied to all items in the financial statements, such as the price-level basis of accounting.

When financial statements have been prepared on a comprehensive basis of accounting other than GAAP, the auditor's report should include all of the information contained in the following example, except that the accounting basis can be different.

We have examined the statement of assets and liabilities arising from cash transactions of XYZ Company as of December 31, 19XX, and the related statement of revenue collected and expenses paid for the year then ended. Our examination was made in accordance with generally accepted auditing standards and, accordingly, included such tests of the accounting records and such other auditing procedures as we considered necessary in the circumstances.

As described in Note X, the Company's policy is to prepare its financial statements on the basis of cash receipts and disbursements; consequently, certain revenue and the related assets are recognized when received rather than when earned, and certain expenses are recognized when paid rather than when the obligation is incurred. Accordingly, the accompanying financial statements are not intended to present financial position and results of operations in conformity with generally accepted accounting principles.

In our opinion, the financial statements referred to above present fairly the assets and liabilities arising from cash transactions of XYZ Company as of December 31, 19XX, and the revenue collected and expenses paid during the year ended, on the basis of accounting described in Note X, which basis has been applied in a manner consistent with that of the preceding year.

Report on Specific Elements, Accounts, and Items

An examination of certain specific elements, accounts, or items such as rentals, royalties, profit participation, or provision for income taxes, may be undertaken by an auditor along with an examination of the overall financial statements or as a separate activity. In reporting on individual items, the first standard of reporting does not apply (individual items do not constitute a financial statement), although the second may if individual items are reported in accordance with GAAP. Also, the concept of materiality must be related to each item being examined and reported upon rather than to the financial statements as a whole.

An auditor's report on individual items in a financial statement should include:

1. An identification of the specific elements, accounts, or items being reported upon and the basis for their presentation
2. A statement that the examination was made in accordance with GAAS and whether or not it was made in conjunction with an examination of the financial statements as a whole
3. An opinion on whether the specific elements, accounts, and items cited are presented fairly on the basis indicated, consistently applied

An example of a special report on the adequacy of a provision for income taxes follows.

We have examined the financial statements of XYZ Company, Inc., for the year ended June 30, 19XX, and have issued our report thereon dated August 15, 19XX. Our examination was made in accordance with generally accepted auditing standards and, accordingly, included such tests of the accounting records and such other auditing procedures as we considered necessary in the circumstances.

In the course of our examination, we examined the provision for federal and state income taxes for the year ended June 30, 19XX, included in the Company's financial statements referred to in the preceding paragraph. We also reviewed the federal and state income tax returns filed by the Company that are subject to examination by the respective taxing authorities.

In our opinion, the Company has paid or has provided adequate accruals in the financial statements referred to above for the payment of all federal and state income taxes, and has provided for related deferred income taxes, applicable to fiscal 19XX and prior fiscal years, that could be reasonably estimated at the time of our examination of the financial statements of XYZ Company, Inc., for the year ended June 30, 19XX.

Ordinarily, an auditor would not issue a special report on individual items in a financial statement if he has issued an adverse or disclaimer of opinion on the financial statements as a whole. Such a report could result in confusion among readers of financial statements as to the position of the auditor.

Reports on Compliance

Companies are often required by regulatory agencies or contractual agreements to comply to externally imposed provisions. For example, a company may be required by a bond indenture to make payments to a sinking fund, to restrict dividend payments during the life of a bond issue, or to maintain certain financial and operating ratio levels.

An auditor may issue a special report on compliance with accounting related terms and conditions of a contractual agreement. This type of special report takes the form of negative assurance by the auditor regarding the contract's requirements. The negative assurance may be given in a separate report or as an addition to the report on the financial statements.

Following is an example of a separate special compliance report on adherence to the terms and conditions of a bond indenture. The negative assurance is given in the second paragraph.

We have examined the balance sheet of XYZ Company as of December 31, 19X1, and the related statements of income, retained earnings, and changes in financial position for the year then ended, and have issued our report thereon dated February 16, 19X2. Our examination was made in accordance with generally accepted auditing standards and, accordingly, included such tests of the accounting records and such other auditing procedures as we considered necessary in the circumstances.

In connection with our examination, nothing came to our attention that caused us to believe that the Company was not in compliance with any of the terms, covenants, provisions, or conditions of sections XX to XX, inclusive, of the Indenture dated July 21, 19X0, with ABC Bank. However, it should be noted that our examination was not directed primarily toward obtaining knowledge of such noncompliance.

Notice that this special report cites the examination of financial statements as the primary focus of the engagement. Further, a statement that the auditor's work was not directed specifically toward determining noncompliance is included.

Prescribed Forms of Schedules

Some regulatory bodies require that specifically worded forms or schedules be filed with them by companies and independent auditors. If the auditor feels that these prescribed reports call for assertions that are not within the bounds of professional standards, he should:

1. Change the wording of the report to reflect his position and assertions, or
2. File a separate report that properly reflects his position and assertions.

In both cases, the guidelines for special reports are followed.

Supplementary Information

Facts, over and beyond those required in basic financial statements, are referred to as supplementary, accompanying, or other information. For example, schedules showing the details of administrative expenses or cost of goods sold, financial ratios, insurance coverage, or calculation of overhead rates. Supplementary information may be included within the covers of a set of audited statements. Instead, financial statements may be included within a larger document, such as an annual report. In the latter case, information in the larger document must be examined for inconsistencies and material misstatements (AU 550). In the former case, when supplementary information is added to the basic financial statements, the auditor must: (1) state whether it has been audited, and if so, (2) express an opinion on it.* An auditor's report in this case would appear as follows:

---

*Supplementary information required by the FASB (e.g., inflation accounting) is treated in a special way. See *SAS 27* and *SAS 29,* par. 15.

CONCEPT SUMMARY

Special Reports and Their Use

Circumstance	Examples	Type of Report
Financial statements prepared on a comprehensive basis other than GAAP	• Basis prescribed by regulatory agency • Basis used for income tax reporting • Cash or modified cash basis • Other basis with substantial support (price-level basis accounting)	Three-paragraph special report with appropriate modifications in the scope and opinion paragraph and an explanatory middle paragraph (see AU 621.05)
Reports on specific elements, accounts, and items in financial statements	• Rentals • Royalties • Profit participation • Adequacy of provision for income taxes	Two-paragraph special report with appropriate modifications (see AU 621.14)
Reports on compliance related to audited financial statements	• Compliance with regulatory requirements • Compliance with contractual provisions	Two-paragraph special report with modifications in the scope paragraph and a negative assurance opinion paragraph or a negative assurance paragraph addition to the standard report (see AU 621.19)
Reports in prescribed form	Reports required by regulatory agencies	Reword the prescribed report or issue a separate special report as appropriate

Our examination was made for the purpose of forming an opinion on the basic financial statements taken as a whole. The (identify accompanying information) is presented for purposes of additional analysis and is not a required part of the basic financial statements. Such information has been subjected to the auditing procedures applied in the examination of the basic financial statements and, in our opinion, is fairly stated in all material respects in relation to the basic financial statements taken as a whole.

It can either be added to the standard report or presented on a separate page. If the information has not been audited, a disclaimer of opinion is issued. Prior to July, 1980 when *SAS 29* was released, this situation was covered in what were called "long-form reports." That phrase has now been dropped from the authoritative literature.

Letters for Underwriters

As a part of the Securities Act of 1933, underwriters of securities and others associated with new security issues are required to perform a "reasonable investigation" of the financial and accounting data of the issuer. This financial and accounting data includes material not covered by the financial statement audit of independent accountants. One way that this reasonable investigation can be carried out on unaudited information is to request a letter of negative assurance from the independent auditors about this information. This negative assurance letter is called a "comfort letter."

Although comfort letters are not required under the 1933 Act and are not filed with the SEC, they are usually an important part of an underwriting agreement. These letters help both the underwriter and the auditor meet their responsibilities under the 1933 Act.

Comfort letters generally deal with one or more of the following areas.

1. The independence of the auditors.
2. Compliance with the 1933 Act as to the form and content of audited financial statements.
3. Unaudited financial statements and schedules included in the registration statement.
4. Changes in selected financial statement items since the last audited financial statements included in the registration statement.
5. Tables, statistics, and other financial information included in the registration statement.

In order to issue a comfort letter, a limited review of the unaudited information in the registration statement must be made by the auditor. The procedures for this limited review are agreed upon by the underwriter and the auditor. They usually include reading minutes and interim financial statements and making pointed inquiries of management. A comfort letter should only be issued by the auditor who has expressed an opinion on the audited financial statements in the registration statement.

A comfort letter should always conclude with the following type of warning as to the use and purpose of the letter (Codification of Statements on Auditing Standards).

This letter is solely for the information of, and assistance to, the underwriters in conducting and documenting their investigation of the affairs of the Company in connection with the offering of the securities covered by the Registration Statement, and is not to be used, circulated, quoted, or otherwise referred to within or without the underwriting group for any other purpose, including but not limited to the registration, purchase, or sale of securities, nor is it to be filed with or referred to in whole or in part in the Registration Statement or any other document, except that reference may be made to it in the underwriting agreement or in any list of closing documents pertaining to the offering of the securities covered by the Registration Statement.

12.4 OTHER REPORTING SERVICES

Independent accountants may perform a number of non-auditing services for a client. These services might include any of the following:

1. Keeping, adjusting, and closing a client's books.
2. Preparing a client's financial statements from information supplied by the client.
3. Reviewing the financial statements of a client to provide a level of assurance more limited than that provided by an audit.

The first service is an *accounting* service; the second is called a *compilation* service; and the third is a *review* service. Guidelines in the compilation and review services area are provided by the Accounting and Review Services Committee, which was formed in 1977. This committee issues *Statements on Standards for Accounting and Review Services* (SSARS).

Compilations and Unaudited Financial Statements

A CPA may be engaged to prepare, or assist in preparing, a client's financial statements. The client may be either a public or a non-public entity depending on whether or not its securities are publicly traded or about to be sold to the public. The term *unaudited* financial statements is used in connection with public entities, whereas the term *compiled* is reserved for non-public entities. Both services are basically the same; financial statements are prepared from the client's data taken at face value. There is no responsibility to perform any audit procedures and no intention to provide the kind of assurance that comes from an audit or review. An engagement letter would normally describe the service, its limitations, and the report that will be issued.

An accountant becomes "associated" with unaudited financial statements when he either prepares them (even on plain paper) or agrees to have the firm's name linked to them. Association requires that the statements be labeled "unaudited" on every page and that a disclaimer be issued, such as the following:

> The accompanying balance sheet of X Company as of December 31, 19...., and the related statements of income and retained earnings and changes in financial position for the year then ended were not audited by us and accordingly we do not express an opinion on them.
>
> (Signature and date
of preparing statements)

If the statements are for internal use only and the client elects to omit the notes or other disclosures, a sentence to that effect is added to the disclaimer.

When an accountant compiles financial statements, he is expected to be knowledgeable about the client and the industry in which it operates. Each page of the statements should say, "See Accountant's Compilation Report." The accountant's report, which carries the date the compilation was completed, looks like the following:

> The accompanying balance sheet of XYZ Company as of December 31, 19XX, and the related statements of income, retained earnings, and changes in financial position for the year then ended have been compiled by me (us).
>
> A compilation is limited to presenting in the form of financial statements information that is the representation of management (owners). I (we) have not audited or reviewed the accompanying financial statements and, accordingly, do not express an opinion or any other form of assurance on them.

Management may decide to omit substantially all disclosures from compiled statements or to exclude a statement of changes in financial position. In that case, a separate paragraph is added to the disclaimer to alert readers.

If, in the process of preparing or assisting in the preparation of unaudited or compiled financial statements, the CPA reaches the conclusion that the statements are not in conformity with GAAP (including adequate disclosure):

1. He should attempt to have the financial statements revised, or if the client refuses,

2. He should disclose the nonconformity and its effect as a part of his disclaimer of opinion, or if the client will not accept the modified disclaimer,

3. He should withdraw from the engagement and refuse to be associated with the statements.

In the final analysis, the independent CPA should refuse to be associated in any way with financial statements that he believes to be false or misleading. This prohibition extends even to typing and reproduction services in connection with the statements.

If an accountant were not independent, his report on the unaudited or compiled financial statements would clearly state that fact.

Reviews of Financial Statements

A review falls somewhere between an audit and a compilation. It provides limited assurance that there are no material modifications required to make the financial statements conform to GAAP.

Reviews are made of the interim (e.g., quarterly) financial statements of public corporations (SAS 24). The financial statements of non-public firms are also reviewed (SSARS 1). Review procedures are basically the same in either case except that a management representation letter is required, and certain inquiries have to be made about the accounting system when a public firm is reviewed.

In a review, internal controls are not evaluated, assets are not confirmed or examined, and tests of the records are not made. Instead, analytical review procedures are performed, and inquiries are made. Examples of inquiries can be found in Appendix A of SSARS 1.

An example of a CPA's report on the review of interim financial information is given below (SAS No. 24).

> We have made a review (describe the information or statements reviewed) of ABC Company and consolidated subsidiaries as of September 30, 19X1, and for three-month and nine-month periods then ended, in accordance with standards established by the American Institute of Certified Public Accountants.
>
> A review of interim financial information consists principally of obtaining an understanding of the system for the preparation of interim financial information, applying analytical review procedures to financial data, and making inquiries of persons responsible for financial and accounting matters. It is substantially less in scope than an examination in accordance with generally accepted auditing standards, the objective of which is the expression of an opinion regarding the financial statements taken as a whole. Accordingly, we do not express such an opinion.
>
> Based on our review, we are not aware of any material modification that should be made to the accompanying financial (information or statements) for them to be in conformity with generally accepted accounting principles.

The report used with reviews of non-public firms (SSARS 1) would be slightly different. The scope paragraph would have a sentence added at the end stating that, "all information included in these financial statements is the representation of the management (owners)." The middle paragraph begins with a clause concerning an understanding of the system. That clause would be omitted. Otherwise, the accountant's reports are the same.

Reports on Internal Control

A CPA may be engaged to report on an entity's system of internal accounting control in conjunction with, or separate from, an audit of its financial statements. An opinion on internal accounting control requires that the scope of an examination be expanded to include all control procedures rather than just those which impact the audit of financial statements. Reports on internal control may be useful to management, regulatory agencies, other auditors, or the general public, particularly in regard to the Foreign Corrupt Practices Act of 1977.

In making a study and evaluation for the purpose of expressing an opinion on the system of internal accounting control, these major steps are taken:

1. Plan the scope of the engagement.
2. Review the design of the system.
3. Test compliance with prescribed procedures.
4. Evaluate the review and test results.
5. Obtain a management representation letter that:
    *   Acknowledges their responsibility for establishing and maintaining the system.
    *   States that they have disclosed all known weaknesses and recent changes to the system.
    *   Describes any irregularities by personnel who are key to the system.

The accountant's report resulting from a special review of a system of internal accounting controls would appear as follows (SAS 30).

> We have made a study and evaluation of the system of internal accounting control of XYZ Company and subsidiaries in effect at (date). Our study and evaluation was conducted in accordance with standards established by the American Institute of Certified Public Accountants.
>
> The management of XYZ Company is responsible for establishing and maintaining a system of internal accounting control. In fulfilling this responsibility, estimates and judgments by management are required to assess the expected benefits and related costs of control procedures. The objectives of a system are to provide management with reasonable, but not absolute, assurance that assets are safeguarded against loss from unauthorized use or disposition and that transactions are executed in accordance with management's authorization and recorded properly to permit the preparation of financial statements in accordance with generally accepted accounting principles.
>
> Because of inherent limitations in any system of internal accounting control, errors or irregularities may occur and not be detected. Also, projection of any evaluation of the system to future periods is subject to the risk that procedures may become inadequate because of changes in conditions or that the degree of compliance with the procedures may deteriorate.
>
> In our opinion, the system of internal accounting control of XYZ Company and subsidiaries in effect at (date), taken as a whole, was sufficient to meet the objectives stated above insofar as those objectives pertain to the prevention or detection of errors or irregularities in amounts that would be material in relation to the consolidated financial statements.

SAS 30 illustrates the report when other situations are encountered, such as the discovery of material weaknesses, scope limitations, and referring to other accountants. When a report on internal accounting controls is an off-shoot of an audit, rather than a special engagement, it is phrased as a negative assurance.

There are no restrictions on the distribution of the CPA's report on internal accounting control when the report results from an engagement specifically to express an opinion. A CPA may, however, report on internal control as a by-product of a financial statement audit or under pre-established criteria by a regulatory agency. In these circumstances, distribution of the CPA's report is restricted to management, regulatory agencies, or specified other third parties. A statement to this effect must be included in the report in the latter two cases.

CONCEPT SUMMARY
Non-Audit Reports and Their Use

Accounting, Compilation, or Review Service	Specific Illustration	Type of Report
Unaudited Financial Statements and Compilations	CPA prepares, or assists in preparing, a client's financial statements.	Disclaimer of opinion which emphasizes that an audit has not been performed, and no opinion is expressed on the financial statements.
	CPA is not independent.	Disclaimer of opinion which emphasizes that the CPA is not independent, that no audit has been performed, and no opinion is expressed.
Limited Review	Interim financial information of a public company. Financial statements for a non-public company.	Descriptive report which: (1) states that the review was in accordance with professional standards, (2) identifies the information reviewed, (3) describes the procedures followed in the review, (4) states that the review is significantly less in scope than an audit and thus expresses no opinion, and (5) states whether material adjustments are necessary for the information to conform to GAAP.
Internal Control	CPA engaged specifically to render an opinion on internal accounting control.	Scope paragraph, explanatory paragraph emphasizing management responsibilities for the internal control system, explanatory paragraph emphasizing the limitations of internal control, and an opinion paragraph.
	CPA reports on internal accounting control as a byproduct of a financial statement audit.	Scope of review limited to audit needs, explanatory paragraph same as above, disclaimer on the system as a whole with a negative assurance, and a paragraph restricting use of the report.
	CPA evaluates internal accounting control based on pre-established criteria.	Scope specified by government agency, explanatory paragraphs same as above, paragraph which comments on the adequacy of the system of internal control, and a restrictive use paragraph.

Key Terms

accounting and review service
change in accounting principle
comfort letter
compilation
emphasis of a matter
except for
explanatory paragraph
fairness
inadequate disclosure
inconsistent application of GAAP
interim financial information
limited review

long-form report
major uncertainty
negative assurance
predecessor and successor auditor
principal auditor
reporting standards
scope limitation
   (client or circumstances)
special reports
subject to
underwriter

Questions and Problems

Questions

12-1 What type of opinion should an auditor issue if the first condition necessary for an unqualified opinion cannot be met? The second? The third? The fourth?

12-2 Distinguish the circumstances that require an "except for" qualification from those that require a "subject to" qualification.

12-3 When the scope of an audit is restricted, describe the differences between the audit report issued when the effect on financial statements is (a) concentrated, (b) widespread.

12-4 What are the sources of GAAP? How does the accounting principle of fairness relate to the body of other accounting principles?

12-5 To what period of time does the consistency reference in the auditor's report apply? Explain the possible types of reports that can result from an inconsistency.

12-6 Define a special report as it applies to auditor communications. Give three specific examples of situations where special reports are appropriate.

12-7 Describe the purpose and use of comfort letters, and indicate the types of information that are usually included.

12-8 How might a CPA become associated with unaudited financial statements? Contrast unaudited and compiled financial statements, and distinguish the respective entities for whom they are prepared.

12-9 Define *limited review*, and discuss how it differs from an audit of financial statements.

12-10 List three circumstances in which an auditor may be engaged to examine a system of internal accounting control, and describe how the CPA's report might differ in each circumstance.

Multiple Choice Questions From Professional Examinations

12-11 In determining the type of opinion to express, an auditor assesses the nature of the reporting qualifications and the materiality of their effects. Materiality will be the primary factor considered in the choice between

 a. An "except for" opinion and an adverse opinion.
 b. An "except for" opinion and a "subject to" opinion.
 c. An adverse opinion and a disclaimer of opinion.
 d. A "subject to" opinion and a piecemeal opinion.

12-12 In which of the following circumstances would an auditor be required to issue a qualified report with a separate explanatory paragraph?

 a. The auditor satisfactorily performed alternative accounts receivable procedures because scope limitations prevented performance of normal procedures.
 b. The financial statements reflect the effects of a change in accounting principles from one period to the next.
 c. A particular note to the financial statements discloses a company accounting method that deviates from generally accepted accounting principles.
 d. The financial statements of a significant subsidiary were examined by another auditor, and reference to the other auditor's report is to be made in the principal auditor's report.

12-13 For which of the following accounting changes would an auditor's report normally not contain a consistency qualification?

 a. A change in principle which does not result in non-comparable statements because the previous year's statements are not presented.
 b. A change to a principle required by a new FASB pronouncement.
 c. A change in principle properly reported by restating the financial statements of prior years.
 d. A change in an accounting estimate.

12-14 Because an expression of opinion as to certain identified items in financial statements tends to overshadow or contradict an overall disclaimer of opinion or adverse opinion, it is inappropriate for an auditor to issue

a. A piecemeal opinion.

b. An unqualified opinion.

c. An "except for" opinion.

d. A "subject to" opinion.

The following applies to questions 15 and 16. Once an auditor has determined that an exception is material enough to warrant qualification of his report, he must then determine if the exception is sufficiently material to negate an overall opinion.

12-15 If an auditor is applying this decision process to an exception based on a departure from generally accepted accounting principles, he is deciding

a. Whether to issue an adverse opinion rather than a "subject to" opinion.

b. Whether to issue a disclaimer of opinion rather than a "subject to" opinion.

c. Whether to issue an adverse opinion rather than an "except for" opinion.

d. Nothing, because this decision process is not applicable to this type of exception.

12-16 If an auditor is applying this decision process to a consistency exception, he is deciding

a. Whether to issue a disclaimer of opinion rather than an "except for" opinion.

b. Whether to issue a disclaimer of opinion rather than a "subject to" opinion.

c. Whether to issue an adverse opinion rather than an "except for" opinion.

d. Nothing, because this decision process is not applicable to this type of exception.

12-17 When a client declines to disclose essential data in the financial statements or to incorporate such data in the footnotes, the independent auditor should

a. Provide the necessary supplemental information in the auditor's report and appropriately qualify the opinion.

b. Explain to the client that an adverse opinion must be issued.

c. Issue an unqualified report and inform the stockholders of the improper disclosure in a separate report.

d. Issue an opinion "subject to" the clients inclusion of the essential information in future financial statements.

12-18 The term "special reports" may include all of the following except reports on financial statements

a. Of an organization that has limited the scope of the auditor's examination.

b. Prepared for limited purposes, such as a report that relates to only certain aspects of financial statements.

c. Of a not-for-profit organization, which follows accounting practices differing in some respects from those followed by business enterprises organized for profit.

d. Prepared in accordance with a cash basis of accounting.

12-19 Whenever special reports, filed on a printed form designed by authorities, call upon the independent auditor to make an assertion that the auditor believes is not justified, the auditor should

a. Submit a short-form report with explanations.

b. Reword the form or attach a separate report.

c. Submit the form with questionable items clearly omitted.

d. Withdraw from the engagement.

12-20 Basic financial statements with supplementary information would not include

a. Exceptions or reservations to the standard (short-form) report.

b. Details of items in basic financial statements.

c. Statistical data.

d. Explanatory comments.

12-21 A CPA is associated with client-prepared financial statements but is not independent. With respect to the CPA's lack of independence, which of the following actions by the CPA might confuse a reader of such financial statements?

a. Stamping the word *unaudited* on each page of the financial statements.

b. Disclaiming an opinion and stating that independence is lacking.

c. Issuing a qualified auditor's report explaining the reason for the auditor's lack of independence.

d. Preparing an auditor's report that included essential data that was not disclosed in the financial statements.

12-22 A CPA would be considered "not associated" with unaudited financial statements when

a. The CPA performed a limited review of a publicly traded company's unaudited financial statements, which are presented in a quarterly report to the stockholders.

b. The CPA assisted in the preparation of the unaudited financial statements.

    c. The CPA completed an audit and rendered a report on the financial statements, which, without the CPA's consent, were part of a prospectus that included unaudited financial statements.

    d. The CPA received all input data from the client, reviewed it, and returned it to the client for processing by an independent computer service company.

12-23 When making a limited review of interim financial information, the auditor's work consists primarily of

    a. Studying and evaluating limited amounts of documentation supporting the interim financial information.

    b. Scanning and reviewing client-prepared, internal financial statements.

    c. Making inquiries and performing analytical procedures concerning significant accounting matters.

    d. Confirming and verifying significant account balances at the interim date.

12-24 A report based on a limited review of interim financial statements would include all of the following elements except

    a. A statement that an examination was performed in accordance with generally accepted auditing standards.

    b. A description of the procedures performed or a reference to procedures described in an engagement letter.

    c. A statement that a limited review would not necessarily disclose all matters of significance.

    d. An identification of the interim financial information reviewed.

12-25 If an auditor's report on internal control is distributed to the general public, it must contain specific language describing several matters. Which of the following must be included in the specific language?

    a. The distinction between internal administrative controls and internal accounting controls.

    b. The objective of internal accounting controls.

    c. The various tests and procedures utilized by the auditor during the review of internal controls.

    d. The reason(s) why management requested a report on internal controls.

Problems

12-26 The auditor's report must contain an expression of opinion or a statement to the effect that an opinion cannot be expressed. Four types of opinions or statements that meet these requirements are generally known as

    a. An unqualified opinion.

    b. A qualified opinion.

c. A disclaimer of opinion.

d. An adverse opinion.

For each of the situations presented below discuss the type of opinion or statement that should be rendered from the above list.

1. Subsequent to the close of Holly Corporation's fiscal year, a major debtor was declared a bankrupt due to a rapid series of events. The receivable is significantly material in relation to the financial statements, and recovery is doubtful. The debtor had confirmed the full amount due to Holly Corporation at the balance sheet date. Since the account was good at the balance sheet date, Holly Corporation refuses to disclose any information in relation to this subsequent event. The CPA believes that all accounts were stated fairly at the balance sheet date.

2. Kapok Corporation is a substantial user of electronic data processing equipment and has used an outside service bureau to process data in years past. During the current year, Kapok adopted the policy of leasing all hardware and expects to continue this arrangement in the future. This change in policy is adequately disclosed in footnotes to Kapok's financial statements, but uncertainty prohibits either Kapok or the CPA from assessing the impact of this change upon future operations.

3. The financial statements of Reid Corporation for the year ended December 31, 1981, were accompanied by an unqualified opinion. Reid wishes unaudited financial statements prepared for the three months ended March 31, 1982.

4. The president of Lowe, Inc., would not allow the auditor to confirm the receivable balance from one of its major customers. The amount of the receivable is material in relation to the financial statements of Lowe, Inc. The auditor was unable to satisfy himself as to the receivable balance by alternative procedures.

5. Sempier Corporation issued financial statements that purported to present financial position and results of operations but omitted the related statement of changes in financial position. (The omission is not sanctioned by APB Opinion No. 19.)

AICPA (Adapted)

12-27 Charles Burke, CPA, has completed fieldwork for his examination of the Willingham Corporation for the year ended December 31, 1982, and is now in the process of determining whether to modify his report. Presented below are two, independent, unrelated situations that have arisen.

Situation I

In September 1982, a lawsuit was filed against Willingham to have the court order it to install pollution-control equipment in one of its older plants. Willingham's legal counsel has informed Burke that it is not possible to forecast the outcome of this litigation. However, Willingham's management has informed Burke that the cost of the pollution-control equipment is not economically feasible and that the plant will be closed if the case is lost. In addition, Burke has been told by management that the plant and its production equipment would have only minimal resale values and that the production lost could not be recovered at other plants.

Situation II

During 1982, Willingham purchased a franchise amounting to 20 percent of its assets for the exclusive right to produce and sell a newly patented product in the northeastern United States. There has been no production in marketable quantities of the product anywhere to date. Neither the franchisor nor any franchisee has conducted any market research on the product.

Required:

In deciding the type-of-report modification, if any, Burke should take into account such considerations as:

— Relative magnitude
— Uncertainty of outcome
— Likelihood of error
— Expertise of the auditor
— Pervasive impact on the financial statements
— Inherent importance of the item

Discuss Burke's type-of-report decision for each situation in terms of the above and other appropriate considerations. Assume each situation is adequately disclosed in the notes to the financial statements. Each situation should be considered independently. In discussing each situation, ignore the other. It is not necessary for you to decide the type of report that should be issued.

AICPA

12-28 Lando Corporation is a domestic company with two wholly owned domestic subsidiaries. Michaels, CPA, has been engaged to examine the financial statements of the parent company and one of the subsidiaries and to act as the principal auditor. Thomas, CPA, has examined the financial statements of the other subsidiary, whose operations are material in relation to the consolidated financial statements.

The work performed by Michaels is sufficient for him to serve as the principal auditor and to report as such on the financial statements. Michaels has not yet decided whether to make reference to the examination made by Thomas.

Required:

a. There are certain required audit procedures that Michaels should perform with respect to the examination made by Thomas, whether or not Michaels decides to make reference to Thomas in Michaels' auditor's report. What are these audit procedures?

b. What are the reporting requirements with which Michaels must comply if he decides to name Thomas and make reference to Thomas' examination?

AICPA

12-29 You are the auditor of X Co. Ltd., a company which at December 31, 1978, had working capital of $200,000, total assets of $2,500,000 and total liabilities of $2,200,000. During the three years ended December 31, 1978, the company has sustained accumulated operating losses totalling $700,000. Management has been informed that current debenture holders will not renew a debenture of $500,000 maturing September 30, 1979 and presently included in long-term liabilities. Although preliminary discussions have already been held with various commercial lenders, it presently appears uncertain as to whether or not X Co. Ltd. will be able to refinance its debt. As X Co. Ltd. has had liquidity problems from time to time, it may be unable to obtain adequate financing both to refinance its debenture and to provide additional working capital. In that case, it may not be able to continue its operations.

Required:

a. outline with reasons possible deviations (if any) from a standard audit report which may be necessary. State your assumptions.

b. outline the minimum note disclosure which you consider adequate in the circumstances. What additional disclosure would be desirable?

CICA (Adapted)

12-30 Roscoe, CPA, has completed the examination of the financial statements of Excelsior Corporation as of and for the year ended December 31, 1981. Roscoe also examined and reported on the Excelsior financial statements for the year prior. Roscoe drafted the following report for 1981.

March 15, 1982

We have examined the balance sheet and statements of income and retained earnings of Excelsior Corporation as of December 31, 1981. Our examination was made in accordance with generally accepted accounting standards and, accordingly, included such tests of the accounting records as we considered necessary in the circumstances.

In our opinion, the above-mentioned financial statements are accurately prepared and fairly presented in accordance with generally accepted accounting principles in effect at December 31, 1981.

Roscoe, CPA
(Signed)

Other Information:

— Excelsior is presenting comparative financial statements.
— Excelsior does not wish to present a statement of changes in financial position for either year.
— During 1981, Excelsior changed its method of accounting for long-term construction contracts and properly reflected the effect of the change in the current year's financial statements and restated the prior-year's statements. Roscoe is satisfied with Excelsior's justification for making the change. The change is discussed in footnote number 12.
— Roscoe was unable to perform normal accounts receivable confirmation procedures, but alternate procedures were used to satisfy Roscoe as to the validity of the receivables.
— Excelsior Corporation is the defendant in a litigation, the outcome of which is highly uncertain. If the case is settled in favor of the plaintiff, Excelsior will be required to pay a substantial amount of cash, which might require the sale of certain fixed assets. The litigation and the possible effects have been properly disclosed in footnote number 11.
— Excelsior issued debentures on January 31, 1980, in the amount of $10,000,000. The funds obtained from the issuance were used to finance the expansion of plant facilities. The debenture agreement restricts the payment of future cash dividends to earnings after December 31, 1986. Excelsior declined to disclose this essential data in the footnotes to the financial statements.

Required:

Consider all facts given, and rewrite the auditor's report in an acceptable and complete format, incorporating any necessary departures from the standard report.

Do not discuss the draft of Roscoe's report, but identify and explain any items included in "Other Information" that need not be part of the auditor's report.

AICPA

12-31 Various types of "accounting changes" can affect the second reporting standard of the generally accepted auditing standards. This standard reads, "The report shall state whether such principles have been consistently observed in the current period in relation to the preceding period."

Assume that the following list describes changes that have a material effect on a client's financial statements for the current year.

1. A change from the completed-contract method to the percentage-of-completion method of accounting for long-term, construction-type contracts.
2. A change in the estimated useful life of previously recorded fixed assets based on newly acquired information.
3. Correction of a mathematical error in inventory pricing made in a prior period.
4. A change from prime costing to full absorption costing for inventory valuation.
5. A change from presentation of statements of individual companies to presentation of consolidated statements.
6. A change from deferring and amortizing preproduction costs to recording such costs as an expense when incurred because future benefits of the costs have become doubtful. The new accounting method was adopted in recognition of the change in estimated future benefits.
7. A change to including the employer share of FICA taxes as "Retirement Benefits" on the income statement instead of including it with "Other Taxes."
8. A change from the FIFO method of inventory pricing to the LIFO method of inventory pricing.

Required:

Identify the type of change that is described in each item above. State whether any modification is required in the auditor's report as it relates to the second standard of reporting, and state whether the prior year's financial statements should be restated when presented in comparative form with the current year's statement. Organize your answer sheet as shown below.

For example, a change from the LIFO method of inventory pricing to the FIFO method of inventory pricing would appear as shown.

Item No.	Type of Change	Should Auditor's Report be Modified?	Should Prior Year's Statements be Restated?
Example	An accounting change from one generally accepted accounting principle to another generally accepted accounting principle.	Yes	Yes

AICPA

12-32 Empire Investments Limited is a large Canadian public company that holds investments in 4 subsidiaries. The company and its subsidiaries all pay combined federal taxes at the rate of 50%.

Three subsidiaries, A Sub Limited, B Sub Limited, and C Sub Limited, are all 100% owned and are audited by CA, who is the auditor of Empire Investments Limited. D Sub Limited is 60% owned and until recently was audited by another firm of accountants.

A Sub Limited is in the publishing business. It publishes several trade magazines, a monthly family magazine and some books, usually of a technical nature.

B Sub Limited prints and sells greeting cards. It also prints calendars, business cards, etc., on a contract basis. In addition, it prints the books published by A Sub Limited.

C Sub Limited has large forestry holdings in Canada. Most of the forests are used for pulp and paper production. The company manufactures many grades of paper and virtually all of the production is sold to A Sub Limited and B Sub Limited. C Sub Limited also produces lumber, much of which is sold to builders near its manufacturing plants, but about 20% of which is sold to D Sub Limited.

D Sub Limited is a real estate development company. It operates around 2 large cities and owns substantial tracts of land near those cities.

For the year ended June 30, 1982, consolidated financial statements had been presented to the shareholders accompanied by CA's audit report, which was unqualified, but contained the standard comments about reliance on other auditors. Reported consolidated net income was $500,000. Shortly after the year-end, CA was appointed auditor of D Sub Limited.

During the course of the audit of D Sub Limited for the year ended June 30, 1983, CA found that one of the company's major building contracts was construction of an office building for A Sub Limited. As at June 30, 1983, $8,000,000 had been incurred by D Sub Limited in construction of the building, estimated to cost $10,000,000 on completion.

CA had known that A Sub Limited was planning a major expansion. Largely, the expansion consisted of converting A Sub Limited's monthly family magazine into a weekly news magazine. To make A Sub Limited more able to compete, the company had to considerably expand its facilities. CA had been under the impression that no progress billings had yet been received with respect to the new building.

On checking into the matter further, CA found that part of the reason for this was that the building qualified for a government grant and that grants of the type involved are paid by the government on behalf of the owner of the building to the builder. On the strength of certain commitments made by A Sub Limited as to the ultimate cost of the building and the number of jobs that would be created, D Sub Limited had, in May,

1982, received $3,000,000 towards the grant, which was equal to 50% of the $6,000,000 cost incurred on the building to that date and 25% of the total contract price of $12,000,000. The building was 60% complete at that date.

Also, prior to June, 1982, D Sub Limited required more money to finance the construction, but instead of sending a program billing to A Sub Limited, it was decided to obtain lumber from C Sub Limited for the houses under construction, but not to pay for it. The price charged to D Sub Limited was $4,500,000 which is the cost of the lumber to C Sub Limited plus a mark-up of 12.5%. The lumber shipments were recorded in the accounts of D Sub Limited by a charge to inventory and the credit was treated as a revenue item.

C Sub Limited then obtained an advance payment of $4,500,000 from A Sub Limited for the large quantities of paper that would be required when the news magazine went into production. This payment was recorded by A Sub Limited as prepaid expense.

D Sub Limited's accounting practice, unlike many development companies, was to present a balance sheet that segregated working capital items from non-working capital items. D Sub Limited used the percentage of completion basis of accounting.

No consolidation adjustments had been made in respect of the building for the year ended June 30, 1982 or the $4,500,000 shipment of lumber.

Required:

What changes do you suggest in the standard auditor's report on these consolidated financial statements, and what additional responsibilities does CA have in this situation?

CICA (Adapted)

12-33 The limitations of the CPA's professional responsibilities when he or she is associated with unaudited financial statements are often misunderstood. Listed below are seven situations or contentions the CPA may encounter in his association with and preparation of unaudited financial statements.

1. A CPA was engaged by telephone to perform write-up work including the preparation of financial statements. His client believes that the CPA has been engaged to audit the financial statements and examine the records accordingly.

2. A group of businessmen, who own a farm managed by an independent agent, engage a CPA to prepare quarterly, unaudited financial statements for them. The CPA prepares the financial statements from information given to him by the independent agent. Subsequently, the businessmen find that the statements are inaccurate because their independent agent was embezzling funds. The businessmen refuse to pay the CPA's fee and blame him for allowing the situation to go

undetected, contending that he should not have relied on representations from the independent agent.

3. In comparing the trial balance with the general ledger, the CPA finds an account labeled "audit fees" in which the client has accumulated the CPA's quarterly billings for accounting services, including the preparation of quarterly, unaudited financial statements.

4. Unaudited financial statements are accompanied by the following letter of transmittal from the CPA:

We are enclosing your company's balance sheet as of June 30, 19X1, and the related statements of income and retained earnings and changes in financial position for the six months then ended which we have reviewed.

5. To determine appropriate account classification, the CPA reviewed several of the client's invoices. He noted in his working paper that some invoices were missing but did nothing further because he felt they did not affect the unaudited financial statements he was preparing. When the client subsequently discovered that invoices were missing, he contended that the CPA should not have ignored the missing invoices when preparing the financial statements and that the CPA had a responsibility to at least inform him that they were missing.

6. The CPA has prepared a draft of unaudited financial statements from the client's records. While reviewing this draft with his client, the CPA learns that the land and building were recorded at appraisal value.

7. The CPA is engaged to review, without audit, the financial statements prepared by the client's controller. During this review, the CPA learns of several items which, by generally accepted accounting principles, would require adjustment of the statements and footnote disclosure. The controller agrees to make the recommended adjustments to the statements but says that he is not going to add the footnotes because the statements are unaudited.

Required:

Briefly discuss the extent of the CPA's responsibilities in each case and, if appropriate, the actions he should take to minimize any misunderstandings.

AICPA (Adapted)

12-34 Loman, CPA, who has examined the financial statements of the Broadwall Corporation, a publicly held company, for the year ended December 31, 1981, was asked to perform a limited review of the financial statements of Broadwall Corporation for the period ending March 31, 1982. The engagement letter stated that a limited review does not provide a basis for the expression of an opinion.

Required:

a. Explain why Loman's limited review will not provide a basis for the expression of an opinion.

b. What are the review procedures that Loman would perform, and what is the purpose of each procedure? Structure your response as follows:

Procedure	Purpose of Procedure

AICPA

12-35 The financial statements of Hiber Company have never been audited by an independent CPA. Hiber's management has asked you, as an independent CPA, to conduct a special study of Hiber's system of internal control for the purpose of expressing an opinion on the system. This engagement will not include an examination of Hiber's financial statements. At the completion of this special study, you have been asked to prepare a report in accordance with the professional standards for reports on internal control.

Required:

a. Discuss the major components and assertions of a report on internal control.

b. Explain and contrast the study of internal control that might be made as a part of an examination of financial statements with a special study of internal control as to
   1. the objectives of the review or study
   2. the scope of the review or study
   3. the nature and content of reports that result
   Organize your answer as follows:

Part of Examination of Financial Statements	Special Study of Internal Control
1. Objective	1. Objective
2. Scope	2. Scope
3. Report	3. Report

c. Discuss the propriety of the external use of a CPA's report on internal control by a client in conjunction with audited or unaudited financial statements.

AICPA (Adapted)

Statistics and
Computer Auditing

13

Statistical sampling

Statistics is a mathematical method for making decisions in the face of uncertainty. By examining only a small sample, statistical techniques can provide a supportable conclusion about the population as a whole. Perhaps the most well-known use of statistics is in public opinion polling: after contacting approximately 3,000 people, the pollster will prepare an estimate of the opinion of the total voting population, numbering some 80,000,000 people.

An important part of auditing involves a similar process of forming a judgement from a sample. For example, after reviewing a sample of accounts receivable, the auditor forms an opinion on the entire accounts receivable balance. Because the auditor needs to support judgements from a sample, statistics is ideally suited to auditing and can be of great assistance to the auditor in his work.

13.1 INTRODUCTION TO STATISTICAL SAMPLING

Articles applying statistical methods began to appear in the 1940s, and the material started to be incorporated into auditing textbooks in the 1950s. In 1962, the AICPA endorsed the use of statistical sampling in auditing, and by the early 1970s most large firms had begun the application of statistics to their audits on a regular basis. The use of statistical sampling is certain to increase in the future.

There are two basic reasons why statistical sampling has taken such a long time to become a standard audit tool. The first is that the traditional statistical techniques developed for other applications were not directly applicable to auditing. The audit samples needed to form a statistical conclusion were so large as to make statistical sampling prohibitively expensive. For this reason, the widespread use of statistics has had to wait upon the development of new statistical techniques specifically designed for auditing. Such techniques are now available.

The second reason for the delay in the use of statistical sampling is that many auditors are unfamiliar with statistics. Because of this unfamiliarity, the first applications of statistical sampling were often invalid. Auditors used the wrong formula or substituted sample items inappropriately—destroying any statistical validity the tests may have had. Professional auditors in the 1980s, however, must become familiar with statistical sampling.

Population

Suppose an auditor is examining the inventory of an audit client. The total book value of inventory is the sum of the book value of the individual inventory items. Statistical language refers to the individual inventory item as a *sampling unit* and the total of all inventory items as the *population*. In general, the population is something about which the auditor wants to make a conclusion. The sampling unit is a component of the population.

Audit Test

In the example of inventory, the auditor wants to decide whether or not the book value is properly stated. To accomplish this task, the auditor

1. Determines how many sample inventory items to examine;
2. Selects that number of items from the population;
3. Audits those items to determine their true (as opposed to book) value;
4. Estimates the true population value from these true audited values;
5. Compares the estimated true population value to the book value; and
6. Concludes that the book value is properly stated or that it is not properly stated.

Typical Population

Exhibit 13–1 gives an example of the book values of the 100 inventory items of Scott Interspacial Industries. These 100 items are numbered from 0 to 99 to make sample selection easier. Though this numbering scheme is a little confusing at first, it will make later work easier.

Histogram

The list in Exhibit 13–1 makes it difficult to get a mental image of the population of inventory book values. For this reason, statisticians often prepare a *histogram* to give a picture of the population. Exhibit 13–2 provides a histogram for the population in Exhibit 13–1.

EXHIBIT 13-1   Book Values

#	Amount	#	Amount	#	Amount	#	Amount
0	41	25	97	50	14	75	134
1	30	26	254	51	39	76	43
2	152	27	100	52	261	77	106
3	16	28	76	53	35	78	193
4	236	29	110	54	41	79	226
5	57	30	87	55	91	80	11
6	42	31	117	56	21	81	201
7	21	32	322	57	20	82	45
8	136	33	200	58	91	83	323
9	41	34	16	59	125	84	32
10	108	35	139	60	104	85	247
11	17	36	29	61	9	86	181
12	207	37	234	62	50	87	25
13	2	38	411	63	339	88	75
14	22	39	329	64	12	89	299
15	88	40	2	65	426	90	583
16	117	41	52	66	219	91	624
17	18	42	202	67	45	92	707
18	102	43	95	68	23	93	880
19	22	44	40	69	49	94	921
20	79	45	66	70	215	95	1601
21	111	46	14	71	129	96	1337
22	175	47	54	72	101	97	1227
23	14	48	156	73	50	98	1066
24	10	49	41	74	243	99	1004

Note: Value of items 0 to 89 $10,000
        Value of items 90 to 99 $10,000
        Total value $20,000

Exhibit 13–2 shows that there are 51 inventory items which have a book value between 1 and 100. There are 22 items with book values between 101 and 200, 11 between 201 and 300, and so on. Exhibit 13–2 is especially important because the shape of the histogram is typical of audit populations. Certainly 100 inventory items is unrealistically low. A retail store can easily have 2,000 items, and a regional wholesaler can have 50,000 inventory items. However, the shape of the histogram will be roughly the same: there are a number of low-value items, with progressively fewer and fewer items as the inventory book values increase.

Statistical Theory

The auditor can then apply the theory of statistics to his task of forming a judgement on the population after only examining a sample of items from the population. The appendix to this chapter presents this statistical theory in an auditing frame-

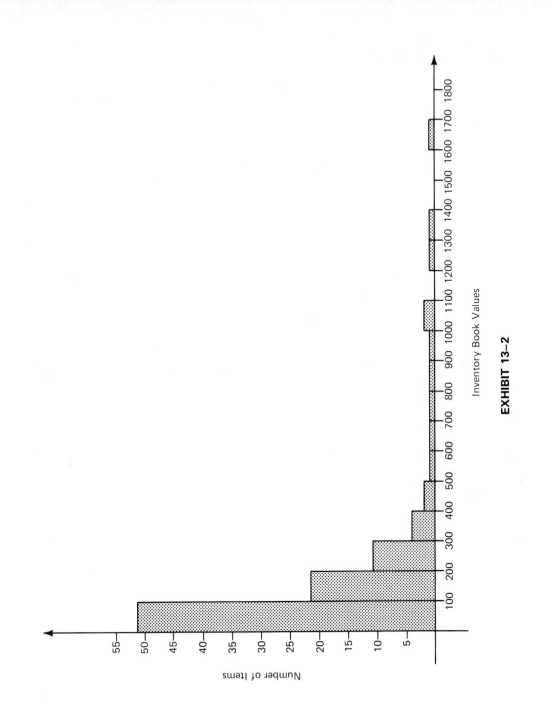

EXHIBIT 13–2

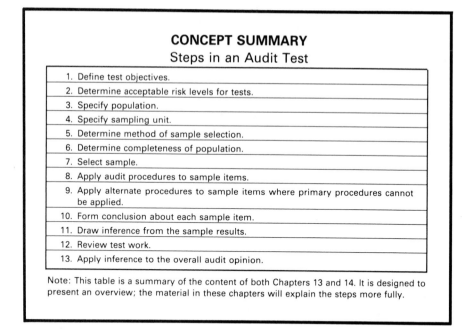

CONCEPT SUMMARY
Steps in an Audit Test

1. Define test objectives.
2. Determine acceptable risk levels for tests.
3. Specify population.
4. Specify sampling unit.
5. Determine method of sample selection.
6. Determine completeness of population.
7. Select sample.
8. Apply audit procedures to sample items.
9. Apply alternate procedures to sample items where primary procedures cannot be applied.
10. Form conclusion about each sample item.
11. Draw inference from the sample results.
12. Review test work.
13. Apply inference to the overall audit opinion.

Note: This table is a summary of the content of both Chapters 13 and 14. It is designed to present an overview; the material in these chapters will explain the steps more fully.

work. This material is covered in introductory statistics courses, but slightly different terminology and examples may be used.

13.2 HYPOTHESIS TESTING

The auditor examines the financial statements of the client to determine if they are fairly stated. In the case of inventory, the auditor estimates a true, audited value of inventory and compares this to the book value of inventory. If the audited value and the book value are sufficiently close, the auditor accepts the book value.

Materiality

The auditor cannot expect that the book value will be precisely correct. The auditor is only concerned if the book value is *materially* incorrect. For example, if the inventory book value is $300,000, but the audited or true value is $299,999, the auditor will accept the book value as materially correct. However, if the book value is $300,000 and the audited value is $100,000, the auditor would say that the inventory value is materially misstated.

The decision of whether or not to accept the book value depends upon what the auditor considers material. For an inventory figure of $300,000, an amount of $1 will always be immaterial, and an amount of $200,000 will always be material. But $200,000 might not be material if the book value were $30,000,000. The exact amount considered material in any particular situation will be set using the auditor's judgement.

Basic Concepts

The auditor's decision is referred to in statistics as *hypothesis testing*. The objective of hypothesis testing is to discriminate between two mutually exclusive possibilities—the *null hypothesis* and the *alternative hypothesis*. The symbol H_0 represents the null hypothesis, and H_1 represents the alternative hypothesis.

In the audit context, the decision is to discriminate between the null hypothesis, that the book value is materially correct, and the alternative hypothesis, that the book value is materially incorrect. The decision to accept or not accept the book value can be written using the following symbols:

BV = book value of inventory

AV = audited value of inventory, estimated from a sample of inventory items

M = materiality in this particular audit test

In symbols, the two possibilities are

$$H_0 : |AV - BV| < M$$
$$H_1 : |AV - BV| \geqslant M$$

Example

In the earlier example, where the book value of inventory is $300,000, materiality might be $20,000. Assuming these figures, the statistical hypotheses are

$$H_0 : |\text{AV} - \$300,000| < \$20,000 \text{ or } \$280,000 < \text{AV} < \$320,000$$
$$H_1 : |\text{AV} - \$300,000| \geqslant \$20,000$$

The auditor can then perform this test. The auditor takes a sample from the population; estimates the true value by the audited value, AV; and determines whether the audited value is within $20,000 of the book value. If AV is within $20,000 of BV, the auditor accepts the book value of $300,000 as materially correct. If AV is more than $320,000 or less than $280,000, the auditor rejects the book value as materially incorrect.

Alpha and Beta Errors

Unfortunately, the hypothesis test in the last paragraph does not control the possibility of being wrong. There are four possible results from this test:

1. The auditor can accept the book value when it is, in fact, correct. This is the proper decision.

2. The auditor can reject the book value as materially in error when, in fact, the book value is correct. This is a mistake, and by making this mistake, the auditor commits the alpha error. (This error is also called a Type I error in some textbooks.)

3. The auditor can accept the book value when it is, in fact, in error by a material amount. This is a mistake, and by making this mistake, the auditor commits the beta error. (This error is also called a Type II error in some textbooks.)

4. The auditor can reject the book value as materially in error when the book value is, in fact, in error by a material amount. This is the proper decision.

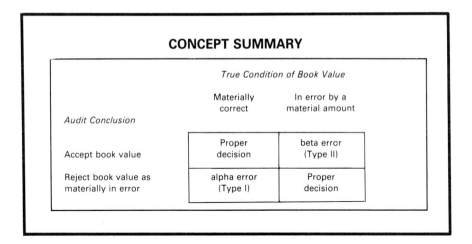

Controlling the Alpha Risk

As in all his decisions, the auditor faces risk. In this particular case, the auditor faces what is called the alpha risk, i.e., the risk that the auditor will reject the book value when it is correct. In other words, the alpha risk is the probability of committing the alpha error.

To have any confidence at all in his decisions, the auditor must have some control of the alpha risk. The consequence of alpha risk is that the auditor will unnecessarily be forced to perform follow-up work when the book value is rejected erroneously. As a result of theoretical considerations, as well as experience in applying statistical techniques, most auditors will accept an alpha risk of 5%. In other words, auditors find it acceptable to reject a correct book value as much as 5% of the time.

Sample Size

The larger the sample of items the auditor selects, the more accurate the result, but the greater the cost. Using the statistical theory in the chapter appendix, the auditor can calculate the proper sample size for his or her desired risk level.

Exhibit 13–3 portrays the auditor's accept/reject decision. For an alpha risk of α, there is an $\alpha/2$ probability in each of the tails of the graph. Thus, if there is a 5% alpha risk, there is a 2.5% probability in each of the tails.

The formula for the sample size, n, is then

$$n = \left(\frac{Z_{\alpha/2} \times N \times \sigma}{M} \right)^2$$

where the meaning and interpretation of the various symbols is as follows:

1. $Z_{\alpha/2}$ is the Z value from Exhibit 13–7, which leaves an area of $\alpha/2$ in the tail. For example, when $\alpha = 0.05$, $Z_{\alpha/2}$ is 1.96, and when $\alpha = 0.01$, $Z_{\alpha/2}$ is 2.58. Thus, *as the alpha risk decreases, $Z_{\alpha/2}$ increases, and the sample size increases.*
2. N is the number of items in the population, such as the number of inventory items. *As the number of items in the population increases, the sample size increases.*
3. σ is the standard deviation of the population, estimated by calculating the standard deviation of the book values. The standard deviation measures the variability of a population, i.e., how "spread out" the values are. The more spread out the values of a population are, the greater is its standard deviation. Thus, *as the variability of a population increases, the standard deviation increases, and the sample size increases.*
4. M is the amount considered material by the auditor for this audit test. *As materiality decreases, the sample size increases.*

Example

Using the above example where the book value was $300,000 and materiality was $20,000, assume that there are 900 inventory items, and the desired alpha risk is 5%. Exhibit 13–7 gives the appropriate Z value as 1.96.

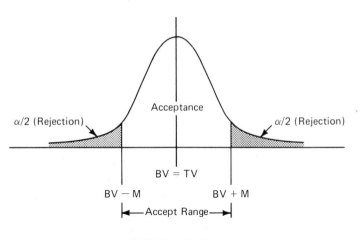

EXHIBIT 13–3

For this example, assume the standard deviation is $140. This gives a sample size of

$$n = \left(\frac{1.96 \times 900 \times \$140}{\$20,000} \right)^2 = 152$$

Assume that the auditor takes a sample of 152 inventory items and determines the sum of those sample items to be $49,146. The sample mean is then

$$\bar{x} = \frac{\Sigma x}{n} = \frac{\$49,146}{152} = \$323.33$$

The audit value is then

$$AV = N\bar{x} = 900 \times \$323.33 = \$291,000.$$

The difference between the book value and the audit value is

$$BV - AV = \$300,000 - \$291,000 = \$9,000$$

The auditor can then accept the book value of $300,000 as materially correct; the difference of $9,000 is less than materiality of $20,000.

Effect of Alpha Risk

The sample size with an alpha risk of 5% is 152 inventory items. This implies that the auditor must examine 152 inventory items in depth. Suppose the auditor can accept an alpha risk of 10%. The sample size is then

$$n = \left(\frac{1.64 \times 900 \times \$140}{\$20,000} \right)^2 = 107$$

But suppose the auditor can only accept an alpha risk of 1%. The sample size is then

$$n = \left(\frac{2.58 \times 900 \times \$140}{\$20,000} \right)^2 = 264$$

Thus, an alpha risk of 1% implies a large sample size, while an alpha risk of 10% implies a smaller sample size. In general, as the alpha risk goes up, the sample size gets smaller. When the sample size gets smaller, the cost of the audit goes down because the auditor must look at fewer items. Conversely, as the alpha risk goes down, the sample size gets larger, and thus the cost of the audit goes up. The tradeoff between cost and risk is quite clear here: (1) reducing risk implies increasing cost, and (2) reducing cost implies accepting a higher risk.

Controlling the Beta Risk

In addition to the alpha risk discussed above, the auditor also has the beta risk—the risk of accepting the book value when it is in error by a material amount. The beta risk is very important because an auditor wants a great deal of assurance that he does not give an unqualified opinion on (i.e., accept) a materially incorrect financial statement.

There is a separate beta risk for every possible misstatement. However, the most important beta risk occurs when the book value is in error by exactly a material amount.

Beta = 0.5

Suppose the decision rule is the same as it was in the previous section: accept book value if the audit value is within ±M of book value, and reject it otherwise. Further suppose that the book value is in error by a material amount. Exhibit 13–4 provides a diagram of this situation.

The audit value will be drawn from the population centered around the true value. The accept range is ±M around the book value, which, in this case, is assumed to be materially overstated (i.e., TV = BV − M).

The shaded area is the area under the curve for the accept range. But this is half the area under the curve. In other words, if the book value is misstated by exactly a material amount, the probability of incorrectly accepting the book value is 0.5 or 50%! This is one chance in two. In statistical language, the situation is described by saying the beta risk is 0.5 or 50%.

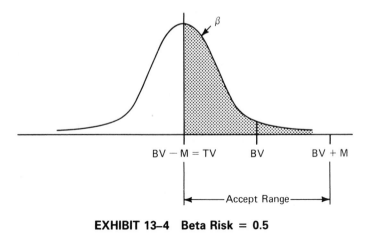

BV − M = TV   BV   BV + M

Accept Range

EXHIBIT 13–4   Beta Risk = 0.5

This is quite a high risk for the auditor to take, but it can be acceptable if there is extremely good internal control. If this is the case, the internal control system will almost surely detect a material error. Assume that the internal control system will detect 90% of the material errors. This implies only 10% of the material errors will not be detected. The probability that: (1) the internal control system will not detect the error, *and* (2) the statistical test will not detect the error is then

$$(100\% - 90\%) \times 50\% = 10\% \times 50\% = 5\%$$

Most auditors will feel that a 5% risk in this case is acceptable.

Beta = 0.05

The auditor can thus accept a beta risk of 0.5 if there is a strong system of internal control. But often the company has poor internal control, and the auditor cannot assume that it will detect and correct any material errors. In this case, the statistical test itself must limit the beta risk to 5% or 0.05. In order to reduce the beta risk to 0.05, the auditor must narrow the accept range. The new accept range is the book value $\pm P$, where P is called the *precision*. (See Exhibit 13–5.)

Thus, in order to control the beta risk, the auditor must reduce the accept range. In addition, the auditor will also have to increase the sample size. Assuming that the auditor desires to control both the alpha and the beta risks, P must satisfy the following equation:

$$P = \frac{M}{1 + \dfrac{Z_\beta}{Z_{\alpha/2}}}$$

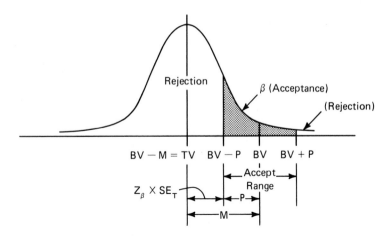

EXHIBIT 13–5 Beta Risk = 0.05

This equation indicates that the precision P will always be less than or equal to M; how much less will depend upon the auditor's decision on alpha and beta risks. If $\beta = 0.5$, then $Z_\beta = 0$, and the precision is exactly the same as materiality. Solving for the sample size gives the following formula

$$n = \left(\frac{Z_{\alpha/2} \times N \times \sigma}{P} \right)^2$$

This is the same equation presented earlier, except that P is in the denominator rather than M. The beta risk does not appear explicitly in this equation, but the beta risk does affect P.

Example

Using the same example as in the last section (with $\beta = 0.5$) will give the same sample size. Assume, then, that β must be 0.05. The precision with $\alpha = 0.05$ will be

$$P = \frac{M}{1 + Z_\beta/Z_{\alpha/2}} = \frac{\$20,000}{1 + 1.64/1.96} = \$10,889$$

The sample size will then be

$$n = \left(\frac{Z_{\alpha/2} \times N \times \sigma}{P} \right)^2 = \left(\frac{1.96 \times 900 \times \$140}{\$10,889} \right)^2 = 514$$

Assume the auditor takes a sample of 514 inventory items, and the sum of all the sample items is $165,051. The sample mean is then

$$\bar{x} = \frac{\Sigma x}{n} = \frac{\$165,051}{514} = \$321.11$$

The audit value will then be

$$AV = N\bar{x} = 900 \times \$321.11 = \$289,000.$$

The difference between the book value and the audit value is

$$BV - AV = \$300,000 - \$289,000 = \$11,000$$

Since the difference of $11,000 is greater than precision of $10,889, the auditor must reject the book value of $300,000 as materially incorrect.

Effect of Beta Risk

With the alpha risk constant at 5%, the sample size has gone from 152 when β = 0.5 to 514 when β = 0.05. This is an extremely large increase, and it illustrates why auditors are so concerned about the evaluation of internal control. If internal control is excellent, then beta can be 0.5, and the sample size for the related substantive test can be small. But if internal control is poor, then beta must be 0.05, and the sample size will be extremely large.

13.3 ADVANCED HYPOTHESIS TESTING

Section 13.2 presented the basic concepts of hypothesis testing. In practice, auditors use hypothesis testing in essentially this way. However, auditors cannot directly use the method as outlined in the previous concept summary for several practical and theoretical reasons.

Finite Correction Factor

The sample size equation assumes that the population has an infinite number of items. While this is true in other applications, audit populations are always finite, even if they are very large.

To calculate the required sample size, it is convenient to do it in two steps. The first step is to calculate n using the same formula as above. The second step is to calculate n', the required sample size, from n using the following formula:

$$n' = \frac{n}{1 + n/N}$$

CONCEPT SUMMARY
Summary of Hypothesis Testing

1. Determine basic facts about the population:

   BV = book value
   N   = number of items in the population
   σ = standard deviation for the population, estimated by calculating the standard deviation of the book values

2. Decide upon the acceptable audit risks:

   M = materiality
   α = alpha risk (usually 5% or 10%)
   β = beta risk (will be between 5% and 50%)

3. Calculate precision and sample size:

   $Z_{\alpha/2}$ = normal table value for $\alpha/2$ (equal to 1.96 for $\alpha = 0.05$, and equal to 1.64 for $\alpha = 0.10$)

   Z_{β} = normal table value for β (equal to 1.64 for $\beta = 0.05$, and equal to 0 for $\beta = 0.5$)

   P = precision = $\dfrac{M}{1 + \dfrac{Z_{\beta}}{Z_{\alpha/2}}}$ (P equal to M for $\beta = 0.5$)

   n = sample size = $\left(\dfrac{Z_{\alpha/2} \times N \times \sigma}{P} \right)^2$

4. Take sample and calculate audit value:

   Σx = sum of audit value of sample items

   $\bar{x}$ = sample mean = $\dfrac{\Sigma x}{n}$

   AV = audit value = $N\bar{x}$

5. Make decision based upon the results of the sample:

   If $|BV{-}AV| < P$, then accept the book value as materially correct.
   If $|BV{-}AV| \geq P$, then reject the book value as materially incorrect.

Where N is the number of items in the population. When N is very large, this equation does not greatly affect the sample size.

Assume that the sample size calculated using the formula for n was 152 items out of a population of 900 items. The required sample size would be

$$n' = \frac{n}{1 + n/N} = \frac{152}{1 + 152/900} = 130$$

This represents a 13% decrease in the sample size and hence a 13% decrease in the cost of this audit procedure.

100% Condition

It is possible that the population has items which individually exceed materiality. For example, assume there are 900 items with a book value of $300,000 and materiality is $20,000. (This is the same example used earlier.) It is quite possible that one or more individual inventory items are each worth more than $20,000.

For this reason, the auditor should always establish a 100% condition, where the auditor will include *all* items above a certain value in the sample. In essence, then, the auditor defines two new populations from the original single population. One of the new populations consists of all items with values less than the 100% condition. The other new population consists of all items greater than or equal to the 100% condition.

Setting the 100% condition involves a tradeoff: (1) the lower the 100% condition is, the lower the standard deviation of the items below the 100% condition and hence the smaller the sample size; but (2) the lower the 100% condition is, the more items will exceed the 100% condition. The goal must be to minimize the total number of items the auditor must examine, whether from the sample population or from the completely examined population.

Setting a 100% condition only makes good audit sense; the auditor would naturally look at all large items. In any case, the auditor would make the 100% condition less than or equal to materiality. The auditor must examine every item which is in itself material because if that item alone were in error, it could cause the statements to be materially misstated.

Stratification

Most realistic audit populations have much higher standard deviations than those given in the earlier examples in this chapter. Even with the sample size correction factor and the 100% condition, the computed sample size will usually be so large as to be unrealistically expensive.

The auditor can reduce the standard deviation σ, and hence the sample size n, by redefining the population into various strata, where each stratum is a smaller breakdown of the population. All items in a particular stratum will be close together, so the standard deviation in that stratum will be relatively small, leading to a reduced sample size.

Example: Nadir Supply, Inc.

Suppose an auditor is examining the accounts receivable of Nadir Supply, Inc., which has 1,073 customer balances and a book value of $700,000. Materiality is $70,000. The alpha risk is set at 5%. The beta risk is set at 50%, so precision equals materiality.

The population standard deviation is $713. The auditor calculates the uncorrected sample size:

$$n = \left(\frac{Z_{\alpha/2} \times N \times \sigma}{P} \right)^2 = \left(\frac{1.96 \times 1,073 \times \$713}{\$70,000} \right)^2 = 458$$

After applying the finite correction factor, the sample size is

$$n' = \frac{n}{1 + n/N} = \frac{458}{1 + 458/1073} = 321$$

The sample is, therefore, essentially 30% of the population, a very large percentage.

However, there is another possibility. The auditor might decide to stratify the population to try to decrease the sample size. A realistic possibility would be to set up three strata: (1) all items below $1,000, (2) items between $1,000 and $3,000, and (3) all items over $3,000. The auditor plans to examine 100% of the third strata.

In this case, the results are summarized below:

	Number of Items	Standard Deviation	Sample Size
Items under $1,000	839	$317	95
Items between $1,000 and $3,000	208	615	38
Items over $3,000	26	—	26
Totals	1,073		159

Thus, by stratification, the sample size goes from 321 to 159. This represents more than a 50% reduction in the sample size. Unfortunately, this text cannot present the calculation of the sample sizes for the individual strata because the computations become extremely complex.

Larger practical applications become even more complex. As a result of both theoretical calculations and practical experience, most large CPA firms use 8 to 10 strata in their audit work. One large CPA firm has an example of a population of 12,222 items where unstratified sampling led to a sample size of 5,710 and stratified sampling led to a sample size of 130.

Cluster Sampling

Consider the following situation. An auditor is examining the financial statements of a large drugstore chain with four large warehouses and 52 widely scattered stores. As part of the examination, the auditor must be satisfied that the statements fairly present inventory.

However, if the entire inventory of all warehouses and all stores is treated as one population, the auditor gets a very unpleasant result. Even with a 100% condition and appropriate stratification, the sample will consist of relatively few items at practically every warehouse and store. Thus, the auditor and his staff must go, at great expense, to many different places and count inventory at all of them.

There is another approach—*cluster sampling*. With this approach, the auditor selects relatively few warehouses and stores to examine, but he samples extensively within those selected warehouses and stores. With the results of the sample, the auditor develops a conclusion on the entire inventory.

The cluster sampling approach is more efficient than the standard approach in this situation, even if the auditor must examine the same number of items, because the auditor can visit fewer stores.

Unfortunately, the mathematics of cluster sampling is too complex to present here. In practice, the mathematics is so complex that it is not often used to draw a *statistical* conclusion on the inventory value. What happens is that the auditor: (1) makes a *judgemental* selection of the warehouses and stores to examine, (2) makes a *statistical* test and conclusion about those individual warehouses and stores, and (3) makes a *judgemental* (nonstatistical) conclusion about the inventory value for the entire company. This approximates a totally statistical conclusion.

The cluster sampling approach does not apply just to the drugstore situation. It applies any time the audit population falls into natural subgroupings. Examples would include:

1. Inventory in many containers where it is expensive to open individual containers.

2. Documents in many boxes where it is difficult to find and open individual boxes.

> **CONCEPT SUMMARY**
> **Modifications Necessary for Hypothesis Testing**
> **To Be Useful In Practice**
>
> | Situation Found in Practice | Solution |
> |---|---|
> | Sampling without replacement from a finite population | Use finite correction factor

$n' = \dfrac{n}{1 + n/N}$ |
> | Some items in the population are individually material | Set 100% condition |
> | Standard deviation of the population is very large | Stratify the population |
> | Population naturally divides into a number of separate groups | Use cluster sampling |
> | Calculations become difficult for a typical sized population | Useful only when there are computerized records |

Necessity of the Computer

The calculations involved in a typical statistical application become quite involved. Section 13.2 presented some of the basic calculations, and the present section has introduced still more. The result is that practical use of hypothesis testing generally requires use of a computer. Further, the accounting records must be on the computer because the book values are used in so many calculations. Chapter 16 discusses the generalized audit software necessary to perform these calculations.

13.4 ESTIMATION METHODS

Suppose that the auditor has rejected the book value of an account as materially incorrect. The question then is: What book value would the auditor accept as correct?

This presents a theoretical difficulty to the auditor. In theory, the client prepares the financial statements, and the auditor accepts or rejects them. Thus, if the auditor rejects the book value, the client should in theory correct the records and develop a new book value which the auditor can examine.

In practice, however, the procedure is somewhat different. Often, the client cannot produce an accurate figure. (If they could have, they would have done so in the first place.) But even if the client could produce a corrected book value, the deadline for issuing the financial statements is often so short that correcting the records is impossible under the circumstances.

Dollar-Value Estimation

Fortunately, the same information the auditor used in the hypothesis test to reject the book value can also produce an estimated value which the auditor can accept. This process is called *dollar-value estimation*.

The auditor will only use dollar-value estimation when he knows the book value is not correct. Since there no longer is a need to test the hypothesis that the book value is correct, the alpha and beta risks are no longer relevant.

The objective of dollar-value estimation is to project, from the sample, the total value of the population within a specified interval. Since an interval estimate is a range of possible values, it illustrates the uncertainty the auditor faces. As a result, the interval estimate is accompanied by a statement giving the auditor's confidence that the true value actually lies within that interval.

To estimate the total value of the population (the point estimate), the auditor uses *mean per unit* estimation:

$$AV = \text{Estimated Audit Value} = N\bar{x}$$

The auditor faces the situation illustrated in Exhibit 13–6. To be able to accept the interval, the auditor must usually be either 90% or 95% confident that the true value lies within the interval. This degree of confidence required by the auditor is called the *confidence level* (CL). Sometimes the degree of confidence is referred to as the *reliability* of the estimate.

The precision, P, is the dollar amount the interval will stretch on either side of AV. The auditor usually sets precision equal to materiality. With precision set, the auditor can compute the confidence interval, which ranges from the audit value minus P to the audit value plus P.

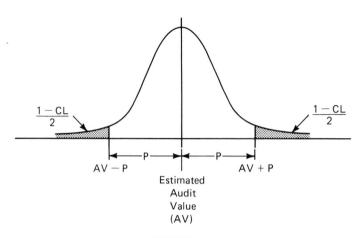

EXHIBIT 13–6

Standard Deviation

In sections 13.2 and 13.3, the auditor could assume that the book values had roughly the same distribution as the sample audit values. Because of this assumption, the auditor could use the standard deviation of book values to approximate the standard deviation of audit values. Therefore, the auditor used the standard deviation of book values to calculate the required sample size.

In dollar value estimation, however, there is either no book value at all or a materially incorrect book value, which the auditor has already rejected. Thus, using the standard deviation of book values is out of the question. There are then two possibilities:

1. If there is no book value, the auditor must (a) take a preliminary sample of 50 to 100 items, (b) calculate the standard deviation of this sample, and (c) use this as an estimate of the standard deviation of the population of audit values. (Calculating a sample standard deviation is illustrated in the Chapter Appendix.)
2. If the auditor rejected the book value by a hypothesis test, the auditor can use the same sample items to calculate an estimate of the standard deviation of the audit values.

Sample Size

Using the estimate, s, of the population standard deviation gives the following formula for the sample size:

$$n = \left(\frac{Z_{(1-CL)/2} \times N \times s}{P} \right)^2$$

This n is the total number of sample items the auditor should examine. If a preliminary sample was taken, those items can be counted toward the necessary total of n items. Similarly, if a sample was drawn for hypothesis testing, it is quite possible that a sufficient number of items has already been examined.

Target vs. Achieved Standard Error

The auditor desires a given amount of confidence that the true value lies within the confidence interval. The sample size is based upon the accuracy that the auditor demands. But the auditor must base the calculation on an estimate of standard deviation of the population, and this estimate should be checked to determine whether it is sufficiently accurate.

The most convenient way to check this accuracy is by: (1) computing a target standard error prior to selecting the sample, and then (2) computing an achieved standard error after the sample has been examined. The formula for the target standard error is

$$SE_T = \frac{P}{Z_{(1-CL)/2} \times N}$$

After examining the sample items, the auditor must calculate the achieved standard error:

$$SE_A = \sqrt{\frac{\Sigma x^2 - (\Sigma x)^2/n}{n(n-1)}}$$

If the achieved standard error is less than or equal to the target standard error, the sample size is satisfactory. If not, the auditor must examine additional items until the achieved standard error meets or is less than the target.

Confidence Interval

The auditor can then calculate the estimated audit value

$$AV = N\bar{x}$$

and the achieved precision (the exact target precision is seldom achieved)

$$P = Z_{(1-CL)/2} \times N \times SE_A$$

The confidence interval is then from $AV - P$ to $AV + P$. The confidence interval is the range within which the true value falls the confidence level per cent of the time.

The client can then enter the estimated audit value into the books and records, perhaps with a valuation allowance, and the auditor can accept this value as materially correct. The client *cannot* use just any value within the confidence interval.

Example

Suppose an auditor wants to estimate an inventory value within $3,000 at 95% confidence. There are 1,000 different inventory items. After looking at 50 items, the auditor estimates the population standard deviation as $20. The target standard error is then

$$SE_T = \frac{P}{Z_{(1-CL)/2} \times N} = \frac{\$3,000}{1.96 \times 1000} = \$1.53$$

and the sample size is

$$n = \left(\frac{Z_{(1-CL)/2} \times N \times s}{P} \right)^2 = \left(\frac{1.96 \times 1000 \times 20}{\$3000} \right)^2 = 171$$

The auditor then selects an additional 121 inventory items (171 required sample items less the 50 already reviewed in the preliminary sample.) The sample of 171 items yields the following results:

Σx = sum of sample audit values $\qquad = \qquad \$34,371$

Σx^2 = sum of squares of sample audit values $= 6,974,854$

$$SE_A = \sqrt{\frac{\Sigma x^2 - (\Sigma x)^2/n}{n(n-1)}} \qquad = \qquad \$1.51$$

Since $SE_A < SE_T$, the auditor can calculate the confidence interval:

$$\bar{x} = \frac{\Sigma x}{n} = \frac{\$34,371}{171} = \$201$$

$AV = N\bar{x} = \$201,000$

P = achieved precision = $Z_{(1-CL)/2} \times N \times SE_A = \$2,960$

The auditor can then be 95% confident that the true value is between $198,040 ($201,000 − $2,960) and $203,960 ($201,000 + $2,960). The auditor wanted precision of $3,000. The achieved precision was slightly more accurate ($2960 instead of $3000) because the achieved standard error turned out to be less than the target standard error.

Ratio and Difference Estimation

There are two more estimating techniques that can be useful under the proper conditions: (1) ratio estimation, and (2) difference estimation. Both are based on audit values and book values for a sample of items. Either the relationship (i.e., ratio) of audit to book values or the average difference between audit and book values is used to estimate the population value. If the conditions are right, a smaller sample (or tighter precision) is possible with the same level of confidence, as compared to that under mean per unit estimation. Another advantage is relative ease of application if manual records are kept. The required conditions are:

CONCEPT SUMMARY
Summary of Dollar-Value Estimation

1. Determine basic facts about the population:
   N = number of items in the population
   s = estimate of the standard deviation of the population as determined from a preliminary sample of 50 to 100 items

   $$= \sqrt{\frac{\Sigma x^2 - (\Sigma x)^2/n}{n(n-1)}}$$

2. Decide upon the acceptable audit risk:
   P = precision
   CL = confidence level (usually .95)

3. Calculate target standard error and sample size:

   $\dfrac{Z_{(1\text{-}CL)}}{2}$ = normal table value for (1-CL)/2 (equal to 1.96 for a CL of .95)

   SE_T = target standard error

   $$= \frac{P}{\dfrac{Z_{(1\text{-}CL)}}{2} \times N}$$

   n = sample size

   $$= \left(\frac{\dfrac{Z_{(1\text{-}CL)}}{2} \times N \times s}{P}\right)2$$

4. Take sample and calculate achieved standard error:
   Σx = sum of audit values of sample items
   Σx^2 = sum of squares of audit values of sample items
   SE_A = achieved standard error

   $$= \sqrt{\frac{\Sigma x^2 - (\Sigma x)^2/n}{n(n-1)}}$$

   If $SE_A > SE_T$, then take additional sample items.

5. When $SE_A < SE_T$, then calculate confidence interval: (if $SE_A = SE_T$, achieved precision and desired precision are the same.)

   $\bar{x}$ = sample mean = $\dfrac{\Sigma x}{n}$

   AV = estimated audit value = $N\bar{x}$
   P = achieved precision

   $$= \frac{Z_{(1\text{-}CL)}}{2} \times N \times SE_A$$

   Confidence interval = from AV — P to AV + P

1. A substantial proportion of the population's members are in error.* In fact, as the incidence of error increases, these techniques become more efficient.

2. A minimum number of errors must show up in the sample (opinions hold from 30 to 50). This minimum number is necessary to get an accurate value for the standard error.

3. There is a book value for every item in the population and their sum equals the total account value.

Desired precision and confidence levels for alpha and beta risks are set by the auditor, as before. The calculation of sample size (and achieved precision) is basically the same as discussed earlier for mean per unit estimation. However, now the estimated standard deviation is of the ratios, or differences, of the population—not of the population itself. Although standard deviation and standard error calculations for the difference estimation technique are basically the same as before, those for ratio estimation are different, being too complex to discuss here. Which of the two techniques to use is dictated by the errors themselves.

Ratio Estimation

Ratio estimation is best to use when a constant percentage of size of error to book value is encountered in a population. For example, inventory item A has a book value of $10, but when audited is found to cost only $8 ($2/$10 = 20%). Item X has a book value of $300 but costs $240 ($60/$300 = 20%). If the difference between the audit value and book value is proportional to the book value—or approximately so—ratio estimation will give the most efficient results.

The audit value of the population is estimated by applying this formula:

$$AV = \frac{\text{mean of sample audit values}}{\text{mean of sample book values}} \times \text{total book value}$$

$$= \frac{\bar{y}}{\bar{x}} \times BV$$

Assume, for example, an inventory of 900 items with a book value of $300,000. A sample of 100 items is drawn having a book value of $42,000. Upon being audited the sample items are found to actually cost $36,000. The total population value can now be estimated:

---

*Some firms carry their inventory records on a FIFO basis and convert to LIFO for tax purposes using these estimation techniques. The term "error" is intended to include any such difference between book value and a second figure.

$$\bar{x} = \$42{,}000/100 = \$420$$

$$\bar{y} = \$36{,}000/100 = \$360$$

$$AV = \frac{\$360}{\$420} \times \$300{,}000 = \$257{,}130$$

Difference Estimation

If the errors in a population tend to be constant in amount, difference estimation is better to use. When approximately the same sized errors occur for items with both large and small book values this technique gives the most efficient results. The audit value of the population is estimated by applying this formula:

$$AV = BV + N\,(\bar{y} - \bar{x})$$

where $\bar{y}$ is the mean of the audited values, $\bar{x}$ is the mean of the corresponding book values, N is the number of items in the population, and BV is their total book value. Using the figures from the previous example, the estimated population value is:

$$AV = \$300{,}000 + 900\,(\$360 - \$420)$$

$$= \$246{,}000$$

CONCEPT SUMMARY
Summary of Statistical Sampling Techniques

Sampling Technique	Principal Objective	Source of Data	Decision Inputs	Strong Points	Weak Points
Hypothesis Testing	To determine whether the book value is materially in error	Usually computerized records	1. Materiality 2. Alpha risk 3. Beta risk	Very effective due to stratification	Difficult to use with manual records
Dollar-Value Estimation	To estimate the value of the population from the sample results	Usually computerized records	1. Precision 2. Confidence Level	Very effective due to stratification	Difficult to use with manual records
Ratio or Difference Estimation	To estimate the value of the population from the sample results	Either computerized or manual records	1. Precision 2. Confidence Level	1. Easy to select sample items 2. Can be used with manual records	Specific error pattern required; auditor needs at least 30–50 errors for effective evaluation

APPENDIX

STATISTICAL THEORY IN THE AUDITING FRAMEWORK

To apply statistics to auditing requires a certain amount of statistical theory. Fortunately, introductory statistics courses cover this basic material in great detail. This section should be a review, with perhaps some different terminology.

Description of Population

Consider the population of inventory items in Exhibit 13–1. The histogram in Exhibit 13–2 gives a picture of the population. To deal with this population mathematically, there must be some numerical descriptions of the population. There are many such numerical descriptions, but the two most useful descriptions are the mean and the standard deviation.

Mean

A mean is an average. Thus, the *population mean* is the average of the population. The mean of a population is usually represented by the Greek letter μ. Calculating the mean involves: (1) adding all members of the population, and (2) dividing by the number of items in the population. In symbols,

$$\mu = \frac{\Sigma x}{N} = \frac{x_0 + x_1 + \ldots + x_{98} + x_{99}}{100} = \frac{41 + 30 + \ldots + 1066 + 1044}{100}$$

$$= \frac{20{,}000}{100} = 200$$

N is the number of items in the population.

Standard Deviation

A measure of dispersion of the population is also useful. This measure gives an indication of how spread out the values of the population are. The population standard deviation is the square root of the average of the squared deviation from the population mean:

$$\sigma = \sqrt{\frac{\Sigma (x - \mu)^2}{N}}$$

For computation purposes, the following equivalent formula is easier to use:

$$\sigma = \sqrt{\frac{\Sigma x^2 - (\Sigma x)^2/N}{N}}$$

For the population in Exhibit 13–1, the population standard deviation is:

$$\sigma = \sqrt{\frac{12,999,942 - (20,000)^2/100}{100}} = 300$$

Sample Statistics

Suppose only a sample of the population were known. The desire is then to estimate the population mean and the population standard deviation from the sample. This involves first the calculation of the

$$\text{sample mean} = \bar{x} = \frac{\Sigma x}{n}$$

where n is the number of items in the sample and the x are the values of the sample items. This sample mean $\bar{x}$ is the best guess of the true population mean μ.

The second step is then the calculation of the sample standard deviation

$$s = \sqrt{\frac{\Sigma x^2 - (\Sigma x)^2/n}{n - 1}}$$

The formula for the sample standard deviation uses n − 1 in the denominator rather than n. Thus, the formula for the sample statistic is not computationally equivalent to that for the population parameter. However, explanation of why n − 1 is used lies outside the scope of this text.

Population of Audited Values

The auditor would like to know the true value of every inventory item. However, this would require auditing every inventory item, which would be extremely expensive. Therefore, the purpose of statistical sampling is to draw a sample from the population and then to estimate the total value of inventory.

This estimation process consists of two steps:

1. Draw the sample and calculate the sample mean, $\bar{x}$
2. Estimate the total audited value of the (inventory) population:

$$\text{Audited Value} = AV = N\bar{x}$$

This process is called *mean per unit estimation*. The sample mean, $\bar{x}$ is an estimate of the average value of the population. Multiplying by the total number of items in the population, N, gives the estimated total value of the population.

Examples of Samples

Consider the following samples taken from the population given in Exhibits 13–1 and 13–2. Assume that the audited value for each item turns out to be the same as the book value. This is not true in general, but it will simplify the work for now.

Samples of n = 2

1. If the sample were the first two items of the population, the sample mean and estimated value would be

$$\bar{x} = \frac{x_0 + x_1}{2} = \frac{41 + 30}{2} = 35.50; AV = N\bar{x} = 100 \times 35.50 = 3,550$$

2. If the sample were evenly spaced throughout the population, the sample mean and estimated value would be

$$\bar{x} = \frac{x_{49} + x_{99}}{2} = \frac{41 + 1004}{2} = 522.50; AV = 52,250$$

3. If the sample were the last two items of the population, the sample mean and estimated value would be

$$\bar{x} = \frac{x_{98} + x_{99}}{2} = \frac{1066 + 1004}{2} = 1,035; AV = 103,500$$

Samples of n = 25

1. If the sample were the first 25 items of the population, the sample mean and estimated value would be

$$\bar{x} = \frac{x_0 + \ldots + x_{24}}{25} = \frac{41 + \ldots + 10}{25} = 74.56; AV = N\bar{x} = 7,456$$

2. If the sample were evenly spaced throughout the population, the sample mean and estimated value would be

$$\bar{x} = \frac{x_3 + x_7 + \ldots + x_{95} + x_{99}}{25} = 228.68; AV = N\bar{x} = 22,868$$

3. If the sample were the last 25 items of the population, the sample mean and estimated value would be

$$\bar{x} = \frac{x_{75} + \ldots + x_{99}}{25} = 485.64; \; AV = N\bar{x} = 48,564$$

Distribution of Sample Means

The examples above should make it clear that the resulting estimate of true value depends critically upon the particular sample items selected. For example, when the sample size is 2, there are 4,950 possible samples, each with a potentially different sample mean and, hence, a different estimate of the total population value. The same is true for samples of 25 items, except that, in this case, there are over 10^{15} possible samples!

There is a distribution of sample means for any given sample size. Exhibit 13–7 provides the relevant distributions. The top distribution is the population distribution; the samples are drawn from this population. This is a continuous, exponential distribution, but it closely approximates the distribution of Exhibit 13–2.

The bottom three distributions are distributions of the sample means. The first is the distribution of sample means when the sample size is 2 (i.e., n = 2). The next is for n = 4, and the third is for n = 25.

Mean

The mean of a distribution of sample means is always the mean of the original population. This is true regardless of the size of the sample. In Exhibit 13–7 an arrow along the x axis points out the mean of each of the four distributions. The mean is the same in all cases and is always equal to μ, the mean of the original population.

Standard Deviation

The standard deviation, however, is different in each case. By looking at the distribution, it is apparent that the standard deviation for n = 25 is smaller than the standard deviation for n = 2. All three distributions have the same mean, but as n increases, the distribution becomes grouped closer and closer around the mean.

The standard deviation of the distribution of sample means is very important, so important that it has its own term. The standard deviation of the distribution of sample means is called the *standard error of the mean*. The standard error of

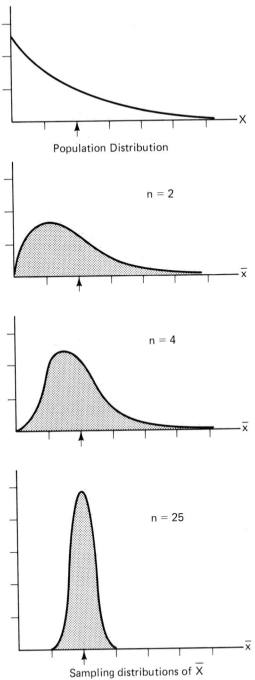

Population Distribution

n = 2

n = 4

n = 25

Sampling distributions of $\overline{X}$

EXHIBIT 13–7
Sampling Distribution of $\overline{x}$ When Population Is Not Normal

the mean is related to the standard deviation of the original population by the following formula

$$SE = \frac{\sigma}{\sqrt{n}}$$

Thus, assume the standard deviation of the original population is 300. The standard error of the mean is 212 for a sample size of 2, 150 for a sample size of 4, and 60 for a sample size of 25. This decrease in standard deviation as n increases is clear from the example samples. For n = 2, the sample means were quite spread apart: 35.50, 522.20, and 1,035. For n = 25, the sample means were much closer together: 74.56, 228.68, and 485.64.

Normal Distribution for n ≥ 25

As mentioned above, the standard error decreases as the sample size increases. But another event occurs as the sample size increases: the distribution of sample means becomes closer and closer to a normal distribution. This fact is stated by the central limit theorem.

If n ≥ 25, then the distribution of sample means is essentially a normal distribution with mean μ (the same mean as the original population) and standard deviation $\sigma/\sqrt{n}$.

Properties of the Normal Distribution

Because of the above result, statistical sampling relies on the normal distribution and its properties. And because of the importance of the normal distribution, statisticians have studied these properties for years. Exhibit 13–8 summarizes most of the properties needed in this chapter.

Tables of Z Values

The graph at the top of Exhibit 13–8 is that of a normal distribution with mean 0 and standard deviation 1. The table gives the area under the curve, as shaded, between the mean 0 and the distance Z along the horizontal x axis. This area represents the probability that a sampling unit drawn from this distribution will be between 0 and Z. For example, the table states that the probability of a sampling unit being between 0 and 1.00 is .3413. This is seen by reading down the left-hand column to 1.0 and over one column for 1.0 + .00. Similarly, the probability of a sampling unit being between 0 and 1.09 would be .3621. These results can be written in symbols as

$$Pr\ (0 \leqslant X \leqslant 1.00) = .3413$$
$$Pr\ (0 \leqslant X \leqslant 1.09) = .3612$$

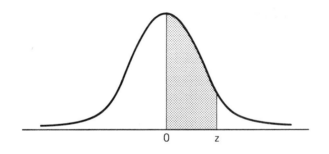

The following table provides the area between the mean and normal deviate value z.

Normal Deviate z	.00	.01	.02	.03	.04	.05	.06	.07	.08	.09
0.0	.0000	.0040	.0080	.0120	.0160	.0199	.0239	.0279	.0319	.0359
0.1	.0398	.0438	.0478	.0517	.0557	.0596	.0636	.0675	.0714	.0753
0.2	.0793	.0832	.0871	.0910	.0948	.0987	.1026	.1064	.1103	.1141
0.3	.1179	.1217	.1255	.1293	.1331	.1368	.1406	.1443	.1480	.1517
0.4	.1554	.1591	.1628	.1664	.1700	.1736	.1772	.1808	.1844	.1879
0.5	.1915	.1950	.1985	.2019	.2054	.2088	.2123	.2157	.2109	.2224
0.6	.2257	.2291	.2324	.2357	.2389	.2422	.2454	.2486	.2518	.2549
0.7	.2580	.2612	.2642	.2673	.2704	.2734	.2764	.2794	.2823	.2852
0.8	.2881	.2910	.2939	.2967	.2995	.3023	.3051	.3078	.3106	.3133
0.9	.3159	.3186	.3212	.3238	.3264	.3289	.3315	.3340	.3365	.3389
1.0	.3413	.3438	.3461	.3485	.3508	.3531	.3554	.3577	.3599	.3621
1.1	.3643	.3665	.3686	.3708	.3729	.3749	.3770	.3790	.3810	.3830
1.2	.3849	.3869	.3888	.3907	.3925	.3944	.3962	.3980	.3997	.4015
1.3	.4032	.4049	.4066	.4082	.4099	.4115	.4131	.4147	.4162	.4177
1.4	.4192	.4207	.4222	.4236	.4251	.4265	.4279	.4292	.4306	.4319
1.5	.4332	.4345	.4357	.4370	.4382	.4394	.4406	.4418	.4429	.4441
1.6	.4452	.4463	.4474	.4484	.4495	.4505	.4515	.4525	.4535	.4545
1.7	.4554	.4564	.4573	.4582	.4591	.4599	.4608	.4616	.4625	.4633
1.8	.4641	.4649	.4656	.4664	.4671	.4678	.4686	.4693	.4699	.4706
1.9	.4713	.4719	.4726	.4732	.4738	.4744	.4750	.4756	.4761	.4767
2.0	.4772	.4778	.4783	.4788	.4793	.4798	.4803	.4808	.4812	.4817
2.1	.4821	.4826	.4830	.4834	.4838	.4842	.4846	.4850	.4854	.4857
2.2	.4861	.4864	.4868	.4871	.4875	.4878	.4881	.4884	.4887	.4890
2.3	.4893	.4896	.4898	.4901	.4904	.4906	.4909	.4911	.4913	.4916
2.4	.4918	.4920	.4922	.4925	.4927	.4929	.4931	.4932	.4934	.4936
2.5	.4938	.4940	.4941	.4943	.4945	.4946	.4948	.4949	.4951	.4952
2.6	.4953	.4955	.4956	.4957	.4959	.4960	.4961	.4962	.4963	.4964
2.7	.4965	.4966	.4967	.4968	.4969	.4970	.4971	.4972	.4973	.4974
2.8	.4974	.4975	.4976	.4977	.4977	.4978	.4979	.4979	.4980	.4981
2.9	.4981	.4982	.4982	.4983	.4984	.4984	.4985	.4985	.4986	.4986
3.0	.49865	.4987	.4987	.4988	.4988	.4989	.4989	.4989	.4990	.4990
4.0	.49997									

EXHIBIT 13–8 Areas Under the Standard Normal Curve

Symmetry

The normal distribution is symmetrical. In other words, half the values are to the right of the mean and half are to the left. This implies that the probability is .5 that a sampling unit is greater than or equal to the mean, and the probability is .5 that a sampling unit is less than or equal to the mean. In symbols,

$$\text{Pr }(0 \leqslant X) = .5$$

But this then implies that the probability of X being greater than 1.00 is equal to .5 less the probability that X is between 0 and 1.00. In symbols,

$$\begin{aligned} \text{Pr }(1 \leqslant X) &= P(0 \leqslant X) - P(0 \leqslant X \leqslant 1) \\ &= .5 - .3413 \\ &= .1587 \end{aligned}$$

The symmetry of the normal distribution has another result: the area under the curve a given distance to the left of the mean is the same as the area under the curve that same distance to the right. In symbols,

$$\text{Pr }(-Z \leqslant X \leqslant 0) = \text{Pr }(0 \leqslant X \leqslant Z)$$

In particular, the area under the curve from -1 to 1 is twice the area under the curve from 0 to 1. Thus,

$$\begin{aligned} \text{Pr }(-1.00 \leqslant X \leqslant 1.00) &= 2 \times \text{Pr }(0 \leqslant X \leqslant 1.00) \\ &= 2 \times .3413 \\ &= .6826 \end{aligned}$$

In a similar fashion,

$$\begin{aligned} \text{Pr }(-1.96 \leqslant X \leqslant 1.96) &= 2 \times \text{Pr }(0 \leqslant X \leqslant 1.96) \\ &= 2 \times .4750 \\ &= .95 \end{aligned}$$

Conversion to Standard Normal Distribution

Exhibit 13–8 gives the area under the curve for the normal distribution of mean 0 and standard deviation 1. This is called the *standard normal distribution* and, hence, Exhibit 13–8 only provides values for the very unusual distribution with mean 0 and standard deviation 1.

Fortunately, it is possible to convert every normal distribution to a standard normal distribution. For the (normal) distribution of sample means, this conversion takes the following form:

$$Z = \frac{x - \mu}{SE}$$

(μ is the mean of the distribution of sample means. SE is the standard error of the mean and is the standard deviation of this distribution of sample means.)

It is important to understand that: (1) the original population *is not* normally distributed, even though it has mean μ and standard deviation σ; but (2) the distribution of sample means *is* normally distributed with mean μ and standard deviation SE $= \sigma/\sqrt{n}$.

What is the probability a sample mean will be between 150 and 175 when μ is 150 and the standard error is 30? To calculate this probability involves first calculating

$$Z = \frac{x - \mu}{SE} = \frac{175 - 150}{30} = .83$$

and then reading the probability of .2967 from the table in Exhibit 13–7. In symbols, then,

$$\Pr (150 \leqslant x \leqslant 175) = \Pr (0 \leqslant \frac{x - 150}{30} \leqslant .83)$$
$$= \Pr (0 \leqslant Z \leqslant .83)$$
$$= .2967$$

Distribution of Audit Values

The earlier discussion mentioned the important result that the distribution of sample means, $\bar{x}$, is normally distributed. Therefore, the distribution of audit values, $N\bar{x}$, is also normally distributed. If the standard deviation of the distribution of sample means is SE, then the standard deviation of the distribution of audit values is N × SE.

Finite Audit Populations

The formula in this appendix for the standard error assumed an infinite audit population. Since all audit populations are finite, the formula for the standard error is the following:

$$SE = \frac{\sigma}{\sqrt{n}} \cdot \sqrt{1 - \frac{n}{N}}$$

As n gets closer and closer to N, the standard error goes to 0. This is natural; if the auditor looked at every item in the population, there would be no standard error of the mean.

This modification of the formula for the standard error leads to the finite correction factor discussed in section 13.3.

Key Terms

accept range
achieved precision
achieved standard error
alpha error
beta error
cluster sampling
confidence level (CL)
difference estimation
distribution of sample means
dollar value estimation
finite correction factor
histogram
hypothesis testing
100% condition

normal distribution
population
population mean
population standard deviation
precision
ratio estimation
sample mean
sample standard deviation
sampling unit
standard error of the mean
standard normal distribution
stratification
target standard error

Questions and Problems

Questions

13-1 Discuss the basic reasons why auditors have begun the widespread use of statistical sampling only in the last ten years. Will the use of statistical sampling increase in the future?

13-2 Define the term *population* as used in statistics. Describe in words and in a picture a typical audit population.

13-3 As an auditor uses hypothesis testing, how does he formulate the null hypothesis? The alternative hypothesis?

13-4 Give the formula for determining the required sample size for hypothesis testing. Explain the impact of the following on the required sample size: (a) book value, (b) number of items in the population, (c) standard deviation of the population, (d) materiality, (e) alpha risk, and (f) beta risk.

13-5 Is stratification of the population required for the use of statistical sampling? What are its costs? What are its benefits?

13-6 It is sometimes said that statistical sampling eliminates the need for an auditor's judgement. Why is this not true? Where, in applying hypothesis testing, must the auditor use his judgement?

13-7 What is a confidence interval? To which value in the confidence interval should the client adjust his books?

13-8 Briefly define dollar-value estimation, ratio estimation, and difference estimation. In which auditing situations would each be most appropriate?

13-9 A typical audit population does not have a normal distribution. How does this affect the distribution of sample means?

13-10 Explain the difference between the standard deviation of the population and the standard error of the mean.

Multiple Choice Questions From Professional Examinations

13-11 Which of the following best describes the distinguishing feature of statistical sampling?

    a. It requires the examination of a smaller number of supporting documents.

    b. It provides a means for measuring mathematically the degree of uncertainty that results from examining only part of a population.

    c. It reduces the problems associated with the auditor's judgement concering materiality.

    d. It is evaluated in terms of two parameters—statistical mean and random selection.

13-12 An important statistic to consider when using a statistical sampling audit plan is the population variability. The population variability is measured by the

    a. Sample mean

    b. Standard deviation

    c. Standard error of the sample mean

    d. Estimated population total minus the actual population total

13-13 If statistical sampling methods are used by a client in the taking of its physical inventory, the CPA must

    a. Insist that the client take a complete physical inventory at least once each year and observe the inventory count if it is reasonable and practicable for him to do so.

    b. Observe such test counts as he deems necessary and satisfy himself that the sampling plan has statistical validity, that it was properly applied, and that the resulting precision and reliability are reasonable in the circumstances.

    c. Either observe a complete inventory count sometime during the year and satisfy himself that the statistical procedures are valid or qualify or disclaim an opinion on the financial statements taken as a whole.

    d. Either observe a statistical inventory count each year or qualify or disclaim an opinion on the financial statements taken as a whole.

Items 14 through 18 apply to an examination by Robert Lambert, CPA, of the financial statements of Rainbow Manufacturing Corporation for the year ended December 31, 1983. Rainbow manufactures two products. Product A requires raw materials that have a very low per-item cost, and Product B requires raw materials that have a very high per-item cost. Raw materials for both products are stored in a single warehouse. In 1982, Rainbow established the total value of raw materials stored in the warehouse by physically inventorying an unrestricted random sample of items selected without replacement.

Mr. Lambert is evaluating the statistical validity of alternative sampling plans Rainbow is considering for 1983. Lambert knows the size of the 1982 sample and that Rainbow did not use stratified sampling in 1982. Assumptions about the population, variability, specified precision (confidence interval), and specified reliability (confidence level) for a possible 1983 sample are given in each of the following five items. You are to indicate in each case the effect upon the size of the 1983 sample as compared to the 1982 sample. Each of the five cases is independent of the other four and is to be considered separately. Your answer choice for each item 14 through 18 should be selected from the following responses:

    a. Larger than the 1982 sample size

    b. Equal to the 1982 sample size

    c. Smaller than the 1982 sample size

    d. Of a size that is indeterminate based upon the information given

13-14 Rainbow wants to use stratified sampling in 1983. (The total population will be divided into two strata, one each for the raw materials for Product A and Product B.) Compared to 1982, the population size of the raw materials inventory is approximately the same, and the variability of the items in the inventory is approximately the same. The specified precision and specified reliability are to remain the same. Under these assumptions, the required sample size for 1983 should be

    a. Larger than the 1982 sample size

    b. Equal to the 1982 sample size

c. Smaller than the 1982 sample size

d. Of a size that is indeterminate based upon the information given

13-15 Rainbow wants to use stratified sampling in 1983. Compared to 1982, the population of the raw materials inventory is approximately the same, and the variability of the items in the inventory is approximately the same. Rainbow specified the same precision but desires to change the specified reliability from 90% to 95%. Under these assumptions, the required sample size for 1983 should be

a. Larger than the 1982 sample size

b. Equal to the 1982 sample size

c. Smaller than the 1982 sample size

d. Of a size that is indeterminate based upon the information given

13-16 Rainbow wants to use unrestricted random sampling without replacement in 1983. Compared to 1982, the population size of the raw materials inventory is approximately the same, and the variability of the items in the inventory is approximately the same. Rainbow specified the same precision but desires to change the specified reliability from 90% to 95%. Under these assumptions, the required sample size for 1983 should be

a. Larger than the 1982 sample size

b. Equal to the 1982 sample size

c. Smaller than the 1982 sample size

d. Of a size that is indeterminate based upon the information given

13-17 Rainbow wants to use the unrestricted random sampling without replacement in 1983. Compared to 1982, the population size of the raw materials inventory has increased, and the variability of the items in the inventory has increased. The specified precision and specified reliability are to remain the same. Under these assumptions, the required sample size for 1983 should be

a. Larger than the 1982 sample size

b. Equal to the 1982 sample size

c. Smaller than the 1982 sample size

d. Of a size that is indeterminate based upon the information given

13-18 Rainbow wants to use unrestricted random sampling without replacement in 1983. Compared to 1982, the population size of the raw materials inventory has increased, but the variability of the items in the inventory has decreased. The specified precision and specified reliability are to remain the same. Under these assumptions, the required sample size for 1983 should be

a. Larger than the 1982 sample size

b. Equal to the 1982 sample size

c. Smaller than the 1982 sample size

d. Of a size that is indeterminate based upon the information given

13-19 If all other factors specified in a sampling plan remain constant, changing the specified reliability from 90% to 95% would cause the required sample size to

a. Increase

b. Remain the same

c. Decrease

d. Become indeterminate

13-20 Precision is a statistical measure of the maximum likely difference between the sample estimate and the true but unknown population total and is directly related to

a. Reliability of evidence

b. Relative risk

c. Materiality

d. Cost benefit analysis

13-21 In estimation sampling for variables, which of the following must be known in order to estimate the appropriate sample size required to meet the auditor's needs in a given situation?

a. The total amount of the population

b. The desired standard deviation

c. The desired confidence level

d. The estimated rate of error in the population

13-22 The reliability (confidence level) of an estimate made from sample data is a mathematically determined figure that expresses the expected proportion of possible samples of a specified size from a given population

a. That will yield an interval estimate that will encompass the true population value

b. That will yield an interval estimate that will not encompass the true population value

c. For which the sample value and the population value are identical

d. For which the sample elements will not exceed the population elements by more than a stated amount

13-23 A CPA's client wishes to determine inventory shrinkage by weighing a sample of inventory items. If a stratified random sample is to be drawn, the strata should be identified in such a way that

a. The overall population is divided into subpopulations of equal size so that each subpopulation can be given equal weight when estimates are made.

b. Each stratum differs as much as possible with respect to expected shrinkage, but the shrinkage expected for items within each stratum are as close as possible.

c. The sample mean and the standard deviation of each individual stratum will be equal to the means and standard deviations of all other strata.

d. The items in each stratum will follow a normal distribution so that probability theory can be used in making inferences from the sample data.

13-24 An auditor selects a preliminary sample of 100 items out of a population of 1,000. The sample statistics generate an arithmetic mean of $120, a standard deviation of $12, and a standard error of the mean of $1.20. If the sample was adequate for the auditor's purposes, and the auditor's desired precision was plus or minus $2,000, the minimum acceptable dollar value of the population would be

a. $122,000

b. $120,000

c. $118,000

d. $117,600

13-25 In estimating the total value of supplies on repair trucks, the LaVigne Company draws random samples from two equal-sized strata of trucks. The mean value of the inventory stored on the larger trucks (Stratum 1) was computed as $1,500, with a standard deviation of $250. On the smaller trucks (Stratum 2), the mean value of inventory was computed as $500, with a standard deviation of $45. If LaVigne had drawn an unstratified sample from the entire population of trucks, the expected mean value of inventory per truck would be $1,000, and the expected standard deviation would be

a. Exactly $147.50

b. Greater than $250

c. Less than $45

d. Between $45 and $250, but not $147.50

Problems

13-26 Identify the factual error in each of the following three statements.

a. In any normal distribution of population values, the mean of the distribution plus or minus one standard deviation includes 25% of the area under the normal curve.

b. To avoid bias in the selection of a sample, every item must have a systematic (every nth item) chance of selection.

c. Assuming the same population size, sample size, and estimated error rate, an increase in the confidence level will result in a narrowing of the range of precision.

IIA

13-27 Ace Corporation does not conduct a complete annual physical count of purchased parts and supplies in its principal warehouse but uses statistical sampling instead to estimate the year-end inventory. Ace maintains a perpetual inventory record of parts and supplies and believes that statistical sampling is highly effective in determining inventory values and is sufficiently reliable to make a physical count of each item of inventory unnecessary.

<u>Required:</u>

a. Identify the audit procedures that should be used by the independent auditor that change or are in addition to normal required audit procedures when a client utilizes statistical sampling to determine inventory value and does not conduct a 100% annual physical count of inventory items.

b. List at least ten normal audit procedures that should be performed to verify physical quantities whenever a client conducts a periodic physical count of all or part of its inventory.

AICPA

13-28 During the course of an audit engagement, a CPA attempts to obtain satisfaction that there are no material misstatements in the accounts receivable of a client. Statistical sampling is a tool that the auditor often uses to obtain representative evidence to achieve the desired satisfaction. On a particular engagement an auditor determined that a material misstatement in a population of accounts would be $35,000. To obtain satisfaction, the auditor had to be 95% confident that the population of accounts was not in error by $35,000. The auditor decided to use unrestricted random sampling with replacement and took a preliminary random sample of 100 items (n) from a population of 1,000 items (N). The sample produced the following data:

Arithmetic mean of sample items ($\bar{x}$) $4,000
Standard deviation of sample items (SD) $ 200

The auditor also has available the following information:

Standard error of the mean (SE) = SD ÷ $\sqrt{n}$
Population precision (P) = N × R × SE

Partial List of Reliability Coefficients

If Reliability Coefficient (R) is	Then Reliability is
1.70	91.086%
1.75	91.988
1.80	92.814
1.85	93.568
1.90	94.256
1.95	94.882
1.96	95.000
2.00	95.450
2.05	95.964
2.10	96.428
2.15	96.844

Required:

a. Define the statistical terms *reliability* and *precision* as applied to auditing.
b. If all necessary audit work is performed on the preliminary sample items and no errors are detected,
   1. What can the auditor say about the total amount of accounts receivable at the 95% reliability level?
   2. At what confidence level can the auditor say that the population is not in error by $35,000?
c. Assume that the preliminary sample was sufficient,
   1. Compute the auditor's estimate of the population total.
   2. Indicate how the auditor should relate this estimate to the client's recorded amount.

AICPA

13-29 You want to evaluate the reasonableness of the book value of the inventory of your client, Draper, Inc. You were satisfied earlier as to inventory quantities. During the examination of the pricing and extension of the inventory, the following data were gathered using appropriate unrestricted random sampling with replacement procedures.

Total items in the inventory (N)	12,700
Total items in the sample (n)	400
Total audited value of items in the sample	$38,400

$$\sum_{j=1}^{400} (X_j - \bar{X})^2 \qquad\qquad 312,816$$

Formula for estimated population standard deviation

$$^sX_j = \sqrt{\frac{\displaystyle\sum_{j=1}^{j=n} (X_j - \bar{X})^2}{n - 1}}$$

Formula for estimated standard error of the mean

$$SE = \frac{^sX_j}{\sqrt{n}}$$

Confidence level coefficient of the standard error of the mean at a 95% confidence (reliability) level

$$\pm 1.96$$

Required:

a. Based on the sample results, what is the estimate of the total value of the inventory? Show computations clearly where appropriate.

b. What statistical conclusion can be reached regarding the estimated total inventory value calculated in (a) above at the confidence level of 95%? Present computations clearly where appropriate.

c. Independent of your answers to (a) and (b), assume that the book value of Draper's inventory is $1,700,000, and based on the sample results, the estimated total value of the inventory is $1,690,000. The auditor desires a confidence (reliability) level of 95%. Discuss the audit and statistical considerations the auditor must evaluate before deciding whether the sampling results support acceptance of the book value as a fair presentation of Draper's inventory.

AICPA

13-30 a. What confidence would an auditor have that the true value lies in the range of $94,200 to $108,860, if the estimated value is $100,000, there are 1,000 items in the population, and the standard error of the mean is $4?

b. What are the 99% confidence limits about the estimated value of $150,000 if there are 1,000 items in the population and the standard error of the mean is $3? 95% confidence limits? 90% confidence limits?

Courtesy of Peat, Marwick, Mitchell & Co.

13-31 An auditor returns your statistical sample evaluation with the comment, "This must be wrong. The total of the errors in the sample shows that the book value is understated, yet you recommended that it be written down. Please recheck your work." Your working paper shows this information:

Stratum	Stratum Includes Accounts	Number in Stratum	Sample Size in Stratum
1	less than $200	800	20
2	$200 or more	50	40

Book value = $100,000
Projected value = $97,000

Sample items in error (all others correct):

Book Value	Audit Value
$ 70	$ 50
80	40
50	30
840	1,000
Totals $1,040	$1,120

Determine whether this situation is possible and explain the reason. (Hint: What happens if you project the differences?)

Courtesy of Peat, Marwick, Mitchell & Co.

13-32 You have been contacted by the engagement supervisor of a very large client engaged in retail distribution. The supervisor tells you he would like to use statistical sampling techniques to verify the gross existence of the accounts receivable account. Due to very tight reporting deadlines, the confirmation procedure (which is the only substantive test designed to establish existence) has always been performed as of the third quarter. Because receivables turn quickly (forty-five days), the supervisor does not anticipate any problems clearing nonresponses. Internal controls have always been evaluated as excellent, but because the engagement is not being staffed until mid-September, the supervisor suggests using a reliance factor of .05 instead of attempting to complete the compliance tests by September 30. He also acknowledges that, because the test is to be run at .05, he will probably get a sample size greater than the prior year's interim judgemental sample sizes. He is not concerned because he plans little year-end work in receivables if the balance at interim is accepted.

What is your impression of this sampling strategy?

Courtesy Peat, Marwick, Mitchell & Co.

13-33 Assume that:

Population per books:

Number of items = 10,000

All items but one are distributed in the range $0 to $1,000; the exception has a book value of $1,000,000.

True (but unknown) values:

There are a few small offsetting errors in the small items, and the $1,000,000 item is utterly worthless.

The auditor takes an unrestricted random sample of 100 items and computes the projected audit value (by difference estimation) and the estimated sampling error.

a. What is the probability the auditor will detect the $1,000,000 error?
b. If the auditor does not detect the $1,000,000 error and projects the following from the sample, how many standard errors will the auditor's estimate be off?

Estimated audit value $4,000,000
Standard error of mean $5

c. What is the probability of being off that number of standard errors by chance?
d. Why did this happen?
e. What general conclusion can be drawn about the use of unrestricted random sampling in auditing?
f. An auditor using hypothesis testing takes advantage of the ability to include selected items in the 100% sample stratum. The criteria below are entered to cause all account balances meeting the criteria to be included in the 100% stratum:

1. Over $10,000
2. Under $ −1,000
3. No collections in last 120 days
4. Credit hold (indicating dispute or delinquency)

5. Processed by one particular billing clerk who is under suspicion
6. Specific account balances selected by the auditor on the basis that they "smelled fishy"
7. Specific account balances that the client's credit manager selected as unrepresentative

For each of these criteria, indicate whether bias will be introduced into the final statistical projections (thus altering the auditor's risk levels).

Courtesy of Peat, Marwick, Mitchell & Co.

13-34 a. Below is an analysis of an accounts receivable population:

Less than − 100,000	20	− 3,117,810
Bet. − 50,000 and − 100,000	22	− 1,511,811
Bet. − 10,000 and − 50,000	92	− 1,200,017
Bet. − 5,000 and − 10,000	511	− 2,651,000
Bet. − 1,000 and − 5,000	2,119	− 2,222,267
Bet. 0 and − 1,000	16,411	− 297,898
Bet. 1,000 and 0	92,081	3,998,109
Bet. 5,000 and 1,000	25,911	29,817,445
Bet. 10,000 and 5,000	4,411	25,911,238
Bet. 50,000 and 10,000	817	25,846,119
Bet. 100,000 and 50,000	114	8,114,133
Grt. than 100,000	41	6,911,142
Less than 0	19,175	− 11,000,803
Grt. than 0	119,364	100,598,186

Using hypothesis testing with no 100% conditions, the sample sizes are extremely large. What is causing the extremely large sample sizes? How could you make this application more efficient and therefore reduce the sample size?

b. You have performed hypothesis testing on accounts receivable and have confirmed each sample item. Assume your rate of nonresponse to accounts receivable confirmations is 25%. You perform alternative procedures on all nonresponding accounts, but for 60% of the non-responses, you are able to verify only 60% to 80% of the balance. You have reviewed the unverified items and found no unusual transactions. What is the correct statistical decision? Why? Would your answer be different if you were able to verify 90% to 95% of the unconfirmed balance?

Courtesy of Peat, Marwick, Mitchell & Co.

13-35 For each of the following situations, suggest a sampling approach:

a. Your client, a wholesaler of leather goods and fashion accessories, maintains inventories at standard prices on manual records. At year-end, management adjusts the actual physical inventory on a global basis to an estimated FIFO cost by formula, making a number of assumptions. You want to verify that the total FIFO cost is correct by selecting a sample of inventory items and computing the actual FIFO cost for each sample item.

b. Your client sells health and beauty aids to mass merchandisers. In the past, you have selected accounts for confirmation on a nonstatistical basis and have had a low response. Specifically, several confirmations to the larger merchandisers have been over 100 pages long. Most confirmations have a small percentage of disputed receivables for short shipments, promotional advertising, freight claims, and other items that have not been paid by year-end and cannot be supported by shipping documents. You intended to use statistical sampling for this year's audit but are concerned about the past history of low response and the number of disputed claims.

Courtesy of Peat, Marwick, Mitchell & Co.

Auditing using statistical sampling

Chapter 13 presented many of the basic concepts of statistics useful in auditing, including the very important distinction between alpha error (rejecting a correct book value) and beta error (accepting an incorrect book value). This chapter will extend these concepts into two new areas: (1) attribute sampling, the statistical evaluation of internal control; and (2) dollar-unit sampling, an easy-to-use substantive test that has important applications when the auditor expects few errors in the population book values.

Hypothesis testing, estimation techniques, and attributes sampling all require a random sample of units from the population. Section 14.3 discusses drawing a random sample and the other approaches to sampling: haphazard, block, systematic, and dollar-unit.

The chapter concludes with a broad overview of statistics, its potential applications in auditing, and its usefulness in clarifying audit decisions. Many auditors believe that the primary usefulness of statistical methods is that they make explicit the basic decisions the auditor must face, such as how much risk the auditor is willing to accept. With nonstatistical methods the risks do not go away, the auditor just does not make them explicit or quantify them.

14.1 DISCOVERY SAMPLING

Chapter 13 discussed evaluating the book value of inventory and accounts receivable. Auditors often refer to this evaluation of an account balance as *variables sampling*. In contrast to variables sampling, the auditor can also use statistical methods to evaluate internal control. Auditors refer to the evaluation of internal control as *attributes sampling*. Variables sampling is thus a form of substantive testing, while attribute sampling is a form of compliance testing.

Multiplication of Probabilities

If someone flips a coin, the probability of a head is 1/2. In symbols,

$$P(H) = 1/2$$

If someone flips a coin twice, the probability of two heads in a row is

$$P(H,H) = P(H) \cdot P(H) = 1/2 \cdot 1/2 = 1/4$$

These probabilities can be multiplied because they are independent.

Precisely this idea is behind attribute sampling. To illustrate, suppose an auditor is evaluating internal control and he wishes to check whether or not the credit manager indicated approval of a sales invoice by initialling it. When the auditor looks at an invoice, it is either initialled or it is not initialled; there are only those two possibilities.

Assume, then, that 4% of the invoices do not have initials on them. If an auditor looks at one invoice at random, the probability is 96% that there will be initials on it. The auditor might write this

$$P(I) = .96$$

If the auditor looked at two invoices, the probability that both would have initials is

$$P(I,I) = P(I) \cdot P(I) = P(I)^2 = (.96)^2 = .92$$

If the auditor looked at ten invoices, the probability that all would have initials is

$$P(I, \ldots ,I) = P(I)^{10} = (.96)^{10} = .66$$

If the auditor looked at fifty invoices, the probability that all would have initials is

$$P(I, \ldots ,I) = P(I)^{50} = (.96)^{50} = .13$$

If the auditor looked at 100 invoices, the probability that all would have initials is

$$P(I, \ldots ,I) = P(I)^{100} = (.96)^{100} = .02$$

In a situation like this, the auditor will call the absence of initials an error because the absence of initials shows that internal control did not work in that instance. So the auditor can make the following statement:

If the error rate (i.e., the absence of initials) is 4%, then the probability of examining 100 invoices and finding none in error is 2%.

Definition of Discovery Sampling

Suppose that the auditor believes there are no errors in the population (i.e., that all invoices have initials) but that the auditor could accept any error rate under 4%. The following sampling plan might then be developed:

Examine 100 invoices. If all 100 invoices have initials, accept internal control as adequate. If any errors are found, reject internal control as inadequate.

This type of sampling is called *discovery sampling* because the auditor examines sample items until he discovers an error. The discovery of *any* error will cause the auditor to reject internal control as inadequate. Discovery sampling is also appropriate when searching for one case or example of an irregularity. e.g., an example of a forged check that would give evidence of fraud.

Alpha Risk

If the true error rate is 0%, there are, in fact, no errors in the population. Then the auditor can never find an error and will never reject internal control. Thus, if the true error rate is 0%, there is no chance of incorrectly rejecting internal control. There is, therefore, no chance of committing the alpha error—the alpha risk is 0.

Beta Risk

If the true error rate is 4%, the probability of finding no errors in the 100 invoices is 2%. But if the auditor finds no errors, he will incorrectly accept internal control as adequate when, in fact, the error rate is an unacceptably high 4%. Thus, there is a 2% chance of committing the beta error—the beta risk is 2%.

Upper Precision Limit/Confidence Level

In a situation like this, the auditor refers to 4% as the *upper precision limit* (UPL) because that is the lowest unacceptable error rate. Any error rates above the upper precision limit are also unacceptable.

Rather than referring to the beta risk of 2%, the auditor usually refers to the *confidence level* (CL) of 98%. Confidence level is $1 - \beta$ and measures the auditor's confidence that an unacceptably high error rate has not been accepted. As in Chapter 13, n represents the sample size. The auditor can then write the above formula

$$(1 - UPL)^n = 1 - CL$$

Sample Size

Suppose an auditor had an upper precision limit of 4% but could accept a confidence level of 95% (beta risk of 5%) rather than 98%. The sample size is greater than 50 because we already know that a sample size of 50 leads to a confidence level of 87% (100% − 13%, as determined earlier).

To get the exact sample size involves solving the above equation for n using the formula

$$n = \frac{\ln (1 - CL)}{\ln (1 - UPL)}$$

where ln represents the natural logarithm.* Solving this equation exactly for a confidence level of 95% and a critical error rate of 4% gives

$$n = \frac{\ln (1 - .95)}{\ln (1 - .04)} = \frac{\ln(.05)}{\ln(.96)} = \frac{-2.996}{-.0408} = 73$$

Simplified Sample Size Formula

Many modern calculators can provide the natural logarithm at the press of a button. But for practical purposes, the above equation can be simplified. The auditor will almost always be concerned with a confidence level of 95%. Within practical accuracy,

$$\ln (1 - .95) = \ln (.05) = -3.00$$

For a critical error rate between 1% and 10%, there is another simplifying relationship

$$\ln (1 - UPL) = -UPL$$

For example, ln (1 − .04) = −.04. The simplified formula for sample size in discovery sampling is then

$$n = \frac{\ln (1 - CL)}{\ln (1 - UPL)} = \frac{-3.00}{-UPL} = \frac{3}{UPL}$$

For an upper precision limit of 4%, the simplified formula gives a sample size of 75, essentially the same as the exact figure of 73. For an upper precision limit of 5%, the sample size is 60 using the simplified formula; using the exact formula, the sample size is 59.

---

*The natural logarithm of a number is the power of e (a mathematical term equal to approximately 2.71828) which equals the number. For example, $e^0 = 1$ and so ln (1) = 0.

Difficulty With Discovery Sampling

Discovery sampling is very efficient if the auditor expects no errors. For example, if the auditor desires 95% confidence and the upper precision limit is 10%, the auditor need examine only 30 items. But the auditor must "pay" for this efficiency—discovery sampling is intolerant of any errors. In other words, if the auditor finds *any* errors, he cannot accept internal control as adequate.

Suppose the true error rate is 2% and the upper precision limit is 10%. This is an acceptable state of affairs since the true error rate is less than the critical error rate. And suppose the auditor were to use discovery sampling, still desiring a confidence level of 95%. The beta risk is 5% (100% − 95%).

The alpha risk is the chance of incorrectly rejecting what is, in fact, an acceptable internal control. In this case, this is the probability of getting one or more errors out of the 30 invoices examined.

To compute this probability exactly requires a certain amount of statistical theory that is beyond the scope of this chapter. But applying this theory gives a probability of 0.45 of getting one or more errors out of 30 invoices.

This means that the alpha risk is 45%. If the expected error rate were higher than 2%, the alpha risk would be even higher than 45%. This is unacceptably high, so the auditor must use a different approach.

CONCEPT SUMMARY
Summary of Discovery Sampling

1. Determine attribute to be tested	Identify a documented internal control feature which is either there or not there; example: initials indicating credit approval of an invoice.
2. Determine upper precision limit (UPL)	Specify the minimum unacceptable error rate; example: initials can sometimes be missing, but it has to be for less than 4% of the invoices.
3. Determine confidence level (CL)	Specify the confidence the auditor must feel that the true error rate is less than the critical error; the confidence level in practice is usually 95%
4. Calculate sample size	The exact formula is n = sample size $$= \frac{\ln(1\text{-}CL)}{\ln(1\text{-}UPL)}$$ In practice the formula for 95% confidence and 1%–10% critical error rate can be $n = \frac{3}{UPL}$
5. Draw sample and evaluate results	If no errors are found, then at the given confidence level, the true unknown error rate is less than the upper precision limit. If one or more errors are found, then the true unknown error rate may be greater than the upper precision limit.

14.2 ATTRIBUTES SAMPLING

The auditor normally expects errors and thus, will not use discovery sampling. When there are errors, attributes sampling is employed. The sample size is first determined for every control (i.e., attribute) to be tested. This sample size will be based upon both:

1. Upper precision limit (the error rate that would lead the auditor to reject the internal control as inadequate).
2. Expected error rate (the percentage of errors the auditor thinks he will find in the population).

Sample Size

Determining the sample size in any given situation can require a great number of trial-and-error calculations. There is no simple formula that will give the sample size. For this reason, auditors use a table that has been computed and checked. This table relieves the auditor of performing involved calculations.

Exhibit 14–1 is a sample size table. Suppose the upper precision limit were 10% and the expected error rate were 2%. The auditor would look in the 10% column and the 2% row to determine the sample size of 50. If the expected error rate were 4% rather than 2%, the sample size would be 90.

All the sample sizes in this table are rounded to make them easier to use. The theoretically correct figure may, in some cases, be somewhat smaller. As discussed earlier, the sample size with an upper precision limit of 4% and an expected error rate of 0% is 73, which is rounded up to 80 for this table.

EXHIBIT 14-1 Sample Size Table

Confidence Level = 95%

Expected Error Rate	Upper Precision Limit									
	1%	2%	3%	4%	5%	6%	7%	8%	9%	10%
0%	300	150	100	80	60	50	50	40	40	30
1		600	260	160	100	80	70	60	60	50
2			900	300	200	140	90	80	70	50
3				400	200	160	100	90	80	80
4					500	240	180	100	90	90
5						500	240	160	120	

Exhibit 14–1 assumes a confidence level of 95%. At a different confidence level, the auditor would need an entirely new table. At 90% confidence, the sample sizes would be smaller, and at 99% confidence the sample sizes would be larger.

Size of the Population

This discussion of attributes sampling assumes that the population is infinite. In most audit situations, where error rates are low and populations are large, the assumption of an infinite population is quite appropriate. This is a useful simplification, since the effect of considering the population size would be small. In contrast, for variables sampling (as discussed in the last chapter), the population size has a very significant effect on the sample size.

Compliance Testing and Evaluating Results

After determining the sample size from the sample size table, the auditor selects and examines those items. Working papers such as Exhibits 14–2 and 14–3 are prepared to record the controls tested, the auditor's judgements, sample sizes, and errors found. When compliance testing is finished, each control is evaluated and the results noted on the working paper (see Exhibit 14–2). The table in Exhibit 14–4 is used to determine the upper precision limit actually achieved. If the achieved precision exceeds the desired precision, the control is rejected as unsatisfactory. The consequences of a rejected control are that substantive tests will be affected and management—and conceivably the Board of Directors—will be alerted.

Evaluation Table

Suppose the auditor looks at a sample size of 50 and finds 1 error. He goes to the row for a sample size of 50 and then across the row to 1. The auditor then reads up to an upper precision limit of 10%. If he found 0 errors, the upper precision limit would be 6%. Other tables are available for a full range of percentages and sample sizes.

The sample size of 50 was based upon an expected error rate of 2%, leading to an expected number of errors of 50 × 2% = 1. If this one error is found, it leads to an upper precision limit of 10%, as was desired. The sample size table and the evaluation table are inextricably linked together.

Definition of an Error

When an auditor is compliance testing, he is trying to determine the error rate of a particular internal control feature. An example of an internal control feature discussed earlier was the indication of credit approval by the credit manager's

W. P. NO.	N-1
ACCOUNTANT	RAS
DATE	1/14/X2

Test No.	Attributes Tested	1 Expected Error Rate	2 Sample Size	3 Errors Discovered (No.)	4 Desired	5 Achieved	
1.	Voucher is supported by required documents and details agree	2	90	1	7 %	6 %	
2.	Account code is correct	3	160	2	7	4	
3.	Voucher and supporting documents are properly authorized	1	160	1	4	3	
4.	Invoice is initialled as being checked for mathematical accuracy	4	100	2	9	7	
5.	Math. is correct (reperform)	1	70	0	7	5	
6.	Voucher and supporting documents are marked "paid"	3	160	8	7	9	(A)
7.	Voucher and voucher register entry agree	2	200	7	5	7	(B)
8.	Voucher and cancelled checks agree as to amount, date, and payee. Signature and endorsement checked.	1	160	0	4	2	

Columns 4 and 5 grouped under heading: Upper Precision Limits (Desired / Achieved)

(See N-1A)

- 95% confidence level specified for all attributes
- Sampling unit: vouchers from population of those issued in 19X1.
  #56,901 through #104,362 = 47,461 total.
- Selection: $\frac{47,461}{n}$ = skip interval with random stab start from table of random numbers.

Decision rule: If col. 5 > col. 4, reject control.

(A) Discussed with management. Compensating control appears satisfactory. Also vouched remainder of sample (n = 200) plus 20 more. No more errors discovered; achieved UPL = 7%.

(B) Discussed problem with management (include in management letter) and reclassified errors — see Note #7 — Expand substantive tests of details by selecting all vouchers ⩾ $5,000 and tracing into voucher register for agreement of details.

FORM-WP-71 COMFORT & CO., INC. N.Y.C.

EXHIBIT 14-2

W. P. No.	N-1A
ACCOUNTANT	RAS
DATE	1/14/X2

VOUCHER No. (errors only)	REMARKS	ATTRIBUTES PER W/P N-1							
		1	2	3	4	5	6	7	8
✓7,003	V/R charged $1,090 - s/b $109.22 *							✓	
✓7,321	P.O. not authorized - immaterial; "$2"			✓					
✓8,060	voucher not cancelled						✓		
✓8,061	" " "						✓		
64,774	" " "						✓		
73,919	requisition missing	✓							
78,164	no initials; math O.K.				✓				
83,605	voucher not cancelled						✓		
83,606	" " "						✓		
88,312	wrong expense A/c coded ¢		✓						
91,422	V/R incorrect $2,000 s/b $2,222 *							✓	
93,159	V/R incorrect $6,500 s/b $65.22 *							✓	
95,098	voucher not cancelled						✓		
96,250	V/R incorrect $1,848 s/b $1,848 *							✓	
97,512	wrong expense A/c coded ¢		✓						
98,341	V/R incorrect $39 - s/b $3,900 - *							✓	
99,003	voucher not cancelled						✓		
101,642	" " "						✓		
101,916	V/R not correct $18,490 s/b $13,490 *							✓	
102,819	no initials; math OK.				✓				
103,909	V/R incorrect $800 - s/b $8.22 *							✓	
	Total number of errors (✓)	1	2	1	2	0	8	7	0

* See AJE #13
¢ See RJE #1

EXHIBIT 14–3

EXHIBIT 14-4   Evaluation Table

Sample Size	Confidence Level = 95% Upper Precision Limit Achieved									
	1%	2%	3%	4%	5%	6%	7%	8%	9%	10%
30										0
40								0		
50						0				1
60					0			1		
70					0		1		2	
80				0		1		2		3
90				0		1	2		3	4
100			0		1		2	3	4	
120			0	1		2	3	4	5	6
140			0	1	2	3	4	5	6	7
160		0	1	2	3	4	5	6	8	9
180		0	1	2	3	5	6	8	9	11
200		0	1	3	4	6	7	9	11	12
300	0	1	3	6	8	11	13	16	18	21

initials on the invoice. If the auditor examines an invoice and does not find the appropriate initials, then that invoice is an error. It does not matter if the credit manager specifically remembers approving the credit for that invoice; if there are no initials, there is an error. The internal control feature must be documented.

A more complicated situation arises when the internal control feature is to: (1) recheck the extensions and footings of an invoice, and (2) initial the invoice indicating performance. The auditor must count an error if either (or both) of these steps is improper. If the initials are not on the invoice, there is an error. Moreover, even if the initials are on the invoice, if the extensions and footings are inaccurate, then there is an error. The internal control feature must not only be documented, it must be performed correctly.

There are then two important conclusions here:

1. *The auditor must reperform the internal control feature, if possible.* This reperformance is impossible in cases such as credit approval, which require judgement. But the auditor can reperform mechanical internal control features, such as checking extensions and footings.

2. *The auditor can only test documented internal controls.* If there is no documentation, there is nothing to test. If the client says that "somebody" checks the extensions and footings, but there are no initials indicating the check, there is no way to distinguish between the initial performance of the task and the internal control step. As a result, the auditor cannot test the internal control specifically. For undocumented controls, the auditor must rely on inquiry and observation audit procedures.

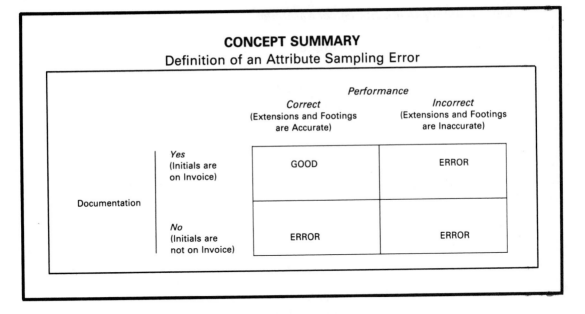

CONCEPT SUMMARY
Definition of an Attribute Sampling Error

	Performance	
	Correct (Extensions and Footings are Accurate)	*Incorrect* (Extensions and Footings are Inaccurate)
Yes (Initials are on Invoice)	GOOD	ERROR
No (Initials are not on Invoice)	ERROR	ERROR

Documentation

CONCEPT SUMMARY
Summary of Attributes Sampling

1. Determine attributes to be tested	Identify a documented internal control feature which is either there or not there; example: initials indicating credit approval of an invoice.
2. Determine upper precision limit	Specify the minimum unacceptable error rate; example: initials can sometimes be missing, but it has to be for less than 10% of the invoices.
3. Determine confidence level	Specify the confidence the auditor must feel that the true error rate is less than the upper precision limit; the confidence level in practice is usually 95%.
4. Determine expected error rate	From past experience and judgement, or last year's audit, estimate the error rate of the sample; example: the auditor estimates that 2% of the invoices will not have initials for credit approval.
5. Find sample size in table	Look up sample size in table, given the upper precision limit, the expected error rate, and the confidence level; example: Exhibit 14-1 gives a sample size of 50 for an upper precision limit of 10%, expected error rate of 2%, and confidence level of 95%.
6. Draw sample and determine the number of errors	Examine the appropriate number of sample items, and decide how many are in error; example: auditor finds one invoice out of 50 that does not have proper initials.
7. Evaluate results using table	Use evaluation table to find the achieved upper precision limit at the given confidence level for the sample size and the number of errors found; example: Exhibit 14-4 gives a rate of 10% for a sample size of 50 and 1 error at a 95% confidence level.

Sequential Attributes Sampling

For a given upper precision limit, the sample size goes up rapidly as the expected error rate increases. With an upper precision limit of 6%, the sample size increases from 50 with a 0% expected error rate to 500 with a 4% expected error. It is easier to distinguish statistically between 6% and 0% than between 6% and 4%.

If the auditor is unsure of the expected error rate, he may not want to immediately examine a sample of 500. If the error rate is low, only a small sample is needed, but if the rate turns out to be larger, a bigger sample is needed. This situation can be dealt with statistically by *sequential attribute sampling*.

With sequential attribute sampling, the auditor examines a sample and then decides to: (1) accept internal control, (2) continue sampling, or (3) reject internal control. If the decision is to continue, the auditor will examine an additional block of items. The auditor then faces the same three choices as before. After examining a maximum of three additional blocks after the original sample, the auditor will achieve a statistical conclusion to accept or reject internal control. Sequential attribute sampling can lead to smaller sample sizes than fixed attribute sampling when the error rate in the population is large.

14.3 DOLLAR-UNIT SAMPLING

Consider an accounts receivable balance of $1,000,000 where there are 4,000 customers. Chapter 13 dealt with this situation by considering the population as having 4,000 items, each customer was an item of the population.

But there is another way of looking at this situation. The auditor can view the population as having 1,000,000 items, each dollar is an item of the population. In this view, the population consists of 1,000,000 units, each equal to one dollar. Each dollar unit is then either correct or incorrect. The dollar is correct if the customer owes the company that dollar, and the dollar is incorrect if the customer does not owe the company that dollar.

Suppose the 1,000,000 dollar bills are laid end to end, and the auditor examines 60 of these dollars at random. If he finds no errors, the auditor can conclude with 95% confidence that the rate of error is less than 5%. The auditor can use attributes sampling concepts, with each dollar a separate unit. The error rate can then be stated in monetary terms and can also serve variables sampling purposes.

Dollar-unit sampling (DUS) thus defines each dollar as a separate unit and gives each dollar an equal chance of selection; the conclusion is stated as a rate of incorrect dollars rather than a rate of, say, incorrect invoices. If in the above example there are 5% of dollars in error, the total error is $50,000 ($1,000,000 book value × 5% error rate).

Upper Precision Limit

The upper precision limit (UPL) is the error rate in the population that the auditor would find unacceptable. He can calculate this UPL using the concepts of Chapter 13:

$$UPL = \frac{M}{BV} = \frac{materiality}{book\ value}$$

The upper precision limit is materiality as a fraction of the book value.

Using the basic concepts of Section 14.1, the formula for the sample size when the auditor expects no errors would be

$$n = \frac{\ln(1 - CL)}{\ln(1 - UPL)}$$

when CL stands for the confidence level.

Assuming a confidence level of 95% gives a simplified sample size formula

$$n = \frac{3}{UPL}$$

Sampling Interval

In dollar unit sampling, the sampling units are the individual dollars that make up the population. The more dollars a physical unit (such as an invoice or account balance) has, the greater the chance that item will be examined. Dollar-unit sampling subdivides the population into equal dollar-value segments and then selects one dollar from each segment. The dollars that are selected act as "hooks" to extract the physical unit that will be examined. The *sampling interval* (SI) is the width of the segments. It is calculated using the following formula:

$$SI = \frac{BV}{n} = \frac{book\ value}{sample\ size}$$

Example

Assume an auditor is examining an account balance of $5,000,000 where he determines materiality to be $150,000. The auditor requires a confidence level of 95%, which in this context is equivalent to setting the beta risk at 5%. The auditor can then calculate the upper precision limit

$$UPL = \frac{M}{BV} = \frac{\$150,000}{\$5,000,000} = 0.03$$

If the auditor expects no errors, the sample size is then

$$n = \frac{3}{UPL} = \frac{3}{.03} = 100.$$

And the sampling interval is

$$SI = \frac{\$5,000,000}{100} = \$50,000.$$

The sample size of 100 is the maximum number of physical units that the auditor must examine. The auditor will examine this maximum number only if each dollar selected is from a different physical unit. Physical units with more dollars than the sampling interval will have two or more hooks in them. If multiple hooks are in one physical unit, the auditor need only examine it once. This would reduce the sample size below the calculated maximum.

Suppose that, after examining the 100 sample items, the auditor determines there are no errors. He can then conclude, with 95% confidence, that less than 3% of the dollars are in error. In other words, the auditor can be 95% confident that the book value is not overstated by more than $150,000 (3% × $5,000,000 = UPL × BV).

Treatment of Errors

Suppose that the auditor determines that one of the 100 examined accounts is worthless. Thus, for a sample size of 100 items there was 1 error. The table in Exhibit 14–4 indicates that the upper precision limit is 5%; this means 5% of the dollars. The auditor can then be 95% confident that the book value is not overstated by more than $250,000 (5% × $5,000,000 = UPL × BV). The same table can be used for evaluation here as in the attributes sampling case because the same concepts apply.

Advantages of DUS

As explained above, DUS is a method of variables sampling. As such, DUS applies in basically the same situations as do the hypothesis testing and estimation methods of Chapter 13. But DUS has some substantial advantages over these methods. To give an idea of the importance of DUS, one major firm uses it in approximately 50% of its variables sampling applications and uses hypothesis testing and estimation methods the other 50% of the time. However, the firm estimates it may soon use DUS in as many as 80% of the cases of variables sampling.

CONCEPT SUMMARY
Summary of Dollar-Unit Sampling

1. Determine basic facts	BV = book value CL = confidence level = 1 − beta risk M = materiality
2. Calculate sample information	UPL = upper precision limit $\quad = \dfrac{M}{BV}$ n = sample size $\quad = \dfrac{3}{UPL}$ assuming 95% confidence SI = sampling interval $\quad = \dfrac{BV}{n}$
3. Draw sample and evaluate results	UPL = revised upper precision limit (using Exhibit 14-4) The auditor can then make the following conclusion at the given confidence level: $\quad$ BV is not overstated by more than UPL × BV. If there are no errors, an equivalent conclusion is: $\quad$ BV is not overstated by more than materiality.

Ease of Use

One of the main advantages of DUS is its ease of use. The auditor can either make the necessary calculations by hand or use timesharing computer programs to ease the computational burden. Section 14.4 will show that selecting the sample is easier for DUS than it is for hypothesis testing.

No Assumptions About Audit Population

DUS makes no assumptions about the audit population. Specifically, DUS does not require an estimate of the population standard deviation, as did the methods of Chapter 13. Statisticians call techniques which make no assumptions about the population *nonparametric methods*. DUS is thus an example of a nonparametric method.

Automatic 100% Condition

DUS will select for audit every item greater than, or equal to the sampling interval. For example, if the sampling interval is $120,000, then every item $120,000 or more will be in the sample. The reason is that, as the auditor adds through the population (by adding the sampling interval successively), it is impossible to start on one side of an $150,000 item, say, and then add the sampling interval of $120,000 and get on the other side of the $150,000 item.

Maximum Stratification

In hypothesis testing, the auditor (with the help of a computer) can stratify the population and make it more likely that the sample includes the larger items. DUS automatically achieves this goal by making the probability of an item's selection proportionate to the dollar value of the item. By its nature, DUS always provides the maximum stratification.

No Computer Required

As discussed in Section 13.3, the complicated mathematics of hypothesis testing with stratification requires that both: (1) the accounting records be on the computer, and (2) computer programs be available for the necessary statistical computations to process the records. Neither of these requirements holds for DUS. The auditor can use timesharing programs to ease the computational burden and to reduce the chance of errors, but the accounting records can be manual.

Ideal When No Errors Expected

In certain situations, an auditor will expect no errors. For example, auditors have examined many savings and loans for years without detecting a single error in the mortgage loan account. Since the transactions are so few and so simple, and since the property is immovable, the auditor can realistically expect no errors in the future. In a situation like this, DUS gives a: (1) small sample size, and (2) a valid statistical conclusion without sophisticated manipulations of the data. From the auditor's perspective, this is almost an ideal situation.

Useful When Book Value Not Known

Suppose the financial statements for an insurance company are being examined. During interim work, the auditor wishes to begin checking the validity of claims that have been approved for payment. The standard procedure would be to compute the sampling interval from the book value. However, this procedure is impossible to perform at interim because the auditor does not know the book value and will not until the end of the year. To get around this problem, the auditor can calculate the sampling interval directly:

$$SI = \frac{BV}{n} = \frac{BV}{\dfrac{3}{UPL}} = \frac{BV \cdot UPL}{3}$$

$$= \frac{BV}{3} \cdot UPL = \frac{BV}{3} \cdot \frac{M}{BV}$$

$$= \frac{M}{3}$$

The sampling interval is thus ⅓ of materiality, regardless of the book value. The auditor can, therefore, begin at the beginning of the year and use this sampling interval all the way up to the interim date without knowing the book value of the account being audited.

Appropriate Uses for DUS

Based upon the above, DUS would be most appropriate for the following audit tests

1. Accounts receivable with credit balances unlikely or where they can be audited separately.
2. Loans, such as mortgages, commercial loans, or installment loans.
3. Investment securities.
4. Inventory price test, where the auditor is testing whether the inventory item is properly valued at its FIFO cost.
5. Fixed asset additions.

Disadvantages of DUS

Although DUS has many advantages, it also has a certain number of disadvantages that make it unsuitable in some circumstances. Also, because many large companies use the computer for accounting, and large CPA firms have computer statistical packages available, the "advantage" of not requiring computerized records may not be important.

No Control of Understatements

The basic DUS assumption is that the dollar is either correct (and should be valued at 1) or incorrect (and should be valued at 0). Even with the sophistication of the "tainted dollar," which this text will not discuss, the value would lie within the range 0 to 1. The relationship between the audit value (AV) and book value (BV) for each item must then be

$$0 \leq AV \leq BV$$

In other words, the audit concern must be one of overstatement. This eliminates the use of DUS for liability accounts, such as accounts payable. But for asset accounts (where the concern *is* overstatement) this is not really a disadvantage.

No Negative Items

It also follows from the $0 \leq AV \leq BV$ equation that DUS will not handle negative items, such as credit balances in accounts receivable. The hypothesis testing approach can often handle these credit items directly, along with the rest of the population. With DUS, the auditor must segregate the credit items and audit them separately. This is not a difficult process, however. When adding through the population, the auditor need only skip all negative items and put them to the side for later review.

Conservative Projection of Errors

Even the most sophisticated versions of DUS make very conservative projections of errors. As a result, DUS is very intolerant of numerous errors in the population, even if they are small or offsetting. The result can be an unwarranted rejection of the book value or adjustment to the book value. This is a fundamental problem with DUS, so for an error-prone population, the auditor should use the hypothesis testing approach.

Inappropriate Uses for DUS

Based upon the above, DUS would be inappropriate for the following audit tests:

1. Accounts receivable where credit balances may be large or frequent.
2. Inventory quantity tests, since the audit amount could be greater than, as well as less than the book amounts.
3. Brokerage customer accounts, since the problem is one of understatement.
4. Accounts payable, where again the problem is one of understatement.

The above discussion of DUS provides an introduction to the topic. A number of details have to be added to these basic concepts before DUS can be useful in practice. Fortunately, the computer programs auditors use in practice build in these details. Entire textbooks have been written about DUS. For our purposes, we do not need to cover this topic in any more depth.

14.4   SAMPLING FROM THE POPULATION

The discussion in the last chapter and a half has covered calculations of the required sample size in various situations and interpretation of the sample results. However, the actual selection of the sample items has been glossed over. There are four basic methods that auditors use to select a sample of a given size from a population. Each of these methods is applicable to both attributes sampling and variables sampling.

Haphazard Sampling

Haphazard sampling is the judgemental selection by the auditor of the items to be audited. In many audit situations this approach is the simplest to apply because the auditor need only review the records and select the sample items immediately.

CONCEPT SUMMARY

Summary of Statistical Sampling Techniques

Sampling Technique	Principal Objective	Decision Inputs	Strong Points	Weak Points
Discovery Sampling	To determine whether the error rate in a population exceeds a given critical value. To discover a case of irregularity	1. Confidence level 2. Upper precision limit	Smallest sample size	Intolerant of any errors
Attributes Sampling	To determine whether the error rate in a population exceeds a given critical value	1. Confidence level 2. Upper precision limit 3. Expected error rate	Tolerant of some errors	May require large sample sizes
Sequential Attributes Sampling	To determine whether the error rate in a population exceeds a given critical value	1. Beta risk 2. Alpha Risk 3. Upper precision limit	Tolerant of small rates of errors	May require large sample sizes
Dollar-Unit Sampling	To test for overstatement of the book value of an account	1. Materiality 2. Confidence level (Beta risk)	1. Very efficient due to maximum stratification 2. Easy to use on manual records	1. Intolerant of numerous errors 2. Very conservative projections of errors

The auditor's hope is that the sample will be representative of the population. Unfortunately, it is virtually impossible for anyone to perform this task completely without bias. Because of past experience, the auditor will tend to select some types of items (such as large ones or those in a particular physical location) to a greater extent than he should.

As a result, an auditor *cannot* use haphazard sampling in any statistical applications. For some applications the ease of doing haphazard sampling can outweigh the theoretical advantages of superior, but harder to use, statistical sampling methods.

Block Sampling

Block sampling is the selection of an entire sequential group to be audited. Usually, auditors use block sampling primarily for tests of transactions details. Examples would include: (1) auditing every cash disbursement in July, or (2) auditing invoices 1101 to 1200.

Block sampling is easier to use than is haphazard sampling. However, if the auditor does not choose the blocks properly, there can be a bias. For example, a different clerk may have worked in July than worked in the other parts of the year. Thus, the error rate for that clerk may not be representative of the error rate for other clerks.

As in the case of haphazard sampling, block sampling is unsuitable for statistical sampling applications because of the risk of bias. For nonstatistical applications, however, auditors use it extensively because of its ease of use.

Systematic Sampling

Systematic sampling is the selection of every nth item in the population to be audited. The auditor accomplishes this by choosing a random starting point and then examining every nth item from that point. For example, if there are 100 items in the population, and the auditor wishes to examine 25 items, he can: (1) start at item 1 and examine items 1, 5, 9, . . . , 97; (2) start at item 2 and examine items 2, 6, 10, . . . , 98; (3) start at item 3 and examine items 3, 7, 11, . . . , 99; or (4) start at item 4 and examine items 4, 8, 12, . . . , 100.

The critical factor in systematic sampling is ensuring that no periodic or cyclic pattern exists in the population related to the characteristic being measured or tested. If such a pattern exists, it may bias the results of the sample. As an extreme example, if there is a separate population item for every day of the year, and the auditor examines every 7th item, he will examine only one day of the week (e.g., only Monday's sales). Before using systematic sampling, the auditor should try to determine the order of the items in the population to be sampled.

In practice, the threat of bias in systematic sampling is relatively slight. As a result, CPA firms often use systematic sampling in both statistical and nonstatistical applications.

Random Sampling

Random sampling is the use of random numbers to choose the items to be audited, thus ensuring that every population item has an equal chance of being selected. The auditor gets these random numbers from either: (1) a random number table, or (2) a computer program that generates random numbers.

Exhibit 14–5 provides an example of a random number table. The auditor would use the computer output in a similar way.

Random sampling using a random number consists of the following steps:

1. Establish a correspondence between the random numbers and the population items (e.g., by invoice or check numbers).
2. Select a random starting point somewhere in the table.
3. Follow the random numbers sequentially from the starting point, and select as sample items those items (e.g., invoice numbers) corresponding to the random numbers.
4. Eliminate any duplicate numbers, and continue looking at the next number.

For example, suppose an auditor wished to draw a random sample from the population in Exhibit 13–1 using the random number table in Exhibit 14–5. This table has 80 columns and 20 rows.

The population items are numbered conveniently from 00 to 99. The auditor, therefore, needs only to look at two-digit numbers from the table. A random

EXHIBIT 14-5 Table of Random Numbers

10097	85017	84532	13618	23157	86952	02438	76520	91499	38631	79430	62421	97959	67422	69992	68479
37542	16719	82789	69041	05545	44109	05403	64894	80336	49172	16332	44670	35089	17691	89246	26940
08422	65842	27672	82186	14871	22115	86529	19645	44104	89232	57327	34679	62235	79655	81336	85157
99019	76875	20684	39187	38976	94324	43204	09376	12550	02844	15026	32439	58537	48274	81330	11100
12807	93640	39160	41453	97312	41548	93137	80157	63606	40387	65406	37920	08709	60623	02237	16505
66065	99478	70086	71265	11742	18226	29004	34072	61196	80240	44177	51171	08723	39323	05798	26457
31060	65119	26486	47353	43361	99436	42753	45571	15474	44910	99321	72173	56239	04595	10836	95270
85269	70322	21592	48233	93806	32584	21828	02051	94557	33663	86347	00926	44915	34823	51770	67897
63573	58133	41278	11697	49540	61777	67954	05325	42481	86430	19102	37420	41976	76559	24358	97344
73796	44655	81255	31133	36768	60452	38537	03529	23523	31379	68588	81675	15694	43438	36879	73208
98520	02295	13487	98662	07092	44673	61303	14905	04493	98086	32533	17767	14523	52494	24826	75246
11805	85035	54881	35587	43310	48897	48493	39808	00549	33185	04805	05431	94598	97654	16232	64051
83452	01197	86935	28021	61570	23350	65710	06288	35963	80951	68953	99634	81949	15307	00406	26898
88685	97907	19078	40646	31352	48625	44369	86507	59808	79752	02529	40200	73742	08391	49140	45427
99594	63268	96905	28797	57048	46359	74294	87517	46058	18633	99970	67348	49329	95236	32537	01390
65481	52841	59684	67411	09243	56092	84369	17468	32179	74029	74717	17674	90446	00597	45240	87379
80124	53722	71399	10916	07959	21225	13018	17727	69234	54178	10805	35635	45266	61406	41941	20117
74350	11434	51908	62171	93732	26958	02400	77402	19565	11664	77602	99817	28573	41430	96382	01758
69916	62375	99292	21177	72721	66995	07289	66252	45155	48324	32135	26803	16213	14938	71961	19476
09893	28337	20923	87929	61020	62841	31374	14225	94864	69074	45753	20505	78317	31994	98145	36168

starting point is chosen, say column 16, row 7. The number is 4, and the two-digit number starting there is 47. Thus, the first sample item is item 47. Reading across the row, the entire sample would then be:

Sample Item #	Random Number	Sample Item #	Random Number	Sample Item #	Random Number
1	47	10	53	19	93
2	35	11	45	20	21
3	34	12	57	21	72
4	33	13	11	22	17
5	61	14	54	duplicate	35
6	99	15	74	23	62
7	43	16	44	24	39
8	64	17	91	25	04
9	27	18	09		

Dollar-Unit Sampling

Suppose an auditor had determined the sampling interval for a dollar-unit sample. To select the sample the auditor would follow these steps:

1. Eliminate all items of the opposite sign (e.g., credits in all asset accounts).
2. Pick a random number from zero to the sampling interval.
3. Subtract this number from zero to start the accumulating process.
4. Add the dollars of each physical unit in the population one at a time until you get a nonnegative number. The physical unit that causes this will be the first item selected. (Zero is nonnegative.)
5. Subtract the sampling interval from the nonnegative accumulated total.
6. Test the new total to make sure it is negative. If not, subtract the sampling interval again. This situation will happen when the physical unit selected has two or more hooks. Keep repeating Step 6 until you have a negative number. Then go to Step 4. Continue selecting items using Steps 4 to 6 until the population is exhausted.

Exhibit 14–6 provides a flowchart of this sampling procedure.

Example

Suppose the sampling interval (SI) was $50,000 and the population was:

A	$20,000	D	$16,000
B	$44,000	E	$105,000
C	$12,000	F	$15,000

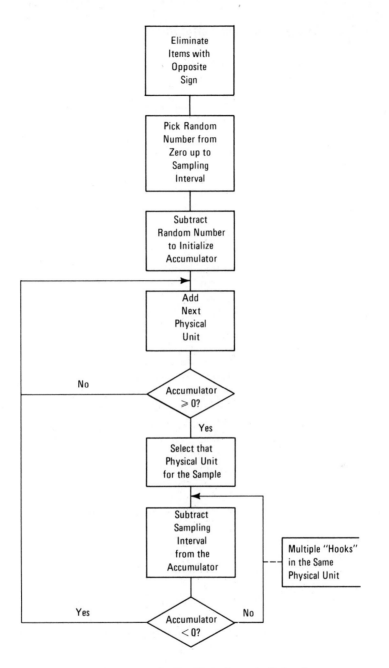

EXHIBIT 14–6   Dollar-Unit Sample Selection

The sampling procedure is:

Step 1.   No credits are present

Step 2.   27,000 (a random number between 0 and SI; it could be
          drawn from a random number table).

Step 3. $0 - 27,000 = -27,000$

Step 4.   −   27,000
          +   20,000   Item A
          ─────────────
          −   7,000
Step 4.   +   44,000   Item B
          ─────────────
              37,000   Nonnegative, B is the first sample item
Step 5.   −   50,000
Step 6.   −   13,000
Step 4.   +   12,000   Item C
          ─────────────
          −   1,000
Step 4.   +   16,000   Item D
          ─────────────
              15,000   Nonnegative, D is the second sample item
Step 5.   −   50,000
Step 6.   −   35,000
Step 4.   + 105,000   Item E
          ─────────────
              70,000   Nonnegative, E is the third sample item
Step 5.   −   50,000
Step 6.   20,000   Nonnegative, so item E has multiple hooks
Step 5.   −   50,000
Step 6.   −   30,000
Step 4.   +   15,000   Item F
          ─────────────
          −   15,000

After adding through every item, the auditor would determine that the sample contains items B, D, and E.

14.5 AUDIT OBJECTIVES AND AUDIT RISKS

The SEC requires all firms registered with it to have an annual audit by a CPA firm and most banks require certified financial statements before lending money to a prospective borrower. It is important always to keep in mind why these requirements exist:

> The overall objective of the attest function is to improve the credibility, and therefore the usefulness, of financial statements by ensuring their material accuracy and the adequacy of disclosure.

This audit objective is the same regardless of whether the auditor uses non-statistical or statistical sampling. Nonstatistical and statistical sampling are simply

CONCEPT SUMMARY

Summary of Sampling Methods

Sampling Method	Description	Application	Weaknesses	Strengths
Haphazard Sampling	Auditor judgementally selects items to be audited	Nonstatistical sampling	May unintentionally bias results; may slight or ignore hard-to-audit items	Easy to use; auditor can concentrate in areas where he feels there are problems
Block Sampling	Auditor chooses one or more groups of population items and then audits every item in those groups	Nonstatistical sampling	May unintentionally bias results; may not be representative	Sample items will be easy to find; easy to use
Systematic Sampling	Auditor chooses a random starting point and then selects every nth item to be audited	Nonstatistical and Statistical sampling	May fall into a pattern or cycle in the population	Usually easy to physically access every nth item
Random Sampling	Auditor makes a correspondence between random numbers and the population items; the random numbers then identify the items to be audited	Statistical sampling	Sometimes difficult to relate random numbers to the physical items	Guaranteed randomness of sample; permits statistical evaluation of results
Dollar-Unit Sampling	Auditor chooses a random starting point and then selects every nth dollar to be audited	Statistical sampling	Only applicable for dollar-unit sampling	Probability of selection is proportional to the item's dollar value

alternative ways to implement audit tests, which accomplish the objective above. The audit objective is never a function of the audit techniques that the auditor uses.

Sampling vs. Nonsampling Error

When the auditor samples the items in a population, there are two basic types of error possible:

1. *Sampling error.* This error arises because no sample is ever going to be perfectly representative of the population. As a result, the projection of sample results to the entire population will always cause a certain amount of error.

2. *Nonsampling error.* This error arises because people make mistakes, devise faulty sampling plans, and do not follow procedures exactly as they should. As a result, the human factor will always cause a certain amount of error.

There is a tradeoff between sampling and nonsampling error. As the sample size increases, the sample becomes more representative of the population, and the sampling error decreases. But, as the sample size increases, there are more audit procedures to follow, and the nonsampling error increases. In addition, as the sample size increases, the cost of audit procedures increases. The auditor's choice of sample size is, therefore, never an easy decision.

Judgemental vs. Statistical Sampling

Nonstatistical sampling is usually called *judgemental sampling*. As the name implies, this approach relies heavily on the judgement of the auditor for the determination of sample size and the evaluation of the sample results. The auditor develops this judgement over years of auditing similar firms or even the same firm. The judgement of auditors is often quite good.

However, studies show that for a given factual situation, two equally experienced auditors can (and do) come up with widely different sample sizes. Sample size for one auditor can sometimes be more than 10 times as large as the sample size for another auditor. These sample size differences are unexplained by the facts of the situation—they result solely from differing judgement.

The Difference Statistical Sampling Makes

The advantage of statistical sampling is that it can both measure and control sampling error. It also provides a more defensible procedure in the case of a lawsuit. The major effects of statistical sampling are that it:

1. Requires the auditor to specify materiality and the levels of risk he is willing to take.
2. Provides a way to relate explicitly the reliance on internal controls to the required amount of audit testing.
3. Tells the auditor how much to audit (i.e., the required sample size) given the specified materiality, risk levels, and reliance on internal control.
4. Permits a quantification of the risks the auditor takes.

Statistical sampling is a formidable tool and every auditor should be familiar with its basic concepts. Specifically, an auditor should consider the use of statistical sampling whenever he must form an audit conclusion about an entire population by examining only a part of it.

Sample Design

Statistical sampling is just a tool that must be used properly to be effective. Without the proper design, the results of the audit may provide no valid statistical conclusion, even if it is done properly. Therefore, the single most important step for the auditor is to create the proper sample design. This step requires audit judge-

EXHIBIT 14-7   Sample Design Considerations

1. Is the objective of the audit test:
   a. compliance testing of the internal controls;
   b. substantive testing of the reasonableness of an account's book value; or
   c. estimating the value of an account, usually inventory?

2. Are the records computerized or manual?
3. Is it possible to define the items in the population in more than one way?
4. Are alternative procedures necessary? If so, how tedious are they? Should this affect the definition of an item in the population?
5. What errors are likely in the population?
6. Can problem areas in the population, if any, be segregated so they can be audited separately?
7. Will all errors have a direct impact on pretax income, or will their effect be reduced by collateral insurance or offsetting errors in other accounts?
8. Is the definition of an error consistent with the audit objectives?

ment, so an auditor must do it—he cannot get a statistician to do it for him. Exhibit 14–7 provides a summary of some of the basic considerations in sample design.

Audit Risks

The ultimate audit risk is the chance that the following four events will *all* occur:

1. A material error occurs

2. Internal controls fail to detect the error

3. Other audit procedures fail to detect the error

4. The statistical test fails to detect the error

Should these events take place, the auditor will issue an unqualified opinion on materially misleading financial statements.

The audit must make the auditor highly confident that there is no material error or, if there is one, that he will discover it. To the extent the auditor can depend on one source of reliance, he need not depend so heavily on another.

Internal Controls

The reliance factor (i.e., beta) for a particular statistical test is related to the risk that a material error might occur and stay undetected by the system of internal controls. This risk is inversely related to the quality of internal control. Good controls will help (1) prevent errors, and (2) detect those that do occur. When controls are good, the auditor's risk is lower, and he can test at a higher reliance factor (i.e., using a higher beta).

The auditor need evaluate only those specific controls he will rely on in setting beta. However, once he decides on those controls, the auditor must test them for compliance and effectiveness. On the other hand, there is no need for a compliance test when controls are undocumented because the auditor cannot rely on these controls.

Other Audit Procedures

The auditor must consider the nature and effectiveness of other audit procedures. There are basically two types:

1. Significantly effective tests, such as most detail tests. These would have a high probability of detecting material errors.
2. Moderately effective tests, such as a well-designed analytical review. These would have a fair probability of detecting material errors.

When the auditor performs other detail audit procedures, or analytical review of ratios and trends, he can reduce his reliance on statistical tests.

If the auditor is relying on other audit procedures, he must carefully evaluate any unusual conditions that any of the tests reveal, regardless of the outcome of the remainder of the tests. The auditor cannot find an unusual condition in one test and then ignore it because the other tests fail to reveal it.

The Effect of Alpha and Beta

For every statistical test, the auditor must set the alpha and beta risk levels that he is willing to accept. In the absence of other factors, the auditor would want both risks to be as low as possible. However, the lower the risk levels are, the larger the sample size, and the greater the cost of the audit.

In many cases, the fee for an audit is fixed and is independent of the risks that the auditor takes. In these situations, the tradeoff is quite clear: the higher the risks, the greater the profitability of the audit. In other cases, the auditor is bidding for a job against other auditing firms and the bid is, at least in part, related to the estimated cost. Thus, in bidding situations, the tradeoff is again quite clear: the higher the risks, the greater the chance of getting the job.

For these reasons, the auditor will usually accept higher risks if he can justify them. Exhibit 14–8 provides a rough guide to the effect of these higher risks on the sample size. The table sets the base sample size of 100% for an alpha risk of .05 and a beta risk of .05, since classical statistics textbooks use those risks as standard.

Most firms now use an alpha risk of at least .10. Exhibit 14–8 shows that this decreases the sample size (and hence audit cost) significantly. Firms often accept an alpha risk of .20, giving a further reduction in sample size of nearly 20%. The

EXHIBIT 14-8   Relative Sample Sizes when Levels Vary

	Alpha Risk		
Beta Risk	.05	.10	.20
.05	100%	84%	66%
.10	81	66	50
.30	47	36	25
.50	29	21	13

rationale is that even if the statistical test incorrectly rejects the book value, the other audit procedures will compensate.

When the auditor can rely on internal control, a higher beta risk is justified. The effect of good internal control is easy to see; when internal control justifies a beta risk of .50, the sample size decreases by more than 70%.

Cumulative Effect of Risks

Ultimate risk is the combination of the risks that material errors will occur and further, will not be detected by the auditor. The first risk is reduced by internal control and the second by statistical and other audit tests. The risk of these adverse events occurring jointly can be viewed as the product of the individual risks and expressed as:

$$UR = (IC)\,(AR)\,(B)$$

Where: UR = Ultimate risk
IC = Risk of internal control failure
AR = Risk of other audit procedures failing
B = Risk of failing to detect a material error (beta)

Key Terms

attributes sampling
block sampling
discovery sampling
dollar-unit sampling (DUS)
evaluation table
haphazard sampling
nonsampling error
random number table

sample size table
sampling error
sampling interval (SI)
sequential attribute sampling
systematic sampling
upper precision limit (UPL)
variables sampling

Questions and Problems

Questions

14-1   Distinguish between variables sampling and attributes sampling. How are they related to the compliance testing and substantive testing of Chapters 5–10?

14-2   Give the five basic steps of discovery sampling. Calculate mentally the sample size necessary for a confidence level of 95% and an upper precision limit of 1%.

14-3   What is the major problem with discovery sampling? Describe attributes sampling, including how it solves the problem associated with discovery sampling.

14-4   Discuss the sample size table and the evaluation table for attributes sampling and show how they are related.

14-5   Explain the basic advantages and disadvantages of dollar-unit sampling as opposed to hypothesis testing. List three audit situations where dollar-unit sampling would be appropriate and three audit situations where it would be inappropriate.

14-6   Dollar-unit sampling makes the assumption that the maximum error for an item will not exceed its book value. Why should an auditor make sure this assumption is valid before using DUS?

14-7   Define the terms *haphazard sampling, block sampling, systematic sampling,* and *random sampling.* Describe the circumstances in which an auditor would be most likely to use each method.

14-8   DUS defines a dollar as the sampling unit. What would happen if the sampling unit were defined as $100 or 1¢? How would an auditor in England have to modify this method?

14-9   Explain the overall objective of the audit. Is it the same whether nonstatistical or statistical sampling is used? What is the distinguishing feature of statistical sampling?

14-10 Give the basic sources of audit risk. What is the ultimate audit risk? Is the beta risk more important to an auditor than the alpha risk? Why?

Multiple Choice Questions From Professional Examinations

14-11 Auditors often utilize sampling methods when performing tests of compliance. Which of the following sampling methods is most useful when testing for compliance?

a. Attributes sampling
b. Variable sampling
c. Unrestricted random sampling with replacement
d. Stratified random sampling

14-12 Which of the following sampling plans would be designed to estimate a numerical measurement of a population, such as a dollar value?

a. Numerical sampling
b. Discovery sampling
c. Sampling for attributes
d. Sampling for variables

14-13 An example of sampling for attributes would be estimating the

a. Quantity of specific inventory items.
b. Probability of losing a patent infringement case.
c. Percentage of overdue accounts receivable.
d. Dollar value of accounts receivable.

14-14 Which of the following best describes what the auditor means by the rate of occurrence in an attributes sampling plan?

a. The number of errors that can reasonably be expected to be found in a population.
b. The frequency with which a certain characteristic occurs within a population.
c. The degree of confidence that the sample is representative of the population.
d. The dollar range within which the true population total can be expected to fall.

14-15 When using statistical sampling for tests of compliance, an auditor's evaluation of compliance would include a statistical conclusion concerning whether

a. Procedural deviations in the population were within an acceptable range.
b. Monetary precision is in excess of a certain predetermined amount.
c. The population total is not in error by more than a fixed amount.
d. Population characteristics occur at least once in the population.

14-16 Statistical sampling generally may be applied to test compliance with internal accounting control when the client's internal accounting control procedures

a. Depend primarily on appropriate segregation of duties.

b. Are carefully reduced to writing and are included in client accounting manuals.

c. Leave an audit trail in the form of documentary evidence of compliance.

d. Enable the detection of material irregularities in the accounting records.

14-17 As the specified reliability is increased in a discovery sampling plan for any given population and maximum occurrence rate, the required sample size

a. Increases

b. Decreases

c. Remains the same

d. Cannot be determined

14-18 A formula for determining the reliability level for substantive tests (S) based upon the reliance assigned to internal accounting control and other relevant factors (C) and the combined reliability level desired from both internal control and the substantive tests (R) is:

a. $S = 1 - \dfrac{C}{R}$

b. $S = R - C$

c. $S = 1 - \dfrac{1 - R}{1 - C}$

d. $S = R - \dfrac{1}{C}$

14-19 If all other factors specified in a sampling plan remain constant, changing the specified precision from 8% to 12% would cause the required sample size to

a. Increase

b. Remain the same

c. Decrease

d. Become indeterminate

14-20 If all other factors specified in a sampling plan remain constant, changing the estimated occurrence rate from 2% to 4% would cause the required sample size to

a. Increase

b. Remain the same

c. Decrease

d. Become indeterminate

14-21 In the evaluation of the results of a sample of a specified reliability and precision, the fact that the occurrence rate in the sample was the same as the estimated occurrence rate would cause the reliability of the sample estimate to

   a. Increase

   b. Remain the same

   c. Decrease

   d. Become indeterminate

14-22 For a large population of cash disbursement transactions, Smith, CPA, is testing compliance with internal control by using attribute-sampling techniques. Anticipating an occurrence rate of 3%, Smith found from a table that the required sample size is 400 with a desired upper precision limit of 5% and reliability of 95%. If Smith anticipated an occurrence rate of only 2% but wanted to maintain the same desired upper precision limit and reliability, the sample size would be closest to

   a. 200

   b. 400

   c. 533

   d. 800

14-23 A CPA's test of accuracy of inventory counts involves two storehouses. Storehouse A contains 10,000 inventory items, and Storehouse B contains 5,000 items. The CPA plans to use sampling without replacement to test for an estimated 5% error rate. If the CPA's sampling plan calls for a specified reliability of 95% and a maximum tolerable error occurrence rate of 7.5% for both storehouses, the ratio of the size of the CPA's sample from Storehouse A to the size of the sample from Storehouse B should be

   a. More than 1:1 but less than 2:1

   b. 2:1

   c. 1:1

   d. More than .5:1 but less than 1:1

14-24 Which of the following is an advantage of systematic sampling over random number sampling?

   a. It provides a stronger basis for statistical conclusions.

   b. It enables the auditor to use the more efficient "sampling with replacement" tables.

   c. There may be correlation between the location of items in the population, the feature of sampling interest, and sampling interval.

   d. It does not require establishment of correspondence between random numbers and items in the population.

14-25 To satisfy the auditing standard to make a proper study and evaluation of internal control, Harvey Jones, CPA, uses statistical sampling to test compliance with internal control procedures. Why does Jones use this statistical sampling technique?

a. It provides a means of mathematically measuring the degree of reliability that results from examining only a part of the data.

b. It reduces the use of judgement required of Jones because the AICPA has established numerical criteria for this type of testing.

c. It increases Jones' knowledge of the client's prescribed procedures and their limitations.

d. It is specified by generally accepted auditing standards.

Problems

14-26 The use of statistical sampling techniques in an examination of financial statements does not eliminate judgemental decisions.

Required:

a. Identify and explain four areas where a CPA may exercise judgement in planning a statistical sampling test.

b. Assume that a CPA's sample shows an unacceptable error rate. Describe the various actions that he may take based upon this finding.

c. A nonstratified sample of 80 accounts payable vouchers is to be selected from a population of 3,200. The vouchers are numbered consecutively from 1 to 3,200 and are listed, 40 to a page, in the voucher register. Describe four different techniques for selecting a random sample of vouchers for review.

AICPA

14-27 For which of these populations should you consider applying dollar-unit sampling? Explain how you would deal with credit balances.

a. Payroll

b. Mortgage or commercial loan receivables

c. Credit card receivables

d. Accounts receivable (magazine subscriptions)

e. Inventory (small manufacturing company without a perpetual inventory system)

f. Fixed assets examination of a utility client

g. Trust assets

h. Claims paid by a state Medicare/Medicaid agency

i. Estimation of LIFO inventory for tax purposes

    j. Evaluating internal control

    k. Estimating revenues

    l. Construction in progress on major construction project

    m. Funds disbursed under a CETA grant

Courtesy of Peat, Marwick & Mitchell & Co.

14-28 a. You are reviewing a compliance test where 59 items were selected for testing. Only 35 were the type of transaction that required the attribute (initials) the audit team was testing. Can we consider the proper absence of initials compliance with the system?

    b. You are reviewing a sampling plan to test the operation of an internal control procedure for the entire year. The plan was designed to achieve a 95% confidence level and a 5% upper precision limit. The attribute sampling plan was drawn and executed, but no statistical conclusion was reached presumably because of a high error rate found in the sample (eight out of fifty-nine). After further investigation, you discover that:

1. All eight errors occurred in the first two months of the calendar year.

2. The person responsible for performing the control feature during that two-month period was terminated on March 1 and replaced by a more responsible individual.

What would you suggest to the audit team?

    c. Would your suggestion to (b) be different if the control procedure was only instituted on March 1?

Courtesy of Peat, Marwick, Mitchell & Co.

14-29 a. You are reviewing the results of an attribute sampling plan that was designed at a 95% confidence level and a 2% upper precision limit. When you initially approved the sampling plan, the audit team told you that 2% was used because of the significance of the control feature being tested to the audit and that substantive procedures were being significantly reduced. You notice, while reviewing the results, that two instances of noncompliance were discovered, and this comment was inserted in the working papers:

"Based on the results of our sample, we can be 95% confident that the true rate of noncompliance does not exceed 4.2%."

You also note the comment:

"The original sample was designed with a CL of 95% and UPL of 2%, so the sampling plan would be tolerant of two errors. The desired upper precision limit of 5% was therefore obtained for this test."

What action would you take, if any?

b. Assume the same situation as (a) above except that twelve compliance deviations were located, and this comment was included in the audit working papers:

"Based on the results of this test, there will be very little reliance placed on this internal control. However, because this control is not critical, no modification of the planned degree of substantive audit procedures will be done."

What action would you take in this situation, if any?

c. You are reviewing an attribute sampling plan that was designed to test the operation of an internal control procedure where the controller initials all journal entries, indicating his review and approval of the entry for propriety and correctness. The test was designed to achieve 95% confidence that the error rate of noncompliance does not exceed 5%. Fifty-nine sample items were reviewed, and the working papers indicate that proper approval was evidenced on all 59 journal entries. You note that substantive audit procedures were performed on each sample item designed to determine the propriety of the journal entry and that the test was labeled a dual-purpose test. The conclusion in the working papers stated:

"Based on the results of the sample, we are 95% confident that the error rate of noncompliance in the control feature and the rate of monetary error in the recording of journal entries does not exceed 5%. Also, based on the favorable results of this compliance test and the fact that our substantive procedures on these 59 sample items revealed no errors, no additional audit work is considered necessary in the journal entry area."

Do you agree with the conclusion? Why?

Courtesy of Peat, Marwick, Mitchell & Co.

14-30 a. Given the facts below, state in precise language the statistical interpretation that can be made. (Solve for the upper precision limit.)

Sample size = 100

Errors in sample = 0

Confidence level = 95%

b. You are selecting an attribute sample using a client's program. The basis is a systematic sample. What precautions would you take?

c. Which of these audit objectives are met by compliance tests:
   1. Labor distribution by project
   2. Expense classification
   3. Account distribution
   4. Correct posting

Courtesy of Peat, Marwick, Mitchell & Co.

14-31 I.M. Poor, Inc., is a shipbuilder with a contract to build six oil tankers for Black Gold Oil Company. A substantial cost overrun has resulted in a major contract dispute and labor negotiations. You have been asked to determine the validity of the total cost of $96 million in direct materials, direct labor, and overhead.

You and the parties involved agreed that you should report with 99% confidence and a precision of $500,000.

The client maintains a basic manual system, except for payroll (direct labor), where daily input is keypunched and maintained on tape. The following records are maintained:

1. Tanker material cost summary is an accumulation of all direct *material* costs from inception by contract number ($43,000,000).
2. Direct *labor* tapes are the total direct labor charges to each ship by contract number ($26,000,000).
3. *Overhead* control is represented by general ledger cards for each account. The general ledger cards itemize the vendor's invoice and journal entries ($27,000,000).

Required:

a. The anticipated error rate in the population is thought to be very small (e.g., .2%). What sampling strategy would you suggest? Why?

b. What would be your population(s) for a dollar-unit sample? What physical sampling unit would you use for each of the three cost categories?

c. Assume a manually applied dollar-unit sampling plan is implemented on overhead costs.
   1. How do you propose to deal with small credits in overhead cost representing adjustments to previously entered assets?
   2. In reviewing the adding machine tapes of overhead cost, you discover that an audit assistant entered a page total of $169,000 in the machine as $196,000. What effect does this have on your dollar-unit sample? What would you do?
   3. Your sampling interval is $40,000, the random starting point is $10,000, and the sampling unit is the invoice. These entries are on the client records:

Overhead control entries (monthly postings)

Entry	Amount
1	$ 1,353.65
2	86,792.32
3	4,210.32
4	1,042.21

Invoice #	Amount
1	$ 1,353.65
65	6,792.32
94	20,000.00
103	46,000.00
641	14,000.00
	$86,792.32
400	1,850.03
760	4.00
761	2,356.29
	$ 4,210.32
800	$ 1,042.21

Compute which entries and which invoices would be selected for testing.

d. If you discovered that the client's detail records did not agree with the general ledger control account, what effect would this have on your sampling plan?

14-32 Design a statistical sampling plan for each of the following situations:

a. As auditor of a distillery, you are planning the audit approach to verify the company's inventory of 53,000 casks of whisky in the three warehouses. The company's computerized inventory file gives the value and exact location (warehouse, area, rack, and number) of each cask. The dollar values of each cask are virtually identical.

b. Your client imports the spare parts for its automobiles in sealed containers from its parent company. The containers remain unopened until the contents are needed, and then the container is completely emptied and the contents taken to the spare parts storage area. At year-end, the total inventory is:

- 2,000 unopened containers
- 4,000 bins, each with unique parts, in the spare parts storage area.

You need to audit the 2,000 unopened containers for which you have only the parent company's invoice. You ask that the company physically count the contents of all 2,000 containers, but both management and the storekeepers object.

c. Your client keeps a manual accounts receivable file with about 150 customers. Five of the accounts make up 60% of the total account balance. The system of internal control is excellent, and no errors are expected. In fact, no errors have occurred through the confirmation procedure for the past five audits.

d. An insurance company's history file of paid claims has a five-year moving average of paid claims and is being used to estimate the claims reserve. The history file of paid claims has been audited on a continuous annual basis by your firm. The calendar year audit has just been completed, and your firm has been engaged to give a limited review of quarterly financial information beginning March 31. The engagement supervisor calls you to ask if a statistical sampling plan can be designed for the year-end audit that will test the paid claims by quarters. Due to the excellent system of internal control, errors are not expected.

Courtesy of Peat, Marwick, Mitchell & Co.

14-33 Assume you are auditing the inventory population given in Exhibit 13–1 and depicted in Exhibit 13–2. You are using random sampling with numbers coming from a random number table. Use the same sequence of random numbers as that given in Section 14.4 for each aspect of the problem.

Assume that the following inventory items, whatever their book values, are in fact worthless. In other words, their audit value is 0:

Item #	Item #	Item #	Item #
15	32	60	79
17	34	67	83
21	37	68	84
23	44	73	91
31	56	77	96

All other book values are correct.

Required:

a. Use an unstratified random sample of 25 items to estimate both the book value of the population and the audit value of the population by mean per unit estimation.

b. For both the estimate of the book value and the estimate of the audit value determined in (a), calculate the standard error of the estimate.

c. Use stratification to estimate both the book value and the audit value of the population by mean per unit estimation. Divide the inventory population into two strata: those items under $500 and those items over $500. Take a random sample of 15 items from the first stratum, and examine all items in the second stratum.

d. For both the estimate of the book value and the estimate of the audit value determined in (c), calculate the standard error of the estimate.

Courtesy of Peat, Marwick, Mitchell & Co.

14-34 Assume the same facts given in Problem 14-33.

Required:

a. Use the unstratified random sample of 25 items in 14–33(a) to estimate the audit value of the population by ratio estimation.

b. Use stratification to estimate the audit value of the population by ratio estimation. Divide the inventory population into two strata: those items under $500 and those items over $500. Take a random sample of 15 items from the first stratum, and examine all items in the second stratum. These will be the same items used in 14–33(c).

c. Use the samples from (a) and (b) to estimate the audit value of the population by difference estimation in both the unstratified and the stratified case.

Courtesy of Peat, Marwick, Mitchell & Co.

14-35 Assume the same facts given in Problem 14-33.

Required:

a. Use dollar-unit sampling to estimate the audit value of the population. Begin with a "random" start of ⟨260⟩ and use a sampling interval of $800.

b. Calculate the upper precision limit at 95% confidence and draw the appropriate statistical conclusion about the book value.

Courtesy of Peat, Marwick, Mitchell & Co.

15

Internal control in a computer environment

Chapters 6 through 10 went into the details of auditing specific manual systems. These chapters only discussed manual systems in order to concentrate on the auditing issues involved. However, increasingly firms are using one or more computers to assist in accounting. The use of the computer will alter: (1) the methods and techniques necessary to implement the elements of internal control, (2) compliance testing, and (3) substantive testing.

This chapter will discuss the nature of internal control in a computer environment and the related compliance testing needed. Chapter 16 will describe the necessary substantive testing for both batch and on-line computer systems.

15.1 BASIC COMPUTER CONCEPTS

Both the auditor's view of the computer and his relation to it have undergone steady, massive changes in the last 20 years. When computers were first used in business, they processed essentially stand-alone applications. The auditor could, at that point, view the machine as a relatively straightforward (though extremely fast) adding and filing machine. As a result, the auditor did not need to understand the computer. Substantive testing could verify account balances generated by the computer just as in manual systems. If necessary, it was a simple, albeit time-consuming task, to manually check the computer's processing of some transactions to verify the computer's accuracy.

Through the late 1960s and early 1970s, however, computer systems became far more integrated. A single order-entry transaction could automatically affect shipping, inventory, customer, and general ledger systems and files. The computer had become an integral part of the accounting system, not just a clerical aid, and understanding the system necessarily involved understanding the computer.

The auditing profession responded to this changed environment by developing *SAS No. 3.* This standard authoritatively stated that, to understand the client's system and evaluate its internal controls properly, the auditor had to deal with the computer. In practice, this has not necessarily meant that the auditor has dealt with the computer and its internal control problems himself. Instead, he has relied on specialists, such as those on the accounting firm's consulting staff, to deal with the computer.

In the foreseeable future, the trend will be toward even greater integration of computer systems and even deeper involvement of the computer in the affairs and activities of business. As a result, reliance by the auditor on computer specialists will become increasingly untenable and unjustifiable. Even now, auditing the accounting system has come more and more to mean auditing the computer system. Because of the pervasiveness of computers in business systems, computer expertise will be required of *all* auditors in order to plan and conduct an audit properly.

Basic Computer Characteristics

The components of a computer system can be conveniently grouped into two major categories—hardware and software. *Hardware* refers to the machines that make up the system. *Software* refers to the entire set of instructions that directs and controls the activities of the hardware. Together these two elements make up a functioning computer system.

Hardware Components

It is possible to generalize about the required hardware components of any computer system. There must always be a hardware device(s) to accomplish each of the following functions:

1. *Input.* These devices receive the instructions to be performed by the computer and the data (numbers, names, symbols, and so on) on which these steps should be carried out. The primary input devices are card readers and terminals.

2. *Processing.* The processor, often called the central processing unit (CPU), actually carries out the instructions on the data provided. Since executing the desired instructions is the most important and difficult responsibility of any computer system, the processor is the most complex hardware unit.

3. *Storage.* Even in the simplest problem, some processing steps must be remembered by the computer so they can be performed repeatedly. Also, some basic data must be retained for the same purposes. Storage devices accomplish these functions. The primary storage devices are magnetic tapes and disks.

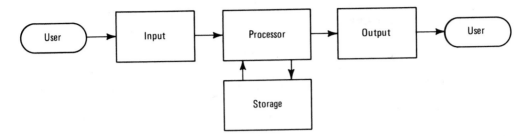

EXHIBIT 15–1   Basic Hardware Components

4. *Output.* These devices convey the results of the processing (in effect, the answer to the processing problem) to those who need to know these results. Processing solutions are received from the computer through these devices. The primary output devices are printers and terminals.

Exhibit 15–1 provides a schematic of these basic hardware components.

Software Components

It is slightly more difficult to generalize about the required software components of a computer system. However, there will always be at least the following software components:

1. A set of internally stored general instructions that control and coordinate the activities of the various hardware devices (input, processing, storage, and output). These instructions as a group are often called the *operating system* and are, generally speaking, supplied by the hardware vendor.

2. A set of specific instructions to the processing unit to perform certain actions on certain specific data and to provide the location of this relevant data. These instructions are called *application programs* because they do specific processing toward a desired result or solution. Application programs are generally thought of when programming or computer programs are discussed. These instructions may be written by the user or purchased from software vendors. These programs are more user-oriented than the operating system because they are designed to instruct a hardware system to accomplish some specific processing task desired by the user. These application programs are written in programming languages. Writing an application program is called programming the computer.

Relationship of Instructions to Computer Hardware— The Translation Process

System users have a processing need or problem and want to use computer hardware to fill the need or solve the problem. Humans would prefer to communicate the necessary steps to solve a problem in their own language (such as English), but computers only understand their own language, which is a series of "O's" and "1's" used in various combinations. For human-computer communication to take place, human language instructions must be translated into machine language instructions to be carried out by the hardware. This translation process involves three steps.

1. The use of a programming language rather than a natural language is the first step in the translation process. All natural languages contain ambiguities that require inference and contextual translation, so it would be impossible for a machine to translate in an exact manner. Programming languages require humans to issue instructions in a precise format using commands, syntax, and structure in a rigidly fixed manner. An application program written in a programming language is called a *source program,* and the language is often called a *source language.*

2. Even programming languages, however, are not understood by computers, so they must undergo a translation into machine language. The rigid syntax and structure of programming languages are translated by a special software component called a *compiler,* which is part of the operating system.

3. The original set of instructions translated into machine language is called the *object program.* It is the object program that is understood by the CPU. The processor interprets each machine language instruction and issues directions to the other hardware components of the system to carry out the processing.

Fundamental Advantages/Basic Requirements of Computer System Design

There are three distinct advantages a computer system has over other processing alternatives:

1. *Computer system hardware (particularly the CPU) is very fast.* Extraordinary speeds are commonplace for all these devices. In the speed of calculations, decisions, and input and output, no processing alternative can match a computer system.

2. *Computer systems possess incredible memory.* Storage devices and the processing unit are able to keep extremely large amounts of data accessible in very small spaces without forgetting any of it.

3. *Computer hardware does exactly what it is told to do.* Since instructions are always followed without deviation and without complaint, computer systems do not make mistakes in their own right. On the other hand, hardware devices must be given instructions in minute detail, will do everything they are told to do (no matter how silly it may seem), and apply no perception, reasoning, initiative or common sense to their activities.

To be effective and efficient, all business processing systems must be able to:

1. *Generate large amounts of data.* All businesses create significant amounts of data in the course of their operations. There is a definite need (sometimes legal) for this information about business activities to be processed accurately. In addition, some of these data must be retained for long periods of time, while other data must be digested into some form of useable output (statements and reports).

2. *Process simple, repetitive events.* Although businesses may engage in all sorts of different events, they experience the same common transactions repeatedly. Business processing time is mostly spent on a few (perhaps a dozen or so) basic events, and the calculations and decisions required to process these events are very simple.

Computer systems are made up of a set of components that are extremely fast, possess an excellent memory, and follow instructions perfectly but which have no imagination or initiative. In business processing, problems require the simple, fast, and accurate processing of very large amounts of repetitive data, so computer systems could not be better suited to the needs of business.

Internal Control Advantages

The introduction of the computer eliminates some major internal control concerns associated with manual systems.

Accuracy

The computer is immeasurably more accurate than any person performing the same calculations. Unlike the human clerk, the computer will not extend invoices incorrectly or foot journals improperly. In addition, the computer will not accept a journal entry that does not balance or post an entry to the wrong account.

Consistency

Once the computer is programmed, it will be consistent in its treatment of transactions. For example, if the program instructs the computer to check the customer's credit limit before a sale, the computer will always consistently check the credit limit.

Motivation

The computer will not have any dishonest or disloyal motivations, since the machine cannot profit from any misstatement. The employee, however, may place his own interests before those of the company.

15.2 INTERNAL CONTROL PROBLEMS AND THEIR SOLUTIONS

Along with these internal control benefits, however, there are a number of internal control problems inherent in computer use. For ease in comprehension, this section presents these problems using the same structure as Exhibit 15–1: input, processing, storage, and output.

Input and Its Preparation

Source Documents are Eliminated

In a manual accounting system, a journal entry is made from a source document, and it ties to that source document. As a result, the audit trail can always go back from the journal to the original document, evidencing the original transaction authorization. In a computer-based system, a terminal operator often makes an entry directly into the computer using the terminal, without a source document. An example would be order entry where an order is received over the phone and entered directly into the system. Another, more familiar, example would be the airline reservation desk, where the operator receives phone calls and makes reservations without a source document.

The problem is, then, that there is no source document to indicate proper authorization, and the audit trail can be lost. The solution to this problem has two aspects. The first is physical control over the terminals so that only those who are properly authorized have access to the terminals. This will ensure that only those who are authorized to initiate transactions in fact initiate them. The second is to tie each transaction back to the operator, terminal, and time where it was initiated. This process will assign responsibility and provide a check on the authorization of transactions.

Sophisticated Tampering Can Cause Unauthorized Actions

A standard approach to data processing is to devise internal controls over the entry of data to the computer system. Then, when the information is in the computer, the assumption is made that the transaction has been authorized. Note that, if someone can surreptitiously enter information into the system by bypassing the various controls, these transactions become, in effect, "authorized." For example, a California man became very familiar with the system of Pacific Telephone. He used the telephone to place orders in excess of $100,000. The company delivered the goods to various sites where he picked them up and resold them. Another example was the programmer who was angered at being fired and added himself to the pension rolls.

In order to combat this problem, the system must ensure that proper authorization is required for all transactions. Additionally, the system must allow the check of all authorizations—another example of the importance of a proper audit trail. If a proper audit trail exists and if an improper transaction is checked, the tampering will come to light. However, if there is no adequate audit trail, an unauthorized transaction will only be discovered by accident or by confession (which is, in fact, how most sophisticated problems are discovered).

There are New Sources and Potentials for Error

A user of a program is generally not intimately familiar with it and will often put in erroneous data or respond incorrectly. All programs should be written assuming that the user will try to use the wrong disk or tape and that all data are very possibly incorrect. Some people frankly enjoy getting the computer to make mistakes. Others will simply make mistakes through inexperience or inadvertence. The computer programs must contain extensive edit checks to detect and help correct errors.

Processing

The Machine Lacks Judgement

Everyone has probably heard stories about computer systems that wrote payroll checks for $20,000 instead of $200 or which sent a truckload of magazines to a startled subscriber. In a manual system, the employees will not do something completely ridiculous; they will realize that something is wrong. The machine, on the other hand, exercises no judgement and will do strange things if told to do them.

However, even though the machine lacks judgement, the computer system can exercise judgement by having it built into the programs. The programs should constantly test the data they are manipulating, always checking to see if the amounts are reasonable or within established limits. For example, when processing hours worked for a payroll system, the program should flag or somehow point out any people being paid for more than, say, 68 hours per week.

Similarly, the program should not process transactions outside of authorized limits. For example, in an accounts receivable system each customer is given a credit limit. The program could check all prospective sales to determine if they are in excess of credit limits; if a sale exceeded the limit, it would be rejected. This check has two purposes: to see that a customer does not buy more on credit than he can pay and to ensure that no unreasonably large sale is processed.

Duties Are Concentrated Within the Computer

The separation of duties is absolutely critical for effective internal control. As a particular example, the duty of journalizing transactions should be separate from the duty of posting the transaction to the ledger accounts. However, in a computer-based system, both of these duties (along with many others) are done by the computer. As an additional example, in a payroll system a computer might keep payroll and personnel records, make the labor distribution, and prepare the paychecks.

In and of themselves, these facts are no particular cause for alarm. Unlike the human employee, the computer cannot divert funds or assets to itself. (Computers with a will of their own, like HAL in *2001, A Space Odyssey*, are purely science fiction and will remain so.) The problem is that, although the computer will not abuse its function, others can.

If a person has unauthorized control of the computer, the standard protection of separated duties will no longer be effective. Examples of this sort of problem abound in computing. In one instance, a programmer modified a bank program that printed out a list of overdrawn accounts; he had the program simply omit his account from the list. He was able to overdraw his account without being detected and was only caught when a machine breakdown required that the list be prepared manually. Another instance involved a programmer who instructed the computer to prepare several paychecks for him. He was caught when other employees noticed the checks piling up on his desk while he was on vacation.

The general solution to this problem is the separation of knowledge and access. Those with knowledge of how the system works (such as programmers) should not have access to the computer. Those with access to the computer (such as operators) should not learn how the system works.

Great Speed Extends One Person's Capabilities

One protective element in manual systems is human limitation; one person is only capable of doing so much. One person can alter only so many checks or change only so many records. With the use of the computer, this limitation no longer exists.

An example of this problem is the computation of interest by banks. When the bank computes the appropriate interest to credit the accounts of its depositors, the computation is made to only a fixed, limited number of decimal places. Thus, there is a small difference between the interest an individual actually receives and the exact interest. The difference is always in the bank's favor. Although it is only a small amount in any individual case, with tens of thousands of depositors, the amount becomes significant in total.

Programmers have taken advantage of this situation and have modified the interest calculation program to credit the difference to their own account. The programmer would then be able to withdraw large sums from that account. Notice the difficulty of detecting this technique; the accounts all balance, and nobody is in a position to detect the irregularity. To protect against this type of problem, the system must provide for: (a) review of all programs by a supervisor, and (b) physical protection of programs from unauthorized modification.

There Are New Sources and Potentials for Error

Manual systems have numerous potentials for error, such as incorrect calculations and mispostings. With computer-based systems, the potentials for error are generally reduced. However, new and different sources and potentials for error are created. There are basically three of these.

First, and generally least important, are vendor-supplied errors. These errors include faulty hardware or errors in the system software, such as operating systems and compilers. These errors are usually quickly apparent and are corrected by the vendor.

Second are errors in application programs. A satellite launch went out of control and had to be destroyed (at a cost of many millions of dollars) because a programmer omitted a minus sign from the control program. When the computer makes a major mistake, there is generally an error in an application program.

The solution to these two problems is extensive and effective testing of programs prior to their use in production. Unfortunately, this is easier to say than do because of the insidious nature of many errors; they often do not become apparent until weeks, months, or even years have gone by.

The third source of error is poor design in either the program or the system. A standard problem in a computer-based system is excessive rigidity in the system; it is too difficult or impossible to handle special circumstances or situations. There have been many articles in newspapers and magazines about people's problems with computerized billing. People receive a bill with an error and fight for months with the system, all the while receiving increasingly abusive letters concerning nonpayment.

The solution is proper system design in the first place; the system should be designed to handle unusual situations and circumstances.

Storage

Records and the Audit Trail Are Invisible

Some writers say that, with a computer system, the audit trail vanishes. This is misleading because, even though it is not possible to see the audit trail, it does exist but in machine-readable form. This invisibility of records and the audit trail means that checking accuracy, cross-checking, and the analysis of support for figures on financial statements are made more difficult. The checking and analysis cannot be done manually; it must be done utilizing the computer. Consequently, the system has to be designed to incorporate the data for all necessary analysis.

Information Can Be Changed Without Physical Traces

One of the great protections of manual systems is that the records are in ink. If someone tries to change any information, the erasures and smudge marks will make it immediately apparent. If someone removes a page, the page numbering will point this up. If someone replaces a page with a new one appropriately doctored, the different tint of the new paper will show up.

There is no similar protection for computer records; electronic information can be changed without a trace. There was a case where a programmer reduced individual credits to various revenue accounts by mere fractions of dollars. The total sum was considerable, however. To keep the system in balance, the programmer withdrew large amounts of cash. The reduction of individual credits simply could not have been done with manual records.

Viewed in another light, this capability of altering records without a trace is a tremendous advantage, since it allows the same storage media to be used over and over again. However, from an internal control viewpoint, this computer capability is a headache.

Another serious problem is the possibility of changing programs. If done properly, a program becomes operational and is used on a regular, production basis only after it has been approved, reviewed, and tested. A sophisticated embezzler could get around this by either modifying the production program directly or replacing it with a new version.

Protection against the problem of change without traces is difficult but most attempts proceed on two fronts: (1) physical controls to reduce access to the computer (in order to prevent manipulation), and (2) cross checks to make sure that all data file changes are backed up by properly authorized transactions.

Concentrated Information Is Easier to Steal

Manual records are often so bulky that stealing them would present serious logistical problems in just moving the vast quantity of material. In addition, the loss of vast records would be immediately apparent. This same problem no longer exists with computer-readable information, vast quantities of information are stored in a small volume and can easily be copied or physically stolen.

In one recent example, investigators of the General Accounting Office (the investigative arm of the United States Congress) walked out of the Social Security System's national computer complex with a cart. The cart alone contained names, addresses, and other information on more than one million beneficiaries. In another example, an insurance company that sold insurance policies by mail spent a great deal of time accumulating names and addresses for a mail solicitation. The mailing failed because a company vice-president stole the names and addresses by copying various computer tapes. He then sold the tapes to a rival firm, which made an earlier mailing.

The solution to this problem is good physical controls over records in electronic form. Only authorized people should have access to the records, and an audit trail should be available to determine who used what, when. The life insurance firm finally uncovered the vice-president's scheme through a tape librarian, who had recorded his withdrawal of certain tapes on a specific date.

Electronic Information Is Easy to Lose

In a manual system, the records are written in ink on substantial paper. The only way to lose the information is to lose the physical records or to have them burn up in a fire. Information written down is essentially permanent.

The situation is completely different with electronic information. As discussed earlier, the information on the computer can be easily changed, leaving no trace of the earlier content. This change often happens inadvertently, and huge amounts of information can be quickly lost.

An example of this problem occurred during a fund-raising campaign. The pledges were recorded on a computer tape as they were phoned in; the names, addresses, and amounts were kept to later collect the money. The information on that tape was accidentally wiped out, so a great deal of money was never collected. The international CPA firm in charge of the system paid several million dollars to the charity to cover the loss.

A somewhat different situation occurred outside of Denver, Colorado where one system kept crashing (i.e., it would stop working in a spectacular fashion) and losing information on the disk. It turned out that, for over a year, one of the operators was shortcircuiting the computer and causing these crashes deliberately. When the police asked him why he did it, he said he had an "uncontrollable urge."

Since electronic information can be lost so quickly and easily it is essential to provide backup capabilities for all data.

Output and Its Use

The User is in Awe of the Computer

The earlier discussions of internal control stressed the importance of outside checks on the system's accuracy. For example, statements of account sent to customers are relied upon to check that the accounting records are correct. It is not uncommon, however, to neglect checking the computer and to simply assume that it is correct.

One computer thief took advantage of that attitude by modifying the payroll deductions for the employees at his firm. He reduced everyone else's deductions by a small amount in each case and added the total amount (large) to his deductions. Thus, the system was completely in balance, but he was going to get an extra-large refund from the IRS at the expense of the other employees. He was caught when a janitor happened to add up his own weekly paychecks for the year and noticed the discrepancy between his totals and the amounts on his W-2 form.

However, very few people add up the totals from their paychecks, completely check their bank statement, or completely check their credit card bill (comparing it to a file of receipts). A similar problem occurs within companies, where the user departments often do not check the output of the computer.

The general solution is to try to provide control totals and other information to user departments to help them check the computer output. It may even be necessary to require active checks by users of the system output rather than simply assume that, if no one complains, it must be all right.

Vast Capabilities Can Create a Different Reality

After a point, the information stored in the computer no longer reflects reality, it becomes the reality. Originally, the computer record simply reflected the operations of the firm. In extremely sophisticated applications, however, the computer record is the operations of the firm. For example, a bank balance is the electronic information stored in the bank's computer; in the life insurance business, an individual policy is essentially the information stored on the computer.

The management at Equity Funding took the final step and created life insurance policies without policyholders. There are two basic questions to explain: (a) why the company would do such a thing, and (b) how the company could get away with it for so many years.

The company created the policies because there is an established reinsurance market where policies can be sold for cash to reinsurers by the primary insurance company. The company could get away with it because of bad auditing procedures. The procedures are somewhat understandable when you consider that a policy is essentially a liability for the insurance company (because of the payout required), and companies rarely overstate liabilities. However, whenever the auditors requested backup evidence on a created policy, the Equity Funding personnel simply claimed difficulty in finding the records and then made up any necessary documents that night.

In any case, with the help of their computers, the management of Equity Funding was able to create a different reality, one that only existed on their computers. The solution to problems of this scale is effective testing of account balances. The amounts in the account balance have to be constantly checked to determine if the computer system (even if it is internally consistent) is consistent with the world outside of the computer center.

CONCEPT SUMMARY

Internal Control Problems Specific To Computer Systems

	Control Problem	*Typical Result*	*General Solution*
Input and Its Preparation	Source documents are eliminated	Loss of audit trail	Physical control on access to terminals
	Sophisticated tampering can cause unauthorized actions	Add name to pension rolls when fired	Ensure proper authorization
	There are new sources and potentials for error	Input incorrect data into the system	Extensive program edit checks
Processing	The machine lacks judgement	Spectacular errors	Build in judgement with reasonableness tests
	Duties are concentrated within the computer	Person in charge of computer can circumvent controls	Segregate duties within data processing
	Great speed extends one person's capabilities	Accumulate round-off error in one account	Review programs, limit access to programs
	There are new sources and potentials for error	Incorrect use of the system	Complete debugging and proper system design
	Records and the audit trail are invisible	Audit trail hard to use, but it is there	Use the computer to analyze records and audit trail.
Storage	Information can be changed without physical traces.	Change account balances without a trace	Use physical controls and cross-checks
	Concentrated information is easier to steal	Social Security has over 1 million records stolen	Physical controls and proper authorization
	Electronic information is easy to lose	Fund-raising loses millions in pledges	Proper backup
Output and Its Use	The user is in awe of the computer	User does not check computer output	Use control totals; check results of the computer
	Vast capabilities can create a different reality	Equity funding creates fictitious policyholders	Independent checks with "real world"

15.3 ELEMENTS OF INTERNAL CONTROL IN A COMPUTER ENVIRONMENT

Many of the same internal control procedures and techniques discussed in earlier chapters will also be applicable in a computer environment. Examples of such essential techniques would include the double-entry system and the audit trail. The double-entry system and the audit trail are specifically mentioned here because it is sometimes claimed that the use of the computer eliminates the need for the double-entry system and makes auditing impossible by eliminating the audit trail. Such claims are baseless, as will be seen in the remainder of this chapter and in the next chapter.

There will be a number of differences between internal control in a computer environment and in a manual environment. However, it will be most useful to use the same elemental breakdown presented in Chapter 4. The elements of internal control are the same; the computer just changes the methods by which these elements are implemented.

Honest and Capable Employees

This element of internal control is essentially the same with computer-based systems as it was with manual systems. If employees are capable and honest, much can be done even in an environment of weak internal control. If employees are dishonest or incompetent, no set of internal controls will be effective. If anything, however, honest and able employees are more important in a computer environment than in a manual system. As discussed earlier, the dishonest or incompetent employee can use the vast speed and electronic nature of the computer to create far more difficulties than would be possible with a manual system, with related human limitations.

Establish a Climate Where Security is Taken Seriously

Many, if not most, computer centers simply do not consider the problem of security to be a serious one. As a result, employees reflect this lack of concern and are not sensitive to potential problems or weaknesses in internal control.

Ensure Proper Training on the Computer

Many of the people using the computer will be unfamiliar with the capabilities and limitations of the machine. It is essential that these people be properly introduced to the computer, so they will be capable of using it well. Even if the people were capable in the manual environment, they will not necessarily be capable in the computer environment.

Check the Background of All Employees and Consultants

Experience has shown that many companies could have prevented problems by looking into the past history of prospective employees to see whether they had been in trouble before and would likely be in trouble again.

Bond Critical Employees

It is important to bond employees because: (a) it is a psychological deterrent, (b) it provides an additional check on the background of employees, and (c) it provides protection against loss in the event something does happen.

Exclude Disgruntled Employees from the Computer Area

Fired employees have manipulated computer records or added errors to the system because of their anger and resentment. At the termination interview, the employee should be asked to surrender keys or other means of access to the computer.

Reduce Temptation

The reduction of temptation will help ensure that the basically honest employees will remain so. Attempts to reduce temptation should include: (1) a policy of having two people present when the computer is in use so that one person will not be alone with his temptations; (2) control over time to reduce the possibility that an employee will engage in illicit activities in addition to his regular job; (3) a mandatory vacation policy to ensure that people will not be able to keep up a consistent fraud; and (4) a policy of rotating jobs so the possibility of personal manipulation of the system will be more difficult.

Clear Delegation and Separation of Duties

Just as in a manual system, there should be a written plan of organization, with clear assignments of authority and responsibility. As this plan is laid out, there should be a conscious effort to prevent any personnel from becoming "essential"; if one employee is unable to do his job (because of resignation, sickness, or termination) others should be able to take over.

The separation of duties in a computer environment, however, will not be the same as the separation of duties in a manual system. The plan of organization must assign independent responsibility for: (1) the accuracy and timeliness of the data; (2) the appropriateness and efficiency of the systems; and (3) the correctness and integrity of the computer programs. Exhibit 15–2 gives some of the basic job positions in data processing.

Next, it is important to separate people who might collude. Thus, the EDP department must be separate from operating departments. In addition, no one in EDP should have custody of assets or should be able to authorize transactions, initiate master file changes, or reconcile output controls. Also, to the extent possible, programmers and accountants should be separated, because a combination of the two skills could be disastrous for internal control.

It is also important to limit the scope of individual programmers. Programmers and systems analysts should not be permitted to use programs they wrote or designed, and they should not be allowed to operate the computer. Their detailed knowledge of the program and its application would allow them to circumvent controls. Users (with guidance and assistance) should specify the functions of programs; the programmer should not be on his own. The programmer's supervisor should review each program the programmer writes, and some other qualified employee should conduct the final testing of the program. Also, one programmer should not write all programs for a sensitive application.

Proper Procedures for Processing Transactions

Proper procedures begin with proper authorization of transactions. Even in a computer system, transactions often begin with "hard copy," such as a check

EXHIBIT 15-2 Basic Job Positions in Data Processing

	Title	Description of Duties
Those with KNOWLEDGE of how the system works	EDP Manager	The top executive in data processing: sets long-range and short-range goals; supervises the data processing staff
	Systems Analyst	Works with users to define data processing projects; formulates problems; defines solutions; develops specifications for programmers
	Applications Programmer	Develops effective, efficient, well-documented programs meeting the specifications set by systems analysts
	Systems Programmer	Maintains the operating system of the computer and adapts its capabilities to the particular company needs; this position is only necessary in large computer installations
Must be separate from	Computer Operator	Runs the programs according to the operating instructions; mounts tapes and disks; loads paper into printers
Those with ACCESS to the computer, documentation and files	Data Entry Clerk	Puts information into computer-readable form, either by keypunching or typing into a terminal
	Data Control Clerk	Compares control totals from the computer with the manually prepared control totals to ensure accurate processing; corrects transactions in error
	Librarian	Maintains the library of documentation, magnetic tapes, and disks (containing both programs and data)

copy or an invoice. Thus, the authorization can be indicated by the written initials of the person authorizing a transaction.

More sophisticated systems often originate transactions in machine-readable form only, eliminating "hard-copy." Examples of this include point-of-sale recorders and remote terminals. In these cases, proper authorization can only be assured by restricting access to the terminals to those responsible for authorizing and initiating transactions.

Since most data go into the computer via terminals, the next step for proper procedures must be proper design of terminal dialog. The dialog should be easy to use and take into consideration both the operator's background and his or her interest. Dialog for a data-entry clerk should be written differently from dialog for analysis used by a manager. The computer should also respond quickly enough to keep the attention and interest of the operator. Finally, the computer should check the entered data for error and notify the operator as soon as an error is determined.

The goal should be to make the system "bulletproof"; in other words, make it impossible to enter errors into the system, even deliberately. This brings up an important, pervasive goal of proper procedures: to ensure that input data are properly recorded on source documents and properly entered into the computer system. In order to do this, the system should develop totals and identify errors as close to the source of the data as possible.

It is also important to require proper authorization of new systems and programs. All new systems should be approved by the user department, an executive independent of EDP, and the systems and programming management. Each new program must be completely tested and authorized. After the programmer writes a program and signs off on it, his supervisor checks and approves it, the control group and users test it, and only then does it come into production.

The procedures discussed above assumed the computer would keep working, but it does not always do so. The system must have procedures to use when the computer breaks down. It is important to note that the computer can break down in the middle of processing. It must be possible, even at the cost of some inconvenience, to reconstruct data lost due to a system crash.

Suitable Documents and Accounting Records

Just as in a manual system, the computer files must contain all necessary information and an effective audit trail. In addition, there are a number of requirements specific to computer systems. These requirements basically arise from the ease of losing electronic information and from the increased importance of proper documentation.

Because information on the computer is so easily lost, there must be tested backup files. No important information should ever exist in only one place; for simple safety, it should also be kept in duplicate somewhere else. To ensure that they can be relied upon, these duplicate or backup files must be periodically tested to see if they can restore lost files.

A critical requirement is for documentation on three levels: systems documentation, program documentation, and operator instructions. The system documentation provides an overall view of the system, how it works and its control features. Program documentation provides the information necessary for understanding and modifying each program. Operator instructions provide information necessary to use the program.

Documentation is far more important in a computer environment than it is in a manual system. In a manual system, the records and their contents can be seen, and it is possible to follow the flow of information through the system—in a sense, the manual system is self-documenting. This is not true in a computer system; documentation is necessary to understand the system and how it works.

The next required documents are written procedures and standards of performance. These should include standards for: (1) documentation, so that documentation prepared by different people at different times will be uniform and easier to understand and maintain; (2) security measures over data files, program libraries, and the computer room, so that policy will be consistent; (3) the authorization of requests for data processing, whether it is a new program, a new system, or a routine run, to ensure that order is maintained and that priorities are established; and (4) operation of the computer and maintenance of the files.

Adequate Physical Control Over Assets and Records

As discussed earlier, erasures, changes, or substitutions in manual records will generally be visually apparent unless done in an unusually expert way, so such records are protected from manipulation. Changes in computer systems are invisible, so physical control over access to the system and records is even more important. Proper controls over access to the computer itself, terminals, and computer records, depend on the particular situation, but the following are basic elements of physical control:

1. It is important to protect programs as well as data. There should be a library of tapes and disks with one person accountable for them. Inventory records should be maintained and checked periodically in order to account for all file movement.

2. The systems and program documentation should be locked to protect them from operator access.

3. The computer room should be locked (with emergency exits for safety's sake) to restrict the access of programmers to the computer.

4. It is often important to regularly change keys, passwords, and combinations to ensure that access is only available to those authorized at that time, rather than to everyone who has been authorized in the past.

5. There should be controls on access to sensitive input and output data. While the input data is waiting for processing or after it is processed, the information should be protected from unauthorized access. Also, after the computer output is generated, it should be protected. It is a good idea to log the distribution of reports to check that everyone who should get the reports does get them, and that only those who should get them do so.

6. There should be physical protection and insurance coverage against theft and loss from catastrophic accidents, such as a fire or flood. For example, fire protection should include a fire extinguisher and a sprinkler system. In particular situations, fire-proof cabinets, on-site storage vaults or off-site storage may be necessary. In all of these cases, there are two costs to keep in mind. The first is the cost of physical loss of equipment, such as computer hardware, tapes, and disks. The second, and often more important cost is that of reconstructing the programs and data files.

7. It is essential to take care of the equipment so that it will function properly. The temperature and humidity should be kept at the proper levels for the particular equipment. Also, there should be proper preventive maintenance by qualified technicians on a regular basis.

Independent Verification of Performance

As discussed earlier, it is possible for a computer-based system to paint a balanced and consistent picture of reality that is completely false. As a result, it is absolutely essential to have independent verification of the system picture. The basic independent verification is to periodically check asset balances to determine if the system balances match with the actual amounts. Another important independent verification is for the system's users to maintain independent control totals of input and review the output of the system. In addition, the system should periodically develop summaries for users to check. For example, gross margin should appear reasonable based on past performance.

Another important independent verification of performance is a check that the written procedures and standards of performance are, in fact, being followed. It does little good to have procedures and standards if they are widely ignored. Physical controls and security measures must be checked, and lax security must be tightened if there is to be effective internal control.

There should be system logs of both transactions and operator actions. This will allow an independent check of transactions using the audit trail. It will also allow a check if errors become excessive for any particular system, terminal, or operator. Excessive errors could indicate faulty system design, poor forms, poor terminal dialog, untrained operators, or attempts at unauthorized access.

Finally, there should be an independent audit. This is an excellent means of checking compliance with established standards and of identifying internal control deficiencies.

CONCEPT SUMMARY
Elements of Internal Control in Computer-based Systems

Honest and capable employees	1. Create climate where security is taken seriously 2. Provide proper training in use of computer 3. Check background and bond employees 4. Promptly exclude fired employees from computer
Clear delegation and separation of duties	1. Develop written plan of organization 2. Do not allow any employees to be essential 3. Assign responsibility for data, systems and programs 4. Separate people who might collude
Proper procedures for processing of transactions	1. Ensure transactions are properly authorized 2. Check entered data for accuracy 3. Use only authorized and tested programs 4. Develop and test procedures for computer breakdown
Suitable documents and accounting records	1. Provide backup files of data and programs 2. Have written procedures and standards of performance 3. Develop documentation of systems and programs 4. Use prenumbered documents and forms
Adequate physical control over assets and records	1. Control access to computer and terminals 2. Protect equipment and data against loss 3. Control access to sensitive input and output 4. Maintain equipment on a regular basis
Independent verification of performance	1. Develop overall system controls 2. Check adherence to policies and procedures 3. Check security and tighten lax security 4. Have audit by independent CPA firm

---

15.4 EVALUATION OF INTERNAL CONTROL IN A COMPUTER ENVIRONMENT*

The evaluation of internal control in a computer environment is done in a slightly different way than in a manual system. Exhibit 15–3 provides a flowchart of the study and evaluation of internal control in EDP systems. This flowchart will guide our discussion.

Perform Preliminary Review

The first step in the evaluation process is to perform a preliminary review of the internal controls.

---

*This section is based upon *The Auditor's Study and Evaluation of Internal Control in EDP Systems*, AICPA, New York, 1977.

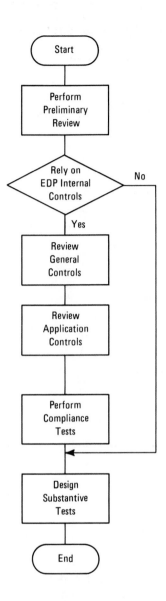

EXHIBIT 15–3   Study and Evaluation of Internal Control in EDP Systems

Purpose

The purpose of a preliminary review is to understand the accounting system, including both its computer and its manual components. In the preliminary review the following should be determined:

1. The information flow through the system. The auditor should make sure that he understands where the input data are generated, the type of processing that takes place, and the output that is developed.

2. Use of the output. The auditor should determine how the results generated by the computer affect the rest of the system and, in particular, determine the significance of the output.

3. Extent of computer usage. The auditor should determine how much the computer is used in accounting applications, again assessing the significance of the computer in the overall system of the company.

4. Basic structure of internal controls. The auditor should gain an overall view of the system's internal controls. He may examine these controls in more detail later, but an overview is sufficient at this point.

Methods

Four basic methods are employed to determine the information collected during a review.

1. *Inquiry and observation.* One of the auditor's most powerful tools is discussion with the employees who actually operate the system, and the corporate officers to whom they report. The auditor should also watch the operations of the firm searching for deficiencies and omissions.

2. *Review of documentation.* As discussed in Section 15.3, documentation is critically important in a computer environment. At this point, the auditor should look over the documentation for the system.

3. *Trace of transactions.* Despite the best possible design and documentation of internal control, the controls are worthless if they do not work properly. The auditor should trace selected transactions through the operations network to check the functioning of internal controls.

4. *Internal control questionnaires and checklists.* To help ensure that he does not overlook important areas, the auditor will often have documents that cover the basic topics relevant to all computer systems. These questionnaires and checklists are very similar to those illustrated in the cycle chapters.

Decision: Rely on Internal Controls?

After the auditor performs the preliminary review, he must decide whether or not the internal controls can be relied upon to reduce substantive testing.

Do Not Rely on Controls

If the auditor decides not to rely on internal controls, he can then proceed directly to the design of the substantive tests. There are three situations where an auditor would arrive at this conclusion:

1. The accounting control procedures may not be good enough to reduce the amount of substantive testing.
2. The effort to complete the review of controls would exceed the benefit of reliance on the controls.
3. The controls within data processing may be redundant since other controls exist.

Rely on Controls

If the auditor decides that he will rely on internal controls, he must then look at them in more depth. To make this decision, the auditor must feel that the accounting control procedures are good enough to warrant reducing the amount of substantive testing.

Review General Controls

Section 15.3 presented internal control in a computer environment using the same six elements of internal controls as in the discussion of manual systems in Chapter 4. However, there is a further breakdown that is useful for the evaluation of internal control.

1. General controls, such as the separation of duties within data processing, which apply to all application areas.
2. Application controls, such as the reasonableness tests built into accounts receivable which apply to one particular application area.

Using the breakdown, the general controls can be evaluated once for all applications. The auditor can then concentrate on the application controls as he focuses on the individual applications in turn.

Basic General Controls

There are five basic general controls:

1. *Organization and operation controls.* These controls consist of the proper separation of duties between the EDP department and the users, and the separation of duties within EDP.
2. *Systems development and documentation controls.* These are controls over: (a) review, testing, and approval of new systems; (b) changes to production programs; and (c) procedures for the development of documentation.
3. *Hardware and operating system controls.* These controls include periodic preventive maintenance on all hardware and the proper authorization of any changes to the operating system.
4. *Access controls.* These are the controls that prevent unauthorized access to program documentation, data files, computer programs, and the computer hardware.
5. *Data and procedural controls.* These controls include: (a) a control group separate from the operator, (b) written procedures manuals in support of the systems, and (c) the capability to reconstruct lost, damaged, or incorrect files.

Weaknesses in any of these five general controls would usually affect all EDP applications.

Purposes

Given these basic general controls, the auditor will review them

1. To identify any internal controls that could be relied upon.
2. To determine how these controls operate.
3. To consider possible compliance testing.
4. To weigh the effect of strengths and weaknesses in internal controls on compliance testing.

Methods

The three primary methods to perform this review consist of:

1. Examining any appropriate documentation in detail.
2. Interviewing internal auditors, members of the EDP department, and user department personnel.
3. Observing the operation of the internal controls.

Review Application Controls

After completing the review of the general controls, the auditor will review those controls that are related to significant accounting applications.

Input Controls

The purposes of input controls are to ensure that data are correct and that the system will reject any incorrect data. The basic input controls include the following:

1. Measures to see that the computer only processes properly authorized data.
2. Procedures to verify the data that are input, including all significant codes.
3. Techniques such as record counts, batch controls, and verification that control data entry.
4. Controls to ensure the correction and resubmission of all errors detected by the application.

Processing Controls

The purposes of processing controls are to ensure that all authorized transactions are processed, that no unauthorized transactions are processed, and that all processing is done correctly. The basic processing controls include the following:

1. Control totals that can be reconciled with the input control totals.
2. Programs containing limit and reasonableness checks.
3. Cumulative totals and record counts for each printout to verify run-to-run controls.

Output Controls

The purposes of output controls are to ensure that the output is accurate and that only authorized personnel receive it. The basic output controls include the following:

1. Output control totals that reconcile to the input and processing control totals.
2. User scanning of the output and testing of it by comparison with source documents.
3. Output that is promptly delivered to only the authorized user(s).

The purposes and methods of reviewing application controls are the same as the purposes and methods of reviewing general controls as given above. For this reason, the purposes and methods are not repeated here.

Perform Compliance Tests

After completing the review of application controls, the auditor can then test for compliance those controls he would like to rely on.

Purposes

As in the manual case, the purposes of compliance testing are:

1. To determine whether necessary controls are, in fact, in place.
2. To provide reasonable assurance that controls are functioning properly.
3. To document when, how, and by whom the controls are performed.

Methods

The methods of compliance testing include:

1. Examining records.
2. Testing the operation of internal controls.
3. Inquiring of client personnel.
4. Observing client operations.

Design Substantive Tests

After completing the compliance tests, the auditor is in a position to design the substantive tests. Every weakness pointed out by the compliance tests must be compensated for by the substantive tests.

Audit Effect of a Weakness in General Controls

The auditor must know and appreciate the audit effect of a weakness in each type of general control.

1. Organization and operations controls. If the organization structure is not adequate for good accounting control, the auditor should have serious reservations about the reliability of system results and substantive testing should expand significantly.

CONCEPT SUMMARY

Evaluation of Internal Controls

GENERAL CONTROLS: Those which apply to all application areas	Organization and operation controls: proper separation between EDP and user departments and separation of duties within EDP
	Systems development and documentation controls: controls over the development of new systems, including related documentation, and modification of production programs
	Hardware and operating system controls: preventive maintenance and proper authorization for changes to the operating system
	Access controls: Prevention of unauthorized access to documentation, files, programs, and equipment
	Data and procedural controls: Separate control group, written procedures, and backup capability
APPLICATION CONTROLS: Those which apply to only one application area, such as accounts receivable	Input controls: Ensure that data are correct and the system will reject any incorrect data
	Processing controls: Ensure that all, and only, authorized transactions are processed
	Output controls: Ensure that all output is accurate and that it is only received by authorized personnel

---

2. Systems development and documentation controls. If documentation is inadequate, it will be necessary to expend substantial effort to obtain an accurate description of the accounting applications. Weaknesses in control over new systems or changes to production programs are serious and will act to expand substantive testing significantly.

3. Hardware and systems software controls. If these controls are weak, the auditor might reduce the reliance he can put on the system output.

4. Access controls. If these controls are lacking, this decreases the integrity of the system and increases the chance of unauthorized modification of files and programs.

5. Data and procedural controls. If these controls are weak, the auditor must reduce his reliance on the system's output. However, the audit consequences are less severe than some of the other possibilities above.

Audit Effect of a Weakness in Application Controls

As presented above, there are three basic types of application controls:

1. Input controls. A lack of adequate input control may permit items to become lost, duplicated, or be entered incorrectly, which could have a serious effect

on the financial statements. A possible audit reaction is to expand the testing of transactions details.

2. Processing controls. A weakness in processing controls may have a serious effect on the data records, possibly causing errors, which would be used in many applications.

3. Output controls. If the control of output distribution is weak, there is a loss of power to detect errors and irregularities. The audit consequences of this loss depend on whether errors or irregularities have occurred, their variety, and the audit area they affect. A range of audit reactions is possible.

Key Terms

application controls	output device
application program	printer
backup	processor
card reader	program documentation
disk	programmer
EDP manager	software
general controls	source language
hardware	source program
input device	storage device
librarian	systems analyst
machine language	systems documentation
object program	systems programmer
operating system	tape
operator	terminal
operator instructions	terminal dialog

Questions and Problems

Questions

15-1 Give the four basic types of hardware devices and their purposes. Contrast the two basic types of software.

15-2 List the advantages of computer systems over manual systems. Describe the characteristics of business processing that make computers so useful.

15-3 Discuss the internal control problems that a computer's lack of judgement cause. What can be done to prevent these problems?

15-4 Why is the audit trail more of a problem in a computer system than in a manual system?

15-5 In what way is the computer's computational ability an internal control benefit? In what way is it a problem?

15-6 Explain why the separation of duties is a different sort of problem in a computer system than in a manual system. What can be done to provide a proper separation of duties in a computer environment?

15-7 Is documentation more important in a computer system than in a manual system? If so, why? Give the basic types of documentation and a brief description of each.

15-8 What are the basic independent checks useful in a computer system? Why is an audit important?

15-9 List and briefly describe the six basic steps of the study and evaluation of internal control in EDP systems.

15-10 Distinguish between general controls and application controls, and give the basic types of general controls and application controls.

Multiple Choice Questions From Professional Examinations

15-11 So that the essential accounting control features of a client's electronic data processing system can be identified and evaluated, the auditor must, at a minimum, have

    a. A basic familiarity with the computer's internal supervisory system.

    b. A sufficient understanding of the entire computer system.

    c. An expertise in computer systems analysis.

    d. A background in programming procedures.

15-12 The auditor should be concerned about internal control in a data processing system because

    a. The auditor cannot follow the flow of information through the computer.

    b. Fraud is more common in an EDP system than in a manual system.

    c. There is usually a high concentration of data processing activity and control in a small number of people in an EDP system.

    d. Auditors most often "audit around" the computer.

15-13 Which of the following best describes a fundamental control weakness often associated with electronic data processing systems?

    a. Electronic data processing equipment is more subject to systems error than manual processing is subject to human error.

    b. Electronic data processing equipment processes and records similar transactions in a similar manner.

    c. Electronic data processing procedures for detection of invalid and un-
usual transactions are less effective than manual control procedures.

    d. Functions that would normally be separated in a manual system are
combined in the electronic data processing system.

15-14 An advantage of manual processing is that human processors may note
data errors and irregularities. To replace this element of error detection
associated with manual processing, a well-designed electronic data processing system should introduce

    a. Programmed limits

    b. Dual circuitry

    c. Echo checks

    d. Read after write

15-15 In both of the next two items, two independent statements (numbered I
and II) are presented. You are to evaluate each statement individually and
determine whether it is true. Your answer for each item should be selected
from the following responses:

    a. I only is true.

    b. II only is true.

    c. Both I and II are true.

    d. Neither I nor II is true.

    I. The control of input and output of accounting transactions to and from
the data processing department should be performed by an independent control group.

    II. An important improvement in recent computer hardware is the ability
to automatically produce error listings.

15-16 Meridian Corporation's EDP department personnel include a manager, a
programmer-systems analyst, three machine operators, a librarian, four
keypunch operators, and a control clerk.

    I. Assuming that employees' activities are strictly limited to their assigned
responsibilities, internal control would not be strengthened by rotating
periodically among machine operators the assignment of individual
application runs.

    II. If work volume expands sufficiently to justify individual positions, it
would be desirable for Meridian to separate the duties of the systems
analyst and the programmer.

15-17 A computer programmer has written a program for updating perpetual
inventory records. Responsibility for initial testing (debugging) of the program should be assigned to the

a. EDP-department control group.

b. Internal-audit control group.

c. Programmer.

d. Machine operator.

15-18 Evaluation of the electronic data processing aspects of a system of accounting control should

a. Not be a part of the auditor's evaluation of the system.

b. Be a separate part of the auditor's evaluation of the system.

c. Be an integral part of the auditor's evaluation of the system.

d. Be coordinated with the auditor's evaluation of administrative control.

15-19 Accounting functions that are normally considered incompatible in a manual system are often combined in an electronic data processing system by using an electronic data processing program or series of programs. This necessitates an accounting control that prevents unapproved

a. Access to the magnetic tape library.

b. Revisions to existing computer programs.

c. Usage of computer program tapes.

d. Testing of modified computer programs.

15-20 Which of the following employees in a company's electronic data processing department should be responsible for designing new or improved data processing procedures?

a. Flowchart editor

b. Programmer

c. Systems analyst

d. Control-group supervisor

15-21 An auditor's investigation of a company's electronic data processing control procedures has disclosed the following four circumstances. Indicate which circumstance constitutes a weakness in internal control.

a. Machine operators do not have access to the complete run manual.

b. Machine operators are closely supervised by programmers.

c. Programmers do not have the authorization to operate equipment.

d. Only one generation of backup files is stored in an off-premises location.

15-22 Some electronic data processing accounting control procedures relate to all electronic data processing activities (general controls), and some relate to specific tasks (application controls). General controls include

a. Controls designed to ascertain that all data submitted to electronic data processing for processing have been properly authorized.

b. Controls that relate to the correction and resubmission of data that was initially incorrect.

c. Controls for documenting and approving programs and changes to programs.

d. Controls designed to ensure the accuracy of the processing results.

15-23 Which of the following is an example of application controls in electronic data processing systems?

a. Input controls

b. Hardware controls

c. Documentation procedures

d. Controls over access to equipment and data files

15-24 An independent auditor studies and evaluates a client's electronic data processing system. The auditor's study portion includes two phases: (1) a review of investigation of the system, and (2) tests of compliance. The latter phase might include which of the following?

a. Examination of systems flowcharts to determine whether they reflect the current status of the system.

b. Examination of the systems manuals to determine whether existing procedures are satisfactory.

c. Examination of the machine room log book to determine whether control information is properly recorded.

d. Examination of organization charts to determine whether electronic data processing department responsibilities are properly separated to afford effective control.

15-25 The auditor looks for an indication on punched cards to see if the cards have been verified. This is an example of a

a. Substantive test.

b. Compliance test.

c. Transactions test.

d. Dual-purpose test.

Problems

15-26 The Lakesedge Utility District is installing an electronic data processing system. The CPA who conducts the annual examination of the Utility District's financial statements has been asked to recommend controls for the new system.

Required:

Discuss recommended controls over:

a. Program documentation
b. Program testing
c. EDP hardware
d. Tape files and software

AICPA

15-27 The following five topics are part of the relevant body of knowledge for CPAs having fieldwork in immediate supervisory responsibility in audits involving a computer:

1. Electronic data processing (EDP) equipment and its capabilities.
2. Organization and management of the data processing function.
3. Characteristics of computer-based systems.
4. Fundamentals of computer programming.
5. Computer center operations.

CPAs who are responsible for computer audits should possess certain general knowledge with respect to each of these five topics. For example, on the subject of EDP equipment and its capabilities, the auditor should have a general understanding of computer equipment and should be familiar with the uses and capabilities of the central processor and the peripheral equipment.

Required:

For each of the topics numbered 2 through 5 above, describe the general knowledge that should be possessed by those CPAs who are responsible for computer audits.

AICPA

15-28 Your client has procured a number of minicomputers for use in various locations and applications. One of these has been installed in the stores department, which has the responsibility for disbursing stock items and for maintaining stores records. In your audit you find, among other things, that a competent employee, trained in computer applications, receives the requisitions for stores, reviews them for completeness and for the propriety of approvals, disburses the stock, maintains the records, operates the computer, and authorizes adjustments to the total amounts of stock accumulated by the computer.

When you discuss the applicable controls with the department manager, you are told that the minicomputer is assigned exclusively to that department and that it, therefore, does not require the same types of controls applicable to the large computer system.

Required:

Comment on the manager's contentions, discussing briefly five types of control that would apply to this minicomputer application.

IIA

15-29 When auditing an EDP accounting system, the independent auditor should have a general familiarity with the effects of the use of EDP on the various characteristics of accounting control and on the auditor's study and evaluation of such control. The independent auditor must be aware of those control procedures that are commonly referred to as "general" controls and those that are commonly referred to as "application" controls. General controls relate to all EDP activities, and application controls relate to specific accounting tasks.

Required:

a. What are the general controls that should exist in EDP-based accounting systems?

b. What are the purposes of each of the following categories of application controls?
   1. Input controls
   2. Processing controls
   3. Output controls

AICPA

15-30 You are involved in the audit of accounts receivable, which represent a significant portion of the assets of a large retail corporation. Your audit plan requires the use of the computer, but you encounter the reactions described below.

1. The computer operations manager says that all time on the computer is scheduled for the foreseeable future and that it is not feasible to perform the work for the auditor.

2. The computer scheduling manager suggests that your computer program be catalogued into the computer program library (on disk storage) to be run when computer time becomes available.

3. You are refused admission to the computer room.

4. The systems manager tells you that it will take too much time to adapt the computer audit program to the EDP operating system and that the computer installation programmers would write the programs needed for the audit.

Required:

For each of the four situations described, state the action the auditor should take to proceed with the accounts receivable audit.

IIA

15-31 You have been engaged by Central Savings and Loan Association to examine its financial statements for the year ended December 31.

In January of the current year, the association installed an on-line, real-time computer system. Each teller in the association's main office and seven branch offices has an on-line, input-output terminal. Customers' mortgage payments and savings account deposits and withdrawals are recorded in the accounts by the computer from data input by the teller at the time of the transaction. The teller keys the proper account by account number and enters the information in the terminal keyboard to record the transaction. The accounting department at the main office has both punched card and typewriter input-output devices. The computer is housed at the main office.

In addition to servicing its own mortgage loans, the association acts as a mortgage servicing agency for three life insurance companies. In this latter activity, it maintains mortgage records and serves as the collection and escrow agent for the mortgagees (the insurance companies), who pay a fee to the association for these services.

Required:

You would expect the association to have certain internal controls in effect because an on-line, real-time computer system is employed. List the internal controls that should be in effect solely because this system is employed. Classify them as

1. Those controls pertaining to input of information.
2. All other types of computer controls.

AICPA (Adapted)

15-32 You are performing an audit of the EDP function of a chemical company with about $150 million in annual sales. Your initial survey discloses the following points:

1. The EDP manager reports to the director of accounting, who, in turn, reports to the controller. The controller reports to the treasurer, who is one of several vice-presidents in the company. The EDP manager has made several unsuccessful requests to the director of accounting for another printer.
2. There is no written charter for the EDP function, but the EDP manager tells you that the primary objective is to get the accounting reports out on time.
3. Transaction tapes are used daily to update the master file and are then retired to the scratch tape area.
4. A third generation computer with large disk capacity was installed three years ago. The EDP activity previously used a second generation computer, and many of the programs written for that computer are used on the present equipment by means of an emulator.

5. You observe that the output from the computer runs is written on tape for printing at a later time. Some output tapes from several days' runs are waiting to be printed.

6. The EDP manager states that the CPU could handle at least twice the work currently being processed.

Required:

a. Identify the defect inherent in each of the six conditions shown above.

b. Briefly describe the probable effect if the condition is permitted to continue.

NOTE: On your answer sheet, show the defect, followed immediately by the probable effect, for each condition.

IIA

15-33 The Meyers Pharmaceutical Company, a drug manufacturer, has the following system for billing and recording accounts receivable:

1. An incoming customer's purchase order is received in the order department by a clerk, who prepares a prenumbered company sales order form on which is inserted the pertinent information, such as the customer's name and address, customer's account number, quantity and items ordered. After the sales order form has been prepared, the customer's purchase order is stapled to it.

2. The sales order form is then passed to the credit department for approval. Rough approximations of the billing values of the orders are made in the credit department for those accounts on which credit limitations are imposed. After investigation, approval of credit is noted on the form.

3. Next the sales order form is passed to the billing department, where a clerk types the customer's invoice on a billing machine that cross-multiplies the number of items and the unit price and adds the automatically extended amounts for the total amount of the invoice. The billing clerk determines the unit prices for the items from a list of billing prices. The billing machine has registers that automatically accumulate daily totals of customer account numbers and invoice amounts to provide "hash" totals and control amounts. These totals, which are inserted in a daily record book, serve as predetermined batch totals for verification of computer inputs. The billing is done on prenumbered, continuous, carbon-interleaved forms having the following designations:
   a. "Customer's copy."
   b. "Sales department copy," for information purposes.
   c. "File copy."
   d. "Shipping department copy," which serves as a shipping order. Bills of lading are also prepared as carbon copy byproducts of the invoicing procedure.

4. The shipping department copy of the invoice and the bills of lading are then sent to the shipping department. After the order has been shipped, copies of the bill of lading are returned to the billing department. The shipping department copy of the invoice is filed in the shipping department.

5. In the billing department, one copy of the bill of lading is attached to the customer's copy of the invoice, and both are mailed to the customer. The other copy, together with the sales order form, is then stapled to the invoice file copy and filed in invoice numerical order.

6. A keypunch machine is connected to the billing machine so that punched cards are created during the preparation of the invoices. The punched cards then become the means by which the sales data are transmitted to a computer. The punched cards are fed to the computer in batches. One day's accumulation of cards comprises a batch. After the punched cards have been processed by the computer, they are placed in files and held for about two years.

Required:

List the procedures that a CPA would employ in his examination of his selected audit samples of the company's

a. Typed invoices, including the source documents
b. Punched cards.

(The listed procedures should be limited to the verification of the sales data being fed into the computer. Do not carry the procedures beyond the point at which the cards are ready to be fed to the computer.)

AICPA

15-34 George Beemster, CPA, is examining the financial statements of the Louisville Sales Corporation, which recently installed an off-line electronic computer. The following comments have been extracted from Mr. Beemster's notes on computer operations and the processing and control of shipping notices and customer invoices:

- To minimize inconvenience, Louisville converted without change its existing data processing system, which utilized tabulating equipment. The computer company supervised the conversion and has provided training to all computer department employees (except keypunch operators) in systems design, operations, and programming.

- Each computer run is assigned to a specific employee, who is responsible for making program changes, running the program, and answering questions. This procedure has the advantage of eliminating the need for records of computer operations because each employee is responsible for his or her own computer runs.

- At least one computer department employee remains in the computer room during office hours, and only computer department employees have keys to the computer room.

- System documentation consists of those materials furnished by the computer company—a set of record formats and program listings. These and the tape library are kept in a corner of the computer department.
- The company considered the desirability of programmed controls but decided to retain the manual controls from its existing system.
- Company products are shipped directly from public warehouses, which forward shipping notices to general accounting. There a billing clerk enters the price of the item and accounts for the numerical sequence of shipping notices from each warehouse. The billing clerk also prepares daily adding machine tapes ("control tapes") of the units shipped and the unit prices.
- Shipping notices and control tapes are forwarded to the computer department for keypunching and processing. Extensions are made on the computer. Output consists of invoices (in six copies) and a daily sales register. The daily sales register shows the aggregate totals of units shipped and unit prices, which the computer operator compares to the control tapes.
- All copies of the invoice are returned to the billing clerk. The clerk mails three copies to the customer, forwards one copy to the warehouse, maintains one copy in a numerical file, and retains one copy in an open invoice file that serves as a detail accounts receivable record.

Required:

Describe weaknesses in internal control over information and data flows and in the procedures for processing shipping notices and customer invoices. Recommend improvements in these controls and processing procedures. Organize your answer sheets as follows:

Weakness	Recommended Improvement

AICPA

15-35 A Company Limited, a food wholesaler, has combined the purchasing, accounts payable, and inventory systems into one integrated computerized system. The file updating process automatically generates reorder messages in a punched-card format. These punched cards are repeatedly processed in the system in order to:

a. Generate the printed purchase orders

b. Update the inventory file to reflect the new orders

c. Serve as the receiving report in the receiving department and

d. Update the inventory file to record the receipts.

The inventory master file contains fields for the following information for each item:

> Inventory code number
> Item name
> Quantity on hand
> Open purchase order—quantity on order
>   —date of order
>   —purchase order number
> Minimum quantity (reorder point)
> Reorder quantity
> Reorder code (automatic or discretionary)
> Vendor number
> Date and purchase order number of most recent shipment received
>
> Number of reorders year-to-date
> Total issues year-to-date
> Total issues last year.

System description (keyed to numbered points on flowchart following):

1. When the quantity on hand plus the quantity on order for an inventory item falls below the reorder point, a reorder message is punched by the computer into a card. If the master file contains an *automatic reorder* code for the item, a routine reorder message is punched which contains the following information, both printed and punched:

> Date
> Inventory code number
> Vendor number
> Standard order quantity.

In addition, a brief name or description of the item is printed on the card.

If the master file contains a *discretionary reorder* code, or if there is no vendor number in the inventory master file, a discretionary reorder message is produced, which contains the date and inventory code number punched and printed, and the item name and standard order quantity printed only. These discretionary message cards are then sent to the purchasing department.

The purchasing department decides whether or not to order, enters the quantity and vendor number on the card, and returns the card to the data processing department, where the additional information is punched into the card.

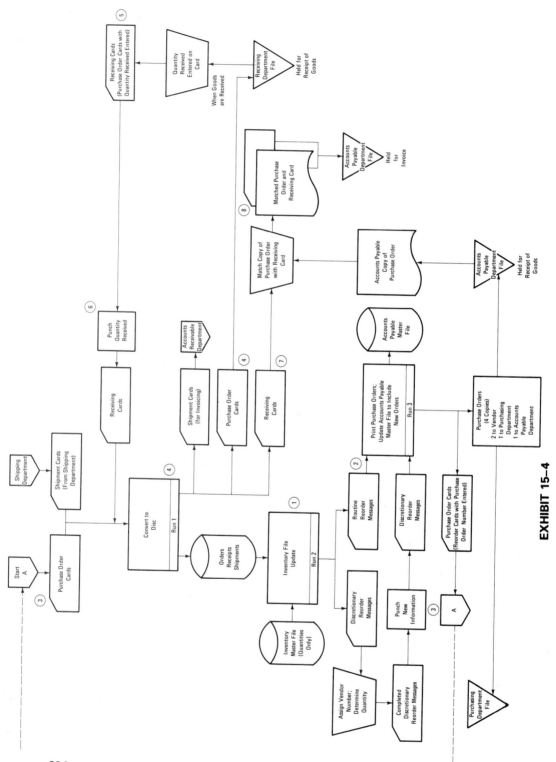

EXHIBIT 15-4

620

2. The routine reorder message cards and the returned discretionary message cards are used as the input to a computer program, which prints 4 copies of the purchase orders and updates the accounts payable master file (on disk) to include the items ordered in the vendor file as "ordered, not received." The vendor name and address are obtained from the accounts payable master file. The copies of the purchase order are distributed as shown on the flowchart. The purchase orders are automatically numbered and dated by the computer, and the purchase order number is punched into the reorder message card, thereby changing it to a purchase order card. No check is made of the numerical sequence of complete or incomplete purchase orders, and no attempt is made to identify missing purchase order numbers or open orders outstanding for a long period of time.

3. The purchase order cards are re-entered into the system in the next day's processing in order to update the inventory master file to show the quantity on order. In addition, shipment cards generated by the shipping department update the inventory file to reduce the quantity on hand and to update the total issues field. Purchase order cards and receiving cards (described below) are processed before shipment cards.

4. After conversion to disk for the updating, the purchase order cards are sent to the receiving department, where they are filed for use as receiving reports.

5. When goods are received, the receiving clerk pulls the card for that order, enters the quantity received (if different from the quantity ordered) and sends the card back to the data processing department, where the quantity received is punched into the card (when necessary) and the card re-enters the inventory updating.

6. Cycle to move the quantity received from the "on order" to the "on hand" field in the master file.

7. The receiving cards then are sent to the accounts payable department where they are matched with the accounts payable copy of the purchase order and

8. Held for receipt of the invoice from the vendor. The receipt and payment of the invoice, and the updating of the accounts payable master file to delete the open purchase order, to enter the invoice, and to record the eventual payment, are all later steps in the processing and are not included in this part of the system description or flowchart.

The auditor has at his disposal a generalized audit software package, which can directly access any of the machine-readable files and perform a variety of standard audit procedures.

Required:

a. Describe the weak control points in this system. For each weakness identified, show what improvement you would recommend.
b. For each weakness identified in part (a), list what compensating audit procedures you would use in performing an audit of the purchasing-accounts payable-inventory area.

CICA (Adapted)

16

Auditing in a computer environment

Chapter 15 discussed internal control in a computer environment and the auditor's evaluation of internal control as part of his examination. The discussion was a general one because it applied to all computer environments.

In order to appreciate the effect of computer systems on auditing, however, it is necessary to become more specific about how a business computer system functions. This chapter discusses and illustrates the two primary types of business computer systems: batch processing and interactive processing. This should help clarify the concepts of internal control in a computer environment. Compliance testing and substantive testing in a computer environment are then described.

16.1 ELEMENTS OF A BATCH PROCESSING ENVIRONMENT

The design of a computer system, to take full advantage of its suitability for business data processing, depends upon the particular information needs of a business, its most repetitive and important processing problems, and the cost of potential equipment. Sections 16.1 and 16.2 discuss the basic configurations used in business processing systems. These discrete examples of successful hardware combinations for particular information and processing needs have been selected from an almost continuous scale of possibilities. The possible configurations that could be used in business data processing are almost endless. Hardware system design is limited only by the imagination of the user.

The first decision to be made in establishing a hardware configuration is what the basic orientation of the system will be. There are two such orientations available: batch or interactive.

Batch Processing

In batch processing systems, data is stored and processed in a specified order and at specified discrete times. Generally, data is accumulated and stored for a certain period of time or until a certain quantity of data is accumulated. Typical examples would include all transactions for a week or all transactions for a day. Then, processing of all data accumulated takes place at once, and output is generated from all of the data. This approach processes data in batches.

It is ideal if information needs are such that timely, immediate processing results are not necessary. The most common use of batch processing is payroll, where checks are printed on a regular schedule, not on demand.

Data is usually organized on some numerical (sequential) basis for batch processing to be most efficient. Data storage in batch systems may be off line since processing takes place only at predetermined times, and data needs are known well in advance. The most useful sequential storage media is magnetic tape, and most batch systems are built around magnetic tape storage, although data may be organized and processed sequentially from disk storage.

Refinements of Batch Processing

Refinements of the sequential batch-processing approach can be made to: (1) the process of converting source documents to machine input form, and (2) the methods of transmitting this converted data to the computer for processing. Exhibit 16–1 gives brief descriptions of two approaches, showing the differences in data conversion and transmission. Both descriptions represent the batch approach to processing and require that: (1) data be susceptible to sequential organization and processing, (2) data be processed at discrete times in groups of similar transactions or events, and (3) management needs for timely or special information do not require that each transaction be processed individually as it occurs and immediate results generated. Sequential orientation and batch processing represent the oldest approach to computer hardware system design and may still be the most widely used approach in business. On computers specifically designed for batch processing, it is the simplest and least expensive approach to processing business data.

How Batch Processing Works

Exhibit 16–2 shows a schematic of how basic batch processing works in processing customer orders. The figure is not a complete flowchart because it does not show the final disposition of all the input used and output generated. But it does illustrate the basic concepts without excessive detail.

The company receives orders, either through the mail or over the phone where a salesman fills out the appropriate form. In any case, there is a source

EXHIBIT 16-1 Two Approaches to Batch Processing

	Basic Batch	*Batch With Remote Data Transmission*
Source documents	Gathered and manually transferred to computer site.	Converted to machine input form at various remote data collection points.
Data conversion	All data is converted to machine input form at computer site.	At certain predetermined times, the data is electronically transferred to the computer site to be stored for processing.
Processing	Takes place in batches at predetermined times.	Takes place in batches at predetermined times.
Output	Generated at the computer site and then manually transferred to users.	Generated at the computer site and may be electronically transferred to remote points to users.
Input and output devices	Punched cards for input and printers for output would be usual in such a system.	Input and output devices and media would probably be a combination of those used in basic batch plus some remote devices such as terminals or remote card readers and printers.
Data storage	Magnetic tape likely for files of permanent or semi-permanent data.	Magnetic tape likely for files of permanent or semi-permanent data.
Costs/benefits	This is the simplest and least expensive large system to operate.	Better turnaround and accuracy would likely result as compared to basic batch, since some manual functions are eliminated. Costs of this system would be higher than basic batch.

document—the customer order. Other copies will trigger shipment of the goods and update various manual files, but one copy of each customer order will go to data processing. Every day, a copy of each customer order shipped that day will be accumulated into a batch. That batch will then go to data processing.

Data processing will keypunch one card for each item on the order. There will be one card per item rather than one card per order because this transaction must update both the customer balance and the amount on hand of the inventory items.

The cards go to the data control clerk who processes them through an edit program which generates: (1) an edit listing of all cards, with any errors identified, and (2) a file of order transactions, with one record for each item on each order. If there are any errors, the data control clerk corrects the cards in error and reruns the edit program, creating another edit listing and another order transaction file. The data control clerk repeats this process until there are no errors in the cards. No further processing occurs until all errors are corrected.

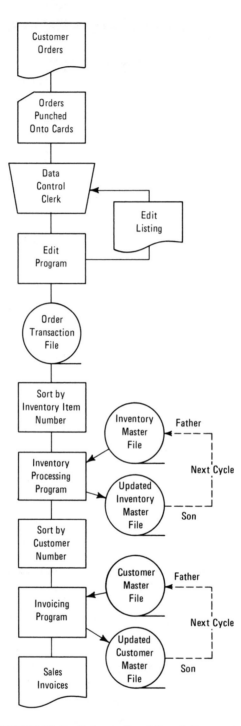

EXHIBIT 16–2 Schematic of Batch Processing

When there are no longer errors, the order transaction file is sorted into inventory item number sequence. This sort is required because the transaction file must be in the same order as the master file since both are accessed sequentially.

The inventory processing program then reads in both the sorted order transaction file and the inventory master file. For every record read from the inventory master file, a record is written to the updated inventory master file. If one or more transactions affect an inventory item, the program updates the item's record by reducing the amount of inventory on hand. The updated record is then written to the updated inventory master file. If no transaction affects an inventory item, an unchanged record is written to the updated inventory master file. The output master file will always have exactly the same number of records as the input master file.

The same order transaction file is then sorted into customer number sequence, the reason being that the transaction file must be in the same order as the master file it will update. The processing of the transactions against the customer master file uses the same logic as given above for the inventory master file. Any customer records with transactions are updated to reflect the new balance owed before writing the record to the updated customer master file. In addition, the invoicing program prints a sales invoice for each customer with transactions.

Grandfather-Father-Son Concept

Typically, a batch processing system updates the master file at the end of each day. For example, on Wednesday night, the master file is updated to reflect Wednesday's transactions. The input master file reflects transactions through Tuesday; the output file then reflects transactions through Wednesday.

It is possible, however, that the input file and the output file could both be destroyed, while the computer is processing them, through operator error, program error, or hardware error. Without backup, the company could lose all of its records on what its customers owe them—an unacceptable situation.

For this reason, batch processing keeps a third, earlier copy of the master file. In the example above, the company would keep a copy of the file reflecting transactions through Monday. If both the Tuesday and Wednesday files were destroyed, the company could recreate the Tuesday file from the Monday file and then process Wednesday's transactions again to create the Wednesday file.

In this process, Wednesday's file is called the "son," Tuesday's file is called the "father," and Monday's file is called the "grandfather." On Thursday, the physical tape used for Monday's file is used for Thursday's file and becomes the "son." Wednesday's file becomes the "father," and Tuesday's file becomes the "grandfather." These three tapes then cycle indefinitely in this manner.

This is called the *grandfather-father-son concept*. Its advantage is that there is always a copy of each master file that is not on the computer. This copy can recreate the current master file if the file is destroyed.

Programmed Controls

Chapter 15 discussed an important element of internal control—proper processing of transactions. In a computer environment, much of the processing of transactions is done by computer programs. But it is not sufficient for a program to process correct data correctly. The program must also identify and reject incorrect data using appropriate programmed controls. Exhibit 16–3 provides a summary of programmed controls used in batch processing.

Programmed controls, as the name implies, are checks built into the computer programs themselves. The appropriate controls for each program, therefore, depend upon the type of processing that a program performs.

The schematic of Exhibit 16–2 shows two types of programs: edit programs and processing programs. These two types of programs will use different programmed controls because:

1. The edit program does not access any master files and, therefore, cannot compare any input data to information on the file. The processing program, on the other hand, does access the file and can make such comparison.

2. The edit program is used immediately by the data control clerk to correct errors; this is not true of the processing program. Thus, the edit program should catch as many errors as possible and not leave them for the processing program to catch.

As a result, edit programs typically contain all of the programmed controls in Exhibit 16–3 that check input wholly within the program or that compare input totals to manually prepared totals. The processing program would not need those checks, since they have already been done. It needs only those controls that compare input to information on the file.

Tape Labels

Even a moderately sized data processing operation can have hundreds of tapes, all physically almost identical. In order for the operator and librarian to tell them apart visually, each tape will have an external label. This label identifies the particular file contained on the tape and gives the date the file was created so that the operator can perform the appropriate grandfather-father-son rotation of tapes.

Even with this external label, it is easy to put the wrong tape on the computer and destroy a valuable tape by mistake. It is also easy to use and update the wrong version of a master file. For these reasons, most tapes have an internal label called a *header label* in addition to the external label. This header label is at the front of the tape and contains essentially the same information as the external label. Before reading a master file or writing an updated master file, the computer uses the header label to ensure that the proper tape is being used.

EXHIBIT 16-3 Programmed Controls for Batch Processing

	Control	Description	Example
Check input wholly within program	Reasonableness	Test whether the amounts are within reason given the situation	Invoice should not exceed $10,000,000
	Validity	Check whether numbers or codes are valid	Month should be between 1 and 12
	Completeness	Determine that all elements of the transaction are included	Date must be included
	Self-checking number	Add digit to item numbers to catch transposition errors	3287 and 3827 are both valid but 32876 is valid and 38276 is not
Compare input totals to manually prepared totals	Control total	Program sums one meaningful item for all transactions to compare with manually prepared totals to ensure all and only proper transactions are keypunched	Person outside of data processing would sum dollar amounts of all transactions. Data control clerk would compare program results given on the Edit Listing to these manual totals
	Hash total	Programs sums one meaningless item for all transactions to compare with manually prepared totals for the same purpose as the control total	Process would be similar to that for the control total except for a sum of part numbers or quantities rather than dollar amounts
	Record count	Program counts the number of transactions to compare with the manual count of transactions	Process would be similar to that for the control total except for a count of each transaction rather than a sum
Compare input to information on the file	Redundancy	Input information about the item in addition to its number to make sure the number is correct	Input the first 5 characters of a customer's name as well as the customer number
	Existence	Ensure item is on the file and active before processing transaction	Customer number should refer to an active customer on the file

---

CONCEPT SUMMARY
Tape and Disk Labels

Type		Description
External label		Label on the outside of the file to ensure that the operator and librarian can identify it
Internal labels	Header label	Label at the beginning of the file to ensure that the correct file is processed
	Trailer label	Label at the end of the file to ensure that file totals and record counts stay correct

---

There is another internal label, the trailer label. The trailer label is at the very end of the file and contains a record count of the file, i.e., how many records are on the file. The trailer label may also contain control totals of the entire file, such as a total balance owed by all customers. Checking the trailer label between runs can help ensure that no information is added to or deleted from the file inappropriately.

Labels can also be used with disk packs and disk files.

16.2 ELEMENTS OF AN INTERACTIVE PROCESSING ENVIRONMENT

Interactive processing systems are characterized by data storage in direct access, by easily accessible media, and by processing, which can take place immediately as transactions occur. In the interactive approach to system design, the data is processed individually and continuously as transactions take place, and output is generated instantly. Since processing in interactive systems takes place in any order as events occur or information is needed, data storage must be in on-line, direct-access form. Disks are the most widely used on-line, direct-access storage, and most interactive systems are built around this media.

Basic approaches to interactive systems can differ in the extent to which processing can be initiated from remote locations as transactions occur. Exhibit 16–4 describes two interactive systems, which differ in the degree that continuous processing is allowed from remote data-gathering locations. The interactive approach to processing requires that: (1) data be always available in direct-access storage, (2) some processing be initiated from remote locations away from the computer system, and (3) management needs for timely information make it impossible for processing to wait while data accumulation takes place. In summary, interactive processing must make fast, up-to-date information constantly available.

Which particular system orientation a company may choose will depend on its overall processing problems and applications, and its information needs. Gen-

EXHIBIT 16-4   Two Approaches to Interactive Processing

Inquiry/Response Only	*With Real-Time Processing*
1. Direct interaction with the computer is possible through remote terminals (I/O devices) for questions and answers.	1. Direct interaction with the computer is possible through remote terminals (I/O devices) for questions and answers, as in the previous system, and also for the processing of data.
2. Normal processing is interrupted as questions come in, and the CPU searches data stored in on-line, direct access devices (disks) to answer questions.	2. Normal processing is initiated from remote input-output devices as transactions occur with data stored in on-line, direct access devices (disks).
3. No processing is done from remote input-output devices, only a question and answer dialogue is possible, and questions are answered using the data available.	3. Since normal processing is continuous there is no time lag between the occurrence of a transaction and the reflection of that transaction in the stored data of the computer system. This is called a *real-time system*.
4. Normal processing is accomplished at the computer site at fixed times using input-output devices and media similar to that used in batch processing systems.	4. Unless errors occur, information is constantly accurate and up to date because computer system data instantly reflects events as they occur.
5. This approach provides much more timely information than batch processing (at greater cost). The information is still not precisely up-to-date because processing is not continuous, and some time lag is necessary between the occurrence of an event and its reflection in the data files of the system.	5. This is a very costly and complex system to implement and operate; however, the movement in computer systems has been toward this design.

erally, however, the necessity for up-to-date, accurate information must be balanced against the extra cost and complexity of interactive systems. Also important in basic hardware design is the level of flexibility in the system. The capacity of the system for change and growth as business processing needs and circumstances change is a critical dimension of any hardware configuration. Clearly observable in the world of business data processing systems is a general trend toward quick response (interactive) systems as competition and customer demands accelerate and hardware costs decrease.

How Interactive Processing Works

Exhibit 16–5 gives a schematic of how interactive processing works in the processing of customer orders. As in the schematic for batch processing, it is not a complete flowchart, but it does illustrate the basic concepts.

The company receives customer orders in the mail or fills them out from phone calls, in which case there is a source document created. A clerk takes the

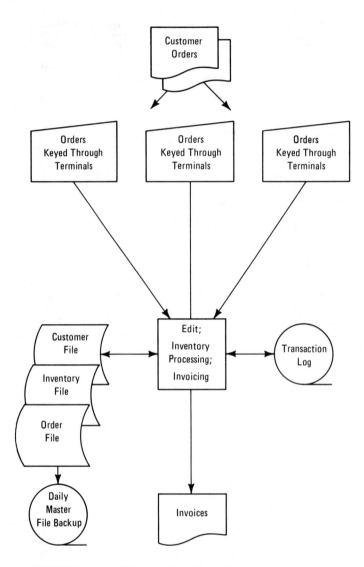

EXHIBIT 16–5   Schematic of Interactive Processing

information from the customer order and keys it into the terminal. For orders received over the phone, it is also possible to key the information directly into the terminal, eliminating the need for a source document. This approach is more efficient because it eliminates a time-consuming step, but it also increases the difficulty of ensuring proper authorization of all transactions, since all transactions no longer tie back to a source document.

The computer immediately performs all program checks, such as reasonableness, completeness, and validity, as the information is keyed into the terminal. In addition, as the customer order is entered, the computer checks available inventory quantities and checks the customer's credit. If the order is accepted, the computer allocates the inventory quantities to that order. When the goods are shipped, the computer invoices the customer and updates the on-hand inventory balances.

Ensuring Proper Authorization

One internal control difficulty with interactive processing is that, in the absence of special measures, anyone with access to a terminal can input data to the system, even without proper authorization. To combat this problem, an interactive system requires a user identification number (user ID) and a password for anyone trying to use the system. The system can limit the activities of specific users to only those transactions with which they are authorized to deal. The system can then display at the system console any attempted security violations. Management can periodically change passwords for all employees and delete user IDs and passwords for all employees who quit or were fired.

Test of Input for Errors

When the operator enters the customer number, the computer displays the customer name and address. The operator can then visually verify the correct customer. Similarly, the computer displays the appropriate description when the operator inputs the inventory item numbers for the order. This control, called *descriptive feedback*, ensures that the correct customer gets the exact items desired.

Because descriptive feedback is possible using interactive processing, two of the programmed controls used in batch processing are no longer needed. The self-checking number catches transposition errors that occur when clerks copy numbers onto forms and ensures that the proper account is updated. Redundancy also helps in seeing that the intended account is updated. But visually checking the customer name or inventory description is more effective, so neither of these batch processing controls are used in interactive processing.

The computer validates all codes by matching them to tables of valid codes. If the computer finds an invalid code, it displays an error message and gives the operator the option of correcting the error immediately or cancelling the order. The system will not accept orders with invalid codes.

The system ensures that the salesperson number matches a valid salesperson. Additionally, the system verifies that the order number is not the duplicate of an order already on file. Again, if there are errors, the system displays an error message and gives the operator the choice of correcting or cancelling the order.

The operator may key in a nonstandard price and thereby override the standard price on the inventory file. To detect a gross keying error, such as a misplaced decimal, the computer displays a warning message if the keyed price is not in the range of 20 per cent to 200 per cent of the standard price.

Credit Checking

The system automatically checks the customer's credit for every order. Exhibit 16–6 gives an example of such a credit check display. There are appropriate warning messages when a customer exceeds his credit limit. The system considers the accounts receivable balance, invoices which have not completed the billing process, and the invoice being processed in determining the customer's balance. If the balance exceeds the credit limit, the system places the order in "hold" status. To release the order from "hold," an operator must input a two-character authorization ID. This capability of the system reduces the work of the credit department, since the department need only review the orders where the customer fails the credit limit tests.

Independent Verification of Terminal Operators

The operator inputs transactions directly into the system, without the backup of an authorized source document. It is therefore necessary for the system to independently verify the performance of the terminal operator. Exhibit 16–7 illustrates an Order Reconciliation report, which can perform this function. A terminal is often called a *workstation,* abbreviated W/S. Various terminals are identified W1, W2, etc.

The Order Reconciliation report shows all orders in the system, including the workstation where they were entered. The report also shows the daily action, if any, for that order. The report points out any orders on "hold" status which were released by entering a two-character authorization ID. In addition, the report points out any orders where the operator overrode the standard price. Control totals are given at the end, as shown in Exhibit 16–8. These totals give the order volume by workstation, thereby measuring operator performance, and ensuring that orders were entered only from authorized workstations.

The totals from the Order Reconciliation report balance to a manually prepared control log, illustrated in Exhibit 16–9. The operator will enter control totals for each order and then develop daily control totals. The information from this log should balance on a daily basis with the sum of the Orders Entered Today and New Open Orders Entered Today amounts, which appear in the Order Reconciliation report totals. This procedure ensures that the system processed all orders that were logged as entered. It also provides assurance that the orders processed were received by the person maintaining the Order Entry Control log.

```
33200151  TOWNE OFFICE SUPPLY                    ORDER 10248 - CREDIT CHECK
                                                                 1 24

   PREVIOUSLY RECEIVABLE FROM CUSTOMER
      ACCOUNTS RECEIVABLE BALANCE                      720.84
      FUTURE CHARGES                                    75.20
      IN TRANSIT TO ACCOUNTS RECEIVABLE                 30.05
                                          TOTAL A/R    826.09
   ORDERS IN PROCESS
      ORDER 10248 - NOT YET INVOICED                   225.77
      ORDER 10131 - NOT YET INVOICED                   107.23
      ORDER  9980 - ALREADY INVOICED                    61.44

      CREDIT LIMIT          1,000.00     TOTAL DUE    1,220.53

   ORDER 10248 PLACED ON CREDIT HOLD     OVER LIMIT BY  220.53

COMMAND KEYS
 1 RESUME ENTRY
24 SIGN OFF
```

EXHIBIT 16–6 Credit Check Display. © 1978, 1979 by International Business Machines Corporation and reproduced with their permission from *System/34 Distributors Management Accounting System II (DMAS II)*.

CONCEPT SUMMARY
Comparison of Processing Alternatives

	Batch	*Interactive*
Data Entry	Punched onto cards off-line and run through the card reader	Typed in on-line through the terminals
Input Validation	Process cards with separate edit run to validate input	Program checks input for errors as the data are typed in
Error Correction	Data control clerk corrects cards with errors and reruns edit; no further processing occurs until there are no errors	Terminal operator corrects errors as they occur
Transaction Order	Because of sequential access, transactions must be sorted and are processed in master file order	Because of direct access, transactions need not be sorted and are processed in the order they occur
Master File Backup	Grandfather-father-son concept; father tapes are saved for backup; son tapes become father tapes in the next cycle	Dump entire contents of all master files to tape on a daily basis
Transaction Backup	Save transaction files even after they have been processed to recreate father and son master files	Create transaction log tape containing every processed transaction

ORDER RECONCILIATION
DMAS CORP.

ORDER NUMBER		CUSTOMER NUMBER	NEW TODAY	CONTROL TOTALS	ENTERED BY	ACTION TODAY	ITEMS	SPEC CHGS	CHANGED TODAY BY	PRICING OVERRIDE	PICK LIST	INVOICE PRINTED	ON FILE		ITEMS	SP/CHGS
5	O/ORDER	12780000	-	-	W1	CHANGED	1	0	SAME W/S	-	-	-		O/ORDER	1	0
9	O/ORDER	21000000	-	-	W1	RELEASED	1	0	-	-	-	-		ORDER	1	0
12510	O/ORDER	11430000	-	-	W4	RELEASED	1	0	SAME W/S	-	YES	-		ORDER	1	2
25111	O/ORDER	11750000	-	-	W3	-	3	1	-	-	-	-		O/ORDER	4	2
25137	O/ORDER	11111800	-	-	W2	CHANGED	3	1	SAME W/S	-	-	-		O/ORDER	1	1
75968	O/ORDER	17640000	-	-	W2	-			-	-	-	-		O/ORDER	1	0
75984	CR MEMO	20000020	NEW -	BALANCED	W3	NEW	4	0	-	-	-	YES				
77993	ORDER	11495000	NEW -	BALANCED	W4	NEW	4	2	-	-	YES	YES				
77996	ORDER	28000000	NEW -	BALANCED	W4	NEW	8	2	-	YES	YES	YES		O/ORDER	1	0
RBK 2970-1 BACKORDER CONVERTED TO OPEN ORDER																
77999	INVOICE	11800010	NEW -	BALANCED	W4	NEW	3	3	-	-	-	YES		O/ORDER	1	0
RBK 2970-1 BACKORDER CONVERTED TO OPEN ORDER																
78186	ORDER	22400000	NEW -	NO ENTRY	W2	NEW	3	0	-	-	YES	YES				
79211	ORDER	16300000	NEW -	FORCED	W3	NEW	3	1	-	-	-	YES				
79212	INVOICE	21000000	NEW -	BALANCED	W3	NEW	5	1	-	-	-	YES		ORDER	1	0
79250	ORDER	17600030	NEW -	BALANCED	W3	NEW	1	0	-	-	-	-		URDER	4	2
80342	ORDER	11750000	-		W1	-			-	-	-	-		ORDER	4	2
80345	INVOICE	11800020	NEW -	BALANCED	W1	NEW	3	0	-	-	-	YES				
80347	ORDER	17600030	NEW -	BALANCED	W1	NEW	2	1	-	-	-	YES		O/ORDER	1	0
80348	ORDER	25000020	NEW -	FORCED	W1	NEW	6	2	YES	YES	-	YES				
RBK 2970-1 BACKORDER CONVERTED TO OPEN ORDER																
80349	O/ORDER	11610000	NEW -	BALANCED	W1	NEW	4	1	-	-	YES	-		O/ORDER	4	1
80350	ORDER	11111800	NEW -	BALANCED	W1	NEW	1	0	-	-	YES	YES				
89000	INVOICE	10100000	NEW -	BALANCED	W1	NEW	1	0	-	-	YES	YES				
89001	ORDER	00000000	NEW -	NO ENTRY	W1	CANCELED	0	0	-	-	-	-				
89020	ORDER	16005000	NEW -	BALANCED	W1	NEW	2	0	-	-	YES	YES		ORDER	1	0
89021	ORDER	11380020	NEW -	BALANCED	W2	NEW	1	0	-	-	YES	YES				
89025	ORDER	11380010	NEW -	BALANCED	W2	NEW	1	0	-	-	-	-				
89026	INVOICE	11400000	NEW -	BALANCED	W1	DELETED	1	0	DIFF W/S	-	-	-		ORDER	1	0
89028	O/ORDER	00000000	NEW -	NO ENTRY	W1	CANCELED	0	0	-	-	-	-				
89029	CR MEMO	00000000	NEW -	NO ENTRY	W1	CANCELED	0	0	-	-	-	-				
98541	ORDER	25000020	NEW -	NO ENTRY	W1	NEW	1	0	-	-	-	-		ORDER	1	0
RBK 1600-1 ORDER IS ON CREDIT HOLD																
98542	ORDER	11630000	NEW -	NO ENTRY	W1	NEW	2	0	-	-	-	-		ORDER	2	0
RBK 2530-1 CL AUTHORIZED RELEASE FROM CREDIT HOLD																

EXHIBIT 16-7 Order Reconciliation Report. © 1978, 1979 by International Business Machines Corporation and reproduced with their permission from *System/34 Distributors Management Accounting System II (DMAS II)*.

ORDER RECONCILIATION
DMAS CORP.

NEW ENTRIES TODAY --	----- NEW ORDERS -----			----- OPEN ORDERS -----		
	ORDERS	ITEMS	SP/CHGS	ORDERS	ITEMS	SP/CHGS
WORKSTATION W1	9	18	3	1	4	1
WORKSTATION W2	3	5	0	0	0	0
WORKSTATION W4	3	15	7	0	0	0
WORKSTATION W3	4	10	2	0	0	0
	19	48	12	1	4	1

RECONCILIATION	ORDERS	ITEMS	SP/CHGS
OPEN ORDERS ON FILE AT START OF DAY	6	12	3
PLUS ... NEW OPEN ORDERS ENTERED TODAY	1	4	1
LESS ... OPEN ORDERS DELETED IN FULL	0	0	0
PLUS ... LINES ADDED/DELETED IN OPEN ORDERS ON FILE		1-	0
LESS ... OPEN ORDERS RELEASED TODAY	2	2	0
PLUS ... PARTIAL RELEASES RETURNED TO FILE	0	0	0
PLUS ... BACKORDERS KEPT FOR LATER RELEASE	3	3	0
OPEN ORDERS ON FILE AT END OF DAY	8	16	4
ORDERS ON FILE AT START OF DAY	1	0	0
PLUS ... ORDERS ENTERED TODAY - EXCLUDES OPEN ORDERS	19	48	12
PLUS ... OPEN ORDERS RELEASED TODAY	2	2	0
PLUS ... STANDING ORDERS RELEASED TODAY	0	0	0
LESS ... ORDERS DELETED IN FULL	1	0	0
PLUS ... LINES ADDED/DELETED IN ORDERS ON FILE		4	2
LESS ... LINES HELD BACK IN PARTIAL RELEASES		0	0
LESS ... ORDERS RELEASED TODAY FOR INVOICING	14	43	12
ORDERS ON FILE AT END OF DAY	7	11	2

15 ORDERS AND OPEN ORDERS ON FILE ... FILE CAPACITY- 190
68 RECORDS IN THE OPEN ORDER FILE ... FILE CAPACITY- 1700
34 RECORDS IN THE ORDER FILE ... FILE CAPACITY- 864

EXHIBIT 16–8 Order Reconciliation Report Totals. © 1978, 1979 by International Business Machines Corporation and reproduced with their permission from *System/34 Distributors Management Accounting System II (DMAS II)*.

Example of Control Log

Order Entry / Billing Control Log entries

1 Order number: The number assigned to the order.

2 Number of items: Count of line items entered for the order. This column total should balance to the corresponding total on the Order Reconciliation report.

3 Total quantity all items: A (hash) total of the quantity ordered of all transactions.

4 Number of special charges: Count of the special charges for the order.

5 Total of special charges: A total of the amounts of special charges.

Order Entry/Billing Control Log

Page No. ____
W/S ____ ID ____ Op. ____

Line	Date	Order number **1**	Number of items **2**	Total qty. all items **3**	No. spec. charges **4**	Total of spec. chgs. **5**
1						
2						
3						
4						
5						
6						
7						
8						
9						
10						
11						
12						
13						
14						
15						
16						
17						
18						
19						
20						
21						
22						
23						
24						
25						
26						
27						
28						
29						
30						
31						
32						
33						
34						
35						
36						
37						
38						
39						
40						
Carry-forward Totals						
TOTALS		*		*		

*Balance to Order Reconciliation

EXHIBIT 16–9 Example of Control Log. © 1978, 1979 by International Business Machines Corporation and reproduced with their permission from *System/34 Distributors Management Accounting System II (DMAS II)*.

It is possible to achieve additional control over unauthorized entry of transactions to the order files by comparing the Open Orders On File At End Of Day (deferred orders) and the Orders On File At End Of Day (active orders) to the corresponding Start of Day totals on the Order Reconciliation report of the next day. This procedure provides assurance that: (1) the system processed the correct files, and (2) there was no change in the number of orders since the run of the previous day.

16.3 COMPLIANCE TESTING IN A COMPUTER ENVIRONMENT*

Compliance testing in a computer environment, just as in a manual environment, involves checking the internal controls to determine if they are functioning properly. In a computer environment, some of the most important internal controls are the programmed controls, such as reasonableness tests. Consequently, these controls must be tested for compliance. At the same time, it makes sense to check that the computer system is performing properly and generating the correct information.

Test Deck

The basic tool for compliance testing in a computer environment is the test deck, a collection of transactions generated by the auditor. The auditor knows what the correct results of processing the test transactions should be. He processes the test deck using the client's programs and compares the results generated by these programs to the previously determined correct results.

Exhibit 16–10 provides a schematic of test deck use. This schematic shows how the test deck can be used to independently verify that the client application programs are functioning as they should. To function properly, the programs should both process correct data correctly and identify and reject incorrect data. Therefore, the test transactions should contain both correct and incorrect data for complete testing.

Suppose the auditor wished to compliance test the file maintenance program, which adds, modifies, and deletes employees from the payroll master file. Exhibit 16–11 gives five test deck transactions the auditor might develop. He would want to see the program reject the first four transactions and process the fifth transaction correctly. If the program does not reject all of the first four transactions, then the programmed controls are not functioning as they should.

---

*This section and the next are based upon *Computer-Assisted Audit Techniques,* American Institute of Certified Public Accountants, New York, 1979.

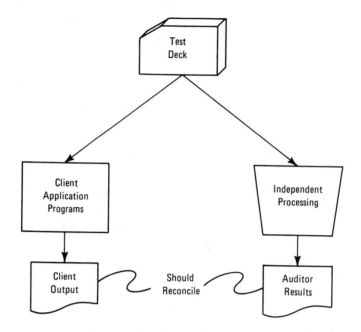

EXHIBIT 16–10 Schematic of Test Deck Use

Advantages and Disadvantages

The test deck approach is most suitable in batch processing systems, where the auditor can make a copy of the client's master file for audit use at night or other low-demand time. Any changes to the auditor's copy of the file are of no consequence. Interactive processing systems typically require all of the computer's resources to process the company's transactions. To process test transactions might destroy part of the client's files.

The test deck is most useful when the number of conditions to test is limited. In complex systems, it becomes almost impossible to design a comprehensive set of test data. For internal purposes, U.S. Steel developed a test deck for its payroll system. Because of the number of plants, the different types of jobs, the union contract, the overtime, and the different pay for different times of day, the test deck contained 10,000 transactions.

Integrated Test Facility

Because test transactions can destroy a client's live data, some companies have added dummy entities to their files (e.g., customers, employees). The auditor can then process transactions against these dummy entities using the client's regular system. This is called an *integrated test facility* (ITF). It is basically an adaptation of the test deck to an interactive processing environment.

EXHIBIT 16-11 Examples of Test Deck Transactions

	Transaction Description	Programmed Control	Desired Result
1	Add an employee with an existing social security number	Compare new social security number to those already on the file	Detect duplicate social security number; print error message; do not update file with new record
2	Add a new employee omitting the required date employed	Check input data for completeness of required data	Detect incomplete data; print error message; do not update file with a new record
3	Add a new employee with both an hourly rate of pay and a monthly salary	Check input data for consistency	Detect inconsistent data; print error message; do not update file with a new record
4	Increase the hourly rate of pay for an employee from $6 to $36, where the normal range of pay is $3.50 to $13.50 per hour	Check input data for reasonableness	Detect unreasonable data; print error message; do not change hourly rate for this employee
5	Increase the hourly rate of pay for an employee from $6 to $7	Print all data that have been changed	Process the transaction; print the hourly rate both before and after the change; change the hourly rate in that one employee's record

The effect of the dummy entities must be removed for reporting purposes. This removal can be done: (1) manually, (2) by reversing the effects of the test transactions, or (3) by special coding in the report program that eliminates the dummy entities.

It is possible for the auditor to obtain a copy of the client's data files and process test transactions, using the interactive processing system, at night or at another off time. The difficulty is that the auditor cannot be sure that the system he is processing at an off time is the same one that the client uses for regular processing. If any unauthorized modifications had been made to the system, the auditor could easily be given an unmodified version. The integrated test facility approach is better because the auditor knows that the system he is using is the one used for regular processing.

Program Tracing

In a manual system, the auditor can follow the flow of transactions from the source documents through the various processing steps. In a computer system, the auditor can also follow the flow of transactions using program tracing. A program trace is a list of the steps a program follows in processing a transaction. The auditor can use this trace to identify exactly what happens to any given transaction.

The capability of generating a program trace may be built into the client's application program because it helps for both audit and debugging purposes. The trace may also be generated by special software.

Review of Program Logic

In a manual system, the auditor can visually review the source documents, forms, accounting records, and reports. These will show him the various processing steps involved and how the final results were generated. In a computer system, such a visual review of the process is impossible because so much of the accounting records and the programs that process them are electronic and hence cannot be looked at directly. But the auditor can review the processing steps performed by the computer system by reviewing the program logic.

The auditor reviews the program logic in two steps. The first step is to collect and review the program documentation to get an overview of the program, its purpose, and its functions. The second step is to examine the source listing of the program to see exactly how the program works. This process makes the auditor intimately aware of the system and how it functions. However, it requires extensive programming knowledge and would be extremely time consuming for complex systems.

Program Comparison

One of the auditor's primary concerns is that all authorized changes to production programs are made and unauthorized changes are not. This check can be accomplished using special software that compares one copy of a program to another, identifying any differences.

One approach is to compare an earlier version of a program, say that of June 30, to the December 31 version. A second approach is to compare a library version of a program to the production version. The auditor should be able to explain any differences as approved, authorized, and tested changes. This comparison can be made for both source and object programs. However, the interpretation of identified differences in object programs is quite difficult.

Parallel Simulation

In some situations, the processing in the client's application programs is so complex that the auditor cannot verify the results with a test deck. For these circumstances, the auditor may use a self-developed program that performs the same key functions as the client's programs. The auditor can then independently verify the results of the client's processing, i.e., perform a parallel simulation. The results of the client's processing and the auditor's processing should reconcile. The auditor's program need not perform all of the functions of the client's programs, only the key functions of audit interest.

Embedded Audit Modules

The client application programs can have audit functions built in, by embedding audit modules into the programs. One approach is to build in audit modules that are only used periodically. An example would be confirmation capability being built in to the program that produces monthly billings. Another approach is to build in audit modules that are used continually. An example would be the "capture" of any transaction that tried to violate an established control. The transaction could then be written to a separate audit file for further examination. Embedded audit modules can, therefore, identify exception conditions as they occur. However, such testing can only identify anticipated exceptions.

Job Accounting Data

Most sophisticated systems develop an activity record of all the programs processed by the computer. The auditor can review this record to determine exactly when production programs were run and how many times they were run. This review can help the auditor determine if the programs were run correctly. For large systems, the activity record may be so vast that it requires special software to generate reports the auditor can interpret.

CONCEPT SUMMARY
Techniques for Compliance Testing*

	Description	Advantages	Disadvantages
Test Deck	Test transaction processed by both the client application programs and independently by the auditor	Requires little technical expertise; effective if the number of conditions is limited	Only tests preconceived conditions; almost impossible to design comprehensive test data for complex systems; time consuming; lacks objectivity
Integrated Test Facility (ITF)	"Dummy" entities against which the auditor can process transactions using the client's regular system	Useful for interactive processing systems; tests system in a regular processing mode; only moderate level of technical expertise required, other advantages parallel "test deck"	Removing test data from system may destroy client files; other disadvantages parallel "test deck"
Program Tracing	List of program steps followed in the processing of a given transaction	Use of actual data; can be more effective when used in combination with ITF	May require special processing logic not normally used; no guarantee that all logic paths are traversed
Review of Program Logic	Review program documentation and the source listing of the subject program	Examines processing logic in detail; auditor is intimately aware of processing code	Very high level of technical expertise required; very time consuming; practical only in relatively simple systems
Program Comparison	Compare a copy of a program that is under the auditor's control to the version currently used in processing	Compliance tests the general controls that all and only authorized changes are made to production programs; enhances auditor understanding of the system	When discrepancies are found, it may be very time consuming to evaluate the results effectively, especially with object programs
Parallel Simulation	Auditor develops program to perform same key functions as client application; compare results of client and auditor programs to ensure proper processing	Allows independence of auditor from client personnel; facilitates examination of a larger number of transactions; only moderate level of technical expertise required	No inference about unexamined data or processing; difficult to do in complex systems
Embedded Audit Modules	Section of program code to perform audit functions; can be either used periodically (e.g., confirmations) or continually (e.g., identification of overrides of controls)	Can detect "exception" conditions when they occur	Detects only anticipated "exceptions"
Job Accounting Data	Review activity record to determine production programs were run at the correct time and run the correct number of times	Can help determine that unauthorized applications were not processed and authorized applications were processed properly	Voluminous activity reports to review; may need special software to generate usable reports

*Cash, Bailey and Whinston, "A Survey of Techniques for Auditing EDP-Based Accounting Information Systems," *The Accounting Review,* October 1977.

16.4 SUBSTANTIVE TESTING IN A COMPUTER ENVIRONMENT

The data files in computer applications often become extremely large. Sears, Roebuck & Co. has millions of customers, and the accounts receivable file will, therefore, have millions of records. To do all the necessary substantive auditing steps manually with a file this size would be extremely tedious and wasteful. The auditor must use the computer to audit the computer system.

Generalized Audit Software

In the case of accounts receivable, the auditor could write an application program that would select and print out the appropriate confirmations. This would avoid the task of selecting the accounts manually and typing the confirmations. However, even this would be time consuming if the auditor had to write a separate program for each audit client.

In the early days of computer auditing, this was the only possibility. To do this, however, required not only writing the program but also debugging it, testing it, documenting it, and running it. In actual cases this process has taken 300 hours, thereby adding substantially to the audit fee.

There is a better approach. The auditor can write one program to work for all audit clients. This program must work with all different types of files, since each client will likely set up the accounts receivable file differently. Because the program must be generalized in this way, it is harder to write, but the savings gained from only writing the program once make this approach worthwhile.

Such programs are called *generalized audit software* (GAS). They are useful in more situations than the one client/one application program would be since they are generalized. Exhibit 16–12 gives a schematic of generalized audit software use. This schematic shows that GAS can provide an independent processing of the client's data to verify the proper processing by the client's application programs.

These GAS programs can be quite sophisticated. Each of the major CPA firms and several independent software firms have developed such systems at the cost of millions per system. Exhibit 16–13 gives the seven basic capabilities of GAS, including examples of their use in both accounts receivable and inventory application.

Inventory Audit Case Study

The purpose of this case study is to demonstrate the use of generalized audit software in accomplishing an audit objective. This is not a real package or a complete application, but it does convey the basic concepts.

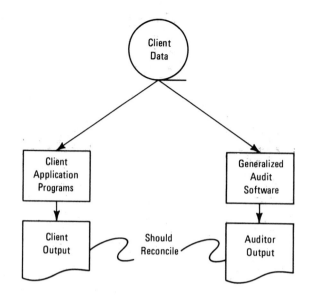

EXHIBIT 16–12　Schematic of Generalized Audit Software Use

EXHIBIT 16-13　Capabilities of Generalized Audit Software

		Examples	
	Capability	*Accounts Receivable*	*Inventory*
1	Select sample items	Customer balances for confirmation	Inventory items for observation
2	Examine records meeting specified criteria	Customer balances over credit limit	Negative or unreasonably large quantities
3	Test and make calculations	Recalculating interest charges	Recalculating inventory extensions
4	Compare data on separate files	Compare change in balance with details on transaction files	Compare current and prior period files to help identify obsolete items
5	Resequence and analyze data	Prepare accounts receivable aging	Resequence items by location to help observation
6	Compare data from audit procedures to company records	Compare customer responses to balances on file	Compare test counts with perpetual records
7	Perform statistical computations	Stratify population and compute the proper sample size	Estimate inventory value and compute confidence interval

Audit Objective

The audit objective is to verify that the client's inventory as of December 31, 19X2, is stated at the lower of cost or market.

Audit Procedures

The client took a physical inventory on December 31, 19X2, and created a magnetic tape file from the physical inventory count tickets. Exhibit 16–14 gives a description of this tape file and a flowchart of the audit procedures that will be followed:

1. Extend the 19X2 physical inventory counts at both the 19X1 standard cost and the 19X2 standard cost. Then, calculate the percentage change in standard costs during 19X2. See Exhibit 16–15.

2. Identify any missing or duplicate tickets and print an appropriate report. See Exhibit 16–16.

3. Sort the file into part number order, and summarize records by part number.

4. Select items for a price test, including all items valued over $100,000 and a random sample of 10 percent of the items under $100,000.

5. Analyze inventory at 19X2 standard cost, and print a report of 19X2 inventory by part number. See Exhibit 16–17.

Data Base Management Systems

Most computer systems, both batch and on line, are conventional file systems. This means that there is a master file supported by a transaction file for each application. For accounts receivable, then, there will be a customer master file and a transaction file containing all sales, collection, and adjustment transactions. The master file will contain the current balance for each customer, while the transaction file will contain the audit trail information which backs up that balance. There would be a similar file structure for other computer applications, such as inventory, payroll, and general ledger.

Problems With Conventional File Systems

Conventional file systems have three major problems:

1. The same transaction may affect more than one file, so each application must separately process the transaction. For example, the same sale might have to: (a) increase the customer's balance with accounts receivable department, (b) reduce the amount of inventory on hand in the inventory control depart-

Client Data File

Field Description	Position on Record		Field Type	Number of Decimal Places
	Starting	Length		
Count ticket	1	6	Character	
Count team	7	3	Character	
Part number	10	5	Character	
Description	15	40	Character	
Quantity at 12-31-X2	55	8	Numeric	0
19X1 Standard Unit Cost	63	7	Numeric	3
19X2 Standard Unit Cost	70	7	Numeric	3
Filler	77	4	Character	

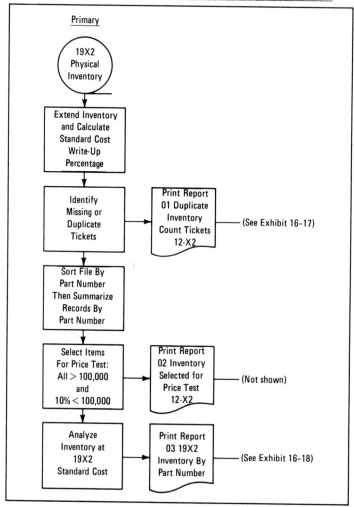

EXHIBIT 16–14 Client Data File and Logic Flowchart. © 1979 by the American Institute of Certified Public Accountants and reproduced with their permission from *Computer-Assisted Audit Techniques.*

Input Function

FN	SEQUENCE NUMBER	INSTRUCTION	FIELD NAME	DESCRIPTION	TYPE	DEC	FIELD LENGTH	START POSITION	LENGTH	DEC	OTHER	ID FIELD
IP	00230	FIELD	TIKET	COUNT TICKET				1	6N			SAMP
IP	00240	FIELD	TEAM	CNT TM				7	3N			SAMP
IP	00250	FIELD	PAXNO	PART NUMBER				10	5C			SAMP
IP	00260	FIELD	DESCB	DESCRIPTION				15	40C			SAMP
IP	00270	FIELD	X2QTY	QUANTITY AT 12-31 X2				55	8NO			SAMP
IP	00280	FIELD	X1CST	19X1 STANDARD COST				63	7N3			SAMP
IP	00290	FIELD	X2CST	19X2 STANDARD COST				70	7N3			SAMP
IP	00300	FIELD	X1VAL	INVENTORY AT X1 COST	N3							SAMP
IP	00310	FIELD	X2VAL	INVENTORY AT X2 COST	N3							SAMP
IP	00320	FIELD	WRTUP	AMOUNT OF WRITE-UP	N3							SAMP
IP	00330	FIELD	PERCT	PERCENTAGE WRITE-UP	N1							SAMP
IP	00340	FIELD	MSSG2	MESSAGE 2	C		20					SAMP

Processing Function

FN	SEQUENCE NUMBER	INSTRUCTION	FIELD NAME 1	2	FIELD NAME 3	FIELD NAME 4	5	CONSTANT AND OTHER 6	7	8	9	10		FIELD
PR	04010	MUL	X1CST	BY	X2QTY	X1VAL								SAMP
PR	04020	MUL	X2CST	BY	X2QTY	X2VAL								SAMP
PR	04030	SUB	X1VAL	FR	X2VAL	WRTUP								SAMP
PR	04040	DIV	WRTUP	BY	X1VAL	WKNO1								SAMP
PR	04050	MUL	WKNO1	BY	CONST	PERCT		100						SAMP
PR	04060	MISDUP	TIKET											SAMP
PR	04070	IF	ERDUP	EQ	CONST		04081	ON						SAMP
PR	04080	PRINT	01											SAMP
PR	04081	FOOT	X2VAL				INVENTORY AT 19X2 STANDARD COSTS							SAMP
PR	04090	SORT												

EXHIBIT 16–15 © 1979 by the American Institute of Certified Public Accountants and reproduced with their permission from *Computer-Assisted Audit Techniques.*

Output Function-Report (System Formatted)

FN	SEQUENCE NUMBER	INSTRUCTION	RPT NO.	REPORT NAME	ID FIELD
OP	1.000.0	NAME	0.1	DUPLICATE INVENTORY COUNT TICKETS 12-X2	SAMP

FN	SEQUENCE NUMBER	INSTRUCTION	FIELD NAME	FIELD NAME	FIELD NAME	FIELD NAME	FIELD NAME	ID FIELD
OP	1.010.0	SORT	TIKET					SAMP

FN	SEQUENCE NUMBER	INSTRUCTION	FIELD NAME	SPACE	FIELD NAME	SPACE	FIELD NAME	SPACE	FIELD NAME	SPACE	FIELD NAME	SPACE DETAIL	ID FIELD
OP	1.020.0	SUBTOT										Z	SAMP

FN	SEQUENCE NUMBER	INSTRUCTION	FIELD NAME	FO.OT	FIELD NAME	FO.OT	FIELD NAME	FO.OT	FIELD NAME	FO.OT	FIELD NAME	FO.OT	FIELD NAME	FO.OT	FIELD NAME	FO.OT	FIELD NAME	FO.OT	FIELD NAME	FO.OT	ID FIELD
OP	1.030.0	PRDATA	TIKET		TEAM		PARNO		DESCB		X2QTY		X2VAL								SAMP

Resulting Report (System Formatted)

```
SAMPLE COMPANY                    CPA FIRM              12-31-X2      01-15-X3  AICPA COMPUTER AUDITOR        PAGE    1
COMPUTER COMMON AUDIT SOFTWARE - VENDOR                 INVENTORY               REPORT 01     RUN   1         TIME 12:46

                                     DUPLICATE INVENTORY COUNT TICKETS 12-X2

 COUNT    CNT    PART                                       QUANTITY AT            INVENTORY
 TICKET   TM    NUMBER   DESCRIPTION                         12-31-X2              AT X2 COST
•••••••••••••••••••••••••••••••••••••••••••••••••••••••••••••••••••••••••••••••••••••••••••••••••••••••••••••••••
     3     204    316    STARWHEELS                            70                   70.000.000

     3     204    326    HOPPER                                75                  187.500.000

    10     201    315    ACME PUNCH DIE                        75                   48.750.000

    10     205    315    AJAX PUNCH DIE                        25                   16.250.000

    17     202    313    WIRE                                  40                   15.000.000

    17     202    327    PUNCH KEYS                            80                  280.000.000

    17     202    327    KEYS                                  85                  297.500.000

    23     203    304    DIRECT IMPULSE HUB                   300                   18.150.000

    23     205    328    FEED HOPPERS                          10                   20.000.000

 COUNT     9                                                                       953.150.000
```

EXHIBIT 16–16 © 1979 by the American Institute of Certified Public Accountants and reproduced with their permission from *Computer-Assisted Audit Techniques.*

Output Function-Report (Auditor Formatted)

OP	SEQUENCE NUMBER	INSTRUCTION	RPT NO.	REPORT NAME	FIELD
OP	3,0,0,0,0	NAME		0,3 19X2 INVENTORY BY PART NUMBER	SAMP

OP	SEQUENCE NUMBER	INSTRUCTION	FIELD NAME	FIELD NAME	FIELD NAME	FIELD NAME	FIELD NAME	FIELD
OP	3,0,1,0,0	SORT	PARNO					SAMP

OP	SEQUENCE NUMBER	INSTRUCTION	FIELD NAME	FIELD NAME	FIELD NAME	FIELD NAME	FIELD NAME		
OP	3,0,1,1,0	SUBTOT					2		SAMP

FN	SEQUENCE NUMBER	INSTRUCTION	AUDIT FIELD	LINE NO.	START	LENGTH	FORMAT	HEADING LINE 1	HEADING LINE 2	FIELD
OP	3,0,2,0,0	COLUMN	PARNO		5			PART	NUMBER	SAMP
OP	3,0,3,0,0	COLUMN	DESCB		40				DESCRIPTION	SAMP
OP	3,0,4,0,0	COLUMN	X1CST		8	N3QE		STANDARD	COST - X1	SAMP
OP	3,0,5,0,0	COLUMN	X2CST		8	N3QE		STANDARD	COST - X2	SAMP
OP	3,0,6,0,0	COLUMN	X2QTY		8	NOQE		19X2	QUANTITY	SAMP
OP	3,0,7,0,0	COLUMN	X1VAL		12	2QE	INVENTORY AT	X1 STD COST	SAMP
OP	3,0,8,0,0	COLUMN	X2VAL		12	2QE	INVENTORY AT	X2 STD COST	SAMP
OP	3,0,9,0,0	COLUMN	WRTUP		10	2QE	WRITE-UP	IN 19X2	SAMP
OP	3,1,0,0,0	COLUMN	PERCT		4	NOQE	PER	CENT	SAMP

Resulting Report (Auditor Formatted)

```
SAMPLE COMPANY                    CPA FIRM              12-31-X2    01-15-X3  AICPA COMPUTER AUDITOR       PAGE    1
COMPUTER COMMON AUDIT SOFTWARE - VENDOR                INVENTORY             REPORT Q2      RUN  1        TIME  12:46

                                    19X2 INVENTORY BY PART NUMBER

   PART                       STANDARD    STANDARD    19X2     INVENTORY AT    INVENTORY AT    WRITE-UP    PER
  NUMBER  DESCRIPTION         COST--X1    COST--X2   QUANTITY   X1 STD COST     X2 STD COST    IN 19X2    CENT
  ......................................................................................................

    301   ACCOUNTING MACHINES    .025       .035        0           0.00            0.00          0.00     0.0

    302   BOND FEED WHEELS      1.125      2.250      1000        1150.00         2250.00       1125.00   100.0

    303   CARD HOPPER          30.375     60.750       200        6075.00        12150.00       6075.00   100.0

    304   DIRECT IMPULSE HUB   40.500     60.500       300       12150.00        18150.00       6000.00    49.4

    305   FORM LIGHTS          50.525    101.000       400       20210.00        40400.00      20190.00    99.9

    306   GANGPUNCH SWITCH     60.594    112.675       250       15140.00        28168.75      13020.25    36.0

    307   HAND FEED WHEELS     70.596     90.250        10         705.96          902.50        196.54    27.8

    308   INTERPRETERS         81.000    100.000        15        1215.00         1500.00        285.00    23.5

    309   JACK PLUG            92.000     98.000        20        1840.00         1960.00        120.00     6.5
```

EXHIBIT 16-17 © 1979 by the American Institute of Certified Public Accountants and reproduced with their permission from *Computer-Assisted Audit Techniques.*

ment, and (c) increase the sales by salesperson for commission purposes in the payroll department. This causes often a major problem of coordination because not all files always get promptly updated. As a result, the information in different departments of the same company may not be consistent.

2. Management requests for information often span more than one computer application. For example, suppose management wants to project the effects of introducing a new product. A proper computer analysis would require information from many different areas of the company, including marketing, inventory control, and accounting. Such cross-application analyses are quite difficult with conventional file systems.

3. The conventional file system does not show the interrelationships between data. For example, one purchase order may be for several different inventory items, while each inventory item may be on several purchase orders. Such relationships are not shown by file systems. The basic data may be there but not the relationships.

Data-Base Approach

Because of these problems, the current trend in data processing is toward the data-base approach. The data-base approach is to develop a consistent, integrated collection of information (called a *data-base*), which provides the data needed for all applications. The data-base stores not only all needed data but also the interrelationships between the data. Additionally, for any transaction all updates are performed at the same time.

What allows the data-base approach to work is the availability of very complex software called *data-base management systems* (DBMS). The DBMS performs all the necessary tasks of building and updating the data base, including both the data and all interrelationships. The DBMS will also usually provide an inquiry capability, so the user can develop reports based upon the information in the data base.

Audit Problems with DBMS

DBMS are one of the most important developments in the history of data processing and will only increase in importance in the future. However, the DBMS presents a difficult problem to the auditor. The primary problem is that the generalized audit software (GAS) cannot access the data maintained by the DBMS.

The GAS is designed to deal with data files maintained by conventional file systems. The data maintained by DBMS are stored in a very complex way, and each DBMS stores its data in a different way.

Auditing in a DBMS Environment

Because of the above problem, the auditor cannot use GAS in a DBMS environment in the same manner discussed earlier in the chapter. There are then two possibilities:

1. Dump the data from the data base to tape and use GAS. This is the most commonly used approach. However, this approach has three shortcomings: (a) special programs must reformat the data before GAS can use it; (b) the data is then stored in the conventional way, and all interrelationships are lost; and (c) the auditor has to rely on the client's system, which could be compromised to dump the data.

2. Use the inquiry capability of the DBMS to perform the audit functions. The selection, calculation, and analysis capabilities of GAS are often available as part of the DBMS to give the user maximum use of the data base. The auditor can then use these capabilities, but again there are major shortcomings: (a) the auditor must rely on the client's personnel and system to access the data base, thus reducing independence, and (b) the auditor often has to use the system during off hours to avoid disruption; he can then no longer be sure that the data and programs tested are the actual data and programs used for daily data processing.

There is currently no perfect solution to the problem of auditing in a DBMS environment. Eventually, perhaps, DBMS vendors will build in audit "windows" so that the auditor's independent programs will be able to access the data base directly. Until such time, however, the auditor should be very conscious of the problem of independence in this situation.

CONCEPT SUMMARY
Techniques for Verifying Results of Processing*

	Technique	Advantages	Disadvantages
1	Custom-designed or special-purpose computer programs	Aids in accessing data stored in machine readable form; forces familiarity with the system	High cost; long lead times for program development; low degree of flexibility
2	Generalized Audit Software (GAS)	Lower cost than special purpose programs; uses business-oriented language; flexible	Designed for use with sequential file structures; typically written for ease of implementation rather than efficiency
3	Data Base Management Systems (DBMS)	Can access more complex data structures; auditor not responsible for access of data	Auditor relies on client's system to generate data for audit; increased level of technical expertise needed

*Cash, Bailey, and Whinston, "A Survey of Techniques for Auditing EDP-Based Accounting Information Systems," *The Accounting Review,* October 1977, p. 827.

Key Terms

batch processing	header label
control log	integrated test facility (ITF)
control total	interactive processing
data-base management	internal label
system (DBMS)	programmed control
direct access	record count
edit program	self-checking number
external label	sequential access
generalized audit software (GAS)	test deck
grandfather-father-son	trailer label
hash total	transaction log

Questions and Problems

Questions

16-1 Give the fundamental characteristics of batch processing. Distinguish between the basic batch and batch with remote data transmission approaches.

16-2 Discuss the grandfather-father-son concept. Why is it useful in protecting data files?

16-3 List the nine programmed controls for batch processing, and give an example of each.

16-4 List the fundamental characteristics of interactive processing. Distinguish between the inquiry/response only and real-time processing approaches.

16-5 Explain the relationship between the Order Entry Control log and the Order Reconciliation report.

16-6 What is a test deck? How is it useful in compliance testing? What are its limitations?

16-7 Describe each of the eight techniques for compliance testing besides the test deck, and give their advantages and disadvantages.

16-8 List the seven capabilities of generalized audit software, and briefly explain how each might be useful in an audit situation.

16-9 Briefly narrate the objective of the inventory audit case study given in the chapter and the procedures followed to accomplish this objective.

16-10 Discuss the data-base approach. Why is generalized audit software not directly useful with data-base management systems?

Multiple Choice Questions From Professional Examinations

16-11 Which of the following client electronic data processing (EDP) systems can generally be audited without examining or directly testing the EDP computer programs of the system?

    a. A system that performs relatively uncomplicated processes and produces detailed output.

    b. A system that affects a number of essential master files and produces a limited output.

    c. A system that updates a few essential master files and produces no printed output other than final balances.

    d. A system that performs relatively complicated processing and produces very little detailed output.

16-12 An electronic data processing technique, which collects data into groups to permit convenient and efficient processing, is known as

    a. Document-count processing

    b. Multi-programming

    c. Batch processing

    d. Generalized-audit processing

16-13 The grandfather-father-son approach to providing protection for important computer files is a concept that is most often found in

    a. On-line, real-time systems

    b. Punched-card systems

    c. Magnetic tape systems

    d. Magnetic drum systems

16-14 Which of the following is not a problem associated with the use of test decks for computer-audit purposes?

    a. Auditing through the computer is more difficult than auditing around the computer.

    b. It is difficult to design test decks that incorporate all potential variations in transactions.

    c. Test data may be commingled with live data, causing operating problems for the client.

    d. The program with which the test data are processed may differ from the one used in actual operations.

16-15 The Smith Corporation has numerous small customers. A customer file is kept on disk storage. For each customer, the file contains customer name, address, credit limit, and account balance. The auditor wishes to test this file to determine whether credit limits are being exceeded. Assuming that computer time is available, the best procedure for the auditor to follow would be to

a. Develop a test deck which would cause the account balance of certain accounts to be increased until the credit limit was exceeded to see if the system would react properly.

b. Develop a program to compare credit limits with account balances and print out the details of any account with a balance exceeding its credit limit.

c. Ask for a printout of all account balances so that they can be manually checked against the credit limits.

d. Ask for a printout of a sample of account balances so that they can be individually checked against the credit limits.

16-16 An auditor obtains a magnetic tape that contains the dollar amounts of all client inventory items by style number. The information on the tape is in no particular sequence. The auditor can best ascertain that no consigned merchandise is included on the tape by using a computer program that

a. Statistically selects samples of all amounts.

b. Excludes all amounts for items with particular style numbers that indicate consigned merchandise.

c. Mathematically calculates the extension of each style quantity by the unit price.

d. Prints on paper the information that is on the magnetic tape.

16-17 General and special computer programs have been developed for use in auditing EDP systems. When considering the use of these computer-audit programs, the auditor

a. Should determine the audit efficiency of using a given computer program.

b. Will find them ineffective for applications containing many records and requiring significant time for testing.

c. Should use them on a surprise basis in order for them to be effective.

d. Will find them economically feasible for any size EDP system.

16-18 The primary purpose of a generalized computer audit program is to allow the auditor to

a. Use the client's employees to perform routine audit checks of the EDP records that otherwise would be done by the auditor's staff accountants.

b. Test the logic of computer programs used in the client's EDP systems.

c. Select larger samples from the client's EDP records than would otherwise be selected without the generalized program.

d. Independently process client EDP records.

16-19 Control totals are used as a basic method for detecting data errors. Which of the following is not a control figure used as a control total in EDP systems?

    a. Ledger totals

    b. Check-digit totals

    c. Hash totals

    d. Document-count totals

16-20 In computer-record data fields, totals of amounts that are not usually added but are used only for data processing control purposes are called

    a. Record totals

    b. Hash totals

    c. Processing data totals

    d. Field totals

16-21 An auditor would be least likely to use a generalized computer-audit program for which of the following tasks?

    a. Selecting and printing accounts receivable confirmations.

    b. Listing accounts receivable confirmation exceptions for examination.

    c. Comparing accounts receivable subsidiary files to the general ledger.

    d. Investigating exceptions to accounts receivable confirmations.

16-22 What is the computer process called when data processing is performed concurrently with a particular activity, and the results are available soon enough to influence the particular course of action being taken or the decision being made?

    a. Batch processing

    b. Real-time processing

    c. Integrated data processing

    d. Random access processing

16-23 Two independent statements (numbered I and II) are presented. You are to evaluate each statement individually and determine whether or not it is true. Your answer for each item should be selected from the following responses:

    a. I only is true.

    b. II only is true.

    c. Both I and II are true.

    d. Neither I nor II is true.

Computer files are usually maintained on magnetic tapes or disks.

I. A principal advantage of using magnetic tape files is that data need not be recorded sequentially.

II. A major advantage of disk files is the ability to gain random access to data on the disk.

16-24 Which of the following is a characteristic of an integrated system for data processing?

a. An integrated system is a real-time system where files for different functions with similar information are separated.

b. A single input record describing a transaction initiates the updating of all files associated with the transaction.

c. Parallel operations strengthen internal control over the computer processing function.

d. Files are maintained according to organizational functions such as purchasing, accounts payable, sales, etc.

16-25 When auditing a computerized system, an auditor may use the integrated test facility technique, sometimes referred to as the mini-company approach, as an audit tool. This technique

a. Is more applicable to independent audits than internal audits.

b. Involves using test decks.

c. Is the most commonly used audit tool for "auditing through the computer."

d. Involves introducing simulated transactions into a system simultaneously with actual transactions.

Problems

16-26 Executive management of Continental Incorporated, a rapidly expanding manufacturing company, has been reviewing a proposal prepared by the manager of the data processing department to update the computer equipment now in use. The present equipment includes a central processing unit, tape drives, a card punch, a card reader, a card sorter, and a line impact printer.

The data processing manager suggests that new equipment be acquired to provide an on-line, real-time capability for inventory stock control and more efficient operation.

Required:

a. Briefly describe the function of each item of equipment now in use.

b. Identify two types of equipment not mentioned above that would be required for the proposed on-line, real-time application.

c. Indicate the principal advantage of each item in Column A over the corresponding item in Column B.

d. Indicate the principal advantage of each item in Column B over the corresponding item in Column A.

A	*B*
1. Magnetic tape storage	1. Disk storage
2. Card reader	2. CRT (visual display) terminal
3. Printer	3. Card punch

IIA

16-27 Linder Company is completing the implementation of its new, computerized inventory control and purchase order system. Linder's controller wants the controls incorporated into the programs of the new system to be reviewed and evaluated to ensure that all necessary computer controls are included and functioning properly. He respects and has confidence in the system department's work and evaluation procedures, but he would like a separate appraisal of the control procedures by the internal audit department. He hopes that such a review would reveal any weaknesses or omissions in control procedures and lead to their immediate correction before the system becomes operational.

The internal audit department carefully reviews the input, processing, and output controls when evaluating a new system. When assessing the processing controls incorporated into the programs of new systems applications, the internal auditors regularly employ the technique commonly referred to as "auditing through the computer."

Required:
a. Identify the types of controls that should be incorporated in the programs of the new system.
b. Explain how the existence of the computer controls and their proper functioning are verified by the "auditing through the computer" technique.

CMA

16-28 A CPA's client, Boos & Baumkirchner, Inc., is a medium-sized manufacturer of products for the leisure time activities market (camping equipment, scuba gear, bows and arrows, etc.). During the past year, a computer system was installed, and inventory records of finished goods and parts were converted to computer processing. The inventory master file is maintained on a disk. Each record of the file contains the following information:

- Item or part number
- Description
- Size
- Unit-of-measure code

- Quantity on hand
- Cost per unit
- Total value of inventory on hand at cost
- Date of last sale or usage
- Quantity used or sold this year
- Economic order quantity
- Code number of major vendor
- Code number of secondary vendor

In preparation for year-end inventory, the client has two identical sets of preprinted inventory count cards. One set is for the client's inventory counts, and the other is for the CPA's use to make audit test counts. The following information has been keypunched into the cards and interpreted on their face:

- Item or part number
- Description
- Size
- Unit-of-measure code

In taking the year-end inventory, the client's personnel will write the actual counted quantity on the face of each card. When all counts are complete, the counted quantity will be keypunched into the cards. The cards will be processed against the disk file, and quantity-on-hand figures will be adjusted to reflect the actual count. A computer listing will be prepared to show any missing inventory count cards and all quantity adjustments of more than $100 in value. These items will be investigated by client personnel, and all required adjustments will be made. When adjustments have been completed, the final year-end balances will be computed and posted to the general ledger.

The CPA has available a general-purpose computer audit software package that will run on the client's computer and can process both card and disk files.

Required:

a. In general and without regard to the facts above, discuss the nature of general-purpose computer audit software packages, and list the various types and uses of such packages.

b. List and describe at least five ways a general purpose computer audit software package can be used to assist in all aspects of the audit of the inventory of Boos & Baumkirchner, Inc. (For example, the package can be used to read the disk inventory master file and list items and parts with a high unit cost or total value. Such items can be included in the test counts to increase the dollar coverage of the audit verification.)

AICPA

16-29 In the past, the records to be evaluated in an audit have been printed reports, listings, documents, and written papers, all of which are visible output. However, in fully computerized systems that employ daily updating of transaction files, output and files are frequently in machine-readable forms such as cards, tapes, or disks. Thus, they often present the auditor with an opportunity to use the computer in performing an audit.

Required:

Discuss how the computer can be used to aid the auditor in examining accounts receivable in such a fully computerized system.

AICPA

16-30 An auditor is conducting an examination of the financial statements of a wholesale cosmetics distributor with an inventory consisting of thousands of individual items. The distributor keeps its inventory in its own distribution center and in two public warehouses. An inventory computer file is maintained on a computer disk, and at the end of each business day, the file is updated. Each record of the inventory file contains the following data:

1. Item number
2. Location of item
3. Description of item
4. Quantity on hand
5. Cost per item
6. Date of last purchase
7. Date of last sale
8. Quantity sold during year

The auditor is planning to observe the distributor's physical count of inventories as of a given date. The auditor will have available a computer tape of the data on the inventory file on the date of the physical count and a general purpose computer software package.

Required:

The auditor is planning to perform basic inventory auditing procedures. Identify the basic inventory auditing procedures, and describe how the use of the general purpose software package and the tape of the inventory file data might be helpful to the auditor in performing such procedures. Organize your answer as follows:

Basic Inventory Auditing Procedure	How General Purpose Computer Software Package and Tape of the Inventory File Data Might Be Helpful
1. Observe the physical count, making the recording test counts where applicable.	Determining which items are to be test counted by selecting a random sample of a representative number of items from the inventory file as of the date of the physical count.

AICPA

16-31 You are reviewing audit working papers containing a narrative description of the Tenney Corporation's factory payroll system. A portion of that narrative is as follows:

> "Factory employees punch timeclock cards each day when entering or leaving the shop. At the end of each week, the timekeeping department collects the timecards and prepares duplicate batch-control slips by department showing total hours and number of employees. The timecards and original batch-control slips are sent to the payroll accounting section. The second copies of the batch-control slips are filed by date.
>
> In the payroll accounting section, payroll transaction cards are keypunched from the information on the timecards, and a batch total card for each batch is keypunched from the batch-control slip. The timecards and batch-control slips are then filed by batch for possible reference. The payroll transaction cards and batch total card are sent to data processing where they are sorted by employee number within batch. Each batch is edited by a computer program that checks the validity of employee number against a master employee tape file and the total hours and number of employees against the batch total card. A detailed printout by batch and employee number is produced that indicates batches that do not balance and invalid employee numbers. This printout is returned to payroll accounting to resolve all differences."

In searching for documentation, you found a flowchart of the payroll system that included all appropriate symbols (American National Standards Institute, Inc.) but was only partially labeled. The portion of this flowchart described by the above narrative appears in Exhibit 16–18.

Required:

a. Number your answer 1 through 17. Next to the corresponding number of your answer, supply the appropriate labeling (document name, process description, or file order) applicable to each numbered symbol on the flowchart.

b. Flowcharts are one of the aids an auditor may use to determine and evaluate a client's internal control system. List advantages of using flowcharts in this context.

AICPA

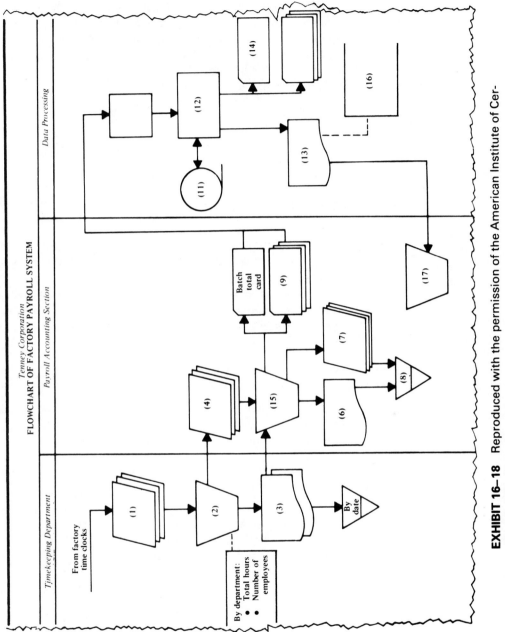

Tenney Corporation
FLOWCHART OF FACTORY PAYROLL SYSTEM

Timekeeping Department | *Payroll Accounting Section* | *Data Processing*

EXHIBIT 16–18 Reproduced with the permission of the American Institute of Certified Public Accountants.

16-32 Roger Peters, CPA, has examined the financial statements of the Solt Manufacturing Company for several years and is making preliminary plans for the audit for the year ended June 30. During this examination, Mr. Peters plans to use a set of generalized computer audit programs. Solt's EDP manager has agreed to prepare special tapes of data from company records for the CPA's use with the generalized programs.

The following information is applicable to Mr. Peters' examination of Solt's accounts payable and related procedures:

1. The formats of pertinent tapes are in Exhibit 16–19.
2. The following monthly runs are prepared:
   a. Cash disbursements by check number.
   b. Outstanding payables.
   c. Purchase journals arranged: (1) by account charged, and (2) by vendor.
3. Vouchers and supporting invoices, receiving reports and purchase order copies are filed by vendor code. Purchase orders and checks are filed numerically.
4. Company records are maintained on magnetic tapes. All tapes are stored in a restricted area within the computer room. A grandfather-father-son policy is followed for retaining and safeguarding tape files.

Required:

a. Explain the grandfather-father-son policy. Describe how files could be reconstructed when this policy is used.
b. Discuss whether company policies for retaining and safeguarding the tape files provide adequate protection against losses of data.
c. Describe the controls that the CPA should maintain over:
   1. Preparing the special tape.
   2. Processing the special tape with the generalized computer audit programs.
d. Prepare a schedule for the EDP manager outlining the data that should be included on the special tape for the CPA's examination of accounts payable and related procedures. This schedule should show the:
   1. Client tape from which the item should be extracted.
   2. Name of the item of data.

AICPA

16-33 L Limited is a dry goods chain selling mainly staples, such as practical clothing for the family, work clothes, shoes, notions, piece goods, and a relatively small amount of housewares. Its 170 stores are distributed across the country. Ten years ago, the president authorized the introduction of a credit card system, and within 2½ years, the company had issued 300,000 credit cards. In 1982, some 450,000 credit cards were in cir-

Master File—Vendor Name

Vendor Code | Rec Type | Space | Blank | Card Code 100 | Vendor Name

Master File—Vendor Address

Vendor Code | Rec Type | Space | Blank | Address—Line 1 | Address—Line 2 | Address—Line 3 | Blank | Card Code 120

Transaction File—Expense Detail

Vendor Code | Rec Type | Voucher Number | Blank Batch | Voucher Number | Voucher Date | Vendor Code | Invoice Date | Due Date | Invoice Number | Purchase Order Number | Debit Account | Prd Type | Product Code | Blank | Amount | Quantity | Card Code 160

Transaction File—Payment Detail

Vendor Code | Rec Type | Voucher Number | Blank Batch | Voucher Number | Voucher Date | Vendor Code | Invoice Date | Due Date | Invoice Number | Purchase Order Number | Check Number | Check Date | Blank | Amount | Blank | Card Code 170

EXHIBIT 16–19 Reproduced with the permission of the American Institute of Certified Public Accountants.

culation of which some 430,000 showed monthly activity. Seventy percent of the company's sales are made on credit, with some 75 percent of the credit sales made to company credit card holders and the other credit sales being made to holders of other credit cards.

The credit card system is one of several computerized systems processed on the company's computer.

Relevant procedures for the computerized credit card system are as follows:

There are 140 stores located in areas other than head office. All credit card purchase, credit, adjustment, and payment documents are batched daily by each store, and record counts represent the input control. The batches are delivered each evening to a local data center for keypunching. After verification and check to the record count, the data is transmitted via teleprocessing on the following day to L Limited's computer.

For the 30 stores in the head office area, the system works similarly except that the batches are delivered directly to head office.

Cyclical billing is done at the head office. Credit card holders have been divided into groups, the size of the group having been determined by dividing the number of customers (credit cards) by the number of working days in the month. Each group is billed once a month.

Remittances received by mail or in person at head office, write-offs, and other adjustments including service charges on overdue accounts are processed at head office.

The credit department at head office is responsible for the issue of credit cards and for a weekly advice to all stores of cards that have been inactive for 90 days and of delinquent credit cards. Credit cards are delinquent as soon as:

a. The customer exceeds his credit limit

b. The customer has made no payments for 60 days since the last billing

c. The credit card is reported stolen

d. The customer has given notice of cancellation

In addition to the above information, the auditor finds the following in the accounts:

Accounts receivable—credit cards . . . . $8,218,374 debit
Allowance for doubtful accounts
(manually controlled) . . . . 1,221,000 credit

During the discussion of the computerized system, the data processing manager indicated that he would be pleased to have one of his programmers write a program to extract information from the credit card master file according to the auditor's specification.

Required:

a. As auditor, assuming you accept the data processing manager's offer, describe with reasons the information you would hope to obtain through the program prepared by the client.

b. How would you control that no account in the credit card master file would be excluded from the program prepared by the client?

CICA

16-34 The primary reason for the use of ITF is that the whole system can be tested—the manual procedures as well as EDP. The auditor can monitor test data from the point of its authorization and input into the system to its final disposition in output. The resulting transaction and file interactions caused by the test data can be reviewed, as can the manual procedures applied.

This problem illustrates the use of ITF for compliance testing with an on-line savings deposit application. The objectives of this audit application are to

1. Determine whether missing, duplicated, or inaccurate data would be detected by the system by compliance testing the functioning of various controls within the system.

2. Determine whether data initiated internally by the system are accurate by comparing generated data to results of manual computations.

3. Determine whether errors are displayed on the terminal for teller review and correction.

4. Determine whether administrative policy and manual procedural controls are being carried out by employees.

5. Determine whether control totals on teller-terminal transaction amounts are generated for teller balancing and supervisory review.

6. Determine whether daily report totals produced off line agree with teller cash reports and terminal transaction totals.

The data elements on the on-line savings master file are defined on page 668.

Required:

Develop three test transactions that would be appropriate in such an ITF application. Organize your answer as follows:

Transaction Description	Manual Control/ Programmed Control	Desired Result

Element Number	Description of Contents
1	Account Number
2	Customer Name
3	Customer Address
4	Social Security Number
5	Account Balance
6	Share Loan Balance
7	Uncollected Funds Hold
8	Miscellaneous Hold Code
9	Passbook Balance
10	Unposted Item Count
11	No/Book Withdrawal
12	Date Last Monetary Activity
13	Date Last Nonmonetary Activity

16-35 The following problem is a simple application showing a higher-level language program in which a trace function is implemented. The input transactions and master file records are presented in Exhibit 16–20.

Exhibit 16–21 represents portions of the client's COBOL program for payroll file maintenance and uses the TRACE verb. Only those statements appropriate for the trace are shown. The purpose of the simple program in this example is to demonstrate how tracing works. In practice, tracing software would usually be used with more complex applications where logic and calculations may be difficult to follow manually (e.g., algorithms for overhead allocation). In this example, the COBOL DISPLAY verb is

Record Layouts

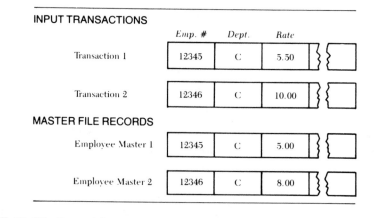

EXHIBIT 16–20   Record Layouts. © 1979 by the American Institute of Certified Public Accountants and reproduced with their permission from *Computer-Assisted Audit Techniques.*

COBOL Program Using Trace

SEQUENCE (PAGE)	(SERIAL)	CONT	A	B COBOL STATEMENT
0001	00			START-TRACE-PARA.
0001	10			READY TRACE.
0001	20			READ-TRANS-PARA.
0002	00			DISPLAY 'TRANS-EMP-NO=' ,TRANS-EMP-NO.
0002	10			READ-MASTER-PARA.
0002	50			IF TRANS-EMP-NO EQUAL MASTER-EMP-NO
0002	60			NEXT SENTENCE ELSE
0002	70			GO TO READ-MASTER-PARA.
0002	80			CHECK-RATE-PARA.
0002	90			IF TRANS-RATE IS GREATER THAN 8.50 OR
0003	00			IF TRANS-RATE IS LESS THAN 2.30
0003	10			GO TO RATE-ERROR-PARA.
0003	20			UPDATE-RATE-PARA.
0003	60			GO TO READ-TRANS-PARA.
0003	70			RATE-ERROR-PARA.
0003	80			DISPLAY 'RATE ERROR FOR EMPLOYEE NO',TRANS-EMP-NO.
0003	90			DISPLAY 'RATE =',TRANS-RATE.
0004	00			GO TO READ-TRANS-PARA.

EXHIBIT 16–21 COBOL Program Using Trace. © 1979 by the American Institute of Certified Public Accountants and reproduced with their permission from *Computer-Assisted Audit Techniques.*

669

used to print the contents of selected data fields. In simple applications such as this one, manual tracing, test data, or some other technique would probably be a preferable approach. By reviewing the trace listing, the auditor can determine whether the transaction has been processed properly.

The trace listing is normally printed as the program is executed. The listing shows the names of all paragraphs executed while the trace function was operative.

Required:

a. Write the output as it would appear when the auditor runs this program. Indicate which of the lines of output would be printed by the COBOL DISPLAY verb.

b. For each transaction, state whether it would be accepted by this program or not. If it would not be accepted, explain why the transaction is in error.

INDEX